DATE DUE

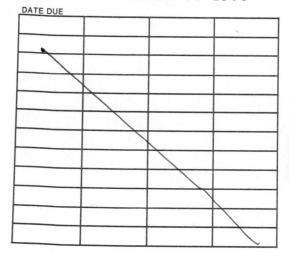

This is a volume in

THE UNIVERSITY OF MICHIGAN HISTORY OF THE MODERN WORLD

Upon completion, the series will consist of the following volumes:

THE SOUTHWEST PACIFIC TO 1900

A Modern History

The University of Michigan History of the Modern World
Edited by Allan Nevins and Howard M. Ehrmann

THE SOUTHWEST PACIFIC TO 1900

A Modern History

AUSTRALIA NEW ZEALAND THE ISLANDS ANTARCTICA

BY C. HARTLEY GRATTAN

Ann Arbor: The University of Michigan Press

TO MY WIFE
Marjorie Campbell Grattan

MY THREE DAUGHTERS
Rosalind, Jacqueline, Jennifer

AND

MY SON
John

Preface

The interest of the history of the Southwest Pacific resides in the fact that it is a story of how men of European origin have, in the course of adventuring in far places under the overhang of Asia and just beyond, built up nations of distinctive character on the Euro-American pattern and otherwise assimilated their area to the West. The history of the Southwest Pacific, like the history of North America, is at once an integral portion of the history of the expansion of Europe and also of the variegated history of nation-building in "new" lands. Up until yesterday the nation-builders of the Southwest Pacific maintained a "psychological distance" from Asia in spite of the geography of their situation. Now in response to the remolding factors at work in Asia and in the world, they are challenged to dissolve that psychological distance and develop intimate economic, political, and cultural relations with Asia. Insofar as they keep their traditional European ties in good heart and also for good and sufficient reasons swing a bit toward the United States as the most powerful Pacific Basin nation of similar character to themselves, the presumption will be that, however relations with Asia increase in intimacy, they intend to preserve their Euro-American character into the future. Because this "issue" has but recently arisen, this book is almost wholly a story of how "the West" became established in the Southwest Pacific. It is this writer's conviction that it is but a prelude to a history which, though differently conditioned from that of the past, will continue indefinitely into the future.

Contents

INTRODUCTION

CHAPTER I

The Area Disclosed: The Explorers

For Europeans, the Southwest Pacific was a theory long before it became a reality. The theory had a history running back to the Pythagoreans of the sixth century B.C., who expounded the proposition that the world was round and had an idea about the probable distribution of land and water on the globe. To keep the globe in balance it was thought there had to be a land mass about equal in size in the south to balance the known land mass of the north. For centuries this idea was affirmed and denied by scholars (muddled in time by the complementary theory that the tropics were so hot that no man could survive a passage through them—no European *did* until 1471), but it was only belatedly put to the test. Geography had to become a science of facts before a test seemed the logical way to deal with a hypothesis. Even after the testing began through exploration, the idea of a large continent in the south persisted; it survived by a process of constantly shifting the location of the land mass. This went on from 1498 when Vasco da Gama proved that it was possible to go around Africa into the Indian Ocean and on to India, thus showing that the southern land mass was not an eastern extension of Africa, to the time in the late eighteenth century when Captain James Cook showed conclusively that the Southwest Pacific consisted of Australia, probably Antarctica, and innumerable islands. The hypothetical land mass was first put on a globe in 1515, on a printed map in 1529; it thereafter recurred on globes and maps for about two and a half centuries.

When Da Gama took advantage of the rounding of the Cape of Good Hope by Bartholomeu Dias in 1488, the Pacific Ocean did not figure in men's calculations. They knew that there was continental land extending considerably to the east of the Levant for Marco Polo had been to China and had even brought back vague news of Japan; they soon knew of land to the west of the Atlantic Ocean from the voyages of Columbus; but they were unaware that the vastest of all oceans separated the new West and the already traditional East. The expectation was that the new and old lands would be connected and that additional new lands would be found (notably what the armchair geographers came to call *Terra Australis Incognita*), but no particularly impressive new oceans. They got their first intimation of a tremendous new ocean when Vasco Nuñez de Balboa sighted it looking south from the west coast of the Isthmus of Panama in 1513. At about the same time on the other side of the great ocean, the Portuguese, who had moved rapidly from the west coast of India along the southern coasts of Asia into the islands of the Indies, had reached the western shore of the new ocean.

It was, however, Ferdinand Magellan who, in 1519–20, first crossed the new ocean, named it Pacific, and demonstrated how huge it really was. After his death his men continued through the Indies and the Indian Ocean to complete the first circumnavigation of the earth. Magellan worked from east to west, or more accurately from southeast to northwest. However, his track was such that he barely touched the Southwest Pacific, for in that area he chanced on only uninhabited Pukapuka, an outlier of the Tuamotus, and Flint Island in the Line group. By sailing around the tip of South America he showed that that continent was disconnected from the anticipated great southern land mass and that there was a large ocean to the west of the west coast of that continent. The theoretical geographers, however, continued to speculate that the land to the south of the strait Magellan traversed was solid to the southern pole and probably was part of the *Terra Australis Incognita* which, they then contended, stretched from somewhere in the western South Atlantic west and north toward Africa. For a long time to come almost every bit of land discovered in this huge area was considered a headland of this hypothetical continent and sometimes cloudbanks were mistaken for headlands. It took many years to get at the truth.

The delay was in part occasioned by the fact that men's minds were fully occupied with the task of finding and exploiting the wealth of the Asiatic East which they thoroughly understood and highly prized, and in part by the fact that what they did by chance learn about the Southwest Pacific either did not excite their cupidity or did not readily satisfy it. Their focus of interest was lands on and to the north of the equator, especially—in the beginning—the East Indies, where the pioneer Portuguese had established themselves by the end of the fifteenth century. The rich lands that interested the Portuguese were approached by way of the Cape of Good Hope, up the west coast of Africa to the vicinity of Madagascar, and east across the Indian Ocean. This route kept them away from the Southwest Pacific. There is no conclusive proof available that they ever had knowledge of Australia or the islands, but as they were a secretive people they may have hidden away their knowledge in their archives. When the Spanish found their way across the Pacific from the east they tried to dislodge the Portuguese from the Indies, but were unsuccessful. Alternatively, they took possession of the Philippine Islands, their heritage from Magellan, where they settled in 1565. To link this Spanish possession with the homeland via America they pioneered a trans-Pacific route from Manila to Acapulco, Mexico, thence overland to the Caribbean, and so to Spain. This was the famous route of the Spanish treasure ships and in both the Pacific and Atlantic oceans the ships that traveled it attracted the fell attention of Spain's enemies. But by the time Spain had established this scheme of trans-Pacific communications, her imperial energies were slackening. They reached a climax in the Americas, not in the Pacific, and what Spain did in the Pacific, aside from the Philippines, was not impressive. She was chiefly satisfied to insist that the Pacific was a closed sea (*mare clausum*) to her rivals and enemies. Nevertheless, Spain was the dominant power in the Pacific for two centuries, and she held the Philippines until 1898.

D3

As far as the Southwest Pacific was concerned the Spanish activities were quickly and enduringly fogged in obscurity, both by the design of the authorities and the low state of the technique for determining geographical locations, especially longitude. The voyages into this area were initiated and often executed in whole or in part by enthusiasts for gold and the salvation of souls, authorized in Madrid, but outfitted in and based upon Peruvian ports, notably Callao. The scattered nature of the discoveries illustrated how vast the spaces of the ocean really were. The earliest voyage of which it is profitable to take notice was that of Alvaro de Mendaña who sailed west from Callao on November 19, 1567, and returned to that port about two years later. He was stimulated to look for islands to the west by tales of the Incas. Eighty days out from Callao, Mendaña discovered the islands (including Guadalcanal)—inhabited by Melanesians—subsequently dubbed the Solomons, which, because of sailors' gossip, were believed to contain rich gold mines. Otherwise, the voyage was not productive or even distinguished, and once the Solomons sank from Mendaña's sight they were not certainly located again for over two centuries—though seen in whole or in part by several voyagers. Mendaña sailed again from Callao on April 9, 1595, and this time followed a more southerly route. In late July he discovered and named the Marquesas Islands, the first inhabited

Polynesian islands ever seen by European men, but the Solomons were his objective. He died trying to find them and command was taken by his chief pilot, Pedro Fernandes de Quirós, who brought the expedition into Manila in February 1596 without further significant discoveries.

Quirós' experience did not give him a vision of an island world, but in some odd fashion it fired in his mind the notion of a great southern continent. On December 21, 1605, he sailed in command of an expedition of his own, with Luis Váez de Torres as chief pilot. By this time Quirós, after a decade of brooding and frustration, was less a practical explorer than an obsessed visionary. After passing through the Tuamotu Islands he encountered a large island in the New Hebrides and was convinced he had found the continent of his dreams. He planned its settlement elaborately, but precipitately abandoned his plans and nevertheless grandly named the place—invoking the home country of his sovereign and also his God—Austrialia del Espiritu Santo. Separated from his chief pilot by contrary winds, Quirós made his way back to America, landing at Acapulco on November 23, 1606, and continued on to Madrid to report his discovery as he misconceived it. He found the authorities in no mood to encourage further Spanish expansion, continental in scope least of all, and for seven years he pleaded in vain to be allowed a new expedition. He died in Panama in 1614 on his way to Peru in the expectation of sailing west again, not knowing that the Peruvian authorities had instructions to humor him but to frustrate his plans. Meanwhile, his pilot Torres had reached Manila after coasting for two months along the *southern* coast of New Guinea, passing through what is now called Torres Strait. It is unlikely, but not impossible, that he saw the continent of Australia. Torres' report of his discoveries was filed and forgotten in Manila and knowledge of the strait was not recovered until 1761, when a note about it was found in papers taken from Manila by the English. After reporting at Manila, Torres disappeared from history, and after the second Quirós expedition the Spanish made no more explorations in the Southwest Pacific until Malaspina's visit at the end of the eighteenth century.

D3

Oddly, the Dutch, who displaced the Portuguese in the Indies, never solved the mystery of Torres Strait—a jumble of islands, shoals, and false channels—and hence never found the most convenient route into the Southwest Pacific from their great base at Batavia (now Jakarta) in Java. They explored the southern coast of the vast island of New Guinea for many miles, looking for gold and trading opportunities, but never broke through. In their frustration they were forced into, or retreated into, the great body of water they named the Gulf of Carpentaria. It was while probing in the Gulf in 1606 (about the time Quirós was at the New Hebrides) that they discovered Australia. This was the accomplishment of Willem Jansz in the ship "Duyfken" ("Little Dove"). The coastal land Skipper Jansz saw was supremely unattractive, and until the middle of the twentieth century it never allowed anything better by way of use than extensive grazing. The Dutch took it to be a southern extension of New Guinea.

In their voyages to the Indies the Dutch, until 1611, usually followed the old Portuguese route. In that year, however, Captain Hendrik Brouwer ascertained that if one continued eastward from the Cape of Good Hope, one would eventually fall in with winds that would carry one swiftly north to the Indies. This considerably shortened the voyage out from the Netherlands and made it quite certain that sooner or later someone following this route would accidentally arrive at the western coast of Australia. As a matter of fact the Dutch made a good many such landfalls in succeeding decades, but they did not have the luck to chance upon country that was at all inviting. On a voyage in 1627 the southern coast of the vaguely perceived country was explored from Cape Leeuwin (Dutch named) eastward to the islands of St. Francis and St. Peter, but it too proved barren. By the early 1640's the Dutch knew something of the coast from Cape York in the east westward around to the islands in the Great Bight. They were not at all sure whether they had outlined a continent or a series of islands lying closely together. They called the vaguely understood country New Holland, a name which continued to be the standard designation into the nineteenth century, and while it was decidedly a new country it proved in none of its parts to be anything like Holland.

The climax of Dutch exploration came under Governor-General Anthony Van Diemen, who took office at Batavia in 1636 and held it until his death nine years later. He began by sending ships to continue exploration of the southern coast of New Guinea in search of a passage into the Pacific which, if found, was to be followed by a tracing of the eastern coast of New Holland and a circumnavigation of the whole land mass. If the strait were not found the expedition was to search for a passage *through* New Holland opening, they hoped, some place on the northern coast. However, the leader of the expedition was murdered by natives in New Guinea, no strait was found, and the expedition added little to existing knowledge. After an incursion into the north Pacific in pursuit of a rich island rumored to be east of Japan, the Dutch turned south again and in 1642 undertook what proved to be

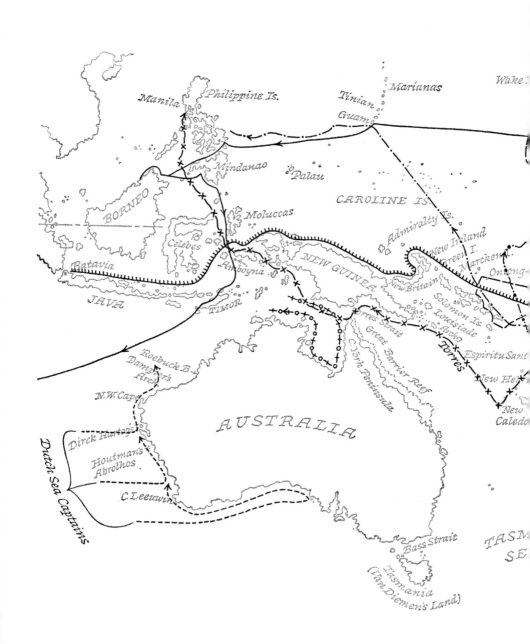

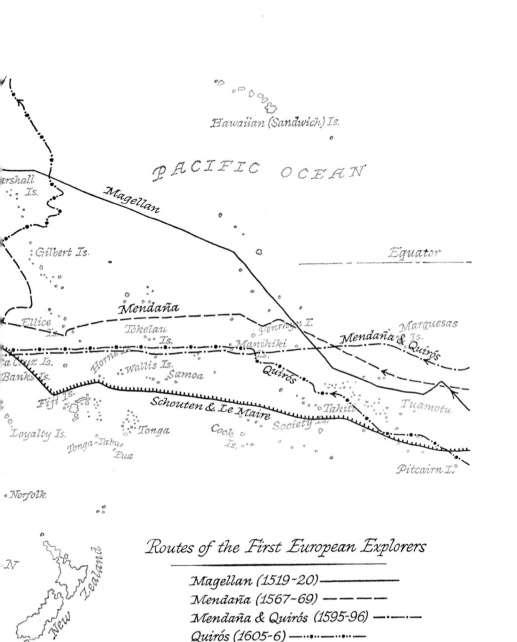

Hawaiian (Sandwich) Is.

PACIFIC OCEAN

Magellan

rshall Is.

Gilbert Is.

Equator

Mendaña

Ellice Is.

Tokelau Is.

Penrhyn I.

Manihiki

Mendaña & Quirós

Marquesas Is.

a Cruz Is.
Banks Is.

Horne Is.

Wallis Is.

Samoa

Quirós

Tuamotu

Fiji Is.

Schouten & Le Maire

Tahiti

Society Is.

Loyalty Is.

Tonga

Cook Is.

Tonga-Tabu
Eua

Pitcairn I.

Norfolk

N

New Zealand

Routes of the First European Explorers

Magellan (1519–20) ————
Mendaña (1567–69) — — — —
Mendaña & Quirós (1595–96) —·—·—
Quirós (1605–6) —··——··—
Torres (1606–7) —×—×—×—
Jansz (1605–6) +o+o+o+
Schouten & Le Maire (1615–16) ⊔⊔⊔⊔⊔⊔⊔
Dutch Sea Captains (1616–50) --------

their greatest voyage of all and a major voyage in Southwest Pacific history. The objectives, aside from ascertaining the geography of the area, were to uncover the trading resources of any new territories discovered and to locate a new and better route for Dutch raiders of Spanish shipping off the coast of South America. To lead this expedition Van Diemen chose Abel Janszoon Tasman as captain, with Frans Jacobzoon Visscher as chief pilot. They were given two ships, the "Heemskerck" and the "Zeehaen." Leaving Batavia, they went to Mauritius, then in Dutch possession, for final preparations, and from there sailed south to pick up the winds that would carry them east, south of the limits of New Holland. At some point to be determined by events, they were to turn north and make their way back to Batavia.

As it happened they turned north at a point that soon brought them to a coast which they named Van Diemen's Land. Whether it was insular or continental they did not ascertain. They explored the new coast only briefly, not finding it of much interest, and while they felt that they were being watched they saw nothing of the natives. This was in November 1642.

The explorers, turning east again in mid-December, came to the western shore of what is today known as the South Island of New Zealand. The Dutch at first called it Staaten Landt and thought it part of a continent, another face of which was the Staaten Landt off the southern tip of South America; however, when the latter was demonstrated to be an island they named their new discovery Nieu Zealande. Because of bad weather and the fierce hostility of the natives, no landing was made. Neither did the Dutch find it possible to circumnavigate the islands—hence their error of assuming it to be continental land. And they did not define Cook Strait which separates the North and South Islands, though they sailed a distance into it. In effect, they merely drew a line on the map.

Leaving this coast on January 6, 1643, Tasman and his crew turned northeast and toward the end of the month came upon two islands, Tongatabu and Eua, of the Tonga group; in early February they were among some of the smaller islands of the Fiji group; keeping to the north and west, they traveled along the northern coast of New Guinea and reached Batavia on June 14, 1643, after an absence of ten months. Tasman had made a complete circuit of New Holland, but always so far from the coast, except when he was at Van Diemen's Land, that he only clarified its position in the roughest fashion.

The next year Tasman was sent out again, this time to tackle the problem of the passage along the southern coast of New Guinea into the Pacific and, if successful in finding a way, to go down the eastern coast of New Holland and so around the southern land. Alternatively, he was to see if a passage through the land opened out of the Gulf of Carpentaria. Tasman accomplished neither objective and hence did not modify the conception of New Holland and its eastern neighborhood which he had established the year before. He was still of the opinion that the eastern coast of New Holland extended from a point in New Guinea southward to link up with his discovery in Van Diemen's Land—a line miles too far to the east—and that New Guinea and New Holland were all one land mass. After the voyage of 1644 Tasman drew a map embodying his knowledge and ideas. He had added more exact knowledge to the store about the Southwest Pacific than anybody to that time. His map was a distinct advance over its predecessors, even if far from accurate by modern standards. It was not separately published at the time, however—indeed it was not so published until 1948—but it was probably used by Dutch cartographers of the Amsterdam Chamber of Commerce in producing charts, atlases, and globes, so its information became public property.

While the Dutch habitually traveled to the Indies by way of the Cape of Good Hope, the East India Company's rights also covered the approach via Cape Horn and across the Pacific. Anybody—particularly any Dutchman—who attempted without authorization to reach the Indies by way of the Horn was guilty of trespass, at least in legal theory. Nevertheless, Dutchmen occasionally took the risk of defying the Company, and their voyages in the Pacific led to discoveries. Two voyages particularly must be recalled: that of Schouten and Le Maire in 1615–16, and that of Roggeveen in 1722. The former resulted in the discovery of Strait Le Maire, a passage to the south of the Strait of Magellan; the naming of Cape Horn (originally Hoorn); the expounding of the theory that Staaten Landt was a continent, to Tasman's confusion later on (that Staaten Landt was an island was demonstrated by Hendrik Brouwer in 1643); and the discovery of islands, probably in the Tonga group. Roggeveen discovered Easter Island, the northern Tuamotus, and Samoa. His voyage made a particular appeal to the imagination of the English, since, in spite of the fact that he discovered only islands, he nevertheless professed the belief that a continent still awaited discovery. Nobody knew what was in the vast stretches of ocean still untraversed, though to our later sense the Dutch were in possession of knowledge that would have allowed them to say that the Southwest Pacific consisted of New Holland and numerous clusters of islands scattered widely over a huge expanse of water.

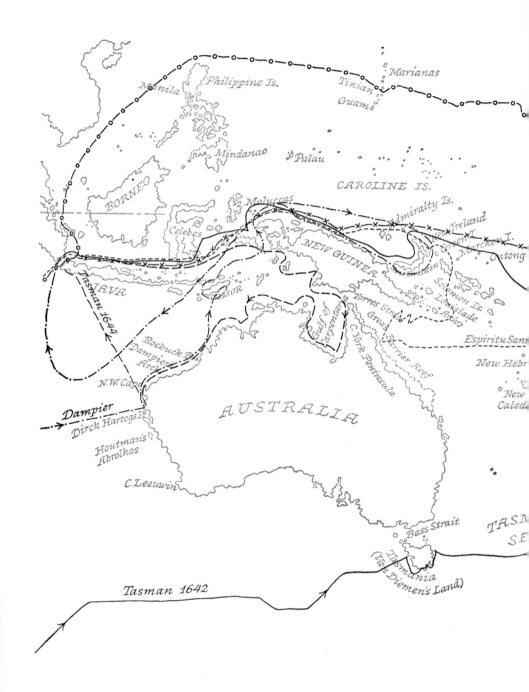

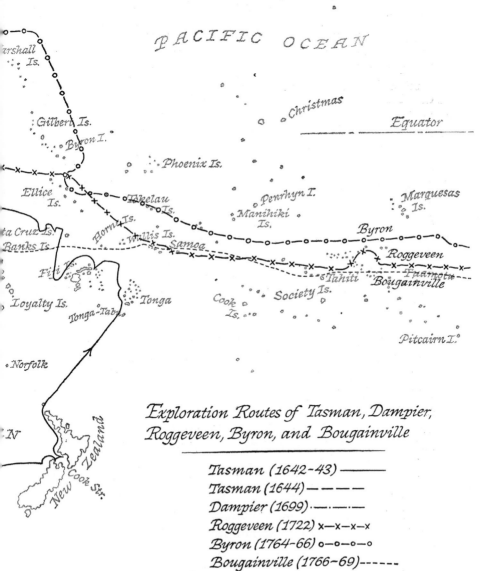

Hawaiian (Sandwich) Is.

PACIFIC OCEAN

Equator

Marshall Is.

Gilbert Is.

Byron I.

Phoenix Is.

Ellice Is.

Tokelau

Horn Is.

Willis Is.

Samoa

Banks Is.

ta Cruz Is.

Fiji Is.

Loyalty Is.

Tonga-Tabu

Tonga

Norfolk

New Zealand

Cook Str.

Christmas

Penrhyn I.

Manihiki Is.

Marquesas Is.

Byron

Roggeveen

Tahiti

Bougainville

Tuamotu

Society Is.

Cook Is.

Pitcairn I.

Exploration Routes of Tasman, Dampier, Roggeveen, Byron, and Bougainville

Tasman (1642-43) ————
Tasman (1644) — — — —
Dampier (1699) ·—·—·—·
Roggeveen (1722) x—x—x—x
Byron (1764-66) o—o—o—o
Bougainville (1766-69) ------

D3

British activities in the Pacific stemmed from imperial ambitions that at one time or another brought them into conflict with every other nation that sought a place in the Pacific sun. In the earliest phase the rival was Spain, and the Pacific aspect of the Anglo-Spanish conflict was an extension of the animosities symbolized in their European phase by such events as the defeat of the Armada in 1588, the War of the Spanish Succession of 1701–14 (which brought the Churchills to fame), and the so-called Seven Years' War between England and Spain and France which culminated in England's great triumph of 1763 and which involved the Americas and India as well as Europe. In the Americas the quarreling was over trade and territory and was largely centered in the Caribbean and South America; in the Pacific it led to the English effort to discover a northwest passage into the great ocean through the Arctic, in which Cabot, Frobisher, and Davis participated, and to actual incursions into the great ocean by way of Cape Horn.

The Pacific phases of the story were initiated by a theoretician of geography named Dr. John Dee who believed both in the existence of a practical northwest passage into the Pacific and also in *Terra Australis Incognita,* the latter on the basis of Marco Polo's remarks about a great land to the south of the Indies which Dee conceived of as stretching across the ocean to the vicinity of the Strait of Magellan. He drew support from the projections of a continent on the maps of such cartographers as Ortelius (map of 1564) and Mercator (map of 1569). Dee definitely aspired to promote a British empire in the Pacific. We should see the great voyage of Sir Francis Drake in 1577–80 against the background Dee provided. He put Dee's ideas to the test both as to *Terra Australis Incognita* and the northwest passage. (The official instructions issued to Drake were substantially—often in the exact same words—repeated to British explorers in the Pacific to the time of Captain Cook.) Drake had some knowledge of Mendaña's first voyage of 1567–69 which was interpreted as supporting the existence of *Terra Australis Incognita.* Drake had a very rough time around the Strait of Magellan, in the course of which he discovered open ocean south of all the known land in that vicinity—an early item in the exploration toward Antarctica—and he deduced from the prevailing winds there that he could not make the hypothetical coast of *Terra Australis Incognita.* He turned north instead of west and raided the Spanish settlements in Peru, spent a month in California which he annexed as New Albion, initiated the English search for a northwest passage from the Pacific side, and sailed for home via the Indies and the Cape of Good Hope, completing his classic circumnavigation on September 26, 1580. His immediate successors, Cavendish and Hawkins, were raiders pure and simple and the capture of Hawkins by the Spanish dampened the English enthusiasm for Pacific adventure. None of these raiders had anything to do with the Southwest Pacific. Soon the national energies were directed primarily to establishing colonies in North America and to gaining control of India or to building the first British Empire and the attendant wars with Spain and France, leading step by step to the great triumph over the Spanish and the French in 1763 and the collapse of the first Empire in 1783 when thirteen of the North American colonies won their independence.

History, however, is not a tidy operation and the second British Empire, with which we have a primary concern here—the building of which led to British dominance in the Southwest Pacific—had its genesis before the Americans broke free. There is reason to accept William Dampier, that strange mixture of buccaneer and scientific observer, as the British precursor in the Southwest Pacific. His voyages into the Pacific between 1681 and 1711, in the course of which he twice visited the Indian Ocean coast of New Holland (1688 and 1699), and especially the books he wrote about his travels stirred up active interest in the Pacific in England once again. But perhaps the true imperial urge found more unmistakable expression in the thinking of Lord Anson. Anson's mind was clear about the territorial strategy of imperial power: he captured a Spanish treasure ship in the Pacific and figured out the rationale of the Manila-Acapulco route, but he chose to act in the Pacific more as a raider than a strategist. It was left to Captain the Honorable John Byron, known as "Foul-weather Jack" from his marked propensity to run into storms at sea (and who was to be grandfather of the poet Lord Byron), actually to act on Anson's reasoning. In January 1765 he took possession of the Falkland Islands which were valuable in helping to control the entrance into the Pacific around Cape Horn. After taking the Falklands, Byron continued into the Pacific, saw something of the Tuamotu Islands, and completed an otherwise rather footless voyage around the world. He ignored his instructions to look for a northwest passage, still considered a necessary alternative, all-British route to the Pacific Ocean. His taking of the Falklands initiated a dispute with the Spanish over their ownership which continues with their Argentine successors to the present day.

The British were now eager for Pacific exploration and hardly was Byron home than they dispatched Samuel Wallis in association with Philip Carteret (who had just returned with Byron) on a joint expedition which, since the ships became permanently separated in a storm at the Strait of Magellan, became two expeditions. They were sent out to look for *Terra Australis Incognita*. Wallis sailed among the Tuamotus south of those Byron had seen and on June 18, 1767, discovered Tahiti in the Society group and thus brought into Western history an island which has enjoyed a supremely romantic reputation ever since. (His men probably introduced syphilis, or was it the French, a little later, under Bougainville?) After a month at Tahiti Wallis sailed west through the Society Islands, turned north for Batavia, and thence went home, where he arrived on May 20, 1768. Carteret meanwhile had sailed over much open ocean, eliminating a large piece of *Terra Australis Incognita* from the charts. He had discovered Pitcairn Island, had seen some of the southern islands of the Tuamotus, and, running north, had passed out of Polynesia into Melanesia and coasted unknowingly through part of Mendaña's Solomons to New Britain and New Ireland, whence he went to the Philippines, visited the Celebes, and reached Batavia with his ship in very bad condition. He arrived in England on March 20, 1769, almost a year after his partner Wallis. Before Carteret got back the next British expedition to the Southwest Pacific, that under Captain James Cook, had left England for Wallis' Tahiti. The English now knew that if one bore west after rounding Cape Horn one would probably find something to one's advantage.

D3

Before turning to Captain Cook's wonderful exploits it is necessary to bring the French directly into the story of the Southwest Pacific. There, as in North America and India, they were at this stage of history keen rivals of the British and, in spite of the great reversal of 1763 in Canada and the still greater disaster of Napoleon's final collapse in 1815, they continued to be rivals of fluctuating strength in the colonial arena until the entente of Britain, France, and Russia was formed to balance the Central Powers during the preliminaries of World War I.

The French announced their interest in the Pacific by dispatching Louis Antoine de Bougainville on a voyage around the world in 1766. Bougainville, then a man of thirty-seven, was a soldier turned sailor. He had served as aide-de-camp to Montcalm at the fateful battle of Quebec, at which Canada had been lost to France. As a naval commander he was to serve under Comte de Grasse in that expedition which the French contributed to the American Revolutionary cause and which notably assisted in Cornwallis' defeat at Yorktown, when the collapse of the first British Empire was tolled. Meanwhile, Bougainville was under instructions to make a circumnavigation of the globe, obviously as a challenge to the English. He opened his voyage, now evaluated as the "most celebrated" before Cook's, by a transaction in the Falkland

Islands. Even before the English, the French had perceived their significance in relation to entry into the Pacific and before Byron had taken possession, Bougainville had established a small outpost there at his own expense. Byron, however, knew nothing about it, not bothering to examine the islands carefully. Now Bougainville was to stage another act in the curious and lengthy drama of the Falklands by handing over his settlement to the Spanish who claimed the group as part of their South American dominions. (In 1770 the Spanish challenged the British pretension to possession and this almost but not quite led to war.)

Bougainville then proceeded into the Southwest Pacific around Cape Horn. He began, in accordance with established precedent, by attempting to find *Terra Australis Incognita* at about the same place as Carteret had sought it and arrived at the identical conclusion: it simply wasn't there. This ritualistic phase of Pacific exploration completed, he also, like Carteret, found himself among the Tuamotus and from there, like Wallis (but not Carteret), among the Society Islands and so to Tahiti, where he landed on the side opposite that visited by Wallis a year earlier —a visit of which Bougainville shortly learned. Tahiti conveyed to Bougainville an impression like that of a painting by Watteau or Fragonard; his later writings had a good deal to do with launching Tahiti on its highly romantic career in the West as the home of the noble savage.

Sailing west from Tahiti Bougainville next came upon Samoa. Then, instead of bearing north like so many of his predecessors, he wisely continued westward and came on land which he wrongly identified as Quiros' Austrialia del Espiritu Santo, although it was of the same island group. From there he continued still farther west, the first explorer since Torres (about whose voyage he knew nothing) to do so, toward the unseen eastern coast of New Holland—what he knew about this simply wasn't so. He continued on until he came to the outskirts of the Great Barrier Reef, approximately 150 miles from the continental coast, and then at last turned northwest. He had not found the coast of New Holland, but he had shown conclusively that Quirós had not found a continental land mass either. His next landfall was New Guinea, and while he thought that there must be a passage along the southern coast into the Gulf of Carpentaria (in which he was essentially right) he nevertheless decided to go in the opposite direction, becoming involved in a time of very foul weather in the Louisiade Archipelago and fetching up among the Solomons (which he did not identify as such), where he named Choiseul and Buka and supplied his own name for Bougainville.

Finally, he reached the destination he had had in mind all along, New Britain, where he was able to repair the ships and get water, though food was terribly scarce. Hunger accompanied the ships to Boeroe in the Indies, where the Dutch succored them, and finally Batavia was reached, twelve days after Carteret had sailed from thence for England. Traveling home via Mauritius and the Cape, Bougainville overtook Carteret off the west coast of Africa and offered him assistance, but was refused. He arrived in France on March 16, 1769.

D3

Captain Cook had left England seven months before, on August 26, 1768, on the first voyage of three that he was to make into the Pacific. Ostensibly scientific in purpose and undertaken at the instance of the Royal Society as part of its program for observing the transit of Venus predicted to occur in June 1769, which the Society had decided could best be studied at three points—Hudson's Bay in northern Canada, Spitzbergen, and some place in the Pacific south of the equator—the voyage was also designed (as shown by secret instructions issued to Cook, the substance of which "leaked" to the London press before Cook's departure) to continue the British effort to solve the geographical mysteries of the Pacific. In the beginning the idea was to set up the observational equipment at either Mendaña's Marquesas or in Samoa (if they could be rediscovered), but on Wallis' return with his news of Tahiti, the location of which he had determined with reasonable accuracy, it was immediately decided to use that place. Cook himself was to be one of the observers. The resulting data would, it was believed, allow the calculation of the distance of the earth from the sun. In this respect the expedition to the Pacific—and all the other journeys for observation—failed; in the end the calculation had to be made from other data entirely, but it nevertheless set the precedent for scientific work in the area which was still extremely lively in the International Geophysical Year of 1957–58.

James Cook, almost universally regarded as the very pattern of excellence as an explorer, was a child of the common people of Britain —of Scottish and English stock, born in Yorkshire, October 27, 1728 —who, in a century when one's status by birth and the amount of influence one could command were more potent determinants of success in one's career than self-generated merit, rose to great heights by virtue of his innate and diligently cultivated talent. The son of a farm laborer whose highest flight in life was to become a bailiff, Cook obtained the least elements of a primary education at the instance of a patron of his father and was first apprenticed to a retail grocer; by his own choice he transferred to the merchant marine to learn the trade of seafarer. He served his apprenticeship in the coastal coal trade, using the slack times of winter for the study of mathematics. Advanced to the point where the next step was to be made a merchant captain, he chose—again by his own motion—to enter the Royal Navy as an able-bodied seaman.

England was just then in the early phases of the Seven Years' War, and apparently Cook calculated that advancement would be rapid. Up to a point—and to a point eminently satisfactory to him—it was. In fairly short order he became a ship's master, the person who had the nautical management of a ship of war. In this capacity he went on the expedition against Quebec in 1759, the climax of which was Wolfe's defeat of Montcalm, and was one of the men who did the marine survey of the St. Lawrence River that made it possible for the British ships to go up to the Canadian capital. Afterward, Cook spent several summer seasons in survey work on the coast of Newfoundland and Nova Scotia and also around the islands of St. Pierre and Miquelon before the latter were turned over to France. His charts were standard for a century. As an incidental undertaking he made a careful observation of an eclipse of the sun and communicated the results to the Royal Society. Cook, then, had become a skilled specialist, though his general culture was not conspicuous. He was not, fundamentally, a deep-sea sailor; he was a coastal man. Most explorers were the former. But he was a man whose mind and activity could not be permanently confined by limitations imposed by specialization of any kind. He had potentialities of growth which circumstances could release.

The requisite circumstances appeared when he was chosen to command the "Endeavour" bark on the expedition to the Southwest Pacific. He was not the first choice for the job and not the Royal Society's choice. The Society's choice was Alexander Dalrymple, a man who has come down to us with a disabling reputation as a crackpot. The bait that trapped his not inconsiderable intellect was *Terra Australis Incognita,* of which he was the last great exponent. He was more than that, however; he was also a close student of voyages into the Southwest Pacific (even if he bent the facts to feed his fixation); he was a lucky researcher, for he recovered from the dustbin of history the report of the voyage of Torres through the strait between New Guinea and Australia; and he was a good enough scientist to become first hydrographer to the Royal Navy, after service with the East India Company in the same capacity. He had commanded merchant ships in the East Indies. His trouble was that he insufficiently appreciated the point that geography was a science of facts, not of armchair theories, and he irredeemably spoiled all his significant qualities by a personality that was both highly

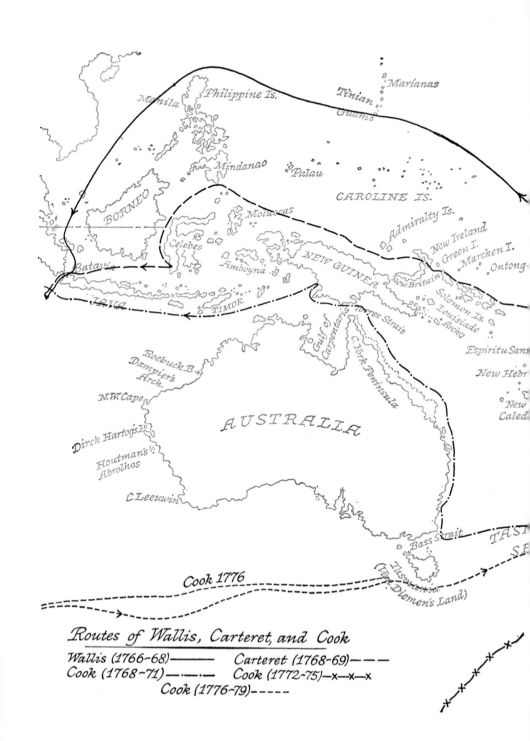

Routes of Wallis, Carteret, and Cook

Wallis (1766-68) ——————   Carteret (1768-69) — — —
Cook (1768-71) —·—·—   Cook (1772-75) —x—x—x
Cook (1776-79) - - - - -

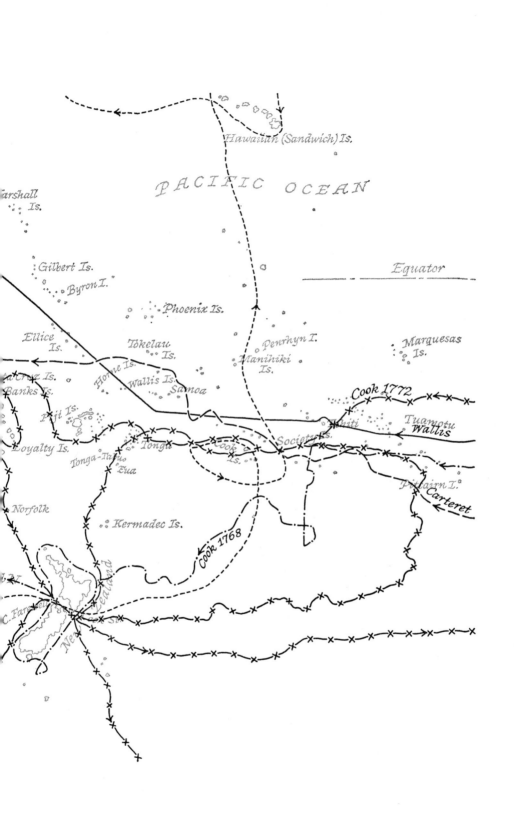

offensive to the public and very immediately offensive to his close associates. This was the man whom the Royal Society put forward. The Royal Navy balked. The Navy men pointed to a flaw in his qualifications: he had not, as the book of rules required, served six years in the Navy. So apparently at the instance of Sir Hugh Palliser the choice fell on Cook, known to the Navy as an excellent marine surveyor and to the Royal Society as something of an astronomer. For the task he was commissioned a lieutenant.

To the contemporaries of the expedition attention was not, however, focused on Cook. His great reputation was made by it and the subsequent voyages. Contemporary interest was in Joseph Banks and Dr. Daniel Carl Solander. Joseph Banks, then a young man of fortune with scientific interests, particularly in botany, was to become the Grand Cham of British science (much after the fashion that his contemporary, Dr. Samuel Johnson, was the Grand Cham of literature), as well as the man whose finger was perpetually in the Australian pie for years after settlement there was first broached. Dr. Solander was a professional botanist, trained under Linnaeus, who was invited to go along by Banks. The Banks party also included other expert assistants, including an artist, Sydney Parkinson. The Royal Society assigned an astronomer with whom Cook was to work both at Tahiti and during the voyage in the determination of longitude, a difficult task before the chronometer came into use. (Cook got a chronometer for his second voyage.) It is thought that Cook's necessarily close association with Banks and the other educated people on board considerably broadened his mind and interests; the voyage was a continuation of his education.

It was in executing his secret instructions that Cook brought imperishable fame to the expedition. The authorities were still interested in the open question of *Terra Australis Incognita* and after finishing the work at Tahiti Cook traversed a considerable area of open ocean seeking it, of course without avail, and then he elected not to attempt a sweep through a larger and more southerly area because of the risk to his now weakened ship. Instead, he chose to elect an alternative open to him and rediscover and examine Tasman's New Zealand. On October 7, 1769, he came to the islands, but on the eastern side, opposite to that seen by Tasman, and in the course of about six months he circumnavigated the group and determined that there was a passage between the two principal islands, now known as Cook Strait. Moreover, he and his people landed at several points, discovered that the language was intelligible to the Tahitian they had with them (thus ascertaining that the New Zealanders were Polynesians), and were impressed by the vigor and fierceness of the inhabitants. The quality of the country they thought good. The charts Cook made were masterly depictions of a land but partly reported hitherto.

His work in New Zealand adjudged to be completed, Cook had the choice between leaving immediately for home via Cape Horn or the Cape of Good Hope, or continuing his explorations. He deliberately chose to attempt to locate that eastern coast of New Holland which had so long eluded travelers. His immediate objective was Tasman's other discovery, Van Diemen's Land. Stormy weather prevented Cook from reaching Tasman's reported land, thus leaving the determination of the exact meaning of that discovery for other and later voyages, and instead he came upon land to the north and west on April 19, 1770. He called the newly discovered country New South Wales. It proved to be the eastern shore of the mainland of New Holland which time would show to be the coast of the economic heartland of the continent. Traveling north Cook spent four months tracing the seaboard to its termination, often in situations of extreme peril, especially after he got into the waters inside the Barrier Reef—the Reef that a few months earlier had kept Bougainville away from the continent. Cook's successful handling of all the problems and disasters he encountered within the Reef is a striking tribute to his consummate seamanship and his power as a leader of men. In meeting the manifold challenges he confronted in turning the geographical unknown into the known and mastered, he showed his full stature, and a considerable part of the perennial fascination of his *Journals* is, in addition to the marvelous story they tell, in the way in which the often laconic entries reveal Cook's growth in stature as a man. He capped his voyage along the coast of New South Wales by discovering a passage through the strait between New Holland and New Guinea—though not Torres' passage. He reached Batavia on October 10, 1770.

Up to this point the voyage had been remarkable for the health of those on board. Cook took a keen and constant interest in the problem of maintaining health at sea, especially in ways and means of combatting scurvy, a vitamin deficiency disease that had reduced many explorers' ships to a shambles of sick, dying, and dead men and was so to reduce many others even after Cook had demonstrated what attention to protective diet could do, and how important, also, it was to keep the ship sanitary and the men clean in person and properly clothed in all weathers. On the first voyage Cook lost no men between England and Batavia by sickness, but Batavia was then a deadly unhealthy port, a killer of men, primitive in public health measures, and there Cook lost seven men to malaria, dysentery, and related diseases and twenty-three more from aftereffects on the journey home, mostly between Batavia and the Cape of Good Hope. He arrived in England on July 13, 1771, and almost immediately was commissioned to lead a second expedition which sailed on July 13, 1772.

D3

The English activities in the Southwest Pacific, challenged by Bougainville, continued to be challenged by the French, and the Spanish took precautionary measures. Even while Cook was still on the coast of New Zealand, a Frenchman, Jean François Marie de Surville, en route to Tahiti (which he never reached) to forestall England's taking possession of the island, was also on the coast and the two passed one another during a storm, but neither saw the other. Surville's venture was a private one, based on Pondicherry in India where he and associates were trying to build a trading enterprise. He entered the Southwest Pacific from the north, via Manila, and because of the desperate condition of his people and his ship by the time he reached New Zealand, he went directly from there to Callao in Peru, in approaching which he was drowned in an accident.

Before Cook set out on his second voyage, another Frenchman was in the Southwest Pacific. This was Marion du Fresne, also a man of private means who financed his own activities. His immediate purpose was to return to Tahiti a native whom Bougainville had taken to France and who had been sent to Mauritius (then in French possession and called Île de France) to be forwarded home when opportunity arose. The native died while Marion was still in the Indian Ocean, but the expedition continued. It arrived on the New Zealand coast on March 25, 1772, after having made a short visit to Van Diemen's Land earlier in the month. Thereupon ensued one of the most tragic dramas of early New Zealand history; while Marion and his men were obtaining supplies from the natives and timber for the repair of the ships and were apparently on the most agreeable terms with the natives, they were set upon and twenty-seven of them, including Marion himself, were killed (and later eaten), for which the surviving Frenchmen took sanguinary vengeance, killing 200 natives. Nevertheless, the country was claimed for France under the name of Austral-France.

The Spanish, for their part, took formal possession of Easter Island —they had much earlier fortified the island of Juan Fernandez, as Carteret had found—and they put Roman Catholic missionaries on Tahiti, only later voluntarily to withdraw them with nothing accomplished. The French voyages showed that the French were determined to keep up competition with the British, but the Spanish activities were mere low-level reflex actions of a dying imperialism. However, the British could not feel that they had finally downed the Spanish claim to comprehensive power in the Pacific Basin until they defeated their pretentions at Nootka Sound, at Vancouver Island, in 1790.

D3

Cook's second voyage, recommended both by Cook himself and by Banks, was chiefly designed to finish the job, well begun, of making sure that *Terra Australis Incognita* did not exist. As long as any considerable body of ocean in the Southern Hemisphere remained unexplored, there the ingenious theoreticians could locate their cherished phantom. When it was understood where Cook had been, that curious process of relocating the elusive land took place, as Cook and Banks foresaw it would. Their own attitude was one of critical skepticism: they did not *know* that the land was a figment of imagination, but they seriously doubted its existence. The only way to resolve the question was to traverse the ocean solitudes. Cook's second voyage was, therefore, chiefly devoted to the exploration of the southern oceans to as near to the South Pole as he could get. His activities among the islands of the Southwest Pacific were to be by way of refreshment between voyages toward Antarctica and to make the best use of time during the bad season in the south.

On this voyage Cook sailed in the "Resolution," and he was accompanied in the "Adventure" by Tobias Furneaux, a competent sailor who had first been in the Pacific with Byron. Although Joseph Banks made elaborate plans to go along, the reconstruction of the superstructure of Cook's ship required to accommodate his party and equipment would have made it unmanageable, so he withdrew and went to Iceland instead. However, he remained on friendly terms with Cook.

The two ships were at the Cape of Good Hope on October 30. Cook knew of the allegedly continental discovery the Frenchman J. B. C. Bouvet de Lozier had made in 1738 in latitude 54° S; he knew, too, of the Spanish discovery of South Georgia, toward South America in the far South Atlantic in 1756; at the Cape he learned that a Frenchman named Yves Joseph de Kerguélen-Trémarec had discovered land far to the south in the Indian Ocean and that another, Marion du Fresne, had also discovered islands (called the Crozets) not too far away from Kerguelen's while on his voyage toward Tahiti.

Cook began his explorations by turning his attention to Bouvet's land and disproved any idea of its continental dimensions without proving how extensive an island it was. He then moved on eastward. On January 17, 1773, the ships crossed the Antarctic Circle a little to the west of what is now called Enderby Land, the first crossing of the circle in history. Here the ice was heavy and menacing. Cook therefore directed the expedition to move northward and eastward until the ships were between the islands of Kerguelen and Marion, but neither group could be found. The expedition then moved southeast to below the sixtieth parallel. At this point the ships parted after appointing a rendezvous in New Zealand. Cook himself continued eastward until the middle of March when the ship was finally directed toward New Zealand.

After refreshing his men for seven weeks at Dusky Sound on the southwest coast of South Island he moved on to the rendezvous with Furneaux at the top of the island. Furneaux had visited Van Diemen's Land and incorrectly concluded it was an integral part of New Holland.

On June 7 the ships went to sea again. In company they ran east between latitudes 41° and 46° S until longitude 133° W was reached, when they turned north. No land of any kind had been seen. They headed for Tahiti which was reached on August 16; the ships remained there about a month. They then turned west and a little south, picked up but did not visit what today are called the Cook Islands, and then rediscovered in turn Eua and Tongatabu in the Tonga group, originally found by Tasman long before. Sailing from there after a very pleasant visit, the ships returned to New Zealand, off the coast of which they parted in a storm never again to be reunited on the voyage. Cook prepared to return to the antarctic region.

Early in his new trip to the south Cook reached 67° 31′ S, beyond the point he had reached earlier in the voyage, and at the end of January he penetrated to 71° 10′ S on longitude 106° 54′ W, where he was stopped by solid ice, an achievement not to be matched for fifty years. It so happened that Cook made this extraordinary southward penetration at a point where the continental coast of Antarctica bends far to the south. He was actually considerably farther south than Palmer Peninsula, the most northerly extension of the continent, to the east. Following this stupendous achievement Cook turned north and east to try to locate the alleged continent of Juan Fernández. It proved to be mythical, like so much else by way of land Cook had had to seek, and, after a visit to Roggeveen's Easter Island, the ship sailed once more to Tahiti. By pursuing a course around to the north of the island, Cook came upon the Marquesas, unseen since Mendaña discovered them on his second voyage, and finally reached Tahiti on April 22.

Sailing on June 4 Cook set out to find Quirós' Australia del Espiritu Santo. Along the way he saw several small islands and revisited Tongatabu. He came on the islands he was seeking on July 16 and set about making a survey of the group, which he named the New Hebrides. Hitherto his South Sea contacts had been with Polynesians; here he first met

Melanesians, and his prejudice, like that of most subsequent visitors, was in favor of the former. On August 25 he found the harbor at which Quirós had played out his strange drama of settlement and abandonment of settlement. Turning back to New Zealand, Cook came on New Caledonia from the north, but had to go on without making a complete survey and, still New Zealand-bound, discovered Norfolk Island on October 10. He reached Queen Charlotte's Sound in New Zealand eight days later.

As the final phase of his task of circumnavigating the world in the far southern oceans—and of making the first circumnavigation ever in an easterly direction—Cook resolved to go straight toward South America along latitudes 54° and 55° and then to examine the far south Atlantic on his way to the Cape. He found no land on the first phase of his journey, passed Cape Horn on December 28, and early in January 1775 began his Atlantic Ocean work. He dropped down to 58° 9′ S long enough to disprove one of Dalrymple's fancies that there was continental land thereabouts, turned north and on January 14, came upon South Georgia and, toward the end of the month, the Sandwich group of islands. (The South Georgia discovery was actually a rediscovery of land reported in 1756.) His next and final concern was to try again to find the land Bouvet de Lozier had reported. In this he failed, so he was at the Cape on March 22 and home again on July 30. He had been away for a little over three years and had so far solved the vitamin problem that not one man had died of scurvy. *Terra Australis Incognita* as conceived by speculative geographers was no more—it now passed to the keeping of the historians of human error—but in a third voyage Cook was to tackle that other snare of the geographical imagination, the northwest passage. Meanwhile, he was appointed post captain, elected to the Royal Society for his work on scurvy, and was granted an administrative sinecure at the Greenwich Hospital for naval pensioners.

The quest for a northwest passage was now suddenly urgent again to the British, as their trade with China was on the increase and a shortening of the voyage between England and China (normally made via the Cape of Good Hope) would be highly desirable. Earlier attempts to find a passage had stopped in Hudson's Bay in Canada in the previous century. No way out of the Bay to the west coast of North America had been found. The Hudson's Bay Company's people had been in the vicinity of the Bay since 1670 and one of them, Samuel Hearn, had recently traveled west from the Bay and then north until he reached the Arctic Ocean, a route which required him to meet with and cross any outlet. He had met with none. The only remaining possibility was that an ice-free passage could be found from Hudson's Bay or Baffin Bay around the Arctic coast to Bering Strait and thence into the North Pacific. It was resolved to send an expedition to search for this passage from the Pacific end. Cook volunteered to lead it, and on July 12, 1776, he sailed in the "Resolution." The companion ship, the "Discovery," left on August 1. A rendezvous was made at the Cape of Good Hope.

The ships sailed from the Cape on November 30 and after determining the nature of the sub-antarctic islands discovered by Marion du Fresne and Kerguélen, touched at Van Diemen's Land (without questioning Furneaux's conclusion that it was part of the continent) and by mid-February were in New Zealand. After a fortnight there the ships moved on to the Tongan Islands among which two months were spent, after which they went to Tahiti, where they arrived on August 12. They finally left for the North Pacific on December 7. Much of Cook's time on this visit to the islands was given over to observations of native customs and the results add great and important substance to his *Journals*. Once away from Tahiti, Cook soon passed out of the area with which we are primarily concerned, but as earlier transactions in the North Pacific have been recounted because of their bearing upon the South, so what Captain Cook did in the North must here be briefly sketched. In due course the northwest coast of North America and the North Pacific Ocean became centers of economic interest to men whose ships passed to and fro through the Southwest Pacific on outward and homeward voyages, and on both occasions they customarily engaged in activities important to the history of the area.

On his northward journey Cook chanced upon Christmas Island, first seen earlier by a Spanish voyager, on December 25 and then on January 18, 1778, discovered the Hawaiian Islands. Although it was long rumored that the Spaniards had discovered these islands as far back as 1527, or alternatively in 1555, it is now generally conceded that the honor belongs to Cook. Spanish traffic in the North Pacific was chiefly confined to the tracks of the ships traveling from Manila to Acapulco, and none seems ever to have gotten as far north as Hawaii. On the other hand, the Russians, active on both the Asiatic and American sides of the North Pacific, had not gotten so far south. But Cook was not primarily concerned with idyllic islands. He was commissioned to work north along the coast from Sir Francis Drake's New Albion into the Bering Sea and Strait in an attempt to reach Hudson's or Baffin Bay. Therefore, by March 7 he was off the North American coast along the shore of what is now the state of Oregon. The Spanish had been this far north and a little farther, and the Russians were at the time working southward from Alaska. Cook was now to fill up the gap between them. He was shortly at Nootka Sound, a place about a decade hence to acquire large symbolic significance in Pacific history. As the ships moved north it was found that the principal articles offered in trade were furs, and Cook's report of this advertised the economic potential of the area. In late May and through June the ships were among the Aleutian Islands. During July Cook followed the coast northward toward Bering Strait and on August 9 he reached Cape Prince of Wales, the westernmost point of North America. The next day he landed across the way in Asia. Crossing to the American side again, he pushed on to reach latitude 70° 44′ N, his farthest point north, where he was stopped by impenetrable ice. Turning south, he coasted along the shore of Asia a while, shifted over to North America, and for three weeks occupied an anchorage at Unalaska in the Aleutians. Here he was visited by the chief Russian trader of the district, and Cook's men visited the Russian settlement.

On October 16 the ships left for Hawaii to recruit, and after some adventures they came to anchor in Kealakekua Bay. Here Cook was taken for and treated like the god Lono by the natives, but when local food supplies ran low there was some anxiety about how long he was going to stay. Aware of the situation, Cook took his departure on February 4, 1779, but he had not gone far when it was realized that his ship was in urgent need of serious repairs. He therefore resolved to return to Kealakekua Bay in spite of the obvious undesirability of the move. The spirit of the place was very different on his return visit.

Thieving, a conspicuous vice of all the natives of the Pacific islands, and one of which Cook had ample experience, reached new heights and Cook was correspondingly exasperated. When the ship's cutter was stolen he resolved to take hostages against its return, his long-standing practice in recovering articles he felt he simply had to have back. He therefore went ashore accompanied by marines to take his hostages and found the natives in an angry mood, inclined to resist. Cook posted the marines at the water's edge and went forward accompanied by their lieutenant. He was just about to give up his plan and return to the ship when the natives learned that one of their chiefs had been killed by some of Cook's men assigned to blockade the bay's entrance. This incensed them, and as Cook and his companion turned to rejoin the marines and retire to the ship, an assault was made on them. Cook, the lieutenant, and the marines fired on the natives and killed some; in turn, marines were killed; Cook had reached the water's edge safely and had turned to face the natives when he was simultaneously stabbed in the back and struck on the head. He fell face down in the water. The natives dragged his body on shore in triumph, while the surviving marines hastened to get back to the ship, and a shocked hush settled over the scene. Captain James Cook, the god Lono, was dead, February 14, 1779.

With his passing a great and marvelous era in the history of exploration was closed. All that happened after in Pacific exploration was like an epilogue.

D3

It is necessary at this point to change the emphasis and pace. Exploration in the Southwest Pacific has continued actively to our day, lately mostly in Antarctica. But as the eighteenth century drew to a close the emphasis began to shift away from that fascinating activity. New discoveries became incidents within a different historical context—the story of how men of the West carried their political, economic, and cultural heritage into the area and began to build new nations there, handling the resources for livelihood in a fashion vastly different from that of the anciently indigenous inhabitants. The indigenes were, in the process, forced onto the defensive and often to the periphery of the drama, and their survival became problematical for many unhappy decades. Two very different places, the continent of New Holland and the islands of New Zealand, proved especially adaptable to the uses of Western men, and in them they rather quickly built up virile Western-style societies. It is with the building of these that we will chiefly be concerned hereinafter.

PART I
AUSTRALIA

CHAPTER II

The British Foothold

When, on August 18, 1786, Lord Sydney, Secretary of State for Home Affairs in the government of William Pitt the Younger, notified the Lords Commissioners of the Treasury that it was His Majesty's pleasure that they help prepare a fleet of vessels to convey 750 convicts to Botany Bay in New Holland, he was putting into execution a plan for solving a vexing domestic problem by making a limited use of the territory of New South Wales discovered by Captain Cook sixteen years earlier. The plan was to set up a principal penal colony—an open-air jail—on the coast and a subsidiary colony on an outlying island.

The pressing domestic problem that required this course for its solution was the large number of convicts under sentence of transportation out of the kingdom who had accumulated in the "hulks" (old ships, anchored and converted into jails) on the River Thames and elsewhere. They had accumulated at this time because they could no longer be sent to the North American colonies.

The sentence of transportation, on the law books since the sixteenth century and periodically revised, required the rapid removal of the condemned out of the country. The "hulks" had been utilized only as temporary places of confinement while a sufficient number of convicts to make a shipload had been accumulated, or until the demand for them from contractors cleared them away. Lately, it had been difficult to get them away to their traditional destination.

For years it had been the practice to sell the government's property right in the labor of the convicts under sentence of transportation to contractors, who thereupon took them to the American colonies along with free persons who had indentured themselves (i.e., pledged their labor for a specified period in payment for a passage) and sold the labor right to the colonists at a profit. At one time or another this traffic fed cheap labor—only a cut above slave labor—into all the North American colonies, but the most capacious receptacles had proved to be the plantation settlements, notably Maryland, Virginia, and the West Indies.

Long before the American Revolution—as far back as 1670—the continental Americans had on occasion objected to the convict element in this labor supply and had sought by law either to limit it by insisting that the convicts be precisely identified or stigmatized or to eliminate it altogether. The British government had ignored the protests. All that the colonists were able to do to stem the flow was to refuse to buy the labor right to known convicts; and in doing this they had considerably spoiled the market for transportees before the Revolution broke out. The traffic nevertheless continued up to the Revolution, and the British government attempted to resume it after hostilities had ceased. It was quickly found, however, that the market for convict labor was poorer than ever, not only in the independent United States but also in the loyal West Indian and Canadian colonies. However, some convicts were "sold" in Maryland after the Revolution, and what appears to have been the last lot dispatched to the United States was landed at Fisher's Island in Long Island Sound in 1788. These people had left England *after* the convict colony at Botany Bay had actually been established. In that same year, however, the Continental Congress passed a resolution that "it be and it is hereby recommended to the several states to pass proper laws for preventing the transportation of convicted malefactors from foreign countries into the United States." The advice was taken, the traffic ceased, but it is worth noting that the legal obstacle was erected about two years after the king had designated an alternative outlet in British territory. On the record, it was a shrinking market for convicts in America, coupled with the cessation of the traffic during the Revolution, that turned the mind of the British government to alternative outlets, not the formal barring of transportees from the United States.

The persistence of the British authorities in continuing transportation in the nineteenth century is sometimes contrasted unfavorably with their early acceptance of the abolition of slavery, but it should be kept in mind that British social morality on the point was not out of line with that of other nations. Transportation was an ancient practice, known to the Greeks, which was continued into the nineteenth century by Spain, Portugal, France, Sweden, Holland, Denmark, Peru, Ecuador, Chile, and, most famously of all, czarist Russia. The system naturally differed considerably from one country to another, and much has properly been made of the cruelties and horrors of the British system, notably in regard to the passage to the land of exile and the severe discipline visited upon the transportees, especially the recidivists. The story of it is unquestionably an ugly passage in British history, but that the system was uglier than contemporary systems has never been established. The British system has simply received far more publicity both during its course and since. The worst that can be said about it—and this was often said during its continuance both by those operating it and by its critics—is that it was closely akin to slavery and had much the same moral impact on the receiving society as slavery. It was particularly macabre in that the slaves were, with rare exceptions, of the same race and nationality (unless the Irish are taken as a separate nationality) as the oppressors. Some American writers, notably Frederick Law Olmsted, were aware of the analogy between Southern Negro slavery and conditions in Australia. Oddly, however, no foreigner was ever moved to make as close a first-hand study of the British system as an American, the elder George Kennan, made of the Russian system as it was in the middle 1880's; and no victim of the system ever wrote so effectively about it as Feodor Dostoevski did of the Russian system in *The House of the Dead*.

The problem to which Lord Sydney addressed himself had been under discussion from 1779, long before it was absolutely clear that convicts could never again be sent to America. In that year a committee under Sir Charles Bunbury considered it, heard of the declining market from the principal contractor trading to Maryland and Virginia, and also heard of Botany Bay as a possible alternative from Sir Joseph Banks. Banks stated that the location met two prescribed requirements: it was very remote and escape from it would be difficult; and it was fertile enough to make self-support likely at an early date after original settlement. The first point was apparently suggested by the frequency with which transported convicts got back to England from America, the second by the government's obvious wish to solve its problem as cheaply as possible. A self-supporting jail was a shining desideratum. Banks underestimated the ingenuity of the convicts and overestimated the immediate fruitfulness of Australia's soil.

During the seven years that followed before a firm decision in favor of Botany Bay was finally made, the questions of what to do with the transportees and what to do about New South Wales were periodically canvassed by legislators, officials, and private citizens. The discussion introduced an element of confusion into the subsequent history of the colony which took a long time to dissipate. On the one hand the idea of a penal colony persisted while on the other hand the idea of allowing free settlers to proceed to New South Wales was introduced. It was suggested that New South Wales be made available to the American Loyalists as a new home, notably by James Maria Matra, one of the breed, born in New York and with Cook on his first voyage. However, the government moved too slowly and the Loyalists, insofar as they stayed in North America, either settled down in the United States or emigrated to Canada and formed a nucleus of a richly landed Tory group in Nova Scotia, New Brunswick, and Upper Canada, with fascinating political results later on. If Matra's idea, which enjoyed the support of Banks, had been followed, Botany Bay might have started out as a colony of free men with convicts playing much the role they had played in North America. Official opinion, however, was biased against this. The British official mind at that time was not favorably disposed toward "settlement" colonies, for the American colonies were of that description—and look what had happened! Rather, opinion favored the kind of colony represented by the West Indies, India, and the East, in which economic and political domination of a large and energetic indigenous, or an imported bond, population was characteristic, and the profit was worked out in lucrative trade on mercantilist principles. Canada, of course, was a settlement colony, at least prospectively, but it was not then very warmly cherished. The idea that settlement colonies inevitably grew to independence, thus making them dubious assets of an imperium, was variously expressed by British political thinkers even after the problems raised in ruling them had found a brilliant solution.

The king's ministers were not in the 1780's interested in the kind of expansion of empire that a new settlement colony in New South Wales would represent. They were interested, narrowly, in a cheap solution of a fundamentally domestic problem in penology. Lord Sydney's letter announced clearly and unmistakably that the government was going to found a *penal* colony, not a settlement colony, and a penal colony only. That is how the colony was officially regarded for half a century thereafter. Australia was thus not in the beginning thought of as a compensation for the loss of the North American colonies. India and its eastern extensions at Singapore (founded 1819) and Hong Kong (founded 1842) can more accurately be said to have played that role in British thinking of the period. The West Indies were thought far more important than Australia until the free trade policy in the middle of the nineteenth century undermined the sugar industry.

Yet somehow the idea that New South Wales should also receive free settlers would not down; within two years of its founding the governor was pleading for free settlers, and within five years the first of them arrived in the country. Moreover, it was inherent in the system of transportation that it should be a manufactory of free men, even if free men of an embarrassingly ambiguous character. It was assumed that time-expired and pardoned convicts would, on regaining freedom, settle down in the country as farmers. Moreover, it was the law that children born of convict parents in New South Wales be free. The British government seems not to have perceived that in sending out free men, and in "creating" free men there, it was inserting the thin edge of a wedge that would eventually destroy the character of New South Wales as a jail and nothing but a jail. It was proved rather early that a society consisting partly of men and women in penal bondage and partly of those who had never been other than free—or who had attained freedom—could not long be contained within the political and economic machinery of an open-air jail. An important chapter of Australian history, therefore, concerns the emergence of a free society from the contradiction in which the country had been entangled by the king's ministers while suffering one of those fits of absence of mind which allegedly account for so much imperial history.

D3

To command the expedition to Botany Bay and become the founding governor of the settlement, the British government (at the instance of Sir George Rose, Under Secretary of the Treasury) appointed Captain Arthur Phillip, a naval officer then on half pay and living as a gentleman-farmer in Hampshire. The appointment of Phillip occasioned mild surprise, but no opposition. It was not a coveted post he got, but equally it was thought that there was nothing in Phillip's record that made him a logical choice for it. Phillip showed himself entirely adequate to the heavy burdens laid upon him, but, like many another man, had he not had greatness thrust upon him he would have lived out his life in quiet mediocrity. Born in London in 1738 of a German father who was a language teacher and an English mother of a family with naval traditions, Phillip entered the navy at the age of seventeen and rose through the ranks, serving in the Mediterranean, the West Indies, and home waters. From 1774 to 1778 he served in the Portuguese navy during a war with Spain. One oddly prophetic item of this service was the task of transporting 400 Portuguese convicts to Brazil. In 1778 Phillip returned to the British navy and continued in the service until 1784, when he went on half pay. The most notable exploit of the latter period of active service was a voyage to Madras. This was his only journey beyond the Cape of Good Hope before going to New South Wales. There was obviously nothing brilliant about this record, but there was some evidence of comfortable competence and—more—that Phillip was a sound example of an eighteenth-century seagoing Englishman. One would not be too surprised to come upon a man of his type in a novel by Tobias Smollett, serving as an example of a *brave homme* of the officer class.

All that was solid and sound in him came out early and late in his work at "Botany Bay" (as the Australian settlement was long popularly known), from his appointment to his retirement. Somewhere along the way he had picked up the kind of knowledge useful to a founding governor. The correspondence he conducted with the various authorities concerned with the preparations showed that he wanted everything ship-shape and in a decent relation to the task ahead. He did not succeed in enforcing his views. Neither with regard to people nor equipment were his sound ideas fully met. The contractors, at that time thoroughly devoted to cheating the government, apparently thought, insofar as they reflected at all, in terms of a six-week passage to America at standards considered satisfactory for black slaves. The jail authorities for their part did not think in terms of supplying convicts prospectively useful in founding a colony, but rather of clearing the overcrowded hulks. The equipment supplied was hardly calculated to make building and farming easy. Phillip tried hard to improve matters, but could not fundamentally change the situation. It is in his letters of request and complaint that one first finds the evidence of his competence for the task set him. The wonder is that a man so well aware of the handicaps being imposed upon him should have persevered with the task. His salary of £1,000 a year—raised from the original allotment of £500—hardly seems an adequate inducement to go on.

The first fleet for Botany Bay sailed from Plymouth on May 13, 1787. It consisted of a warship, HMS "Sirius" 500 tons, converted from a ship built in 1781 (this was Phillip's own ship), an armed tender of 170 tons, the HMS "Supply," six transports: the "Alexander" 452 tons, the "Lady Penrhyn" 333 tons, the "Charlotte" 335 tons, the "Scarborough" 430 tons, the "Friendship" 274 tons, and the "Prince of Wales" 350 tons, and three storeships: the "Fishburn" 378 tons, the "Golden Grove" 375 tons, and the "Barrowdale" 275 tons. All the ships were loaded to full capacity, but it is still a matter of doubt exactly how many people were aboard at sailing, how many died on the voyage, and how many actually landed in New South Wales. A "return" on personnel dated April 15, 1787, gave the following figures: 211 marines (160 of whom were privates), plus 30 wives and 12 children (7 males and 5 females), and 718 convicts of whom 565 were males and 153 females, plus 11 children (6 males and 5 females), a total of 982 persons. Governor Phillip and his suite were additional. A conventional figure for those who debarked in New South Wales is 1024 (which certainly implies an excellently managed voyage), of whom about 700 were convicts, while the balance manned the government at various levels, or were dependents. This is as good a place as any to take notice of the fact that the early history of Australia involved very few people. The population did not pass 50,000 until 1830, and the million mark was not reached until the late 1850's.

Throughout Australian history there has been a persistent disproportion between the size of the population and its accomplishment in mastering what proved to be a puzzling and disconcerting continent, in area about the same size as the United States.

Captain Phillip had his fleet together in Botany Bay on January 20, 1788, eight months after its departure from England. It had traveled to its destination via the Canary Islands, Rio de Janeiro, and the Cape of Good Hope, and at every point, especially the last, it had added commodities, including livestock, for the welfare of the people. Phillip had tried to arrive several days in advance of his companions to make plans for disembarkation, but he actually arrived only forty hours ahead of the others. But Phillip immediately saw that Banks had seriously misdescribed and misevaluated the Bay and its environs; it was obviously no proper place for a settlement. Earlier, while still in England, Phillip had foreseen this possibility and had hinted at an alternative, the harbor slightly to the north—the entrance to which Cook had seen but had not explored. Phillip promptly investigated it and found it ideal. Port Jackson, as it was called, proved to be one of the great natural harbors of the world and one of the most beautiful, ranking with Rio de Janeiro and Naples. By January 26 Phillip had his ships around to the new harbor and on that day the people landed. By February 7 affairs were sufficiently in order for the ceremonies incident to the formal initiation of government to be held. The place was named Sydney, after Lord Sydney.

On January 24 two ships of a French expedition of exploration under Comte de La Pérouse had entered Botany Bay, where they remained until March 10. When the ships were sighted approaching, the first reaction was that they were probably Dutch, sent out to forestall the English occupation of the country. La Pérouse was in the Pacific to explore and to look into the possibilities of whaling and the fur trade. He had left France in 1785 in utter ignorance of British intentions in New South Wales and had no political motive in appearing at Botany Bay when he did. (On the other hand, Phillip had been informed that La Pérouse was in the Pacific.) La Pérouse had entered the Pacific via Cape Horn and immediately proceeded to the fur country on the northwest coast of North America where he did some excellent detailed survey work, had then gone to Manila to recruit, visited the coast of Asia and followed it north to Kamchatka, clearing up some geographical confusions, dropped down to Samoa, and from there had proceeded to Botany Bay to rest his men. When he sailed from Botany Bay his apparent intention was to test a theory of his countryman Buâche as to the location of the long-lost Solomon Islands of Mendaña, but whatever his intentions, he actually sailed away to oblivion. Only after thirty years were authentic relics of the expedition discovered. The mystery of the Solomons was solved in 1792 by La Pérouse's countryman, Bruni d'Entrecasteaux.

Captain Phillip set up a government which was autocratic in character, tempered one way and another by the character of the man temporarily the despot. The scheme was not totalitarian, but rather was so imperfectly devised that the military could, and rather soon did, joust with the governor. Within the colony the governor's authority was in theory very nearly absolute, if he could maintain it, but he was nevertheless subject to instructions from the Secretary of State for War and Colonies—an official responsible to Parliament—and all his acts were subject to review and approval by the Secretary. He could be removed from office by the Secretary, with or without explanation. The internal stresses and strains created by contention between some of the military and the governor, especially after the former acquired economic roots in the country, produced passages of history unhappy and spectacular. The governor nevertheless held in his hands the executive and legislative powers, and he had also much influence over the judicial machinery.

It was a nice question how far the military was within the governor's ambit of authority and how far the military was a voluntarily co-operating co-ordinate power. The disputes between the two authorities, often incredibly trivial not to say idiotic in the general circumstances of the settlement though usually deadly serious in inner meaning, eventually came to a focus in the courts, which from the beginning could only function with the co-operation of the military. The courts became the forums for the politico-economic disputes in the absence of alternative places, such as legislative bodies and newspapers, in which to air and settle opinion and power clashes. When free settlers of substance appeared and allied themselves with the dissident military, the confusion was naturally more confounded. The first "solution" was to refurbish the despotic powers of the governor, but in the long run the British authorities were forced to take steps to bring government more into line with the practice of the home country.

The excuse for this experiment in autocracy was that the settlement was a jail. In law, as it happened, it was nevertheless largely illegal. The power exercised was in theory derived from the king, but the king by this time had no right to grant such power. He had had the right in the seventeenth century when American colonies were autocratically ruled, but it had passed to Parliament toward the end of that century. The government set up in Australia by Pitt's associates was not sanctioned by Parliament. Of course, the stresses and strains between the governor and the military men and their allies had little to do in their origins with the point about the legality of the governor's authority. That point was first made by lawyers. In the earliest days the government was run without lawyers, but when they were introduced to "assist" in operating the machinery of government, they soon turned upon the governors the weapons of their profession, largely to escape from the effects of the autocracy and to provide a firm foundation on which to found challenges to specific measures he had taken or wished to take. The club the lawyers uncovered was handed to dissident Radicals and Whigs for their use on the Tory governments of the time. The most celebrated of those who picked up the club were the redoubtable Jeremy Bentham, always a critic of transportation as a punishment—he favored incarceration in penitentiaries at home—who took up the point about the illegality of the governor's powers as early as 1803; Sir Samuel Romilly, the criminal law reformer; William Wilberforce, the antislavery spokesman; and H. G. Bennett, an ambitious but not too brilliant Radical politician.

As a matter of fact, neither the general public nor the parliamentarians, speaking generally, were much interested in New South Wales for some years after its founding; not until 1812 did a parliamentary group attempt an investigation of its affairs and this effort was largely ignored by the secretary, probably because it was a frustrate performance handicapped by inability to gain access to full and up-to-date information. It was not until circa 1820–25 that reasonably full information about New South Wales was freely available in England. Up to that period even parliamentarians chiefly relied upon ex parte statements contained in letters from participants in the interminable quarrels with the governors. By that time, however, the fundamental question could be intelligently asked: "Is this place to be a jail or a colony in which free men can have the rights of Englishmen?"

For the convicts the argument in all its various phases was academic, except insofar as they might expect to achieve freedom by conditional or full pardon or by serving out a sentence. It was upon them that the weight of the jail rested most heavily. During the continuance of the system, 160,000 convicts were sent to Australia and any generalized statements about what manner of men, women, and children—for women and children were transported—they were, cannot fail to be to a certain degree imprecise. Not only did they vary widely in character at particular moments in the six decades they were sent to eastern Australia and the two decades after when they were sent to western Australia, but as social conditions and law changed in Britain, so the character of the whole body of convicts sent abroad changed.

It is a historical fact that the criminal code of England in the late eighteenth and early nineteenth centuries was incredibly severe, and many crimes were then punished by transportation which at a later time would have drawn but a short sentence in a local penitentiary. Moreover, the vexed question of the relation of poverty and crime—for terrible poverty was rife in Britain during practically all the years of transportation to Australia—must be faced and the guilt of those driven to crime by utter poverty somehow evaluated. Were fundamentally decent but poor people driven to crime in considerable numbers in those decades? Did they leaven the criminal lump? Australian writers are inclined to answer "Yes." There is also the problem of weighting the importance to the population of transportees of those guilty of political crimes in causes long since won and those guilty of what criminologists now call "white collar crimes," such as forgery. The political transportees were, against the total group, relatively few but notably conspicuous by reason of the attention paid to them contemporaneously and historically. The Scotch, the Irish, the English, and the Canadians all contributed political transportees whose cases have a place in the political histories of that time. Many of them were very fractious prisoners, though most of them conformed to the discipline to which they were subjected; and the "politicals" managed some, but not all, of the more spectacular escapes, occasionally with the assistance of American ships. Several of the "white collar" transportees contributed notably to Australian life, and this has led to attempts at minimizing their lapses from strict observance of the law of the time. Exercises in classifying the convicts according to schemes which mitigate or "explain away" their criminality have been very common and widely and sympathetically received in Australia for a good many years, but they have mostly been fairly desperate efforts to wash out the "birthstain" of pioneer criminality, to eliminate by ex post facto argument the "shame" Australians have felt about the distressing circumstance that their history began in a jail.

The cold, hard fact is that the majority of the transportees during the entire period of transportation were professional criminals of the cities and towns, mostly of working-class origin, or *lumpen proletarians,* highly various as to trades, or practicing no trade at all. The larger part of the rest were of rural origin, though not always farm laborers, the small balance being white collar offenders and political prisoners. The crime for which most of the adults and children of England, Scotland, Wales, and Ireland (for Ireland contributed heavily to the stream from 1791) were transported to Australia was theft or some other offense against property rights. There was justice in the contemporary impression that Botany Bay was a "thief colony." This was a period in British history when— of the Lockean trinity of life, liberty, and property—life and liberty were recklessly sacrificed to the protection of property. (The Irish constituted about one-third of all the convicts, the numbers sent annually suddenly multiplying about four times during the famine of 1845; and as one would suppose from the character of Anglo-Irish relations circa 1790 to circa 1865, there was a steady Irish contribution to the minority of political prisoners.) A significant portion of the transportees are known to have been recidivists in the homeland, as one might guess from the fact that the criminal element heavily predominated; as time passed cases of men sentenced to transportation a second or even a third time appeared, and some of these were colorful persons indeed. The worst disciplinary excesses were, however, visited on transportees who committed crimes within the convict colonies. A terrible tradition of execution for crime was early established in Australia. The first man executed lost his life for stealing thirty days after the colony was founded.

Most of the people transported were sentenced for seven years (the minimum for transportation); fourteen years appears to have been fairly common, while "for the term of your natural life" was the least common. The idea was that once they were bundled off to Botany Bay, they were out of England for good, no matter how long the actual sentence. It was assumed in the beginning that escape during sentence was impossible, but this idea soon proved false and escapees rapidly dispersed over the Pacific islands, including Hawaii, to India, to the east coast of America, and back to England. Two convict women (but no convict men) established the precedent of escape by getting away on La Pérouse's ships in March 1788. No official assistance was given to time-expired convicts to go back to England, but they did return. What the prisoners experienced will be looked at later on. The gist of the matter is that, while the system was designed to be condignly punitive, to later judgment punishment was all too commonly far in excess of the crime. The idea of reformation of the condemned was always there, but it was all too often drowned in a sea of punitive measures administered by men always stern and self-righteous and sometimes sadistic; and one of the nastiest of the early political arguments turned on whether or not rehabilitation was, after all, morally possible. The prevailing view of the time was that reform by harsh punishment was possible, by kindness it was an appalling improbability. There was more than a hint that it was then believed by many that a disposition to crime was hereditary. The convict era was, without a doubt, nasty and brutish. Fortunately, it was relatively short.

D3

Governor Phillip's fundamental task during the five years he spent in the colony was to fend off starvation. The firm discipline he imposed was designed to support that struggle. Phillip's role resembled that of Captain John Smith in Virginia in getting men to work that they might eat. Phillip was a man of Smith's quality, two centuries after. Instead of a couple of years, as forecast, it took at least sixteen before the colony became anything like self-supporting and a severe drought could even then endanger self-sufficiency in the basic essentials. Supplies from outside were, in the beginning, absolutely required for survival, and their nonarrival from England confronted the people with utter disaster. Voyages for food were early made to the Cape of Good Hope (via Cape Horn and around the world because of lack of knowledge of winds and currents to travel directly west to Africa), Batavia in the Dutch Indies, and India. Some food was obtained in the islands—salt pork from Tahiti, for example. The early diet of the convicts and their keepers alike resembled that characteristic at the time on shipboard: salt meat, especially pork, and wheaten flour were basic ingredients, with rice and vegetables added when available. This diet was obviously lacking in a sufficiency of the protective foods with which Captain Cook had experimented. It was probably also deficient in vitamin C. The caloric intake sank below 2,000 per day for considerable periods. The bad diet reduced the convicts' energy and thus impeded progress toward a better condition.

The energies of the convicts, such as they were, were directed toward building and agriculture, but the limitations on their powers in building were less important than they were in farming, particularly since there were no persons among them or their masters who were skilled at it. Phillip was a gentleman-farmer, not a practical farmer. The convicts were organized into gangs under a superintendent—the first superintendent being a free man from Phillip's own household—with the task of raising food on government farms for the public stores. The environment was utterly different from that of England, and in addition to learning farming they had to learn how to farm in Australia. The aborigines offered no hints; they were not agriculturalists but food-gatherers, and what they gathered, aside from some animals, birds, and fish, all in limited quantities, was of small use to Europeans. What was of use was never more than a minor supplement to supplies. The incoming Europeans had to bring into the country all the economic plants and animals they needed for their subsistence. Australia offered but minor bits and pieces; the aborigines, with dietary practices far below European tolerance, could survive and even thrive, but Europeans could not do so from indigenous resources.

The convicts and their masters had trouble finding soil that was at all promising, for at the point of settlement the land was obviously sterile.

They finally located some at Parramatta, about 15 miles away, and in 1789 located still better country on the banks of the Hawkesbury River, even farther from the principal settlement. They had to learn, too, how to cope with the erratic rainfall and early experienced that great Australian menace, drought. It took over a decade to work up to the use of the plow, chiefly because of the roughness of the fields and the absence of draft animals: horses and bullocks. (A few plows were brought out by the first fleet.) Early farming in Australia was therefore a hoe-culture, a matter of scratching the ground between the stumps of recently felled trees. In the absence of animal manure or mineral fertilizers, it was also a soil-mining operation. Vegetables grew quite well, but it took a good while to get supply and need into a reasonable relation. The earliest success in cereals was with maize, the Indian corn of the Americas, and then wheat. The settlement began with but a limited supply of livestock— 136 animals of all kinds, 74 of which were pigs—and it was several years before slaughtering for consumption was permitted.

Early in February 1788 Phillip dispatched part of his people, under the charge of Philip Gidley King, to Norfolk Island (five miles long, three wide, 800-odd miles east of Sydney), according to plan. This settlement was a little more successful than the one on the mainland in achieving a measure of self-support. Later on, in a moment of desperation, Phillip assigned convicts to the island in numbers sufficient to give it just about as many people as the mainland colony. They pulled through.

In spite of periodic bouts of a near-starvation diet and the recurrent threat of complete exhaustion of supplies—the month of April was usually the hardest of the year to get through—Phillip retained an optimism about the future which it is often difficult to relate to the objective facts he confronted. He had an unshakable conviction that New South Wales was a country which would give rich returns once its peculiarities were mastered, and he was confident that they could be mastered, perhaps not by convicts, but certainly if free men were sent out to lead the way. He asked that some free farmers be sent out, but none arrived in his time. He had to make do with the human materials at hand.

The first person to set up as an independent farmer was a time-expired convict named James Ruse. Ruse's undertaking was in accordance with the scheme in the minds of the British authorities who envisaged the Botany Bay colony. They laid it down that time-expired convicts who elected to stay in the colony, those granted pardon on condition that they stayed in the country, and those granted full pardon who elected to stay— the three groups eventually to be known collectively as the "emancipists"—were to be granted thirty acres of land—ten more if married, and ten for each child—for farming. Apparently, the idea was that these people would become *peasant* farmers whose limited surplus would find its market at the public stores, supplementing the produce from the convict-manned government farms. Thus would the jail become more self-supporting. It proved impossible to confine the people of New South Wales within this pattern and the struggle to find another caused trouble.

Meanwhile, Phillip's difficulties were multiplied by the arrival of more convicts in the second and third fleets. The harbinger of the second fleet was "Lady Juliana," which arrived at Port Jackson on June 3, 1790, with 222 female convicts, described as mostly streetwalkers. Skepticism about the virtue of the women convicts was for years endemic in New South Wales. The ordinary presumption was that they were whores. The sex life of the convicts, female and male, was stated to be lurid indeed, and their example allegedly infected the soldiers and settlers to a degree that was adjudged scandalous. The "Lady Juliana" brought the news that a storeship, the "Guardian," due at Port Jackson the previous February, had struck an iceberg east of the Cape of Good Hope and while the ship was salvaged, only a fraction of her cargo was in a condition to be forwarded from the Cape. Phillip thus got more convicts at a time when he was without the food the home authorities assumed he had received. On June 20 the four ships of the second fleet, only one of which was a storeship, arrived. The three convict carriers brought in 930 male and 78 female convicts and 109 members of a new military guard called the New South Wales Corps, together with thirty wives and children. This corps was a fateful acquisition indeed. The second fleet was perhaps the worst managed example of convict-carrying of all; the people arrived in a perfectly appalling condition. A captain of the corps wrote that "the slave trade is merciful compared to what I have seen in this fleet." Not only were the convicts crowded but their quarters were not properly ventilated, the captains held back food to increase their profits, and cooking arrangements for what food was issued were bad. Discipline was merciless, punishments inhuman. Over a quarter of the convicts embarked in England died on the voyage and of the thousand-odd landed almost half were sick, commonly of scurvy or dysentery, and a quarter of these died within a few days. Phillip's complaints about this calculated inhumanity led to reforms, but it took years for a sound system of ship management to be worked out. A major contribution to this end was eventually made by the emancipist doctor, William Redfern. Even though Phillip managed the visitation of the second fleet as wisely as any man could have under the circumstances, it is no wonder that there was famine again in April 1791.

And then on July 9, 1791, the third fleet began to arrive. It was to consist of nine ships on which were over 2,000 convicts, perhaps 300 of them women. The ships came in at intervals from July to October. The HMS "Gorgon," which arrived in September, brought only a few convicts but a number of very useful civil officers and many official papers, including a formal authorization of conditional and unconditional emancipation by the governor. Then in April 1792 the annual food crisis inevitably occurred. In June, however, the arrival of the storeship "Britannia" signalized (as appeared ex post facto) the beginning of the end of recurrent famine. Supplies thereafter came forward more regularly. And in November a new element was injected into the situation when the first foreign trading ship put into Port Jackson, the "Philadelphia" of Philadelphia in the United States. It made its visit on speculation, suggested to the captain by a conversation with Philip Gidley King at the Cape of Good Hope the previous year. From the visitor Phillip bought salt beef, pitch, and tar.

The new military organization, the New South Wales Corps, was not complete until the arrival of its commander, Major Francis Grose, on the ship "Pitt," a convict carrier in very bad order, on February 14, 1792. The marines, replaced by the corps, had created difficulties for Phillip from the beginning, chiefly about the ways in which their services could legitimately be employed but also by being insubordinate and "tumultuous," largely because of boredom and resentment at such a distasteful assignment. The corps to replace the marines was especially recruited in England, supplemented by marines willing to remain in New South Wales and even a few emancipists. Grose had had the management of recruiting. He had served in the American war at Bunker Hill and elsewhere and, having been wounded, had been invalided home. Much has been written about the poor quality of the men recruited and of the officers also, and certainly some of them were shabby and soiled individuals, but others were men of ability, and some continued to obtain promotion after service in the penal colony. The most forceful indictment of them is the role some of them essayed to play in New South Wales, that of using the country as the nabobs had used India: as a place in which to get rich quick, notably through private trading (a practice forbidden men in official positions in India by Lord Cornwallis in 1786). These soldiers were unscrupulous as to means, though perhaps no more so than their Indian counterparts; but what they did was the more reprehensible in that they did it while wearing the king's uniform. As it turned out, their plans were facilitated by the fact that their commander, like the marine commander before him, was also commissioned lieutenant governor.

On December 11, 1792, Governor Phillip sailed for England, a sick man but not a disillusioned one. Shortly after his arrival home, he resigned his governorship and resumed his naval career. Once again he showed himself comfortably mediocre, but he rose in rank until he became Admiral of the Blue in 1814. That same year he died at Bath, his passing clouded by the rumor that he had committed suicide. He was one of the few men who ever enhanced his reputation by service as governor of New South Wales in the "earlies." Above all he had left the colony securely founded, and that was neither a mean feat nor one ever likely to be forgotten by posterity.

D3

Major Francis Grose succeeded Phillip in office and continued in the place until December 1794 when he too left for England because his old wounds were bothering him. He was in turn succeeded by Lieutenant Colonel William Paterson, second in command of the corps who, in his turn, went on sick leave to England on the arrival of the next regularly appointed governor, John Hunter. Hunter arrived on September 11, 1795. Civil and military authority were thus combined for about three years, between the departure of Phillip and the arrival of Hunter. What happened in that interval deeply influenced the course of events for the ensuing thirty years.

The corps had shown its intentions even before Phillip left the colony. On their arrival the officers who had traveled in the "Pitt" had offered for sale trade goods they had brought with them on speculation. They knew demand exceeded supply by a good margin and asked and obtained high prices. Apparently, on the strength of this success the officers then banded together to hire the "Britannia" to go to the Cape for a cargo of goods. Phillip pointed out to them that this was a violation of the rights of the East India Company which held a trading monopoly covering the entire Pacific basin. However, the soldiers persisted and the scheme was successfully carried through. This was the beginning of that wing of the officers' economic "system" which eventually did great damage to the community; this was the beginning of their effective monopoly of the import trade. (The export trade was at this time entirely insignificant.) The other wing of the structure they built was their adventure in landholding and agriculture. Under Phillip commissioned officers were not able to get land grants; they were assigned plots for "subsistence" and that was all. Noncommissioned officers and privates, on the other hand, were allowed grants. The commissioned officers of the New South Wales Corps early began to campaign for grants and shortly they were authorized. This opened the way to large-scale farming by the officers. To provide the necessary labor power, Grose assigned convicts to them, reducing the numbers employed on government farms to do so, but continuing to feed and clothe them from government stores. This in effect was a subsidy of £20 per annum per convict assigned, aside from the worth of the work performed.

Thus, the officers were launched into what was at the place and time large-scale agriculture. They were soon the principal producers. At the same time the small producers, almost all emancipists, continued to increase in numbers. But there was only one market in the colony, the government store. The officers, therefore, became chief suppliers to the government store. They were paid with receipts of the storekeeper which, in the absence of a regular money supply, served as a local currency. Periodically, the receipts could be consolidated into bills on London. The officers were, of course, in a strategic position to gather up the lion's share of these bills. These they used to maintain their stranglehold over imports, for which bills were the principal means of payment. Controlling imports, and in a position to command monopoly prices, they could exploit the small producers who had to obtain their supplies from them. The officers were wholesalers of the imports, but they effectively controlled the retail trade as sole suppliers. Many of the goods available at Sydney were brought in by American vessels (until the War of 1812) en route to the Northwest coast or China, for they could ignore the prohibition of trade by the East India Company which the London merchants, for their part, could not afford to overlook.

The situation was worsened when it was discovered that there was a very active market for "rum" (a term which appears not only to have covered rum per se—mostly of inferior grade—but all high-proof intoxicants then commonly in circulation). This was not unexpected if it is kept in mind that the eighteenth century in England was a time of hard-drinking, which Hogarth, Rowlandson, and their fellows vividly depicted, and that drinking debauches were especially fancied by the class of men and women who made up the convict and emancipist populations—though it was not they who justified the locution, "drunk as a lord." With the arrival of the third fleet, "rum" in quantity was conspicuous among the imports from England and it was also conspicuous among the goods brought from India and those sold at Sydney by the American traders. In the absence of an effective currency, it was one of the commodities which was "bartered." As an import, its price was readily inflated. The combination of its high price, the monopolization of the supply by a small group, and the association of that group with the system of exploitation the corps patronized and participated in, led to the identification of the system with rum. An understandable exaggeration of its significance in the economy led to the historical myth that rum was the explanation of all that was evil in New South Wales from circa 1792 well into the 1820's. Actually, the period, or part of it, is better understood as a time of rather crude and unscrupulous profit-taking and capital accumulation by a strategically placed minority. In three years the "system" was firmly enough founded to last about a decade and a half, coming to a climax in an episode known (again that symbolism) as the Rum Rebellion, after it had begun its slow retreat under the effective challenge of competitive capitalists of a different background. Oddly, it was later inadvertently but completely destroyed by its principal architect.

This was John Macarthur, as fateful a figure as has ever trod the stage of history in Australia and one to whom Shakespeare's words do not apply, for both the good and the evil he did lived after him. Indeed, historians have shown a rather stronger disposition to blame him for the harm he did than to understand his creative accomplishments. It is not too clear that he himself knew one from the other, in which he resembles the pioneer entrepreneurs of industrialism in England and the United States. Macarthur's field was agriculture, his great contribution was to pastoralism, and his economic attitude was that of a parvenu capitalist. In government he favored a landed oligarchy of himself and a very few like-minded friends, tempered by personal anarchy. He firmly believed that what was good for John Macarthur was good for New South Wales.

Macarthur was born in England in 1767 of a family of Scottish origin. His father was a dealer in army clothing and his brothers were naval and marine officers. The family could pretend to some gentility, but it had very little money. He himself elected an army career and at fifteen obtained an ensign's commission in a regiment recruited for service in the War of the American Revolution. This regiment never saw service, and Macarthur went on half pay, during which period he married rather above himself. His first effort at any army career after marriage seems to have been directed toward gaining a chance to serve in India, perhaps to take advantage of the opportunities which made nabobs, but since this did not work out he obtained a commission in the New South Wales Corps in June 1789. His rank was that of lieutenant, and he was twenty-two; subsequently he was promoted to captain. He arrived at Sydney in the "Scarborough" of the second fleet in 1790, but he had sailed in the "Neptune" of the same fleet, transferring in midocean because of a violent quarrel with the captain of the "Neptune." This forecast one aspect of his subsequent career: he was a fantastically quarrelsome man in an era when the British were a very quarrelsome people, and verbal and physical violence were freely used in defence of something called "honor," a quality which in practice was often a perverted *amour propre.*

Macarthur even managed to quarrel with the mild and magnanimous Governor Phillip. His personality was authoritarian. He was a skilled manipulator of men, whom he mostly assessed to be fools or rogues or both, and those he could not manipulate he set about to smash. Unquestionably he was neurotically irritable (he ended his life insane), but he had enormous energy, considerable powers of mind, notable pertinacity in carrying out plans (including malignant ones), a steady eye for the main economic chance, and striking insight into Australia's potentialities.

His positive abilities were little employed in strictly military affairs. The general direction of his interests was indicated by the fact that he was the prime mover behind the plan for chartering the "Britannia" for private trading and by the fact that he got one of the earliest land grants (100 acres) made to officers by Major Grose. It was he who seized the opportunity provided by Phillip's departure to bilk the civil power and consolidate all power in the hands of the military, at the same time contriving an economic base for the military power which it had hitherto totally lacked. He and certain of his fellow officers made it almost impossible for civilians to survive in any important economic way without tacit tolerance of, or active collaboration in, the new order of things. He and his associates did their job so well that what under Phillip had been a weak dissident element in an autocracy in which the balance of power rested with the governor, became so strong that it was able to challenge and defeat three successive governors before the British authorities bothered to ascertain the point of the situation and send out a man fitted to reassert the governor's power against the oligarchy Macarthur had contrived.

CHAPTER III

Search for a Viable Economy

The three governors who wrestled with and were defeated by the curious system Macarthur and his cohorts had created were John Hunter (1795–1800), Philip Gidley King (1800–1806), both of whom had arrived in New South Wales with the first fleet, and William Bligh (1806–8), then already imperishably associated with the mutiny of the "Bounty." All three, like Phillip before them, were acquaintances and correspondents of Sir Joseph Banks; and Bligh was appointed to office on Sir Joseph's insistent recommendation. One reason that it was possible for three governors in sequence to founder without the British government paying any significant heed was that during these years Britain's thoughts and energies were concentrated on the struggle with Napoleon. What went on in New South Wales was of very little importance.

Thus, when Hunter, an amiable man and an excellent naval officer, applied for the governorship, it was given to him, but when his administration burst into a blaze of emotional and vindictive charges and countercharges, it was easier to set aside the tedious task of ascertaining the rights and wrongs of the situation, recall Hunter, and send out King, a stronger personality; and when King got into difficulties similar to those of Hunter, to recall King and send out Bligh. Until 1812, it should be remembered, there was no well-organized Colonial Office to deal with such matters, and, in wartime, nobody was particularly interested in doing so. Hunter had but an imperfect understanding of what needed to be done and effectively bungled his own well-meant scheme. King attacked the misuse of subsidized convict labor with some success in an effort to stop public support of convicts in private employment and tried also to distribute the convict labor more fairly among claimants. He tried price control on the rum trade and attacked the monopoly of imported trade goods by introducing government imports, only to spoil his efforts by snarling them in red type. Bligh followed up King's schemes and attempted some moves of his own.

The essence of the trouble was consistently the same: the dissident entrepreneurs, usually with Macarthur in the lead, challenged the authority of the governor. This crowd was able to get rid of Hunter and King by some dirty infighting, but Bligh was a man of very different character and he forced a spectacular showdown. Like his principal opponent, Macarthur, Bligh was also an authoritarian personality; his authoritarianism was that of the quarterdeck—he expected his orders to be obeyed with alacrity; when he was "bucked" he blustered. His task in New South Wales, like that of Hunter and King, was to reassert the authority of the governor. A conspicuous part of the task was to break up the trading monopoly, including the traffic in rum, at which Hunter and King had both hacked in their times. Bligh also tried to improve the position of the small farmers, in his day concentrated along the Hawkesbury River. Inevitably, Bligh collided with Macarthur who, equally authoritarian, was always able to trick out a defense of private power and privilege as a defense of freedom against tyranny and to carry with him the military and civilians who were convinced, or could be deluded into believing, that their interests were identical with his. The collisions, mostly in the courts, between these two oddly similar personalities, exacerbated by tactlessness on Bligh's part toward all and sundry who did not respond in a lively enough fashion to his often ill-advised orders, led step by fatal step to armed rebellion. The military arrested and deposed Bligh on January 26, 1808, just twenty years after the founding of the settlement, in an action which has come down in history as the Rum Rebellion. Lieutenant Colonel George Johnston took over the government and was succeeded in turn by Colonel Joseph Foveaux and Lieutenant Colonel William Paterson. These men administered the settlement until the arrival of Bligh's successor, Governor Lachlan Macquarie, at the beginning of 1810.

D3

The period from the departure of Phillip to the arrival of Macquarie was one of very slow progress. In 1792 the total population of New South Wales was 3100 of whom eight out of ten were convicts; in 1809 the population was over 11,000 of whom perhaps three out of ten were convicts. The explanation for the declining proportion of convicts was not the immigration of free settlers, but the fact that transportation slackened during the Napoleonic wars. Once they were concluded in 1815 convicts were again transported in numbers and became about four out of ten of the population. Only a very few free immigrants had arrived up to 1810—probably not more than three to four hundred outside of soldiers and civil officials, of whom almost all were well-to-do. The nonconvict population was at that time largely emancipist. The ingredients of the society were (1) the tiny minority of free people who had never known any other condition, some former military men like Macarthur, who had resigned from the corps in 1804, (2) the native-born, in all cases, regardless of parentage, born free (the first generation of this group was just coming of age when Macquarie took office), (3) the emancipists, consisting of time-expired convicts (also called expirees) and holders of conditional and full pardons, (4) the ticket-of-leave people who were convicts but were at large on probation and responsible for their own support (often men of superior education or social status or both), and (5) the convicts actually in bondage.

Probably the best index of actual economic progress was the acreage under cultivation. In 1797—after the military oligarchs had made their initial efforts—Governor Hunter reported the figures as follows: wheat 3361 acres, corn 1527 acres, barley 26 acres, potatoes 11 acres, and vines 8 acres. Vegetables were grown in garden plots and a variety of temperate and tropical climate fruits in small orchards. Wheat had by then displaced maize as the principal grain crop. Production by individual cultivators exceeded that on the government's farms. By 1808, when the Rum Rebellion had been consummated, the position was: wheat 6874 acres, corn 3389 acres, barley 544 acres, oats 92 acres, peas and beans 100 acres, potatoes 301 acres, turnips 13 acres, orchards 546 acres, and flax and hemp 37 acres, with garden plots of vegetables additional. After a burst of enthusiasm for crop agriculture, especially wheat-growing, during which they reached a maximum production of over half of all that was produced, partly by sharply reducing public production, the officers turned their energies chiefly to trade, where the profits were greater, and in Macquarie's time, to his disgust, used much of their land for the grazing of cattle and sheep. (King and Bligh had opposed pastoral developments; King, Bligh, and Macquarie all had their eyes and policies fixed on cropgrowing on small and moderate-size farms.) As the interest of the officer-entrepreneurs in cropgrowing faded, the small farmers became responsible for the greater part of the annual crop. Most of these were emancipists. In Macquarie's time an emancipist farmer was thought to be doing about what could be expected if he netted £60 a year. Macquarie's opinion that the emancipists were the principal support of the economy of the country was thus related to his policy of favoring crop agriculture.

However they used their land, the officers were for a time the most important landowners. In 1803, for example, whereas 35 officers (now a mixture of military and civil officers) held 18,412 acres, of which the largest individual holding was 3400 acres, 548 small holders had only

24,965 acres, about half of them having but 20 acres each. One objective of the officers was to aggregate as much land as possible. They acquired small farms by foreclosure of mortgages, thus bringing into their possession cleared land, the most valuable kind. The proportion of land owned by the small group of officers reached a peak at 42 per cent and then began to decline. This is probably an indication that their grip on the economy was loosening as competitive capitalists became established; and it seems likely that the Rum Rebellion was in a sense a last ditch effort of the officer group to maintain itself, rather than a demonstration of its indisputable power. Nor did the shift in landownership mean the end of large holdings. Actually, the new land economy that began to emerge in Macquarie's time required broad acres for its efficient functioning, and crop agriculture itself was in due course found to function best on large acreages, not small holdings. But in its initial phase, the land problem in Australia was a matter of large holders versus small holders in a struggle in which land was a fundamental element of economic power. The land problem was to prove a durable item in Australian history.

D3

As these early phases of Australian history involved few people, so the action took place on a very confined stage. Practically nothing was known about the continent when settlement was first undertaken. Its exact size and shape were both unknown; it was not even certain that it was a continent—possibly it was a collection of islands; and nobody had surveyed all the coasts by close circumnavigation. As pointed out, Phillip had to ascertain for himself the character of Port Jackson before locating the initial settlement there. That Van Diemen's Land was an island was not known, for Cook had accepted Furneaux's report that no strait separating it from the mainland existed. What the interior contained was a total mystery. When Phillip left for England the people's knowledge of the country was of an area only about fifty miles from Sydney in any direction, in spite of fairly persistent explorations, begun by Phillip himself and called "excursions." The discovery of the Hawkesbury River, on the banks of which the colony's first "breadbasket" developed, was one result of these efforts. A thorough knowledge even of the limited area penetrated was not gained. Early in Phillip's administration some cattle had escaped into "the woods"—the term "bush" came into use later—and they and their progeny were not found until late in 1795, though the pasture was quite close to Sydney. West seemed the logical direction in which to proceed, but progress in that direction was blocked by rugged and complex, though not very high, mountains which long proved impossible to cross. The dominant motive for inland exploration was nevertheless early established: it was and long remained a search for economically useful land—new, "good" country—farther out.

By sea the record of exploration was more impressive. Up to 1795, however, the coast had been little examined save immediately to the north and south of Port Jackson. In that year the celebrated navigator, Matthew Flinders, arrived at Sydney with Governor Hunter. Joining forces with George Bass, a ship's surgeon, Flinders found or made time to undertake explorations. The partners began by closely examining a river flowing into Botany Bay and went on, at a later date, to explore a harbor that had been observed south of the Bay, eventually called Port Hacking. Late in 1797 circumstances made it possible for Bass, working alone, to lead an expedition to settle a point of long standing: Was there, or was there not, a strait separating the mainland and Van Diemen's Land? In January 1798 Bass and his party established the existence of the strait. It was given the explorer's name. In October of that same year Bass and Flinders joined forces again, this time to make the first circumnavigation of Van Diemen's Land, completed in January 1799. After this Bass turned his attention to commercial voyages of a speculative nature in the islands and shortly disappeared utterly on a voyage to South America.

Flinders for his part went to England and, with the assistance of Sir Joseph Banks, obtained a small ship to carry on his coastal explorations in New Holland. He also got married. Arriving at Cape Leeuwin from England early in December 1801, he proceeded eastward along the southern coast making detailed surveys as he went. While off the mainland coast in the vicinity of Kangaroo Island on April 8, 1802, Flinders encountered the ships of Nicholas Baudin, a French explorer, who was on a voyage authorized by Napoleon to complete the earlier work of La Pérouse and D'Entrecasteaux. From this encounter, its ramifications, and the subsequent fate of Flinders arose the story that Napoleon was bent on seizing a portion of New Holland as a site for a colony, a conclusion given some color of reality when the French published a map designating the coast Baudin had surveyed Terre Napoleon and giving French names to features Flinders had first surveyed. At the time, however, Flinders and Baudin had some agreeable conversations, and Flinders recognized Baudin's priority in surveying the coast a good distance to the east of their point of meeting—until, indeed, he overlapped with the discoveries made by James Grant in December 1800 while on the first voyage from England to Sydney via Bass Strait. While examining the coast Grant had traveled, Flinders chanced on what was soon called Port Phillip, today the port of Melbourne, and was briefly under the impression that he had made an original discovery. However, Port Phillip had actually been discovered in the previous January by John Murray while following up Grant's work from Sydney. Flinders reached Sydney on May 9, 1802. He had further discussions with Baudin and his people when they visited Sydney shortly afterward.

In July Flinders traveled northward along the coast, surveying as he went, passed through Torres Strait, skirted the shores of the Gulf of Carpentaria, and continued on until he had circumnavigated the continent, reaching Sydney again on June 9, 1803. This was the first true circumnavigation, for Tasman had rounded the continent too far to sea for it really to count.

Flinders' vessel was now worn out, so he was provided a passage to England to get a new one, but the ship was wrecked about 700 miles north of Sydney. Returning to that port by small boat, Flinders was given a vessel of twenty-nine tons for his trip to England and again he started out north around New Holland. His ship was leaky and to make repairs he put in at Île de France (Mauritius), then a French possession. There he was made a prisoner of war and was detained until 1810, when he was released (partly because of Sir Joseph Banks's representations to the French), only to die in 1814 at the age of forty. (He left his wife, and a small daughter who became the mother of Flinders Petrie [1853–1942], the celebrated Egyptologist.) Flinders was considered second in ability and enterprise only to Cook among the explorers who worked on the Australian coast in the "earlies"; and there is no doubt that he was one of the most attractive personalities of his time in New South Wales. He it was who proposed that the continent, the coasts of which he had so closely studied, be called "Australia." However, the Admiralty opposed the idea and would not even allow Flinders to call the narrative of his discoveries "Voyage to Australia," so he had to use *Voyage to Terra Australis*. New Holland continued to be the official name for the continent for some years after Flinders' proposal of Australia, with New South Wales the name of the portion under the authority of the British governors.

D3

It was suspicion of what the French might do in New Holland, stimulated by Baudin's activities and the nervousness of the British authorities in India about French activities any place east of the Cape of Good Hope, that led to the establishment of the first new settlements after Sydney, its satellites, and Norfolk Island. The initiative was taken by Governor King about the middle of 1803 when he sent Lieutenant John Bowen,

R.N., temporarily at Sydney and a volunteer for colonial service, with about fifty people to establish a settlement in Van Diemen's Land at Risdon Cove on the Derwent River. The following year this settlement was abandoned—its brief history was one of turbulence that forecast failure—when another and larger establishment was planted at Hobart on the same river. The latter came about rather fortuitously, but it proved to be of immense importance in the early history of Australia. Lieutenant Colonel David Collins was a marine who had been loyal to Governor Phillip in the disputes with the military. He had continued at Sydney until 1796 when he returned to England. Late in 1802 the British government decided to establish a convict settlement at the newly discovered Port Phillip, and Collins was offered command of it with the rank of lieutenant governor. (King at Sydney, to be Collins' superior, had no knowledge of this until much later.) Collins arrived at Port Phillip with 300 convicts and a marine guard on October 9, 1803, but circumstances prevented him from locating or occupying a suitable site for a settlement there and he was given permission by Governor King to transfer to Van Diemen's Land. There he occupied the site of Hobart on February 20, 1804, and on August 9 the Risdon Cove settlement was amalgamated with Collins' establishment. Collins' settlement started out well, but suffered from neglect during its early years.

A third settlement in Van Diemen's Land was made at Port Dalrymple in November 1804. This was done at the direction of Governor King acting on specific orders from Britain. The officer in charge was Lieutenant Colonel William Paterson, commander of the New South Wales Corps and lieutenant governor of New South Wales. This settlement took root and eventually grew, after curious vicissitudes marked by migrations in pursuit of a suitable site for a town, into the present city of Launceston. Early in 1807 an overland route from Paterson's settlement to Hobart was opened. This raised the question of the desirability of combining the two settlements under one government, a project not carried out until 1812, when Governor Macquarie (acting on instructions) made the settlement at Port Dalrymple a dependency of Hobart. The new government thus controlled the whole island. It was headed by a lieutenant governor subordinate to the governor of New South Wales.

D3

Lachlan Macquarie, a slightly Anglicized Scotsman, was forty-eight years old when he arrived in New South Wales as governor. He was an example of a type that became common after the union of Scotland and England in 1707; he was one of those Scotsmen who made careers helping to run the British Empire. He had joined the army at sixteen and had served in Nova Scotia, Jamaica, India—longer there than anywhere else—Egypt, and Ceylon. He had visited China. His rank at the time of his appointment was lieutenant colonel. His first wife had died in China, but he had remarried and was accompanied by his second wife to Sydney. By training authoritarian after the military manner, Macquarie was by disposition paternalistic, after a Scottish laird's manner, ordinarily sympathetic and kindly, rather lacking in imagination, and humorless to a degree. He was generally recognized to be a gentleman, even by those in New South Wales whose joy in life was to scourge governors. He prized order. He liked pomp and ceremony and insisted upon it as it attached to his position. As an executive he was quick and decisive, although quite capable of departing from the book of rules, even after he himself had made the rules; or he could stick by rules even after the secretary in London had disapproved them. In most of his conceptions he was highly conventional, but he was not without ideas and when he got hold of any, he stayed with them through thick and thin. He soon had ideas about New South Wales.

He was a second choice for the governorship. His commanding officer was the first choice and Macquarie was to go along as commander of the troops, but his senior fell sick, and the choice devolved upon Macquarie. The determination of the government was to send a soldier as governor—all the other governors had been sailors—and to send with him troops loyal to him. The New South Wales Corps was at long last to be recalled. Many of the corpsmen elected to stay in the settlement or were soon drawn back to it by their economic interests, but as a military unit the corps ceased to be.

Macquarie's first tasks were to re-establish legitimacy by restoring Bligh to office for a brief period and to pacify the turbulent people. These things he did easily enough—acquiring mixed feelings about Bligh as a man—for Johnston and Macarthur were in England. Johnston stood trial, was found guilty of mutiny, and was cashiered; Macarthur, equally guilty but a civilian, was thought sufficiently punished by detention in England. He did not get back to New South Wales until 1816. His very competent wife Elizabeth managed his affairs while he was absent.

In Macquarie's time the population of the Australian settlements reached 30,000 (1820), but if there were more people and proportionately more acres of land were occupied than earlier, neither the pattern of the government nor of the economy changed markedly. In effect, an economic skeleton in existence at the beginning of his regime was progressively fleshed out. Actually, and most unfortunately, Macquarie turned a cold eye on the men and activities that were destined to provide the country with a truly dynamic and viable economy, and he also betrayed confusion about changes in the structure of government that would have adjusted it best to changing circumstances. Essentially, what Macquarie tried to do was to guide into being as best he knew how a society that would stay within the confines of a jail but which would nevertheless allow careers for those emancipists who appeared to have been sufficiently reformed by their experience of bondage to live rewarding lives. Socially these men were to be recognized and rewarded by admittance to the dining table at Government House, traditionally a powerful cachet of respectability; politically they were to be available for appointment as civil magistrates and to other important posts within the autocracy; and economically they were to find fortune—some indeed did—in agriculture, commerce, banking, and the professions. The trouble was that Macquarie's program for the emancipists provoked the opposition of many of the most powerful free settlers and the economy he favored was not dynamic enough to satisfy the aspirations and needs of the energetic people of any of the cliques and classes.

In seeking a secure future in society for the emancipists, Macquarie precipitated with those who opposed his program a quarrel that ramified in every direction. In the end one could hardly find a question of public policy in which it did not figure. The opposition was called the "exclusives" or the "exclusionists." They held that any man who had ever been a convict was tainted for life. Nothing he could do would eliminate the taint. It was often implied, indeed, that he passed the taint to his descendants. The exclusives were therefore opposed to meeting emancipists socially, as at the governor's table, or to allowing them to serve the government in judicial or other capacities that impinged significantly upon the determination of law or policy—they *could* be clerks, or surveyors, or constables, or artists, etc.—or to their assuming or being granted rights that would raise them above the level of second-class citizens. In effect, then, the exclusives elected themselves a "ruling circle" of the colony and, since the governor who had actual possession of the machinery of government was following a policy they condemned, they became the governor's opposition. Small a group as they were, they proved very potent, and in the long run were able to bring the governor down. The question posed was not resolved until after Macquarie's time when there emerged public issues about which exclusives and emancipists essentially agreed. Economics and politics conquered malignancy and snobbery.

Macquarie's point of view was that if the exclusives could not accept the terms and conditions of life in New South Wales they could go back where they came from, and anybody knowing them in advance and not prepared to accept them could stay away. Actually, no more than 800 adults of all classes arrived free in the settlement from 1810 to 1820; and at the end of Macquarie's time the free settlers totaled no more than 2000 men, women, and children. The men were mostly men of capital, as Macquarie preferred them to be, but only when they went into agriculture did they really meet with his approval. Many of them were, if the governor's remarks are sound, of the type later called "remittance men," or feckless or disgraced members of good families sent to the colonies to be out of sight. The governor liked these moneyed wastrels rather less than poorer people who were prepared to work hard. Macquarie would probably have had to tolerate more free immigrants had not political conditions in England operated against the establishment of a public policy favoring emigration. Pressure of population—evidenced by widespread poverty—was building up in those years, however, and to relieve it and divert emigration from the United States to British possessions, a change of policy was inevitable. It was to reduce dangerous social pressures that Britain eventually was induced to turn once again to building settlement colonies overseas, first Canada, then South Africa, then Australia, and eventually New Zealand.

As Macquarie favored the emancipists socially, so he regarded them as the men who contributed most economically. This was because they were mostly farmers—some were tradesmen and professional people—and farming was to the governor not only the basic economic activity in the society as he found it but the one that, he felt, should by plan and autocratic cajolery continue to be basic into the future. Yet while production increased in Macquarie's time, it cannot be said that farming was ever in a healthy state. His journals of his tours of the colony are full of complaints about sloppy culture methods, bad rural housing, and generally disgraceful conditions. Australian farming, by Macquarie's notes, was nearly rotten before anybody could consider it ripe. It was not merely that successful farming was difficult in the area occupied, by reason of indifferent soil, erratic rainfall, and inefficient methods of cultivation, but also because the market was too limited to encourage vigorous expansion. The government's store was the principal market, and while a private market was encouraged by Macquarie it did not provide an outlet of sufficient magnitude to justify free expansion of cropgrowing. This point was vigorously made by William Charles Wentworth in his important book published in England in 1819. Wentworth thought—and Macquarie favored this too—that a solution of the problem of a market for grain could be found in distilling, then illegal in

New South Wales, but when distilling was authorized it proved irrelevant. What Macquarie had was a subsistence agricultural economy propped up by imperial expenditures on jail operations.

The fundamental economic need—clearly perceived by John Macarthur—was for a satisfactory export commodity. In the beginning there were no exports from New South Wales and the ships that brought convicts, stores, or merchandise for general sale to the colony had to leave empty. Many, beginning with the first fleet, went to China or India under charter to the East India Company to pick up cargoes for England. (It was because first fleet ships were scheduled for backloading at Canton that the American consul there learned of the plan for a settlement in New South Wales a year before it was actually planted.) Then, for a number of years, exports were a miscellany in relatively small quantities: whale oil and bone, sealskins, timber (mostly of New Zealand origin), and other indigenous commodities of the nearby seas and islands. Some of the whale and seal produce was obtained by colonial enterprisers in colonial vessels, but such activities were of doubtful legality and in any case of less significance than what was accumulated at Sydney by enterprisers working out of British ports. (Actually only a proportion of such produce passed through Sydney; much of it went "home" directly from its place of origin.) The colonials also participated in a trade to China in sandalwood, *bêche-de-mer,* and other minor island produce, but as they could not legally go to China as traders themselves, much of the produce reached Canton in American vessels. But the legal obstacles in the way of a colonial export trade were of less importance than the absence of a really satisfactory export commodity, or a combination of several, which would allow of a real impact on the British market. Moreover, by 1813 the East India Company's monopoly in the Pacific, by then considerably compromised, was finally abolished, and although the China monopoly continued to 1834, the China trade was never any more than a useful minor market for New South Wales.

To break out of the confines of their limping economy the enterprisers needed an export in active and constantly expanding demand in England, an export as important as tobacco had proved to be in insuring viable settlement in Virginia. By a series of experimental moves, Macarthur arrived at the export commodity that was not only to solve a temporary economic difficulty but which was also to serve as the basic Australian export far into the twentieth century. This was fine wool. Woolgrowing, however, did not rescue Macquarie's agricultural economy manned by emancipists within the confines of a jail system, but rather came to serve as the basis of a free economy manned by free capitalists working within the global economy as it focused on Britain during the nineteenth and twentieth centuries.

Macarthur was not, of course, the only man of his time to experiment with sheep. Among the contemporary experimenters were the Reverend Samuel Marsden, William Cox, and others, but these others were either interested in sheep for meat or as dual purpose animals, whereas Macarthur rather singlemindedly concentrated on the fleece. He had the singular good fortune in this quest to obtain from their importers (who had brought them from the Cape of Good Hope) some Spanish merinos, the finest wool sheep of the time. By selective breeding Macarthur arrived at an animal wonderfully adapted to Australian conditions which produced good wool. And not only did he attend to the production of a good fleece, he also paid special attention to the technique of "classing" the fleeces, packing them for shipment, and marketing the wool in England. In the latter undertaking he was favored, once the quality of his wool was established, by the fact that he was offering a source of supply within the empire for a product then obtained from Spain and the Germanys. Wool was first exported from New South Wales to Britain in 1806 (245 pounds), but it did not become a significant factor in the market until the middle 1820's, after Macquarie had departed. Macarthur conducted his experiments with sheep along with cropgrowing; indeed, his first economic success was as a farmer, but the new industry he pioneered was best conducted on a pastoral basis. It was as a pastoral enterprise that it spread far and wide across country which, when Macarthur began his work, was unknown to man. The first experiments in pasturing animals to feed and fatten on the native grasses of Australia were with cattle, but sheep were soon added. Macquarie regarded the pastoral life as a lazy man's way of earning a living and opposed its development.

It was the need for more land for pastoral purposes, triggered by drought in the occupied area, that led to the solution of the problem of how to cross the Blue Mountains which had fenced the colony in on the narrow coastal plain. The first assault on the mountains was made as early as 1789, but after twenty-three years of intermittent effort, no one had succeeded in crossing them. The difficulty was that no pass leading through them could be found. Then early in 1813 Gregory Blaxland, feeling acutely the need for more grazing land for his stock, persuaded William Charles Wentworth (visiting his father in Sydney from school in England) and Lieutenant William Lawson to join him in an assault on a new principle: they would travel along the ridges. Between May 11 and June 6 they got across and returned by the method suggested. Macquarie immediately sent his assistant surveyor to follow the route and prospect the country on the other side of the mountains. His report was highly favorable and in the second half of 1814 William Cox directed the building of a rough road along the route the explorers had followed. Macquarie himself traveled this road to the new country in 1815 and characteristically viewed the new country as a field for the expansion of agriculture. However, it was the pastoralists who first occupied it, explored its potentialities, and passed beyond it into still newer country. Only in time did Macquarie's farmers get possession and then mostly of those parts they could incorporate into their wheat belt. Pandora's box was opened, but Macquarie did not see what was in it.

Macquarie's great contribution to New South Wales was to impose a certain order on what was inherently a disorderly society. Sometimes his conception of order was beside the mark, as in his heavy emphasis on crop agriculture; sometimes it became trivial and cruel, as when he had a free man lashed for trespassing on the grounds of Government House; sometimes it became slightly comic, as when his passion for naming natural features led him to overemploy his own names, those of his wife and son, and those of features of his native Scotland; and on occasion it got him into serious trouble as when he spent freely on public works while under pressure from England to economize.

He imposed order as an autocrat, and since the autocratic method suited his temperament and he had but a limited understanding of law, he was often guilty of acting illegally. A new Charter of Justice was promulgated in 1814. One consequence of this was the bringing into the administration of men trained in the law—two brothers, Ellis and Jeffrey Hart Bent. These two men, especially the latter, came into conflict with Macquarie over the legality of his actions to the point where, instead of facilitating and improving the administration of justice, they impeded it. The position of the emancipists was at stake, in this case the propriety of allowing emancipist lawyers to practice in the courts, and the governor's legislative powers, more particularly as they involved the collection of money as taxes and fees. The British government was not, however, ready to deal forthrightly with the situation. It recalled the Bents and upheld the governor, though rebuking him. The new appointees—one of whom was the celebrated Barron Field (Charles Lamb's "distant correspondent")—also could not accept as legally trained men the implications of the autocracy, so in the end the issues simply had to be faced. Preliminary to grappling with them a full-scale investigation of the situation in New South Wales was authorized and carried out.

Two considerations seem to have led Macquarie to pursue his public works policy so systematically and diligently against repeated warnings from England that he was going too far. He had a reasonably correct hunch about the immediate and prospective needs of the community, and he was under compulsion to find work for convicts whom the agricultural economy could not absorb. Macquarie tackled and made notable progress with the provision of roads; he was the pioneer of adequate inland transport. He had a passion for building—convict and military barracks, churches, law courts, etc. At Macquarie's direction the earliest buildings were erected that are now regarded as part of Australia's aesthetic inheritance. He delighted in town planning: he tried to straighten out the chaos into which Sydney had fallen after Phillip's original effort at a plan in 1792 and established a sixty-foot width for streets; and he selected sites for and laid out agricultural villages, some of which, alas, failed utterly to materialize. But perhaps as significantly interesting as any contribution he made to order was his patronage of the beginning of private banking in Australia.

The idea that New South Wales needed a bank was suggested to Macquarie before he left England and it was confirmed by his personal study of the banking arrangements at the Cape of Good Hope. When he arrived in Sydney he found a monetary chaos with which, perforce, he had to deal. The situation he confronted was immensely complicated. Several media of exchange were in use simultaneously, including the documents issued by the government in payment for foodstuffs and supplies, arbitrarily valued copper and other metallic coins, not always British, and promissory notes of small denominations, often dishonestly issued and sometimes forged. There was also a good deal of barter— chiefly in wheat and rum. Two systems of evaluation were applied: the media convertible at par into Treasury bills on London (i.e., the documents issued by the government storekeeper) were called *sterling*, those not so convertible were called *colonial currency,* or simply *currency. Currency* was constantly at a fluctuating discount against sterling which was always in short supply. The shortage of sterling was tied up with the absence of exports in quantity and the dependence of expenditures on jail maintenance.

Late in 1816 it was apparent that the situation was out of hand. Macquarie was convinced that only a bank could fundamentally improve matters by allowing the establishment and maintenance of a comprehensive sterling standard. *Currency* should be abolished. But, unfortunately, the secretary of state had forbidden the governor to establish a bank. Macquarie and his legal officers had therefore to find— mistakenly it turned out—a legal basis in his powers as governor which would allow him to do what he wanted to do. A bank was chartered on March 22, 1817, and opened for business on April 8. It was called the Bank of New South Wales, and it has continued to operate to this day in spite of the flaw in its original charter. (The first bank in New South Wales to have a sound, legal charter was established in 1834.) The Bank, unfortunately, did not solve the monetary problem; it was not able to eliminate *currency*. But its success otherwise was fairly reasonable evidence that a capitalistic economy sufficiently vigorous to support a banking institution was in existence.

D3

The inquiry into the state of affairs in New South Wales which was conducted during the latter months of Macquarie's administration was instituted at the suggestion of Earl Bathurst, secretary of state for War and Colonies. It was about this time that the Colonial Office began to take modern shape. The task of inquiry was given to John Thomas Bigge, an Oxford-educated lawyer, thirty-nine years of age, who had been in the imperial service since 1815 as chief justice of Trinidad. Both Bathurst and Bigge were Tories. Bigge's secretary while in Australia was Thomas Hobbes Scott, his brother-in-law, lately graduated from Oxford.

The two men arrived at Sydney on September 25, 1819, on a convict-carrier and sailed for home on February 14, 1821. Between these dates they found time to visit Van Diemen's Land.

Bigge produced three reports, one on the convict establishment, one on the judicial establishment, and the third on agriculture and trade. They were printed between June 1822 and March 1823, after Macquarie had left office, and were well received by Earl Bathurst. Numerous specific recommendations in them had to be carried into execution by Macquarie's successor, Sir Thomas Brisbane. But they were ill received not only by Macquarie, who felt them to be terribly unjust, but by W. C. Wentworth and other knowing observers. Not only was their factual accuracy impeached, but many of the matters discussed were adjudged to be on the level of dirty gossip rather than of high public policy, and the influence of John Macarthur on the reports was regarded as deplorable.

Bigge's reports were certainly not great state papers, but it is difficult to see how they could have been when it is considered that Earl Bathurst had candidly stated his prejudgment of the whole situation in instructing Bigge before he left England. On January 6, 1819, Bathurst wrote Bigge as follows: "You are aware of the causes which first led to the formation of the settlements in New Holland. As they are peculiar in themselves, these settlements cannot be administered with the usual reference to those general principles of colonial policy which are applicable to other foreign possessions of His Majesty. Not having been established with any view to territorial or commercial advantages, they must chiefly be considered as receptacles for offenders. . . . So long as they continue destined by the legislature of the country to these purposes, their growth as colonies must be a secondary consideration, and the leading duty of those to whom their administration is entrusted, will be to keep up in them such a system of just discipline as may render transportation an object of serious apprehension." Thus in effect, Bathurst carefully excluded the possibility that Bigge might report in favor of policies which would encourage the further growth of a free society within the jail society which Bathurst correctly stated was originally intended and which he obviously thought should be perpetuated. Bigge, therefore, was cued to take up a particular point of view, and he did so.

His recommendations were almost uniformly designed to make New South Wales and its dependency Van Diemen's Land better jails; and conversely he attacked policies and practices of Macquarie which by accident or design pointed in a different direction or appeared, consciously or unconsciously, to reflect a different assumption. Bigge sought to make convict discipline harsher, not easier. He attacked Macquarie's policy with regard to emancipists, he thought Macquarie's buildings too elaborate for a jail society, he opposed much liberalization of judicial practices, and in fact most of his policy recommendations were designed to meet Earl Bathurst's prescription that the very idea of transportation should inspire terror in the criminal population of the United Kingdom.

But if in these respects he could play the sedulous ape to Bathurst, he could not completely ignore the fundamental paradox of society in New South Wales. This was the paradox arising from the presence in the country of free men—their freedom variously achieved—engaged in economic activities for private profit and beginning to ask for the social and political privileges of free Britishers as they existed at home and in other colonial communities. Bigge, following the cue given by Macarthur, suggested only minimum concessions; and in the event the British government at first granted only minimum concessions. Recognizing that the situation in New South Wales was in truth anomalous, a sympathetic and perceptive commissioner could have given a far more creative lead than Bigge offered. The development of such a lead was, as we shall see, left to William Charles Wentworth and his political associates.

Bigge was also in difficulties, which he did not resolve, over his perception that the economic future of New South Wales lay in woolgrowing. He owed this insight to John Macarthur, but like Macarthur himself he was blind to the socially explosive implications of such a development. He was sociologically obtuse in believing, as he apparently did, and Macarthur certainly did, that somehow a large pastoral industry could be successfully built up by a few wealthy free men within the confines of a harshly administered jail and a political autocracy. In the very year that Bigge went to New South Wales, Wentworth had given effective notice that this was impossible. He saw that much, even though in some respects he also was a man of blurred vision.

Bathurst and Bigge attempted to settle the future of New South Wales by misconstruing the very factors and forces in existence in 1819–21 which were most instinct with the future. It fell to Sir Thomas Brisbane, Macquarie's successor, to impose the Bathurst-Bigge program on the colony. Brisbane was, however, not a leader or even a strong administrator. He carried out his orders; he was not of a disposition to bring large policy questions into sharp focus. He in effect temporized, leaving to his successors the battle which he must have perceived (for he was an intelligent man) was bound sooner or later to break out.

CHAPTER IV

Toward Continental Occupation (1)

The three decades between the departure of Macquarie in 1821 and the discovery of gold in 1851 were years of great accomplishment. Macarthur's vision of a pastoral economy supplying wool to the British mills was translated into reality on a scale far beyond even his acute sense of its possibilities. As the needs of the pastoralists for virgin grasslands had stimulated the successful crossing of the Blue Mountains, so their need for ever more land "farther out" stimulated further adventures in exploration which opened up vast areas constituting practically all of "economic" Australia. British capital, even if but a small fraction of the total of that which was then flowing overseas, supported the pastoral development. In the old colonies of New South Wales and Van Diemen's Land the convicts provided the bulk of the labor force. At various points around the coast new settlements were made, establishing the outline of a scheme for attacking the most recalcitrant of continents and reducing it to the needs of European mankind. The new colonies were founded by and for free men, and in the older convict colonies the numbers of free men were increased by plan—not only free and "emancipist" capitalists but also free workingmen. It proved the case that a society partly free and partly convict-slave could not long endure; the abolition of transportation to Australia began in its original seat, New South Wales. Nor could the participation of free British subjects in the management of their public affairs be denied: the march toward self-government advanced rapidly and the voice of democracy was heard in the land, though it was strongly deprecated by the ruling pastoral oligarchs. Altogether the record constitutes a striking tribute to the nation-building capacities of the British people.

D₃

From 1786 to 1825 the western boundary of that portion of New Holland which the British claimed under the name of New South Wales was the 135th degree of east longitude, in effect a straight line across the continent from north to south just west of the Gulf of Carpentaria in the north and Spencer Gulf in the south. This claim covered about half the continent. In 1825, incidental to settlement efforts on the north coast, the line was shifted west to the 129th degree. The following year a claim to the continent to the west of the 129th degree was lodged at King George's Sound in the southwest, where a small precautionary penal settlement was being attempted, and in 1829 the claim was reiterated more formally at the mouth of the Swan River preparatory to settlement at that place. In the 1820's, of course, there were vast tracts of territory on the continent about which absolutely nothing was known or which were only in the vaguest sense within the realm of practical knowledge. Two closely related activities began the resolving of this ambiguity: exploration and the founding of new settlements. Exploration was required to spy out the land and make a useful guess about its economic value; settlement, or occupation, was necessary to make the British claim to the vast territory good in international law. Aside from the settlement in the far west beyond the official boundary of New South Wales, and abortive attempts at settlement in the north, the new settlements were within the old territory of New South Wales and when they were set up as colonies, their territories were carved out of New South Wales.

The early inland exploration of Australia was dominated by the problem of the rivers. W. C. Wentworth in 1819 speculated about the existence of a great river flowing through vast stretches of useful country and reaching the sea—where? Once the Blue Mountains had been crossed, this fixation on rivers dominated the activities of the explorers. Slowly it was revealed that the Australian continent was warm, dry, remarkably level over vast stretches, and of prevailingly low elevation. The ultimate implications of this were not immediately understood and but slowly accepted when understood, roughly paralleling the reactions of the Americans to the dry country west of the 100th meridian. More of Australia proved analogous in character to territory in the United States west of the 100th meridian than east of it. Not only was the rainfall low over enormous stretches of country, but it was variable. The early inland explorers quickly passed beyond the twenty-inch rainfall line. They early experienced drought conditions. There could be seasons when vast quantities of water flowed in the river channels; there could be seasons when the channels were dry, or at best pocked with pools of drinkable water at intervals only. The vegetation had adapted to the prevailing climate, and country traversed in a year of good rainfall would have a lush covering, edible by grazing animals, while in a drought year it was discouragingly bare. These things the explorers had to learn, and those who were to occupy the country had to learn how to accept and "live with" them.

The first probings beyond the Blue Mountains took place in what in later wisdom would have been called "good" years. When Macquarie sent G. W. Evans to follow up the Blaxland-Wentworth-Lawson crossing of the mountains, he got a hundred miles beyond their farthest point and found the country excellent. Macquarie then directed that a road be built over the mountains and in May 1815 the town of Bathurst was founded, the first inland town on the continent. From this town, a few days after its founding, Evans left on another exploratory journey which was similarly successful. The rivers encountered held water. The obvious line was to follow them along their courses in the expectation of finding more good country.

The task was begun by John Oxley in 1817. It was his luck to find that the river he had chosen disappeared into what appeared to be an impenetrable swamp, a fact which raised the speculation—ultimately proved false—that somewhere in the interior was a vast lake into which all the rivers drained. What had been uncovered were really certain elements of a very complicated drainage system, the most important on

Some Significant Explorations of AUSTRALIA

Sturt 1830 ×××××××××
Eyre 1841 o—o—o—o—o
Leichhardt 1845 x—x—x—x
Stuart 1862 —.—.—.—
Forrest 1874 — — — — —

the continent, though with a use-potential far less than its complexity seemed to forecast, which eventually reached the sea. The man who discovered the organization of the river system was Charles Sturt, probably the greatest of all the inland explorers of Australia. Sturt began his work in 1828–29, when in a year of drought (deliberately chosen in the hope of finding the swamps dry) he reached the Darling River, only to find it salt. The following year, 1829–30, Sturt again tackled the problem by traveling overland to the Murrumbidgee River (discovered by Charles Throsby in 1821) and putting a boat on the river to follow it to its mouth. This proved an inspired move, for the Murrumbidgee carried him into the Murray (actually discovered higher up a little earlier and differently named) and the Murray carried him to Lake Alexandrina, from which the river drained into the sea by several channels. The lake had been discovered earlier by sealers, but the connection with the river was demonstrated by Sturt. He speculated—and Sir Thomas Mitchell later proved—that the Darling River flowed into the Murray. Thus to Sturt fell the honor of establishing the nature of the principal drainage basin of Australia, the Murrumbidgee-Murray-Darling system, by far the most important riverine resource of the dry continent.

Following this exploit, Sturt was fully occupied with the business of being a settler and public official until 1845–46, when he made a classic and tragic expedition northward of South Australia west of the Darling River in an effort to ascertain the nature of the center of the continent. He swung as far east as he did in order to get around the dry, salt lakes, probed by—among others—Edward J. Eyre, which appeared to block progress directly north. On this occasion Sturt and his companions suffered terrible hardships, for they got into desert country, dry with very high temperatures, and for many months were immobilized at an isolated waterhole, unable to move forward or back. Although Sturt got a considerable distance north, he found nothing at all encouraging. If the interior of Australia contained any "good country," it was not to be sought in the area he covered. Ironically, he traveled along the Barrier Range which, years later, was found to contain fabulous mineral wealth.

Reverting to earlier times, notice must be taken of the exploits of Allan Cunningham, botanical collector sent out by Kew Gardens in London, who, after learning bushcraft, probed to the north from Bathurst and first discovered Pandora's Pass to the Liverpool Plains in 1823 and then the Darling Downs in 1827. In 1828 Cunningham proved that the Darling Downs could be reached from the sea via Moreton Bay. Working south from the limits reached by local explorers like Throsby, the discoverer of the Murrumbidgee River, Hamilton Hume, a native-born bushman, and W. H. Hovell, a sea captain turned pastoralist, made a famous journey from Hume's property on Lake George (near present-day Canberra) across the upper Murray (which they named for Hume, since he first saw it), and on to the coast at Corio Bay, an arm of Port Phillip. These explorations pointed the way from old New South Wales to the areas later to be known as Queensland and Victoria.

Sir Thomas Mitchell, a proud soldier of the Peninsula campaign become a rather contumacious public servant, sought the privilege of leading exploring expeditions for the glory he expected of them, as contrasted with Sturt—of whom he was jealous—whose passion was geographical revelations. Mitchell was a maker of grand traverses. After an abortive journey to the north in 1832, when his food supply failed, he went in 1836 to the Darling River to trace its course and prove or disprove Sturt's hypothesis about its debouchment into the Murray. He did not quite complete the task on this first try, but showed that the country to the east of the Darling, even beyond the twenty-inch rainfall line, was good pastoral country in an ordinary season. The next year, after ascertaining that the Darling *did* join the Murray, he crossed that river and made a sweep southward to the coast, uncovering a pastoral country so rich to his eye that he dubbed it Australia Felix. Mitchell capped his activities as an explorer in 1846 by a long journey north into the west of what was to become Queensland in search of a river that flowed north to the sea. His identification of the river was mistaken, as was shortly proved by another, but he again uncovered vast tracts of potentially useful pastoral country.

The explorers moving north, south, or west from the Sydney-Bathurst axis were often troubled by the roughness of the country but only Cunningham reached "mountains" and these averaged only 3000 feet in height. It was reserved to a Pole, Paul Strzelecki, to locate and name the highest peak in Australia, Mount Kosciusko, 7316 feet. After traveling in the islands and New Zealand, Strzelecki visited Australia in 1839–40 while on a trip around the world collecting "specimens," chiefly geological, for sale at a profit to the museums of Europe. He eventually settled in London and became a British citizen and something of a public figure. After collecting around Sydney, Strzelecki undertook a journey to the south in 1839–40 which carried him into what became Victoria. But his journey differed from others in the same direction in that he kept in the coastal mountains a large part of the way, and this led to the discovery of Kosciusko and to a traverse of Gippsland, a heavily forested region later to be rich farming and grazing country. Strzelecki's journey through Gippsland was important, but he must share credit for uncovering its possibilities with a less romantic figure, Angus McMillan, a hardheaded Scot, who penetrated into (but not through) the area about the same time with the practical purpose of finding pasture for cattle.

The contrasting motivations of Strzelecki and McMillan in wrestling with the problems of traveling in Gippsland can be taken as symbolizing a persistent contrast in motivation of the Australian explorers in general: the scientific motive and the practical motive; and sometimes the two found lodgment in the same person. Sturt as an explorer seems to have been dominated by the scientific motivation, whereas Mitchell was, in terms of results if not basic purpose, of the practical school. He sought "good" pastoral country as much as the solution of geographical puzzles. Moreover, there is another abiding contrast, that between the men who made major traverses of considerable tracts of country and those who pushed back the margin of the unknown by "local" expeditions. By and large the men whose exploits are noticed here are of the former type, but McMillan and Throsby are of the latter. Only in most detailed studies of the opening up of inland Australia do all the Mc-Millans and Throsbys get full credit for their exploits.

Before leaving eastern Australia, notice must be taken of the work of the German, Ludwig Leichhardt, a man whose motivation was scientific (botanical) but who was also moved by a dark, obscure, romantic passion for travel into unexplored country. No bushman, when Australians evaluated explorers in the light of their bushmanship, yet in 1844 he successfully led a party from the Darling Downs northward, west of the coastal mountains, to the base of the Gulf of Carpentaria, and around the Gulf to Port Essington at the top tip of Arnhem Land. His passion for the unknown unappeased by this resounding feat, Leichhardt next planned an expedition to cross the continent east to west through the center. He started out in 1846, but shortly returned frustrated. In 1848 he tried again, this time to disappear utterly from the ken of man and thus to provide one of the abiding mysteries of Australian history. What *was* Leichhardt's fate? Because he was not a Britisher, but rather a proud, mysterious German, the record of his career has ever since been combed over in detail, often with shocking rancor, and if Sturt is the "parfit gentil knight" of Australian exploration, Leichhardt has been the unlucky butt of disapproval, a fate he by no manner of means courted or deserved.

Meanwhile, hardy and daring men were assessing the character of the west of the continent. It was on the northwest coast of this segment of New Holland that Dampier in the late seventeenth century formed his low opinion of the continent and its inhabitants; and the Dutch before him, having touched the coast at many points, had seen nothing that exactly fascinated them. George Vancouver, on his way to the northwest coast of North America had examined King George's Sound in the south of Western Australia in 1791. Flinders had examined the northern, western, and southern coasts on his circumnavigation. The French explorers, notably Bruni d'Entrecasteaux and Baudin had been on the western and northern coasts. But the first reasonably detailed examination was made by Phillip Parker King, son of Governor King of New South Wales, who was already well launched on a career as a scientific officer in the Royal Navy. King was commissioned to follow in the footsteps of Flinders (whom he had known), and since he was a skilled hydrographer his charts were for a long time standard. Between 1817 and 1822 King surveyed the continental coast from Hervey Bay to Torres Strait in the east and from Cape Arnhem to Cape Leeuwin in the north and west, together with other portions not before satisfactorily examined and recorded.

None of these people seem to have thought of what they observed in the west as anything but "geography," and the first seriously to regard it as a possible home for men was Captain James Stirling who arrived in Sydney in 1826 to carry out a necessary errand to the north coast of the continent and, finding the voyage unwise during the rainy season in those parts, proposed that he look at the coast of western Australia between Shark's Bay and Cape Leeuwin with a view to ascertaining if it was fit for settlement. He saw great advantages in a settlement at that position. Stirling was sent to make observations and gave particular attention to the Swan River area. He and his party were at the Swan River in April 1827, and Stirling viewed what he saw with great enthusiasm. His favorable judgment was supported in full measure by the botanist of the party. He forthwith became a confirmed advocate of settlement at the Swan River. Subsequent inland exploration of this portion of western Australia seriously tempered Stirling's optimism. Coming over from South Africa in 1838 and 1839 Captain George Grey, who later became a distinguished proconsul, made two rather profitless explorations to the north of the Swan River, proving it was dry and repellent country, as had all along been understood. The most memorable result was the first discovery of aboriginal rock paintings.

The explorations described, together with the numerous lesser efforts which filled in details, left the greater part of the continent still unknown. However, the great and valuable southeastern segment of the continent formed by a line drawn from Moreton Bay across country to Spencer Gulf was mostly quite well known or its character fairly accurately suspected. This, time was to show, was really the "heart" of the continent as far as its usefulness to man was concerned. It was clear, too, that the southwestern portion of Western Australia had potential economic value. Something was known about the northern coast, though little that was encouraging, but very little was known about what lay behind that coast. Leichhardt had connected the "heart" country with the far north. It remained to connect the "heart" with Stirling's west. This, it turned out, involved crossing some of the most arid and difficult country of the continent along the shores of the Great Australian Bight. The feat was accomplished with incredible fortitude and inspiring heroism almost wholly by a single man, Edward John Eyre, in 1840–41. As an example of sheer courage there is nothing to surpass Eyre's feat in the annals of Australian exploration. But it really only defined a problem which has haunted the Australian people for many a long year: how firmly to attach the western Australian area of good country firmly to the richer parts of the continent in the east. Although on the same land mass as the eastern good country, the intervening desert turned western Australia into a kind of "island." And the desert distances involved emphasized its remote and insular character.

D3

The effective occupation of the continent—the explorers of this period and later times revealed—continues to be the prime task of the Australian people to the present day. What might well be called the politics of occupation is perhaps the most basic politics of all, ramifying obviously into land policy, transport, development, immigration, and many other questions. Begun at Sydney in 1788 and extended to Van Diemen's Land in 1803, the 1820's and 1830's saw the general pattern of attack firmly established, though nobody would be tempted to say that planning played much of a role in the total operation, however well or ill individual moves may have been executed. As a matter of fact, the moves were made rather haphazardly, often with only the most reluctant cooperation of the British government, which appears to have been more anxious to guard the public treasury from expense than to confirm possession of Australia by adventurous settlement.

The earliest moves arose partly out of the necessities of convict discipline and partly from political and economic motivations, to forestall possible competitors. In 1825 a convict settlement was made at Moreton Bay at the site of present-day Brisbane for the reception of transported men convicted of crimes within the colony. The Brisbane River, flowing into Moreton Bay, had been discovered in 1823, first by runaway convicts and shortly after by John Oxley on an official expedition. The British government first approved the establishment at Moreton Bay and then withdrew its approval in favor of private enterprisers, but the New South Wales government persisted in its plan and maintained a convict establishment at Moreton Bay until 1839, when it was abandoned and the area was shortly thrown open to free settlers. The first land sales were held in 1842, but squatters had reached the Darling Downs of Cunningham, inland from the Bay, two years before. Late in 1826 fear of the designs of the French and the Americans (represented by sealers and whalers) on western Australia led to the dispatch of a small military force and a few convicts to establish an outpost on Vancouver's King George's Sound. This effort had but a short and rather miserable history; the settlement was abandoned early in 1831. The area of its location was by then an integral part of the territory of the Swan River colony.

The colony at Swan River, founded in 1829, was the direct consequence of the enthusiasm of Captain Stirling, who was, indeed, the founding governor. He had had the persistence to argue the case for settlement with successive British governments. He had alleged that a settlement at Swan River would be useful in the trade with India and the East Indies, but that argument was deprecated. The effective argument for action was the British fear that the French might, unless the west of Australia was in some fashion occupied, achieve occupation themselves and thus establish a claim, very difficult to rebut, to all of the continent to the west of the 129th parallel. (There was a subsidiary suspicion that the Americans might also take a similar step.) The government therefore ordered the dispatch of a naval vessel from the station at Capetown (under British sovereignty since 1814) to claim (or reclaim) the territory. This task was carried out by Captain Fremantle only a little in advance of the arrival of Governor Stirling and the first settlers from England.

From the bright cloud of optimism on which the settlers rode to Swan River from England, there was a quick descent to harsh and acutely discouraging realities when the people and their possessions were dumped on the shores of the new port, shortly to be named Fremantle. The settlers expected to be granted land in liberal proportion to capital invested, with a generous interpretation of what was relevant capital, on certain conditions as to development of properties within the first ten years. But on their arrival no surveying had been done, and there turned out to be insufficient land available near the river which even to inexperienced eyes looked good, so that excursions far into the bush had to be made to locate more. Claims in some instances were sizable, and it was quickly apparent that some settlers would have to go far afield from the center of settlement and government, at Perth, a few miles upriver from Fremantle. Dispersion, with its inevitable hardships, was absolutely required. Nor were the people properly prepared for their task even when they got land: it was not generally realized that the seasons were the reverse of those in England, few had brought out truly useful equipment, and the need for acclimatization of plants and animals had been overlooked. But what really was discouraging was that the time it would take to get established in the country was grossly underestimated. The settlers mostly expected quick results, and in many instances they expected the work for these results to be done by hired laborers, while they played the role of landed proprietors. The laborers brought out were not a good selection; they quickly perceived that labor was in short supply and exploited the situation to raise wages, and many elected to work for themselves rather than for others. The problem of labor supply was to plague Western Australia for many years. The aborigines proved more troublesome than at any other Australian settlement. Eighteen ships, none larger than 500 tons, arrived from London in 1829, and the flow of people into the colony was greater in 1830, by which time the population was 1800. But when Governor Stirling retired at the end of 1838 there were still fewer than 2000 people all told.

Stirling's accomplishment was securely to found the colony; he did not succeed in making it prosperous, nor was he able to supply a program for rapid development. All told he did a very creditable job and if he became mildly unpopular, it was because he was the victim of the frustrations of the settlers. These could be traced back to Stirling's original overoptimism about the country rather than any gross mismanagement. His successors up to 1850 did not see any very impressive structure raised on the foundations he laid.

At the beginning of 1832 the practice of granting land against capital investment was discontinued and the policy of selling land at a fixed price, progressively raised in the ensuing years, was instituted. The wrangle over land policy, a feature of Australian politics in every colony as we shall see, was thus begun, for like Australian settlers elsewhere, the western Australians dissented from imperial policy, often violently. The people came into the colony to farm, but only a minority found prosperity in farming in the first two decades; it took that long to bring 7500 acres under cultivation. Consistently for many years imports far exceeded exports. The struggle to find profitable exports was comparable to that in New South Wales. The western Australians exported whale oil and bone, sandalwood, native hardwoods, and wool. There was a year in which they exported sandalwood to a higher value than wool. But it was wool that came to be the fundamental reliance. Wool was first a significant export in 1833; by 1850 exports exceeded 300,000 pounds. From the middle 1830's it was recognized that the predictable future of Western Australia lay in the pastoral industry, not in crop agriculture. But the perception was no more made and acted upon with vigor than depression ensued. It was not until 1846 that the colony began once more to revive and go forward, haltingly but forward. In depressed and good times the settlers diagnosed their troubles chiefly in terms of a radically mistaken land policy and the chronic shortage of labor. Nothing much could be done about the land policy by the colonists, but they thought they saw a solution of the labor problem.

The solution was to turn Western Australia into a convict colony. It had been established with specific provision that it be a colony of free men and the convicts at King George's Sound had been sent away for that reason. But hardly had they gone than individuals began to speculate on the uses of convict labor in getting acutely needed public works constructed and perhaps in manning private undertakings as well, not to mention the uses of the money the imperial government would spend on a convict establishment. Early suggestions that convicts be introduced were rejected, but in the late 1840's the idea was viewed with greater favor. As the eastern convict colonies were agitating for the discontinuance of the convict system, Western Australia was becoming more favorably disposed toward it. The year 1846, with economic revival clearly underway, seems to have been the time of decision. The case was put to the imperial government. It was assumed that enough progress had been made in convict management for the worst evils of the system to be avoided. What the imperial authorities proposed was to send out only men who had already undergone a period of punishment in prisons in England or in hulks at Bermuda or Gibraltar, who would land in Western Australia as ticket-of-leave "exiles," subject to close surveillance as to place of residence. In a later statement, the imperial government offered to set up a fund for sending out free settlers to balance the convicts introduced. With some final caveats, the people of Western Australia accepted the situation. On May 1, 1849, Western Australia was designated a place to which the British government could send convicts, and by the end of the year the necessary local legislation was passed. The first transportees arrived June 1, 1850, twenty-one years after the first settlers had landed on the sands at Fremantle harbor.

D3

British activities on the northern coast of the continent—an area of tropical heat, a wet-dry seasonal climatic pattern with unreliable monsoonal rains, the mostly bad soils useful only in patches, and the aboriginals bothersome—were at this time motivated by rivalry with the Dutch. This was the region where Asiatics had been exploiting the fisheries of the coastal waters for an unknown number of centuries, bringing the Australian aborigines into contact with Malayans and Indonesians, with cultural and genetic consequences measurable by latterday anthropologists, where Chinese may possibly have landed while on their voyages toward Africa, and where the Dutch explorers had been active from early in the seventeenth century. Captain Flinders had been on the coast in the early 1800's, and Captain Phillip P. King a little later. In attempting settlement in the 1820's, the English were not thinking of penetrating inland on the continent, but rather of establishing posts from which to harass the Dutch in the East Indies. The activities in northern Australia were related to those of Sir Stamford Raffles, whose galvanizing motive was to advance English commerce to the east of India and strengthen the British position on the road to China. It was Raffles who, during the Napoleonic wars, had taken Java from the Dutch and ruled it until 1816. In the peace settlement the British gave Java back to the Dutch and Raffles went to Sumatra, where he governed from 1818 to 1823, when he once again had to give way to the Dutch. In 1819 he achieved what proved to be the solution of his problem, the establishment of a trading port on Singapore Island at the foot of the Malay Peninsula. But it was not immediately apparent, however, that Singapore *was* the solution.

In 1823, therefore, when a trader to the Indies named Barns suggested that it would be useful to have a base in Australia from which to enter the trade in the Dutch Indies, his reasoning was supported by the East India Company and accepted by the British government. The essence of the scheme was to establish a settlement to which the Malayan trepang fishermen would be attracted, trade with them and cultivate their friendship, and then extend the resulting trade into the islands to the north. About the same time that Barns made his proposal, the government received Captain King's reports. What he had to say supported Barns's proposal, and he pointed to a harbor he had named Port Essington, on the tip of the Coburg Peninsula, the northernmost extension of Arnhem Land (so named by the Dutch in 1623), as the likeliest place for a settlement, although his narrative, published in 1827, made it plain that this was the judgment of a seaman assessing a harbor, not a landman assessing the hinterland.

The British effort was directed at Port Essington, but the first and second tries to form settlements were finally not made there. On the first try, after a look at Port Essington and a failure to find a suitable supply of fresh water, a settlement was made on Apsley Strait, the narrow waterway running between Melville and Bathurst Islands, just to the west of Coburg Peninsula. This was in 1824. The location on Melville Island was west of the 135th degree of east longitude (as indeed was Port Essington), the western boundary of New South Wales; this was the immediate cause for the transfer of that boundary to the 129th parallel in 1825. The settlement, created as a military post and supplied with a labor force of convicts, was anything but a success; the Malayan fishermen did not find their way to it.

It was continued interest in the matter that brought Captain Stirling to Australia. His assigned task was to find a better location for the post and to stand by until the new settlement was securely founded. His choice fell on Raffles Bay (so named by Phillip P. King after Sir Stamford) on the Coburg Peninsula. The settlement was made late in 1827, after Stirling's visit to Swan River. He had evidence that the Malayan fishermen resorted to this bay, but this did not guarantee the success of the settlement. In May 1828 the abandonment of the establishment on Melville Island was ordered, the people and what was salvageable being transferred to Raffles Bay. However, before the year was out the order had been written in London for the abandonment of the Raffles Bay settlement also.

Less than a decade later the effort to establish a settlement on the northern coast was resumed. The will-o'-the-wisp of Eastern trade was still involved, but the immediate motivation was the frustration of French designs. A settlement was at last actually made at Port Essington in 1838. Although this post remained in existence for eleven years, no real effort was ever made to develop the place or its hinterland; it was managed in a very unimaginative fashion strictly as a trading and military post, but it developed no trade and served no obvious military purpose. The only concrete evidence that the French at this time had designs on this part of Australia was the fact that Dumont d'Urville's ships conducted surveys in the vicinity in 1839.

By mid-century, the British had not solved the problem of settlement on the northern coast but they had securely established a pattern of failure which was to stand as a model for some years to come.

D3

Returning now to the progress of settlement in eastern Australia, attention must first be directed to the island of Van Diemen's Land, then to the south of New South Wales, where the colony of Victoria was to emerge, and to South Australia, finally returning to New South Wales for a review of events of significance, not only to the oldest colony, but to the whole of Australia.

Van Diemen's Land was settled from a mixture of motives, but primarily the intention was to establish a new penal colony. But as in New South Wales the situation was early complicated by the appearance of free settlers, either men who had known no other status, or ex-convicts who had rewon the status. These people introduced into the jail society the economic and political ideas of free British subjects, with consequences that were not very intelligently foreseen by the British authorities, but which ex post facto seem practically inevitable.

In the beginning the economic function of the free settlers employing assigned convict labor was much the same as that of the government officials in utilizing the convict labor force remaining in their charge: to contribute to making the jail community self-sustaining in foodstuffs. Additionally, the government had the responsibility for public works. The market was restricted to government demand, but within a dozen or so years, a significant export trade was feasible, chiefly grain and salt meat sent to Sydney, and between 1820 and 1850, Van Diemen's Land was transformed from a penal colony into a free capitalist economy with some of the political institutions of freedom, but still burdened with the task of taking care of British convicts. The progress was not even and steady but rather punctuated with booms and depressions in a rather complicated pattern.

When Commissioner Bigge was in Van Diemen's Land he pointed out that the probable resources for agriculture and grazing were not then fully explored, let alone exploited. At that time there were 5,468 persons in the colony, approximately half of whom were convicts in bondage. Probably two-thirds of the free were ex-convicts, leaving a rather small minority of settlers who had always been free. The population was increasing, within two decades the usable land was fully occupied, and tentative glances had been cast at the land in the south of New South Wales where the colony of Victoria was to rise. Thus, while the economic growth in Van Diemen's Land was as rapid as in any colony of Australia during this period, the fact that it took place on an island with limited resources early led to a feeling that an outlet on the continent was indispensable. The definitive moves to establish this outlet came in the middle 1830's.

Between 1810, when David Collins, the founding governor of Van Diemen's Land died in office, and 1850 the island had a number of governors of varying capacity. Collins' immediate successor was a disaster, one Thomas Davey, a dissolute man of questionable probity in money matters. His successor, William Sorell, was good enough to win the approbation of his contemporary and superior, Governor Macquarie of New South Wales. But the first governor of distinction was Sir George Arthur, who held office for twelve years, from 1824 to 1836, and was the first to rule Van Diemen's Land as a separate colony (from 1825). Arthur was a skilled administrator and a stern disciplinarian and if he made a fortune dealing in land that was not particularly held against him. What Arthur did was to take seriously the position that Van Diemen's Land was a penal colony and to order its affairs so that it really was. This naturally required him to subordinate the interests of the free settlers. Arthur believed in the system of transportation as he found it, administered it in Van Diemen's Land with remarkable singleness of purpose to realize its ends as he saw them, and brought the system to a kind of macabre perfection. Moreover, when the system came under fire in England in the late 1830's, he defended it against its critics, notably as their views found expression in the report of Sir William Molesworth's Parliamentary Committee of 1838. Rarely has such excellent service been rendered so dubious a cause. Sir George's obvious deficiency was a lack of imagination, a gap in his equipment which did not prevent him from being a highly successful servant of the Empire.

After Arthur to 1850, the governors of Van Diemen's Land were Sir John Franklin, Sir John Eardley-Wilmot, and Sir William Denison. Sir John Franklin had first been in Australia with Matthew Flinders (his cousin), and he had already engaged in the polar explorations to which, after he retired from his governorship, he returned and contributed one of the great tragedies of the field, his disappearance in 1845. Lady Franklin was a woman of force and imagination, one of the earliest of the governors' wives to leave a mark on a colony in which her husband served. The Franklins governed creatively, rejected Arthur's singleminded conception of Van Diemen's Land as a penal colony, but fell afoul of a subordinate official in such a fashion that Sir John, after six years in office, was recalled. Eardley-Wilmot served but briefly and unluckily. Sir William Denison served beyond 1850 to 1855 and saw the colony through the abolition of transportation (a change he opposed) and the transition to responsible government. He then went to New South Wales to govern that colony under the new system.

The growth of the economy of Van Diemen's Land to 1850 can best be illustrated by attending to the fundamental facts about the pastoral industry, agriculture, sealing and whaling, and commerce. However, the story is meaningless if torn from the context of convictism. It is necessary to emphasize the successful transition from an economy circumscribed by the markets offered by the convict establishment to a capitalist economy centered upon a free, public market, including the export markets of other Australian colonies (notably New South Wales) and England, primarily, but also those of India, Mauritius, and the Cape of Good Hope. But all that was accomplished was achieved as the shabby drama of convictism was played to its bitterest end in Van Diemen's Land.

The earliest sheep kept in Van Diemen's Land were unimproved animals whose value was as meat vendible to the government stores. The wool was mostly thrown away, or sold for very little as stuffing for mattresses. But in the decade 1820–30 wool exports increased from practically nothing to a million pounds a year; and it was in this same decade that powerful efforts to improve the sheep as wool producers were made by importations of stock from New South Wales, England, and Germany. Whereas in 1830 there were, in round numbers, 681,000 sheep in the colony, in 1840 there were 1,712,300, or as many as the island carried for almost a hundred years into the future. In accordance with the usual pattern of development of the Australian colonies in the pastoral period, the advance of agriculture in Van Diemen's Land was not nearly so spectacular, even though agriculture was more important there than in any other colony save South Australia. Agricultural practice in England in this period was poor; in Tasmania it was "slovenly." By 1829 there were a little over 34,000 acres in crops, almost two-thirds in wheat. Van Diemen's Land early had a wheat surplus; it first exported to New South Wales in 1815, and for some years it was the granary of Australia, but at the end of the period when total acreage cropped had reached 166,200, wheat had only increased to 64,700. The bulk of the territory occupied was used for pastoral pursuits. The pastoralists' contempt for the crop agriculturalists was fully expressed: farmers were a "despised class," for the money was in wool.

It was in Governor King's mind that the people sent to Van Diemen's Land in 1803 might make something of sealing. This proved to be a reasonable expectation. They also in due course made a good thing of whaling, both "bay," or onshore, and deep-sea whaling. Sealing and whaling were conducted out of Sydney from the early 1790's and while the products of both enterprises were in the early days of great economic significance to the people of New South Wales, the focal port for both industries became Hobart. The colonial operators were independent of the British who were also active in both industries but especially whaling, and both the British and the colonial enterprisers were in competition with the Americans. As sealers the Americans were in Australian waters as early as 1803, and there is a record of an American whaler on the western Australian coast in 1792, but the American whalers were most commonly seen at Hobart in the 1840's and after, when they were granted special privileges with regard to port charges. However, Australian waters were of but subsidiary interest to American whalers at any period, for while they worked all the grounds of the Pacific and Indian oceans, they were chiefly interested in those of the North Pacific. From the North Pacific grounds, they worked south in season through the Pacific islands to New Zealand and Australia, or vice versa, as the time of their arrival in the Pacific from Nantucket, New Bedford, and other whaling ports might dictate.

Sealing as an active industry was practically over by the 1830's, though it lingered on in a minor way for many years. The Bass Strait rookeries, where Australian sealing began, were practically exhausted within two or three years of the founding of Hobart, and the Van Diemen's Landers were forced far afield. They found their way along the southern coast of the continent to King George's Sound, they worked the New Zealand rookeries, and they pioneered the Australian association with Antarctica by sealing on sub-Antarctic islands. Bay whaling began in Van Diemen's Land in 1806 and spread westward along the southern coast of the continent to the Swan River and east to New Zealand. It began to dwindle by the early 1840's. By that time the Van Diemen's enterprisers were in deep-sea whaling and by the end of the decade Hobart was the principal deep-sea whaling port of the entire British Empire. The industry persisted to the end of the century. Like the sealers, the Hobart deep-sea whalers ventured beyond the established grounds near the coast into the sub-Antarctic region.

However romantic these activities were, or may appear in retrospect, they were always subsidiary to the land industries. The sea, for Australians, has always been of significance mainly in terms of carrying the products of Australian land industries to market and bringing in imports from overseas, notably from the United Kingdom. While Australians have produced their quota of sailors, especially for the vital coastal trade, overseas transport has predominantly been a preserve of United Kingdom enterprisers, a part of the great British system of ocean-going transport that has traditionally helped tie the Empire together.

Until the 1830's the merchants were the dominant economic group in Van Diemen's Land, but in that decade they merged with, or associated themselves with, the large pastoralists. The most conspicuous individual enterpreneurs, however, were active in several directions at once, as in whaling, wholesale merchandising, and pastoral pursuits. The great merchants engaged in both importing and exporting, sending colonial produce, especially and increasingly wool to the United Kingdom and foodstuffs to other Australian colonies, and importing a full range of consumer goods, including sugar, tea, and so on, from tropical markets. The wholesalers supplied the imported goods to retailers on credit, as they had obtained them from their sources, and the retailers supplied them on the same basis to their customers; the accounts were liquidated as colonial produce was seasonally marketed, in this phase of the movement the wholesale merchants either buying up the produce for export, or acting as agents for its sale to their correspondents in other colonies or the United Kingdom. As the economy became more complex, the banking functions of the merchants were split off and developed as true banking. The first bank in Van Diemen's Land was established in 1823, and before 1850 ten local banks had been formed, some of which had brief careers, but one or two lasted into the twentieth century. United Kingdom banks began to establish branches in Australia in the 1830's. Similarly, local insurance companies were formed beginning in 1835, shortly joined by United Kingdom companies. It was through the merchants first, then the banks and insurance companies, that British (and Indian) capital found its way to Van Diemen's Land and to investment, chiefly in pastoral enterprises, but more to finance the waiting period while wool was actually produced than for investment in fixed capital assets.

All through the period to 1850 the expenditures on convict maintenance and management were an important item of income. It was only as the net economic gain from convictism became less important than the charges on revenue, and far less than the moral losses the system occasioned, that a campaign against it was launched. Anticonvictism (or antitransportation) was largely a moral agitation, though closely mixed up with the inherent conflict between free and "slave" labor; those who had a clear economic stake in cheap labor, notably the pastoralists, tended to defend the system to the end. Systematic and effective agitation against the system began in Van Diemen's Land in 1847.

CHAPTER V

Toward Continental Occupation (2)

The Van Diemen's Landers began to feel the need for more land for pastoral expansion than the island appeared to afford in the late 1820's, but no significant action, leading directly to a major invasion of the continent, took place until the middle 1830's. Interestingly enough, these years in New South Wales were also a time when the acute need for new pastoral country led to a spread of the pastoralists farther and farther afield. It was not long before the two movements coalesced. Both movements involved the occupation of lands under the jurisdiction of the government of New South Wales and the violation of the prohibition against occupation and use of the land taken. Under imperial instructions, the New South Wales government was still attempting to keep the pastoralists within defined bounds of settlement, centered on Sydney. The political struggle over the land had entered a new phase.

It was easy enough to decide that a migration onto the continent was the logical next move for the Van Diemen's Landers, but from what coastal base should the occupation be launched? Collins' abortive effort to establish a colony at Port Phillip had deflected attention from that point of approach. For something over a decade Western Port, just east of Port Phillip, had been thought of as the proper place, in spite of a succession of adverse official reports on the quality of the country thereabout. For years sealers and whalers had been at work on this coast without attention being directed to any alternative, although they were optimistic in general about the value, as pasture, of the country all along the coast. In 1827 no less than three applications of permission to occupy land at Western Port had been made by private enterprisers, including John Batman, who finally promoted the decisive move from Van Diemen's Land. It was at Western Port that Hume and Hovell aimed their famous probe of the country south from Lake George, though through a miscalculation they ended their effort at Corio Bay, Port Phillip. The authorities had tried to establish a settlement at Western Port in the late 1820's. In November 1834, Edward Henty established a settlement at Portland Bay, to the west of Port Phillip. His large and enterprising family had gained experience in sheep-breeding in England and had put a good deal of money, hired help, and energy into the Swan River colony without satisfactory results; they had thereupon established themselves in Van Diemen's Land as pastoralists and merchants, but had not found enough land there for their needs. Portland Bay was a well-known place of bay-whaling and the Henty family engaged in that activity while looking for sheep runs and doing a minimum of crop agriculture. But though the Hentys seemed to be successful enough, they had not been at Portland Bay long enough to establish it as a point of entry in the public mind.

The ideal place proved to be Port Phillip, and in its first phase the area was named the Port Phillip District (of New South Wales). On May 27, 1835, John Batman, a pastoralist, freeborn son of free immigrant parents in New South Wales (but with a convict wife), having formed a loose association of supporters, sailed for the continental coast. About seven months earlier Edward Henty had simply set out to occupy land at Portland Bay, leaving it to subsequent legal action to establish his position as a claimant of land in an area closed to settlement, but Batman and his associates proposed to acquire title to land by negotiating a treaty with the aborigines, a tactic used time and again by the North American pioneers in getting land from the Indians. Actually, the Batman device was no more serviceable in dealing with the toughminded authorities than simple "squatting," but it was a fascinating flourish. Under the treaty, Batman and his associates claimed 600,000 acres. If they did not succeed in engrossing for their profit so large an area, they did determine the correct ingress to the country. Batman came on the Yarra Yarra River, flowing into Port Phillip Bay, and with considerable skill chose a site for a town a few miles from the mouth which later comers also agreed was the most desirable. (In his diary Batman wrote: "This will be the place for a village," one of the most famous remarks in Australian history.) By noting the occupations of Batman's associates in his enterprise, one has an excellent idea of the types then willing to participate in pastoral pioneering: a banker, eight government officials of various ranks, a lawyer, three retail merchants, and a retired army officer. Of these the most active were the lawyer (who prepared the draft of the treaty), a surveyor (a government official) who had traveled in this country, and the banker.

Leaving behind a small party at Port Phillip, Batman returned to Van Diemen's Land and initiated his long and unsuccessful effort to have his claim officially recognized. Meanwhile, in August, John Pascoe Fawkner of Launceston, publican son of a convict, brought to Van Diemen's Land as a small boy by his free mother who accompanied her husband into exile, sent out an expedition aimed at Western Port or Port Phillip, which came to rest at the latter. Fawkner himself arrived at the Port Phillip "Settlement" (for at this stage it had no other name) on October 11 and settled down; Batman did not get back to his "place for a village" until November 9. Who was the "father" of the Port Phillip settlement? Undoubtedly Batman, if justice is done, but Fawkner made more notable contributions to the development of "the Settlement." Batman died in 1839.

When Batman's statement of his proceedings reached Governor Sir Richard Bourke of New South Wales through Lieutenant-Governor Sir George Arthur of Van Diemen's Land, Bourke took the only possible step. On August 26 he issued a proclamation at Sydney declaring Batman's treaty "void and of no effect against the rights of the Crown," and went on to point out that all persons at Port Phillip were trespassers on the vacant lands of the Crown and would be dealt with accordingly. But at this stage the effort to keep trespassers out of the vacant lands of the Crown or, in reverse, to keep settlers within defined boundaries of permissible settlement was breaking down. Bourke himself in reporting the matter to England made it clear that he had no expectation that his proclamation would drive anybody away from Port Phillip or keep anybody out. And a little over a year later, on September 9, 1836, Bourke issued another proclamation authorizing settlement at Port Phillip under the land regulations of New South Wales. A police magistrate was sent to "the Settlement" to represent the colony's government. Early in 1837 Governor Bourke himself visited Port Phillip. Every step he took while there was obviously based on the assumption that the new settlement was to be both permanent and, in due course, of considerable magnitude. He authorized a plan for "the Setttlement," named its principal streets after persons associated with the history of the district, the king, and himself, and gave it the name of Melbourne, after the prime minister of the day in the United Kingdom (whose family name, with poetic appropriateness, was Lamb). Within three years the district was put into the hands of an official called a superintendent, who exercised the powers of a lieutenant governor under the governor of New South Wales. The task of government was given to Charles Joseph La Trobe who retained it into the 1850's. La Trobe was a man of literary talent who had traveled widely in Europe and North America and written travel books. He had been a companion of Washington Irving on the famous "tour of the prairies."

While the Van Diemen's Landers were busy transporting a great many sheep and some cattle to Port Phillip, Sir Thomas Mitchell made his celebrated sweep through the country back of Port Phillip from the Murray River to Henty's Portland Bay Settlement and from there to the Murray again and to Sydney. He climbed an eminence he named, by an interesting process of association, Mount Macedon—Phillip and Macedon!—and surveyed the bay but saw no sure signs of the occupation. When Sir Thomas' results became known, as they quickly did, it was made abundantly clear that the good pastoral country was not confined to the general vicinity of Port Phillip but probably extended to the Murray River to the north and west. This stimulated migration into the new district from New South Wales. An overlanding party, including Joseph Hawdon, brought down cattle from the Murrumbidgee River at the end of 1836; the first sheep from New South Wales arrived the following March. The Port Phillip District was thus settled and stocked from Van Diemen's Land and New South Wales, and the influx of men and animals from New South Wales eventually overwhelmed the Van Diemen's Land contribution. A good many men expecting quick profits from sheep came directly from England. Occupation for pastoral purposes was completed within a decade and a half.

The history of the Port Phillip District to 1850 was, then, a story of the very rapid growth of a pastoral society, from gestation to maturity. As Sydney was the governmental and economic focal point of its district, and early took on urban characteristics, so Melbourne quickly assumed the same relationship to Port Phillip District. Scattered far and wide outside the city were the pastoral establishments, just at this period beginning to be generally called "stations" (instead of sheep-runs or "walks" as hitherto—the Spanish-American term "ranches" was never employed). Characteristically, they encompassed considerable areas, depending on the number of sheep depastured and the quality of the country, but in any case requiring a relatively small labor force for successful operation, though what labor was required was keenly needed indeed, so that in the early period there was a very active demand for workers. From this extensive utilization of the coveted resource, the natural grasses, in which the sheep was the basic machine of production, and the required labor minimal, it followed naturally that the "services," governmental and economic, would tend to be concentrated at one particular center for a large area. In such cases the favored center was normally a seaport, or a place having fairly immediate access to a port, to which imports could be brought and from which they could be distributed and through which the exports (chiefly wool, of course) could be dispatched to the United Kingdom, the needed ancillary services clustering around. Thus, the first great system for exploiting Australian resources on an extensive basis allowed the rise of small cities, while the total population needed (urban and rural) remained relatively small. Crop agriculture was never in this period able to keep up with local demand. Thus did Port Phillip develop.

The great political achievement of the people of Port Phillip in the first decade and a half was winning separation from New South Wales and establishment as the colony of Victoria. The pioneers seem to have suffered a good deal of confusion about the political status of the district, acting as though they half believed that the vacant lands they occupied were located in a political vacuum. Yet it was clear enough that the area was an integral part of New South Wales and therefore subject to being governed from Sydney. Batman and his associates tried to play off the government of Van Diemen's Land, from which they anticipated sympathetic treatment, against that of New South Wales, and Governor Arthur was strongly tempted to accept the hint. However, he did not do so, as is made clear by his reference of Batman's documents, including the celebrated treaty, to Governor Bourke at Sydney. Bourke's proclamation was, in essence, an assertion of his jurisdiction over the area. To Bourke the pioneers were trespassers on Crown lands. But it so happened that trespassing on the Crown lands was also going on in other parts of New South Wales. The year 1835 has been set as the conventional date for the beginning of the great spread of pastoral activities beyond the bounds of settlement to which the imperial authorities wished to confine it. How to deal with this almost universal propensity to trespass was a crucial question of the time. As Bourke foresaw, the declaration that the Port Phillip pioneers were trespassers was merely *pro forma;* it was unlikely to halt the movement into the district. The alternative was acquiescence in the movement and administratively to assimilate the new district to the government of New South Wales. This is what happened, first through a police magistrate, then through a superintendent.

The people of Port Phillip, however, did not at any stage welcome assimilation to New South Wales. Not only were they discontented with imperial policies, especially with regard to land, equally under challenge in the older parts of New South Wales, but they felt that the way in which Sydney administered the land policy at Port Phillip encouraged outrageous speculation in land values. The Port Phillip people felt that they could handle the land problem more equitably, though they never

The "Attack" on AUSTRALIA

demonstrated how they could do so under the existing regulations. What they said emphatically was that government from Sydney was undesirable because Sydney was five hundred miles away, a considerable distance in the days of slow travel, and little understanding of local problems could be expected. They were vocal, too, about the demonstrable fact that not all locally produced revenue was being expended on local improvements; the surplus was going into the Sydney treasury. When in 1842 Port Phillip was given six representatives (one from Melbourne, five for the rest of the district) in the Sydney Legislative Council, it was pointed out that the six were a minority in the Council and unable to make the Port Phillip point of view effective. The Port Phillip six could regularly be outvoted. Moreover, there was the point that too few qualified persons at Port Phillip could afford the time and expense of serving at Sydney. Most of Port Phillip's early representatives were Sydney men. To underline their opinion that representation in the Sydney Council was useless, the Melbourne voters in 1848 elected Earl Grey, the colonial secretary in the London government, to office, although they must have known that the action was of highly questionable legality and could be interpreted as a calculated insult to authority.

Yet while Port Phillip's political anger was first focused on Sydney, it was, in the final analysis, only in London that the difficulties could be resolved. Hence much of the political activity in favor of separation took the form of petitions to the Queen, either originating in local public meetings or from the Port Phillip representatives in the Legislative Council at Sydney. They all made essentially the same case, but perhaps the most sophisticated version was that of December 1844. This originated with the six legislative representatives of Port Phillip at Sydney (all Sydney men at that time) and was composed by Reverend John Dunmore Lang, a Presbyterian clergyman who cut an enormous and highly controversial swath through Australian history from the moment of his arrival in 1823 to his death in 1878. (He was in turn and often simultaneously a Presbyterian clergyman, an educator, a promoter of immigration, a journalist, pamphleteer, and poet, a politician, a parliamentarian, a fervent advocate of new colonies, a spokesman for "democracy," a republican, a forecaster of Australian independence.) This petition traversed both local and imperial history, citing American precedent for carving up large colonies into smaller ones (the case of Virginia), and adducing comparative statistics of population and area to justify the creation of a new colony, as well as repeating the familiar arguments against rule from Sydney.

What the people of Port Phillip long did not know was what effect their petitions were having in London. They acted on the assumption that the Sydney government had greater influence and that it was exerted in favor of continuing the existing arrangement. Actually, the London government was alternately for and against the idea of setting up a new colony. In the end the question was considered as part of the larger problem of providing a new form of government for the Australian colonies generally. Not until 1846 did the people of Port Phillip learn that the British government was favorably disposed to separation. In that year it requested the Sydney government to examine the Port Phillip representatives, and other competent persons, on the point. This clear indication of attitude led the Sydney group to modify its opinion and report in favor of the change. However, Britain and Europe were politically disturbed in the late forties—the culmination was Chartism and the revolutions of 1848—and it took time to get legislation through Parliament. The separation of Port Phillip was provided for in "An Act for the Better Government of Her Majesty's Australian Colonies" of August 5, 1850. The people of Port Phillip first heard about the act in November and were delirious with joy, celebrating for a full week, but they had not clearly understood that "separation" was part of a complex act and that the implementation of the reference to Port Phillip was in Sydney's hands. Actual separation was not accomplished until July 1, 1851.

D3

The settlement of the Port Phillip District was generated and supported by forces at work within the Australian colonies themselves, but the settlement of South Australia, which went on simultaneously, is only explicable by reference to conditions in the United Kingdom.

Considered as an accumulation of variegated pieces of real estate inhabited by a wide variety of peoples, the British Empire went right on growing after the American Revolution, but there was a minimum of interest for a time in "settlement" colonies which might be systematically built up into nations by the emigration of men and capital. It took time for the British even to admit that it was wise to allow free emigration overseas; it was felt that somehow it weakened a country to allow an outflow of population. The difficult social conditions after the Napoleonic wars, characterized by what appeared to be a chronic unemployment at all levels of society summed up as a redundancy of population, led to a reconsideration of the matter. Thomas Malthus appeared to have explained the condition; the task was to find a method of correcting it. The first response which had reference to emigration was that conspicuously promoted by Wilmot Horton, who argued voluminously from about 1815 in favor of sending people overseas, particularly to Canada. Because of the types of individuals he favored sending and eventually actually sent in numbers, Horton's activities were dubbed "pauper shoveling," an epithet long applied to the assisted migration of the disadvantaged classes. Horton's idea was that settlement colonies were valuable "vents" for excess home population. He and his supporters had little concern about what happened to the people overseas.

A far more sophisticated set of ideas was synthesized in the 1830's and 1840's by an associated group of men who are known to history as the Colonial Reformers. From the "condition of England"—and quickly going beyond Horton's "pauper shoveling"—they evolved, by borrowing ideas, generating new ones, and combining relevant proposals commonly closely associated with one or another of the group, what may be called an ideology of settlement colonization. As propagandists, politicians, and practical administrators they set out to convert the nation to their program and, not unnaturally, they directed much of their most vigorous negative criticisms of the *status quo* policy at the Colonial Office and the government generally, feeling that established policy was not only incompatible with theirs but also actively hostile to it. In this they were in the very beginning probably right, but they persisted in hostility to the Colonial Office long after official policy had changed in their direction, partly because they had acquired the habit of opposition and more because nobody in the Colonial Office was permitted publicly to refute their canards. The reformers thus established the common nineteenth-century conviction that the Colonial Office could do no right. The most conspicuous Colonial Reformers were Edward Gibbon Wakefield (remotely related to the great historian), Charles Buller, and Lord Durham. Their principal butt was a permanent official of the Colonial Office, Sir James Stephen (father of Sir Leslie Stephen, grandfather of Virginia Woolf).

What the Colonial Reformers sought was a policy, or cluster of policies, which would build up in the areas of the British Empire open to settlement by British people thriving colonies which would ultimately greatly profit the Empire, economically and politically. They sought ways and means of bringing capital, capitalists, and labor together on the vacant lands of the Empire. Their vision was of agricultural societies of a structure as close to that of England as could be managed, with a small landed ruling group, governing by themselves their own internal affairs, and a landless laboring class able, by diligence, to rise into the ruling group. They wanted, in short, to export the rural British society more or less intact, but minus the social ills that were debilitating it at home. By removing idle capital, frustrated capitalists, and underemployed workingmen to the colonies, the risk of serious social disorders at home would be lessened. By exporting a social structure rather than atomistic individuals they expected to be able to avoid the colonialism of colonial societies (exemplified so notably by the United States) and bring into being "civilized" (i.e., British Isles) societies of a kind already pleasantly familiar to them. As sociologists of national growth they were fantasists, as the histories of the colonies they promoted show, but mixed in with fantasy were viable ideas. Their chief impact as builders of colonies and on colonial policy was in Australia and New Zealand.

Taking a cue from the United States, they argued that the public lands should not be granted by favor and for nothing, but sold at a price. On this question their chief theorist was E. G. Wakefield. He argued that the price of land should be "sufficient" and thus out of the early reach of laborers, who would remain landless long enough for capitalists to bring the land into full production with the laborers as employees. By fixing a uniform price for all land no matter where located there would be no sense in going far afield for land, since it would be no cheaper, and this would eliminate dispersion, the prime cause for the barbarization of colonial societies. With the money taken in by sale of the land to the capitalists, laborers could be brought out from Britain. Since one cause of trouble in colonies was the difficulty of governing them from a distance (or from the Colonial Office in London), colonies on reaching a certain population should be granted full charge of their domestic affairs, only strictly imperial questions being reserved to the home government. Thus, it was expected that strong British communities would arise overseas, closely and permanently associated with the Empire. The theorists were so convinced of the coherent excellence of their theory that they thought that if they could get firm control of all the elements, keeping the Colonial Office out, colonies would rise on wastelands with noble inexorability.

Edward Gibbon Wakefield was *par excellence* the theorist of land policy among the Colonial Reformers and he was, indeed, the principal exponent of their ideology in all its phases. He was a clever pamphleteer. However, Lord Durham, by an accident of circumstances, became the most impressive exponent of the idea of granting colonists political control of their domestic affairs. And Charles Buller achieved immortality in greatest part by a classic blast at the Colonial Office. It was he who attached to the office the opprobrious epithet, Mr. Mothercountry, the alleged misruler of the Empire.

Wakefield embodied his views in a series of books and pamphlets of which the most famous were *A Letter from Sydney* (1829) and *The Art of Colonization* (1849). He was, unfortunately, a man who lived his life under a cloud; he wrote his *Letter from Sydney,* not from Sydney at all, but from a jail in England where he was confined for abducting a young heiress. He never quite washed that stain from his escutcheon. He therefore did most, though not all, of his work behind the scenes and anonymously. He was, or perforce became, an inveterate wirepuller and manipulator of other, and often far better, men. He knew nothing of colonial life before he entered upon his career as sociologist and economist of colonies, but when he did acquire some first-hand knowledge, the experience did not cause him to revise his notions. He never understood that land is not uniformly valuable regardless of its quality and location; he never corrected his bias in favor of speculation in land values, whether by resident or absentee landholders; and he never grasped the significance of pastorial pursuits in the settlement of Australia and New Zealand. Even in his special field of land policy, he was a doctrinaire incapable of discriminating between sound ideas and mistaken notions. He even resented it when his sound ideas were taken up and used by the Colonial office simply because the mass of fustian in which they were embedded was put to one side. After his truly monumental labor in favor of new colonies was over he himself left England for the colonies. He died an immigrant in Wellington, New Zealand, in 1862, at sixty-six, convinced to the end that justice had never been done to his ideas, failing entirely to perceive how colonial realities had shown some of them mistaken.

Lord Durham, who before his untimely death at the age of forty-nine in 1840 knew and worked with Wakefield for several years, stands today as the decisive exponent of the idea of extending self-government in domestic affairs to colonial communities, reserving to the Crown a defined list of imperial subjects. This idea he gave form in his celebrated *Report on the Affairs of British North America,* published in 1839. The *Report* embodied his observations and conclusions about the problems of Canada as they had been brought to a head by the celebrated armed rebellion of 1838. In making his study and report, Durham had the assistance of Charles Buller as his chief secretary and E. G. Wakefield as back-room-boy specializing in land problems. Based on hints derived from Canadian political leaders, notably Robert Gourlay and Robert Baldwin, Durham with assistance from Buller and Wakefield developed the idea of colonial self-government as his central contribution to the solution of a complex problem in imperial management. From this seed grew the ideas about the autonomy of associated governments which came to flower in the middle of the twentieth century in the Commonwealth of Nations. Durham's *Report,* now generally regarded as a magisterial state paper, at least in those parts dealing with the idea here emphasized, was not well received at the time either by the Whigs or the Tories, but it won acceptance within a remarkably few years. Instrumental in publicizing the idea expounded, in addition to Wakefield and Buller, both of whom wrote significantly about it, was no less a personage than John Stuart Mill, friend of all the left-wing Whigs called Radicals, of whom Durham was one. When Durham was dying he expressed the hope that Canada would do justice to his memory. It has, and so has the whole Commonwealth.

Buller's role in his short life—*he* died at forty-two in 1848—was chiefly that of parliamentary and journalistic spokesman for his fellows. He brilliantly rephrased the idea of Durham's *Report* and met criticisms of it, and he went on to compose the famous bravura passage against the Colonial Office. Wakefield liked it so much that he reprinted it in a book of his own; it colored opinion of the Colonial Office for decades as the invective was echoed by others.

How the ideas of Wakefield, Durham, and Buller were translated into public policies in a general way will sufficiently emerge in due course, but here we must consider Wakefield's role in the settlement of South Australia. In addition to being a doctrinaire theoretician, Wakefield also thought of himself as a practical promoter, or supplier of ideas to promoters, of specific efforts at building colonies. But like most passionate theoreticians of social policy he set as great store by the details of his thinking as by the generalizations in it and was never satisfied to have a general idea, however valid, abstracted from *his* context and placed in the context of established colonial life and administration. He wanted his ideas applied *in toto,* but circumstances never quite allowed that. He must often have been tempted to remark, "Je ne suis pas Wakefieldiste." His first important experience in trying to have his scheme for establishing viable colonies applied in reasonable detail was in South Australia. It was an exasperating experience.

South Australia as a site was fixed upon largely because of testimony from Captain Charles Sturt, who believed that there was good country to the west of the Murray River near its mouth, supplemented by information coming from the early coastal explorers and the sealers and whalers (who had made extensive use of Kangaroo Island), and "confirmed" by the findings of Captain Collet Barker's expedition to the mouth of the Murray in 1831. Actually, the information accumulated prior to settlement was quite vague and contradictory. The settlers had little sound advance knowledge of the country to which they were directed, and as at Swan River they had to learn how to use the country after they got to it. As a matter of fact, most colonists have "gone blind" to the colonies of their choice through all history, not merely Australian history. Rumor and "sales talk" have been more important than exact factual knowledge.

It took Wakefield and his successive associates seven years to send colonists to South Australia. The campaign for the establishment of the colony opened in 1830 when Wakefield in association with some wealthy young men recently down from Cambridge founded the National Colonization Society. Harkening back to the efforts of Wilmot Horton to remove some of the redundant labor of England overseas, Wakefield and his associates proposed also to remove some unemployed laborers and some capitalists to South Australia. But whereas Horton had handed over his people to whatever government existed at their destination, the Wakefieldians proposed to keep the people under the Society's care until such time as they were numerous and prosperous enough to govern themselves. This effort was a total failure. Wakefield next tried to form a chartered colony in association with some Whig bankers. They styled themselves the South Australian Land Company, but their proposals were rejected by the Colonial Office because they appeared to cover a land speculation and because the authority of the government was too rigorously excluded. There was then formed the South Australian Association, made up of Wakefield and a miscellany of philosophical radicals, some of whom were members of Parliament. This group succeeded in getting through Parliament the South Australian Act of 1834 authorizing a colony, but under most peculiar and disadvantageous conditions.

The act was a clumsy attempt to combine the authority of the South Australian Association and the government in such a fashion that the financing of the venture would fall wholly on the Association. The British government was not interested in incurring expense to acquire a new colony on the vacant lands of Australia. The Association was required to gather a guarantee fund of £20,000 and to sell land to the value of £35,000 (at £1 an acre) before it could send out settlers. The money taken in from land sales was to be used, as Wakefield had proposed, to take workers to the colony, and it was from the proceeds of land sales in the future that further increments in population were to be financed. No convicts were to be sent to South Australia (as had also been the agreement with regard to Swan River). The Association had a managing committee of twenty commissioners, one of whom was to go to the colony as resident commissioner and manage the economics of the effort, while the government sent out a governor to handle its interests. By plan, authority in the colony was divided; and so, also, almost by plan, crippling quarrels were practically inevitable. However, the preconditions were so onerous that the Association almost failed to reach the point of dispatching colonists. It gathered the £20,000 guarantee, but it could not sell enough land, sight unseen, at a pound an acre, to return £35,000. The situation was saved when the South Australian

Company, a commercial enterprise aiming to engage in whaling (at which it failed), port building, landholding, and banking (at the latter two of which it had a great success), founded by a devout and philanthropic Baptist, George Fife Angas, bought up all the land remaining for sale, at twelve shillings an acre. But the Association had not sent out anybody, expert or not, to make a close study of the area selected, or anybody to survey the country sold preparatory to its actual occupation. A highly competent surveyor, William Light, finally reached the country after the first settlers had arrived, with about two months in which to do two years of work. Early in 1837 he chose the site of the capital city, called Adelaide (instead of Wellington as Wakefield had proposed), and laid out an admirable plan for the city on the greenbelt principle, then an unprecedented innovation. Light was bitterly criticized for his choice of site, but time triumphantly vindicated him as he hoped it would. However, he could not survey fast enough all the country actually needed, and from this circumstance flowed trouble for all concerned.

Settlers began to arrive in South Australia in July 1836. The South Australian Company actually landed almost a hundred persons in the colony before the first ship dispatched by the commissioners arrived. All told 546 persons reached the colony before the end of the year, 275 of them before Governor John Hindmarsh arrived on December 28. The colony was then formally proclaimed.

The settlers congregated in the capital city of Adelaide, suffering a kind of compulsory urbanization because the surveyors could not mark out the countryside fast enough to permit orderly occupation. Dwelling unproductively in the town, they consumed their capital in maintaining themselves on foodstuffs imported from England or brought from Van Diemen's Land, in any case only to be had at high prices. The workers, finding their services in active demand for various purposes in Adelaide, forced up wage rates. To earn *something,* the capitalists indulged in land speculation—land they could not occupy and use. Escaped convicts and ex-convicts from New South Wales infiltrated the settlement and, while highly useful as instructors in bush life, sent up the crime rate. Joseph Hawdon and Charles Bonney, pioneers of overlanding from New South Wales to Port Phillip, pioneered an overland route from New South Wales and the Port Phillip District along the Murray River to Adelaide and brought in cattle and sheep, introducing the pastoral idea. At the end of 1838 about 5000 people were pent up in Adelaide. Trading on the disillusion with Canada occasioned by the rebellion there, the commissioners in London chose this moment to sell 250,000 acres of land and send out 15,000 settlers.

The quarrels between the resident commissioner and the governor, mostly mutual recriminations about the chaos of the settlement, led to the recall of the governor and the deposition of the commissioner. Without abolishing the system, the two offices of authority were combined in the person of a single officer, called the governor. In October 1838 Colonel George Gawler arrived to take the composite position.

Gawler saw very clearly that the solution of the colony's difficulties was as rapid settlement on the land as could be managed. The speculative boom must bust. He therefore arranged that the work of surveying be speeded up. By the end of 1839 people began to move into the bush. Gawler also instituted a program of public works, building roads in the country, erecting government buildings in Adelaide, and also improving the facilities at Port Adelaide. But immigrants poured in faster than it was possible to absorb them into private enterprises, and Gawler's development program became in part a way of dealing directly with unemployment. It cost large sums. When his bills were presented to the commissioners in London, they could not meet them. The British government in the end arranged that they be paid and the total sum charged as a debt on the colony, to be met in installments. The cumbersome dual system of control was then abolished; South Australia became a regular Crown Colony; and Captain George Grey was sent from Western Australia to bring order into the settlement.

Grey, who entered the history of the Southwest Pacific as an explorer, and had then turned administrator, received his first exacting test in the latter respect in South Australia. He succeeded so well that he went on to an extraordinary career in New Zealand and South Africa and again New Zealand. In South Australia Grey followed a deflationary line, ruthlessly paring down public expenditures, but forcing the pace of land occupation. Pastoral activities expanded, but the most striking and, in the Australian context, unusual early success was in wheat growing. The cost of preparing the virgin land, which had very few trees or shrubs on it, was low and yields per acre were reasonably good. Most of the early wheat farmers planted but a few acres and harvested by hand. Prices were uncertain and in 1843, when a surplus over local requirements was achieved, the industry appeared to falter. But in that very year a mechanical harvester called a "stripper," a device for taking the heads off wheat standing in the field and threshing them, was devised in principle by J. W. Bull and the building of a model was financed by John Ridley. This device substantially lowered costs once the farmers adopted types of wheat the heads of which stood firmly upright when ripe. Furthermore, under the leadership of Governor Grey and a colonist named F. S. Dutton, the use of fertilizers to increase yields was commenced. The problem then was marketing; it was gradually solved by exports to Australian colonies not producing all their requirements—New South Wales, Port Phillip, Western Australia—and abroad to Mauritius, New Zealand, and Singapore. By the beginning of the 1850's the English market, until then but a tantalizing possibility, began really to open up. For Australia, South Australia led the way to it, but the country as a whole did not enter the international market for wheat in a serious fashion until the 1870's.

Captain Grey left the colony in 1845 to take up his first appointment in New Zealand as a "trouble shooter." He was the last of the important governors of South Australia in the period of original settlement. The colony was, as he left, just about earning its way. Unique among the mainland colonies, crop agriculture was a major segment of the economy. But at Grey's departure it was not apparent how the colony would get off dead center. What saved it from a stagnation like that of Western Australia was the discovery of base metal deposits, especially of copper, a most unexpected development which in a curious way forecast what was to happen on a larger scale in other colonies later on. The first significant discovery of copper was made at Kapunda in 1842—F. S. Dutton made a comfortable sum from this—but in 1845 a far richer deposit was discovered at Burra Burra. By 1851 at least thirty mining companies were active. The ores were carried to the seaboard in wagons drawn by bullocks and dispatched to England. Mining and transporting ore were important employment resources. By 1847 it was possible to resume regular immigration into the colony, and by 1850 the total population was 63,700, a remarkable number for a colony only a decade-and-a-half old.

CHAPTER VI

The Pastoral Economy

Imperial policy was decisive in this period and while imperial policies were criticized and resisted in Australia, the criticism and resistance were effective only if they registered in London. Imperial interference in colonial affairs reached its height in the 1830's and 1840's. The purpose of resistance to it was to adjust the imperial policy in some reasonable fashion to local conditions. "Government from a distance," to which Jeremy Bentham had taken exception and to which the Colonial Reformers were opposed, was proving increasingly difficult, and this in itself was an argument for colonial self-government. However, the Colonial Reformers, as Durham made plain in his *Report* on Canada, favored the reservation to the imperial authorities of several matters, and the transfer of these to the colonies was not to be allowed too readily.

Among the reserved matters was land policy, the focus of Wakefield's interest. From the time of Governor Phillip to the 1830's practically all the Crown lands were disposed of by grant. This resulted in the parcelling out of considerable quantities of land at a rising rate as the economy developed, not always to people able and willing to make economic use of it. When grants passed from the hands of their original holders by purchase or chicanery, large tracts of land were accumulated in private hands. It was the contrast between large areas held and minimum development in terms of land cropped that inspired disquiet. The thinking about land use, including Wakefield's thinking, was dominated at the time by crop agricultural considerations. But as it turned out, the important use of land in Australia in the first great period of development was as pasture. This Wakefield never clearly understood, but nevertheless his ideas about land policy had tremendous influence. They seemed to show the way to using the imperial domain for the welfare of the living generation and of posterity.

Although some of the imperial domain had been sold before 1831, and the idea of sale had appealed to Bigge, Macquarie, and Wentworth, chiefly in parcels to supplement grants, it was in that year that the principle that the imperial domain could *only* by disposed of by sale was introduced into Australia. A price of five shillings per acre was set as an upset price at auction. This was the equivalent of the $1.25 the American government asked for its land. (The authorities shilly-shallied on the auction principle in later years.) Subsequently the price was raised to twelve shillings (1839) and then to one pound (1842). The increases raised the price of land beyond what the local people considered fair and shut off sales for periods of time, especially in times of economic depression when the going price was naturally down. As the principal use of the money taken in from land sales was to subsidize immigration (as Wakefield proposed), this also had the effect of cutting down the inflow of people.

In New South Wales only such land was for sale as fell within the so-called limits of occupation (or location), or nineteen counties to the north, south, and west of Sydney, outlined first in 1829, but not fully surveyed until 1834. The area designated contained 34,505 square miles (as contrasted, for example, with the 1450 square miles that was considered the open area of the colony in Bligh's time); it consisted of a rough semicircle based on Sydney, touching the coast north and south of the city and reaching inland to a few miles west of Bathurst. It was Sir Thomas Mitchell's great professional achievement to carry through the survey and to build arterial roads to serve the area, something he did not accomplish without difficulties—with the task itself and with his superiors and critics. This area might have proved sufficient for all purposes for a good many years had crop agriculture been the basis of development, but by the time it became a practical question of confining the people within the boundaries, pastoral pursuits dominated and land-hunger was driving them far afield. In any event, the limits of occupation proved as futile a demarcation for authorized settlement as that laid down for the North American settlers in the Proclamation of 1763.

The pastoralists flowed over the limits in all directions, especially after the middle 1830's, moving south and west into Port Phillip, reaching the Darling River in the west of New South Wales, and the Darling Downs to the north in what was to become Queensland. This movement was unauthorized, and while unauthorized settlement by pastoralists had been known even within the limits of location, outside it was the universal practice. Moreover, the general character of the people guilty of unauthorized occupation changed; whereas in earlier days they were squatters in the derogatory sense familiar in the United States, and mostly had the character of such squatters, being only too often unreformed ex-convicts, by the early 1830's they were usually men of substance and

often of excellent social background, who engaged in "squatting" because of an irresistible urge to find pasturing ground for sheep so that
from their wool and increase they might accumulate fortunes. Shortly
the term squatter acquired an aristocratic overtone, and the squattocracy
which the squatters composed as a collectivity was the oligarchy of
Australia.

As we have noticed, Governor Bourke was convinced as early as
1836 when he had to deal with John Batman's claim at Port Phillip that
it was hopeless to expect that the pastoralists could be confined within
the limits of occupation. Several subsequent governors also adverted to
the futility of it all in their struggles to explain the local situation to the
imperial authorities. But even if it was a hopeless effort, it was obviously
impossible to leave the situation unregulated. An endemic disease demands attention as much as an epidemic disease. Squatting raised the
land problem in a new form, and as the Australians have never let a
chance for argument over land policy go by default, a violent altercation ensued. It fell to the lot of Governor Sir George Gipps of New
South Wales, in office from 1838 to 1846, to deal with the squatting
problem, and in the process he acquired a monumental unpopularity
with the squatting interest (the most powerful and vocal interest in the
community) which led to the evaluation that he was the "worst" governor to his time. This was a manifest injustice, for if he refused to give
the squatters exactly what they wanted, he also stood his ground against
any extremist views proposed by London. Gipps's misfortune was to have
to try to do justice to a local interest that did not know the meaning of
moderation. Moreover, there was more to his administration than the
squatting question.

The first step in legalizing the position of the squatters was taken by
Governor Bourke when in 1836 his Legislative Council passed an act
under which Crown land outside the limits could be occupied in any
quantity for a payment of ten pounds annually. This law was administered on the basis of defined squatting "districts." Since the scheme was
inadequate on the administrative side, an addition was made in 1838. A
"border police" was established to keep order in the squatting districts
and to pay for it a tax was levied on the basis of sheep possessed. But
the simple right to occupy land and a minimum of order in the police
sense did not satisfy the squatters. They wanted more. They wanted
property rights in their stations: specifically they wanted by law to be
able to command compensation for any improvements they had made
on their stations if they had to relinquish them, they wanted security of
tenure (not to be had under annual license), and they wanted pre-
emptive rights over the land they occupied when the question of purchase

arose. To gain these points the squatters stirred up a perfect din of agitation both in Australia and in the United Kingdom and even had their case argued in the newspapers of India.

Squatting in its aspect of land-taking was a catch-as-catch-can operation, a matter of first come, first served. The land the squatters occupied in the first instance was not only not surveyed, it was often in the literal sense unexplored.

After the first arrival in a district had staked his claim to a station, the later comers fitted themselves around him according to their fancy. Boundaries between runs were natural features, often notably imprecise to a surveyor's sense. The coveted natural feature next to or even above grass was water, preferably *permanent* water, not the easiest thing to find at an otherwise desirable point in outback Australia. Occupying both sides of a running stream could make many square miles of country away from the stream quite useless. The basis for determining the size of a station property was ideally the number of sheep one actually brought with one, or proposed to accumulate by natural increase. It was, normally, a matter of three sheep to the acre, but the natural richness or poverty of the country and the expected water supply (including rainfall) actually determined how many acres to the sheep should be allowed. Late-comers found themselves constricted by the unavailability of land, regardless of the other considerations. Moreover, there was often nothing in the early years except lack of capital and employees to prevent an adventurous man from taking up several stations on a single license. In one district in 1844 stations ranged in size from 40,000 to 140,000 acres. The license fee was the same no matter what the size of the holding. By the early 1840's the squatters had occupied about all the country then thought to be desirable. (Ideas changed at later stages.)

The squatting life produced a copious literature, and reading the numerous narratives one is impressed by the wide variations in the type of man attracted to it. Basically, it was a speculative venture and the great depression of the 1840's wiped out hundreds of precariously founded enterprises. While the families who pioneered woolgrowing in Australia had representatives among the squatters, many more were adventurous types from England, or India, or elsewhere, often retired army or navy officers, who had little personal knowledge of sheep and wool. All they knew was that wool was considered a "good thing." Many of the squatters did not conceive of themselves as permanent settlers, either in the outback or elsewhere in Australia, but rather were seeking to make money quickly and retire to England. Great emphasis was put, in advertising opportunities in squatting, on the large profits to be expected. The basic money investment was in sheep and "outfit"; part of the money was often borrowed; and speculative shares in squatting ventures were taken by urban merchants and professional people.

The life was hard and, in the early days especially, exceedingly rough. As the squatters moved farther and farther out, the transport problem became more and more difficult, both as to bringing in supplies and taking out the wool. The cost of transporting supplies from Sydney to a "station" was often more than their purchase price in Sydney. Transportation also was slow; the pace was set by bullocks, the favorite draft animal. The diet was limited: mutton, tea with sugar and damper (unleavened bread cooked in wood ashes). Many squatters were too indifferent to the niceties even to grow green vegetables for their own tables. Housing was the coarsest imaginable: usually it began as a rough shed covered with bark. It was a man's life; in the early days few women lived on the stations. Labor, of which there never seemed to be enough, was at first convict and ex-convict, mostly unskilled, leavened in later days by some free skilled workers, but always the basic qualification was that elusive skill called bushmanship. Naturally, different men responded differently to the life. Some rapidly lost their standards, lived dirtily in the omnipresent dirt, while others strove mightily to keep up the standards they brought with them, but as long as the squatters felt no security, this was difficult and in any case an "unnecessary" expense. Highly educated squatters can be depicted cherishing their books in a bark hut. A good many squatters contrived to spend as much time as they could in Sydney or Melbourne where life, if not exactly brilliant, was nevertheless a lot easier and measurably more "civilized." Squatting in its first burst may have been the most romantic episode in all Australian history, but it was a rough-and-tumble episode generally comparable to the occupation of the cattle country in the American West. Fundamentally, it was a "big man's" frontier enterprise; it took more capital to set up even the smallest station than a workman was likely to accumulate in those days. The workman who moved on the squatting frontier was ordinarily a member of a rural proletariat, a fact which had a profound influence on the history of Australia. Only in time did the pastoral life acquire a *mystique* and only later was it alleged that the pastoralists had something of a culture of their own discernibly different from that of crop farmers and urban entrepreneurs. In the beginning squatting was a way of making a fast pound fast.

This being the situation it is not surprising that the squatters acted on the principle that what was good for them in the immediate present was good for Australia in perpetuity. Essentially, what Governor Gipps sought to do was to make the occupation of the land easy for squatters and to make the fees they paid on the land occupied equitable, while at the same time not making it unduly easy for them to acquire ownership of the land. He wanted to keep them from a position in which the mere occupation of land would give them a right to purchase which would wholly contravene the established practice of selling land by fully competitive auction. He opposed the so-called pre-emptive right they asserted; he wanted to keep the road to ownership wide open, not impeded by a "right" based on mere occupation. In April 1844 Gipps, after consultation with the Legislative Council, issued new regulations on squatting which provided that each station be licensed separately, limited the size of stations, defined the number of sheep which could be kept on a station of the specified size (and specially taxed sheep kept in excess of that number), and provided for orderly procedures, including fees, for transferring stations and setting up new ones. Attention was also paid to protecting access to water. Separately, he sent to England for approval proposals dealing with the purchase of station land. Gipps suggested that after five years' occupation the occupier was to have the right to purchase 320 acres of land at the established rate per acre, presumably including the station home and outbuildings, such as the shearing shed, and the best permanent water on the property. An assessment for improvements would be allowed against the purchase price, thus giving the right to occupy the rest of the property for a period of eight years, when another purchase of 320 acres should be made, and so on indefinitely. If the occupier refused to buy, the property should be auctioned, the occupier only recovering from the sale price the assessed value of the improvements. On learning of these regulations and proposals, the squatting community exploded in indignation, set up with the landowners a pressure group called the Pastoral Association, and devised political machinery for going over Gipps's head in London. The landowners (who were often squatters too) joined in the clamor against Gipps because of their resentment of the price of land; they sank any differences they had with the squatters for the pleasure of taking a swipe at Gipps. The pastoralists generally saw themselves confronted with ruin or rebellion. But they were met both by Gipps and the imperial authorities with firmness, for in opposing the pastoralists both felt that they were defending the rights of the Crown in the "waste" lands.

Yet in the end the squatters triumphed. A new imperial act, the Waste Lands Occupation Act of 1845, opened the way for an Order in Council, dated March 9, 1847, which provided that within the old limit of occupation (a terminology now abolished in favor of "settled districts") leases of one year's duration only would be allowed, while in "intermediate" districts leases might run for eight years, and in the rest of the country, denominated "unsettled districts," leases could run for fourteen years.

The "unsettled districts" were in essence the true squatting districts. During the currency of a fourteen-year lease, only the occupier could buy the land. He was to pay an annual assessment based upon the animals run upon the area. This gave the squatters what they wanted, pre-emptive rights in the land. They promptly reassorted their ideas and transformed themselves from rebellious pioneers of the outback into privileged landtakers supporting the constituted authorities against all innovators.

D3

Closely allied to the land question was the labor question, for plainly occupation could not go forward without an adequate supply of labor both in the land industries and the ancillary productive activities and services. Through the 1820's the primary labor supply consisted of convicts, but during the next decade the immigration of free labor began, the supply of native-born free labor increased, and a dual system, bond and free, arose. The story thereafter was of the displacement of the mixed system by a free labor system whose triumph was confirmed by the abolition of transportation.

It was a fundamental principle of transportation that the government had a property right in the labor of convicts. In Australia the government transported the convicts to the country (or had contractors take them out) and maintained control over them there. The question of how the property right in their labor was to be exercised was in practice only decided there, even if by direction from London. In the earliest days, the convicts were mustered in gangs for labor on government projects, either on public works in the ordinary sense or in agriculture; and as long as transportation lasted, the government utilized some of the convict labor on its own account. But as soon as a private demand for labor arose, the practice was established of "assigning" convicts to private employers. From Governor King's time the majority of the convicts were normally "assigned." In the first phase of "assignment" the government continued to feed and clothe the convicts, thus doubly subsidizing the private enterprisers from public funds, but a change was soon made to requiring the employer fully to maintain his convicts, thus reducing the cost to the government of the convict establishment. One of the first private enterprisers fully to maintain his assigned convicts was John Macarthur. The condition of the convict worker was early regulated: he labored for his employer for fixed hours weekly. At no time could the employer himself punish a convict for breaking discipline. Such a convict had to be sent before a magistrate, or board of magistrates, charged with meting out punishments in the form of specified numbers of lashes (ranging from 25, 50, or 100 lashes and even several hundred in extreme cases) with a cat-o'-nine-tails on the bare back and bare buttocks while the convict was trussed up. Women convicts were "assigned" (chiefly for house or farmyard work) and disciplined in the same fashion. In early years the supply of convict labor exceeded the demand, leaving many of the convicts on the government's hands, but as time wore on the demand exceeded the supply, and this, as much as anything, opened the way for free labor. Free workers were sent out to fill a gap in the labor supply, not, however, with the idea in the beginning of displacing convict labor completely—that was an inadvertent result.

The convicts left in government employment were partly skilled tradesmen, whose condition was quite good, retained on arrival in the colony for work on building projects such as those undertaken with such brilliant results by Governor Macquarie, and partly men in very bad condition, returned from private employment for extreme or constantly recurring infractions of discipline, apparently not correctable by the lash. These latter were employed in building roads or at other hard labor, often in isolated places, under harsh taskmasters who had no reluctance to have the lash applied and who sometimes took an obviously sadistic pleasure in seeing it done. However, this was not the ultimate degradation for the convicts, for those who were convicted of crimes within the colony were sent to special penal stations for recidivists where labor was not only terribly hard—in coal mines and timbering enterprises—but discipline was fantastically severe. These were variously located over time, but included Norfolk Island off the coast, Moreton Bay, Newcastle (coal mines), and Port Macquarie in New South Wales, and Macquarie Harbor and Port Arthur in Van Diemen's Land. Of these, the real hellholes of Australian convictism, Macquarie Harbor had by far the most noisome reputation, with Norfolk Island in its time the runner-up. In these places men were driven by despair to *actes gratuits* (including murder) to insure their own deaths by hanging.

On any balanced assessment, however, the history of transportation as a system of punishment, macabre and revolting as aspects of the story are, is of lesser significance than its history in terms of labor supply on the one hand, and of the moral impact of the system on Australian society and its influence on politics on the other. The Committee on Transportation of 1838, under the chairmanship of Sir William Molesworth who, as a Colonial Reformer started out with a strong bias against the system in all its aspects, gave the system the most intensive scrutiny it ever had. It recommended the abolition of the system after fifty years of history, and the point was made that the terrors of transportation had been considerably mitigated by the use of the convicts under assignment because there was always the chance that a convict would get a good and kind master prepared to mitigate the punitive aspect by indulgences designed to command the convict's loyalty and improve his efficiency. (On the other hand, there were, of course, many in New South Wales to whom Clytemnestra's observation in *Agamemnon* applied: "For they who reap an unexpected growth of wealth, are harsh to slaves beyond the line of a well-tempered rule.") The committee did not play down the horrors of the lash, or of the receptacles for recidivists, but it played up the actual condition of the average convict in private service. It pointed out that the punishment of transportation had lost its terror in England because of knowledge and rumor about the actual condition of assigned convicts and emancipists in Australia; and it concluded that the only remaining terroristic aspects of the system were *exile* and *slavery*. But exile was, in effect, the lot also of free working-class immigrants, few of whom, in contrast to their betters who were often inveterate travelers, ever got home again. Exile, while in a sense a punishment, was rather chiefly to be thought of as a traumatic experience common to all immigrants of the lower class, both voluntary and compulsory. Slavery was the peculiar lot of the convicts, a temporary slavery perhaps, but slavery in essence as long as the convict was in bondage. No reformatory element was found in it.

Slavery was indictable not only for its effects upon the slaves, but upon society at large, both while the convicts were in slavery and after they had been emancipated or freed. This indictment the committee drew in considerable detail and while in the nature of the case it is impossible to accept their drawing as an entirely accurate portrait of Australia circa 1838, it was nevertheless reasonably close to reality. Australia had developed the stigmata of a slaveholding society, and Henry Parkes, who arrived in New South Wales in 1839 and rose to political eminence later on, was on the mark when he invoked the image of pre-Civil War Virginia to illustrate what the situation was like, with the difference that emancipated slaves in Australia were rising in the social hierarchy. Much was made by Sir William Molesworth and his associates of the general lowering of moral standards in New South Wales as a consequence of convict slavery, but his evidence, while not impeachable as detail, was not fully balanced by counter-evidence. The indictment was deeply resented by many in New South Wales and the realism of those who supported it was questioned by Governor Bourke, while others accepted it only insofar as it could be interpreted as a criticism of the emancipists and their influence, while rejecting it insofar as it appeared to apply to themselves and their selected fellows. Whatever its detailed accuracy, the indictment had obvious political importance, for as long as the convict system continued it could be used to impede the progress of self-government in Australia.

The indictment of transportation was, then, chiefly a moral indictment. The system was assessed a failure both in terms of punishment and reformation; and it corrupted all society by its very existence. Opposition to it found its earliest forceful and politically influential expression in England. The moral indictment was important in Australia, but there the question was also viewed as a problem in economics—labor supply. The pastoralists favored the continuance of the system because they felt they needed the cheap labor it supplied even though they were well aware that not enough convicts could be sent out wholly to meet their requirements. From self-interest they argued for the retention of the convict element in a mixed labor system. On the other hand, the free workingmen and their allies (chiefly city dwellers) argued against transportation in moral terms, obviously in the hope of improving the position of the free workers by removing a degraded and degrading competitive group—a line that was a mixture of morality and economics. The disputation had curious political effects.

In 1837 the imperial authorities ordered the discontinuance of assignment, but it took four years to bring it to an end. This, of course, meant that the pastoralists were progressively deprived of convict labor. The convicts were to be employed solely by the government on public works. Then in an Order in Council dated May 22, 1840, the list of places beyond the seas to which convicts might be sent was revised to exclude New South Wales. Only Van Diemen's Land and Norfolk Island in Australia were named as places for the reception of convicts, and the only other place in the British Empire so designated was Bermuda.

But while the Order in Council of 1840 apparently removed the problem wholly to Van Diemen's Land, it did not in fact entirely eliminate it from the mainland for, apart from the carry-over of convicts already in New South Wales and escapees from the island, the British authorities were not, it turned out, yet ready to give up the idea of sending convicts to New South Wales. The effect on Van Diemen's Land was disastrous and Norfolk Island provided little relief but rather, indeed, became itself a vile hell-hole. Van Diemen's Land soon became oversaturated with convicts, and experiments in discipline, chiefly designed to provide incentives for reform to the ticket-of-leave stage, did no real good. As the convicts multiplied, the inflow of free immigrants, which had been strong in 1840 and even included people from South Australia and New Zealand, practically ceased. Even earlier times provided no precedent for the predicament of the free settlers; they now really learned what it meant to live in a jail.

To relieve the pressure on Van Diemen's Land, the British authorities turned once again to New South Wales. In April of 1846 William Ewart Gladstone, as secretary of state for colonies, addressed a dispatch to Governor Sir Charles Fitzroy of New South Wales in which, after suggesting that it was merely a "promise" that no more convicts would be sent to New South Wales, he asked the governor to feel out his Legislative Council on the possibility of receiving some convicts of a special character before the penal establishments, then still functioning, were broken up. If opinion was favorable, he proposed to send from England and transfer from Van Diemen's Land men who had served part of their sentences under severe discipline and were now ready for tickets-of-leave. These he thought could be received into private employment and thus relieve any labor shortage that might exist. The proposal, when it became public knowledge, immediately divided opinion in New South Wales: the squatting interest, dominant in the Legislative Council, reacted favorably and alleged as one reason for doing so that it would tend to lower wages, while the public at large, including the free workers, was intensely hostile. Not proceeding at this time to challenge the opposition by action, the British authorities let matters rest for about two years and then in December 1848 Earl Grey, now the responsible minister, forwarded to Fitzroy an Order in Council which designated New South Wales once again a place for receiving persons sentenced to transportation, and he announced the dispatch of a ship loaded with what he called "exiles," or persons who had already served sentences in British jails but who were not thought ready to be let loose on society in the United Kingdom. This was a clear case of giving greater weight to the opinions of the squatting interest than to those of the rest of the population. At the same time that a ship was dispatched to Sydney, another was sent to Port Phillip, and a third to the Cape of Good Hope. At all three points a fierce agitation against the landing of the "exiles" was carried on, provoking in New South Wales an invocation of the American Revolution by Henry Parkes. In the event the convicts were sent to Moreton Bay and the far outback of New South Wales. This was a final effort of the English authorities.

Van Diemen's Land was therefore in an appalling position. Earl Grey backed and filled as to his intentions. He hinted he might abolish transportation to the island; he announced his resolve to continue to send out convicts because, after all, the colony had been founded to be a convict colony. The attitude of Governor Sir William Denison was equally unhelpful. He began by favoring transportation, and he ridiculed the antitransportation people in his dispatches—after all convict labor was still in active demand—but then he began to back water. After 1847 the antitransportation group had a strong organization which extended to the mainland, where its position was vigorously defended as of importance to all Australia. The elected members of the Legislative Council were all antitransportationists. But for all the agitation it was not until December 1852 that the British government finally announced that transportation to Van Diemen's Land would cease as soon as the necessary legislation could be passed. Even then Sir John Pakington, to whom it fell to make the announcement, felt it necessary to comment wistfully on the fine market for convict labor that still existed. His clinching reason for giving up the system was neither moral nor in the strict sense economic; he referred to the discovery of gold on the mainland and commented on the senselessness of sending convicts to that part of the world at no cost to themselves while thousands of free men were laying out hard cash to get to the same destination! The people of Van Diemen's Land celebrated their "liberation" on August 10, 1853, but men who had originally arrived as transportees lingered on into the 1870's and 1880's. To signalize the change, the name of the island was changed to Tasmania, an alternative usage for some years, and the change became official in 1856. Only in the distant and isolated west did transportation continue; and it was thought so far away as hardly to matter. Eastern Australia was free of the incubus and the process of rationalizing this singular "blot" on Australia's first fifty years could begin. It was to prove endless.

D3

During the first four decades of Australian history the free immigrant to Australia was, with rare exceptions, a "capitalist," not a workingman. The immigrant's claim to the possession of capital might be more than a little fraudulent and the capital actually possessed might be remarkably small, but by pretension and expectation it was to the capitalist class that he belonged. Nor was any other class of person wanted, even though the governors often complained, frequently naming names, about the capacity, interests, and activities of the free capitalists who came out. When Governor Phillip declared his conviction that some free farmers would be of immense use to him in establishing the colony, he was plainly asking for men of managerial capacity who could direct convict labor in crop agriculture. By 1807 the indispensability of this class of free persons was so obvious that Governor Bligh, in a dispatch to London describing the colony in detail, recommended that the policy of encouraging only "capitalists" be made explicit. His proposal was accepted and from that time to about 1830 practically no deviation from it was allowed. Even in the 1820's when the flow of free immigration was greater than any hitherto known, the people were capitalists and their dependents. They were needed to direct the labor of the convicts whose numbers were also increasing as crime increased in the disordered society of post-Napoleonic Britain.

It was in the 1820's, however, that attitudes and needs changed, both in the United Kingdom and Australia. The idea that it weakened a country to allow its people to emigrate lost ground in the United Kingdom, and the idea that the country was overpopulated and that relief from overpopulation was needed gained ground. The law putting obstacles in the way of skilled workmen who wanted to emigrate was repealed. Voluntary emigration to North America, particularly the United States, swelled in volume. In Australia, on the other hand, the shift from a condition of surplus of convict labor to a shortage took place. On March 31, 1826, Governor Sir Ralph Darling addressed a dispatch to London about the situation, asking for more convicts *and also* for "a number" of skilled agricultural and building workers in terms not markedly different from those employed by Governor Phillip years earlier. Governor Darling got his convicts—they had already been dispatched, as a matter of fact—but he did not get his free skilled workers. The government considered that it would be too difficult and costly to assemble, select, and send out free workers. In short, the situation in New South Wales was favorable to the reception of free workingmen, but the British government was not then prepared to help in satisfying the need.

The need in New South Wales was little likely to be satisfied by self-financed emigration from Britain. It was not only that prospects in North America were better, and much more favorably known to the working class of Britain, while Australia was "Botany Bay," but also that North America could be reached for five pounds, whereas it cost up to forty pounds to get to Australia. Even after competition brought down the rates, it still cost at least twenty pounds to get to Australia in the meanest accommodations. Therefore, the superior, or better understood, attractions of North America and the lower cost of reaching the Eldorado put Australia at a competitive disadvantage. The only way to offset this disadvantage of cost was to "assist" the emigrants by offering free or very low-cost transportation to the Australian colonies. Although immigrants paying their own way to Australia were from the beginning of the movement reasonably numerous, the assisted immigrants were always markedly more numerous up to 1851, except in years of economic difficulty in the colonies, when such immigration was temporarily discontinued. (Even after 1851 and to the present day, assisted immigration has been a major constituent of all immigration.) It was assisted immigration that chiefly built up the free population of Australia before 1850.

The Colonial Reformers were active proponents of free working-class emigration. They were, as already noted, hostile to transportation and the use of convict labor under assignment. Their scheme, as exemplified in the South Australian project, posited a free working class. They were thus an important factor in encouraging the facilitation of the emigration of free workers from the United Kingdom to Australia. But even before Wakefield's ideas took hold, experiments in assisting emigration to New South Wales were mooted, including a scheme for obtaining the money by taxing convicts, but none was satisfactory. It was in 1832, the year after Wakefield's policy of selling land at a fixed minimum price was introduced into New South Wales, that the use of the funds derived from the sales to assist immigration was also introduced. Such funds were long a principal, but not the sole, reliance. Various other sources were tapped.

The Colonial Reformers favored the emigration of couples not more than thirty years old, preferably without too many children. But in New South Wales the sex ratio, under the convict system, had traditionally been radically unbalanced. Convict women were hopelessly outnumbered by convict men and the same imbalance existed among the free. This was offered as an explanation of the prevalence of sexual looseness in the colony, evidenced by much casual and professional prostitution, a preference for readily discardable mistresses over wives, and the high illegitimacy rate. The provision of single women was considered a necessary task. Assisted immigration began with experiments in sending out single women, presumably of a character fit to be wives in due course, but at first useful as houseworkers. Many unseemly wrangles occurred over the character of the women sent out. But assisted immigration soon settled down to the provision of workers, male and female, married or unmarried, accompanied by children if married. Up to 1836 numbers exceeded 1000 in only one year (1833), after which the totals rose irregularly and suddenly jumped to a peak of over 20,000 in 1841. In 1843 and 1845–47 assisted immigration was suspended because of depressed conditions in New South Wales. From 1848 through 1851, however, over 30,000 people were brought out, over 15,000 in 1849, for a total of about 90,000 persons from 1832 to 1851, both inclusive. In the same period about 30,000 unassisted immigrants arrived. The total population of New South Wales in 1851 was a little over 260,000; that was about two-thirds of the total population of all the Australian colonies.

Almost all these immigrants were British: English, Scottish, and Irish. Although a group of Germans fleeing from religious troubles in Prussia was admitted to South Australia in 1838, and some Germans reached New South Wales for employment in the vineyards (as also some Frenchmen) between 1847 and 1851, immigration of non-British peoples was insignificant in this period, and indeed uncharacteristic of Australia until after World War II. But from the comments upon them and the struggles of the United Kingdom and colonial authorities to insure a proper selection among the people offering to emigrate, notably through the establishment of the Colonial Land and Emigration Commission in London in 1840, it is painfully apparent that from the point of view of the employers of New South Wales they were never wholly satisfactory. What seems not to have been adequately understood was the radical adjustment required successfully to transfer oneself from a position in the lower ranks of British society, where one had not been too successful, to a well-founded position in the lower ranks of the vastly different Australian society. Few people made enviable reputations in managing the peopling of Australia; perhaps T. F. Elliot who managed the Colonial Land and Immigration Commission in England did best at that end and Caroline Chisholm at the Australian end. In the early 1840's Mrs. Chisholm performed an enormous service to the immigrants into Australia by way of care on arrival and placement in jobs, particularly to the female immigrants.

These people, whether English, Scottish, or Irish, were uprooted from vastly disturbed societies—everywhere in the British Isles agriculture was declining, urban industrialism in England was rising—and replanted in a quite rough and ready young pastoral society. In the earlier years of the immigration they were flung into a mixed labor system, partly free and partly convict, and even up to 1850 they lived under the shadow of convict competition. The labor laws applicable to them were still pretty much those formed at a time when the relation of free master and convict servant strongly colored the standards. The legal position of the free worker was not good; the master and servant legislation gave the master the whip hand. These laws were written by and for the squatters, the dominant people and principal employers of the colony. The work they offered was not only hard in itself; it often had to be performed in the outback under conditions of physical isolation and climate wholly unfamiliar to the newcomers. The marvel is that so many immigrants actually achieved the miracle of adaptation, not that some of them failed.

The squatters, however, felt that altogether too many of the immigrants settled down in Sydney (or Melbourne) and by that very fact showed they were poor stuff. The squatters failed to understand that urbanization in Australia stood in a symbiotic relation to the development of the rural areas and that the growth of the cities was an inevitable consequence of general economic growth, not a consequence of the perversity of immigrants. Probably many true failures, and some chronic malingerers, took refuge in the cities, but plainly they did not swell the population of Sydney to its 50,000 by 1850. They, along with people who never tried rural life, provided the urban labor force the pastoral economy demanded in order to operate efficiently. But the real animus of the squatters against the immigrant workers was that in spite of the fact that they augmented the pool of workers, wages nevertheless remained high—"too high," in the view of the employers. In making this judgment the squatters seem never to have taken into account the general opinion, stated by Governor Darling for example, that a single good free laborer was as productive as three convicts, especially in the case of skilled tradesmen. The squatters, therefore, deprecated free labor and desired convict labor even when free labor had come in in quantity; and whenever a labor shortage could be alleged to exist, they sought not only convicts but actually talked of bringing in Chinese or Indian coolies or Pacific Island natives. As late as 1848, in declaring in favor of bringing in convicts, the squatters expressed the hope that this would bring down wages. Thus, to the end of the period when any other alternative was in any degree possible, the principal employers deprecated the virtues of the free labor system. That was what the free immigrant workers were up against. All in all they appear to have stood up manfully to the onerous situation in which they found themselves. Not unexpectedly their political views, and those of men sympathetic to them, savored to the oligarchs of "democracy."

D3

In general terms, the economic structure elaborated in New South Wales was comparable to that of Van Diemen's Land, sketched earlier. The earliest capitalists were military officers, or ex-officers, who combined wholesaling of imported merchandise with crop agriculture in a pattern apparently suggested by John Macarthur. All hands were given to diversifying their investments by ventures in sealing, whaling, sandalwood gathering, distilling, and so on. The ex-convict entrepreneurs conformed more or less to this pattern. One of the earliest and most famous of these was Simeon Lord; he was a leading merchant by 1804. As the pastoral industry developed, the capitalists shifted into it from crop agriculture; and as more and more men took to the pastoral life, some differentiation of function took place, but the merchants, and also civil servants, supplied credit to and took shares in pastoral enterprises. This was particularly true with regard to *squatting* enterprises. As banking developed the shareholders were also normally a mixed group: merchants, pastoralists, civil servants. This was especially true of locally financed banks, not so true of the banks whose head offices were in London but which had local boards of directors. These, which became popularly known as "the Anglos," began to appear in New South Wales in 1832 and were shortly followed by British mortgage and insurance companies, thus being obviously related to the rise of squatting into which they channeled United Kingdom investment funds. The incoming British banks established the practice of branch banking, ever since characteristic in Australia. At this time, also, the company form of business organization began to be far more widely used than hitherto, not only in banking and insurance, but also in land and water transport, mining, flour-milling, and so on.

All this capitalistic development was ultimately founded on a single commodity: wool. As John Macarthur had perceived, an export commodity, highly valued in Britain, for which there was an expanding market at the mills of Bradford and Leeds, was the key to economic success in Australia. Wool from Australia could be fitted without too much trouble into the "old colonial" trading system, for it would lessen Britain's dependence upon foreign sources for wool, notably Spain and Germany, in mercantilist thinking a prime desideratum. However, the Australians were never completely easy under the "old colonial" system, though they were never as involved in the commodity aspects of it as the Canadians were with their timber and wheat and the planters of the West Indies with their sugar. For wool it was chiefly a matter of getting duties on the colonial product reduced or removed.

What bothered the Australians in the early days was the East India Company's monopoly of the trade of the Pacific Basin, but that came to an end in 1813, save for the China trade which held to 1834. The China trade by that time had ceased to be important to the Australians —it chiefly related for them to the trade in sandalwood, a wasting commodity. Until 1813 the Company's monopoly made it impossible for the United Kingdom merchants to enter freely into trade with Australia; it was during this period that the Americans were briefly the chief suppliers of the Australian market.

Under the restrictive legislation the Australians could not solve their problem by building vessels large enough to trade with the United Kingdom, the prescribed size being uneconomic for colonial enterprisers. The laws about shipping (or in the terms then employed, "navigation") really embarrassed the Australians, and they took an active interest in easing these restrictions. This was largely accomplished by 1819. After that date the burdens were never onerous enough, as they bore on Australia, to slow the rise of the wool trade, and in 1849 the navigation laws were radically liberalized. By that time it was apparent that the "old colonial" system was wholly doomed, though it survived in vestigial fashion to 1860. The wool trade, however, had already attached Australia so closely to the United Kingdom as a dependent economy that regardless of any theory—mercantilist or free trade—Australia was thereby in any case firmly integrated into the imperial trading system.

Although the fundamental trend of the Australian economy, once it got underway on the basis of wool, was upward from strength to strength, that economy was, of course, subject like all its capitalist fellows of the nineteenth century to booms and slumps, panics and depressions. Drawing a distinction between the painfully slow rate of growth that early became characteristic of Western Australia, and the kind of crisis that was engendered in South Australia by the abrupt termination of Governor Gawler's policy of heavy public spending, and what are ordinarily called booms and slumps, the latter occurred in this period in the late 1820's and again in the 1840's. That of the 1820's affected New South Wales and Van Diemen's Land (the other colonies were not yet founded) while that of the 1840's was in some degree Australia-wide, though not as severe in South Australia, where wheat-growing served to moderate it, and Western Australia, as in Van Diemen's Land and New South Wales.

The difficulties of the 1820's, which were at their height about 1828, were associated at the time with excessive speculation in stock, sheep, cattle, and horses. At that time there was a veritable boom in land grants. The largest ever made was that of a million acres in New South Wales in 1824 to the Australian Agricultural Company, a venture backed by the Macarthurs, and almost as impressive was the 350,000 acre grant to the Van Diemen's Land Company the next year. The new land grants all had to be stocked, so local speculators gambled heavily on a rising market for sheep, cattle, and horses. Much of the British capital coming into the colonies arrived as merchandise to be sold at auction; and the excellent market attracted also purely trading consignments as well. But then the price of wool, for complicated reasons associated with the depression of 1825 in England, began to fall. The market became glutted with imported merchandise, and prices at auction went down. A drought caused the failure of the wheat crop in New South Wales and that caused an increase in the costs of woolgrowing as the wheat price rose. Credit became tight, bankruptcies ensued, and the first Australian "bust" had occurred.

The difficulties of the 1840's, at their most acute, 1841–43, were rather differently based. The expansion of the 1830's had been based on the idea that the occupation of new land for sheep stations could go on indefinitely: that an open-ended expansion was feasible. Then, however, overseas wool prices began to decline, wages and other costs (including transport costs as the stations spread farther and farther afield) continued to rise, the quality of the sheep available for stocking new stations declined, lowering the wool yields, and it began to be realized that indefinite geographical expansion was not, after all, possible, for the kind of country then thought necessary for stations was running very short. The profitability of the industry obviously declined. There was, therefore, a parallel shrinkage in expectations. Credit was consequently tightened and a sharp recession ensued. Assisted immigration, sensitive to economic changes in Australia, was suspended. Banking difficulties were a conspicuous expression of the troubles. The imperial authorities gave guidance to the governor in judging local banking legislation. Like the Americans, the Australians have a long history of banking troubles associated with the loose use of credit in periods of expansion when entrepreneurial optimism has run very high. Both countries have ridden the prevailing upward trend in economic development over the bumps of bankruptcies.

CHAPTER VII

A Struggle for Free Government

Taking a large view of what is politics, it can be said that political activity began in Australia in Governor Phillip's time as a struggle between the civilian and the military authorities over questions of responsibility and authority and widened into a struggle for the control of the government as the effective means of advancing economic interests between the early "monopolists," civilian and military, and the autocratic governors. In this sense the first Australian politician of distinction was John Macarthur, and the culminating political event of the first twenty years was his overturn of Governor Bligh's administration. Under an autocratic system of government, opposition politics was necessarily tainted with subversion; the Rum Rebellion was a triumph of subversives, as the record shows. Insofar as the United Kingdom authorities dealt with the principals in the rebellion against Bligh, this was their verdict too. The difficulty with politics under an autocracy is that there is no formal forum for political activity, and tolerance of *ad hoc* expressions of political views is decidedly adventitious.

In the struggle with Bligh, the opposition solved the problem to its own satisfaction by using the courts as its forum, and practically all of the significant maneuvering took the form of court cases. But the issues could not be settled in the courts and of necessity the opposition, when defeated in the courts, had either to accept that defeat or resort to the use of force. By virtue of the fact that many of the military gave allegiance to the opposition, Macarthur was able when the moment came to command the support of the only important organized force in the community, the military garrison. He summoned it to action, with the result that the legitimate government collapsed. Legitimacy was restored by Macquarie.

Macquarie also restored autocracy and, indeed, expressed the hope that no other kind of government would be instituted in New South Wales. He was unable, however, to stifle opposition politics; indeed he inadvertently, in pursuit of quite other ends, divided the people into two factions, one of which, the emancipists, he attached to himself, and the other, the exclusionists, opposed both him and the emancipists. The exclusionists proved, in Macquarie's time, to be the stronger of the two political groups. The Bigge reports represented a triumph for them. In the continued absence of any formally constituted public political forum under Macquarie, there was resort to intrigue both in New South Wales and London (focused there on the Colonial Office and the House of Commons), and to these techniques of politics were added, with Macquarie's watchful tolerance, public meetings and petitions for the redress of grievances. The first really significant use of the public meeting and of a widely signed (over 1300 signatures) petition was made by the emancipists in seeking to establish and defend their civil rights against adverse court decisions. The meeting occurred on January 23, 1821, and Governor Macquarie forwarded the petition to London with his full support. To advance their cause the emancipists named Edward Eagar their political agent and sent him to London. He was an emancipist lawyer, a pious Methodist, who, as it happened, had been the principal figure in the disastrous court cases. The adverse decisions had been made by Barron Field, judge of the Supreme Court of Civil Judicature. At that time the emancipists far outnumbered the settlers who had arrived free, and collectively they held far more property. Their defeat in the courts, in the person of Eagar, called into question the validity of locally issued pardons and thus placed in jeopardy their pretension to the full civil rights of free men. It was a major political reverse and a triumph for the exclusionists, who thus saw reinforced in law the ostracism they were trying to enforce socially.

The emancipists thus entered public politics in defense of their civil rights, and for a time this was the whole of their concern. They obviously were numerically a considerable political force. It was patent that a leader prepared to embrace their cause would have a ready-made following of great importance. He could advance himself with their backing a considerable distance toward important political power.

The man who clearly perceived this was William Charles Wentworth. Although it was apparent that he was after bigger game than the emancipists were then prepared to stalk, he became one of their leaders. Wentworth was a freeborn native son of New South Wales, the first native-born political leader of his country. He was born on Norfolk Island in 1790, the son of D'Arcy Wentworth, a medical man in the public service, who had voluntarily come to the colony after brushes with the law involving charges of highway robbery. His mother was a convict. D'Arcy Wentworth prospered both as a public servant and as a private person, but socially his position was ambiguous. He brought up his son to suppose that he was an exclusionist. The son was long an intimate of the Macarthur family, and at one stage hoped to marry a Macarthur daughter. William Charles was educated in England and did not learn the nature of the cloud under which his father lived until he was a mature man. It was while visiting New South Wales between educational experiences that he participated in the first crossing of the Blue Mountains. He qualified as a lawyer and attended Cambridge University. While in England, at the suggestion of the Macarthurs he wrote his famous book, but the ideas on government he expressed displeased John Macarthur and confirmed a rift between Wentworth and the family. What Wentworth proposed was that the Canadian constitution of 1791, itself closely modeled on prerevolutionary constitutions of the former North American colonies, should be granted to New South Wales, including a liberal franchise which should be extended to emancipists. This unwonted liberalism outraged the Macarthurs, whose central political purpose was to exclude emancipists from participation in government even if this meant the defense of autocracy. They regarded concessions to the emancipists as too high a price to pay for *representative* institutions. (At this stage neither Wentworth nor his opponents were thinking of *responsible* government.) The emancipists, however, were not for their part even thinking of *representative* government, but of civil rights only.

The politics of this period first came to a focus in the discussions and negotiations in London incident to the preparation and passing in July 1823 of an act for the better administration of justice and more effectual government in New South Wales. This act was an effort by the imperial authorities, in the person of Wilmot Horton, to solve problems of law and government in New South Wales which had plagued the settlement for some years. It was founded on the acknowledged assumption that the time had come to assimilate New South Wales in some degree to the status of a regular Crown Colony instead of continuing to regard it wholly as a jail. Quarrels which had beset the Macquarie administration were to be resolved; the fundamental basis for their resolution was to be the findings and recommendations of Commissioner Bigge. This involved both the reformation of the courts and the provision of a system for giving advice and assistance to the governor.

Eagar participated in the discussions and seems to have been an effective advocate of the emancipist cause. Some of the questions he raised were settled separately from the act, others in the act. The act elaborated the system of courts, partially removing established abuses, defining the position of judges in relation to the governor, and made a tentative move toward trial by jury. The emancipists had asked for trial by jury as far back as 1819; actually it was introduced piecemeal over a number of years. The net effect was to strengthen the position of the courts, though the difficult problem of getting first-class justices for service in Australia remained. As to the governor, as early as 1812 it was recognized by a committee of the House of Commons that the governor of New South Wales needed some kind of advisory council, and as the government structure of New South Wales became more complicated, governors of necessity obtained advice informally from senior public servants and important persons of the general community. The Act of 1823 formalized practice by providing for a Legislative Council, consisting of five principal public servants. Little power was granted to it. The governor remained an autocrat, subject to a minimum of restraint. Nevertheless, the Legislative Council could be regarded as a tentative step toward representative government, for conceivably nominated *unofficial* members could be added to give representation to the uppercrust of the general community. A greater restraint upon the governor than the Council was the power given the chief justice; he was to certify that legislation was not repugnant to the laws of England, a kind of check, however, that was not long continued.

To W. C. Wentworth the Act of 1823 was but a sop. His sharpest printed criticisms were directed at the inadequacies of the new system of courts; he took satisfaction in what slight clipping of the governor's power he could detect; he had remarkably little to say about the question of representative government. Plainly, he was taking his cue from the emancipists: they were not interested in representative government; they were not in a political position to make a bid for it; but they were concerned about civil rights and their eyes were on the courts. Trial by jury was the principal boon they sought. Wentworth declared for trial by jury; he thought it would be granted when the Act of 1823 came up for revision in five years' time. Actually, the most far-reaching change in 1828 was the provision for the application of the laws of England in the colonial courts—the transit of the common law to Australia, an important factor in making the situation of Australia "normal" as a Crown Colony.

The emancipists were not leaderless when Wentworth returned to New South Wales in 1824. He did not occupy a political vacuum, and he was never their sole leader, but in retrospect he seems somehow the most important individual associated at the time with the emancipist group. For at least five years before 1824 and for many after, Sir John Jamison, a free settler of distinction, gave patronage and leadership to the emancipist cause. Wentworth himself placed a very high valuation on the contributions of Dr. William Bland, a medical man transported for killing a man in a duel, who began his political career by baiting Governor Macquarie. And there were others.

Wentworth's unique contribution to the emancipist cause was to lend it the power of his vigorous and well-instructed mind and to guide it away from the limited objective of civil liberties to the support of a campaign for representative government. He began his contribution by adding a new weapon to the political arsenal, the newspaper. With Robert Wardell, a doctor of law and a journalist, whom Wentworth had met in London, he established *The Australian,* the first *independent* newspaper in the colony. The first newspaper, *The Sydney Gazette,* founded in 1804, was subject to official censorship. Governor Brisbane was favorably disposed to a free press. On establishment of *The Australian* he freed the *Gazette* from official control, but the verbal violence of *The Australian* got it into trouble under his successor, Sir Ralph Darling. So virulent was *The Australian's* criticism of him that he tried to bring it under control by a heavy stamp tax on each copy to limit its circulation, but this act was disallowed by the chief justice. Harassing suits for libel against the editor were also defeated. By 1827 freedom of the press was firmly established in Australia.

Aside from this innovation politics continued to employ the weapons of public meetings, testimonial dinners, and petitions. Wentworth used these for all they were worth to demand not only trial by jury but also representative institutions. His point was that as a matter of law and right the free people of New South Wales, including the emancipists, were entitled to the full benefits of the British Constitution. Less than three years after his return to the colony his fighting platform was widely accepted by a large body of people, including emancipists, who could be described as "the Gentry, Merchants, Landholders, Yeomen, Traders and others..." Wentworth was behind the forceful petitions sent to London in 1827 and 1833. An important outgrowth of the latter, and a major political development, was the Australian Patriotic Association, formed in 1835, to advance the cause of representative government. This organization enlisted the aid of important advocates in the House of Commons, notably Charles Buller.

The position of Wentworth and his friends and collaborators was decisively compromised by the existence of the convict element in New South Wales and its constant replenishment by transportation. As long as the emancipists were the principal component of the body of free men, and men in bondage, from among whom future additions to the emancipist group would be made, were both numerous and constantly

being added to, it was possible to oppose the extension to New South
Wales of both trial by jury and representative government. Not only
did the local exclusionists take such a position, but many people in England, otherwise well disposed toward colonial self-government, did so
also, including Charles Buller and the Colonial Reformers generally. In
their minds the political future of New South Wales turned upon an
increase of the number of free immigrant settlers and the cessation of
transportation. The increase in the numbers of free immigrants began
in the 1820's, as we have seen. This was favorable to Wentworth's cause,
and he approved it. But he made his position more difficult than it
needed to be when he opposed the moves to abolish transportation.
This he did in pursuit of his interests as a pastoralist concerned to insure a supply of cheap labor.

The position of the exclusionists was vigorously put by James Macarthur and his friends, using the device of petitions as Wentworth did,
as well as private activities including intrigue, both in the colony and
in London. In the year 1837 the exclusionists succeeded in an especially
brilliant job of publicizing their case in the United Kingdom. That year
three general works on New South Wales which discussed the political
situation and included important documentary evidence were published
in London. One was by James Macarthur himself (or was ghost-written
for him by Edward Edwards), another was by a man with extensive
experience in New South Wales, James Mudie, and the third was the
first edition of four of Dr. John Dunmore Lang's celebrated history,
autobiography, and polemic. These works, all of which emphasized the
alleged danger of granting free institutions to a community in which
convictism continued and the emancipists were numerous, made an
enormous impression. They appear to have gone a considerable distance toward establishing, or confirming, the opinion among even the
liberals of Britain that only when the free immigrants were clearly dominant and convictism abolished could free institutions properly be established.

Wentworth seems never to have acknowledged the force of this line
of argument. He had, since 1819, ignored it, and he continued to ignore
it to the end. Even when it was known to be the considered opinion of
the agent of the APA, Charles Buller, Wentworth showed no sign of
acknowledging its strength and importance. But it was perfectly obvious
that it left the tactical advantage with his opponents and that as long
as it was the established position, all Wentworth and his friends could
hope for were fringe benefits, such as the progressive extension of the
right to trial by jury. By 1830 this right was effectually established by
administrative rulings under an order in council. In spite of some tinker-

ing in 1828, the constitution of the colony was little altered from 1823 to 1842.

D3

As the years passed, the economy and society of New South Wales changed considerably and Wentworth himself underwent a change of ideas. The essence of the change in him was a mounting suspicion of the political ideas of the common man. His ideas about a liberal franchise, formulated in 1819 when he was a young man, now began to appear dangerous to him. He shifted toward a more limited franchise, the limitations expressed in property terms. He became alarmed by what he termed "democracy" and impressed by the necessity of rule by a propertied oligarchy. In effect he was returning to his origins—to a position close to that of the Macarthurs and their friends—but in so doing he opened the door to the charge that he was betraying the common man. At one stage even the newspaper he had founded attacked him mercilessly for his alleged defection. This is the origin of the allegation that, in Australian political slang, Wentworth finally "ratted" on the people.

Since his return to the colony in 1824 Wentworth had built up a lucrative law practice, had inherited considerable property when his father died in 1827, and had invested heavily in pastoral enterprises, both within and without the limits of location. He was both a landholder (i.e., he owned property in freehold) and a squatter. At one stage he was alleged to be in control of 250,000 acres. In 1835 he dropped his law practice—he had long since withdrawn from the newspaper—and took up his position as a great and influential pastoralist.

But if he repudiated his youthful ideas about the franchise, he did not abandon the emancipists nor, above all, his advocacy of representative government. Rather he shifted toward *responsible* government, at least as his ultimate goal. The publication of Lord Durham's report on Canada as a serial in the Sydney press gave intellectual support to his position. Charles Buller's brilliant pamphlet, *Responsible Government for Colonies,* was also aid and comfort. Social changes in New South Wales had reduced the significance of the emancipist element in his following. As free capitalist immigrants came in greater numbers, they tended to support Wentworth's demand for political freedom. But even though he must have been fully aware that his British allies on the constitutional question made their support turn on the abolition of transportation, Wentworth stubbornly defended that system. His economic interests as an employer of cheap labor triumphed over his grasp of political realities.

Wentworth was, of course, not unique in this. He had powerful support in his protransportation position, but it was support from people by whom for many years he had been opposed. The fight over transportation helped confirm his identification of his primary interests with the great pastoralists. As much as by his revised ideas on the franchise, Wentworth alienated his following among "common men" by his stand on transportation. He carried the Australian Patriotic Association with him, but such popular support as it had had promptly evaporated. The antitransportation position was taken up in New South Wales by the popular elements, free working-class immigrants and middle-class persons who did not identify themselves with the pastoralists, both mostly urban types resident in Sydney. The defeat of transportation, insofar as it was accomplished in Australia, was one of the earliest triumphs of town over country interests. The richer emancipists, heavily engaged in pastoral activities, could go along with Wentworth on this question for economic reasons, however paradoxical it may have appeared for them to support the basis of their moral disability.

Wentworth also found himself identified with the pastoral interest on land questions. He opposed the introduction of the Wakefield principle of sale of land and especially the successive increases in the price of land. He was, in the great arguments that developed around squatting, consistently prosquatter.

Step by step Wentworth and his followers moved to a position quite close to that of their opponents, the exclusionists. But whereas the exclusionists insisted that representative (to say nothing of responsible) institutions should not be introduced into New South Wales while transportation continued, Wentworth argued, as he long had, that they could and should. When Sir William Molesworth and his friends engineered the great inquiry into transportation in 1838, they drew from James Macarthur, then in London, the admission that he would favor political change if New South Wales could be "purified," by which was meant the drowning out of the emancipists by free immigrants. He thus was made to appear closer to the Colonial Reformers, and in their eyes more sensible than Wentworth! As a matter of fact, Buller actually had a meeting of minds with Macarthur on a constitution.

But Wentworth and his friends reacted violently against the committee's findings, denied the correctness of its moral indictment of New South Wales society, and argued for the continuance of transportation. They opposed the abolition of assignment, they opposed the abolition of transportation, and in due course they argued in favor of Earl Grey's effort to revive transportation on a new basis, all in terms of labor supply. They even supported old-style assignment after James Macarthur was for giving it up in favor of employing the incoming convicts exclusively in land development and public works. The political career of William Charles Wentworth is replete with paradoxes, but none is more astonishing than his insistence on keeping in existence the system that "tainted" the very emancipist group of whose political interests he was so long the exponent to the jeopardy of the prize of responsible government.

Wentworth only won his representative institutions *after* free immigration had reduced the importance of the emancipists and *after* transportation was abolished. By that time the situation had taken such a shape that Wentworth and James Macarthur were in essential agreement on most aspects of public policy. They were close together in the discussions that preceded the granting of the constitution of 1842. In forwarding the act to New South Wales, the colonial secretary candidly stated: "Looking at the great increase of the free population, and the cessation of transportation, Her Majesty's Government have not thought it necessary to introduce into the Act any exceptional provision in reference to emancipists." In other words, Wentworth had something resembling what he wanted *in spite of* the policies he had advocated. Wentworth was in the not uncommon political position of a man who had triumphed in spite of himself. But as it happened his triumph in 1842 was in his own eyes a very temperate affair.

Wentworth had all along advocated the establishment in New South Wales of a constitution modeled upon the Canadian constitution of 1791. By the time the British authorities began to write a new constitution for New South Wales, there had been an armed rebellion in Canada against the very constitution Wentworth recommended. This naturally made the British doubt the wisdom of introducing such a constitution into another colony. Rather, they chose to build upon the representative elements in the earlier constitution of New South Wales, and, while Wentworth had moved toward responsible government, they chose to keep closely within the confines of the representative form and, moreover, to place restrictions upon the power of the representatives. Under a governor, a Legislative Council of thirty-six was constituted, with powers comparable to those of the House of Lords in England. Of the thirty-six members, six were to be civil servants nominated by the governor, and six citizens-at-large also nominated by the governor, while the remaining twenty-four were to be *elected* under a high property franchise (higher than that in vogue in England) for the electors and a still higher property qualification for members. An essentially aristocratic Council was thus guaranteed; the pastoral oligarchy could feel secure. Emancipists could vote, but it seemed improbable that any could gain seats on the Council. But even this was not the end of the safe-guards the British government threw around the government. The governor could veto bills, he could also *reserve* bills and send them to Britain for the home government to accept or reject, and he had complete control over the Crown land and the revenue arising from its sale. (The British government could also veto bills even though the governor had approved them.) Moreover, the act established the so-called "Civil List" or a schedule of expenditures for salaries of certain officers (appointed in England), the administration of justice, and the subsidization of religious worship, which totaled about a third of all local revenues. This further accented the independence of the governor. The net effect of the act was to give the elected representatives of the pastoralists limited control over the purse and the government but to insure that the governor would still be in a position to enforce the views of the British authorities and carry on essential activities regardless of the opinions of the legislators. By limiting the legislature's power over the purse and wholly denying it a role in land policy, the act was an obvious challenge to the politicians of New South Wales. It was soon clear that government of this kind could not satisfy the aspirations of Wentworth and his followers. At the end of 1844 Wentworth used his position as chairman of a Committee on General Grievances of the Legislative Council to start a powerful drive for *responsible* government under which the executive would come under the control of the legislature.

Up to 1847 the steam behind the drive for responsible government was provided by the struggle over land policy between Governor Gipps and the squatters led by Wentworth. As we have seen, the squatters finally triumphed, or thought they had triumphed, on the land question with the Order in Council of 1847. This, however, left the question of responsible government where it was. Some squatters, being satisfied by the Order in Council, lost interest in responsible government. But Wentworth did not, apparently because he regarded it as a good thing in itself, not merely a provocative gambit in a quite different argument. He therefore continued to campaign for it. He was supported by his successors in the leadership of the "popular" groups, Robert Lowe, a brilliant lawyer, writer, and speaker transiently in Sydney (later a successful political figure in the United Kingdom and Viscount Sherbrooke), and Henry Parkes, who was to achieve great political power in New South Wales in the next period. But these men only supported Wentworth on the *principle* of responsible government; they rejected his effort so to organize it that the primacy of the pastoral oligarchy was secure. The "popular" interest wanted responsible government and a temperate democracy; Wentworth wanted responsible government and oligarchy, for he feared and abhorred "democracy." It is interesting that both Lowe and Parkes sought to assist themselves to political power by establishing newspapers, Lowe the *Atlas,* Parkes the *Empire.*

The fruit of the excursions and alarums of the eight years after 1842 was an Act for the Better Government of Her Majesty's Australian Colonies, dated August 5, 1850. It was a carefully thought out act— the *Report of Committee for Trade and Plantations of Privy Council on Proposed Australian Constitution,* dated May 1, 1849, on which it was based is a justly famous state paper—but while elements of it were pleasing in themselves to the colonies or peoples to whom they applied, the failure to bring in responsible government in New South Wales immediately gave it a poor reputation, and as parliamentary critics of the act such as Sir William Molesworth emphasized, it did not really represent a rethinking of the problem of colonial government; it was essentially a somewhat liberalized version of the Act of 1842. It satisfied the residents of the Port Phillip District by providing for the erection of the District into the separate colony of Victoria. It satisfied the Victorians, the free residents of Van Diemen's Land, and the people of South Australia, by extending to them the system of government in existence in New South Wales, with some liberalization. The liberalizations of the Act of 1842 pleased some of the people of New South Wales, since one of them increased the authority of the Legislative Council over the so-called Civil List, though checks were still retained, and another halved the property qualification for the franchise and extended the franchise to holders of squatting licenses. But to more people the incompleteness of the power over the Civil List, the failure to give the colony's legislature full power over the appropriation of revenue raised in the colony (not to mention power of appointment of men receiving salaries from the colonial revenue), and the keeping of land policy with its offensive Wakefieldian character out of the hands of the Council were widely deplored. From the point of view of the proponents of responsible government of all schools the only really good thing about the Act of 1850 was that it gave the colonial Legislative Councils the right to amend the constitution themselves, subject to confirmation of the changes by the imperial authorities. The immediate response to the act in New South Wales was a vigorously expressed *Declaration and Remonstrance of the Legislative Council,* dated May 1, 1851. While Earl Grey responded to this with a scholarly critique chastising its exaggerations, it was a signal to W. C. Wentworth to launch himself upon a campaign for responsible government with which he at once crowned his career and sealed his political fate.

CHAPTER VIII

A Transit of Civilization

At mid-nineteenth century it was customary to speak of "the Australian colonies"—at that time four in number—but to indicate their common geographical location rather than to imply anything in the way of nationality. The several colonies were segments of the overseas frontier of the United Kingdom, frontiers of raw material producers, all fairly primitive pastoral societies, the oldest still entangled in or only lately disentangled from convictism and but on the verge of self-government. A few far-sighted leaders—W. C. Wentworth was one—recognized that even at this early stage they had common political interests and said that provision might profitably be made for machinery of government to deal with them. But when Earl Grey, during the preliminary discussions of the constitution of 1850, made tentative proposals for limited federation, there was more apathy than enthusiasm and the proposals were dropped.

There was practically no sense of Australian nationality in any other terms either. Such expressions of national thinking and feeling as found their way into print in this period were clearly more in the nature of private literary exercises than expressions of even the most inchoate common thought and emotion. The colonists did not at first easily think of themselves as Tasmanians, or New South Welshmen, let alone as Australians, but rather as loyal subjects of Queen Victoria temporarily domiciled in remote places. Colonies were extensions of the United Kingdom, and whatever significance or value might be attached to the life in them by the residents, it was universally judged to be inferior to life in the home country. As provincial life was there adjudged inferior to London or metropolitan life, so colonial life was a long step down from provincial into the ultimate cultural abyss, colonial parochial. A colony did not, in the thought and feeling of many, even acquire the dignity of being home; Home (capital H) was the United Kingdom. It took time for the colonists to acquire a sense of being Australians, and longer for them to acquire a pride in so being, whether politically or culturally. In 1850 the colonists in Australia had hardly begun their search for a national identity.

D3

The Australian continent was the nearest thing to a cultural *tabula rasa* encountered in that swarming of human beings which was the expansion of Europe. The aborigines were so few and so widely and thinly dispersed and possessed a culture so much more primitive than that of the intruding whites that resistance was minimal. Compared with the troubles experienced in New Zealand, or the protracted difficulties with the Indians in North America, what happened in Australia was hardly trouble at all. There was, too, a minimum of borrowing from the aborigines and a striking failure creatively to influence the aboriginal culture. By taking the land, the whites disrupted and often destroyed both the foundation and the superstructure of aboriginal life, but before 1850 it is improbable that anyone felt very deeply disturbed about that.

It was the duty of the governors to protect the aborigines, and the outlook of the British authorities was definitely humanitarian, becoming more so under missionary influence. But whatever the governors did by way of carrying out their instructions, the settlers, and especially their employees, acted very differently. The settlers at best pushed the aborigines aside with thoughtless, if sometimes kindly, indifference about what became of them, while at worst they destroyed the natives as though they were vermin. The differences between the settlers and the aborigines usually arose over the occupation of the land and over the use of the animals depastured. By and large, the aborigines were a "nuisance" rather than a menace, and violence between the whites and the aborigines never achieved the scale of "war," even in Western Australia where difficulties were most trying. The violence was a matter of nasty affrays, usually called "massacres," involving few people on either side, and close to murder in character. The governors tried to prevent such affairs, but when they occurred, the whites who obviously were the aggressors were punished. Efforts to civilize the aborigines systematically by giving them religious instruction and some training in the simpler trades normally failed. Frustration was the reward of the few men who undertook the task. And whatever was done for the aborigines in good will was usually corrupted by the conviction that it was in the nature of things that they would die out in contact with white civilization, not successfully adapt to it. However, the aborigines survived, mostly on the periphery of white settlement, to become subjects for the anthropologists and a prick to the consciences of later generations of white Australians.

It is difficult to exaggerate the isolation of the pioneers, especially since their point of reference was the United Kingdom. It has been noted that the first fleet took eight months to make the trip out. As knowledge of winds and currents improved, the time required was reduced, but up to 1849 the standard time was never less than 140 days. The early clipper ships then cut the time down to 90 days. Prior to the coming of the clippers at the very end of the period, the average size of the sailing ship employed was 300 tons. Ordinarily, the voyage out was made by way of the Cape of Good Hope and the return voyage to England by way of Cape Horn. There were no regular scheduled services. The frequency and pace of sailing ships determined the speed of communications, including the transmission of news and other information and instruction.

Inland transportation was at the pace of the horse for the unencumbered traveler and at the pace of bullocks for the movement of heavy loads. The first "made" road was built in 1794—Sydney to Parramatta—and one of Macquarie's contributions was to improve inland transport with 300 miles of road, including a road over the Blue Mountains. Sir Thomas Mitchell was an active surveyor and builder of roads, and with him was associated as bridge-builder David Lennox, whose work is now much admired by architectural critics. Outside the areas served by "made" roads, tracks were the sole reliance. After 1821 coaches operated as common carriers connected the principal settlements. The longest run was that from Sydney to Melbourne, 560 miles. Until 1850 bullock teams alone carried supplies inland to the remotest stations and brought out the wool.

Because the colonies were spotted around the coast, and because of the great difficulties of overland transport, it was inevitable that coastal shipping should become a principal reliance. Even within colonies, as between Sydney and Newcastle, carrying by sailing ships was long of primary importance. It is indicative of the importance of coastal shipping that the first steamship seen in Australian waters was imported for that service in 1831. It was twenty years before a steamer entered the service between Australia and England.

The earliest settlers had a sufficiently difficult problem with the mere provision of shelter not to bother too much with its architecture. How to use the indigenous materials had to be learned by trial and error, and since the available trees, the gums or eucalypts, were mostly hardwoods subject to warping and splitting unless carefully seasoned they gave much trouble. Gums were used for framing, while siding was provided either by setting the trunks of cabbage trees closely together and plastering the outside with clay, or by weaving a mat of twigs and plastering that. Since wattle (*Acacia*) twigs proved best adapted for siding, the twig-and-plaster method became known as "wattle and daub." From observation of the aborigines, who did not "build" but put together crude shelters, use was made of sheets of bark for roofing and siding. Roofs were also thatched with rushes, but soon it was found that serviceable shingles could be made from the she-oak. The crude huts thrown together from indigenous materials were put up by the settlers wherever they went and these huts were the ancestors of the characteristic dwelling of the country: a single-story house of very few rooms, no cellar, a pitched roof, and a veranda on one or more sides to keep off the hot sun. The prevailing warmth also dictated that the kitchen be removed from the living quarters, often into a separate building. The single-story house, no matter what materials or architectural flourishes were employed, became the standard of the country and still is.

Since the indigenous timbers were so hard to handle, it was a happy discovery that the local clays could be worked up into bricks and tiles. The first brickmaster was James Bloodsworth, a convict, who rendered such notable service that he won emancipation in 1790. In May 1788 Bloodsworth began work on the first important brick structure in the colony, a house for Governor Phillip. It was occupied and dignified with the name of Government House in 1790; it remained in use until 1845. Little more than a box architecturally, it had a remarkable feature: a staircase. Few dwellings other than the most pretentious had two stories before 1850, though public buildings did, and three-story buildings were exceedingly uncommon. The tallest structures erected were churches. The embryonic towns consisted of a nucleus of two-story buildings in their business centers, surrounded by an ever-widening sea of single-story dwellings. However, the "capitalists" usually signified their prosperity by erecting dwellings, sometimes in the bush, of considerable architectural pretensions, often in two stories. In 1815 Governor Macquarie established the rule that all government buildings should be constructed of brick or stone. The same materials were commonly used for dwellings, though wooden houses probably predominated.

The settlers at Sydney showed a profound reluctance to keep to any town plan. The place became an attractive town more because of its natural setting on the beautiful, multi-armed harbor and the practice of setting the dwellings in gardens than because of skillfully planned land use. Towns established later were normally planned, at least at their centers, usually by the employment of the nineteenth-century "grid." Adelaide was unique in that the central city grid was surrounded

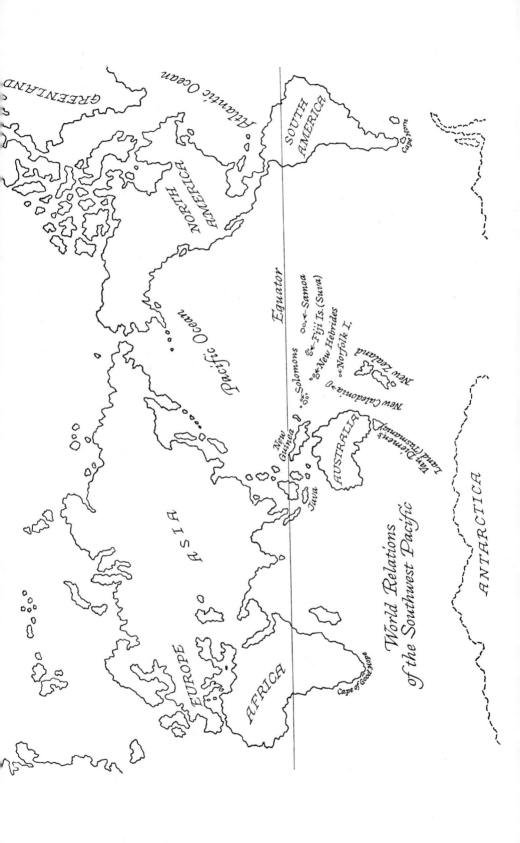

World Relations
of the Southwest Pacific

by a green belt. Other cities later relieved the monotony of the grid by developing parks. Of these Melbourne was an excellent example. Governor Macquarie reserved a notable park now near the central business area of Sydney.

Until Macquarie's time there were no architects in the country, but in 1814 three arrived, one a free settler, one an army man, the third a convict. Of the three, the greatest was the convict, Francis Greenway. Before falling into obscurity, Greenway as architect to the government created numerous lovely buildings of which perhaps a dozen still survive, most of them altered and mutilated, which provide the country's architectural classics. In style and taste, Greenway was a Late Georgian. An architect named John Lee Archer made a similar bequest to Van Diemen's Land. By 1850, however, architectural Victorianism had begun to lay its fell hand upon Australian buildings.

It has already been noted that the technology of farming remained backward in the Australian colonies, save in South Australia, for a long time. In the pastoral industry the situation was mixed, for clearly John Macarthur's experiments in breeding sheep for wool were of immense importance. However, the care of the sheep on the stations followed methods not much changed since Biblical times. The sheep were in the care of shepherds who in effect lived with the animals. The wool was removed from the sheep with handshears (known as "the blades"). It was not until the period 1850–1900 that a technological revolution overtook the wool industry. In miscellaneous ways, however, the colonists contributed to the establishment of the tradition of quick adoption of technological innovations in Australia. It has been noted that the steamboat came into use in 1831. Prepayment of postage charges on letters was introduced in New South Wales in 1838, eighteen months before it was adopted in the United Kingdom. Sydney streets were lighted by oil lamps from 1826 and by gas from 1841.

Most of the early scientific work was closely associated with or related to exploration; it was done, in effect, as part of the general task of gathering the data needed to define the special character of the new land. Unfortunately, as there is no history of science (nor of technology) in Australia, it is impossible to deal with the subject systematically. It was natural for explorers to make notes on vegetation, bird and mammal life, geology and mineralogy, and the aborigines. An occasional explorer might possess expertise in one or another of the relevant sciences, but more commonly he was an amateur, though in a day when amateurs were quite likely to make important contributions to knowledge. As exploration became less casual, it became the practice to attach one or more scientists to the expeditions.

Because Sir Joseph Banks, the patron of Australia, was particularly interested in botany, much of the early scientific work was in that field and the closely associated sciences. Banks encouraged such members of the governing group as had a special interest or who wished to please him to send materials to him in England. As early as 1800 he had George Caley, a professional botanical collector, sent out, and the next year he saw to it that Flinders was accompanied by Robert Brown, a professional botanist. Phillip Parker King, who followed up Flinders' work, was accompanied by Allan Cunningham, a collector who worked in New South Wales from 1817 to his death in 1839 and made his own contributions to exploration. The explorers and the professionals collected more than botanical specimens; they also collected birds. Caley and Brown attended to the bird life almost as systematically as to the plants. Captain Charles Sturt collected birds when on his famous trip down the Murray. Indeed, a book devoted to Australian ornithology was compiled and illustrated by J. W. Lewin, an engraver by profession, as early as 1808. Nevertheless, it was not until the 1830's that fundamental work was done in ornithology. Arriving in 1838, John Gould, who stands in the same relation to Australian ornithology as John James Audubon does to American, systematically collected the materials embodied in *Birds of Australia,* published between 1840 and 1848 in thirty-six parts, making seven volumes. In 1845–63 he brought out *The Mammals of Australia.* However, systematic zoology trailed botany and ornithology, as also did entomology. Geology in this period hardly got beyond the collection of "specimens," but a systematic account of mineralogy was first attempted as early as 1833. The most important discoveries in economic geology were coal in New South Wales in 1791 —worked from 1801—silverlead, and especially copper in South Australia. Systematic geological surveys waited upon the gold rushes.

Astronomy began with the strictly practical task of determining exactly where on the globe Australia was located. The Board of Longitude commissioned Lieutenant Dawes of the marines of the first fleet to carry out this chore, and he set up an observatory for the purpose. It was, however, Governor Sir Thomas Brisbane who really established astronomy in Australia. He had an observatory built and equipped at his own expense to study the stars of the Southern Hemisphere, and from the data accumulated William Richardson of the Royal Observatory at Greenwich compiled *A Catalogue of 7835 Stars, Chiefly in the Southern Hemisphere,* published by order of the Lords Commissioners of the Admiralty in 1835.

A natural outgrowth of the early cultivation of botany was the early establishment of botanical gardens. The gardens were partly designed to give pleasure, partly to study indigenous plants, many hundreds of which were eventually domesticated for garden use, and partly for the acclimatization of imported plants. However, the government gardens did but part of all this work, for amateurs were exceedingly active. It was the amateurs who played a large role in acclimatizing unfortunate imports that subsequently ran wild and ruined vast tracts of useful land (as we shall see later). Much amateur and also professional effort went into acclimatizing the basic economic plants and even various other plants (and birds and mammals) intended to "humanize" the country by establishing favorite examples from England. Giving way to nostalgia, people attempted to transform the peculiar native vegetation and bird and animal life by giving it a British veneer. The curious aspect of the business was that while the indigenous vegetation was being intensively studied and, when it was pasture, intensively exploited, it commonly suffered emotional and aesthetic rejection by alienated immigrants. An important phase of the making of Australians was the achievement of a reconciliation to the environment even in its most extravagantly non-European expressions.

D3

Since religion and education were closely intertwined in the United Kingdom at the time of the settlement of Australia and for a good while after, it is to be expected that they should be intertwined in Australia also. A chaplain for the penal colony—the Reverend Richard Johnson of the Church of England—was appointed on October 24, 1786, but no schoolmaster was appointed. Johnson was expected to take care of both religion and education. He accompanied the first fleet to Sydney and remained in the colony until 1800. He does not appear to have been an especially strong personality, but he was evidently a "good" man, for casehardened convicts testified that he was. He had a hard time and little was done to make his way easier. He even had to finance the building of his own first church—a wattle-and-daub affair—and then some miscreant burnt it down. He was the sole ministrant of religious consolation, and all convicts regardless of denomination had to attend his services.

Johnson worked alone until 1794 when he was joined by the Reverend Samuel Marsden. Religiously, Marsden was far less sensitive than Johnson, but he was a far tougher personality and hence better qualified for success in a penal colony. He was the senior clergyman until 1824. On the departure of Johnson, Marsden was alone until the next year when he obtained the services of the Reverend Henry Fulton, holder of a B.A. degree, transported from Ireland as a political prisoner. Marsden wanted the colonial church placed under the Bishop of London, but finally, in 1814, it was put under the Bishop of Calcutta, an interesting indication of how the British then saw the imperial structure. Ten years later, in 1824, Thomas Hobbes Scott, secretary to Bigge in the investigation of Macquarie's regime, was appointed archdeacon of Sydney, but he was a tactless man and lasted but four years. His successor, William Grant Broughton, was a complete success, at least with regard to the organization and administration of the church. He was raised to bishop of Australia in 1836; and in 1847 he became bishop of Sydney and metropolitan of Australia. A conference of bishops was held in Sydney in 1850 by which time there were bishops for Sydney and Newcastle in New South Wales, Hobart in Van Diemen's Land, Adelaide, and Melbourne. Up to the 1850's, the Church of England was "official" but not "established"; after that time it ceased to be even "official."

The forced attendance of all convicts at Church of England services was most disturbing to the Catholics. There were enough Roman Catholics even in the first fleet for two priests to petition the government for permission to go out with it and accept as their lot whatever befell the convicts, but they were refused. By 1800, however, Roman Catholic priests appeared among the transportees from Ireland, and the first mass was said in Australia in 1803. However, no official recognition was given Roman Catholic clergy, and one who arrived without authorization was deported. In 1819 New Holland was included in the vicariate apostolic of the Cape of Good Hope, and late that same year two Irish priests, John Joseph Therry and Philip Connoly, sailed from Cork for Sydney with official letters from the colonial secretary to Governor Macquarie; on May 3, 1820, they established the Roman Catholic Church in Australia.

The Catholic Church had a rapid growth. The emancipation of the Catholics in England in 1829 was of material assistance. Although Catholics appeared as high appointed officials of the administration and were conspicuous among the economically successful emancipists, most of the Catholic communicants were among the poor and many of them were convicts. This circumstance gave the Australian Catholic Church a strong bias in its social thinking and an early identification with anti-transportation, representative and responsible government, and, as time passed, with social reform through legislation. A vicar apostolic for New Holland—Dr. John Bede Polding—was appointed in 1835, and between that date and 1848 episcopal sees were created in Hobart, Adelaide, Perth, and Melbourne, as well as Sydney. Dr. Polding became archbishop in 1842.

The Presbyterians built their first church in New South Wales in 1809 and maintained a regular clergyman from 1822. The Methodists received a missionary clergyman in 1815, the Reverend Samuel Leigh, who at a later stage pioneered the missions to the Maori in New Zealand and to the Tonga Islands. The Baptists built their first church in Sydney in 1836. The Lutherans were established in South Australia in 1838. Jews were sufficiently numerous in Sydney to build their first synagogue in the 1840's. From 1836 all impartially received subsidies from the government in support of their religious purposes. The Church of England and the Roman Catholic Church were the first and second churches by numbers of communicants, as they have ever since remained.

Most of the churches took a hand in education, notably the Church of England, the Roman Catholic, the Methodist, and the Presbyterian. The pioneering was done by the Reverend Richard Johnson with the help of convict teachers and support from the Society for the Propagation of the Gospel. The first nonconvict teachers were refugee missionaries from the islands. No professionally trained teacher was available until 1809, and persistently for the next forty years the unavailability of trained teachers was a problem.

Attention was chiefly directed to elementary education: reading, writing, and arithmetic. The various churches, seeking to serve and conserve their communicants, tended to duplicate facilities and thus instead of a single sound school in a district, two or three indifferent schools existed. Moreover, no systematic coverage of needs was achieved any place, and at no time up to 1850 were all children of school age in attendance at schools. Constant complaints were made that the churches collectively were failing in their task, in spite of special subsidization by the government. And it was felt that education, particularly in its aspect as moral discipline, was peculiarly required in a society in which convictism existed.

The successive governors took an interest in education if only as part of their concern for the moral condition of the children, since so many of them came from homes of doubtful stability and dubious morality. As the children constituted the native-born population on which the future would much depend, it was naturally a matter of concern that they not lapse, because of official neglect, into the ways of their forebears. Since the churches were not reaching all—and probably not reaching precisely those most in need of their assistance—it was natural that thought should be given to supplementing or supplanting the church-based system by a "national" system controlled by the government.

The first governor to suggest such a solution of the problem of elementary education was Bourke in 1833. Apparently, because it was familiar to him, but also because it offered a way around the sectarian question, he proposed to introduce the so-called Irish system. It was acceptable to the Roman Catholics, a very important consideration. Bourke was defeated by the adamant opposition of the Protestants, led by William Grant Broughton. Returning to the problem, since it would not brook neglect, Governor Gipps proposed the British and Foreign Society system, but this also was opposed by Broughton, and it was, moreover, not acceptable to the Roman Catholics. By that time, however, it was apparent that Broughton was primarily interested not in preserving education for the churches in general but in achieving a monopoly of education for the Church of England. This split the Protestant opposition to governmental action, especially when John Dunmore Lang pointed his accusing finger at Broughton. Nevertheless, Gipps felt it unwise to force a program on the colony. In 1844 the question was examined by a select committee of the Legislative Council, headed by Robert Lowe. After pointing out that at that time only half of nearly 26,000 children between the ages of four and fourteen in the colony were receiving any kind of education at all, and laying this at the door of the churches, the committee recommended the Irish system for adoption. This stirred up controversy well enough, but it was a clear indication that sooner or later the denominational schools would have to face competition from government schools. Representative Protestants and Catholics alike now spoke in favor of the Irish system. Bishop Broughton, as though tired of controversy, quickly accommodated himself to the emerging compromise solution of the vexing school problem.

Competition became the order of the day in 1848 when a dual system came into operation. The denominational schools continued under a Board of Commissioners, but alongside it was established a Board to direct so-called National Education (the Irish system), both using public funds. At mid-century New South Wales still had an unsatisfactory system of primary education, but the seed from which the future system was to grow had been planted. A weak compromise could hardly endure forever, but the environmental circumstances of the compromise were fair warning that any move by a government wholly to take over education would stir the sectarian fires.

Secondary education was and continued to be for some time a field for both private enterprise and denominational efforts. The first secondary school, a private enterprise, was established by Dr. Laurence Halloran, sometime clergyman, transported to New South Wales for forging a frank worth ten pence. Halloran established his school in 1817 and made much of his success in the classics. The Church of England began its efforts in secondary education in 1830; and in 1832 the Presbyterians, led by John Dunmore Lang, opened a most impressive secondary school, the Australian College. All these efforts and many others of much the same character, various as to quality, mostly had but short lives, though a few survived this period to become the fashionably "public" schools of the country. The mortality among secondary schools was attributable to undernourishment in finance, absence of qualified teachers, and social troubles caused by acceptance of children of emancipists.

Thus it happened that there was no solidly based primary and secondary education in existence when the Legislative Council, under the leadership of William Charles Wentworth, founded the University of Sydney in 1850. In the language of the act of incorporation, the University was designed to advance religion and morality and promote useful knowledge, to "hold forth to all classes and denominations of Her Majesty's subjects resident in the colony of New South Wales, without any distinction whatsoever, an encouragement for pursuing a regular and liberal course of education." The denominational question was evaded by banning all theological studies. Three chairs were established: classics, mathematics, and chemistry and physics. Of the first professors, one was from Oxford, one from Cambridge, and one from Aberdeen. Classes began in 1852 with twenty-four undergraduates. The policy of drawing senior staff from the United Kingdom was long continued. Complementing it, the practice of sending Australian-educated candidates for advanced degrees to the United Kingdom was also early initiated. This insured that the colonial elite should remain British. Often the desired enculturation was doubly insured by sending boys to England for their education from the public school level on, according to the example set by William Charles Wentworth himself.

D3

Culturally, there seems to have been no sharp and unwavering line between the convicts and the emancipists and the free. The groups shaded into one another, with an occasional convict clearly able to claim a place among the cultural elite. Nevertheless, in the mass there was sufficient difference between the bond and the free for it to be true that there was a "popular culture" (in the sociological sense), chiefly in the early days to be identified with the convicts and the working-class, and an "elite" culture, chiefly to be identified with the aristocracy and the governing group. However, since all these people lived in a small and rather intimate society the elite groups undoubtedly shared even more than they commonly do elsewhere in the popular culture.

Convict jargon words, we know, gained general currency. It is difficult to say which group supplied the nomenclature of the basic occupations, such as sheep farming, who discovered aboriginal designations for birds, beasts, and flowers, or gave them British names on analogical reasoning, or discovered and used aboriginal place names. (It is clear that governors, explorers, and upper-class settlers were freely given to labeling the countryside with British names for natural features until, for example, of the three principal rivers of the country's greatest river system only one today has an aboriginal name.) Ballads were a constituent of popular culture and were popularly adapted to Australian themes, only later to be imitated by literary men and thus assimilated to the elite culture; later still these popular ballads became an active academic interest. Broadsides, important in popular culture in England, were produced also in numbers in Australia. The lower orders had no monopoly of the composition and distribution of "pipes" —scurrilous verses aimed at individuals in the governing group and distributed by dropping them where the friends of the victim would find them. We know, for example, that W. C. Wentworth once composed a "pipe."

Sport, so conspicuous an element of Australian popular culture in later times, whether in its participation or spectator aspects, with regard to its associated gambling, or with regard to the journalism and literature that developed around it, seems to have been initiated by the military garrison and to have spread from the soldiers to the general population. Competition in team sports was often between the soldiers and "the natives," but whether the natives were always only native-born is not clear. The soldiers introduced cricket (and Marylebone Club rules) in 1803, and soon soldiers were competing with "natives" for a purse, while side bets were being laid in coin, timber, foodstuffs, and what not. Oddly, cricket also early spread to the aborigines. The military introduced football in the late 1820's. Naval officers stationed in Australian ports introduced sailing as a sport in those years also. Horseracing, *par excellence* a sport immediately engaging the interest of the whole community—the record is clear about this—was begun in 1810. On the other hand, a sport like hunting had an ambiguous character, for while all and sundry could go out for kangaroo, dingo, and emu, hunting with hounds was definitely aristocratic, patronized by the governors. By contrast bare-knuckle boxing, introduced in 1817, was subject to police interference if a bout in progress was discovered. Competitive swimming came in the 1840's, as did the game of bowls, and even golf. By the middle of the century the "sportin'" character of the colonials was firmly established, and Australia was well on its way to becoming one of the great sporting countries of the world.

From its inception the country inspired the production of a voluminous written and pictorial record. The governing group of the first fleet produced several narratives which rank in interest, if not in moral intensity, with such American colonial documents as Bradford's *Plymouth Plantation*. These books initiated the literature of Australian experience. They are reportorial in character, usually autobiographical in considerable part, and designed for the utilitarian purpose of telling the curious world something about a presumably exotic country. Books of this general description not only first satisfied the world's curiosity about Australia, but they have continued to be the most popular kind of reading matter about it to the present day.

Although printing began in Australia in 1796, at first exclusively for official purposes (after the press brought out in the first fleet had lain idle for eight years), and although many independent newspapers were published after 1824, as well as an assortment of shortlived periodicals (the first appeared in 1821), most of the early writing about the country was published overseas, chiefly in London. Up to 1850 there was no regular book publisher established in Australia. The few books produced locally were casual productions. (The first, brought out by the government press, was *The New South Wales General Standing Orders* in 1802.) This heavy dependence upon London for the production of books continued for many decades and has not been wholly overcome even in the middle of the twentieth century. When to this is added the practice, also dating from this period, of drawing heavily on London for books in general, we have interesting evidence of a material kind of how the cultural ties between Australia and the homeland were maintained at strength.

The settlers brought books with them and when they went off into the bush they often took their books along. The probability is that all the "standard" writers of the eighteenth century were soon available at Sydney and that current publications were coming out from London. We know that the reading capacity of the settlers soon outran their personal resources of books. At Sydney in 1822 a kind of "union catalogue" of private collections was made and in 1826 the Australian Subscription Library was founded under the patronage of Governor Darling. As it proved rather difficult for private persons to obtain books from London, bookselling as a trade became established in Sydney as early as 1828, and by 1850 there were a dozen dealers in business. These men also handled magazine subscriptions. In 1833 a library of less exclusive character than the ASL was established in connection with the Mechanics Institute, and it gave the form to the libraries established in country towns.

When it comes to making discriminations among the books that pretended to aesthetic qualities and were produced in Australia during the early decades one suffers the embarrassment that always afflicts the student of the literary beginnings of overseas countries. The colonial and frontier milieu was, with its heavy emphasis on building the material foundations of personal and social success, hostile to the aesthetic attitude, and local readers, however ardently they conned imported books, were reluctant to give any time to local productions. Those who had, or thought they had, the capacity to do themselves and the country credit in poetry and literary prose were even more decidedly odd men out in early Australia than they normally are in more mature societies. Working without precedents, without a local tradition, their minds disciplined only by imported ideas and attitudes and forms, lacking genius, they could hardly be expected to exceed mediocrity in results.

Poetry tempted most of the pioneers of Australian literature, and poetry has ever since been the primary literary preoccupation, overshadowing prose. Yet it was not until 1845 when Charles Harpur, farmer and grazier, stimulated by the English Romantics, published his initial volume that any verse was written that pleases present-day critics. Before Harpur's time credit goes only to those who were responsible for "firsts," like Barron Field, the literary judge who published in 1823 the first book of verse, and Charles Tompson, clerk of court and legislature, who in 1826 became the first native-born poet to have a book of his work published.

A novel of sorts written by Henry Savery, transported for forgery, was published in Van Diemen's Land in 1830. However, it was not until 1843 and the publication in London of Charles Rowcroft's *Tales of the Colonies* that prose fiction of Australian reference of wide appeal appeared. Rowcroft, a free sojourner in Australia, published other stories later on, and all his books were reprinted in New York for the American trade. But by far the most remarkable novels of this period were *Ralph Rashleigh,* composed as a memoir by a convict named James Tucker, probably about 1845 but not published complete until 1952, and *Settlers and Convicts* by Alexander Harris, originally presented as personal reminiscences in 1847. These two works, each an indeterminate mixture of reportage, reminiscence, and fiction, came closer to giving the authentic flavor of the life in Australia within their purview than any others of their time.

How to use Australian materials in the drama proved the most difficult of all literary problems, not only in the early days but for many decades after. Nobody before 1850 managed anything more than a closet drama. This was not because there was no theater. The theater in Australia had a long and checkered history dating from a dramatic performance put on by the convicts at Sydney on June 4, 1789. A regular theater was opened in 1796. Theatrical firsts in the other colonies were Hobart 1833, Adelaide 1838, Perth 1839, Melbourne 1841. Starting out with an amateur status, and lapsing back to that rather frequently, the theater first achieved something approaching professional status in Sydney in the 1830's under an entrepreneur named Barnett Levey. Before 1850 the commercial theater was strong enough to import players from London and to offer opportunities to French vaudevillians and Italian jugglers on tour. All the early productions were local versions of plays from overseas, chiefly from London, classics interspersed among plays of the day. Dancing came in with plays. Before 1850 the basic pattern of the theater in Australia was laid down, even to the export of talent to the United Kingdom and America.

The settlers took a keen interest in music as a performing art, though they achieved no original compositions. The first music heard publicly was that of the regimental bands of the garrison troops. In general, however, the settlers began by favoring singing over instrumental music, though a piano was landed in 1791; they had choral and glee clubs and organized singsongs before they had chamber music and orchestral societies. Yet by 1836 a wandering English musician named Wallace, later to have a career in New York, London, and Vienna, established the first school of music in Sydney and for a few years was a conspicuous and successful teacher and performer. That same year the first visiting artist arrived, an English singer named Mrs. Chester. Also, the Deane family of Van Diemen's Land began a career in music that lasted several generations. Music, more than the theater, profited from the patronage of the governors.

Most of the early painting done after settlement was of a kind known as "topographical," a variety of pictorial reportage, which performed the same function that photographs did later on and complemented the reportorial prose of the time. Thomas Watling who arrived in 1791 under conviction for forgery was the pioneer. In the 1820's a convict named Joseph Lycett made a series of Sydney views of more than ordinary quality, but perhaps the most meritorious of all examples of the genre were those executed by J. Skinner Prout, a free visitor, who did a beautiful series of Sydney scenes in 1842–43, published with useful letterpress by John Rae. A convict artist of uncommon personal interest was Thomas Griffith Wainewright, subject of Oscar Wilde's famous essay "Pen, Pencil and Poison," but his Australian work, chiefly portraits, is rather cloying in manner and effect. Far more interesting aesthetically is the work of another convict, William Barlow Gould. Gould did flower pieces of unusual skill in his earlier days, but finally eroded his talent away with drink. Probably the most accomplished of the early immigrant artists was John Glover, a man of English reputation, who retired as a free settler to Van Diemen's Land when in his sixties. He had no particular influence on Australian art. That comical-tragic Victorian artist Benjamin Haydon noted along with other curious things that British colonials had an active affinity for portraits. This is certainly borne out in Australia. The first *professional* portrait painter to work in Sydney was the free immigrant Robert Read who arrived in 1814; it is to Read that we owe the sharp visual image we have of Macquarie. By far the most important artist, historically speaking, who established himself in Australia before 1850 was Conrad Martens who arrived as a free immigrant in 1835 and continued to work in Australia until his death in 1878. Martens, with all his skill, did not wholly achieve the transition from the iconographic to the aesthetic; he did not discover how to get the image of "Europe" out of the artist's eye in favor of an accurate image of Australian vegetational and other forms, let alone discover how to render Australia's vivid light; but he nevertheless did make very interesting pictures from Australian materials as he saw them. In the course of earning a living he made many pictures of the country seats of the "capitalists." Martens was born in London, was trained there, and went to South America in 1832. He served for a time as artist on the "Beagle," gaining the enduring friendship of Charles Darwin. Leaving South America, he emigrated to Australia via Tahiti and the Bay of Islands, of both of which he made fascinating pictorial records. More than any other figure of this period, Martens established painting as a major element of the Australian creative tradition.

NEW ZEALAND

CHAPTER IX

New Zealand in Polynesia

Whereas what may be called the "prehistory" of Australia as a part of the European political-economic-cultural world consists wholly of the story of its discovery and ends rather abruptly with the settlement of 1788, the prehistory of New Zealand covers seven decades, or from Captain Cook's exploratory visit of 1769, to 1840 when systematic European settlement began. Between 1769 and 1840 New Zealand was essentially an island group in Polynesia which, after 1790, drew to it Europeans of varied types, from disgusting wastrels to noble philanthropists, including sealers, whalers, timber-getters, flax-collectors, food buyers, traders, adventurers, and missionaries, most of whom also appeared in the other Polynesian groups. These people discovered and advertised the economic potential of the place—even missionaries had an eye for this—and New Zealand, the only island group in Polynesia wholly within the temperate zone, was early sized up as a likely field for large-scale colonization. The delay in action was partly caused by unfavorable attitudes toward such an enterprise in the United Kingdom and partly by fear of the Maoris, whose cannibalism inspired horror. In the 1830's, however, land hunger led to a discounting of Maori powers of resistance to incoming whites. It was guessed that New Zealand could be settled without serious "trouble." This proved to be wrong, and in the end the Maoris had to be crushed by force. But by the time it came to bush-fighting between whites and Maoris, the die had been cast and New Zealand had been irrevocably wrested from Polynesia and incorporated into the Western world.

D3

There was no visit to New Zealand for the purpose of exploiting its resources until after the settlement at Sydney, but within four years of the arrival of the British in New South Wales, commercial visits began, and thereafter for several decades the primary (but not sole) foreign impact on the country came from or via New South Wales. New Zealand was, thus, with the other islands of the Southwest Pacific, a wilder frontier of a frontier. The visitors in the first ten years were after seals, whales, or timber, or were concerned with flax or food (especially potatoes). Inevitably, these early visitors had contacts with the Maoris and traded with them, continuing the introduction into the Maori culture of iron and European textiles, as well as domesticated plants and animals.

The very first known commercial visitor arrived in January 1792. He was Captain Bunker (a displaced Nantucketer in the service of the British) in command of a whaler out of Sydney. The following year another British ship put a party of sealers ashore in the South Island. In 1793 also, one of Vancouver's ships, en route from the northwest coast of North America to Sydney, put in at New Zealand, according to instructions, and kidnapped two Maori men whom it took to Norfolk Island to instruct convicts in the working of flax which grew wild there. They, however, professed ignorance of the art, saying it was women's work (and, as a matter of fact, the Maori women did chiefly process the flax), but Captain Philip Gidley King, in command at Norfolk, treated his visitors kindly and later in the year returned them himself to New Zealand. On this trip, King, in addition to other gifts, supplied the Maori with seed potatoes. The potato proved a revolutionary contribution to the Maori economy and diet. Its culture was rapidly dispersed throughout the islands, and it became a staple food, perhaps too much so for the good of the Maori people. Within two years of King's momentous visit, the timber trade began when a ship called in for a cargo of spars, a resource recommended to attention by Captain Cook. Before the century was out the first white man (an escaped convict) was living among the Maoris and very early in the 1800's the first half-caste (a girl-child) was pointed out to visitors.

The Bay of Islands in the northeast of North Island early became the principal port. It seems to have been so established by the very early 1800's, and when the deep-sea whalers were really active among the islands it was the southern counterpart of Honolulu in the north, though very much smaller. As the Americans gained predominance in deep-sea whaling, they too tended to dominate the life of the Bay of Islands. American ships calling there far outnumbered the British in the 1830's, and in 1839 it was so important a port-of-call for Americans that the United States government appointed a consul there (an English resident named Clendon). However, when the British took sovereignty in New Zealand in 1840, the Americans soon shifted to Hobart in Van Diemen's Land rather than pay the port charges and put up with other annoyances introduced by the British authorities. The authorities at Hobart were more generous in their policies.

In its heyday, however, Bay of Islands, or Kororareka as the town was called, was a fairly typical place of "refreshment." British writers customarily refer to it as a veritable Alsatia (after a privileged sanctuary for wastrels and criminals which existed in London for many years, abolished 1697), and one of the few Americans who left a record of his reactions was equally repelled, but it seems to have been no worse and no better than other such resorts of its time. Its evil reputation grew up around the drinking and fornication that went on, but neither appears to have been more flagrant than was characteristic in other "red-light" districts of that day and age. The Maori chiefs set up in business as keepers of bawdyhouses, or suppliers of temporary wives to the more fastidious (usually captains of the ships). As was natural, the commercial morality was low. In the earlier days the Maoris were the merchants, offering potatoes and pork for European trade goods, including muskets, and they often were outrageously cheated. When the volume of trade increased, white merchants set up shop and stood to an extent between the Maoris and the visiting buyers; their commercial morality was better but far from good; they drew supplies of manufactured articles from Sydney. Moreover, deserters from the ships contributed a low element to the population, and the practice of getting them dead drunk and delivering them for a fee to captains filling out a crew preparatory to sailing did not improve the tone of the place. Petty thievery was rampant. Murder, arson, and malicious demolition of buildings occurred. But account must be taken of three facts in judging Kororareka: it grew up in a country where western notions of orderly government were nonexistent; it was a place of resort of many white men (and a few white women) at war with conventional morality before they got there; and contemporary judgment upon it was passed chiefly by missionaries, not the most tolerant of witnesses. New Zealand was not uniquely victimized by its Kororareka; rather Kororareka was simply what New Zealand offered as an Alsatia in the days when Alsatias were common around the Pacific. It was, moreover, an Alsatia which had a church; and from 1814 missionaries had headquarters nearby.

When white men—the Maoris called them pakeha—began to infiltrate the islands, the Maori reputation for fierceness was already well established. Until 1840 a very few whites dealt with a great many Maoris, especially as the Bay of Islands was fairly central to the portion of the North Island where the Maori population was most dense. In the earlier years it is probable that there were upwards of 200,000 Maoris in the

North Island, and even in 1840, after fifty years of decline, it is generally assumed that nearly 100,000 still remained. (The South Island
Maoris probably at no time numbered more than 10,000 to 15,000,
most of them to be found close to Cook Strait.) The contact of cultures
nevertheless proceeded in a surprisingly peaceful fashion. To be sure,
whites lost their lives at Maori hands, but it would be unjust and un-
candid to blame this on every occasion on the Maoris. It is usually
possible to discern the provocation that led them to extreme action;
and even when they apparently killed without a provocation that made
sense by Western standards, it is often possible to reconcile the actions
to Maori morality, especially by reference to the Maori idea of vengeance on the tribe of the offender rather than on a specific individual or
group of individuals. The Maori custom that most offended the incoming whites was, of course, cannibalism. But the Maoris never made a
point of eating whites. Their cannibalism was associated with the eating
of slain enemies. They only ate whites when the whites were slain enemies. During the first fifty years of active contact between the races,
far more Maoris died by Maori violence than by white violence, because
the contact had brought the Maoris into possession of the musket, and
they turned it, for Maori purposes, on one another. Moreover, a heavy
toll of Maori lives, taken by introduced diseases, including venereal diseases, the deleterious effect of changes in diet and clothing, and the bad
consequences of changes for the worse in the location and character of
Maori housing, must be laid to the white men's account. All in all, it
is not so remarkable that the Maoris killed some white men as that they
killed so few and killed most of the few with so much show of reason.

The fact is the Maoris rather tended to welcome than repel the incoming whites because they were appreciative of the advantages of having whites among them. They, like most peoples in their stage of evolution, welcomed iron. The superiority of the musket over their stone
weapons in war was early understood. They had no difficulty in making
the pig and the potato part of their diet and in maintaining the supply
by their own efforts as well as a surplus for trading. They proved adept
at agriculture in general, including cereal growing, when it was introduced among them. It was chiefly on the technological level that the
missionaries first made progress. It was, of course, an appalling misfortune that in learning good and useful things the Maoris also learned
bad and destructive things. But the Maoris were in no position either
to select the whites who settled in New Zealand nor to choose with discrimination from among the things and practices the whites offered. If
they could discern the good of new agricultural crops and techniques,
that was net gain, but if they lacked a scale of values that would allow

them to reject the musket as an almost unmitigated evil to their society, that was bad luck. Cultural contact is normally a disorderly process at whatever level of development the givers and the receivers may be. On the whole, the Maoris felt they had won a net profit from the whites until the whites began to engross the land.

Although the whalers and sealers both first appeared in New Zealand in the 1790's, it was not until the decade 1810–20 that sealing in the islands reached its zenith and not until the 1830's that whaling (both deep-sea and shore) was at its maximum. The sealers began to move into New Zealand after the rookeries in Bass Strait were exhausted. They were chiefly active in the South Island, especially on the southern coast around Foveaux Strait. Most of the New Zealand sealers were employees of Sydney entrepreneurs, though some were from Hobart. As sealing declined in productivity, it was replaced, chiefly along the east coast of South Island and in Cook Strait, by bay whaling, or the practice of killing whales as they came into the bays to calve. This activity was also chiefly controlled in New Zealand by entrepreneurs located in New South Wales. It was still going on, though in its declining phase, when systematic colonization began. Since bay whaling, like sealing before it, was a seasonal operation and the workers lived ashore, the tendency was to establish small semipermanent settlements. This was more true of the bay whalers than of the sealers. The men were a very rough lot, given to excessively hard drinking of rum, but far from all bad. They intermarried with the Maoris and brought up families of half-castes. Around their little settlements they established garden plots and even on occasion brought over cattle and sheep from New South Wales. Almost by inadvertence they were settling New Zealand, though if bay whaling had completed its decline before the systematic settlers arrived, it is doubtful if many of the whalers would have stayed on. As it happened some of the more substantial whaling settlements lasted into the period of colonization and assisted notably in helping the newcomers get established. An example of this was the settlement in the far south of South Island directed by John Jones of Sydney, a self-made capitalist of no mean ability. He himself found no difficulty in completing his career in the New Zealand of post-1840 in spite of the frustration of his notable efforts in collaboration with Wentworth as a land shark.

Similarly, the timber and flax trades led to the permanent establishment of individuals and groups of white men in New Zealand. At first in the nature of hit-and-run operations, dependent wholly on short-term Maori co-operation for success, they tended to become fairly continuous operations in the late 1820's. The flax trade, a business of buying the product after it had been cut and prepared by Maori women to the point where it could be made into rope and canvas, began with casual visits to the sources of supply, either taking up what was available or waiting while the supply was prepared, and then was stabilized with a willing tribe by stationing a white man to superintend production. (This apparently was the origin of the pakeha Maori, a white man permanently resident with a tribe and regarded by the tribe as their particular white representative in trading and other negotiations.) After a crisis in the flax trade, marked by a sharp drop in price about 1830, the trade declined for a time. The timber trade was transformed by the sawmill. When the timber was prepared for market in New Zealand rather than exported in the rough, a settlement tended to form around the mill. An especially famous early settlement of this kind was Hokianga on the northwest coast of the North Island, about forty miles overland from the Bay of Islands. Here, as in other places also, small ships for the colonial trade were built of the local timber, with a significant political consequence, as we shall see.

D3

While the commercial approach to New Zealand was almost wholly exploitive, and what good the Maoris derived from it was incidental, the approach of the missionaries was different. It was based on the proposition that the Maoris were an intelligent, upstanding people obviously ready to receive the blessings of Christianity and civilization. The emphasis was on the good of the Maoris, not on the good of the white intruders. The missionaries set about reducing the language to written form, teaching the people to read and write, printing portions of the Bible and tracts in Maori, teaching the practical arts, particularly agriculture, and encouraging the Maoris to divert their energies from war to peaceful pursuits. The missionaries offered a very different version of Western civilization to the Maoris from that offered by the exploiters. They had to do so, however, in an environment obviously strongly influenced by the example of the exploiters and the choice between the two versions of civilization was plainly up to the Maoris. It is hardly to be wondered that the Maori response was mixed and confused; it is rather remarkable that in the long run the missionary version (speaking in the large) won out. The great failure in New Zealand, as in most countries where a comparable conflict of cultures took place, was that it proved impossible to achieve the victory at a time and in a form that would allow the Maoris to maintain their position as an independent sovereign people, masters of their own house. It was the white intruders who took over New Zealand and, once they consolidated their victory by defeating the Maoris in war, defined the conditions on which the

Maoris could survive—as a minority people in a predominantly white community. It was, in time, a reasonably generous definition, conspicuously including elements the missionaries had emphasized, a kind of dependency looking toward equality. Many individual Maoris have achieved equality.

The inspirer and guide of the missionary effort was the Reverend Samuel Marsden, senior (Church of England) chaplain of the penal colony of New South Wales. Marsden was a remarkable character, a man obviously prisoner of the ideas of his time (he saw no irony in holding up the situation in New South Wales as "civilization" to his Maori charges). Religious *pro forma* but with an ecumenical outlook, he was eminently skilled in secular arts, particularly farming, and entertained a wholesome prejudice in favor of the Maoris as human beings. He saw the Maori virtues with a discerning eye, believed that teaching the practical arts was a necessary preliminary to the success of Christianity among them, and guided his agents in the way they should go with a hand that was always firm and occasionally overly severe. His mind had been directed toward the missionary field in the islands by the missionaries who had abandoned Tahiti and taken refuge at Sydney in 1798, and in a remarkably short time he was counseling the Church Missionary Society on general policy and specific questions. He early gained knowledge of the Maoris from Maori visitors to Sydney (the first voluntary visitor was in Sydney in 1803) and conceived the idea of a mission to New Zealand long before it was adjudged practical. One of the early Maori assaults upon the whites, the so-called massacre of the "Boyd," which occurred at the Bay of Islands in 1809, a disaster which the whites quite clearly brought upon themselves and which they avenged with a characteristic lack of discrimination, delayed Marsden for some years. Marsden and others under his influence early perceived that an urgent task in the islands was, in addition to missionizing the people, to protect the natives against white aggression. In 1814 Marsden at last obtained permission from Governor Macquarie to establish a mission in New Zealand and on December 22 landed at the Bay of Islands. He was then by no means a stranger to the Maoris and indeed his hopes for the future were based upon the friendship he had established with them in Sydney. He preached the first missionary sermon from the text, "Behold, I bring you tidings of great joy."

From the end of 1814 until his death in 1838, Marsden made no less than seven voyages to New Zealand on mission business and on the earlier visits, when he was a strong and active man, he made long journeys through the North Island that rank as explorations. Characteristically, his conversations with the Maoris were as much concerned with from Australia

North Cape

Bay of Islands

from "Overseas"

The "Attack" on
New Zealand

North Island

Hauraki Gulf

Bay of Plenty

from U.K.

New Plymouth
Mt. Egmont

Hawke Bay

Karamea
Bight

Tasman Bay

Kapiti I.

Cook Strait

Wellington

1840 from U.1

Nelson

Port
Nicholson

South Island

Marlborough

Christchurch

from U.K.

Canterbury
Bight

PACIFIC OCEAN

Dunedin

from U.K.

Foveaux
Strait

Stewart I.

preaching the virtues of what he called "civil society" as with preaching Christian doctrine; in his mind the two concepts were intimately intertwined. His assistants were, as might be expected, a mixed bag, and he had his difficulties with them. It was not easy, in the beginning, to staff the mission wholly with ordained clergymen, and in New Zealand as in the other Polynesian islands much use was made of pious craftsmen of one kind or another, some of whom were men of unusual ability. The failures were not related to the social status or education of the missionaries but to character defects which could afflict men of any preparation. Few of them had anything resembling an anthropological approach to the Maoris, but some of them, notably Thomas Kendall and William Yate, both of whom had to be dismissed for derelictions from duty, had a greater capacity than ordinary for observation and understanding. Kendall took a leading role in reducing the Maori language to written form, while Yate wrote a perceptive book on the country and its people. On the other hand, men like Henry Williams, Octavius Hadfield, and the mission printer William Colenso, who began publishing in Maori in New Zealand in 1835, had long and distinguished careers in New Zealand extending into the period of organized immigration. It was the Reverend Henry Williams, a former naval officer, who finally changed the emphasis from teaching crafts to teaching religion after his arrival in 1823. His secular preoccupation was inducing the Maoris to keep the peace among themselves, a task which kept him constantly on the move in the North Island.

In 1822 the Wesleyan Methodists established a mission in New Zealand with the full co-operation of Marsden's people. The leader was the Reverend Samuel Leigh, who had pioneered Methodism in Australia. The first effort, established at the site of the massacre of the "Boyd," was driven out by native disorders, but in a few years the mission was reestablished and took firm root.

Before 1840 the Church of England missionaries had nineteen establishments, all but two of which were in the north of the North Island, and the Methodists had eight, all located there. Both groups united in opposing the coming of the Roman Catholic mission under Bishop Pompallier in 1838. The Catholic mission, led by the Bishop Apostolic of Western Oceania, Pompallier, was interpreted religiously in the "Scarlet woman of Rome" fashion and also politically as a spearhead of French imperialism, both equally abhorrent to the British clerics. But by 1840 the Catholics had two mission stations well established. Sectarianism had been avoided before the arrival of the Catholics, but after their coming it was unavoidable. The Catholics emphasized that the Protestants were heretics. At a later stage the Maoris showed themselves highly adept at the detection and cherishing of theological differences.

It was ten years after Marsden's first visit before any formal conversions took place. Up to that time the missionary influence was almost wholly secular in character. As in all tribally organized societies, the key to success was the chiefs. Although from the beginning Marsden enjoyed the favor of chiefs, it is apparent that in the beginning the chiefs coveted secular skills, not divine revelation. But once the chiefs began to be converted, the missionaries could make real progress, for the people followed their leaders. Great progress was made in the 1830's, but simply because of the way in which it occurred, there were arguments about the depth and meaning of the shift in outlook, especially among those who felt that acceptance of Christianity was in large part a way of gaining access to the obviously superior mana of the whites. Not unexpectedly, a crisis in Maori religion accompanied the Maori-pakeha wars of the 1860's.

Although the effort was made, it never proved entirely possible for the missionaries to keep out of either Maori politics (chiefly the violent politics of war) or Maori-pakeha politics, also deeply tinged with violence. In Maori politics the principal missionary effort was to keep the peace among the tribes by diverting their energies into agriculture and, when war inevitably broke out, to arrange a peace of reasonable justice. It was the misfortune of the missionaries to live and work at the very time that Maori warfare achieved a new universality and destructiveness through the introduction of the musket. In dealing with Maori-pakeha relations, that is, the relations of the nonmissionary pakeha and the Maori, the missionaries were quite consistently pro-Maori. For a good portion of their first quarter-century in New Zealand they were opposed to organized white settlement, hoping that a strong, progressive, and stable Maori nation under their influence could be evolved, but toward the end of the period they—and Samuel Marsden himself as early as any—accepted the inevitability of British sovereignty and white immigration. Their position then was pro-Maori in the sense that they hoped and worked for justice for the Maori within the framework of a British government and society. The missionaries played a conspicuous role in the final British domination.

As the missionaries could not entirely keep out of politics, so they could not keep from getting involved in economic activities. Marsden took a hostile view of missionary participation in trading, but it went on nonetheless, and, worst of all, some missionaries on occasion even supplied Maoris with muskets. But time showed that their most ill-advised economic activity was the acquisition of land. Of course the missionaries could hardly avoid acquiring title to some land on which to live and farm for a living and on which to demonstrate to the Maoris how to farm. (When Charles Darwin visited New Zealand in 1835 while on the "Beagle" voyage, he was deeply impressed by missionary success at farming. It was a missionary who first used a plow in New Zealand—in 1820.) Marsden himself negotiated the purchase of the land on which the original mission was established. But when the missionaries began to buy land on their personal accounts it was a very different matter. The usual excuse was that they were in many cases men with large families for whom they must somehow provide in a country of limited opportunities for acquiring material wealth. Especially in the case of boys, land was a very useful inheritance for with it they could take up farming. But as soon as it became known that the missionaries were buying up land, they were harshly criticized for it (as for instance by the Australian Presbyterian, Reverend Dr. John Dunmore Lang), and in the end they found themselves very close to being on all fours with the Australian landsharks, including William Charles Wentworth, who bought up huge tracts from the natives in the 1830's in anticipation of large-scale white immigration. They were disastrously involved in trying to prove the validity of their titles in the British land courts after sovereignty had been assumed in the islands.

D3

From 1821 to 1838 the almost constant tribal warfare in New Zealand for peculiarly Maori reasons, usually involving *utu* ("revenge"), was productive of exceptional horrors from the use of guns obtained from the white intruders. Not only were tribes driven from their traditional lands, thus forcing them into occupation of the lands of others, causing chain-reaction fighting, but also many tribes were reduced to unimportant remnants which survived only because they were few. The wars were initiated by Hongi, chief of the Ngapuhi tribe, owners of the Bay of Islands. He had grasped the infinite superiority of guns over the stone weapons of old, of which he was a skilled user, around 1818. He had been to Sydney (1814) and was a friend of Marsden's, but while favorably disposed to the missionaries, he was little interested in their religious teachings. He rather coveted their material power as expressed in guns. In 1820 he and a relative went to England in the company of the missionary Kendall and was a primary resource of the English philologist, the Reverend Samuel Lee, in his pioneering work on the Maori language; he was introduced to King George IV; and while he received a great variety of presents, his interest was clearly in guns, for which he exchanged many of his other presents, and in Sydney on his way home he acquired more. In 1821 he was able to resume his career of warfare with a supreme advantage in armaments and was unchallengeable on fair terms until such time as his opponents also acquired guns. Between 1821 and 1827 he practically devastated the Maori world in the north of the North Island, but in the latter year he was accidentally shot in the back in battle by one of his own men and shortly died.

Hongi's place as pre-eminent warrior of New Zealand was taken by his most formidable adversary, Te Waharoa of the Ngati-Haua, whose lands lay to the south of those of the Ngapuhi. Te Waharoa relied less on the strength of his own tribe, which was relatively poor in fighting men, than upon alliances with neighboring tribes, either calculated to keep them quiet while he pursued his own course, or to gain their active support in fighting. He successfully defied Hongi's men, in spite of their guns, by making use of fortifications—in the building of which the Maoris were enormously skilled. His own animosities were directed against the Arawa people who lived around the hot-spring country at Rotorua and against the tribes on the shore of the Hauraki Gulf. Among his allies against Hongi and in his depredations on the Hauraki were the Waikatos. When Te Waharoa aged and ceased to be the warrior he once was (he died in 1839), his place as premier warrior was taken by Te Whero Whero of the Waikatos.

The chief concern of Te Whero Whero was to wage war on the people of Taranaki, as the bulge of the country in the southwest of the North Island, centering on Mount Egmont, was called. Already pressures from the north had led some of the Taranaki people to migrate south under the leadership of Te Rauparaha, who established himself on Kapiti Island in Cook Strait as early as 1819. Te Whero Whero's pressure was so tremendous that in spite of the fact that the Taranaki people had the aid of whites and of artillery in defending their *pa* (or fortified stronghold) and executed many of Te Whero Whero's warriors, it was adjudged unwise to try to hold the position. The Taranaki people joined Te Rauparaha at Cook Strait. In turn, Te Rauparaha crossed the strait and harried the Ngaitahu people in the north of South Island.

In the course of two decades the effects of Hongi's initiative, based on the possession of guns, had disturbed the balance of Maori life from the Bay of Islands in the North Island to South Island. During the fighting probably 20,000 Maoris lost their lives; and the complications of the already complicated Maori system of land tenure (based on collective tribal ownership) were intensified, to the subsequent confusion of all concerned with land ownership in New Zealand.

It should be noticed that the warfare was carried on while the pressures of the white intruders on New Zealand were intensifying. The fighting chiefs ordinarily did not harry the resident whites, even when they participated, as pakeha Maori, in the warfare; and least of all did they bother the missionaries, though the missionaries were both menaced and outraged by the terrible slaughter and general disorder. The highly ambiguous view a leader like Hongi took of the missionaries, rejecting as he did their Christianity while admiring their technological contribution, was exasperating perhaps, but not menacing. As the disorder intensified, moreover, the religious influence of the missionaries increased, for it was in the 1830's that widescale conversions began. The wars also, far from depressing trade, actually stimulated it, especially the business of traders able and willing to supply guns. The flax was intensively exploited by the Maoris in the effort to obtain firearms. The wars finally died down largely because the prospective contenders had more or less reached parity in firepower. It was something like peace by "equality of risk," a situation not unknown among the nations of the west. It was, however, a Maori world disorganized by twenty years of warfare that faced the systematic colonizers of the 1840's. Hardly had the immigrants landed than they thought they saw signs that the Maoris were destined to disappear and began to express the nauseating opinion that their task was to "smooth the pillow of a dying race."

CHAPTER X

Toward British Sovereignty in New Zealand

Well into the 1830's the British backed and filled on the question of the legal position of New Zealand. In the early years the Sydney people, especially those who undertook commercial ventures in the islands, assumed that the British authorities had jurisdiction there, and the authorities in Sydney sometimes acted as though they also thought they did. Then London repudiated the assumption and made it clear that New Zealand was outside His Majesty's dominions. In a loose way the London authorities acted as though they were trying to apply the doctrine of native sovereignty to New Zealand, for they raised no objections to acts of their local agent which certainly pointed in that direction. The Maoris, however, never got as far on this assumption as the Tahitians or the Tongans or, later on, the Fijians. As the pressures for immigration into New Zealand built up in the 1820's and 1830's, the London authorities began to shift their ground. By 1839 they were prepared to authorize the assumption of sovereignty in New Zealand.

The first interest of the governors of New South Wales in the islands was not sovereignty but law and order. The penetration of the islands by adventurers, commercial and otherwise, was accompanied by violence of all kinds. It was Governor Macquarie who, in 1814, made the first effort to regulate affairs in New Zealand. He sought to control the recruitment of Maoris for service on visiting ships and the discharging of white sailors at New Zealand, thus on the one hand regulating the departure of Maoris from New Zealand and, on the other, bringing under control the introduction into New Zealand of white settlers. He appointed Thomas Kendall, the missionary, a justice of the peace and proposed that three named chiefs of the Bay of Islands area grant or withhold permission to settle. Strictly speaking, all the actions of the governors, necessary as they were in terms of law and order, were illegal. The governors simply did not have jurisdiction in the areas they aimed to bring under control. The London government made this clear in 1817.

The moves, moreover, solved nothing, for even as measures to curb disorders they failed from the inability of those favorably disposed to order to exert any authority over the reckless, the heedless, and the criminal types that infested New Zealand. It was impossibly difficult to lay charges, to get the accused to Sydney, to bring over witnesses, and get the case tried. Only very uncommonly was anyone tried at Sydney for crimes in New Zealand, and some of the worst villains who did come to trial gained acquittal. It was after 1817 that Kororareka acquired most of its evil reputation.

During these years the activities of whites in New Zealand increased and the resident population multiplied. The Maoris exhibited no capacity for maintaining law and order themselves and the missionaries, as the principal group likely to take an interest in the matter, had not achieved sufficient influence to encourage them to take steps in that direction. A fatal flaw in Maori organization was the absence of any central authority. Tribal decentralization ruled. It has been alleged that Hongi intended through war to become king of New Zealand, but if he entertained that idea, which is unlikely, he certainly failed of his objective. Yet the London authorities could not see that they should take any initiative to establish *British* authority in New Zealand. The government was full of benevolence toward the natives, but the situation in actuality was less a native problem than a white problem. The only feasible way to solve the white problem was to take sovereignty in the islands.

By the early 1830's it was apparent that *something* had to be done. The pressure of the whites on New Zealand was intensifying. In 1825–26 the first attempt at founding a settlement of immigrants brought directly from Britain was made and though it was a failure, it was a significant portent. Governor Darling of New South Wales thought it would be wise to appoint a British agent in New Zealand, and he favored Charles Sturt, the explorer, for the position, but the British government chose James Busby. He was put on the New South Wales payroll and under the authorty of the governor (by that time, Bourke).

Busby was one of the sons of a civil engineer of New South Wales. While the father was a civil servant, his sons were pastoralists. James held land and in addition to sheep and wool was vastly interested in viticulture, to the establishment of which in Australia he made notable contributions. He also aspired to a career in the public service, but suffering frustrations he journeyed to London to make his case for a substantial appointment. The fruit of his effort was appointment as resident in New Zealand.

Unfortunately for Busby's later reputation, the British government was not prepared to give him any real authority. In fact, they failed to deliver to him even the limited authority promised, for the laws embodying it were never put through Parliament. Such power as he was allowed, he had to obtain for himself in collaboration with the missionaries, and it was to be in the nature of "influence," chiefly influence over the Maoris rather than the resident and transient whites. Throughout his period in office he lacked any legal authority over the whites, as they well understood, and most of them both ignored and ridiculed him, even men who should have known better. Such advice and counsel as he gave the few whites prepared to recognize him was always tempered by his own recognition of his powerlessness and hence was largely ineffective. Although he was himself favorably disposed to the missionaries, and they to him, he never achieved an authoritative stature among them, and he complained that they were headstrong in their own purposes. The fatal difficulty was that he had a weak and unimpressive personality and was equally unimpressive in person and on paper. On paper he proved unable forcefully to impress his ideas upon his superiors in Sydney and London; in person he could not forcefully impress himself on his contemporaries in New Zealand. The wonder is that he accomplished anything at all, but he did.

Busby arrived at the Bay of Islands on May 5, 1833. He represented to the Maoris that his arrival and assumption of the position of resident was a response to a letter they had addressed to King William (with the assistance of the Reverend William Yate of the Church Missionary Society) two years earlier expressing fear that the French ("tribe of Marion," as the Maoris called them) intended to annex New Zealand and take away their lands, complaining of the conduct of the commercial element in the islands toward them, a poor people having nothing but "timber, flax, pork, and potatoes," and asking to be taken under the king's protection. At a public meeting Busby read a letter from the secretary of state for colonies which stated that the danger of French annexation had passed, that the British valued the trade with New Zealand and hoped it would increase, and that Busby would investigate all complaints about the conduct of the traders and other British residents and visitors and address especial attention to keeping out escaped convicts and other undesirables. In a characteristically wordy gloss on this which he also read, Busby emphasized that the British had the utmost good will toward the Maoris, that they desired peace with them and among them, and that the Maoris should listen to the Word of God as expounded by the missionaries, work hard at producing timber, flax, potatoes, and pigs, trade with the traders, provision the visiting ships, and grow rich. He did not read Governor Bourke's instructions to him, for they recited the troubles which from time to time had occurred in the islands between the whites and the Maoris, not to mention among the whites themselves, emphasized carefully that the resident had no legal power to act in relation to them, and directed him to a life of observation and the cultivation of "influence," with the obligation of making full reports on everything interesting that went on, particularly in agriculture and commerce. What the British government wanted was a kind of peace and good order in New Zealand that would favor the growth of commercial relations.

Busby bought a piece of land (with his private funds) on a stream called the Waitangi for his place of residence. Rather significantly it was removed from both the resident commercial whites and the missionaries, as if to illustrate that he represented a third force in New Zealand. His first positive act was to arrange, with the concurrence and co-operation of Governor Bourke, that there be a flag of New Zealand. This was necessary because ships built in New Zealand (as at Hokianga) had been refused registry at Sydney on the ground that they were foreign built. The adoption of a flag would permit the establishment of a New Zealand registry. The ceremony of raising the new flag, attended by Maoris and whites, was held at Waitangi on March 20, 1834. A few weeks later the powerless position of Busby was illustrated when some Maori ruffians attacked his residence for purposes of robbery. The whites at Kororareka quickly saw that Busby could not sustain his position unless he took summary action to discover and punish the robbers. They wrote Busby to that effect. He had to reply, rather ambiguously, that he must rely on the action of the friendly chiefs. This exchange seems to have started the rapid deterioration of Busby's prestige among the whites. Nor were the authorities concerned to strengthen his position. In 1835 they appointed as additional British resident the head of the Hokianga settlement, an impulsive ex-naval man who persistently acted in a fashion contrary to Busby's best judgment of the situation.

In the year 1835 Busby took his second positive step to strengthen the position of the Maoris. He had received notice of the imminent arrival in New Zealand of an Anglo-French adventurer (he claimed dual citizenship) who styled himself Baron de Thierry. Thierry had purchased a block of land in New Zealand from Hongi and his companion when they were in England in 1820, or arranged that it be purchased on their return. Now he was coming out to claim and occupy it and assume, so he alleged, the title of sovereign chief of New Zealand, and rule for the benefit of the natives. Already he had taken the title of king of Nukuhiva (in the Marquesas). He was at the moment in Tahiti (whence he had traveled from Panama in an American ship), and he would travel to New Zealand by way of Sydney. The whole business was as fantastic as it sounds, but it alarmed Busby. Thierry carried out his program; he arrived in New Zealand in 1837 accompanied by ninety followers, but within a few months he had exhausted his capital and was only enabled to live at all by sufferance of the Maoris, who allowed him a small plot of land, and by virtue of his ownership of a saw mill. Busby, however, thought, or pretended to think, that Thierry might succeed in subverting the Maoris and even some of the whites, thus destroying British influence in New Zealand. He therefore convened a meeting of chiefs at Waitangi and on October 28, 1835, had prepared and signed a declaration of Maori independence. The new state was designated "United Tribes of New Zealand"; it was to be governed by the chiefs in annual assembly at Waitangi, and the declaration prayed that the king of England would be the parent of the "infant state" and protect it against "all attempts upon its independence." On its executive side, the new state was to be a mixed white and Maori operation, presided over by the resident. But no executive ever functioned, for neither the Maoris nor the whites saw any way to make it work. The European witnesses to this extraordinary document were two missionaries and two merchants from Kororareka. Busby appeared as signer of the certification that the copy he forwarded to London was an accurate version of the original.

Two years later the Kororareka whites outlined the New Zealand situation as they saw it in a petition to the king. They recited the total lack of firm authority in the islands, emphasized that armed robbery and other disorders were endemic, noted that nevertheless the residents (some of whom had now been in New Zealand for twenty years) were accumulating property, particularly land, at an accelerating rate, that more and more ships were visiting New Zealand, and that settlers were arriving from Australia and England in increasing numbers. (The total white population at that time was, however, only around 2000, with the largest single settlement still Kororareka.) The situation clearly called for action, but the petitioners quite obviously did not know exactly what to recommend, perhaps because they had no inkling of what was being thought in London. The document concluded: "Your humble petitioners would, therefore, pray that your Majesty may graciously regard the peculiarity of their situation, and afford that relief which may appear most expedient to your Majesty." In May 1838 the residents of Kororareka tried to solve the problem themselves by forming an association which was to deal with crimes against property by levying fines at the discretion of an armed posse and, in an extremity, tarring and feathering serious offenders. Busby favored the association until it revealed its methods. Obviously, His Majesty would not regard this as an expedient way of handling the situation in New Zealand.

D3

Just when England began to think of New Zealand as a suitable country in which to plant colonies in any systematic way is unclear. However, in 1825, a group undertook to promote a small settlement in the islands for the purpose of engaging in the timber and flax trades and to send out a group of carpenters, sawyers, blacksmiths, and flax-dressers to found the original settlement. A royal charter for the company was tentatively promised by the government, and in 1826 the settlers were dispatched in a vessel commanded by Captain James Herd, who had experience on the New Zealand coast in the timber trade. But although a few of the men established themselves in New Zealand, the venture was not a success, the promoters lost £20,000, no charter was ever granted, and in the end the remnants of the company were merged into a later venture in which E. G. Wakefield took a conspicuous part.

E. G. Wakefield definitely transferred his attention to New Zealand when the South Australian enterprise took a shape of which he could not approve. He felt that his principles had suffered a disabling perversion; he disapproved of the influence of the government in the enterprise and of its management by the commissioners; and he therefore abandoned it in favor of an effort in the islands. As a matter of fact he had been thinking of New Zealand as a desirable place for settlement for some years before he took action to promote colonization. As early as 1833 he was pointing to New Zealand as a logical and attractive place for British settlement, but it was not until 1837 that steps to organize for the purpose were taken. In that year Wakefield and his associates formed the New Zealand Association, although he himself at this stage kept behind the scenes.

The association was promptly engulfed in the politics of colonization. It set out to obtain a charter from Parliament which would give it comprehensive economic and governmental authority in the new settlement, more or less on the pattern of certain seventeenth-century colonies in America. When approached, the government countered that it could not approve such a scheme but if the association would turn itself into a joint stock company it would take a favorable view. The association took the action the government asked, or said it did, and renamed itself the New Zealand Colonization Company, but the bill for a charter was defeated in Parliament. What had happened? The Colonial Office alleged that the modifications made were not thorough enough. Wakefield thought this but a subterfuge and expressed the suspicion that the leaders of the missionaries in London, who were known to be opposed to planned colonization of New Zealand, had interfered. This was a reference to Dandeson Coates, secretary of the Church Missionary Society, and obliquely to Wakefield's old opponent, Sir James Stephen of the permanent staff of the Colonial Office, who was believed to be under missionary influence. There was something in this. It may also have been that somebody recalled that New Zealand was not then a part of the king's dominions.

At that time the consciences of the English humanitarians were troubled by the treatment aboriginal peoples were receiving at the hands of British subjects in various parts of the world. A full-scale examination of the question was undertaken by a parliamentary committee in that very year of 1837. The missionaries were, naturally enough, deeply concerned; it was their view that it was best to prevent a great influx of white settlers to allow ample time for the missionaries to Christianize the natives and build up a native state. Mr. Coates customarily put the case for this course in a rather extreme form and was firm in opposing those who advocated planned white settlement. His zeal often outran that of missionaries on the ground, as in New Zealand. Sir James Stephen—allegedly under missionary influence but really more accurately described as a man heavily influenced by the same general climate of opinion as the missionaries inhabited—sought all his official life to promote and protect the interests of the poor, the downtrodden, and the pigmented in the British colonies. He was unquestionably highly critical of Wakefield and Wakefield-inspired schemes, but not so much because they were settlement schemes as because Stephen disliked Wakefield's methods. Stephen saw Wakefield as a speculative real-estate manipulator, none too scrupulous in his promotional, sales, and organizational methods, and obviously given to attempting to grab more political power in his proposed colonies than any British government could conscientiously concede. Stephen knew perfectly well that the situation in New Zealand was approaching a crisis. He hoped to solve it by governmental action with justice to all concerned.

When Wakefield returned from Canada in 1838 (where he had gone with Lord Durham) he threw himself with great vigor into the New Zealand promotion. Early in May 1839 Wakefield and his friends formed the New Zealand Land Company with Lord Durham as governor, as successor to the New Zealand Colonization Company. The new company, shortly called simply the New Zealand Company, took over land purchased in New Zealand by its predecessors and generally pre-empted the field. It approached the Colonial Office for approval of its organization, board of directors, and program but failed to win acceptance, chiefly because of its wish to assume so much governmental authority in the projected colony, and also because it was going to carry out its activities *in a foreign country.* Failing to win co-operation from the government, the company resolved to carry out its scheme in New Zealand as a private enterprise. It dispatched the ship "Tory" to New Zealand with a small party headed by Colonel William Wakefield, E. G.'s brother, to buy land from the natives on a land-shark basis. The "Tory" arrived on the New Zealand coast on August 16, 1839, and reached Port Nicholson (harbor of the future city of Wellington), where the company's center of operations was eventually set up, on September 20. Land-shark operations on an enormous scale then ensued. The first vessel carrying company-sponsored settlers arrived at Port Nicholson on January 22, 1840.

Meanwhile, the British government had matured its plans for the future of New Zealand. It has often been said that Wakefield and the New Zealand Company *forced* the government's hand, but this is doubtful. The government had been considering the New Zealand problem for some time, and the Wakefield proposals in their successive forms were but factors in a complicated situation. If anybody forced the British government's hand, it was the Australian adventurers who, before the company came into existence, had pioneered the occupation of New Zealand and made its eventual absorption into the British system inevitable. One might properly say that the government had been searching for a viable New Zealand policy since 1833 when it sent Busby to the Bay of Islands. It is worth noting that it accepted the measures Busby took to stabilize the situation, and it studied his recommendations for future policy and action. In 1837 Governor Bourke of New South Wales sent Captain William Hobson in his ship "Rattlesnake" to New Zealand to survey the situation. Hobson had been posted to Sydney from the Indian Station of the Royal Navy and had accompanied Governor Bourke on his visit to the new settlement at Port Phillip. Hobson consulted with Busby, the missionaries, and native chiefs introduced by one or the other and made the policy proposal of setting up a series of "factories" on the Indian model for thus acquiring limited sovereignty in the islands. This came to nothing, but it was nevertheless grist for the official policy-making mill. Under the date of December 1, 1838, Lord Glenelg, minister in charge of the Colonial Office, notified Governor Gipps of New South Wales that it was proposed to replace the resident in New Zealand by a consul, and in February 1839 just before his retirement, he recommended that sovereignty be acquired in New Zealand.

This recommendation was made three months before the sailing of Wakefield's "Tory." The questions remaining were whether or not to take sovereignty over all of New Zealand or only selected parts of it, and how in any case to take over sovereignty in such a fashion as to protect native interests, especially in the land. Stephen in a lengthy memorandum debated these issues with his customary acute insight, but he did so in the light of the fact that taking sovereignty was a closed question and, by extension, white settlement of New Zealand also. In mid-June Lord Normanby, Glenelg's successor, arranged that the boundaries of New South Wales be extended to take in such parts of New Zealand as might later pass to the British; and on July 1 Captain Hobson, then in London, was appointed consul to negotiate with the Maori chiefs over sovereignty and at the same time was given a commission as lieutenant governor of New Zealand under the governor of New South Wales. Hobson sailed for Sydney in late August (before the "Tory" had reached New Zealand) and arrived in December. Thus, the British government's policy in New Zealand was fixed before the New Zealand Company's agent in the "Tory" actually set foot at Port Nicholson.

Hobson had extended consultations with Governor Gipps in Sydney. They discussed and fixed the form of government Hobson would set up, recruited in Sydney the original body of civil servants for New Zealand, arranged that Hobson get an advance of money from the New South Wales treasury, considered land policy, and defined the nature of Hobson's subordination to Gipps. In Hobson's commission it was stated that the British government would not recognize as valid any title to land that was not derived from or confirmed by a grant made in the Queen's name or on her behalf. This was designed to undercut land-sharking activities in New Zealand, including the company's, then prospective. Gipps had legislation passed in New South Wales to implement this policy, a step which brought him into direct conflict with the land sharks, especially W. C. Wentworth. The subordination of Hobson to Gipps was destined to be short-lived, however, for on May 3, 1841, New Zealand became a separate Crown Colony. Apparently, the device of acquiring New Zealand through the government of New South Wales was chosen for purposes of convenience and speed, taking especially into account the assumed greater familiarity of Gipps with conditions in New Zealand than that of the authorities in London. Once the objective had been achieved, the tie could then be cut.

Hobson arrived at the Bay of Islands on January 29, 1840. The next day he read a succession of documents before the inhabitants assembled in the church at Kororareka, setting out the essential facts about his position and purposes in New Zealand. Oddly, he set himself up as lieutenant governor *before* he dealt with the matter of British sovereignty in New Zealand, but he quickly enlisted the help of James Busby and the principal Church of England missionary, Henry Williams, in handling the rather delicate negotiations. An invitation was sent to all chiefs within a reasonable distance of the Bay of Islands to meet with Hobson at Waitangi on February 5. Utilizing all the pomp and ceremony at his command and taking great care to have his remarks translated into Maori by Henry Williams, Hobson explained to the assembled chiefs why he was in New Zealand and laid before them for consideration a treaty which would, he alleged, transfer sovereignty to the Queen while protecting the rights of the Maoris, especially in the land. The treaty was drafted by Busby from papers handed him by Hobson which reflected the thinking of Sir James Stephen.

Partly of their own motion, but partly in response to the persuasion of the missionaries, as well as some of the commercial settlers, the chiefs accepted the treaty and signed it on the sixth. There was, however, a decided undercurrent of objection, both on the part of Maori chiefs and some of the more raffish white men. The treaty was not completed at Waitangi for many Maori chiefs were not present there. To insure the future of the treaty, Hobson dispatched agents (mostly missionaries) throughout the North Island to collect additional signatures. Although many of the chiefs signed, others did not, a point that had significance later on. It was impossible to deal with the South Island in the same fashion but Hobson sent Colonel Thomas Bunbury, whom Gipps had sent across from Sydney to support him, on a tour of the South Island by ship. Bunbury visited Akaroa (to forestall any French move), Puapuka on Foveaux Strait at the bottom of the island, Cloudy Bay at the top of the island, Kapiti Island in Cook Strait, and called in at Port Nicholson. On June 17 the task of establishing British sovereignty was adjudged complete. However, it is from the February ceremonies at Waitangi that the history of New Zealand is now usually dated.

THE ISLANDS

CHAPTER XI

The Islands as No Man's Lands

When the British officials drew up Arthur Phillip's commission as governor of New South Wales and thus had an opportunity to define British territorial claims in the Southwest Pacific, they indicated exactly the northern, southern, and western boundaries of the area over which he was to exercise authority, but they left the eastern, or seaward, boundary vague. They defined the western, or landward, boundary by a degree of longitude (the 135th), but they selected no line for the eastern. Rather they referred to "adjacent islands," which could mean only coastal islands, but confused that by specifically recommending settlement at Norfolk Island a thousand miles to sea. Moreover, they also referred to such things as obtaining women in the islands for the comfort of the convicts (an outrageous suggestion never acted upon), and they made a point of the utility of exploiting the wild flax which, by implication at least, referred to New Zealand. (Phillip himself once mentioned the idea of marooning recalcitrant convicts in New Zealand and leaving them to their fate among the cannibals, a macabre idea that, fortunately, was only a passing fancy.) But the whole business of the scope of British claims in the islands to the east of New South Wales was left extremely vague, and vagueness permeated official attitudes for a good many years after. The free colonists, too, were vague about the matter, but assumed that the islands far and wide south of the equator were really under British jurisdiction. Even after it was established by imperial action that they were not, colonists occasionally argued that they were and early developed the position that, whatever the legal technicalities of the matter, Britain certainly had an obviously superior position in the islands and that all others who coveted or claimed them were intruders upon an imperial preserve. This attitude was detected by French observers at Sydney as early as 1813, and early in the twentieth century André Siegfried phrased it as "Oceania for the Anglo-Saxons." This attitude permeates the writings of many British historians of the islands, and the genesis of the foreign policies of both Australia and New Zealand is to be found in this possessiveness toward them.

It was in seeking to assist the governors of New South Wales to keep order in the islands that the London government, whether by inadvertence or design is not clear, definitely put the islands outside British jurisdiction in 1817. The law in question sought to deal with murders and manslaughters committed in places "not within His Majesty's dominions" and also outside the dominions of any other government, defined specifically as referring to Honduras and the islands of the South Pacific. These places were assimilated in legal character to the high seas, and it was specified that the crimes named, when committed in them, could be tried in British courts having the requisite maritime jurisdiction. In 1823 the list of crimes was extended to include treasons, piracies, felonies, and robberies. Interesting as these laws are as evidence of the British wish to support law and order in no man's lands, their larger importance was in the disclaimer of sovereignty even when, as was sometimes the case, a claim based on discovery could have been alleged. These acts of the imperial government neither solved the problem of crime in the islands nor the problem of the status of the islands in international law. About all they did was to transform the attitude of the Britons resident in the Southwest Pacific from one of confident belief in British sovereignty in the islands eastward to Tahiti, into one of imperialist insistence that Britain formally take sovereignty in various groups successively to forestall other powers, designated "intruders."

D3

As our chief concern in this history will be with the incorporation of the islands into the Western economic and political systems, it will be well to pause here for a few observations on early voyages of different motivations into the islands, especially in view of the fact that the islands have throughout their history been regarded as proper stages for romantic adventure and fields for the accumulation of specialized knowledge. At the time the economic and political penetration began, the islands were but imperfectly known, even in terms of navigation. And as no persons of any nationality devoted themselves wholly to gathering knowledge about the islands in all their aspects, what knowledge was accumulated, and it rapidly became considerable, was necessarily fragmentary. No single expedition could possibly cover all the island groups, and the various expeditions undertaken were, of course, not planned in such a fashion that their reports, taken together, would cover the entire field. There was much duplication, much omission, even to the present day.

Probably the most commonly visited island of all was Tahiti. Very early also it became almost habitual for travelers of all nationalities to pay visits to Sydney in Australia and many called at the Bay of Islands in New Zealand. Otherwise, the tours were utterly unpatterned. In the period to 1850 most attention was given to the eastern islands, all except Fiji, inhabited by Polynesians. Melanesia, with its different and allegedly more savage people (though the Polynesian Maoris of New Zealand and the Melanesians of Fiji were more or less on a par in their fame as cannibals), was less observed, studied, and exploited. Following the precedent of Captain Cook, some of the more famous scientific expeditions ventured into Antarctica as well as the islands, usually basing their departure and return on Australian ports, or visited the islands before or after a visit to Antarctica.

Several ships of the first fleet to New South Wales went on to China to obtain a backload for England. One, the "Lady Penrhyn," traveled via Tahiti and discovered some of the Kermadec Islands while approaching the island from Sydney, and also discovered Tongareva while en route from Tahiti to China. The "Scarborough" and the "Charlotte," traveling in company north from Sydney, made some minor discoveries in Melanesia, the "Alexander," traveling alone, gained some new information about the Solomons, and the Gilberts and Marshalls north of the equator were investigated and named after ships' captains. This kind of detailed work was characteristic for several decades thereafter— even the commercial visitors, including British, French, and American sealers and whalers, made many such discoveries, for the number of South Sea islands is almost literally infinite. As the technology of communications became more complex in the nineteenth and twentieth centuries and lent special value to specks of land in the infinite ocean, some of the small and isolated islands, discovered by the merest chance, assumed remarkable importance and even became the objects of international diplomacy. As sovereignty over them was rarely completed by occupation, first discovery became a matter of considerable importance, though in international law it was not considered decisive for sovereignty.

In the field of romance by far the most famous of the early expeditions into the islands is that of Captain William Bligh in the "Bounty" during 1788 and 1789. Bligh was sent out to Tahiti by the British government on the advice of Sir Joseph Banks to gather breadfruit-tree seedlings and take them to the West Indies where, it was hoped, the breadfruit would provide a welcome and cheap addition to the dietary of the Negro slaves on the sugar plantations. This remarkable venture into economic botany and plant acclimatization was in the end a failure, for while the trees were, after difficulties to be specified, transferred in

Polynesia, Melanesia and Micronesia

Easter I.

Marquesas Is.

Tuamotu Arch.

POLYNESIA

Society Is.

Hawaii

Kermadec Is.

Chatham I.

Samoa

Cook Is.

Tokelau Is.

NEW ZEALAND

Tonga Is.

Marshall Is.

Gilbert Is.

Ellice Is.

Fiji Is.

MICRONESIA

Solomon Is.

New Hebrides

New Caledonia

Marianas

MELANESIA

NEW GUINEA

AUSTRALIA

good order, it became known that the Negroes did not like breadfruit, preferring bananas.

The great fame of the voyage does not, however, rest on that curious fact but on the circumstance that as Bligh was traveling away from Tahiti among the Tonga Islands, his crew mutinied. The mutineers set Bligh and a few loyal companions adrift in a small boat with a limited quantity of food and gear. After an utterly incredible voyage of six weeks through unknown seas, Bligh brought his company to Timor in the Indies and eventually got them to England. After leaving the vicinity of the Tonga Islands, Bligh and his company passed through a reef-protected group of islands, a circumstance which established his claim to being a principal discoverer of the Fijis, earlier encountered but not penetrated by Tasman and Cook. The mutineers, meanwhile, got the ship back to Tahiti, where a portion of them settled down, while the rest, accompanied by Tahitian women, retired to Pitcairn Island, the isolated speck of land discovered by Carteret years before. The skill and heroism of Bligh in his desperate situation at first overshadowed in public interest the question of the rights and wrongs of the mutiny and the disappearance of some of the mutineers, but historically far more words have been expended on the latter two themes than on the first. The mutiny, in fact, is one of the imperishable scandals of the sea, the establishment at Pitcairn being sufficiently remarkable to have engaged the close attention of latter-day anthropologists. For the mutiny Bligh has suffered frequent condemnation, including that contained in a Hollywood movie, but this shows little regard for the facts of the matter, including the point that Bligh successfully weathered an official investigation at the time. Bligh, one of the unluckiest men in history, has paid heavy penalty for an unfortunate personality and a brutal tongue. While Bligh was occupied in England with the official investigation of the mutiny, Captain Edward Edwards was sent to Tahiti in the "Pandora" to apprehend such of the "pirates" as he could reach. On the return voyage to England the "Pandora" was wrecked and four of the mutineers and thirty-one of the ship's crew were lost. The survivors, including ten mutineers, reached England via Batavia. Then in 1791–93 Bligh, with two vessels, the "Providence" and the "Assistance," carried out his original commission to the letter. The mutineers at Pitcairn remained undiscovered until an American sealer named Mayhew Folger chanced upon them while pursuing his lawful occasions in 1808.

Of lesser fame, but hardly less romantic, was the adventure that befell a practical Irishman, Peter Dillon, in 1827–28. Dillon was primarily a commercial operator, gathering local produce in the islands for sale in India. In the course of a voyage from New Zealand to India with a cargo of timber he called at the island of Tikopia in the Santa Cruz group (where Mendaña had died many years previously) and was shown a silver guard from a sword. This suggested that it was a relic of the La Pérouse expedition which had disappeared in 1788. With the backing of the government of Bengal, Dillon made a special voyage to follow up the matter and established that the vessels of La Pérouse's expedition had foundered with all hands on the reefs of the island of Vanikoro, near Tikopia in the Santa Cruzes. For solving this great mystery Dillon was made a chevalier of the Legion of Honor and granted a pension by the French government.

D3

In the organized pursuit of knowledge of the islands to 1850, the British were definitely second to the French and the Americans. No British traveler made any such contribution to knowledge as was made by the Frenchman Dumont d'Urville on his two voyages of 1826–29 and 1837–40, and none as great as that of the American, Charles Wilkes. However, Captain Frederick Beechey in 1825–28 carried out extensive surveys in Polynesia, chiefly by exactly locating earlier discoveries but also including a close study of native life on Mangareva, as an extended interlude in his primary task of keeping a rendezvous at Bering Strait with the Arctic explorers Parry and Franklin, neither of whom in the end succeeded in reaching the Pacific. The visit of Captain Robert Fitzroy to Tahiti, Bay of Islands, and Sydney in the "Beagle" in 1835, with his famous passenger Charles Darwin, was but a brief episode in a far more comprehensive maritime enterprise actually centered on the coasts of South America. Captain Sir Edward Belcher, of the "Sulphur," for his part, included some work in the South Sea islands (where he had been earlier with Beechey) in 1840 as an interlude in his primary task of a close hydrographic survey of the western coast of the Americas, on which he spent four years. In 1849 and 1850 Captain John Erskine made short tours of islands in the western Pacific, starting from Sydney. His voyages were focused somewhere between the gathering of knowledge and observation and supervision of native-white relations.

The French, on the other hand, were indefatigable knowledge-gatherers though they by no manner of means neglected economics and politics. In 1791–93 the Frenchman Bruni d'Entrecasteaux, whose work has been mentioned earlier, operated entirely outside the pattern suggested above by closely investigating much of Melanesia from the north in search of clues to the fate of La Pérouse. Freycinet in 1819 and Duperrey in 1824 were concerned with magnetism and meteorology as well as geography. Freycinet was more occupied with the North Pacific than the South, while

Duperrey investigated in Melanesia as well as Polynesia. Both visited Sydney, and Duperrey also called at the Bay of Islands. Dumont d'Urville, the premier French explorer of the time, made his first voyage into the South Seas in 1826–29, arriving by way of the Cape of Good Hope and beginning his work with a visit to Sydney. He then proceeded to New Zealand, went on to Tonga, made a survey of the Fijis, swung northwest to New Britain and New Guinea in Melanesia, visited in the Dutch Indies, and went home via the Indian Ocean. On his second voyage in 1837–40, by which time France's interest in the economics and politics of the South Seas was very lively, Dumont d'Urville had added a concern with the whale fisheries to his other interests and on at least one occasion acted in concert with France's political agent in the Pacific, Admiral Dupetit-Thouars. He made an even more comprehensive swing through Polynesia than on his earlier journey, spent some time in Melanesia, and as he had begun his voyage by an incursion into Antarctic waters, so he made another important entry into them from Hobart in Van Diemen's Land. Again his reports were comprehensive and have become classic. His copious remarks about New Zealand, visited on both voyages, have in very recent years been translated into English as valuable primary sources.

Russian activities in the Pacific in the first half of the nineteenth century were concentrated in the North Pacific and were transacted not only in Asiatic Russia but also across the way in Alaska. Insofar as they had anything to do with Polynesia, they chiefly focused on the Hawaiian Islands in which at various times the Russians considered founding a settlement. But because land communications between European Russia and the Pacific littoral were long and difficult—the journey ordinarily took two years—it seemed reasonable to establish a link by sea to Alaska, using Capes Horn or Good Hope, and in doing this the Russians arrived at the islands of the South Pacific. The sea-link between European Russia and the North Pacific outposts was pioneered by Captain A. J. von Krusenstern in 1803–6. His vessel was accompanied by a companion ship commanded by Captain Urey Lisiansky. After rounding Cape Horn the ships made a rendezvous at the Marquesas, which von Krusenstern reached first, and at Washington Island, of which his people prepared an elaborate description. Lisiansky, for his part, made a visit to Easter Island en route to the Marquesas. In company, von Krusenstern and Lisiansky proceeded from the Marquesas to Hawaii. About a decade later (1815–18) another expedition was dispatched to the Russian settlements in the North Pacific. Although on the business of the fur trading company, and manned by the government, the expedition was financed by Count Romanzoff, the imperial chancellor. In command was

Lieutenant Otto von Kotzebue, son of the German dramatist and writer, August F. F. von Kotzebue, of whom Czar Paul I was patron. Young von Kotzebue had been with von Krusenstern. On this voyage minor discoveries were made in the Tuamotus and, north of the equator, in the Marshalls of Micronesia. Later on (1823–26), von Kotzebue made a second voyage along the same general route, including this time a visit to Tahiti, during which he made a few minor discoveries, but mostly verified minor discoveries of others. But the best remembered Russian voyage to the South Pacific is that made by Admiral Fabian Bellingshausen in 1819–21. This was not a voyage to the Russian settlements in the North Pacific, but a purely scientific expedition to carry out explorations in Antarctic waters in which the island activities were an interlude. After three months in the Antarctic area, Bellingshausen reached Sydney in March 1820 and from there made a long loop to the east beyond Tahiti, visiting New Zealand on the outward voyage, making discoveries in the inexhaustible Tuamotus and elsewhere and some in the Fiji Islands on the return toward Sydney. He sailed back to the Antarctic from Sydney in November.

Apparently, the Russians found the long voyage from the Baltic via Cape Horn to Alaska and Asiatic Russia hardly a profitable substitute for the overland route, for after von Kotzebue's second voyage, no more Russian visits to the South Pacific were made. As remarked, the only part of Polynesia they ever coveted was Hawaii in the north. It bore a rational relation to their holdings on either side of the North Pacific Ocean at that time.

The Americans were enormously active in commercial pursuits in the islands from the earliest days, surpassing even the British and the colonials in certain lines and, of course, completely outclassing the French. It was the far-flung American economic interests, particularly whaling, that provided the political support for the great United States exploring expedition of 1838–42, commanded by Charles Wilkes, U.S.N., an enterprise engendered from controversy, continued throughout in controversy, and productive of controversy to the present day. Wilkes himself was a notably controversial figure, as one might expect of the nephew of the British radical politician, "That Devil" Wilkes; and when the expedition was behind him, he engendered new controversies, as in the "Trent" affair during the Civil War. The islands of the Southwest Pacific were but a fraction of the land and sea covered by the Wilkes expedition, which also figures in the history of Antarctic exploration and of the islands of the North Pacific including Hawaii and of the northwest coast of America. Having five ships at his disposal during most of the voyage, Wilkes followed the practice of assigning ships for special duties, so not all of them engaged in all of the activities of the expedition. He also usually allowed time for scientific work in the hinterlands of the ports he visited. The publications arising from and associated with the expedition are rich and voluminous—a bibliography of them runs to 150 pages; a well-informed British student of the Pacific has assessed the official publications as "up to the standard inaugurated by Captain James Cook."

Although the Wilkes people made some discoveries, all minor islands, their important contribution was through exhaustive study of islands already known and the exact location of them on charts. Much work was done soon and late, after the expedition got into the Pacific, in the much-examined Tuamotu Archipelago. Tahiti was visited. Considerable time was spent around the Tonga Islands. Samoa was carefully examined and the great value of the harbor at Pago Pago was pointed out. An especially careful study was made of the Fiji Islands and a chart prepared which was an enormous advance over any hitherto produced. It remained standard for a long time. Using Sydney as a base, Wilkes and some of his men made an incursion into antarctic waters. Some of the ships visited the Bay of Islands where Wilkes's people witnessed the taking of sovereignty by the British. The scientists made investigations around all the ports visited. Eventually, all the ships were withdrawn from the Southwest Pacific and work was concentrated on the northwest coast of North America, but not before important tasks were carried out in Micronesia and the Hawaiian Islands. In the Southwest Pacific the Wilkes expedition made the richest collection of data of varied kinds assembled in the first half of the century.

D3

The Polynesian islands, the first really known, made an enormous appeal not only to the explorers but also to the imaginations and minds of the European intelligentsia. The impressions and information the explorers brought home were woven into a kind of sociology-*cum*-ideology which was more important as a critique of Western society than as an exact report on island society. Diderot's *Supplement to Bougainville's 'Voyage,'* written in 1772 and published in 1796, was an early example of this. Quite apart from its literary, artistic, and political effect, this curious sociology was the context given to the allegedly admirable "natural man"—that is, man before he was corrupted by civilization, as Rousseau and others saw him. It was, too, the foundation of the idea that life in the islands was superbly and exceptionally romantic, an idea which long survived the chances and changes of both island and Western society and even enjoys a measure of vigor in the middle of the twentieth century. Here we are not concerned with this curious influence of the islands on the West—for it is properly the affair of historians of ideas, students of literature and art, and those concerned with man's charming follies—but with the impact of the West on the islands.

Between the 1790's and 1840, when the British initiated the division of the islands among the powers by taking sovereignty in New Zealand, the islands mostly experienced the impact of the West at two cultural levels: the culture as exemplified by deserters from ships, survivors of wrecks or attacks, and runaway convicts, sandalwood, food (pork, arrowroot, etc.), *bêche-de-mer,* and pearl-shell gatherers, sealers and whalers, visiting and resident traders, and planters on the one hand; and the culture as exemplified by Christian missionaries on the other. The islands also, as noted, continued to be visited by explorers accompanied by or doubling as ethnologists, geologists, hydrographers, anthropologists, and so on through the panoply of sciences relevant to the investigation of island life; and they were visited also by representatives of Western governments in the persons of captains and crews of men-of-war engaged in gunboat diplomacy, eventually to back up the resident consuls who began to appear toward the end of the period.

It was relatively uncommon for the missionaries to be the first visitors to any island; they were usually preceded by whites of a less reputable character. It was not easy even then to discriminate among the pioneers as to their character as men. Many were doubtless called convicts who were not, for the common sailors of those days were hardly models of propriety. Nor was it always easy to discriminate between a deliberate deserter and a man who found himself the survivor of a shipwreck or a massacre. Some of the most horrifyingly destructive careers in the islands and also some of the most affectingly pathetic were those of survivors of wrecks. At any rate, hardly any important islands escaped the influence of these types, and the impact was all too commonly of evil consequence. Many of these people arrived in the islands directly from Europe or America but more by way of Sydney, then the port in the general vicinity that stood for "civilization" in the area. It was both the principal port of entry to the area and the refuge of those who survived marooning in the islands and chose to escape when opportunity offered. The nationalities chiefly active in the islands at this time were the British and the Americans, with the French a fateful third group, but the intruders always arrived in ships, and ships in those days were manned by an extraordinary mixture of nationalities, European-American and Asian. By taking service on visiting ships, voluntarily or by kidnapping, the island natives were themselves scattered far and wide, not only among the islands but also to Europe and America. An islander named Queequeg became a famous character in a great American novel published in 1851.

When the London Missionary Society's pioneer group of fieldworkers landed in Tahiti from the ship "Duff" on March 6, 1797, they found three white men already in residence there. The origin of two of these —Swedish by nationality—is obscure but the third, who opposed the missionary influence, was a deserter from one of Captain Vancouver's ships that had touched at Tahiti on a voyage from the northwest coast to New Zealand and Norfolk Island. The "Duff," after leaving Tahiti, put ashore a lone missionary in the Marquesas and a party at Tonga. The Tonga party found two deserters already there. The "Bounty" episode, already recounted, was the classic example of desertion compounded with mutiny, but really only the most dramatic and memorable one of many. However, the dispersion of deserters and survivors through the islands was more the byproduct of commercial enterprise than of government-authorized activity like Bligh's, and the convicts usually reached the islands by stowing away on commercial ships or by being recruited as crew by unscrupulous captains. These people became more numerous as time passed, but considerable numbers of them appear to have been attracted to the Californian and Australian goldfields at the end of the period.

The earliest commercial ships to arrive in the islands were sealers, traders to the northwest coast of America and China, traders for food from Sydney, and gatherers of sandalwood and *bêche-de-mer* for the China trade. The sealers who gathered their products in the subantarctic and temperate parts of the South Pacific stopped at the islands while en route to China to dispose of their skins. This was especially true of those who had operated in Australian and New Zealand waters, but also occasionally true of those who had gathered their skins on the South American side of the ocean. The first American sealer to visit Sydney en route to China arrived in 1792. The American sealers normally carried an excess of supplies for trading, including rum, and these they exchanged for food as the occasion offered, hence their interest in the islands.

Similarly, ships engaged in the fur trade between the northwest coast of America and China stopped at the islands en route from Europe or the east coast of America via Cape Horn to the coast; the first ship to visit Tahiti after the arrival of the missionaries was a British vessel out of Macao in China which had failed to reach the northwest coast and was trying to make the sealing islands near the southern tip of South America. These ships normally traded for food, not the least attractive item they offered being guns. An American ship, the "Hope" commanded by Joseph Ingraham, out of Boston for the northwest coast, chanced on the Marquesas in April 1791, traded with the natives, and discovered some new islands in the group. Josiah Roberts, also from Boston, spent three months at the Marquesas in 1792–93, traded extensively, and even built a small vessel from local materials. Edmund Fanning of Stonington, Connecticut, in charge of a sealer, was there in 1798 and not only dealt with the natives but plucked up the spirits of the London Missionary Society missionary. Étienne Marchand, the pioneer French fur trader, was at the Marquesas in June 1791.

The first duty of the deserters and of the survivors of wrecks and other disasters in the islands was to insure their continued survival, not the easiest thing to manage, for the natives normally killed most survivors. Continuation in this world normally involved adoption by a tribe or group; the most fortunate were adopted by chiefs. (Women, of whom a good many were involved over the years, appear to have had the roughest time, but survive some of them did.) Survival depended on the usefulness of the white to the natives. To be useful the white man naturally tended to conform to the local mores and folkways; he tended, that is, to decivilize himself rather than civilize the natives; and there is, indeed, abundant historical testimony that the former has always been a far easier undertaking than the latter whenever Europeans and savages have been in contact.

As war was an ancient native occupation, the natives early perceived the use of guns, which quickly gained a higher value as articles of trade than alternative metal implements and cloths. Again and again in island records the role of whites among the natives as teachers of the use of firearms recurs. Handling guns was probably the first Western technique the islanders sought to master. This meant an enormous intensification of the destructiveness of war, but that appears to have disturbed few of the commercial adventurers. Some highly reputable men of the time traded guns to the natives; for instance George Bass, discoverer of Bass Strait, while getting together a cargo of pork for the Sydney market, did so at Tahiti in 1801. But the white waifs did more than demonstrate the technology of firearms; they also intensively continued the introduction of a wide variety of diseases, including sexual diseases, begun by casual visitors such as the explorers. Among the diseases introduced were dysentery, whooping cough, mumps, measles, and jaundice, the natives proving as vulnerable to the so-called childhood diseases as any others. Thus, by firearms and disease the process of depopulation was begun. And these people also began the business of miscegenation. A white of this period in Fiji aspired to have 100 children; he got up into the nineties, but failed of his goal. However, it would be wrong

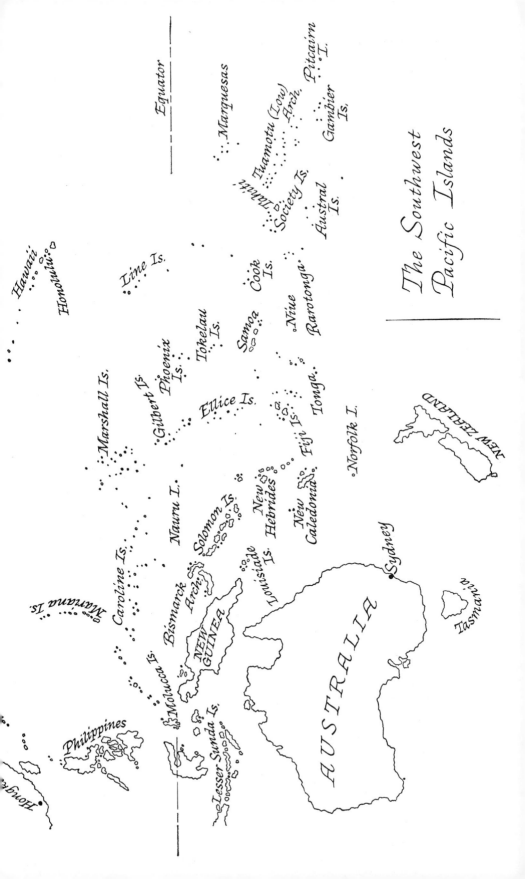

The Southwest
Pacific Islands

to convey the impression that the whites were all designing scoundrels, for some were exceedingly observant and lived among the natives with no harm to themselves or their hosts. The classic example of this type is Will Mariner, who spent several years in Tonga in the early 1800's and whose ghost-written account of his experience is a classic of island literature.

The sealers normally did some trading, as was noticed, chiefly to obtain food, and thereby introduced a considerable variety of Western articles—knives, axes, cloth, clothes, guns and gunpowder, beads, etc. —into the native culture. They began that peculiar process of creating wants only to be satisfied from Western sources that has bedeviled native life ever since. They also began the practice of dealing unscrupulously with the natives, violating every law of fair trading ever heard of, and manipulating prices (or values) with an utter lack of morality. Generally speaking, the natives took readily to trade with the whites; it was a process of which their own culture gave them some foreknowledge, though some groups knew more about it than others. But they were in the beginning no match for whites in trickery, and when they did learn to match the whites, they suffered summary punishment for their audacity, often liquidation on the spot. The whites not only ruthlessly manipulated prices, but they extracted goods from the natives and then refused to pay for them. They exploited native labor in the preparation of products and then sailed away without making even the ludicrously unfair payment promised. On the side of the natives, their worst ingrained attitude was an insouciance about property rights. They were, as the earliest explorers found out, exceedingly skilled thieves; London pickpockets were heavy handed as compared to these light-fingered fellows. Captain Cook died as a consequence of the native disposition to steal. While this made trading precarious, it never seems to have made it impossible.

The early itinerant white traders were not under any discipline but their own, and it was simply the discipline of cupidity. They matched fault for fault with the natives; the results were often horrendous. Almost all the ships cut off in the islands by natives suffered that fate because either the traders in the ship, or in an earlier one, had dealt harshly with them. Of all the commercial people of the earliest days, the sandalwood gatherers acquired the worst reputation, though just why is not entirely clear; it may be simply a matter of fairly ample documentation. Almost any group can be convicted of very nasty practices. Most of the people who came to gather natural resources, such as sandalwood, *bêche-de-mer,* and coconut oil, seemed to regard the islands much as shoplifters regard a rich, unguarded shop; the stuff was there for no other reason than to be "lifted."

Until 1815 whalers who participated in this invasion of the islands were waifs and strays, either American or British, who were operating on the Australian-New Zealand side of the ocean. The richest known grounds of the earlier years were the so-called onshore grounds quite close to the west coast of South America. These grounds were exploited by the British and the Americans from the 1790's, and it was only after the War of 1812 that the offshore grounds westward toward the islands were discovered by an American. It was to attack the British whalers on the onshore grounds that Captain David Potter brought the first American ship of war into the Pacific during the War of 1812. He established a base at Nukuhiva in the Marquesas and claimed the islands for the United States, but his ships were destroyed outside Valparaiso by the British. By the 1820's, however, the whalers were operating all over the Pacific; the Americans were rapidly winning overwhelming predominance in the trade. *Circa* 1840 Charles Wilkes, the American explorer, plotted fifteen whaling grounds, of which eight were south of the equator, most of them described as "in the neighborhood of" one island group or another: the Society Islands (Tahiti), the Samoan Islands, the Fiji Islands, the Gilbert group, and New Zealand. As the whales were migratory, their pursuers developed knowledge of when they were most likely to be on particular grounds in numbers, and thus there grew up something of a routine of visiting the grounds seasonally in turn or sequence. Within the Pacific, which they normally entered and left by way of Cape Horn, they worked from south to north, or vice versa, this in either case bringing them among the islands on their normal occasions. While in the islands, they traded, recruited, and dropped off "hands," regularly lost a quota of men through desertion, and sometimes deliberately abandoned men to avoid payment of wages. A well-founded whaler, particularly an American ship, was supplied with a stock of trade goods: guns, rum, hardware, dry goods, notions.

It was said of the whalers that they "hung their consciences on Cape Horn," for their conduct in the Pacific all too often left much to be desired. As food could be obtained at almost any but the smallest, poorest, or most fanatically savage islands, whalers after food had the most widespread contacts of the time. (Islands regularly visited by whalers sometimes, after whaling declined, were so far off regular routes for other trade that they sank back almost into their original isolation. Rarotonga is an example.) The captains varied as widely as to honesty in their dealings as assorted human beings normally do, but a good many of them, American, British, and French, left a bad odor behind them wherever they went. Their morality was on a par with that of the other commercial enterprisers. The missionaries, their principal contemporary judges, took an ambiguous view of them: on the one hand they appreciated the advantages to the natives of the trade, especially if it brought coin into native hands (for the coin found its way into missionary contribution boxes), and some of the whalers were sufficiently decent to offer missionaries free transport between islands or to America or Europe at a time when transport was scarce, to say nothing of offering a postal service, but the missionaries disliked the habit of the whalers of trading guns and rum to the natives. Trading hard liquors tarnished their reputations irretrievably. It earned them more hostility than their free and easy view of sex. Since the American whalers were so much more numerous than any others, it was the Americans who got most of the blame, though French whalers were not far behind. Since the missionary judges were British, they tended to write less of British derelictions, though enough to keep the British within the whaler fold. One contemporary observer ironically suggested that the missionaries would be better employed in attempting to convert the whalers than in praying over the natives. The crews of American whalers were normally a very mixed bag; one analysis reported American Indians (probably mostly Gay Head Indians of Nantucket), runaway Negro slaves (New Bedford was an abolitionist town), renegade British sailors, Irishmen, Dutchmen, Portuguese and "Bravas," Hawaiians, and, of course, a goodly assortment of Massachusetts men, including a quota of farm boys seeking adventure.

Liquor was even put ashore surreptitiously on islands where the missionaries had good reason to feel they were in full command. The role of firewater in the contacts of disparate cultures is an ancient one, amply documented; the Americans from of old were active and ingenious in the firewater trade with primitive peoples—the Indians at home and the Africans abroad. It was hardly surprising, therefore, that they engaged in the trade in the South Sea Islands. The missionaries expended much passion in recording their hatred of the trade, and they were especially provoked with American ships, usually captained by Quakers, that advertised themselves as "temperance ships," but which nevertheless traded liquor whenever possible. A "temperance ship" was apparently often simply one on which no liquor was available to the crew while it was at sea and prosecuting its proper business of hunting the whale. It nevertheless carried liquor which it was prepared to trade when an occasion arose. The evidence is that the whalers amply earned their bad reputation as liquor traders, but it is also obvious that liquor was never the sole item offered in trade: it figured along with guns, hardware, and textiles.

While the whalers neither initiated nor concluded the trade in sex in the islands, they were certainly avid participants in the traffic. The missionaries also found this trade very obnoxious, though they wrote about it less copiously than about liquor. They could freely remark on the evil of getting natives drunk, but sex was a hopelessly indecorous subject for them and they scrupled about emphasizing fornication with native women. But the missionary inhibition about freely discussing the matter did not mean that they were any the less offended by the sexual indiscipline of the visiting whites or of the native women. It was a heavy cross for them to bear.

Though sex figured in the relations of whites and natives at any island visited, it is particularly associated with the ports of call at which more elaborate "refreshment" was sought. The word "refreshment" refers to a highly ambiguous concept. It was invented by the explorers and taken over by other seafaring people who kept crews at sea for long periods. "Refreshment" covered all kinds of onshore activities of the crews, including desirable variations of diet, opportunities for seeing new faces, and the re-establishment of the customs of civilization, as well as (and equally) the chance to swill liquor until bestially intoxicated and to visit amateur and professional whores. Among the ports that were particularly famous for providing "refreshment" during this period were Honolulu in Hawaii, Papeete in Tahiti, and Kororareka in New Zealand. All of them were freely resorted to by mariners of all nations, but Honolulu and Kororareka were more highly regarded by the Americans than Papeete (though goodness knows enough of them visited it), for the more cautious and observant captains concluded that sexual diseases were more rife there than was tolerable.

Taken together these activities of a commercial nature had a widespread impact on the islands, though some of them are associated especially with particular groups, like sandalwood and *bêche-de-mer* gathering with the Fijis, or pearl shell with the Tuamotus. However, it should not be assumed that the islanders came equally and directly into contact with the white intruders. Some islands acquired a reputation for exceptional savagery (one was actually named Savage Island) and were avoided. The impact was never even throughout *any* island group taken as a whole. In the islands visited, the natives living on the coast, particularly around any indentation making a natural harbor, had far more contacts than natives living elsewhere on the same island, especially in a mountainous interior. Sometimes, too, the psychological distance of enmity was added to the physical distance of geography as a separation between the natives, this definitely slowing down the diffusion of Western artifacts and influences. Many of the larger islands were only known coastally in this period; they were not explored inland until later. The natives living away from the favored point of contact tended to receive the impact of the intruders once, twice, and thrice removed and only as it sifted through the hands and minds of other natives, by which process it acquired a new "meaning." A similarly removed relation existed between the primary contact and natives living in the outer islands of island groups. There were in 1850 survivals all through the islands, even in the best-known groups, of examples of native society hardly at all influenced by the ways and values of the intruders. It was where towns, or apologies for towns, grew up that the fullest impact of the intruders was experienced, and in them and their immediate vicinities the dissolution and recasting of native society went furthest fastest. Conversely, it was in the towns (and because of the forces radiating from the towns) that the conditions were created forecasting and supporting the absorption of the islands into the Western politico-economic system. Sometimes these towns proved transient, as other and better *points d'appui* for Western penetration were discovered, but sometimes those established very early survived the chances and changes of time. Honolulu and Papeete survived; Kororareka did not.

D3

Of all the outside influences working on the islands in this period none was more massive in its effects than the missionary. Where the missionaries took hold, there the strongest efforts were made to transform native society by plan, not by inadvertence as in the case of the commercial interlopers, and in the process to assimilate it to the West. The missionaries were beset with a vision of at once saving souls and of bringing into being a new native society with the values of Bible Christianity and the British lower middle class, modified only by unconquerable native resistance. It was an extraordinary effort by anybody's standards and worthy of a wry respect even by those who must ex post facto regard it, both as an effort and an accomplishment, more than slightly ridiculous and, to minds steeped in anthropological thinking, reprehensibly destructive. Too much disposition to find it ludicrous can result in a failure to understand it truly as a thing in itself and, above all, as an extremely important phase of the absorption of the islands into the Western world.

The London Missionary Society, which sponsored the first missionary enterprise in the South Seas, was founded in 1795. Its founders were dissenting clergymen closely associated with the world of small business enterprise just then rising above individual artisanship and petty shop-keeping. It was a lower middle-class project. It had no real connection with the aristocracy and the world of fashion and none with the world of learning, either in its religious or secular phases. Most of its field-workers, with whom we are concerned here, were skilled tradesmen (who had served apprenticeships) with meager formal schooling. Only a minority were ordained clergymen and even they were hardly learned. However, a considerable number of them were highly articulate, both with tongue and pen, though their writing was fusty with religious cant. They cultivated only those secular interests which they had intimately related to their religious concerns, and indeed they feared to let their minds roam in other directions. They mostly saw the world of the natives darkly and disapprovingly (detecting the spoor of Satan in it); they were all but immune to the aesthetic emotions that the South Sea islands almost invariably stimulate. They were long on the Bible and the secular arts associated with production and trade, but they were short on anything we might call cultural understanding or anthropological insight. They had absolutely no understanding of the relativity of their own queer mixture of values, either in time or space, and therefore put on the same plane the absolutes of their supernatural religion and the values of the class from which they came. They believed with equal fervor in God, the Bible as divinely inspired law for personal and social salvation, diligence in secular work, the acquisition of wealth through trade, regular churchgoing, the wearing of the costumes of contemporary England, continence except within monogamous marriage (they were great child-begetters), and sobriety. They hated nudity, dancing, sex (except within monogamous marriage), drunkenness, anything savoring of *dolce far niente*, self-induced penury, war (except in God's cause), heathenism in all its protean manifestations, and Roman Catholicism. Sex and drunkenness gave them a very great deal of trouble. About both they were far more intolerant than their aristocratic fellow countrymen; their attitudes reflected a class puritanism; but they were nonetheless convinced of their position for that reason. Their enterprise was a stupendous effort to *impose* their values by moral suasion on a people utterly alien by race and culture.

The first LMS missionaries arrived at Tahiti on March 5, 1797, after a long voyage out via the Cape of Good Hope and to the south of Australia and New Zealand. There were thirty-nine persons in the party of whom six were wives and three children. Of the thirty workers, only four were ordained ministers; among the rest were a draper, a butcher, a weaver, a hatter, a shopkeeper, a domestic servant, a cabinetmaker, a tailor, a harness maker, a bricklayer, and a carpenter. Although it was not discernible at the moment, the most remarkable character of all was the bricklayer, Henry Nott. The Tahitians received these ambassadors of God and English artisan culture with characteristic politeness, allowing them to settle in, and proceeded about their own peculiar business. War played a large part in that business, and after about a year the missionaries found themselves not only inconvenienced by it but menaced. The climax came when the missionaries and a group of the natives disagreed on how to handle the trading with a visiting ship. In fear of their lives all but five of the missionaries, and the wife of one of these who was too ill to travel, precipitately abandoned the island and sailed to Sydney. Among those who remained was Henry Nott. Some of the refugees eventually returned, but others were forever lost to the missionary cause. Yet there was an important net gain from the contretemps, for the Tahitian refugees greatly interested the Reverend Samuel Marsden, principal chaplain of the convict establishment, and in a few years he was recognized as a principal adviser to South Sea missions. His own missionary work was done in New Zealand. (See Chapter IX.)

After the establishment of the principal body of missionaries at Tahiti, the "Duff" proceeded to Tonga, where the missionaries were attracted by Captain Cook's circumstantial account of the amiable character of the people, and established a small party there, and then to the Marquesas where a single missionary, the domestic servant, was left. In 1800 all of the Tonga party except one were taken off the island and transported to Sydney, and the adventurer of the Marquesas, after a manly struggle to survive, first shifted his post from one island to another, and then went home to England on a whaler. The man left behind at Tonga had, unfortunately, gone native and was, at the moment of evacuation, some place in the hinterland engaged in goodness knows what. He eventually made his escape to England and reassumed his religious character. The one who abandoned the Marquesas turned up later in New South Wales, where he made a career as a schoolteacher.

In July 1801 a second group of mission workers arrived at Tahiti from England. Meanwhile, Nott had learned the Tahitian language, giving the missionaries direct access to the native mind and laying the indispensable foundation of one of the characteristic, enduring, and valuable missionary enterprises, the bringing of literacy to the natives. In the England of those days (and to an extent in the United States also) there was an intimate association between teaching reading and the propagation of religion. The poor were taught to read so that they could read the Bible and religious tracts. The same principle was applied in the South Seas. First the language was mastered, as Nott mastered Tahitian, then it was reduced to writing, and shortly sections of the Bible (eventually all of it) were printed and the people taught to read. Along with reading went writing. The missionaries invariably established schools to propagate literacy, and the spread of literacy was unquestionably one of their most worthwhile accomplishments. At first works in Tahitian were printed at Sydney, but in 1817 a press was set up in the islands. Printer-missionaries were commonly men of especial distinction, conspicuously gifted members of the creative brotherhood of wandering printers. The great pioneer of printing at Tahiti was William Ellis, who also became a wise student of South Sea life.

Within two years of the arrival of the second party of missionaries they made a discovery of the first importance, though one which forced them into a compromise with native realities. The missionaries discovered that there would be great profit to them if they could command the allegiance of whoever had a claim to be king. The monarchical principle in the South Sea islands was directly derived from the idea of chieftainship. As a rule to establish a king on any particular island, the missionaries had to select and back, even to civil war, the chief who appeared to have the best chance of gaining general dominance. No island group had come under the sway of a single "king" before the arrival of the missionaries and the kings (and queens) who figure in the subsequent annals of the islands were ordinarily promoted to that eminence by the missionaries and, sometimes, other interested whites. Such kings were usually men of exceptionally strong personalities; often they had notable records of savagery in war and government; and to back them at all the missionaries had to overlook a great deal of conduct that was anything but Christian. In 1803 at Tahiti Henry Nott struck up an alliance with a pretender to kingship who styled himself Pomare II.

The Nott-Pomare alliance was fruitful, but its progress was not invariably peaceful. Step by step Nott built up a theocracy with Pomare (and his successors) as figurehead, the missionaries manipulating the government from behind the throne. It can hardly be said that they did this secretly; the fact of missionary power escaped the notice of no visitor. A conspicuous element of the missionary program was the formal conversion of the king to Christianity, this guaranteeing on the one hand that the laws promulgated by the king would conform to the missionary idea of a proper social order and that the people, in fear of the king and desirous of following his example, would also flock to the church. Pomare II was baptized in 1812; the general conversion of the people followed, and in 1819 Pomare formally promulgated a code of laws the missionaries (chiefly Nott) had devised. They were of the kind called "blue," derived from the Bible as interpreted by the missionaries, and designed to enforce the Levitical code of morality to which they subscribed. As long as, and to the extent that, they were enforced they guaranteed that Tahiti would be a puritan land in the South Seas. For about two decades the missionaries had the upper hand, making allowance for the casual weakness of Tahitian flesh and purposeful revolts, the worst involving liquor. After that the missionaries fought a rearguard action. In the missionary version they were done in by the French and the Roman Catholics.

Just as Henry Nott was moving toward his theocratic triumph there arrived in Tahiti a dedicated man named John Williams who was to become, on any accounting, the exemplary LMS missionary. Williams was born in 1796 and at fourteen was apprenticed to an ironmonger and showed equal interest in the counter, the desk, and the workship —he was a natural-born mechanic. In 1814 at the age of eighteen he was converted, after a period of exceedingly mild indulgence in the pleasures of London apprentices, and at the end of 1816 he left for Tahiti as a worker for the LMS. His specific preparation for the work had been a fairly even mixture of religious instruction and training in crafts. Williams was a man of enormous and unflagging energy. He saw his task as on the one hand converting the natives to his version of Christianity and on the other transforming their lives on the secular level by enforcing his outlook toward clothing, housing, work, and trade. Like the missionaries generally, Williams drew no very sharp distinction between the religious and the secular aspects of his work; they were complementary aspects of the fundamental task: to "elevate" the people. He made the natives literate to convert them to Christianity; he sought to support them in Christianity by converting them to the lower middle-class ethic with regard to labor and its fruits. Everything he did fitted together in a neat package, tightly tied.

While it was clear enough what the missionaries were after, their concern with secular affairs introduced fatal ambiguities into their proceedings. When they forced the natives to adopt English clothes, they were eliminating the perfectly adequate native clothing because they associated it with a high degree of nudity which to them was revolting, all the more so because they strongly felt the sexual element in it. To them adoption of English-style clothing symbolized *spiritual* progress. When they forced the natives to adopt a more English style of housing, abandoning native housing, they also were largely motivated by symbolic reasoning. They felt it would be more Christian to live in English-style houses because English Christians did. But they also felt that native-style housing, being open and airy, led to altogether too public a life; and as with clothing, they favored concealment over revelation. What they overlooked was that native clothing was highly perishable and therefore frequently discarded, rarely worn dirty, and therefore hygienic, whereas English clothes were durable, became decidedly dirty long before they were discarded, and that this had distinctly unhygienic consequences. Similarly with housing. The tidy English-style houses were anything but open and airy; their occupants tended to contract diseases whose incubation can be traced directly to the housing they occupied. The missionaries never heard of the principle of adapting dress and housing to climate; least of all did it occur to them that the prevailing native practices might embody wise adaptations. In their zeal for native welfare, as their obsessed minds saw it, they contributed directly to the decline of the natives. While they were glad to see native *society* decay, they did not intend to eliminate the natives with it. This was an ambiguous consequence of their ambitions.

With regard to trade they bumbled into other ambiguities that involved themselves as well as the natives. It is not an ex post facto discovery of suspicious-minded historians influenced by Weber and Tawney that the missionaries deliberately stimulated trade relations with the outside world. They fully professed that that was one of their primary motives in engaging in missionary work. They strongly felt, John Williams not least, that if the natives could be converted to Christianity *and also* to the economic ethic of the English entrepreneurs, this would lead to the provision of new "vents" for English manufactures. In 1836 a committee of the British Parliament accepted this as a principal reason for applauding missions. To gain access to English goods, the natives plainly had to produce tradeable commodities. This required a revolution in their ideas of work. The missionaries believed in work as one of the principal therapeutics against wayward or evil conduct. If the natives worked systematically, they would have less opportunity for indulging in their offensive pastimes. The missionaries often began implanting the idea of systematic work by having the natives bring in tradeable commodities (palm oil, arrowroot, etc.) as contributions to the church in lieu of nonexistent coin. These things were then sold on the church's account and the proceeds applied to the support of the mission and the missionaries. This institutional trade designed to make the mission self-supporting was thought laudable. (Ironically, however, the missionaries soon discovered that many natives were stimulated to their most extravagant bouts of work not by loyalty to the mission but to satisfy wants the missionaries violently attacked: guns and liquor.)

When the missionaries occupied an island which had been visited by white traders, a body of wants only to be satisfied from European sources already existed. The missionaries confirmed and elaborated those wants. But who was to satisfy them? The missionaries both hoped for visits from traders, whalers aiming to trade for food, and other itinerants with goods at their disposal, and were repelled by the conduct of the visitors and some of the items they offered. Moreover, it often happened, even on the largest islands, such as Tahiti, that the demand was greater than the native supply of desired commodities; or, in other islands, the natives produced more tradeable commodities than the irregular visits of purchasers could absorb. When individual missionaries stepped in to supply the deficiency at either end of the equation, or took advantage of opportunities both ways, they were involved in trade and their participation was frowned upon both by their principals in England and by their more rigid-minded associates. The mission as an institution could rightfully engage in trade, the missionaries as individuals could not. Yet many of the missionaries who left distinguished names behind them were personally involved in trade to some extent or other. They offered a variety of specious excuses for the involvement, but never seem to have emphasized that the official missionary attitude toward trade was ambiguous. Why should trade be something missionary activity would by plan stimulate but something in which individual missionaries should not engage? Why should missionaries be denied a wide-open opportunity to provide through trade for their often very large families? Many missionaries concluded that trade by a godly man was a godly trade, and they laid up considerable treasures on this earth as a consequence.

John Williams, an exemplary missionary, was not only a man of multiple and very mixed purposes, but he was also notably restless. However hard he might labor at his duties while in charge at a particular island, his thoughts were constantly on untouched islands "out there." He was in the South Seas from 1817 to 1839, with a break of four years in England from 1834 to 1838; the number of places on which he made a deep impression in his eighteen years in the island is astonishing. He died actively seeking pastures new. His restlessness led him inexorably to his doom.

"Our daily employment," he wrote in 1825, "is as follows:—Every morning, Saturday excepted, at school from six o'clock to eight. Monday evening we have conversation meetings; Wednesday evening, preaching; Friday evening, we have a full meeting of the members and the baptized, when, after singing, prayer, and a short exhortation, the natives speak. . . . On Saturday, the judicial proceedings of the week are settled, which generally occupy two or three hours . . . On Sabbath days, you know, perhaps, that we are fully employed. The natives, at six o'clock hold a prayer meeting. At nine o'clock we have regular service. After this, Mrs. Williams reads aloud some interesting work for our spiritual edification, except any vessels are here, when I always preach in English. At one o'clock the bell rings again, when we have a kind of catechetical service on the sermon preached in the forenoon. In the afternoon, there is another regular service. . . ." The empty spaces of weekdays were filled with secular labors: getting the people to work on dwellings, church building, crops, at processing vendible resources, and so on. Any spare time left the missionary spent in writing voluminous letters and reports to England, translating into the native tongue, and planning future activities. This mixture of activities clearly implies a mixture of motives, and at one point Williams' pious biographer was at pains to emphasize that, appearances to the contrary, Williams kept them in a harmonious relationship. It was an extraordinary tour de force.

Within six months of his arrival at Tahiti, Williams was off to the island of Huahine, where he was properly initiated into missionary work, and then three months later passed on to Raïatéa. There he settled down to the kind of routine just outlined and really developed his missionary character. He labored mightily at saving souls, attacked the clothing and housing problems, and planned the development of production and trade. It was at Raïatéa also that his passion for islands beyond the horizon developed. A chief from the island of Rurutu, which was having trouble, appeared at Raïatéa to solicit missionary help. This suggested to Williams' mind that *all* the South Sea islands were ripe for the plucking. What was needed was a boat to get from island to island.

Although it was ostensibly to consult with doctors about his wife's poor health that Williams went to Sydney in 1821, it was equally to obtain a boat for voyages among the islands and to encourage a regular commercial shipping service between Sydney and the islands which would carry native produce to market. On the way to Sydney he put some native teachers—converted natives adjudged fully enough fortified to undertake preaching to heathen natives—on Aitutaki in the Cook Islands. His boat obtained, Williams began to get about among the islands, working from Raïatéa as headquarters. It was while visiting Aitutaki on one of these occasions that he heard of the island of Rarotonga in terms that peculiarly excited his imagination. It was not until May 1826 that he actually found it, believing that he had in literal fact discovered it. However, we now know that it had been visited by explorers and commercial visitors before Williams' time.

At Rarotonga Williams carried through the missionary program with classic thoroughness. From the history of the island practically every aspect of missionary endeavor touched on in the present discussion can be illustrated; and if there is an example of what missionizing an island meant, that example is Rarotonga. Yet it was but an episode in Williams' career; other men actually spent more time there than Williams himself, notably Aaron Buzacott.

For Williams' heart was always yearning toward the beyond. In 1830 he visited Samoa, held a love feast with the Methodist missionaries already there, but resolved to invade the islands nevertheless, and returned for a second visit in 1832. Always on his visits he left behind native teachers—if indeed he had not sent them on before him—and he followed them up by having missionaries from England assigned to the territory he had opened up. His ambition was boundless, and as early as 1821, when he was negotiating for his first boat, he projected a comprehensive tour of the islands. By 1827 he was writing specifically about the invasion of Melanesia, though all of Polynesia had not been occupied and the depth of the conversion in the islands longest occupied was questionable, as Williams sorrowfully acknowledged.

His protracted visit to England (1834–38) was simply another and very necessary phase of his campaign for comprehensive conversion of the natives, a phase of drumming up support, moral and financial, for the effort. It was while engaged in this work that he snatched time from the making of hortatory speeches to the pious and the worldly alike (for to the one he would preach of the compelling need to spread Christianity and to the other of the expected good consequences in terms of trade) to compose his classic missionary autobiography, *Missionary Enterprizes in the South Sea Islands* (1837) which, in its time, was a best-seller. He returned to the islands well fortified both spiritually and materially, accompanied by new recruits for missionary service.

He made his headquarters not at Rarotonga but at Samoa, specifically at Fasetootai on the island of Upolu, for his ambition was still directing him to the west. In 1839 he embarked at last for Melanesia. He had developed the theory that if he could establish a successful mission in the New Hebrides he could work from there south into New Caledonia and north into the Solomons and New Guinea. En route to the New Hebrides he called in at Rotuma, at that time a kind of crossroads of the island world where one could expect to find not only the usual motley assortment of resident whites but also, perchance, natives of islands otherwise unknown or little known to outsiders. Just possibly he would find a few from the New Hebrides who might be helpful to him on his projected visit. He first reached his goal at the island of Tanna and was vastly encouraged to find that nothing out of the ordinary transpired, but when he moved on to Erromanga his luck turned. The visit began easily enough, and inspired by an excess of trust in superficial signs of a friendly welcome he started inland with a party to visit what promised to be a substantial settlement, when suddenly the natives in the train turned upon him and cut him down. On November 20, 1839, John Williams achieved the immortality of martyrdom. Governor Gipps of New South Wales sent a ship of war to recover the bones, and all that remained of the mortal John Williams was interred at Apia in Samoa. The news reached England on April 6, 1840. In Polynesia John Williams flourished, but Melanesia took life from him at the early age of forty-three.

§3

The missionaries of other sponsorship or denomination followed in general the London Missionary Society pattern of action, but seem not to have carried it to such extremes, either because native resistances were greater where they worked or because the will to undertake an absolute transformation of the native personality and mode of life was weaker or lacking. The later arrivals were as keen as the LMS people to substitute Christian values and practices for native beliefs and customs, that the natives might be saved, and they therefore made as intensive onslaughts on what they regarded as the evil-doings of the natives as their predecessors, but the Samoans and the Fijians, for example, while eventually Christianized, were not subjected to such heavy pressures as the Tahitians and the Rarotongans to become lower-class Englishmen in all respects. That aspect of the missionary effort was early revealed to be quite futile. The natives might, to save themselves, have to accept new ways and new social values, though reluctantly, but they did not really have to become indistinguishable from the intruders in dress, housing, manners, work, and expectations in life. The result was that with all the missionary effort, not to mention the other influences at work upon them, the natives were progressively freer to maintain themselves as natives. Even after over a century of contact, cultural anthropologists today find it immensely profitable and stimulating to study the particular cultural syntheses the natives have evolved and continue to our time to elaborate. They changed and so also did the outlook of the missionaries.

At the same time that the Methodists joined Marsden's Church of England missionaries in New Zealand they also began work in Tonga. Later, they gained some influence in Samoa, but abandoned that field to the LMS at the solicitation of John Williams, and accepted the assignment of Fiji, although it was universally recognized as difficult. The

Methodists began to work in Fiji in 1835, but the real effort was initiated in 1838 when Fiji was constituted a separate "district." Although men of high character and ability were sent to Fiji, progress was very slow. It was not until as late as 1854 that the historically important chief, Cakobau, was finally converted. Meanwhile, in Tonga the Methodists had had a great if peculiar success when Methodism became the state religion under King George Tabou, with consequences to be examined later.

As long as the Roman Catholics kept out of missionary work in the islands there was sufficient ecumenical spirit among the Protestants for them successfully to work in harmony by dividing up the field. But when the Catholics appeared, a fanatic bitterness was engendered. From their side, the Catholics not only would not recognize any division of the field (even when it was suggested by a British foreign secretary), but rather deliberately sought to invade Protestant preserves for the purpose of rescuing the poor natives from intolerable heresy. Since it was impossible for the Protestants to view themselves as heretics and since they on their side viewed the Church of Rome as an abomination, this attempt to invade their territories was regarded as a terrible affront. Moreover, the Roman Catholic missionaries were French and the British Protestants suspected, quite rightly as the French historians now candidly admit, that they were as much agents of French imperialism as of true religion. The Protestant case against the Catholics was complete when the French government acted to protect and advance the Catholic cause in the islands. The first climax came at Tahiti.

The French government, from a study of the reports of explorers, arrived at the opinion that it should acquire "establishments" in the islands as early as 1822. The opinion was strengthened by a study of Dumont d'Urville's account of his voyage of 1826–27, and Duperrey's report of the activities of the Protestant missionaries at Tahiti as he had observed them in 1824 directed attention to the use of missionaries in island politics. At that time no Catholic mission was giving any particular attention to the islands, but in 1825 the Pope charged the Congregation du Sacré-Coeur de Jésus et de Marie (or Picpusiens) to evangelize Hawaii, and priests landed there in 1827. Two years later Irish Catholic Peter Dillon, the discoverer of the relics of La Pérouse who became an exponent of French and Roman Catholic interests in the islands, denounced the English Protestant missionaries to the French government and advocated sending out priests and merchants. The fall of the Bourbons prevented action, but the July Monarchy took up the matter, and in 1835 two vicariates were created, divided by longitude 158°, that to the east assigned to the Picpusiens, that to the west to the Marists, an order founded in 1816. The Picpusien fathers had landed in the Gambier Islands, where they established a headquarters in 1834; they moved on to Tahiti in 1836 and to the Marquesas in 1838. The Marist fathers landed at Wallis and Futuna Islands in 1837, went to New Zealand in 1838, to New Caledonia in 1843 (before any Protestants had been there), and to Fiji and Samoa in 1844. Thus, by the middle 1840's the battle for the souls and bodies of the Polynesians was joined. John Williams and the Marist fathers had indicated that an identical battle was going to be fought over the Melanesians also.

CHAPTER XII

The Islands Enter World Politics

The penetration of the islands was ineluctably productive of domestic disorders, even when the agents of the Western world came to the islands crying "Peace!, peace!" From the disorders stemmed the politics of the times. In the beginning the prime political question was who was responsible for the maintenance of the public peace between whites and natives, natives and natives, and whites and whites. The relations between natives and natives were, except as the missionaries or reckless whites might take a hand, left to the natives. In the earliest years, as we have seen, the British authorities in Australia believed that they had at least some right and obligation to help in maintaining law and order on the tacit assumption that the British held sovereignty over the islands. In this period justices of the peace were appointed on the authority of the government of New South Wales and visits of imperial ships of war were advocated to support the authority of the justices. When the assumed British sovereignty was repudiated (or, rather, treated as though it had never existed) by London in 1817, and the islands thereupon became no man's lands in law, fundamental responsibility for law and order was transferred to the natives under the theory of "native sovereignty." "Native sovereignty" was used by both missionaries and resident whites engaged in business as a basis on which to build native governments which, when missionary inspired and controlled, became theocracies. The intruding governments sent ships of war to engage in "gunboat diplomacy" in support of, or to discipline, residents of the same nationality as the ships, and in this same context began to appoint officials called residents, commercial agents, and consuls to give permanence and continuity to national representation, the ships of war supporting them by visits.

The development of this system, loose as it was, was clear evidence that the nations conceived themselves to have interests in the islands worth protecting and advancing. Whether they would proceed to the length of assuming sovereignty over an island group depended, however, on other factors than the mere decision to use diplomatic agents. The Americans, though they often had large economic interests in various groups and early appointed diplomatic representatives, were not interested in acquiring sovereignty, though since, in the international morality of the time, this was so obviously the ultimate objective of virile powers with regard to backward territories they were persistently suspected of scheming to that end. The utterances of politicians and others at home with regard to the American drive to the Pacific coast of North America, and their assertions about what this would mean in Pacific basin affairs, lent a certain color of reason to the suspicion. The British, with substantial economic and also important religious interests, not to mention the wish to acquire new overseas outlets for settlement, eventually led the way in taking sovereignty in the islands, beginning with New Zealand. The vigor of British activity was, however, largely determined by the colonies of the area, Australia and New Zealand, rather than by the United Kingdom government. The French, with smaller accumulated economic interests than either the Americans or the British, but exploiting a religious interest, were more motivated by the spirit of nationalistic competition with the British on the one hand and hopes of future economic growth on the other and followed the British example. The partition of the islands began in the 1840's.

D3

By an odd quirk of history the islands were no man's lands in practice before they were in theory. The intruding whites in the islands who scorned the law mostly acted on the assumption that its long arm could not reach them. The Sydney authorities were naturally annoyed by this and tried to arrange that it would. Writing home in April 1805 Governor Philip Gidley King, after giving a lurid account of what appeared to be going on in the islands and offering dire predictions about future developments—he forecast an outbreak of piracy—made a suggestion:

To prevent these growing Evils, I would respectfully suggest the propriety of Two or Three Sloops of War being stationed here for the purpose of preventing too great a number of bad Characters from establishing themselves on the Society Islands, and to prevent many abuses and irregularities on the part of Americans as well as for the protection of these Settlements generally.

(King was much upset at that time about the aggressive activities of American sealers and traders.) No action was taken on this by the home authorities who thus initiated a policy of resisting colonial suggestions about island policy which long continued in force. The British idea was to postpone action as long as possible.

Actually, no naval vessel was sent for service in the waters of New South Wales until 1821, in Governor Brisbane's time. A ship was then sent from the India station and was available, on instructions from the governor, for service in the islands. Later on, ships from the British naval station on the west coast of South America were also sent on errands into the islands. In 1826 the ship on the New South Wales coast first made a visit to New Zealand, initiating an annual tour of inspection. In 1830, however, the Reverend Samuel Marsden suggested to Governor Darling that a ship should be permanently stationed on the New Zealand coast and the governor supported the suggestion in a dispatch to London. The home authorities, however, rejected the idea. In 1829 a regular annual tour of the islands was instituted. In the beginning, in addition to New Zealand, the islands visited regularly were Tahiti and Tonga. This scheme was followed for several decades, with adaptations to the changing situations in the islands.

The first effort to station government officers in the islands on a continuing basis was made by Governor King. In 1802 he appointed one of the LMS missionaries in Tahiti a justice of the peace. This had no particularly significant results, however, but except for putting vessels trading from Sydney to the islands under a good conduct bond, King could think of nothing better to do in respect to law and order short of regular visits by ships of war. Neither could Governor Macquarie. In 1813 he was forced to face up to the problem, primarily as it existed in New Zealand, where the Australian involvement was greatest. At the end of that year Macquarie issued a general order requiring a good conduct bond of the substantial sum of £1000 from all ships trading in the islands, and the next year he appointed Thomas Kendall, one of Marsden's missionaries, justice of the peace in New Zealand. However, the Imperial Act of 1817 destroyed what tenuous legal basis the appointments of justices of the peace had, and while it provided for dealing with crimes committed by British subjects in the islands, it failed to provide an adequate machinery for apprehending and bringing to trial other villains involved in crime. In effect the maintenance of law and order was left to the natives, assisted by some of the resident whites. A sad job they made of it, even with the best intentions.

Fundamental reliance simply had to be placed on visits by ships of war. The visits produced all kinds of results from what one might call routine to what were certainly extraordinary. Under the circumstances, the routine visits were the most useful, but their usefulness was limited because the commanders of the ships had few legal powers, were normally ignorant of the local situations, could rarely fully investigate any episode, let alone a series, and could not pause to follow through on any verdict rendered. They spent most of their time attempting to arbitrate quarrels and seeking redress for native outrages on the persons and properties of British nationals. Some damages cases dragged on for years and grew from trivial into substantial claims. On the whole, however, the commanders seem to have rendered rough justice, even though they occasionally took revenge on the natives rather than meted out judicial sentence.

Under this system a great deal depended on the character of the commander. The commanders mostly appeared to have in mind upholding the authority of the more responsible resident whites (notably in Polynesia, the missionaries), commercial people when they were respectable, and of course, the official government representatives when they appeared on the scene. In general the missionaries, never sparing of judgments on island affairs, approved the visits of ships of war, not only because they normally fortified their position, but because they believed in the effectiveness of overawing difficult natives and reckless whites with such impressive evidences of *British* authority. If any outside authority was to be exerted in the islands—and this was an open question with the missionaries for several decades—the British missionaries favored the assertion of British authority. Except for the incorrigible rascals, and there were several, the British commercial people and the beachcombing riffraff felt the same way. Like the British generally, these far-strayed sons of the Empire found it difficult to conceive that any other authority was, in a proper sense, "legitimate."

Two episodes, one in New Zealand and one in Tonga, well illustrate the extraordinary results gunboat diplomacy could produce. In 1834 the ship "Alligator" was dispatched from Sydney to New Zealand to rescue survivors of the wreck of the "Harriet," forcibly detained by the Maoris. The master of the "Harriet," a man named Guard, who had escaped, was an ex-convict engaged in bay whaling; his wife, who was among the detained, was a woman whose reputation for chastity was far from unsullied. Although instructed not to use force against the Maoris, the commander of the "Alligator" had soldiers aboard his ship. After negotiations with the Maoris and after all the captives had been recovered except one of the Guard children, the soldiers attacked the Maori *pa* and many Maoris were killed. The rights and wrongs of the affair from its beginnings were hopelessly complicated, but one point was clear: the use of force on the Maoris at that stage was wanton, calculated only to worsen relations with that particular tribe in the future. The action was, therefore, a crime, not a mistake. It was fervently condemned in England and questioned even in New South Wales where harsh treatment of natives usually found apologists if "rights" of whites could be alleged to be involved.

Equally extraordinary was the episode in Tonga. The natives of Tonga in 1840 were divided into two hostile factions by religious differences. One faction was Methodist, the other, still heathen, was listening to the Roman Catholics. Charles Wilkes attempted unsuccessfully to reconcile the factions when he was in the islands. When Captain Crocker, fresh from recovering John Williams' bones at Erromanga, visited the islands in the "Favorite" he was induced by the Methodist missionaries, on considerations unknown, to assist the converted natives in an armed attack on the heathens. Apparently, Crocker made the common error of underestimating native fighting power, for in the clash he and two seamen from his ship were killed and twenty of the crew wounded. This did not enhance either Methodist or British prestige. The missionaries had to be hurriedly removed to another island. The ship retreated with its wounded to Sydney.

The British were slow in appointing diplomatic officers to the islands. The first British consul appointed to any Pacific group was Richard Charlton at Hawaii in 1824. He had jurisdiction also in Tahiti and Tonga, but he had little occasion to use it. The appointment illustrates that the real focus of interest for the foreign powers in the Pacific at this time was the North, not the South Pacific. In 1833 James Busby became British resident in New Zealand and in 1835 Thomas McDonnell, additional British resident there—appointments which illustrated the predominance of New Zealand among the South Pacific islands as far as the British were concerned. Both the representatives in New Zealand were attached to and paid by the government of New South Wales, indicating that London saw the islands as appendages of the Australian settlements rather than as of direct imperial concern. The situation quickly changed though, for in 1837 London appointed the Reverend George Pritchard, a LMS missionary, consul at Tahiti, with jurisdiction also in Tonga and Samoa. When Pritchard was ousted from Tahiti under extraordinary circumstances shortly to be recounted, he was sent as consul at Apia in Samoa in 1845. By that time the British had a consul general in the Pacific (1843) in charge of the representation in Hawaii, Tahiti, and Samoa. The men were all formally or informally accredited to the native governments of the groups to which they were assigned. While they unquestionably represented a great nation, in their immediate situations they were personally powerless, dependent on the influence they could acquire over the natives and the prestige they could command among their resident fellow nationals and resident foreigners. In the last analysis their positions were impossible unless they could prove their power by invoking the *national* power in an outward and visible form. Their favorite way of doing this was to have a man-of-war call at the port at which they were stationed. (These considerations applied to all consuls, not to the British alone.) The coming of the consuls and other government officers did not particularly change the situation in the islands; it merely signified that the national interests were assessed as of greater importance than earlier. They put a new face on an old structure, and as Governor King had early perceived, unless it was clear that there was an engine of power behind the façade, not much of consequence could be accomplished. In addition to the islands where consuls were stationed, other island groups in which interest was mounting by the 1840's were the Fijis, the New Hebrides, and New Caledonia. But what the British government really sought, through all the chances and changes, was to maintain the status quo. British pressure for change was largely colonial.

D3

The American penetration of the islands was of much the same pattern as the British. It was rather more aggressive commercially, however, and in whaling the American interest surpassed both the British and the colonial. The Americans were also important in the miscellaneous trades of gathering sandalwood and *bêche-de-mer,* as for example in the Fiji Islands, where they (particularly men from Salem, Massachusetts) were dominant until the middle of the century. But it was whaling that really gave the United States an "interest" in this remote part of the world. That interest was maintained from ports in New England, around Cape Horn. It was not until the end of the 1840's that the United States was established on the Pacific coast. By the accident of the richness of the North Pacific whaling grounds, and by virtue of the China trade which in origin predated whaling, the American interest in the Pacific early became centered in the *North* Pacific. The theoreticians of America's future in the Pacific all had their eyes on the Orient, not on the Southwest Pacific. The latter figured in the American dream of expansion, aside from its role in whaling, only as it was on the road to the North Pacific and the Orient. It is an odd but important fact that some of the American activities in the Southwest Pacific, notably the gathering of sealskins, sandalwood, and *bêche-de-mer,* were justified commercially because of the market for these things in China. It is highly significant that when the Americans did acquire territory in the Southwest Pacific it was in terms of a coaling station for steamers traveling toward and from the North Pacific. The progress of the technology of steam navigation and the digging of the Panama Canal, soon and late, lessened the importance of that holding to negligibility. At no time was the Southwest Pacific exactly a cynosure of American ambition in the Pacific Basin; rather it was at best a fascinating byblow.

The moves of the United States in the game of the islands are, therefore, not to be viewed in quite the same light as those of the British and the French. The Americans' primary interest was to keep open the channels of trade and the opportunities to exploit natural resources. Until the Samoa question arose in the 1870's there was never any inclination on the part of the United States government to play the island game to the point of taking sovereignty, whatever stray individuals may have thought or advocated. But as the rules of the game required certain moves, regardless of how one thought of the ultimate stakes, what the United States did was all of a piece with what the British and French did. The British and the French thought mistakenly that the Americans were doing it for the same reasons as themselves. The United States, too, appointed official agents in the islands and supported them by ships of war.

Since Americans were commercially active in the Pacific from 1784, when the ship "Empress of China" arrived in Canton, China, from New York with a cargo of ginseng to exchange for China goods, especially tea, and Major Samuel Shaw, a veteran of the Revolutionary War, was appointed consul at Canton in 1786, it is rather surprising that no person of diplomatic status was appointed to an *island* post until September 19, 1820, when Secretary of State James Monroe designated John C. Jones agent for commerce and seamen at Honolulu. It was, however, entirely logical that Jones, like Shaw earlier, was appointed to a post in the North Pacific. As to the South Pacific, the Americans first sent diplomatic personnel to the countries on the west coast of South America, where their whalers and traders were being victimized by pirates. The first consuls appointed in the islands of the Southwest Pacific were at Tahiti in 1835 (two years before the British moved), at New Zealand in 1838, while the British were satisfied with a feeble-powered resident, and Samoa in 1839, where the British then had no resident representation at all. The consul at Tahiti, a Belgian named Moerenhout, later deserted the American service at an awkward time to join the French as their consul; the consul at Kororareka, New Zealand, was an Englishman, James R. Clendon, a trader who favored British sovereignty and later joined the British colonial service; and the man at Samoa was another Englishman, son of John Williams the missionary. Charles Wilkes caustically criticized this habit of appointing foreigners official United

States representatives, though he himself was responsible for Williams' appointment.

Wilkes saw more of the American consuls and agents in the islands than any other American naval person to his time. Until Wilkes's visit which, of course, was not primarily for that purpose at all, the naval people did little by way of gunboat diplomacy in the islands of the Southwest Pacific, and that little mostly at Tahiti. They were far more interested in Hawaii. It was not until the War of 1812 that the first American ship of war had entered the Pacific Ocean, over a quarter century after the first commercial vessel plowed its waters. However, as early as 1817 the U.S. Navy sent a ship into the Pacific to assist American commercial vessels in difficulties, chiefly arising from the disorders of the revolutions and wars in the Spanish colonies of the west coast of South America. By 1821 a naval "station" had been established, with responsibility for everything from Cape Horn to the Columbia River, but primarily to deal with pirates and other depredators on the coast of South America. Headquarters were made at Valparaiso, Chile, and Callao, Peru. From this "station" the ship "Dolphin," commanded by Lieutenant John Percival, was detached late in 1825 to look for the mutineers of the whaleship "Globe." He found them in the Marshall Islands of Micronesia and, having called in at the Marquesas (thereby setting a fashion) en route, he went on from the Marshalls to Honolulu where, early in 1826, his was the first American ship of war to show its colors in that port.

During 1826–27 Captain Thomas ap Catesby Jones (later on to play a curious role in the taking of California by the Americans), commanding the ship "Peacock," sailed among the islands offering treaties of commerce and friendship. His was the first American ship of war to visit Tahiti, and the United States was the first government to offer to make a formal treaty with the native government. Jones went on from Tahiti to Honolulu, his principal objective, where he successfully offered his treaty to the native government there and also took steps to counteract what he regarded as excessive British influence over the native authorities. Somehow the British had managed to convey to the native mind the idea that the United States was a dependency of Britain like New South Wales! Jones's tour was obviously dictated by pressure from the American commercial interests in the islands. Captain William B. Finch in the U.S.S. "Vincennes" visited the Marquesas and Tahiti in 1829 before going on to Honolulu, his real objective, where he brought his authority and prestige to the support of the missionaries and the native government against the antimissionary traders. At Tahiti he dealt with Pomare Vahine I (Queen Pomare) and was given an affecting letter, an odd mixture of friendly sentiments and commercial information, for the President. While on his way home from Sumatra, where he had gone to strengthen American prestige in the pepper ports, Commodore John Downes in 1832 visited Honolulu and Tahiti.

This record would seem to imply that after Honolulu, the Marquesas and Tahiti were the important islands in American eyes during the late 1820's and early 1830's, but while Tahiti *was* important, the visits to the Marquesas seem to have been due to an accident of geography—they were readily accessible to ships approaching the islands from the South American coast. They had a certain interest for American whalers and sandalwood gatherers, but other groups were even then far more important. After Honolulu and Papeete, Kororareka was already the most important port for whalers in the Pacific islands. Shortly, however, Commodore Downes, now in command of the Pacific squadron, was given orders to visit all the whaling ports of call systematically, and slowly the American flag was seen farther afield in the Southwest Pacific.

The climactic American voyage of this period was not a venture in gunboat diplomacy but in scientific exploration, Charles Wilkes's voyage, already described. Wilkes had little to say about politics in his published report—he may have had more to say in papers sent home and still unpublished—but he did comment in a hostile fashion on the transfer of sovereignty in New Zealand (the ceremonies at Waitangi which some members of his party had witnessed). He expressed his dislike of French aggressiveness in the islands, to an account of which we are coming, and he was not above performing such a routine duty of a gunboat commander as punishing natives for aggressions against Americans, some of them years old, as in Fiji. But on the available evidence he was less interested in the politics of the islands than in the politics of Oregon which, after all, was much more heated. But in regard to both, his concern was that the American entrepreneurs—whalers, gatherers, traders—should not be crowded unduly by the British. He resented their action in New Zealand because he foresaw—correctly—that it would cramp the American style in that country. He felt that Consul Clendon had let the Americans down. And he viewed the doings of the French in much the same light.

D3

Under the rather brummagem monarchy of Louis Philippe and his famous minister, François Guizot, France made an effort to recover her old position as a great imperial power, lost in the Napoleonic disaster. She avidly sought new territory around the world but especially in the

Mediterranean (Algeria), the Indian Ocean, and the Southwest Pacific. In the latter area, a French gesture at New Zealand was unofficial and weak but it was nevertheless the case that possessions that would be useful to her navy and her traders were warmly coveted. The French had large visions of the economic and political changes that would be wrought in the Pacific by the construction of a canal across the Isthmus of Panama, an already old proposal then under active discussion. They were therefore looking for islands prospectively useful in communications to and from the Isthmus and Australia and New Zealand. The logic of this reasoning led them first to the Marquesas and Tahiti. What other Southwest Pacific islands it might be profitable to take could be left for future conjunctions of interest and opportunity.

France had but a tiny economic stake in the Marquesas and Tahiti so she had to make a case out of the bad treatment given Roman Catholic missionaries and the few French civilians at Tahiti. However, the posture of international affairs in Europe was such that the French did not dare jeopardize Anglo-French relations for the sake of Southwest Pacific islands. A great deal depended, therefore, on the British attitude toward Tahiti.

Although Spanish Roman Catholics had attempted a mission to the natives of Tahiti long before the Protestants arrived, they had quickly abandoned the field, and the Protestants by 1835, after almost four decades of activity, felt that Tahiti was "theirs," all the more so because they wielded such great influence over the native government. The central figure at Tahiti was, therefore, not the native monarch, but the LMS missionary who was also the British consul, the Reverend George Pritchard. In the situation that developed in Tahiti, Pritchard had two objectives in mind: to prevent the Roman Catholics from gaining a foothold in the kingdom and also to prevent the French government from taking over the country. The two objectives were very hard to distinguish.

The French Roman Catholic missionaries, established in the Southwest Pacific in 1834, first knocked at the door of Tahiti in 1835. The man they sent to the island found himself forbidden to stay on the ground that he did not have proper permission to do so, but really, as Pritchard candidly told the British government, because he was a Roman Catholic whose activities would menace the Protestant religious monopoly. The London authorities took no notice of this episode. In 1836, however, two Roman Catholic missionaries were expelled under the same circumstances and it was impossible to ignore the matter. The British were nevertheless not disposed to make too much of it and mildly suggested that the Roman Catholics accept the convention under which missionaries kept out of territory already occupied by a rival. Neither the Catholic missionaries nor the French government were inclined to accept this kindly suggestion. Rather they believed that as French citizens the missionaries had a right to undertake their work where they pleased. They did not intend to be denied that right by the fanatic intolerance of the Protestant missionaries. Plainly, the French government intended to make political capital out of a religious dispute.

This became clear in 1838 when Captain Dupetit-Thouars appeared in the area in the "Venus." He first took two Roman Catholic missionaries to the Marquesas, where British Protestants were working, thus indicating rejection of the British government's suggestion about dividing the field, and he then proceeded to Tahiti where he demanded 2000 Spanish dollars of the native government as indemnity for the ill-treatment of French nationals (the two priests expelled in 1836). The money was raised and paid. Dupetit-Thouars thereupon offered a convention providing for perpetual peace between Tahiti and France and the exchange of promises of most favored-nation treatment all around. This represented a defeat for the Protestants and the Reverend George Pritchard. It was Pritchard, as chief adviser to the Tahitian government, who was setting the Tahitian line.

The Tahitians sought to recover ground by asking London to make Tahiti a British protectorate. At the same time they passed a law making LMS Protestantism the official state religion and prescribing deportation for anyone who came to Tahiti to disturb that religion. The British did not in any case want a protectorate over Tahiti; they specifically did not want a protectorate with a law excluding Roman Catholics. Britain's interest in Tahiti was principally the LMS interest there; its economic interest was relatively small, and its strategic interest turned upon how the defense of Australia was conceived. Moreover, the official mind was currently fully occupied with the problem of New Zealand. London therefore temporized, suggesting that what was needed was a strengthening of the Tahitian native government.

For their part, the French continued the pressure on Tahiti. They forced the repeal of the anti-Catholic law; their missionaries were admitted and gained influence, assisted by the Belgian Moerenhout who chose the moment to change from being consul for the United States to being consul for France. Consul Pritchard resisted every French move as best he could and sent London a steady stream of demands for support in the form of visits from ships of war, accompanied by arguments that the French objective was annexation and by demonstrations of how great the British interest in Tahiti was, correctly conceived. The British government, however, remained passive. It saw the whole business as a quarrel between rival missionary groups and did not detect (or acknowledge) the political use the French were making of the situation.

A new act of the drama began in 1842. The French government had had its attention particularly drawn to the Marquesas by Dumont d'Urville. They fitted well into its scheme of possessions useful to naval vessels and merchants in the Southwest Pacific. The Roman Catholic missionaries left at the Marquesas by Dupetit-Thouars in 1838 had established themselves, and the Protestant missionaries had withdrawn at the end of 1841. In May 1842 Dupetit-Thouars, working out of Valparaiso where his squadron made its headquarters, went to the Marquesas and proclaimed French sovereignty. The native chiefs, whose co-operation he had sought, felt Dupetit-Thouars had tricked them and soon had the French penned up in coastal settlements, but as far as the French were concerned their end was achieved. (It proved a barren prize in the long run.) In September 1842 Dupetit-Thouars appeared at Tahiti. For mistreatment of French nationals he demanded an indemnity of 10,000 Spanish dollars, in default of payment of which he would take "more rigorous measures" (that is, bombard Papeete). Not having 10,000 Spanish dollars (the American consul, who could have raised them, decided not to provide them on the grounds that his government would prefer to see Tahiti go to the French rather than the British), the Tahitian government had no choice but to submit to whatever terms the French chose to lay down. The terms were that Tahiti become a French protectorate. This was soon effected. The French government formally accepted Dupetit-Thouars' arrangement in April 1843. The day that the protectorate government began Herman Melville landed at Papeete from an Australian whaler on which he had traveled from the Marquesas, where he had witnessed the taking of sovereignty by the French. He immediately detected Tahitian unrest.

The British government, though surprised at the French action, was disposed to accept the *fait accompli*. Tahiti qualified as a faraway land about which it knew nothing. But there were Britishers—missionaries and Australians (the angry voice of John Dunmore Lang rose loud and clear) to whom the change was highly unwelcome. Consul George Pritchard returned from a sick leave in England early in 1843, landing at Tahiti from a ship of war sent from Sydney by the governor of New South Wales to investigate recent events. Pritchard, the commander of a British ship of war, Captain Toup Nicholas, who kept his ship at Papeete for six months, and other interested Britishers acted on the assumptions that the French government would probably disavow Dupetit-Thouars' action and that the British government was duty bound to protect the Tahitians against French aggression, and so kept the political pot boiling. But in October 1843 Dupetit-Thouars returned to Tahiti with the news that the French government had accepted the protectorate. Finding the Tahitians following Queen Pomare's leadership, which was sustained by Pritchard, disposed to repudiate earlier agreements, Dupetit-Thouars was driven step by step to move beyond a protectorate, depose Pomare, and proclaim French sovereignty. This latter step the French government repudiated, reverting to the protectorate. But regarding the Reverend George Pritchard as the source of all their troubles, the French at Tahiti decided to get rid of him. He was arrested and deported. After a protracted correspondence Pritchard was paid money damages by the French government. In ignorance of the French action in Tahiti the British government also concluded that Pritchard had outlived his usefulness as consul and sent him instructions to move to Samoa.

When the French tried to extend their protectorate to islands of the Society Group beyond Tahiti and beyond the traditional domain of Queen Pomare, they again encountered resistance both from the natives and from LMS missionaries. After some discussion with the United Kingdom the French agreed not to extend the protectorate beyond Queen Pomare's domain, and later they agreed to allow Tahitians to migrate to the free islands if they so chose. Then in 1847 an Anglo-French agreement, called the Declaration of London, was signed which in effect re-established the status quo in the islands of the Southwest Pacific. It was, however, not a *status quo ante* 1840, but one which involved acceptance of British sovereignty in New Zealand and French sovereignty in the Marquesas, as well as the French protectorate over Tahiti. It was not, however, to last very long, for not only were the French looking for new opportunities to acquire presumably valuable island territories, but the colonial British in Australia and New Zealand were soon giving expression to large ambitions for British dominion in the Southwest Pacific islands. Some of the richest and most important of the island groups were at stake.

ANTARCTICA

CHAPTER XIII

Quest into Antarctica

On his second great voyage Captain Cook crossed the Antarctic Circle
three times, but he neither discovered nor visited any land beyond the
circle. The islands he examined, or sought for, were all subantarctic.
By his voyages below the circle he pioneered maritime exploration of
Antarctica, but in subantarctica he had predecessors. Those mentioned
in our narrative were, of course, all Europeans, but it is likely that the
ultimate pioneer was a Polynesian who figures in legend as having
reached the pack ice to the south of the islands about 750 A.D., the
southern limit of the great voyages which dispersed his people over the
enormous triangle, the points of which are Hawaii, New Zealand, and
Easter Island.

As Captain Cook was completing his work in the far south he committed to paper a speculation about what he had and had not seen which
had all the evidences of reason and logic but proved to embody one
of the few striking errors he ever made, especially in its aspect as a
forecast of the future. He wrote:

> ...I firmly believe that there is a tract of land near the pole which is the
> source of most of the ice that is spread over this vast Southern Ocean. ...
> It is true, however, that the greatest part of this southern continent (suppos-
> ing there is one) must lie within the polar circle, where the sea is
> so pestered with ice that the land is thereby inaccessible. The risk one
> runs in exploring a coast, in these unknown and icy seas, is so very
> great, that I can be bold enough to say that no man will ever venture farther
> than I have done; and that the lands which may lie to the south will never
> be explored. Thick fogs, snow-storms, intense cold, and every other thing
> that can render navigation dangerous, must be encountered; and these diffi-
> culties are greatly heightened by the inexpressibly horrid aspect of the coun-
> try; a country doomed by nature never once to feel the warmth of the sun's
> rays, but to lie buried in everlasting snow and ice. The ports which may be
> on the coast are, in a manner, wholly filled up with frozen snow of vast
> thickness; but if any there should be so far open as to invite a ship into it,

she would run the risk of being fixed there for ever, or of coming out in an ice-island. The islands and floats on the coast, the great falls from the ice-cliffs in the port, or a heavy snow-storm attended with sharp frost, would be equally fatal . . . After such an explanation as this, the reader must not expect to find me much farther to the south. It was, however, not for want of inclination, but for other reasons. It would have been rashness in me to have risked all that had been done during the voyage, in discovering and exploring a coast, which, when discovered and explored, would have answered no end whatever, or have been of the least use, either to navigation or geography or, indeed, to any other science.*

In this remarkable fashion Cook showed that he underestimated the interest that would be taken in his reports of seals on the islands he had visited and the risks men would take to gather so profitable a commodity as their skins represented and discounted too heavily the likelihood of the sealers pursuing their restless quest still farther to the south. He ignored also the extent to which the springs of adventure could inspire men to endure hardships and take chances far beyond the level of his own remarkable tolerance. He miscalculated the importance of the scientific findings that might be made even in so desolate a country as he envisioned. Pursuit of economic advantage, the call of sheer adventure, one of the strongest of human motivations, and the unconquerable urge to understand and control which underlies science, all played their parts in proving Cook wrong about Antarctic prospects.

The sealers, as a matter of fact, followed Cook with remarkable rapidity. There were sealers at South Georgia in 1778 and shortly after the American Revolution they began their extraordinarily swift progression across the southern Pacific and Indian oceans. The ships and crews were chiefly American and British, including Australian. By the 1790's the American sealers were in Australian and New Zealand waters and from the sealing grounds made their way through the South Sea islands to the China market for their skins.

It was a marked characteristic of a really successful sealing captain to be constantly on the alert for the discovery, or report of discovery, of new islands where unexploited rookeries were a reasonable expectation. Sealing involved the most ruthless exploitation of the seals when found, as though they were an inexhaustible resource, even though it was early observed that this was not so. The easy and quick depletion of the rookeries caused a premium to be placed upon new ones, where the process could be repeated. It was this search for unexploited rookeries that led the sealers far and wide, not any disinterested concern for exploration as such. It is to be supposed that they sometimes made

* For this passage as it came from Cook's hand, see J. C. Beaglehole, ed., *The Journals of Captain James Cook* (London, 1961), II, 637–38.

discoveries they did not immediately report, or did not report at all. However, the leaking of information by crew members whose tongues were loosened by liquor or cash bribes made complete secrecy hard to maintain, and once "leaked," information traveled fast.

In 1810 an Australian sealer named Frederick Hasselburgh, working out of Sydney, chanced on Macquarie Island, 800 miles southeast of Van Diemen's Land and 900 miles from the Antarctic continent. It proved to be the southernmost of a number of subantarctic island groups, all the rest now attached to New Zealand, including the Bounty Islands (discovered by Bligh in 1788), the Chathams (discovered by Broughton in 1791), the Antipodes (discovered by Waterhouse in 1800), the Aucklands (discovered by Bristow in 1806), and Campbell Island (discovered by Hasselburgh in 1810 immediately before he came upon Macquarie). Most of these islands had seal rookeries that were promptly exploited, but their subsequent history is rather limited, mostly known from shipwrecks, since vessels proceeding from Australian ports to Cape Horn passed through this area. The Chathams, however, were the home of a Polynesian people called Moriois. They were largely exterminated by the Maoris in the 1830's, with the connivance of a disreputable white. The place of confinement for Te Kooti and other Maori rebels during the wars of the 1860's, they were subsequently incorporated into the New Zealand pastoral economy. Macquarie Island figures at a later time in the history of scientific work in the Antarctic region.

A classic case of rapid diffusion of knowledge about a new sealing area occurred in 1819. In February of that year an Englishman, Captain William Smith of the ship "Williams," while on a trading voyage from Montevideo to Valparaiso swung far to the south of Cape Horn in search of favorable winds and chanced on some hitherto unreported, and presumably undiscovered, islands. On his arrival at Valparaiso he reported his find to the captain of the British warship on the station, but was brushed aside. Captain Smith tried to reach the new islands on his return voyage and did not succeed, but traveling again from east to west he not only reached them but landed and claimed them for Great Britain. This time his report was taken more seriously, and a sailing master of the warship was sent south with Smith in his ship, the "Williams," to make a survey of the new discovery. This was Edward Bransfield. He carried out a partial survey of the group which was named the South Shetlands. It was found to be separated from other land to the south by a strait over sixty miles wide. This was named Bransfield Strait. Bransfield named the "other land" beyond the strait Trinity Land—it became customary to use the term "land" when the exact character of a discovery was not immediately ascertained. This was in January 1820.

At Valparaiso Smith had confided his information to a mining engineer, John Miers, for whom he contracted to do some carrying, and Miers embodied it in a communication to the *Philosophical Journal* of Edinburgh in Scotland. Miers mailed his letter in January 1820, and it appeared in print before the end of the year. In Montevideo, Captain Smith's east coast base, the news "leaked"; it was communicated by letter via England to interested parties in the United States and it also came into the possession of Argentines of Buenos Aires who had sealing interests. From the latter it reached the American sealer, Captain James Sheffield at the Falkland Islands, who followed the Argentines to the South Shetlands for sealing in the 1819–20 season (while Bransfield was there surveying). The discovery was highly welcome since the known rookeries of the general area had been badly thinned out. Information about the South Shetlands reached Australia by September 1820. During the next season, that of 1820–21, several American sealers went to the South Shetlands from Stonington, Connecticut (Captain Sheffield), New York, New Haven, New Bedford, Nantucket, Boston, and Salem, as well as some English ships, and the "Lynx," captained by Richard Siddons, from "Botany Bay" in New South Wales. It was promptly rumored that American sealers had been visiting the South Shetlands for at least a decade before Smith's discovery.

The convergence of the sealers on the South Shetlands, then not exhaustively surveyed, in a geographical location which we now know to be close to other land, led inevitably to the construction of an entrancing geographical and historical mare's nest. The sealers not only had to find satisfactory harbors in which to set up headquarters, they also very soon faced the difficulty that the known rookeries had passed into the hands of rivals, forcing them afield to search for new ones. Pitched battles between sealers were sometimes fought for possession of a populous rookery. In searching for new rookeries the sealers inevitably discovered new land, and the question arose as to who first discovered the great peninsula off which the South Shetlands were located—tantamount to the first discovery of the continent of Antarctica—though it is customary to draw a distinction between first discovery of the peninsula and first discovery of the main continent. The question has been debated for over a century, occasionally with great fierceness, especially between American and British geographers.

The British support the claims of Edward Bransfield. It was toward the end of January 1820 that Bransfield was in the vicinity of Trinity Land. While it is established that part of this land was really an island (now named Trinity Island), the island is so close to the peninsula that it is argued to be highly improbable that Bransfield did not see the land back of it. As a matter of fact, a coast was indicated on a chart that could only be the coast of the peninsula. Unfortunately, however, Bransfield indicated the coast with a broken line, reflecting the fact that he felt insecure about its character (or existence) for he was prevented from making a proper examination of it by bad visibility, a common Antarctic hazard that recurs again and again in the story of Antarctic exploration. But time proved that Bransfield's coast was no illusion. However, it is far from clear that Bransfield even guessed that the coast was peninsular, let alone continental, in character.

The Americans long supported the claim of Nathaniel Brown Palmer, making an especially strong case for him in the late 1930's and early 1940's, but it is now considered that Palmer's claim as first discoverer of the peninsula is unsound, though he certainly made notable contributions to knowledge of the geography of the area. However, on American charts the peninsula is still labeled Palmer Peninsula; the British call it Graham Land, for a reason which will emerge shortly. Palmer was first at the South Shetlands with Captain Sheffield in the 1819–20 season as second mate of Sheffield's ship, the "Hersilia." He returned for the historic 1820–21 season as captain of the "Hero." It was while exploring the area in the "Hero" that, it was long believed, Palmer discovered the peninsula and recognized it as continental. It now seems improbable that he did so. But other American vessels in the South Shetlands at the time also were forced far afield in search of rookeries, and it is established that on February 7, 1821, Captain John Davis of the ship "Huron" of New Haven, Connecticut, actually sent a landing party onto the coast of the peninsula, making these men (names uncertain) the first actually to set foot on the continent of Antarctica. Davis wrote in his log, "I think this Southern Land to be a Continent." On February 16 Captain Christopher Burdick of the ship "Huntress" of Nantucket also sighted land which he "supposed to be continental." Thus, if Bransfield left the question astutely asked but not at all firmly answered, the Yankee sealers, especially Captain Davis, were prepared to answer it very firmly indeed. However, it was not finally established that the peninsula was *unquestionably* a part of the continent of Antarctica for over a hundred years. British and American explorers were responsible for the determination which was productive of a good deal of controversy.

D3

Leaving the sealers for a short time to their own extraordinary devices, it is necessary to introduce a Russian naval officer, Fabian von Bellingshausen, whose exploits in Antarctic maritime exploration rank with those of Cook to which they were designed to be complementary. Bellingshausen, who had been with Adam J. von Krusenstern on the first Russian circumnavigation of 1803–6, was indeed an intense admirer of Cook and of the British maritime tradition. He was assigned two ships; his flagship was the "Vostok" (meaning "Orient") and as consort there was the "Mirnyi" (meaning "Pacific"), commanded by Lieutenant Lazarev. At the same time two ships were assigned to attempt a passage from west to east through the Russian Arctic, starting from Bering Strait. The two expeditions left on their assignments almost simultaneously, the Antarctic party sailing from Kronstadt on July 16, 1819. The ships called in at Copenhagen to pick up supplies and in expectation that they would be joined by two German naturalists. Unfortunately, the Germans did not arrive. The next stop was Portsmouth, England. The two commanders went up to London to buy maps, charts, and nautical instruments and enlisted the help of Sir Joseph Banks in looking for naturalists to go on the voyage, but Banks was unable to induce anybody to go on such short notice. Bellingshausen then sailed for Rio de Janeiro, and from there he proceeded directly to the island of South Georgia which was reached on December 27.

At South Georgia Bellingshausen began his task of complementing Cook's activities by surveying the south coast, as Cook had surveyed the north. Taken together the two surveys made a complete record which was standard for many years. Bellingshausen then sailed east and shortly discovered a group of volcanic islands. He named them for the Marquis de Traversey, Russian minister of naval affairs, but the group's name has now been Anglicized as Traverse. Next he visited Cook's South Sandwich Islands. He first crossed the Antarctic Circle on January 27 and the next day the ships were within twenty miles of the Antarctic continent without knowing it. Turned back by the ice, but observing Bellingshausen's resolution to traverse ocean not sailed by Captain Cook and when possible always to the south of his track, they were again within the circle and within sight of land in the middle of February, but the commander dismissed what he saw as great icebergs. This was a common Antarctic error in reverse, for more explorers have mistaken icebergs for land than land for icebergs. Continuing eastward, Bellingshausen successfully kept his track south of Cook's, finding open sea throughout. In mid-March a rendezvous was appointed for Sydney and the two ships parted company, each traveling a different route in the seas south of Australia. Bellingshausen reached Sydney in the "Vostok" on March 28, 1820; the slower sailing "Mirnyi" came into the harbor on April 18. At that stage the ships had been half way around the world, mostly south of the sixtieth parallel and had been three times within the circle. At Sydney Bellingshausen found the two ships of the Arctic expedition pursuing their leisurely way to the point of departure for their attempt at the Arctic Passage. Governor Macquarie was thus suddenly host to numerous Russians; he did himself proud. Not the least gracious act he performed was to allow them to erect a Russian-style steam bath on shore.

After refitting, the "Vostok" and the "Mirnyi" went on the tour of the islands described earlier (see Chapter XI) and after further refurbishment at Sydney were ready on November 12 to return to the Antarctic. While at Sydney Bellingshausen received a dispatch from the Russian minister at Rio de Janeiro telling him of the discovery of the South Shetlands the previous year, and the fact was confirmed by an East India captain recently arrived from England.

After a call at Hasselburgh's Macquarie Island, where sealing operations were carefully observed and described, the Russians sailed south of the sixtieth parallel on December 9 and for over sixty days thereafter, while covering over 7000 miles and dipping four more times below the circle, always on the edge of pack ice, were constantly in the far south. However, they saw nothing but sea and ice until on January 22, 1821, they discovered Peter I Island (named for Peter the Great, founder of the Russian navy) at 68° 55′ South and 90° 50′ West, the southernmost land found to that time; and a week later and slightly to the south came on land again and named it, for their czar, Alexander I Land. (Alexander I Land eventually proved to be a huge island nestled close to the great peninsula and the main continent at their junction on the Pacific side.) On the thirtieth they sailed north, forced by a storm off a course which would have brought them to the peninsular coast.

On February 4 the southernmost South Shetlands were sighted, thus confirming the expectations raised at Sydney, and two days later the Russians saw the first of the numerous sealing ships they were to observe in the group. It was under the command of Nathaniel Brown Palmer; he was invited aboard the "Vostok" for a talk with Bellingshausen.

All the rest of his life (he did not die until 1877, by which time he had added to his Antarctic laurels a distinguished career in clipper ships, both in the United States coastal and China trade), Palmer was to repeat the story of this extraordinary encounter, and the anecdote became of historical importance because Palmer embroidered it with the assertion that he had told Bellingshausen of his discovery of continental land to the south (that is, the peninsula). It was in considerable part on the basis of this assertion that the Americans built their case for Palmer as the discoverer of Antarctica. It was presumed that confirmation of Palmer's assertion would be found in Bellingshausen's journal, which was not, for many years, accessible. It was in Russian and a rare book. When Bellingshausen's narrative became available it was found that while the encounter with Palmer was carefully related, nothing was included about a continental discovery. Since Bellingshausen was a meticulous man, this was taken to mean that Palmer had never made such an assertion to him. If he had, it is argued, Bellingshausen, a dedicated explorer, would very likely have taken immediate steps to confirm it and at the very least would have included such important information in his records. He did neither. Restudy of the log of the ship "Hero" showed that Palmer had not recorded a continental discovery in it, and as he knew nothing of Bransfield's map it appears almost certain that as the years passed Palmer's memory played him tricks and he injected into the Bellingshausen anecdote information which only came to him at a later time. Such things are constantly happening without prejudice to the general honesty of the witness, though rarely with such spectacular consequences.

After working a while longer on a survey of the South Shetlands, the Russians paid a visit to South Georgia, thus completing their circumnavigation. As the ships were now rather shaken by all the rough treatment they had received from the elements, a course was set for Rio de Janeiro, where repairs were made, and on July 5, 1821, they were back at Kronstadt. During an absence of 751 days, they had been at sea for 527. Although Bellingshausen had at no point penetrated as far south as Cook, he had spent much more time below the sixtieth parallel, had crossed the Antarctic Circle over twice as often, had traversed a great deal of ocean that Cook, in his comings and goings into Antarctic waters, had never traveled, and had circumnavigated the continent. He himself was scrupulous not to claim as a certainty to have sighted continental land, but a hundred years later it was shown, particularly by the Norwegians, that several of his sightings were actually of land. It was the Soviet Russians who, writing very dogmatically, made the claim of discovery for Bellingshausen. For a long time the world knew little about the Bellingshausen expedition. His journal was published in Russian in 1831, but it was not until the beginning of the twentieth century that the first comprehensive summary became available in any Western European language, and not until the middle of the century that the book was completely translated.

D3

In returning now to the sealers and their doings, attention must be paid once again to the activities of Nathaniel Brown Palmer, both alone and in collaboration with others, and especially to those remarkable sealing captains, the Englishmen James Weddell, John Biscoe, and others. Palmer, as we have seen, regarded exploration as but an incident in the hunt for seals. While pursuing his trade in the South Shetlands and along the west coast of the peninsula working south, he had found numerous islands, one group of which still bears his name, the Palmer Archipelago. During the 1821–22 season he teamed up with the British sealer George Powell and together they discovered and charted the South Orkney Islands to the east of the northern tip of the peninsula in the South Atlantic Ocean. Unluckily, there were no seal rookeries there. And in 1829–30 he joined his old friend Benjamin Pendleton (with whom he had been associated during the 1820–21 season) to take two ships, the "Seraph" and the "Annawan," on a scientific cruise through the South Shetlands. This expedition was a private venture designed to locate new sealing grounds as well as allow scientists a chance to make observations. On board one of the vessels was one of the patrons, J. N. Reynolds, an indefatigable traveler, collector of data on the discoveries of sealers and whalers, and student of logbooks, who was a principal figure in the protracted promotion of what eventually became the Wilkes expedition to Antarctica and the Pacific at the end of the decade. On the "Annawan" was the geologist James Eights of Albany, New York, who gained the permanent esteem of Antarctic scientists by his accurate scientific observations and his astute interpretations of the phenomena he observed. At the South Shetlands he not only found and exactly described a "new crustacean animal" but also found the first fossil ever located in the far south—a tree section—and correctly interpreted the presence of boulders on icebergs as indicating that the ice had been formed on land. The "Seraph-Annawan" enterprise, and the voyage of the Briton, Henry Forster, to the South Shetlands in H.M.S. "Chanticleer" in 1828–31 to make magnetic and pendulum observations, signalized the beginning of scientific work in Antarctica. With this nearest approach to formal exploration that he made, Palmer took leave of Antarctica.

James Weddell was the first British sealer to reach the South Shetlands after Smith's discovery of them. He was there for the great season of 1820–21. Weddell was, like James Cook, of working-class origin, son of an upholsterer, and after serving an apprenticeship in the merchant marine had been sent into the Royal Navy to learn discipline—he had assaulted his captain. He became a commended ship's master. Paid off in 1816, he turned sealer in 1819 and soon showed that he had the explorer's temperament. In the 1821–22 season he cruised through the South Orkneys, unaware that he was following in the wake of Palmer and Powell. It was during the next season, however, that he achieved imperishable fame. On February 5, 1823, in the ship "Jane," accompanied by his sealing partner Matthew Brisbane in the "Beaufoy," he voyaged south on the Atlantic side of the peninsula, ostensibly looking for seals, but with total lack of success. The compensation, however, was the explorer's reward, for, favored by a good season for open water, Weddell reached 74° 15′ South in what became known as the Weddell Sea, scene of so much Antarctic drama of the future. Weddell's mark was 1° 50′ beyond Cook's farthest south, away to the west, and broke Cook's record after it had stood for fifty years. Weddell's record was in its turn to stand for twenty years. Returning from the far south to South Georgia, Weddell and his associate wintered in the Falkland Islands and the following season obtained full cargoes of skins in the now familiar South Shetlands. He therefore went home commercially solvent, as well as having achieved a very peak of glory as an explorer—truly a virtuoso's performance. Nevertheless, he continued in the sealing trade.

Equally intimately related to sealing were the voyages of John Biscoe, Peter Kemp, and John Balleny in the 1830's. All these men made landfalls of significance, particularly Biscoe and Balleny. They were employees of the famous British sealing and whaling company, Enderby Brothers, whose ships had been active in the south and the Pacific from 1785. One of the Enderby brothers was an active member of the Royal Geographical Society from its founding in 1830, and his company was willing to underwrite voyages which were a mixture of ordinary commerce and adventurous exploration.

John Biscoe sailed on such a voyage in November 1830. His commercial interest was in sealing and the discovery of new rookeries, but it was expected that he would use his ship even more freely in the cause of exploration than Weddell had done with the "Jane." He entered far southern waters via the Falkland Islands, visiting the South Sandwich group, where no seals were found, and then proceeded eastward on or within the Antarctic Circle. The farthest south he reached was 69°. On February 28, 1831, he made the first landfall in history on the main Antarctic continent, at 66° 25′, but was quite unable to get ashore. He named his discovery Enderby Land. Both of his two small ships and their crews were now in utterly terrible condition and a course was shaped for New Zealand, but later they shifted to Hobart in Van Diemen's Land, where Biscoe arrived on May 10, while his consort made land on the continent near where Melbourne was later to rise. At Hobart he found James Weddell still actively engaged in sealing. Recruiting his men and replacing those who had died, Biscoe went across to New Zealand in October to gather cargoes of sealskins and oil. He operated on the New Zealand coast and at the Chatham and Bounty islands and by January 1832 was ready to continue his voyage to the east. His idea was to follow Cook's track—he knew nothing of Bellingshausen's—and in February he was in the vicinity of the peninsula of Antarctica. On the fourteenth

AUSTRALIA
Sydney
Melbourne
Hobart
TASMANIA
Wellington
NEW ZEALAND
Stewart I.
Chatham Is.
Bounty Is.
Antipodes Is.
Auckland Is.
Campbell I.
Maquarie I.
PACIFIC OCEAN
INDIAN OCEAN
ATLANTIC OCEAN
150°
150°
40°
40°
60°
60°
80°
30°
30°
Pack Ice in August (Extreme Limit)
Pack Ice in January (Extreme Limit)
Balleny Is.
Cape Adare
ROSS SEA
Ross I.
Mt Erebus
ROSS DEPENDENCY
TERRE ADELIE
ROSS ICE SHELF
ANTARCTIC CIRCLE
SOUTH POLE
ANTARCTICA
ENDERBY LAND
WEDDELL SEA
Peter I I.
Alexander I I.
Adelaide I.
Palmer Penin.
S. Shetland Is.
Joinville I.
S. Orkney Is.
Cape Horn
Falkland Is.
SOUTH AMERICA
Montevideo
S. Georgia I.
S. Sandwich Is.
Heard I.
Isles de Kerguelen

ANTARCTICA

of the month he reached Adelaide Island and, not knowing about Bellingshausen's Peter I and Alexander I discoveries, thought he had found the southernmost land to date. A few days later he discovered the group now called the Biscoe Islands, to the north of Adelaide Island. Both discoveries were south of Palmer Archipelago, and while significant were of lesser importance than the sighting of the main continent. Biscoe clearly saw what he took to be a mainland behind his new islands, and it was he who gave it the name of Graham. Sir James R. G. Graham, then first lord of the Admiralty, is always described by British writers as a notably unpopular politician, not to mention one who was famed for his destructive ineptitude. Nevertheless, the British extended the designation Graham Land to cover the whole of the peninsula, ignoring both Nathaniel Palmer, whom the Americans have favored, Bransfield, and all other claimants. Biscoe spent a month sealing in the South Shetlands and returned to England in January 1833. His voyage incurred a loss commercially, but its geographical importance was great indeed.

The second of the Enderby series of voyages can be disposed of more summarily. Peter Kemp, sealing for the Enderby company in the Kerguelen Islands, undertook a voyage due south from them and on November 27, 1833, came on Heard Island, located about equidistant between Australia and South Africa and 900 miles from the Antarctic continent. Heard Island thereupon entered sealing history and at a much later time became a famous *point d'appui* in continental Antarctic exploration. Kemp went on south from Heard Island and asserted that he had seen land at 67° South, east of Enderby Land.

The final Enderby man of the sealing era to make his mark in exploration was John Balleny. In 1838 he was sent to New Zealand and given instructions to sail as far south from there as he could. After sealing at the South Island, Balleny went to Campbell Island (where he met John Biscoe, still active in the trade) and from there went south. Early in the morning of February 9, 1838, Balleny came to a group of small islands, all very difficult of access, which are now known as the Balleny Islands. This was the first land found within the Antarctic Circle south of New Zealand. Along with Biscoe's Enderby Land and Kemp's sighting, these islands supported the hypothesis that there was a continent to be found.

D3

As the 1830's wore on the need of the sealing industry for a constant replenishment of its resources by the discovery of new rookeries lost its force. The industry went into a decline and although sealers were active in southern waters as late as the season of 1912–13, they were never again as vigorously important as in the 1820's and 1830's. The decline of the industry was marked by a shift from the emphasis on sealskins to an emphasis on the less profitable oil obtained from the blubber. In this phase, the elephant seal was the most important economic animal and most of the later sealers were after it. This change removed a powerful economic incentive for continued Antarctic exploration. When Antarctic whaling developed it generally stimulated interest in Antarctica and significant links between whaling, exploration, and science developed, particularly in the cases of the Norwegians and the British. However, personal adventure and scientific interest remained even then the forces moving most of the men.

Before the curious lapse of fascination with Antarctica of the latter part of the nineteenth century, roughly 1845–70, called by a historian of the subject, "the generation of averted interest," three men led expeditions which more or less set the pattern of the future: the Frenchman Dumont d'Urville, the American Charles Wilkes, and the Englishman James Clark Ross.

Jules Sébastien César Dumont d'Urville had made an extended voyage in the Southwest Pacific when he succeeded in breaking out of an unhappy and unprofitable retirement to make a second. His personal interests were primarily linguistic and ethnological and were best satisfied in the islands, where he spent most of his time on the second voyage, but to get to go at all he had to pay heed to a suggestion from King Louis Philippe. The king, apparently cued by Baron von Humboldt, who was intimate with him, insisted that the expedition give attention to Antarctica; specifically it was to make an attempt to surpass the southern record of the Englishman James Weddell. Dumont d'Urville himself was far from keen about Antarctica; his ships, the "Astrolabe" and "Zelée," were not properly fitted for adventures in the ice. The expedition sailed from Toulon on September 7, 1837, and began its activities with a survey of the Strait of Magellan. It then turned to the problem of Weddell. The ice proved an insuperable obstacle and D'Urville was irritated enough (he was made somewhat bad tempered by gout) to express skepticism about Weddell's claim. The incursion resulted chiefly in the discovery of a large island to the east of the tip of the peninsula, which D'Urville called Joinville. (It was later proved to be two islands, the smaller of which was given the name of D'Urville.) He then made for the South Seas where he spent two years.

Dumont d'Urville knew of the plans of Wilkes and Ross, and this eventually stimulated his patriotism sufficiently to make him resolve to compete with them. He decided on a second and unscheduled incursion into Antarctica, selecting the area south of 60° and between 120° and

160° East longitude, or just about where his rivals would also operate if they followed their plans. He knew nothing of Balleny's discovery in this area. He might, he thought, find the Magnetic Pole. Sailing from Hobart in Van Diemen's Land on January 1, 1840, with his crew filled out with English sailors of whom he had grave suspicions, he headed southeast and encountered the first ice at 60°. At 66° 30′ South he found land running east and west along the circle, named it Terre Adélie after his wife, as some compensation, he said, for her patience with his protracted absences from home, and took possession of it for France. It was apparent that the Magnetic Pole could not be far away, but it could not be reached. (It was actually on the land and its location awaited the era of land exploration.) While coasting the new land, he had a momentary glimpse of a strange ship, a very surprising sight in such remote waters, and from its flag knew it to be one of Wilkes's, but by a most unfortunate accident the ships did not stop for conversation, with unhappy consequences. On February 1, 1840, D'Urville left Antarctica and no more Frenchmen appeared there during the nineteenth century. He was home in early November and applied himself to the preparation of his reports—among the most appealingly literary of all such writings. One day in May 1842 his wife and son induced him to take a holiday from his labors and accompany them to Versailles to see the fountains in play. On the return journey to Paris the train was wrecked and D'Urville, his wife, and his son were burned to death in the debris, a frighteningly ironic end to a wonderful career in far and dangerous places.

Wilkes's activities in the Antarctic which also embraced the area around the peninsula and that far to the west, south of Australia and New Zealand, were but episodes in the program of the United States exploring expedition. Like Dumont d'Urville, Wilkes suffered frustration in the peninsular area. He himself took charge of the work on the southeast side of the peninsula, but accomplished nothing, and he sent two ships to the west to attempt to reach Captain Cook's farthest south, but this also was unproductive. However, over a century later it was clear that one of the vessels, the "Flying Fish," had made a surprisingly near approach to the continent and at an appropriate point a mountain range was named for Walker, its commander. Wilkes then took four of the six ships with which he had started—one had been lost with all hands, another was sent home as a hopelessly bad sailer—and went to the islands. In November 1839 he was at Sydney to prepare for a second incursion into the Antarctic.

Wilkes's ships were even less adapted for work in the south than Dumont d'Urville's. They were neither reinforced against the ice nor insulated against the cold, and provision for the crew by way of clothing was equally poor. But Wilkes felt he had to go to Antarctica, not only to keep to his instructions, but to vindicate the national honor. In his own ship, the "Vincennes," accompanied by the "Peacock" and the "Porpoise," Wilkes sailed south on December 26, 1839. The ships encountered ice at 61°, but managed to stay together to 66°. Land was first discovered on January 16 and a series of discoveries, or supposed discoveries, were made between the middle of January and February 21, when Wilkes took his ship north. That Wilkes did discover land is now considered beyond dispute and a tract in Antarctica bears his name, but that he also reported land very imprecisely, is also indisputable. He suffered much from the rancorous way in which his errors of technique and judgment were exposed and publicized. Wilkes was far too competent an officer to be wholly mistaken, even in the difficult task of identifying land from a ship's deck in the trying sea and atmosphere of Antarctica. His severest critic, James Clark Ross, was himself not invariably accurate in his conclusions, as time made clear. Part of the land Wilkes saw had also been seen by Dumont d'Urville. In general, Wilkes demonstrated that it was likely that there was continuous land from near the Balleny Islands to Enderby Land. He concluded his personal work in the Antarctic by attempting to reach Cook's farthest south in the Indian Ocean, and he was back in Sydney on March 11. Meanwhile the "Porpoise" had spent its time quite fruitlessly fighting the ice and storms until the crew and minor officers protested the dangerous discomforts and persuaded the captain to take the ship to the appointed rendezvous, the Bay of Islands in New Zealand, where the scientists of the expedition, after some work in Australia, had been taken in the fourth expedition ship, the tiny "Flying Fish." The "Peacock" shared in some of Wilkes's discoveries, though not in company with his ship, saw but did not speak with the French, and then had a dangerous collision with ice, the danger enhanced by the rottenness of the ship's timbers. However, the crew successfully navigated the "Peacock" back to Sydney where repairs were put in hand. The work was well along when Wilkes returned. Shortly, they resumed their studies in the islands.

Wilkes was deeply offended by the strong appearance of calculated discourtesy in the encounter with Dumont d'Urville in the deep Antarctic. Common humanity required at least an exchange of greetings. He said so in plain terms. But the discourtesy was unintentional. Neither ship correctly interpreted the actions of the other, and they were parted before the error could be rectified, as D'Urville later made clear. A difficulty with Ross was differently based, and the acrimony was not so readily drained away. As a magnanimous gesture to a fellow explorer, Wilkes sent Ross a letter and a tracing of a map of his discoveries, including on the map an indication of the location of the Balleny Islands. The tracing was inaccurate as to the Ballenys and was more precise about other points than the facts warranted. Ross asserted in anger that Wilkes had sought deliberately to mislead him by making claims that did not stand up. Unquestionably, Ross's remarks, passed around by Wilkes's American enemies, hurt Wilkes, but their tone and temper was a reflection on Ross. He was not an easy man with whom to get along; his psychology was much complicated by disdain for foreigners, a common fault among Victorian Britishers, especially rife in the Royal Navy. He felt that not only Wilkes but also Dumont d'Urville had sought to affront him and the British nation by conducting explorations in an area he had marked out as his own. It later turned out that Ross had not tested Wilkes's claims at all.

James Clark Ross, captain in the Royal Navy, was of a family with a notable naval tradition, and he had had extensive personal experience in Arctic exploration before he was chosen for service in the Antarctic. He had been with Sir Edward Parry on the attempt to reach the North Pole from Spitzbergen, and under his uncle Sir John Ross he had participated in the location of the North Magnetic Pole on June 1, 1831. Although scientific work figured largely in Ross's Antarctic expedition, he himself was not a scientist. The most notable scientist who went with him was Dr. Joseph Dalton Hooker, the distinguished botanist. Most of the scientific work was carried out by skilled amateurs from the ranks of naval men. It covered a very wide range: terrestrial magnetism, geodesy, tides, meteorology, oceanic depths and temperature, astronomical phenomena, geology, zoology, and botany. Most attention was given to magnetism, about which Ross himself knew a good deal, both within the Antarctic and particularly without. However, in attitude Ross was essentially the explorer as a man of adventure.

The expedition left England on September 30, 1839, in two ships. Ross himself commanded the "Erebus," Commander F. R. M. Crozier was in charge of the "Terror." Both of these ships had seen service in the Arctic, but they were thoroughly reconstructed for Antarctic service, with especial attention to reinforcement against ice. Just before leaving England, Ross had a conversation with Balleny about his newly discovered islands in the quadrant on which Ross had his eye. Pursuing a leisurely course and devoting much time to magnetic work, the expedition reached Hobart in Van Diemen's Land on August 16, 1840. Here they were welcomed by Governor Sir John Franklin, himself a famous Arctic explorer and amateur of science. (A few years later Crozier was to join Franklin in an Arctic expedition in the "Erebus" and "Terror" on which all hands perished and of which relics were only recovered after extensive international co-operation in the search.) At Hobart Ross learned details of the activities of Dumont d'Urville and Wilkes. He was annoyed. He decided to move the focus of his interest to the east.

On November 12 the "Erebus" and "Terror" left Hobart and after calling at the Aucklands and Campbell Island, proceeded south, getting into the ice pack on January 5 and making their way through it to open water on January 9 at 69° 15′ South and 176° 15′ East. This was an epoch-making achievement. Ever since 750 A.D. ships had had to regard the ice pack as an insuperable obstacle. Now it was demonstrated that the pack could be conquered. The elaborate preparation of the "Erebus" and "Terror" thus paid rich dividends. Having gotten through the pack, Ross was well on the way to great achievements. He saw land, Cape Adare, early in January, and thus had the satisfaction of returning to Britain the kudos of discovering land farthest south. Shortly, he was in what today is called the Ross Sea and was soon coasting the Ross Ice Barrier. He had uncovered one of the great entry ways to the Antarctic continent. He named landmarks subsequently of enormous fame: the volcanoes Erebus and Terror, and McMurdo Sound (after one of his lieutenants). He scattered the names of admiralty men, politicians, and patrons of exploration over the visible mountains. He placed the name of Parry on a range that was subsequently proved not to exist. He sailed beyond Weddell's farthest south and reached 78° 4′ South. He landed on an island and took possession of his discoveries—Possession Island at 71° 56′ South, and named the new land for Queen Victoria. (It is now called the Ross Dependency of New Zealand.) But he did not, any more than Dumont d'Urville, find it possible to reach the Magnetic Pole as he had hoped. All told he spent 145 days in the Antarctic, 63 south of the Antarctic Circle. He arrived back at Hobart on April 6, 1841.

Although Ross went twice again to Antarctica before he took his expedition home, he never again had the supreme fortune of his first voyage. At Van Diemen's Land his people carried out geological and botanical studies for two months, then moved to Sydney for a month, and went from there to the Bay of Islands in New Zealand where they spent three months. At the Bay of Islands the commander of a French ship gave Ross a chart of Dumont d'Urville's discoveries; and Captain Aulick of the American ship "Yorktown" picked up the gossip that Ross had sailed over Wilkes's discoveries and gleefully put it into circulation. This allegation was entirely false. From the Bay of Islands, Ross returned to Antarctica on November 23, 1841; he reached the ice pack on December 18, and crossed the circle on January 1, 1842. His objective was the great Barrier at a point which would allow him to continue to trace it farther east. But on this trip, in spite of the fact that he reached a point farther south than in the previous year, 78° 9′ 30″ South, a record for sixty years, he saw no land. En route to the Falkland Islands to make winter headquarters, the ships collided in a storm, while trying to avoid an iceberg. Their rigging became entangled, but no structural damage was incurred. After getting free of the "Terror," the "Erebus" found itself confronted with two huge icebergs obviously about to collide with one another and barely had time to skim between them before the collision took place. One hundred and thirty-seven days out of New Zealand the Falklands were reached without any more difficulty.

The ships were refitted at the Falklands, partly with materials brought down from Rio de Janeiro. Ross selected the site of the town of Stanley, now long the capital of the Falklands. On December 17, 1842, he left for a final season in the Antarctic. The objective was to get beyond Weddell's farthest mark in his Sea. But Ross found himself up against the same obstacle that had defeated Dumont d'Urville when he tried to beat Weddell: ice. Ross made some minor discoveries of land along the east coast of the peninsula south of D'Urville's, but after spending considerable time in the ice, finally headed for Capetown, South Africa. That port was reached in April and the ships returned to England on September 23, 1843.

Then came a generation during which interest in Antarctica was remarkably slack.

PART II
AUSTRALIA

CHAPTER XIV

The Gold Rush Decade

In 1859, after considerable agitation, that part of the old, original New South Wales north of 29° South became the colony of Queensland (named after Queen Victoria), as allowed in the government Act of 1850. This left an oddly shaped tract of country, then of unknown worth and still of highly problematical value, nowhere contiguous with New South Wales as finally constituted, an orphan on the continent. In 1861 the western boundary of South Australia was shifted west to run with the eastern limit of Western Australia, thus cutting off a southern extension of the orphan country; the next year the inland boundary of Queensland was shifted west to absorb some more of it; and in 1863 the Imperial government passed control of what remained—from 26° South (South Australia's northern boundary) north to the Arafura Sea—to South Australia. The orphan acquired the name of Northern Territory (of South Australia).

Thus was the political geography of Australia fixed in a pattern which has continued to the present day, except for the eventual reassignment of responsibility for Northern Territory. From north to south along the Pacific coast were the continental colonies of Queensland, New South Wales, and Victoria. Occupying the western third of the continent facing the Indian Ocean was Western Australia. On the southern continental coast facing the Great Australian Bight was South Australia. And in the Pacific Ocean across Bass Strait from Victoria was the island colony of Tasmania. This was a congeries of colonies, each a separate and distinct governmental unit, and they so remained until federated as the Commonwealth of Australia in 1901.

The period of 1850–1901 with which we are concerned here was a time when the history of Australia was more or less a composite of separate colonial stories in which the actors thought of themselves as Victorians, or South Australians, or Queenslanders, and not often as Australians, citizens of a continental domain. Obviously, it would fragment a narrative unduly to detail the histories of six colonies and a territory within a short space, but as there are elements common to all the stories and the tendency toward national integration was constantly at work (even if much of the time below the political surface), it is possible to write of *Australia* as though it were already an integrated whole. Developments peculiar, or almost peculiar, to particular colonies can be seen and reported in relation to the national pattern as it eventually emerged. However, it will be necessary constantly to refer to the separate colonies and occasionally to emphasize their separateness. A compensation for references to what may seem parochial history is the fact that the colonies in all instances correspond to the states of the commonwealth as eventually constituted, and as it is still not possible to write of the United States wholly without reference to sectional differences, so it is impossible to write of contemporary Australia without some attention to state differences which as often have their roots in colonial history as in geography. This part of the story lays the foundation of an understanding of the Australian Commonwealth as it was when it emerged in 1901.

D3

Gold had been discovered in Australia as early as 1823 and several times during subsequent years, but no public announcement had ever been permitted because it was feared that it would provoke a convict uprising and that, as Governor Gipps remarked, peaceful citizens would be murdered in their beds. It was not then believed that any truly creative consequences could follow. By mid-century, however, conditions had sufficiently changed to make supportable any disruption of the public peace a rush might occasion, and there was the example of California to show that gold was a valuable economic adrenaline.

The great California rush had its impact on the Australian colonies in 1848 and 1849, when it took away enough people seriously to disorganize the local labor market. While some of the men who had been attracted across the Pacific were no great loss to the colonies, particularly those ex-convicts who were to figure in California annals as the "Sydney ducks" and to give the Vigilantes much work to do, others were men whose constructive energies were sorely needed. It was great good fortune, then, when two men more or less of the latter description were driven by indifferent luck in California to reflect that the American gold country was very similar to country they knew in Australia. Returning to the colonies, on the same boat oddly enough, and fortified with a knowledge of a simple method of winning surface alluvial gold, they prospected country they thought likely and in 1851 discovered payable fields. In New South Wales the first discovery was made by Edward Hargraves, who in February panned out a small quantity of gold at a site later named Ophir, in the valley of the Macquarie River near the town of Bathurst; in Victoria the first discovery was made by James Esmonds near Clunes in June.

The discovery in New South Wales induced a rush which affected not only that colony but the others as well; the Victorian discovery was much richer however, and was quickly followed by even more promising finds at Mount Alexander, Ballarat, Bendigo, and other places of subsequent high renown, so that the flow of diggers was soon mostly concentrated in Victoria. The Victorian fields attracted an especially large number of men from South Australia and Tasmania, including from the latter a considerable quota of shady characters lately in bondage. By September 1851 the news of the discoveries had reached London and by the end of the year gold seekers began to arrive from overseas. The next year saw a rush to the Victorian fields comparable in magnitude to the California rush of 1849. The colonial gold fields were quickly thronged by overseas gold hunters, mostly British by nationality, including a good many Irish, but also representatives of most of the nationalities of Europe, especially Germans, as well as numerous Americans, and considerable numbers of Chinese. (The presence of the latter had a fateful influence on immigration policy, to be examined later.) The majority of the newcomers came directly from Europe, galvanized into strenuous activity by hard times, political unrest, and expectations of sudden wealth. On the basis of the high cost of a passage to Australia, it is a reasonable assumption that a large proportion were middle-class persons, some professionals and better off skilled workers, in any case mostly young men, few of whom knew by experience how to "work the earth." Some, especially the Americans, were from the California fields; the peripatetic gold hunter of the latter half of the nineteenth century had begun his career.

Probably not more than half of the immigrants who arrived in the Australian colonies in the 1850's ever went to the gold fields, even temporarily. At least that proportion went directly into conventional occupations, most of them in the "golden" colonies, though some in every one, as the growth of the colonies in the decade shows. New South Wales, South Australia, Tasmania, and Victoria continued during the decade to "assist" immigration, Victoria receiving more assisted immigrants than any other colony. The rushes were, in other words, a powerful stimulant to general immigration into the colonies. They both redistributed and then rapidly multiplied the total population, with Victoria the principal beneficiary of both changes. From 400,000 in 1850 the total colonial population rose to 1,146,000 in 1860, while the population of

Victoria rose from 76,000 to 538,000. Thus, Victoria became the most populous Australian colony, containing almost 200,000 more people than the parent colony of New South Wales (348,500), completely overshadowing its historical contemporary South Australia (125,500), outclassing Tasmania entirely (90,000), and leaving slow-growing Western Australia (15,000) and the new colony of Queensland (28,000) far behind. For the rest of the century the population steadily increased until in 1900 the colonies had 3,765,000 residents, of whom 1,360,000 lived in New South Wales, again the most populous colony, 1,196,000 in Victoria, 494,000 in Queensland, 357,000 in South Australia, 180,000 in Western Australia, at last roused from chronic doldrums, 173,000 in Tasmania, and 4800 in Northern Territory. This growth implies a good deal of development, and the distribution of the population on the continent implies accurately enough where the resources for development had chiefly been found. Development was the principal preoccupation of both the politicians and the private enterprisers throughout the period.

At the discovery of gold, the sudden diversion of so high a proportion of the workers of town and country from their regular employments into a new industry located at sites which had a strong tendency to shift and change as new discoveries were made, mostly away from established centers of population, naturally disturbed the established routine; and when in 1852 contingents of gold seekers began to arrive from abroad in great numbers, the dimensions of the apparent chaos were enlarged. There was an immediate and acute shortage of labor in the old lines of endeavor—in the pastoral industry, in farming, in trade, in government service—and commodity shortages all along the line. Wages and prices rose rapidly. But the chaos was not as fundamental as contemporary observers believed, for the basic economic pattern persisted and the established industries somehow adapted themselves for survival and resumption of growth: the sheep were somehow cared for, the wool shorn and dispatched to Britain, the total quantity actually increasing in 1851–54; the crops were somehow gathered, and by 1856 foreign suppliers began to be displaced from the market; and the merchants, old and new—prime beneficiaries of the uproar—imported heavily on literally golden expectations.

Many men early perceived, and more did as time passed, that gold hunting was a tremendous gamble with very long odds and that money was perhaps more certainly to be made by catering to the needs of the gamblers than by getting into the game with them. Established merchants, for example, were quick to perceive their advantage, and some men followed the rushes with no other purpose than to be storekeepers to the miners. Squatters found it profitable to enter the new market by supplying meat and even, when fields developed near their properties, vegetables. And it was only a matter of some two years before it was made evident to all hands that the gold-created market had limits like any other. There was a sharp economic decline in 1854. The so-called chaotic phase of the gold rushes was definitely over by 1855. The peak of gold production was passed in 1856.

The fields went through all or part of a cycle, depending upon the resources uncovered: first there was the discovery of gold either by planned prospecting or lucky accident, then a helter-skelter rush to get in on the find early and exploit its richness or reveal its poverty, a matter of dealing with surface alluvial, carried out chiefly by informal associations of miners called "mates" in Australia (as "partners" in California), then exploitation of the deep alluvial, usually by small companies, and finally the raising of deep-mined quartz for crushing by companies which required substantial capital, the latter two enterprises bringing to the fields the miner on wages. It was surface alluvial that attracted and justified the presence of large numbers of diggers. The other phases required less manpower. The signal that surface alluvial was either playing out or had attracted more men than it could profitably support, or both, was the decline in average annual earnings. However, the lure of gold was so strong and enduring—the hope of a big killing through finding a nugget or a "pocket of gold," rather than a rational calculation of regular, steady earnings—that it kept men on the surface diggings and following the successive rushes long after the economics of the occupation ceased to ratify their presence. Moreover, many men found that they liked the roving, improvised life of the gold fields and the recurrent rushes, regardless of economic returns.

The peak of employment on the Victorian fields was not reached until 1858, but the decline of average earnings began earlier. In 1852 individual annual earnings ran to perhaps £260 ($1300), while in 1858 the annual average was down to £69 ($340). As in all speculative employments, Lady Luck showed her face only to the star-kissed few. Those whose luck was out—and who were candid enough to admit it—turned to alternative ways of earning a living: they went on the land (though the difficulties in the way of this caused bitter feeling), they became laborers on the new railways, they drifted into pastoral occupations, they found employment in the big towns. Gradually, gold mining as a permanent occupation fell into the hands of men who made it a wage-earning trade like any other, of the curious types called "fossickers" who gained a poor living poking around worn-out fields, and of the types imperfectly rooted in ordinary life ready to drop everything on hearing a rumor that a rich find had been made, no matter where, especially in times of depression. All three types became permanent fixtures on the national scene. Consistently after the finds of 1851 Australia was a gold producer of world significance. Gold production showed a useful tendency to rise in a compensatory fashion in times of economic adversity. Between 1851 and the end of the decade Australia produced 25 million ounces, or 40 per cent of the world's output for those years. In the next decade it contributed 30 per cent. Today it ranks below South Africa, U.S.S.R., Canada, and the United States as a producer, and contributes about 4 per cent of world production.

The history of gold in Australia after the 1850's is a combination of alluvial rushes and deep mining for gold-bearing quartz, the latter being responsible for most of the production. After 1860 deep mining dominated in Victoria. There were important alluvial rushes in New South Wales as late as 1893. South Australia and Tasmania never experienced major rushes. Queensland, however, had a succession of rushes in the 1870's and 1880's, but none attracted the huge bands of miners that followed the fields in the southern states and most of the gold produced was deep mined. The climactic gold discoveries of this period—and perhaps in historical perspective, of all Australian history—were those at Coolgardie-Kalgoorlie in Western Australia in 1892–93. These finds signalized the discovery of the greatest and most enduring deep mines of all, those on the "Golden Mile." They still account for the greater part of Australia's gold production in the middle of the twentieth century.

The color of life on the gold fields of the 1850's is chiefly what made them romantic. In Victoria the prospective diggers were dumped ashore at Port Phillip Bay to find their way to, or at least through, Melbourne to the fields up the country. Melbourne grew fiercely, and while its leading citizens early initiated public works that showed they had a proper sense of its future as a great metropolis, the seat of government, and the economic nerve center of the colony, it was for a time a rather rough town with only improvised amenities, surrounded by suburbs of tents and shacks. Travel to the fields from Melbourne was in the beginning largely by shanks' mare, with the heavy gear and stores hauled over the impossible tracks by bullock power. But one of the byproducts of the rushes was the introduction by Americans of light vehicles able to negotiate bad roads, developed on their own frontiers. A stagecoach service established by an American named Freeman Cobb spread far and wide through the colonies and to New Zealand. The coach services of Cobb & Company were celebrated in song and story and only disappeared in the face of ramifying railways.

On the fields—Ballarat and Bendigo are the most redolent names—there assembled a fantastic variety of types of men. The fields were men's worlds, for not many wives accompanied the diggers, and of the few women there, entertainers, whores, and washerwomen were the most conspicuous. The men were wildly mixed as to personality and temperament and in knowledge of how to live on diggings. The fundamental pattern of adaptation was established and maintained by the colonials, many of whom were professional bush workers. They were equaled only by the Californians for expertness in "getting along." The men dressed in coarse and often gaudy pants, shirts, and headgear, either outback "colonial" or pseudo-Californian in style, and housed themselves in tents and rough shacks. At their work the necessary occupation was to find pay dirt; practically everybody, whether working alone or in a team, was engaged in digging holes, raising the dirt in buckets on windlasses, sifting it in cradles, and washing the residue to clean the gold, if any. A gold field was a conglomeration of holes and piles of sifted earth, a dangerous place at night for a person unfamiliar with the lay of the land, or drunk.

General stores, housed in tents or slab shanties, and hotels—of which the bar was the principal equipment—were the rendezvous in off hours, unless resort was had to a "sly-grog" or speakeasy for a drink. Gambling was the common delight, and the stakes high, normally wildly disproportionate to apparent resources. Most of the men were orderly within a rough and ready definition of orderliness evolved from experience of needs, but physical violence and robbery occurred that "smelled of California," usually attributed to the ex-convict gentry from Tasmania. There were the traditional displays of exuberance with their winnings by the gold miners, both on the fields and when on holiday in Melbourne, including showy drunkenness on fine wines and liquors, "shouting" the crowd and breaking the glassware to make the bill worth paying, gaudy displays of jewelry, extravagant weddings, and Veblenian conspicuous consumption of all kinds. Melbourne holidays were especially favored at Christmas time, the height of the Australian summer, when there was also the excuse that water was short on the fields. Entertainers, singers and actors, good and bad, male and female, were freely patronized by the diggers. One improviser of topical songs, Charles R. Thatcher, won enduring fame among students of Australian ballads. Places of entertainment were normally closely associated with drinking establishments. A kind of peak of theatrical history was reached in 1855 when Lola Montez, the great nineteenth-century courtesan, visited the gold fields in a dancing act. In lieu of flowers, the miners showered the performers with small nuggets.

At first gold was shipped to Melbourne for sale. It was moved under government protection in what was called an "escort." The banks bought it at a rate 30 per cent below the London price, thus insuring themselves lush profits. But the Adelaide business leaders, determined to draw gold to their colony, offered to buy it at a 10 per cent discount on London and thus benefited themselves and the miners. The situation was stabilized by the establishment of a mint at Sydney in 1853. Naturally, gold was stolen, whether from miners' tents or by "bailing up" the escort, even from ships at anchor in the harbor. When branch banks were established on the fields, *they* were robbed. Gold lures in more than one way.

In the first phase of the rushes law and order on the gold fields was represented by a commissioner, assisted by police. In the well-established Australian tradition, the rank and file police were often even more dubious in character than the worst of those they were set to watch and protect. The first Australian police were ex-convicts. And whatever their quality, they were regarded balefully by the colonial diggers, who quickly communicated their hostility to newcomers. The miners were required to take out a license costing thirty shillings a month and to produce the license on demand. From the first there were those who tried to avoid the cost of a license, and as the actual earnings from digging declined the license fee became an issue between the miners and the authorities. The miners soon saw the fee as an exorbitant, unfair tax, laid by a government in which they were not represented. It was the police tactic to conduct "digger hunts," or to organize swift descents upon groups of miners in search of licenseless diggers. When found without a license, a digger was jailed and fined and a portion of the fine went to the officer turning him in. This naturally intensified antagonism between diggers and the police. When in addition police and court justice on the fields did not in other connections correspond with digger conceptions of propriety, the antagonism grew even more. A reduction of the fee in 1853 did not allay the ill will. Making their tortuous way through a thicket of disagreements with the police, the courts, and the political authorities up to the governor (from June 1854 Sir Charles Hotham), the miners on the great fields became more and more militant.

They sought redress of grievances through organization. They demanded not only changes in the administration of the gold fields but also in political matters: they asked for the vote and facilitation of the acquisition of land for farming. At Ballarat their leaders included a Welshman, some Irishmen, a German, an Englishman, and an Italian (whose chronicle of the movement became a classic). Relations with the commissioner and the police on the field rapidly worsened. The men elected Peter Lalor, a well-educated Irish engineer, their supreme leader and adopted as their flag the Southern Cross of stars on a blue field. On the motion of Frederic Verne (a German) they signalized their "rebellion" by burning their licenses. They then established a military organization, gathered weapons, including pikes, and built a stockade which they called Eureka. To the end, however, the men hoped to solve their problem without violence. They were, however, disappointed in this, for on Sunday, December 3, 1854, Eureka Stockade was attacked early in the morning by a mixed government force of 280 soldiers and police. Perhaps 150 miners were on duty inside the slab fortifications. In fifteen minutes the rebellion was over, with six government men and twenty-two miners dead. Of the large number of miners captured, thirteen were held for trial for treason and rewards were posted for three others, including Lalor, who had escaped. All the Americans involved are believed to have been released at the request of the United States consul at Melbourne. On trial a sympathetic jury refused to convict the miners, and Lalor, who had evaded capture, was never even tried, and reappeared to make a distinguished career in politics after an amnesty had been proclaimed. The gold fields administration stood condemned. The government abolished the licensing system, substituting a "miner's right" at a pound a year, and obtained its revenue from gold by an export duty of two shillings and sixpence an ounce. The fields were put in the charge of wardens (instead of commissioners), and special gold-fields courts were constituted to deal with grievances.

This flareup of armed violence, obviously a consequence of maladministration of the fields, was in itself both insignificant and rather pointless. It would today hardly be noticed as against far more serious and fateful disorders involving the Chinese on other fields at later dates, if the radical democrats of Australia, especially democrats of the labor left, had not subsequently seized upon Eureka and turned it into a symbol of their own militancy. Eureka thus entered into political folklore, and the folklore of politics cannot be destroyed by analysis. The intrinsic and extrinsic significance of Eureka Stockade will thus be far apart for evermore, and the flamboyant narrative by the Italian Carboni Raffaelo will maintain its position as one of the cherished Australian classics.

D3

The gold rushes did not divert the political leaders from their appointed rounds and the sudden presence in the country of thousands of miners, a mixed crew of old and new hands, had only incidental influence upon their ideas. The prime political interest during the early and middle 1850's was not in the politics of gold seeking, but in constitution making. The establishment of self-government in the form of "responsible" government held first place on the agenda. In this New South Wales was in the vanguard, and W. C. Wentworth, now in the final phase of his active career, was the central figure.

A dispatch from Sir John Pakington, secretary of state for colonies, dated December 15, 1852, gave an official statement of opinion on contentious questions and a carte blanche for the replacement of the Act of 1850 with constitutions devised by the political leaders of the several colonies, subject to final ratification by the imperial authorities. The recent liberalization of the constitutions of the Canadian colonies, where Lord Elgin was astutely guiding the establishment of responsible government, and the liberal constitution just granted to New Zealand made it impossible to withhold parallel rights from the Australians. The question was, rather, how advanced the Australians really were. The issue was not whether or not they should assume full control of their domestic affairs, including the land, but in which section of the community decisive political power should be lodged.

W. C. Wentworth, the most distinguished constitutionalist in Australia, took the initiative in writing a constitution for New South Wales. His ideas about where political authority should rest provided a focus for controversy. Wentworth saw politics as essentially a conflict of great interests, economic in basis with profound social implications, and the constitutional problem as less a matter of the provision of a machinery of government than the fortification in a position of supreme authority of the interest he favored. Wentworth favored the squattocracy, a term which had come to include both the squatters as such and the large freeholders as well, whose economic sustenance was drawn from the wool-growing industry, a natural oligarchy from its beginnings, now to be transformed by constitutional means into a permanent political aristocracy. The conception had its nostalgic overtones: it was obviously rooted in a vision of the British landed aristocracy as it was before the political reforms of 1832, and in a curious way it was related to the illusions of E. G. Wakefield, another sufferer from nostalgia, about a proper colonial ruling class. Wentworth proposed to install his landed aristocracy in an appointive Legislative Council, to grant hereditary titles to selected members of the squattocracy, and to give them the right to elect members of the Council from among themselves in the future, thus avoiding wholly hereditary seats in the Council while insuring continuity of class representation. The political position of the squattocracy was further to be fortified by a distribution of seats in a lower house, or Assembly, which favored rural residents, but with a reasonably liberal property franchise. Plural voting would strengthen the hold of property on the Assembly.

Opposed to Wentworth's conception of a proper distribution of political power, though in agreement with him about responsible government and most of the "machinery" aspects of the constitution, was the "democracy." In a famous public paper of 1853, undoubtedly drafted by Wentworth, a committee of the Legislative Council frankly declared: "They [the committee members] have no wish to sow the seeds of a future democracy . . ." Wentworth saw the constitutional requirements of the "democracy" as "Yankee notions"; he defined his conception of how democracy would work out by quoting Tocqueville extensively, and, significantly, he quoted Calhoun, the great political theorist of the slaveocracy, in defense of his own position. But the "democracy" was far less monstrous in actuality than it was in the fevered imagination of Wentworth. Essentially, at that time it was the political expression of the urban middle class of Sydney of which the backbone was the city merchant. In a classic passage with strong physiocratic overtones, Wentworth indicated his utter contempt for the merchants, denying them any creative role in the community, especially as compared to squatters. As envisaged by such an ardent spokesman of the "democracy" as Henry Parkes, later long dominant in New South Wales politics, the democracy embraced not only the city merchants but also the farmers and the manufacturers, though in 1850 the latter two groups were more incipient than actual, though sure to emerge in the future if economic evolution followed an expected path. The "democracy" was chiefly opposed to Wentworth's scheme to install his aristocracy in power permanently and to give out titles, not to the idea of appointing rather than electing the members of the Council, and to the planned under-representation of the urban residents in the Assembly rather than to the property franchise (which in any case was moderate). They ridiculed Wentworth's titled aristocracy as a "bunyip" aristocracy—a bunyip being a fabulous animal of the aborigines, allegedly resident in water holes. In the end they succeeded in blocking the proposals for a titled landed aristocracy. Otherwise, they accepted Wentworth's constitution, but with full knowledge that it could be amended in due course to serve their own purposes. In this fashion Wentworth won a great victory and suffered a great defeat.

Since conditions in no other colony were exactly like those in New South Wales, and none other had a towering figure like W. C. Wentworth, the course of constitution making nowhere followed exactly the pattern set in New South Wales, but everywhere a "democracy" was the opposition to oligarchical tendencies. At this stage it tended to focus on the rejection of the Canadian model of a nominated, or appointed, upper house. In Victoria, for example, provision was made for an elected Legislative Council, but the position of the house was fortified by high property qualifications for members and a franchise for electors that had a markedly higher property qualification than in the case of the lower house franchise. Similarly in Tasmania an elected Council was favored. And so also in South Australia, though only after a bid was made for a single-chamber legislature. Democracy ran strongest in South Australia at this time. Western Australia was not, at this stage, ready for responsible government.

Tasmania and South Australia did not write completely new constitutions, though the latter made an effort in that direction. Rather, these colonies settled for amendments to their 1850 constitutions by local acts to meet their requirements, though the resultant documents were regarded popularly as new constitutions.

In the political climate of the time an elected upper house savored of republicanism, even when the property guard on membership and the franchise was formidable. It suggested American practice. A true and proper upper house should be a colonial analogue of the House of Lords, but the democratic colonists were not prepared to follow the analogy all the way. They, in that generation, accepted the principle that a lower house, even one elected on a property franchise, required a check on its likely exuberance. Only a section of the South Australians seriously questioned this. Even when elected the colonial upper houses were expected to be more conservative than the lower houses and to act in defense of "tradition" and property interests. As it happened the economic structure of the country practically guaranteed that the upper houses would be largely populated by landed persons, very wealthy merchants, bankers, and lawyers. As time passed the practice of the principles of an upper house aroused bad feelings between the houses and between the upper houses and the "democratic" people. All the colonies had "upper house trouble" and solved their problems in various ways, but for special reasons struggles between the houses were most spectacular in Victoria. The political task was to change the composition of the upper houses to make them more amenable to lower house political and economic purposes. When the labor left came into politics, it inherited this animosity against the upper houses and it advocated total abolition, aiming at unicameral legislatures. However, abolition was carried out only after federation and in only one state. In the federation the bias against an upper house came to operate against the Senate.

By much the same reasoning, the lower houses were supposed to be close analogues of the House of Commons. It was in them that the primary political struggle was to come to focus; they had the right to initiate money bills; from them the premier would come, as well as most of his cabinet. Democracy, as we shall see, rather quickly took charge of them.

The position of the governors, representatives of the imperial authority in the colonies, was less defined constitutionally than worked out of the hazards of politics. A representative of the crown and therefore a viceregal personage, the governor was nevertheless appointed by the Colonial Office to which he was responsible for his acts. What exactly was his role in a self-governing colony? The drift early became toward reducing his role and defining his position in terms comparable to those which applied to the Queen in Great Britain, but this was impossible to achieve in detail as long as the governors represented the government of Great Britain in the colonies as well as the crown. When the two functions were separated, it became far more feasible, but this did not occur until the middle 1920's. It was the fact that colonial criticisms were uncommonly directed at the crown; they were customarily directed against the Colonial Office, believed generally to be the real master of governors. There were few republicans and few of them were of any political importance. The monarchical principle was never seriously called into question.

D3

Up to the time of the gold rushes of the 1850's, the explorers had, as it turned out, uncovered almost all of economic Australia, but nobody had penetrated to the center of the continent and little was known of the north and the northwest inland from the sea. Leichhardt's expedition of 1840 from the Darling Downs to Port Essington had revealed something about the inland north, but his attempt to cross the continent from east to west had ended in utter disaster. Sturt's effort to reach the center and north had been frustrated by terrible drought. Eyre's east-west crossing was along the seacoast and told nothing certain about the interior. To reach the center, to cross the continent from north to south and east to west, or vice versa, were the challenges still confronting the adventurous. And in the Australian tradition, even those who came closest to wanting to cross territory simply because it was there hoped that in accomplishing a mission they would find "good" country. Alas, they found only an extraordinary land of shreds and patches, low rainfall pastoral country in the center, difficult wet-dry pastoral country in the north, and utter deserts scattered all about—country obviously destined always to be only tributary to the economic heartland, a kind of permanent frontier, even when, as in due course they were, its mineral resources were uncovered and exploited.

In the twenty years between 1856 and 1876 the fundamental riddles were solved. In 1855–56 A. C. Gregory, a surveyor by profession (later Sir Augustus Gregory), who had learned the trade of explorer by local expeditions in Western Australia, went by sea from Sydney to the mouth of the Victoria River, in Northern Territory near the boundary of Western Australia, accompanied by a well-provided party which included the famous botanist of the colony of Victoria, Ferdinand von Mueller. After examining the country to the south until they came to desert, Gregory and his party proceeded overland to the east through Arnhem Land and skirted the Gulf of Carpentaria south of Leichhardt's old track, clearing up some of his errors and ambiguities, continuing until a far outback station was reached on the Dawson River near present-day Rockhampton. This journey suggested that parts of Northern Territory might in due course be assimilated to the southeastern pastoral areas; it contributed nothing to the solution of the old problem of a *point d'appui* for settlement of the north which would link Australia with the East, a matter then still in the minds of the imperial authorities.

Two years later Gregory was sent to search for relics of the lost Leichhardt expedition, a journey which took him southwest from Moreton Bay toward Adelaide which he reached in good order. He found no certain traces of Leichhardt, but he began resolving the mystery of the inland water courses, an intricate system only fully functional in the very occasional times of flood. He visited the Barcoo which Mitchell had identified as a river likely to reach the Gulf of Carpentaria and showed it to be a headwater of Cooper's Creek; and went on to show that Cooper's Creek flowed, when in flood, into the great salt lakes of South Australia. He thus linked the inland explorations of Mitchell and Sturt, for Sturt had been on the Cooper in 1845.

Among Sturt's companions on the 1845 journey was John McDouall Stuart, a draftsman who, between 1858 and 1862, working from Adelaide, put to use his knowledge of exploration in a series of journeys to the north. Those of 1860–62 aimed at a south-north crossing of the entire continent. On the first journey he reached the center of the continent, but as it was in flat country, he named a hill about two-and-a-half miles away Central Mount Sturt (later changed to Stuart in his honor). ("Sunday, 22 April [1860] . . . Today I find from my observations of the sun 111° 00′ 30″, that I am now camped in the center of Australia.") On a second journey he got still farther north, and in 1862 he found a track across the continent on which water was available all the way. He reached the sea at Van Diemen's Gulf, just east of the mouth of the Adelaide River, July 25, 1862.

However, while Stuart had found what proved to be the best south-north route through the center, and the one which became the basis of communications and settlement, his party was not the first to reach the sea from the south. This honor had been won, in dubious fashion, by an expedition of the Victorian government, led by Robert O'Hara Burke, a military man (Austrian army) turned gold-fields policeman, with W. J. Wills, a surveyor, second in command. Leaving Melbourne on August 20, 1860, the expedition went north via the Darling River to Cooper's Creek. Growing impatient while in camp on Cooper's Creek awaiting the arrival of supplies, Burke resolved to make a dash for it. Taking Wills and two other companions, he made straight north and without actually seeing open water, reached the Gulf of Carpentaria at a point where access was made impossible by mangrove swamps. On the return journey one of the men died. The three survivors arrived at Cooper's Creek the day the small base party had evacuated the camp after overstaying the appointed waiting time by a month. Believing themselves now too weak to catch up with the party, Burke and his companions attempted a short cut to a police outpost, but Burke and then Wills died of malnutrition, leaving a single survivor who kept body and soul together by the charity of aborigines, until rescued by a relief expedition under A. W. Howitt. (All told four relief expeditions were sent out, but other than Howitt's their contributions were chiefly by way of assessment of the worth of the country for pastoral purposes.) By far the worst managed expedition in Australian history, Burke's disastrous triumph was ever after a prize example of a collapse of common sense and total absence of even elementary bushmanship. To cap the climax, the route Burke found was useless except in the wettest of seasons such as the one in which he pioneered it.

Far away in the west, F. T. Gregory (brother of A. C.) in 1861 led a party to Nichol Bay on the northwest coast of Western Australia for exploration inland. Up to that time it had been assumed that the country in those parts was arid and worthless, but Gregory reported otherwise. In the vicinity of the Ashburton, Fortescue, De Grey, and Oakover rivers he found some 2,000,000 acres suitable for grazing and 200,000 perhaps useful for tropical agriculture. There was no denying that the country was dry, but it was not barren. In the coastal waters he found pearls and pearl shell. The economic roads forward in this hitherto disregarded country were thus clearly pointed out.

In August 1872 a telegraph line between Port Augusta, South Australia, and Darwin, the new coastal capital of Northern Territory, was opened, linked at Darwin to a cable to Java and Europe. The overland telegraph followed essentially Stuart's track, and it had the effect of dividing the continent into two parts: that to the east which could be taken as explored, and that to the west, largely unknown. It was to probe the unknown country between the telegraph line and Western Australia that three famous expeditions were mounted between 1872 and 1876.

The first was led by Major Peter Egerton Warburton, a former Indian army man turned police commissioner and militia commander in South Australia. In September 1872 he led a party north to Alice Springs near the center of the continent—he originally intended to base on Central Mount Stuart—and from there struck out southwest through unknown country toward Perth. The men were mounted on camels supplied by Sir Thomas Elder, the South Australian pastoralist who in the 1860's pioneered the importation of the beasts for use in transport in the dry interior. This saved their lives. Almost from the moment of their departure they were in difficulties about water, for not only was the country through which they were attempting to travel naturally very dry, but 1873 was a drought year. Instead of steadily trending southwest, they were inexorably forced more and more northwest as they made their way precariously forward from water to water. Provisioned for six months, they were out ten, and at the end of their journey were weak from undernourishment. Finally, they made, by heroic effort, the Oakover River which Gregory had first examined only a dozen years earlier. Some of the stronger members were sent forward to look for pioneering pastoralists. All were rescued and taken to the infant town of Roebourne, far to the north of their objective. But they had indeed made the crossing.

Moving in the opposite direction John Forrest, later a famous Western Australian and Commonwealth political leader, then only twenty-five, in 1874 made a very successful but tolerably difficult crossing on a course running from Geraldton on the coast to the Peake telegraph station, near Lake Eyre. In the early stages, Forrest passed through good pastoral country, but inevitably he encountered true desert. Remarkably enough, Forrest made his crossing with horses, the only explorer ever to do so. A native-born Australian, familiar from boyhood with the bush, Forrest was excellently prepared to deal with the country he traveled. Earlier he had followed Eyre's old coastal track from west to east also, and also with horses.

Warburton's exploit was born of desperate necessity, Forrest's of calm competence in the face of admittedly difficult circumstances, but the two crossings of Ernest Giles—east-west and then west-east—were definitely of the nature of romantic jousts with fortune. Already experienced in desert travel, and well knowing what he would be up against, Giles in 1875 undertook to travel as nearly due west from the telegraph line to Perth as he could. Using camels he made the journey of 2500 miles through some of the toughest country in the world, and then, after a rest of eight weeks, made the return crossing from Geraldton, swinging north to the headwaters of the Murchison River and traveling almost straight east to the telegraph line. Giles knew very well that he, at least, had no "good country" to offer the gods of economics. Sardonically, he wrote: "The successful penetration of such a region must have its value, both in a commercial and geographical sense, as it points out to the future emigrant or settler those portions of our continent he should rigorously avoid."

CHAPTER XV

A New Economic Pattern

After 1860 as before, wool growing remained the premier industry of the Australian colonies. This was true whether the measure was the quantity of land utilized, capacity to absorb investment capital, or power to generate income in terms of colonial gross product, or, even more importantly, as export returns. The expression was "Australia lives on the sheep's back." It long continued to do so. However, in view of the constant enlargement of the population by natural increase and immigration, the pastoralists were early challenged as users of the best land by the proponents of crop agriculture. As it became clear that agriculture could not be developed as fast as its proponents hoped, or exactly in the way they envisioned, other lines of endeavor became significant as outlets for enterprise and labor, notably mining and manufacturing. In the general strategy of development public works were centrally important, chiefly railways, the building of which created much employment and absorbed a high proportion of the investment on public account. The urbanization of Australia, which proceeded apace, created employment in building and took up much private capital investment. Both on private and public account capital from the United Kingdom flowed freely into Australia, especially in the 1880's. The ratio of private to public investment was about 60 to 40. After a slow start in the 1860's, the pace of development increased in the 1870's and reached a climax in the 1880's, culminating in a land boom. Late in the 1880's the inward flow of capital slowed down and in the early 1890's there was a sharp financial panic. Low wool prices and disastrous drought then reduced income. But before the end of the 1890's, a measure of recovery was achieved. Over these same years great political, social, and cultural changes took place. From a congeries of colonies, Australia became an emergent federated nation.

D3

The number of sheep in Australia, 20.1 million in 1860, rose to a peak of 106 million in 1891 and then declined to 53.6 million in 1902. Wool production rose from 58.9 million pounds in 1860 to 634 million pounds in 1891 and in 1902 stood at 408.3 million pounds. Although in the period 1861–65 Victoria had the most sheep of all the colonies, an important fact of the subsequent decades was the emergence of New South Wales as the premier sheep-running colony and the rise of Queensland to second position. Victoria never had more than 10 million sheep in any year, but at its peak in 1891 New South Wales had 61 million, while Queensland's peak was 21.7 million in 1892. South Australia reached 6.9 million in 1893, Western Australia 2.7 million in 1902, Tasmania was steady throughout the period at 1.7 million, while Northern Territory had no sheep at all until 1880 and never more than 73,000 in these years. In the peak year of 1891, New South Wales produced 60 per cent of the wool of the Australian colonies.

The forty years after 1860 were years of constant change within the wool-growing industry. The wool interests, in association with the bankers and the merchants, were the most important single economic interest in all the colonies except possibly South Australia where the wheat farmers were strong. Yet the wool growers were constantly under pressure, not only as users of land, but by drought, pests, increasing need for money to buy land and make improvements, high interest rates for the money, and, after 1872, declining prices for wool.

To retain their hold on the country with the best rainfall—and hence best pasture, attained they thought in 1847—they had to fight off the crop farmers who enjoyed a strong political support infused with a strong antisquatter bias. They were assisted in their resistance by the fact that in spite of political belief in the potentialities of crop agriculture the time was not ripe for a rapid rise of farming. While the success of their resistance varied from colony to colony, it was a victory usually bought at the heavy price of investing large sums of money to obtain the freehold of the properties. In this they were aided by the banks and other money-lending institutions, a disastrous alliance for many squatters, however indispensable at the moment of crisis. However, the buying of freehold did not insure enough land, in spite of intensification of use, to satisfy the expansionist impulses of the pastoralists. These had to be satisfied by locating stations farther and farther beyond the reasonably good rainfall country in the truly dry country, such as the west of New South Wales and western Queensland, where leasehold was the rule. This lowered capitalization, but did not decrease the expense of improvements or general costs. The sheep men thus continued to perform their historic function of extending the outer fringes of settlement. When they got beyond tolerable limits for sheep, defined in their minds at this time largely in terms of transport costs, they proceeded still farther out with cattle. They went to the far west and north of Queensland into Northern Territory and across it to the northeast of Western Australia where they met the Western Australians coming up from the south. So important was this exploration of the far outer marches with cattle that whereas in 1861 Queensland had only 432,000 cattle, Northern Territory none at all, and Western Australia but 32,000, by 1900, in spite of drought losses, Queensland had over 5,000,000—it surpassed New South Wales in 1881—Northern Territory 250,000, and Western Australia 300,000. There thus arose out of a struggle over the use of the heartland of Australia in the southeast of the continent a pattern of use of the tributary country of the continent which eight decades later, in spite of active exploration of other uses in the intervening years, still remains the basic pattern. The tributary country has proved to be Australia's permanent frontier, static for long years, as will emerge, but always there for more intensive use as science and technology advanced. The fundamental growth of Australia was in the heartland.

The 1870's and 1880's were times of pastoralists with tremendous holdings of land and vast flocks of sheep or herds of cattle, or both. They were mostly independent operators, but there were some "companies," groups of individuals holding one or several stations. This was the period when wealth was closely associated with ownership of land, or its control through leasehold, and sheep and cattle—both wealth derived therefrom and as the cachet of wealth otherwise derived, the latter in the ancient British convention that the landholders were the only really true-blue respectables. Wealth derived from urban activities went into stations, often "show" stations, while wealth derived from pastoral activities found its way into mining, banking, and urban real estate. This was the period when men like Sir Samuel Wilson (1832–95), Sir Samuel McCaughey (1835–1919), James Tyson (1823–98), and Sir Sidney Kidman (1857–1935) assembled vast holdings and vast flocks and herds and in good seasons possessed vast wealth. Such men as these and their runners-up were in their heydays the "tall poppies" of the pastoral industry and the colonies. Some of them built fairly palatial homes on their stations and lived expansively. They built, too, impressive city homes. Only in the far outback was station living any longer hard and crude for the owners and their families.

On the other hand, there were those pastoralists, some operating in a substantial way, who, under the pressure of drought, the struggle to meet the capital costs of intensifying production, and low wool prices fell into the hands of the banks and other money-lending institutions. By a convention firmly supported by the literary people of Australia, it was during the 1870's and 1880's that the pastoralist became the enemy of his employees and those who served him as independent contractors, while he himself was a prime victim of the urban financiers. After 1870 the pastoralists began to borrow from banks, wool-broking concerns, stock and station agents. In New South Wales about fifteen lending institutions were active in this business, with the Bank of New South Wales the most conspicuous and deeply involved. The effect with regard to leasehold stations was to change the position of the lessees from one in which in 1866 over three-quarters of the stations were held by individuals and another fifth by groups of individuals (or 99 out of a 100 stations were in the hands of private persons) to one in which less than half the stations were held by individuals and less than a fifth by groups of individuals by 1890. About 40 of every 100 properties passed into the hands of the banks and other lending institutions in a quarter century. The institutions increased their holdings in the next fifteen years. Theoretically, borrowers could pay off their obligations and resume full control of their stations, but this was difficult to accomplish in these years of falling prices and drought. Rather, once a station was encumbered it tended to stay encumbered and the pastoralist tended to become a manager for the lender. In 1905 a writer in a country journal could refer to "the 'Company' or the 'Bank' " as the "modern prototype" of the "old-time squatter," implying a very sweeping elimination of the independent. On the available evidence it is clear that many squatters did become tied to their financial backers both for long-term loans and operating money and to some degree became subject to their direction in station management, but a complete takeover of the industry by the financiers was never achieved. The successful independent widely survived. One might generalize that around 1870 the pastoral industry began to change from the highly promising speculation it had been for three decades to a very difficult industry for men working on a narrow financial base when wool prices were down and seasons bad. High cost borrowing could then easily be fatal to independence.

The pastoralists of this time led the way toward intensification of production in the land industries which has ever since been a principal way forward in Australia. This has always been most feasible within the Australian heartland. In spite of the extension of the area devoted to sheep, most of the sheep in Australia at any given moment were always, and still are, to be found within the heartland. Before the gold rushes only three significant technological innovations, aside from developing new sheep types by breeding, were instituted: "boiling down" started about 1840 as a way of disposing of excess sheep in times of low prices by rendering out the tallow when that was the most profitable utilization; "ring-barking" trees to increase the growth of grass, an Australian adaptation of the practice of girdling trees which the American pioneers had borrowed from the Indians, also started about 1840; and fencing started about 1850 utilizing logs and split rails, and with wire about 1855.

With fencing we come into the present period; and in fact it was the loss of labor by the stations during the rushes that really stimulated fencing. Quite logically it was first carried forward vigorously in Victoria in the 1860's, while the fencing boom took place in New South Wales in the 1870's. When shepherds left the stations for the gold rushes it was noticed that the sheep were really little the worse for unrestricted wanderings, but it was obviously necessary to restrict them somewhat, so large areas, called paddocks, were enclosed. Thus, instead of three workers per 1000 sheep—two shepherds and a hut-keeper—several thousand sheep could be run in a fenced paddock of suitable size with only one worker, a boundary rider to see that the fence was in good order. As long as the paddocks were not overstocked, the sheep did better, raised larger fleeces and had cleaner wool, and more lambs survived. It also made feasible the broadcast sowing of grass-seed, initiating pasture improvement in a new fashion. Moreover, fencing tended to revolutionize the whole operation. Before fencing a squatter of substance ran 30,000 sheep. After fencing, in the Riverina district of New South Wales, a good property of 130,000 acres would run 50,000 sheep, water supply permitting. Naturally, capitalization also increased. However, as mixed farms growing wheat and running some sheep increased in numbers—in South Australia and Victoria in the 1860's and 1870's, in New South Wales later—the size of average flocks was pulled down.

Water was a crucial factor and shortage of it through drought a recurring menace. Much money was sunk in this period into water-gathering and conserving devices called "dams" and "tanks" which represented investment since they involved the construction of earthworks. They were equally vital in "good" and "bad" country, for no country suitable for sheep could be wet, high-rainfall country; and wherever the sheep were run they were in areas subject to drought. Droughts could affect small or large stretches of country, could be localized within colonies, or be intercolonial. In this period they culminated in the drought of 1895–1903, the worst on record to that time. The effect on the sheep and cattle population was devastating. Pastoralists might escape the consequences of a drought covering a limited area by moving the animals to an area which still had feed and water—this was one argument for owning stations in various areas; the alternative was to buy access to grass and water, a practice called agistment. In the late 1870's, a new source of water was tapped. An artesian well was drilled at Kallara Station in the northwest of New South Wales in 1878. This initiated a study of the artesian basins of Australia, subsequently shown to underlie a vast area. More artesian wells—called "bores"—were drilled by private persons on their properties than by governments for common use. The first deep bore in Queensland was drilled at Blackall in 1885. Here again, a support of production was only to be gained by capital investment.

Experimentation with the basic machine for wool production, the sheep, a preoccupation of Australian pastoralists from the beginning, continued. The professional experimentalists, called stud-masters, developed types for sale. In this period the primary concern was still with the capacity to grow a fine fleece of increased weight. The most famous of the creative stud-masters of this time were the Peppin brothers who bred for types adapted to life on the great interior plains on their property in the Riverina of New South Wales. In this trade mistakes could easily be made. One such was made by Sir Samuel McCaughey who imported heavily wrinkled merinos from Vermont in the United States in the late 1880's, but while the breed was widely dispersed, especially in New South Wales and Queensland, it came to be reckoned inappropriate to Australian conditions and in some respects a disaster in spite of the production of a heavy, greasy fleece.

The sheep diseases most commonly mentioned in this period as seriously menacing the squatter's productivity were "scab" and pneumonia. "Scab" was dealt with by "dipping" the sheep in a solution of lime, sulphur, and tobacco, expensive but efficient. By 1890 "scab" was largely a thing of the past in eastern Australia. The most devastating disease among the cattle was the tick which, introduced from India at Darwin in 1872, spread east and south into Queensland and west into Western Australia in the ensuing quarter century. But disease was only one of the hazards. There were indigenous animals such as the dingo which preyed on sheep, or the kangaroo which as a herbivorous animal competed for grass with both sheep and cattle. And above all, an introduced animal, the rabbit, also competed for pasture but on a scale far beyond the effort of the kangaroo. Against all of these competitive animals the pastoralists waged war, campaigns in which the colonial governments joined them. In Queensland in 1887–89, 3,700,000 kangaroos and 60,500 dingoes were killed. The story of the rabbit is, however, a classic case of what happens when an imported animal establishes itself in a land in which its enemies are too few to do it serious harm. Only the dingoes preyed on the rabbits. The rabbit was brought into Australia in the early days, but while it bred freely, it did not make a successful get-away into the interior plains. The rabbits which eventually accomplished this disastrous feat were imported in 1859 by a squatter named Thomas Austin who lived near Geelong, Victoria. From Geelong they spread north and west, crossing the Murray River into New South Wales and South Australia by 1880. Within six years they had crossed New South Wales to enter Queensland and South Australia to enter Western Australia. The rabbit eventually established itself all over Australia south of the Tropic of Capricorn. The invasion of the grazing areas by the rabbit was a great disaster to the pastoral industry. The "eating out" of the country in competition with the sheep or cattle was a catastrophe which fell heavily upon the squatter by reducing the carrying capacity of the land. The squatter was also put to the expense of fighting back in an attempt to control or destroy the enemy. This was chiefly done with "rabbit proof" (mesh) fences, a very expensive method which was not successful. This was also the era in which that figure of Australian story and painting, the rabbiter, a man employed to trap or poison the beasts on the stations, made his appearance; and the squatter's poison cart also roamed the paddocks. Rabbit skins and rabbit meat became articles of export, but they did not return anywhere near enough to compensate for the damage done. Rabbit-proof fences, sometimes heightened to make them also dingo-proof, were built by individual squatters, or groups co-operatively, and on a vaster scale by the colonial governments. In 1886–89 the New South Wales government built a fence for 346 miles along the border of South Australia. Queensland and Western Australia built even longer ones at later dates, the Western Australian fences eventually running a total of over 2000 miles. All proved less important in keeping rabbits out than in slightly facilitating efforts at control within, and in hampering the movements of dingoes, emus, and kangaroos. Not for 90 years was any truly effective way of dealing with the rabbit pest discovered.

Until the 1890's the wool was taken from the sheep by "blades" or handshears, an implement resembling the old-fashioned grass clipper used in trimming lawns in America. The record for shearing with the blades was made at Alice Downs, near Blackall, Queensland, in 1892—321 sheep shorn in 7 hours and 40 minutes. However, in the 1880's a standard day's work was 110 sheep, though more to protect the sheep from cutting than for any other reason. Experimentation with machine

clippers for shearing, reasoning from the analogy of horse clippers, began in the late 1860's, but it was not until 1888 that Frederick York
Wolesly in collaboration with John Howard had developed a practical
machine. The first shearing entirely done with machine clippers was
carried through at Dunlop Station, west of the Darling River in New
South Wales, a property belonging to Sir Samuel McCaughey, in 1888.
A general change-over to machines began in that very year. The advantage of the machines was not so much in the number of sheep a man
could handle, as in the closeness with which a sheep could be shorn,
thus adding to the weight of the fleece. In the early days the sheep were
washed before being shorn, reducing the weight of the wool to be shipped
to market, an important consideration when the wool had to be hauled
many miles to the seaports by bullock teams, but in the 1870's the wool
began to be handled "in the grease." Though the weight of the wool
was increased, the cost of washing, and the cost of constructing washing-
pools, was saved. The wool was "classed" in the sheds by a skilled professional, a practice introduced in the late 1840's. Progress in baling
the wool chiefly involved more efficient pressing of the bales to reduce
the bulk and facilitate handling. The baled wool was hauled to the ports
by bullock teams operated by contractors who also normally brought
in the station supplies. As the railways moved inland, haulage was shifted
to the railheads. It is difficult to say how long a haul was economic,
but in western Queensland in the early days hauls of nine months' duration were not unknown.

By the 1860's the old practice of selling the wool to merchants at
the ports, who thereupon sent it to the London auctions, had been replaced by an arrangement whereby agents at the ports consigned the
wool to London at the grower's risk. About four-fifths of the annual
production was handled that way. In the 1870's and 1880's there was
a definite shift in favor of auctioning the wool at the Australian ports,
a development much favored by continental and American buyers. By
1900 at least half of the Australian wool was disposed of at colonial
auctions and only 30 to 40 per cent was consigned to London. The
growers felt they obtained better returns in this fashion.

It was out of this business of getting the wool marketed that there
arose firms specializing in wool marketing on the one hand and in the
supplying of the station owners with foodstuffs, equipment and money
on loan on the other hand. Some banks also participated in wool marketing and finance. It was during this period that such famous specialist
wool firms as Dalgety's, Goldsbrough, Mort, and Elder, Smith took their
rise.

D3

The progress of crop agriculture was disappointing. As late as 1901 an acute observer noted, "Taken as a whole, [Australia] may be said to be in the first phase of agricultural settlement; indeed, several states have not yet emerged from the pastoral stage." Since the establishment of farmers on the land was a steady aspiration, expressed chiefly in complicated land legislation and railway building programs, this failure to achieve satisfying results constituted a major frustration of the time. It is usually interpreted in terms of a struggle between the squatters and the aspiring farmers over the land, with the squatters blamed for purposefully defeating the agriculturalists. In this context it was often hard to disentangle antisquatter from profarmer sentiment. The optimism about the prospects of agriculture was founded in an inflated conception of Australian resources untempered by any recognition of the harsh realities of the most recalcitrant of continents.

The struggle between the squatters and the farmers was fiercest in New South Wales where progress in agriculture was slow. New South Wales remained a fundamentally pastoral colony until the end of the century. The struggle was generated out of a political aspiration to accomplish two related objectives: to settle respectable yeomanlike farmers on the land, and thus open up opportunities for employment of labor and small capital and enlarging the middle class; and to diversify production in the land industries by providing an alternative to grazing. The politicians who thus viewed the matter were not themselves farmers, though some were landowners, but rather were mostly urban types politically opposed to the pastoral oligarchs. Since access to the land was the indispensable prerequisite, and the land, especially that useful to farmers, was in the hands of the pastoralists, the politicians largely concentrated on legislation designed to shake the grip of the pastoralists on the land and release it to the aspiring farmers. The pastoralists fought back, not only in the legislatures, but extra-legally once legislation menacing to them was on the books. There was much talk about how the moral climate deteriorated at this time, especially in New South Wales, as it did during the rancher-nester struggle in the American West. Since in New South Wales the favored method of "unlocking the land" after 1861 was "free selection before survey," thus giving the prospective farmer the right to "select" a piece of land anywhere as long as it was not freehold, the person not really interested in farming but knowing a good racket when he saw one, selected land he knew the squatter would buy from him to protect his station, while the squatter to protect his station would, on his side, anticipate the holdup by getting "dummies" to "select" the key areas on his station, with the transfer of title to him to follow in due course.

The process of picking out the choice spots on the stations was known as "peacocking." Clever peacocking could damage or protect a station very effectively. In Victoria where at various times survey either before or after selection was the rule, dummying was also rife. South Australia and Tasmania, because of variant land systems, largely escaped the evil. While in New South Wales it was not until 1884 that a serious attempt was made to clear up the difficulties, in Victoria the situation was pretty much under control after 1869. But reformist land legislation continued to be a legislative staple for many years.

In the heyday of "selection" far more land was selected than was farmed. In New South Wales in 1861–84 perhaps not half of the selections were legitimate. This, of course, is another way of saying that the pastoralists fought back very successfully, if corruptly. But there is another side to the coin. It is obvious that farmers cannot farm without land; that access to land is the indispensable first step; and that the struggle to unlock the land was therefore an unavoidable necessity. But it must also be noted that even with land available the impediments to successful farming in Australia were formidable, so formidable that in this period the Australian farmers could barely get started on their way. The problems were both agronomical and economic. They, as much as the squatters, defeated the farmers in this first great effort to make agriculture a major industry.

The spearhead crop was wheat. The first aspiration in each colony was to achieve domestic self-sufficiency, the second, to export grain and flour. South Australia was already successful in both respects. In 1861 South Australia was the premier wheat-growing colony, having long since displaced Tasmania. It was growing 35 per cent of all Australian wheat on 43 per cent of the acreage devoted to it, while Tasmania had fallen to 14 per cent of the production on 10 per cent of the acreage. The challenging colony was Victoria which was now growing 34 per cent of the wheat on 25 per cent of the acreage, but it was nevertheless a long way from self-sufficiency, let alone an export surplus. New South Wales was in 1861 producing only 15 per cent of total production on 20 per cent of the acreage, while in both respects Queensland and Western Australia made negligible contributions. All told, the colonies were producing about 10,250,000 bushels on 644,000 acres. To meet consumption needs the colonies with deficiencies imported from California and Chile.

From its beginnings, wheat growing was a farming-for-market type of operation. It is an important fact that farming in Australia was to be really successful only when it was conceived of as a commercial operation. A successful commercial or entrepreneurial farmer was, under the conditions, only by courtesy a yeoman, however middle class he might become in economic and political outlook when he was successful. Neither farming for subsistence nor on a peasant basis with a small surplus for market was ever to be found practical under Australian conditions. Rather, success was only to be achieved by producing crops for market—on a considerable scale—as a primary purpose. Australian farmers have consistently been entrepreneurs; farming has been a business—as it should be. Yet because of the bias of the profarmer politicians and the inherited British tradition, this had to be learned the hard way. Throughout Australian agricultural history this conflict of ideology and reality has gone on—and still goes on.

In 1861 the wheat industry faced—in addition to the problems of access to the land and quantity of land per enterpriser, which figured so largely in the political arena—the need to learn how to handle the Australian soil for crop growing, how best to conserve the moisture which was normally in short supply, the questions of what varieties of wheat could best be cultivated, and how to get the crops to market. The history of the thirty years after 1861 is largely the story of how these challenges were dealt with, though some of them were not solved within this period. Australia as a wheat producer of significance in the world market was a creation of the twentieth century. It is indicative of the slow progress in the nineteenth century that Victoria did not achieve an export surplus until 1877, New South Wales until 1898.

When the period opened, the continental colonies, except South Australia, had hardly begun the occupation of the areas best adapted to wheat growing. Wheat was still being grown chiefly in the ill-adapted coastal areas, whereas the true wheat country was beyond the "dividing" coastal hills and mountains. In South Australia the existing wheat growing area could fairly easily be pushed north from the vicinity of Adelaide, though in the end this was done most successfully to the east and west, but in Victoria and New South Wales the hills and mountains had to be crossed. It is illustrative of the situation that the bitter selector-squatter struggle in New South Wales was focused on the western slopes of the mountains. This was country of relatively low rainfall and subject to drought. Since it was early found that a haul to market of more than twenty or thirty miles was impossible to manage, transport was a major question. The answer was railways. Once any belief in the old saw that rain followed the plow—most prevalent in South Australia—had been lost, the culture methods of fallowing were pursued. There was no understanding of chemical fertilizers. Once the delusion that small acreages could support families was dissolved, holdings became larger and *extensive* farming became the rule, aided by facilitating machinery. Wheat farmers took out income insurance by running sheep on the unplowed portions of their holdings (they were cut out of pastoral country). However, the prevailing climate of opinion was not conducive to rapid progress. True to their character the world around, the farmers were stubborn adherents to their traditions, traditions mostly not relevant to Australia but to very different Great Britain, and resistant to suggested innovations, most of all to innovations proposed by academic agriculturalists. They were notorious for sloppy methods. In the tradition of the farmers about whom Governor Macquarie complained in the 1820's, their housing was crude, farm amenities poor, and the small towns built as service centers were dreary. On the other hand, the wheat farmers suffered declining yields and low prices on the world market until about 1895. The former they could to an extent combat by improved culture methods, better seed, and increasing the acreage sown—one of the factors increasing the size of holdings was the need of the individual farmer for more acreage on which to try to achieve a viable operation with low yields—but the latter delayed entry into the world market, insofar as it acted as a depressant on efforts to achieve an export surplus.

The failure of the proselector politicians to perceive the importance of capital and operating credit for the aspiring farmers is difficult to understand until it is recalled that apart from using the state power to open up the *opportunity* to farm, they were largely unconcerned with assisting the farmers, taking a laissez-faire position from that point on, except with regard to transportation. It evidently was thought that a farmer could establish himself on, say, 160 acres—half a 320-acre selection—with £220. But he normally had to put down an initial payment of 5 shillings an acre against the total price of £1, or for 320 acres, £80, and find the money for the balance within a few years. Clearing costs, which varied from place to place, perhaps averaged £3 per acre or £480 for 160 acres. The rough temporary hut (slab and bark) cost perhaps £25; a permanent wooden house cost about £50 per *room*. He had to purchase animals—bullocks, horses, sheep, cattle; he had to find his machinery. Since his farm was usually established in grazing country, he ran some sheep on the portion of the farm not put under plow. And the farmers normally had to buy their food from stores. So it is apparent that with all the prospective farmer might wring out of himself and his family in labor, he needed a good deal more than £200 to get established. In Victoria in the mid-1870's about four out of ten selectors were farmers by trade—many from South Australia

—and two out of ten were laborers. The rest were skilled tradesmen—butchers, blacksmiths, and so on, and a very few professional people. These people were divisible into "boss," or well-to-do, farmers and "cockies," or poor farmers. The poor farmers ordinarily worked as laborers for their richer farmer neighbors and the pastoralists. It was not uncommon for poor farmers to clear land, sell it to the well-to-do for the capital gain, and buy unimproved land elsewhere. Poor men thus accumulated capital, while the rich aggregated land holdings. But the much needed credit was difficult to come by and very costly. Until the 1890's no experiments were made with state advances and so farmer borrowing was mostly from their well-to-do neighbors, store-keepers on a line-of-credit basis, and petty professional money lenders. Interest was normally usurious. The farmer's lot was not a happy one.

The progress of wheat growing in the principal colonies can be briefly illustrated. In South Australia, while the acreage was nearly doubled by extending the old area northward, the total expansion was by six times, most of it in new divisions of the colony to the east and west of the old area. In New South Wales production in the coastal divisions practically faded away, while on the inland locations it showed an increase of 70 per cent. Victoria exhibited the same pattern: while production declined in the old locations, it increased 98 per cent in the inland.

The increase in average acreage of farms, least pronounced in South Australia, was clearly apparent in Victoria, where wheat growing throve in this period, and New South Wales, where the potential was greatest. In Victoria before expansion began only one-sixth of the farms had acreages of over 500, while in 1891 just short of half did so. Figures for New South Wales show that average holdings rose from 315 acres in 1876 to 862 in 1890. It became a common belief that a wheat farm should have 1000 acres.

Larger units made fallowing more feasible and allowed the compensation of low yields by an increase in the acreage sown. The early Australian wheat farmer tended to practice soil mining by cropping the same area over and over again. Fallowing was an alternative to this and was supported by the assumption that it conserved moisture and allowed the soil to recuperate. The latter assumption was later supported by scientific knowledge of nitrogen fixation, assisted in South Australia, beginning in the late 1880's, by the dispersion of subterranean clover, which had entered the country as a stowaway. A point to be made is that in this period there was little knowledge of soils in a scientific sense. In essence, fallowing was the Australian version of what in America became known as "dry farming." When after the turn of the century knowledge of American dry farming methods reached Australia, it was quickly seen that the farmers had little to learn from it. The introduction of artificial fertilizer came significantly late in the period. When J. D. Custance came out from England to the Roseworthy Agricultural College in South Australia, he soon concluded that phosphate was the fertilizer the wheat farmers should use. His successor at Roseworthy after 1887, William Lowrie, took up the idea and elaborated a prescription. It was not until the end of the century, however, that the use of phosphatic fertilizer—what the Australians call superphosphate—really caught on.

South Australia pioneered the machine harvesting of wheat. It was one of the reasons why it continued to enjoy pre-eminence as a wheat-producing colony in the face of low yields per acre. In the other colonies, harvesting machines spread as the wheat areas were established in the dry inland and the farms grew in size. They were a prime factor in allowing farmers to compensate for low yields by increasing their acreage. The harvested wheat was then put through threshing machines and bagged for market. The wheat was classified for export purposes as f.a.q. ("fair average quality") on the basis of its milling value, a practice which originated in South Australia in 1888 and was adopted by Victoria in 1891 and New South Wales in 1899.

In 1884 Hugh Victor McKay of Victoria invented a combined machine capable of stripping, threshing, cleaning, and bagging the grain. It was put into factory production in 1891. Plowing, a large item in farm costs, was made cheaper by increasing the number of shares per implement and shifting from bullock to horse power. Steam plows came in from England. British, American, and Canadian farm machinery was imported into Australia from the 1880's onward but as a rule Australian-invented machines of comparable kinds were produced before the imported versions were brought into use, ordinarily because of some supposed technical superiority. Not only did the Australians invent and develop the machinery necessary for normal farm operations, but also they were ingenious about meeting the requirements of special situations. As the lightly wooded savannah-like country, so well suited to wheat growing, was exhausted in South Australia in the late 1870's, country covered with scrub was invaded and later on similar country in Victoria was exploited. To facilitate the preparation and use of such country, a settler named Mullens devised a roller from a steam boiler which was *pushed* through the scrub by horses, thus leveling the scrub. This was done in the late winter. At the end of the summer the rolled country was burned over and wheat sown. However, stumps remained and to meet this difficulty another South Australian farmer named Richard Bowyer Smith devised, in 1876, a plow which would ride over the stumps when encountered and re-enter the ground afterward—a "stump-jump" plow.

From 1861 to 1881 all the colonies except Tasmania, which experienced a steady decline, increased their wheat acreage. After 1880 there was a general lull, but at the end of the 1880's the wheat lands again began to be extended. In 1891 South Australia still remained the colony with the greatest quantity of land in wheat, 1,553,000 acres, while Victoria was a close second with 1,333,000 acres. New South Wales lagged far behind with 357,000. Queensland had about 20,000, Western Australia about 27,000 acres. On this basis production was distributed as follows: Victoria 13,629,000 bushels, South Australia 6,436,000 and New South Wales 3,964,000.

D3

The expansion of wheat farming dramatized once again the fact that water was normally a scarce resource under Australian conditions. The point was periodically underscored by droughts. The wheat farmers, like the pastoralists, early showed a tendency to spread their activities into new untried areas in times when the rainfall was good and to be caught there when the years of rainfall deficiency came and no culture techniques or limited water conservation schemes successfully could counter the scarcity of moisture. Like the pastoralists, the farmers were deceived again and again by "good seasons" which they either from ignorance or hopeful stubbornness considered would last indefinitely. Land use constantly outran knowledge of meteorology and continued to outrun it even after it was accumulated when it contradicted the prevailing optimism about the Australian potential. The former situation was inevitable—a price paid to get Australian resources into use; the latter is an Australian chapter of the history of popular delusions, still unfinished.

Water conservation as a capital cost of land use was initiated by the pastoralists with their tanks, dams, and "bores" and was continued by the farmers, but whereas the pastoralists to a large degree took care of themselves, the farmers came to depend on the governments to finance the works. The colony of Victoria pioneered the field.

The Victorian pioneering began in 1865 with a scheme for providing a water supply for inland towns that had grown up around gold fields. Responsibility rested with the local governments which could strike rates to support water works, while capital funds at interest could be borrowed from the colonial government. This scheme was of small use to sparsely settled farming areas, and it tended to be discredited as the gold towns faded away. In the 1870's Hugh McColl (1819–85), whose first experience was with the local government schemes, began a campaign to introduce into Victoria the idea of water supply and irrigation by private companies on the pattern then flourishing in the west of the United States. Frustrated in this, McColl entered politics and sought action by the central government. Slowly emphasis shifted from water supply, interpreted as the supply of water for human consumption and stock, to irrigation.

At this stage Alfred Deakin entered the picture. As minister for Water Supply and commissioner of Public Works in the government of Premier James Service he confirmed local government responsibility for water works in the form of "trusts," but added irrigation in support of *extensive* farming—pioneered in the Goulburn River valley—as an additional possibility and then went on to pioneer irrigation for *intensive* farming. A drought in the early 1880's convinced Deakin and his political associates that the water problem was urgent. In 1884 Deakin resigned his cabinet post to head a royal commission on water supply.

Although the Australians were informed about irrigation in India, Egypt, and Spain, it was to western United States that they looked for guidance, in large part because of the climatological analogy that could be drawn. When Deakin went to California in 1884, he had been preceded by Australian newspaper correspondents reporting on American irrigation, one of whom accompanied him on his journey. It was the royal commission's first progress report, *Irrigation in Western America* (Melbourne, 1885), written by Deakin himself—he was a skilled journalist, formerly on *The Age* newspaper—that was the most influential part of the report. Moreover, it was from California that two Canadians, the brothers George and W. B. Chaffey, founders of Ontario, California, eventually came to establish a California-style irrigation settlement in Victoria.

George Chaffey arrived in Melbourne early in 1886. After protracted negotiations with Deakin, now once more a minister, an agreement was drawn up to govern the formation and development as a carefully guarded private enterprise of an irrigation settlement at Mildura on the Murray River in the dry northwest of Victoria, over 150 miles beyond the nearest railhead, fundamentally dependent upon the river for transportation, remote from the small colonial markets for the fruit it was proposed to raise. Fundamentally an engineer and promoter, not a trained agronomist, though a wonderfully shrewd judge of possibilities, George Chaffey, assisted by his brother, W. B., had a technical success but a financial failure at Mildura. Simultaneously they had a parallel experience at Renmark in South Australia, 150 miles downriver. The Chaffeys demonstrated the practicality of intensive orchard and vineyard irrigation agriculture, but in 1897 George returned bankrupt to the United States. Subsequently he played a vital role in developing California's Imperial Valley. W. B. lived out his life at Mildura. What defeated George Chaffey in Australia was a practically unanalyzable compound of technical difficulties in water distribution, the drying up of investment money in the crisis of 1893, trouble with marketing produce, and the depredations of agitators animated in some degree by hostility to private enterprise in resource development (or a bias in favor of state action).

The Chaffey accomplishment at Mildura and Renmark was, at the end of the century, unique in Australia, though at that time it was in a highly uncertain condition. Nowhere else was anything comparable done in *intensive* agriculture under irrigation. Neither was anything done about supporting *extensive* agriculture by irrigation outside Victoria's Goulburn Valley. Irrigation as a support of agriculture was a development of the twentieth century. In 1884–87 a royal commission studied the problems in New South Wales and pointed to the uses of the waters of the Murrumbidgee River, but nothing was undertaken. Intensive agriculture did not catch on. It was unpopular with the extensive agriculturalists and the irrigation settlements were in large measure inhabited by people direct from the United Kingdom, attracted by one of the most elaborate promotional brochures in Australian history, *The Australian Irrigation Colonies* (15″ x 11″, 129 pages, illustrated, clothbound). Outside Mildura and Renmark, the commonest examples of intensive agriculture were the market gardens cultivated on the outskirts of the cities and towns, mostly by Chinese, and fruit orchards in South Australia and Tasmania.

D3

Along the coast, between the mountains and the sea, from northern New South Wales to the far north of Queensland, were river valleys and coastal plains where tropical agriculture could be carried on. Although pastoralists and gold seekers, looking for convenient points of entry to the back country, pioneered most of this country, it was farmers who settled it and began its intensive exploitation, chiefly on the basis of sugar-cane growing, with pineapples, introduced from Java, and bananas as lesser products.

Sugar had been produced in New South Wales as early as 1823 by Thomas Scott (1777–1881) on the basis of cane originally brought in from Tahiti. The industry failed to take firm root, chiefly because the country chosen for canegrowing was not really suitable. It was not until the 1860's that canegrowing and sugar production took a firm hold.

From small beginnings in the early 1860's, there was steady progress in acreage under cane until the middle 1880's when a plateau was reached at around 15,000 acres. The acreage declined in the 1890's. It was then concentrated in the Richmond River valley. Many of the growers cultivated cane as one of a variety of crops.

Meanwhile canegrowing was established in Queensland. A very small quantity of sugar was produced experimentally at Brisbane in 1859. By 1863 Captain Louis Hope had established near Brisbane what is considered the pioneer plantation. The cane stock was imported from Java and Mauritius. The government encouraged the industry by a liberal policy of land grants and by permitting the importation and use of Kanakas from the islands for labor, a development whose consequences have been examined earlier. By 1880 canegrowing had been extended north in Queensland as far as Cairns and all the subsequently important canegrowing districts of the colony had been pioneered. Expansion was briefly checked by cane diseases in the middle 1870's, but suitable disease-resistant varieties were discovered and in 1879 a veritable boom developed. The boom collapsed in the middle 1880's when prices fell as beet sugar production in Europe increased. To strengthen the industry, a change was made in the organization of cane milling. Until this time the mills had been small and usually owned by individual planters. Now "central" mills began to be established with government help, the planters of a district taking shares. This system had taken firm hold by the middle 1890's with the application of steam power; the mills became larger and their numbers decreased. They early ceased to make sugar for market, but sold their product to refiners. The famous Colonial Sugar Refining Company Ltd. (founded 1855) of Sydney came to dominate sugar refining in Australia. The new milling system led to a change in the organization of the industry from sizable plantations to small holdings. Large holders began to break up and sell off their estates in relatively small units. By 1895, the average cane farm was of forty-nine acres and instead of being dispersed, the farms tended to cluster around the central mills. There was a boom in canegrowing in the middle 1890's on the new basis. The systematic search for and development of new varieties of cane began in the 1890's, initiated by the government when experts were sent to New Guinea in 1893 and 1895. A study of the industry by an expert from Hawaii in 1900 found the needs to be pest and disease control, fertilizing, and irrigation. As a direct result, the first state supported sugar experiment station was established. By the end of the century Queensland was overwhelmingly dominant in the production of sugar cane. However, domestic production of sugar did not meet local demand and Australia was still dependent upon imports, mostly from Java but also from Mauritius, Fiji, and other countries.

D₃

A fascinating bequest of the gold rushes of the 1850's were the wandering prospectors who combed the Australian colonies for new alluvial fields and reefs. They went almost literally everywhere and anywhere, led on by hopes, victimized or rewarded by rumors of new strikes. Anyone, including aborigines, who knew, or alleged he knew, of payable gold was listened to and his directions followed. Though often tried, secrecy about a gold strike was quite impossible to maintain. No country was too remote, none too difficult of access, too dry or too wet, if the glint of gold had been seen in it. And if no fields of a Victorian richness were found in the thirty years after 1860, and if frustrated refugees from impossible places were commonplace figures, enough gold, alluvial and reef, was found to keep hopes vividly alive and the game going. Probably the most important gold *mine* opened in this period was Mount Morgan in Queensland in 1882, but lesser mines and alluvial fields were discovered in many places. Gold production, though sadly shrunken from the great days, was still important in Victoria, New South Wales, and Queensland. After 1885 Western Australia was prospected over a wide area, eventually with stupendous results.

It was the gold seekers who led to the discovery of other minerals. As a group they rarely knew much about minerals other than gold; they were even capable of passing by rich deposits of gold if it was in a form with which they were not familiar and of uncovering rich deposits of other minerals by accident while all the while firmly believing that it was gold they were pursuing. By the same token, important mines could be accidentally located by men not competent or experienced in mining gold and utterly mistaken about the mineral they thought they had found. And only very uncommonly did the prospectors who found the profitable mineral deposits make much out of the mines in the long run. There seemed to be a complete differentiation of talent between discovery, promotion, and extraction. There was absolutely nothing "scientific" about this first extensive exploration of Australia's mineral resources.

Profitable mineral mining had been initiated in South Australia before the gold rushes. It was also in South Australia that the first important discovery of a mineral other than gold was made after the gold rush decade, copper at Moonta in 1861. Copper was found widely dispersed over eastern Australia in this period, usually in small deposits quickly worked out, but in 1883 a large, rich deposit was located at Mount Lyell in Tasmania. The silver-lead-zinc complex, first discovered in South Australia in 1841, was uncovered in the far southwest of New South Wales in the middle 1870's and abundantly at Broken Hill in the same locality in 1883. The previous year an important discovery had been made at Mount Zeehan in Tasmania. The Broken Hill find proved to be the richest of its kind on the continent and one of the world's greatest. Discoveries of tin, widely dispersed like the copper "shows," were made beginning in the 1870's, first at Inverell in New South Wales. Before the Malayan and Bolivian mines were opened, Australia was an important world source of tin. The richest body of tin ore was found in Tasmania at Mount Bischoff in 1882. While this diversification was going on, production of coal in New South Wales was expanding at the Hunter River deposits around Newcastle, both for the domestic market and export. Originally a government monopoly integrated into the convict disciplinary system, the monopoly was transferred to the Australian Agricultural Company in 1831. The Company lost its monopoly in 1847 and the great expansion of production in the last half of the century was the work of various private enterprisers, notably the Brown family, conspicuously after 1887, John Brown. In the 1870's a western field was opened in the mountains behind Sydney, and, after earlier failures, a field to the south of Sydney served by Port Kembla became firmly established in the 1880's. By 1897 production on the three fields had reached 4.5 million tons, about 70 per cent from the Hunter River field. In the other colonies only 500,000 tons were produced, chiefly in Queensland and Victoria. New South Wales exported coal—60 to 70 per cent of its production—to the other colonies, New Zealand, California, and the Far East, and it bunkered British steamers trading to Australia.

In spite of the immense amount of energy that went into prospecting and mining, the feverish speculation in mining shares—a heritage of the gold period which reached a frenetic peak in the 1880's when the Broken Hill mines were opened up—and the attraction of Australian mining shares for English speculative investors, mining accounted for but a small percentage of the private capital formed in Australia in this period. It was less important by far than pastoral enterprises and agriculture and even than factory industry. Of course mining bulked large in the thought and imagination of all who were in any way touched by it, from prospectors to brokers to speculators. Mining stocks were the principal items traded on the exchanges, especially the Melbourne exchange. Mining was a "fever" as well as an industry. Contemporaries had extreme difficulty in differentiating critically among the innumerable mining companies floated. Not only was it difficult to know which company had been founded to exploit an ore body of size and durability, capable of engendering fantastic profits, and which owned a body which would peter out quickly leaving behind nothing more remarkable than a hole in the ground, but every variety of fraudulent practice associated with mining was rife in Australia in those days, as contemporaries have recorded in their memoirs. Investment in mines was a gamble, often "fixed." Those who gambled on what proved to be in the long run a good thing often lost faith before proof was to hand, and sold out. There was no way of being sure. "Imprudent" mining speculations could become so commonplace as to be remarked by colonial treasurers reviewing economic conditions, as in New South Wales in 1872. Disinterested advice on mines was excessively hard to come by. In 1900 *The Economist* referred scornfully to "the mere hysterical gush which, in Australia, passes current for mining criticism." It seems absolutely certain that in Australia at this time the old saw that far more money has been put into mines than has ever been taken out was amply illustrated. Nevertheless great quantities of profits were earned by *some* mines, such as Broken Hill, Mount Lyell, and Mount Morgan.

When a sizable and durable ore body was located, important consequences followed. Broken Hill, in the arid country of southwestern New South Wales, illustrated that mining was going to supplement grazing as a way of utilizing the dry outback. Mount Lyell showed that the Tasmanian west coast had economic significance after all. A sound and enduring mine of course created employment. A town grew around it. Suppliers of goods and services, including transportation, to the mines and the miners (and their families) created more employment. Capital, which migrated from Broken Hill, still with its pastoral associations to Mount Lyell, eventually migrated from Broken Hill into heavy industry, and contributed strategically to the rise of modern Australia. Mining was at this time primarily an export industry—only of coal was a substantial proportion of production locally absorbed. Diversification of exports was much needed, a contribution to economic strength. Minerals helped tie Australia into the world trading system. But successful mining, once the discovery of a significant ore body was made, was a "big man's game" and the rise of great mining enterprises, as at Broken Hill, confirmed the pattern of the time: it was in line with the prevailing differentiation of the Australian population into a small but integrated group of capitalists on the one hand and a large body of wage and salary workers on the other, with a rather insecure middle class in between. This had highly significant implications for politics.

D-3

Manufacturing, loosely defined, stimulated by the natural protection of distance, the availability of cheap locally produced raw materials, and a market, appeared very early in Australia, certainly by 1815. In New South Wales just before the gold rushes a considerable miscellany of "factories" existed, mostly small. Over half of the 400 establishments recorded were flour mills, 62 were tanneries, 51 breweries, 30 produced soap and candles, and 27 were foundries. The rest were 2 distilleries, 8 potteries, 7 rope walks, 5 saltworks, 2 sugar refineries and 4 places where hats were made. The rushes disorganized this activity and some of the establishments had to close down. After the rushes, an identical pattern of production began to assert itself once again. Out of the pre-rush sugar refineries emerged the Colonial Sugar Refining Company, Ltd. It lived to become one of the leading Australian industrial concerns.

While some manufacturing was conducted in all the Australian colonies between the end of the gold rushes and the early 1890's, and while it tended to increase spasmodically in all, it became important in only two, New South Wales and Victoria. South Australia was a weak third contender. The story is considerably complicated by the fact that Victoria experimented with "protection" from 1869, while New South Wales was "free trade." South Australia adopted protection in the 1880's. However, the "fiscal" question, though it assumed great importance in the minds of contemporaries, proved to have a relation to industrial growth subsequent students have found very hard to define, for Victoria with protection and New South Wales without it had, by the 1890's, industrial structures very much alike. The difficulties over protection versus free trade can best be discussed as a phase of the politics of economic policy. However, a greater percentage of the Victorian employed population found work in factories than in New South Wales, so factory industry was more important to Victoria than New South Wales. Victorian factories tended to be a trifle larger on the average than those in New South Wales, measured by number of hands, but in both most factories were small and of the back yard type. The lighter industries, such as clothing, employed large numbers of female workers. In both there was a heavy concentration on consumer goods—boots and shoes and clothing, especially.

In the 1880's even these industries were still so immature that they were entangled in a good deal of "outwork," or the partial manufacture of the products in homes, as clothing by women, boots and shoes by men. This tended to compound the ill effects of bad factory housekeeping which was characteristic. Victoria had to pass factory legislation as early as 1873 to try to discipline the small capitalists in the interest of labor and the general welfare. In a sense, this early emergence of factory industry as a significant provider of employment was a phase of the intensive urbanization of Australia already underway, a consequence of relatively high productivity in land industries extensively organized but of low direct employment potential which nevertheless supported a considerable structure of services at the ports. Factory industry was both supported by and helped support urbanization. Victoria sought to force the pace with protection, while New South Wales was content to take what came under free trade. Both were inordinately proud of their so-called "secondary" industries at this time.

Victoria's leading industries were boots and shoes and clothing but it also had tanneries and fellmongeries and factories producing woolens, soap and candles, mining and agricultural machinery and implements, and iron and tin wear. Similarly New South Wales had tanneries and fellmongeries, boot and shoe and clothing factories, a variety of metal foundries, coach and wagon works, and sugar refineries. Brickyards and sawmills were common to both. So were flour mills. Both had facilities for building and repairing machinery for ships, Sydney better facilities than Melbourne. But what really distinguished New South Wales from Victoria was that it had the potential of heavy industry—the possession of coal and iron. This point appears not to have been perceived at the time. It is nevertheless historically highly significant that the first experiments in iron smelting were conducted at Mittagong, New South Wales, beginning in 1850 and continued for thirty years thereafter; and that a blast furnace was built at Lithgow in 1875. These ventures failed and Lithgow reverted to rolling and casting scrap. It was at Lithgow in 1900, however, that a Siemens-Martin open hearth furnace for making steel came into production. This was looking to the future, but it is significant that while in both New South Wales and Victoria the industrial techniques were highly enough advanced for local concerns to build small locomotives and primitive rolling stock for the early railways, railway building nevertheless did not stimulate the rise of steel-rail production in Australia. Iron rails were offered, but for price and technical reasons the railway engineers rejected the local in favor of the imported product. The railway workshops became the most highly developed engineering establishments in the colonies, but the railways somehow failed to provide that stimulus to iron and steel production they provided in other rapidly developing countries. The workshops were chiefly devoted to repair and maintenance of rolling stock.

D3

Between 1860 and 1900 Australia underwent a technological revolution in transportation and communications, both internally and externally, that profoundly influenced economic development, politics, and culture.

It was early perceived that the continent posed difficult problems arising from the vast spaces and distances characteristic of it when the continent had been divided into six political units, for the units themselves remained large even by European standards for nations. Victoria and Tasmania were small only by comparison with New South Wales, Queensland, and Western Australia. All, large or small, had uneven developmental potentials, particularly in terms of rainfall. The areas favorable to close settlement were relatively limited, and intensity of use, though subject to change as technical mastery of the difficulties was achieved, tended to diminish as one proceeded inward from the coast. The nature of the country and the nature of the use and development to which it was susceptible dispersed the population sparsely over great areas from a *point d'appui* on the coast. The rivers were of little use as natural highways into the interior. Except in the enigmatic north, the rivers reaching the coast arose on the coastal side of the "divide" —did not penetrate the coastal hills and mountains to reach the sea from sources inland. Even the Murray system, the most important of the continent, reached the sea so tortuously that entry into it from the sea was practically impossible, and this best of river systems had but a brief, though colorful, history as a significant transportation artery. The internal transportation and communications problems were inescapably difficult.

Up to and during the gold rushes internal transportation was based on horses and bullocks. Road making to facilitate their use was early initiated but space, distance, and dispersed exploitation of resources prevented the development of an adequate system. Roads were often so bad that bullock teams were slowed down to three or four miles a day, and transportation costs per ton mile within a colony were far in excess of the costs from Europe to the port of entry. As late as 1886 an expert observer could write, "Nothing less resembles an English highway than an ordinary Australian road. Fences, for the most part, do not exist, and the only indications visible of the existence of a road are frequently the deep cut tracks of cartwheels on the surface of the ground." Made roads, in the formation of which Australian engineers acquired considerable skill, were ordinarily found only near the cities and towns, and even trunk roads were such by designation rather than by consistent condition. The existence of toll collecting stations had nothing to do with the state of the roads—they might be literally unusable between stations, the distance negotiable only by taking to the bordering country. Internal transportation costs early established themselves as an Australian problem. The gold rushes, however, occasioned a vast improvement in the transportation of passengers and the movement of mails on inland routes, an accomplishment of Cobb and Company with its multihorsed Concord-style coaches. But it is no wonder that railways were early assessed as the solution of the transportation problem. As their mileage increased, bullock and horse transportation retreated inland beyond the railheads or in the earlier phases of railway building, between the widely separated lines as "feeder services." So completely was the railway to become the chosen instrument of internal transportation that road making was neglected between its coming and the arrival of the automobile in full force after the turn of the century.

Although the idea of a horse-drawn tramway between Sydney and Parramatta was discussed locally as early as 1833, it was not until the late 1840's that the idea of railways was seriously canvassed. In 1846 Mr. Gladstone, the colonial secretary, sent a circular dispatch to all colonial governors transmitting the Standing Orders of the House of Commons with regard to the laws and regulations to govern the construction of railways. One recommendation was that the 4′ 8½″ gauge, already standard in England, be adopted. Two years later Earl Grey, as colonial secretary, sent a supplementary dispatch repeating the recommendations as to gauge on the authority of the commissioners of railways of Great Britain. This, he pointed out, would facilitate the joining together of them within and between colonies. Earl Grey also pronounced in favor of government building and operation and of financing them out of the proceeds of land sales. Already in the Order in Council of 1847 laying down land policy it had been provided "that nothing in these regulations, or in any lease to be granted . . . shall prevent the . . . Governor . . . from disposing of . . . such lands as may be required . . . for the construction of . . . railways and railway stations . . ." And when discussing the possibility of a federal system for Australia in connection with the Act for Government of 1850, Earl Grey suggested that the House of Delegates have the function of controlling "the formation of roads, canals or *railways* traversing any two or more of such colonies." It is apparent that the London authorities were not only thinking of railways but were thinking of them as an instrument of continental integration. The colonists took up the idea of railways but they ignored the idea of continental integration. They also bungled the gauge question.

It is extremely interesting that the first concrete plans for railways in Australia were made before the gold rushes to serve a pastoral economy. However, none was actually built until after the rushes had begun. The first railway company of Australia was the Sydney Railway Company, incorporated in 1849. Shareholders' liability was limited to their investment, while the government guaranteed 5 per cent interest for 10 years. The first sod for its railway from Sydney to Parramatta was turned on July 3, 1850. Before the line could be completed and opened in 1855, the gold rushes had supervened. This allowed South Australia and Victoria to get in ahead of New South Wales. Both opened short railways in 1854, the South Australian horsedrawn but the Victorian had a locally built steam engine. South Australia opened a steam railway in 1856. The other colonies entered the field later, Queensland in 1865, Tasmania 1871, Western Australia 1879, Northern Territory 1889. Except in South Australia, the pioneering of the railways was done by private enterprise (and even in South Australia private companies were authorized; they failed to perform). Only in Western Australia were railways of any length or continuing public importance built by private enterprise and only there did a considerable railway remain in private hands for long. The relatively few private railways in Australia have characteristically been mining and timber railways. The land grant method of assisting private enterprisers, mentioned as a possibility in the earliest discussion of railways in New South Wales, was employed extensively only in Western Australia, though it became a public issue in Queensland in the 1880's. The general hostility to the aggregation of land in private hands prevented the free use of the land grant method of finance. Rather there was more disposition either to invest public money in privately owned railways or to guarantee a return on capital, or both. The pioneer companies found it difficult to raise sufficient private capital; they tended to underestimate the capital costs; and they drew in more and more public money if they could—or faded away if they couldn't. They were also discouraged by the difficult engineering problems confronted.

The colonial governments were therefore ineluctably drawn into the railway business, taking over the existing lines and then extending them. New South Wales was in the railway business by 1855. Victoria entered the field in 1856, after discussions begun in 1854, by an act of the Legislative Council on the final day of its existence before the establishment of responsible government. However, private lines continued to be operated for a time but were gradually absorbed into the government system. South Australia which never had any really important private railways, aside from mine-owned lines, was also in the railway business before it achieved responsible government. Tasmania entered it in 1873 but the system was a private-public mixture until 1890 and even after that date there were important mine-owned lines in the west. Queensland entered the business to build the first line in 1863 after a private company had failed to find money for the venture. Western Australia was in the railway business from 1873 but developed its system as a public-private mixture. In every case the colonial decision to enter the railway business was pragmatic, having nothing visible to do with the theory of state socialism. At the time there was a widespread conviction that railways would solve the urgent internal transportation problem. Schemes for extending the railways into the interior were under discussion in New South Wales and Victoria before the take-over decisions were made. Private enterprise appeared highly unlikely to perform this task. So it fell to the state to provide this solution of the transportation problem since it alone could command the capital and the engineering skills. The governments acted in relation to railways as they traditionally had in relation to roads. Often in the early days both railways and roads—all works, as a matter of fact—were under a single administration. Other rationales for government-owned railways were ex post facto.

The colonists originally thought of their railways as strictly colonial enterprises, not in continental terms. They thought that any linking of colonial systems was a remote possibility. Actually the systems began to link up about a quarter century after the first lines were opened, an interesting commentary on the speed of Australian development. This limited vision of possibilities accounts in large measure for the failure to recognize the wisdom of the imperial government's suggestion that a common gauge be adopted. In the first instance New South Wales selected the 4′ 8½″ gauge, but a persuasive Irish engineer convinced the New South Wales builders that the 5′ 3″ gauge, used on the lines of Ireland, was more suitable and the Victorians and South Australians accepted it also. However, the Irishman did not actually build the line and his successor persuaded the New South Wales people to revert to the 4′ 8½″ gauge. The Victorians and South Australians, having accepted the 5′ 3″ gauge, refused to follow suit. The question was referred to the imperial government, well known to favor a uniform gauge, but it refused to interfere and referred it back to the colonies. No agreement could be reached and building on different gauges proceeded. Later, in search of cheap railways, Queensland, Tasmania, and Western Australia adopted still another gauge, the 3′ 6″. South Australia, also in the interests of cheapness, built part of its system 3′ 6″ and part 5′ 3″. The cheapness of the narrower gauge was technically questionable; the greater cost arose from the compounding of the gauge confusion.

Railway building began slowly and reached its nineteenth-century climax in the 1880's in the eastern colonies and in the 1890's in west Australia. Investment in railways was the principal public investment of the colonial governments in the decades after the gold rushes and the climax of spending on them in the 1880's was strategic in fostering the boom of that decade. In 1860 there were only 215 miles of railways in the colonies; by 1870 the total mileage was still under a thousand (994); by 1880 it had reached 3,675; while in the next ten years the systems were rapidly extended to 9,757 miles by 1890. The rate of growth then slackened, but by 1900 a total mileage of 12,955 had been achieved, or roughly half the mileage eventually built.

The railway problem of each colony was different in particulars, but a roughly similar pattern can be discerned in the continental colonies. In all the lines were built outward from seaports toward the thinly populated peripheries of settlement where they ended, not having passed through any considerable towns en route. Although in every colony building began from more than one point—in New South Wales from Sydney and Newcastle, in Victoria from Melbourne and Geelong—the tendency was to link the systems together, though this might take some time. The New South Wales system was not unified until 1889. Queensland built its railways inland from several coastal points and did not link them together until the second decade of the twentieth century. The lines were basically goods—or freight—carriers. Everything depended upon the capacity of the country traversed to develop freight for the lines to carry. Hence the effort to divert traffic from the Murray, Darling, and Murrumbidgee rivers to the railways. The Murray River traffic had been pioneered by South Australia in the 1850's; its first railway was built to carry goods, which could not reach the sea through the river's difficult mouth, overland to deep sea water; and while the service was important to the outback areas of New South Wales and Victoria, colonial jealousy was such that any inward and outward traffic to their territories which benefited South Australia was resented. Hence the Victorians built a line to the Murray River at Echuca as early as 1865 and the New South Wales railways reached the Murrumbidgee at Hay in 1882 and the Darling at Bourke in 1885. The line to Hay captured traffic from the Murrumbidgee and carried it to Sydney, whereas it had previously gone to Melbourne via Echuca. This initiated a steady decline of freight carrying on the Murray. The development also illustrated the use of the railways to integrate the separate colonies on a particularistic basis, with the integration focused on the principal seaport and capital city.

Within the colonies the railways came to be conceived of as instruments of development. It was not only sought to divert existing traffic to them but to use them to open up country and thus create traffic, this reasoning particularly applying to areas with an agricultural potential. The utility of railways as a support for agricultural development was first demonstrated in Victoria in the 1870's; their extension accounts in considerable measure for the shifting of Victoria's wheatbelt from a north-south axis through Ballarat to an east-west axis along the Murray River. In the end this resulted in the establishment of the densest outback networks in each colony in the agricultural areas, with lines running from them out into the pastoral country. Once the decision to build lines for developmental purposes had been made, the systems ceased to be commercial undertakings and became government owned and operated services to private enterprisers. Inevitably lines were built into areas where the demand for railway transport failed to reach remunerative levels. Lines were provided on a "pork barrel" basis in response to the pressure from legislative representatives of the districts. The losses were socialized and rationalized by reference to the general level of development. Although the railways were built to integrate the colonies separately, their extension to the borders of a colony early brought them into contact with neighboring systems. With regard to the New South Wales lines, the Victorian border was reached at Albury on the upper Murray in 1883, while the Queensland border was reached at Wallangara in 1888. The Victorian and South Australian lines met on the lower Murray in 1889. Thus by the end of the 1880's the eastern colonies were in contact with one another by railway but the breaks in gauge prevented the integrative effect from being fully realized. The first proposal to unify all lines by adopting a single gauge was made in 1889. An attempt to achieve unification in connection with federation failed.

The railways, even after intercolonial connections had been established, were complemented as carriers of both goods and passengers by intercolonial coastal shipping services, first sail and then steam. For the movement of goods of any great weight or bulk between colonies, ships were favored over railways. This was also true within colonies, as, for example, the movement of coal from Newcastle to Sydney in New South Wales. Thus it was that the quantity of shipping employed on the Australian coasts tended throughout the nineteenth century to increase proportionately to total trade, rather than to decline as the railways developed.

Parallel to the revolution in transportation there was a revolution in communications occasioned by the introduction of the telegraph. The telegraph lines were strung both in advance of the railways and beyond the railheads. Introduced into New South Wales in 1851, Victoria 1854, South Australia 1856, Tasmania 1857, Queensland 1864, and Western Australia 1869, Sydney, Melbourne, and Adelaide were linked in 1858 and Western Australia, isolated from the east as far as railways were concerned for a long time to come, was linked to eastern Australia by telegraph in 1877. During the forty years from 1861, 110,000 miles of wire were strung and Australia not only rapidly built a widely ramifying system, but it quickly achieved a leading place among the nations of the world in messages per head per year. The telegraphs were built and operated as a public utility by the post office departments of the several colonies. Much more directly than the railways, the telegraph helped tie the continent together.

The application of steam to ships and the development of the undersea cable reduced Australia's sense of remoteness from "the world." Not only did the tonnage of shipping visiting Australian ports after the gold rushes steadily increase decade by decade, but the proportion of steamships rapidly increased, although the Australian trade was a stronghold for the sailing ships into the twentieth century, especially for the carrying of wheat. But whereas in 1881 about 60 per cent of the tonnage visiting Australian ports was still sail, by 1900 the percentage had declined to about 17. Under sail the usual voyage to Australia was made via the Cape of Good Hope outward bound and via Cape Horn homeward bound, but under steam it was made via the Cape of Good Hope both ways. Passengers and mail reached Australia via the Mediterranean and the Red seas, transhipping through Egypt, even before the opening of the Suez Canal in 1869, but by the end of the 1870's this was the established route for the scheduled steamers carrying passengers, mail, and cargo of high value. This brought London within thirty-three days of Sydney. Freighters handling cargo to meet London marketing seasons, or of a perishable kind, usually came out via the Cape of Good Hope and went home via Suez to save time. Alternatively, London could be reached in thirty-five days across the Pacific by American steamers to San Francisco and thence by rail to the Atlantic seaboard, a route established in the early 1870's but consistently of only supplementary importance because of the failure of Australian-American trade to develop satisfactorily. A revolution within the shipping revolution was the introduction of refrigerated ships in the 1880's, but whereas the Americans had from 1874 been shipping *chilled* meat across the Atlantic, the Australians, like the New Zealanders, took up the *frozen* meat trade, of necessity at that time because the ships had to pass through the tropics to the London market. The full impact of the trade was not felt in Australia, unlike New Zealand, until around 1905, yet the frozen meat trade was a significant element in the diversification that helped the Australian colonies —New South Wales and Queensland especially—find relief from the depression of the 1890's. In Victoria butter was the commodity that played a parallel role.

The shipping serving Australia was overwhelmingly British—in this period about nine vessels out of ten—with the Peninsular and Oriental and the Orient lines most conspicuous. Of the small contingent of foreign flag visitors, German ships were most numerous, followed at a distance by French and American. The Messageries Maritimes line began a regular service to Australia in 1881, North German Lloyd in 1886. Wool carrying was the stimulant and the original support; the Germans became important in the metals trade.

Customarily approaching Australia from the west and departing westward when following the Cape route, or coming from and going to the north when using the Suez Canal, the ships usually called at a Western Australian port—Albany to the end of this period, then shifting to Fremantle, and at Port Adelaide, Melbourne, and Sydney, where the turnaround was made. Hobart and Brisbane were left out under this routing. The figures for ships entered and cleared somewhat distort the picture of trade, but it is reasonably clear that during this period Sydney displaced Melbourne as the leading trading port of Australia and Queensland ranked third by 1900, most of the trade passing through Brisbane. Brisbane was served by ships traveling inside the Barrier Reef and via Torres Strait to Singapore. The pattern of a principal port in each colony was early established, with the shipping at outports only of significance for such obvious reasons as the coal trade at Newcastle, New South Wales, and at this time there was a definite tendency for outports to decline in significance rather than increase—a reflection of the powerful centralizing forces at work in every colony.

The undersea cables, like the land telegraph, dramatically conquered time. Whereas before cable connections were established communication was mostly at the speed of sailing ships, the cable reduced communications to a few hours even before the steamship had shortened the trip to London to a few weeks. The first cable connection with Europe involved the prior building of an overland telegraph from Port Augusta to Darwin through the center of the continent, a South Australian enterprise of great difficulty and daring. This line was a single iron wire to 1899, when a second line of copper was added. To Darwin the Eastern Extension Telegraph Company Ltd. laid a cable from Banjoewangi, Java, from where via Batavia, Singapore, Madras, and Bombay connection could be made to London. Since Adelaide was connected by telegraph to all points in Australia, this meant that from October 1872 the eastern colonies—from 1877 Western Australia also—were closely linked to Europe telegraphically, with the obvious consequences to government, business, and journalism. An alternative cable connection with Java and Europe was made in 1888 from Broome, Western Australia. In 1876 cable connection was made with New Zealand; and in 1893 a French company laid a cable between New Caledonia and Queensland. As early as 1879 a trans-Pacific cable was proposed, designed to establish a service between the Southwest Pacific and London via Canada—an "All Red" line touching none but British territory. Such a line, built by the interested governments, running from Southport, Queensland to Norfolk Island (where there was a branch to New Zealand), Fiji, Fanning Island, and Banfield, British Columbia, was opened for business at the end of 1902. Meanwhile in 1901 a cable from Western Australia to England via the Cape of Good Hope and up the west coast of Africa was completed. Rates per word were reduced in the 1890's as competition increased, and government subsidies compensated for any losses incurred. In consonance with Australia's established political, economic, and cultural connections, all cables, even the trans-Pacific, led to London and confirmed the country's deep involvement in the Empire, for along them not only went commercial transactions but political and cultural intelligence, both domestic to the United Kingdom and Australia and with regard to the whole world, including Australia's geographical neighbor, the Far East. The cables deepened Australia's Britishness and its London view of the world.

Telephones first came into use in Melbourne in 1878. In their beginning privately owned, the services were taken over and developed by the post offices of the several colonies. Sydney and Melbourne were linked by telephone in 1907.

D3

As the complexity of the economic organization of the Australian colonies increased, so did the intensity of urbanization. In this period, however, there was a steady increase in the numbers classified as rural as well as the numbers classified as urban. A drift to the cities from the rural districts had not yet set in. But as T. A. (later Sir Timothy) Coghlan, the statistician of New South Wales, pointed out in the late 1880's the degree of urbanization was then not only intensifying but had even then surpassed anything to be found in Europe or the United States, especially since in Australia the pattern was for there to be but one great urban center in each colony.

The constantly intensifying degree of urbanization achieved 1861–1901 in the several colonies is reflected in the following table:

Percentage of Population in Capital Cities

	1861	*1871*	*1881*	*1891*	*1901*	*Population 1901*
Sydney	26.7	27.3	29.9	33.8	35.9	487,900
Melbourne	25.8	28.2	32.8	43.	41.	494,129
Brisbane	*N.A.*	12.5	14.5	23.7	23.7	119,428
Adelaide	*N.A.*	23.	37.	41.5	44.7	162,261
Perth	*N.A.*	20.	19.6	16.9	19.7	36,274
Hobart	*N.A.*	18.7	18.2	22.8	20.	34,626

Source: T. A. Coghlan, *A Statistical Account of the Seven Colonies of Australasia—1901–2* (Sydney, 1902)

At this point we are not concerned to re-examine the causes of the phenomenon and even less to resume speculation on the consequences, but rather to point out that the building of these cities was an extremely important economic activity, absorbing much private and public capital, and much labor, in the construction of houses, shops, offices, warehouses, churches, hospitals, and other private structures, government buildings, streets, tramways, water works, street-lighting, and so on. In the general strategy of development, urban development was an immensely important tactic, as was starkly revealed when the boom burst.

Architecturally these cities were Victorian and the building boom gave them an appearance which they in large measure retained for years after. In Melbourne especially there was a weakness for constructing buildings of a massiveness that warranted calling them "piles"—for example, Parliament House. Until around 1885 business blocks were rarely more than three stories high, but in that year the Otis elevator reached Australia from the United States and structures up to nine stories were subsequently built. It has been pointed out that in Melbourne the use of basalt stone gave the buildings a "low" tone, whereas in Sydney they used such stone as Hawkesbury sandstone and achieved a golden tone. The most admired buildings exhibited to the full a "wealth and multiplicity of ornament that sometimes reached fantastic levels." A Melbourne building was described in a publication of the 1880's thus: "It is a five-story edifice, the architect of which has adopted the style of the French Renaissance. . . . A somewhat narrow front—consisting of three divisions, the center one recessed, so as to admit of the introduction of an effective bay, is enriched with polished columns and pilasters of red granite—is ornate with carvings in freestone, embracing caryatides, foliated ornament on panels, and a certain elegance of detail. . . . The leading characteristic of the building before us is what would be described, if feminine beauty were being spoken of, as 'a distracting prettiness' . . ." Sydney had the advantage of a superb site on a truly lovely harbor, but its streets were narrow and the city center crowded. Melbourne compensated for its less spectacular natural environment by making its principal streets broad, developing elegant parks close to the central city, and making the most of, while fondly disparaging, its Yarra River. The homes of the well-to-do in this period were, at their most pretentious, Baroque "mansions," the homes of the poor were frequently jerry-built terrace, or row, houses, say seventeen feet wide, the rooms arranged on a "tunnel" plan one behind the other along a hall running completely through the structure, one side of which was blind. Much use was made of cast iron lace-work ornamentation to disguise architectural poverty and provide pleasant relief for the discriminating eye. Public sanitation was bad. Sydney suffered a bubonic plague in 1900. In social tone the cities were, in varying degrees, provincial. Only Melbourne thought of itself as metropolitan. During the boom there was a good deal of pretentious "high living," spiced with vice. Of all the cities Melbourne took the most exuberant pride in itself: "Marvellous Melbourne."

D3

In the late 1880's and early 1890's the whips of adversity lashed the backs of the Australian colonists. At some point not precisely identified, but along in the 1880's, investment of capital for development, both on private and public account, passed from sound investment to overcapitalization in relation to obtainable returns from production and thence in certain areas into rank speculation, as in urban land and buildings. In fact the climate of business became increasingly speculative as the years passed, embracing the pastoral industry, mining, manufacturing, and real estate. The free availability of money from Britain was very important in giving the final disastrous fillip to the widespread miscalculation of economic possibilities, as it had earlier given a fillip to the attainable rate of sound growth. The situation was based upon excessive Australian optimism about the potential of the country and an acceptance of that optimism by the British investors in colonial securities and enterprises. This British optimism about colonial, or overseas, prospects was not exclusively directed to Australia, but was applied more or less simultaneously to, for example, Canada, Argentina, and the United States. But the Australians were nevertheless able to take advantage of it to borrow more heavily on a per capita measure than any other of the developing overseas peoples. So widespread and confident was the British optimism that the Australians were able to draw money out of the British Isles, especially Scotland, in the form of time deposits in pseudo-banks (really building and land speculation organizations) and orthodox trading banks, even after borrowing by Australian public authorities on the London money market had become difficult.

Overcapitalization, for example, became characteristic of the pastoral industry, a fact revealed as attainable returns from wool were reduced by declining prices and as recurring droughts reduced flocks, the money-earning factors in the pastoral complex. It was also shown by drought that the insurance of income by overstocking stations was a highly dangerous expedient, more likely to jeopardize the station's economic structure than to sustain it by increasing its wool clip. An excess of sheep in relation to carrying capacity, representing an intensification of investment, really increased vulnerability, not to mention the havoc it wrought on the pastures.

The symbiotic relation between the growth of the cities and the progressive development of the bush was perceived but it was only loosely understood and out of this failure of understanding arose a radical misassessment of urban prospects. On this misassessment were founded the land and building booms in Sydney and especially Melbourne. The economic autonomy of the cities was, under the conditions actually obtaining, grossly exaggerated. The urban boom, fed by British money, was promoted by the building and land companies, some of which put up the façades of banks. The boomers, for example, re- and overbuilt the City of Melbourne—the inner business area—and subdivided suburban areas and overbuilt them too in a speculative binge which exhibited all the classic stigmata of land booms, including champagne luncheons for prospective customers, notably those only available to the salesmen on Saturdays. A similar but less gaudy outburst also occurred in Sydney.

Public overinvestment was centered on the railways, to their permanent disadvantage. It was perceived by the politicians in the middle 1880's that the railway boom was getting out of hand. In both Victoria and New South Wales an effort was therefore made to depoliticize them by handing them over to independent commissioners, but in Victoria, while this led to improvements on the operation side, it transferred pressure for authorization of new lines, the crux of the matter, from the parliament to the commissioner's office. Unluckily the commissioner proved as susceptible to pressure, or as deeply bitten by the boom psychology, as the parliamentarians, so extension of the system went merrily on until the boom collapsed. In New South Wales, which followed Victoria in adopting the commissioner approach, Sir Henry Parkes had the astuteness to separate the two phases. His commissioner operated the railways, and Sir Henry resolutely defended his independence, but decisions about new lines were made by a parliamentary committee. This had the effect of somewhat disciplining the local members by publicity and delay and in the end left New South Wales in a better position than Victoria when the time of troubles arrived.

Under the stimulation of the inflow of capital, the colonies were over-importing, but the Victorian government was bound to suffer more from a drop in imports because of its heavy dependence upon customs revenue for income. Victoria, therefore, not only pushed the boom farthest and had the most devastating bust, but also was most prostrate in the aftermath.

As the deflationary pressures began to be felt, the entrepreneurs tried to fortify their shaky positions by resisting the demands of the trade unions. This led to a series of catastrophic strikes in which the unions were defeated. The strikes added a special quality of crisis, a new dimension, to the economic difficulties.

Since the underlying trouble was that development had been overcapitalized in relation to the obtainable export returns of the principal industries, and a similar overcapitalization of basic services such as railways, there was under the existing conditions no escape from a financial crisis if the inward flow of capital diminished and prices continued downward. The real estate boom was in this context fuel for the flames. A warning of what was in store, a little obscured by accompanying corruption, occurred in South Australia in 1886 when the Commercial Bank of that colony suspended as a consequence of overinvestment in pastoral properties progressively being weakened in value by drought and declining wool prices. This event sobered Adelaide and tempered optimism in Sydney, but it was ignored in Melbourne. Another warning came in 1891 when the Bank of Van Diemen's Land, a relatively ancient institution, failed. But the crucial warning came from Britain, or should have come—the Melbourne optimists tried to override it—when, as a result of rising interest rates at home and such events as the failure of Baring Brothers as a result of overinvestment in the Argentine, the British investors became skeptical of *all* colonial prospects. A slackening of the flow of money from Britain to Australia was perceptible from 1889. It caused the land and building boom in Melbourne to falter and unemployment in the building trades rapidly to mount. When the British depositors in Australian pseudo-banks began to ask for their deposits back, and this evidence of failure of confidence was communicated to local depositors, the moment of crisis had arrived. The building societies and land banks began to fail in Melbourne and Sydney in 1891 and failures continued during 1892. Personal bankruptcies, some for farthings in the pound, multiplied. Plainly if this lack of confidence were communicated to the orthodox trading banks, a general collapse would ensue. The upshot depended not upon the technical solvency of the orthodox banks but upon the confidence in them of their depositors, overseas and local. Lacking confidence, or their confidence weakened by rumors, runs could be set off. The individual positions of the banks were worsened in that there was no central bank, only the loosest of interrelations among some of them, and no understanding of the situation in the government. The positions of the trading banks depended to an extent upon the depth of their involvement with the building societies and the land banks and the proportion of their deposits held by British owners. The first orthodox bank failed in 1892, victim of its unlucky associations, but the general crisis came in 1893. The Victorian government, ill-advisedly, tried to deal with it by declaring a five-day bank holiday. The government of New South Wales, led by Sir George Dibbs, did much better by making all bank notes legal tender and putting the government's resources behind them. Of twenty-five banks doing business in Australia at the beginning of 1893, fourteen suspended payments. Melbourne money was peculiarly "tainted," as was remarked at the time. The banks with headquarters in Sydney proved much stronger. The majority of the banks that suspended were "reconstructed" rather than liquidated, a process which involved freezing the deposits until such time as they could be paid off through earnings. This the reconstructed banks in New South Wales and Queensland began to do in 1895, in Victoria in 1896, but the Victorian banks took longest to complete the process.

Generally speaking the colonies proved surprisingly resilient. Although they were blighted by the worst drought in their history from 1895 to 1903, with the consequences to the pastoral industry already adverted to and the reduction of wheat production per acre to fantastically low levels, it can nevertheless be said that by 1895 recovery was underway. Export prices which declined steadily from 1889 to 1894 began to rise in 1895. While New South Wales and Queensland proved more actively resilient than Victoria and South Australia, nevertheless by 1898 Victoria, even under the cautious and parsimonious regime of Sir George Turner, was able and willing to resume borrowing for development through railway extension. Victoria, to be sure, had given up population in its desperate search for viability, exporting its unemployed to New South Wales and more particularly to Western Australia which at this time had a boom based on rich gold discoveries, and even to South Africa. Not only did Western Australia absorb people from the depressed eastern colonies, she also provided a providential market for their industries, foodstuff, and manufacturing. If South Australia, for example, profited from Western Australian demand for foodstuffs for the incoming miners, Victoria profited from the demand for manufactures. As a matter of fact the Victorian recovery was chiefly founded upon the continued growth of manufactures and their expansion into intercolonial trade, the rise of the butter industry in Gippsland and the export of butter under refrigeration, a revival of gold mining, the rise in wool prices, and the expansion of wheat acreage. The significant resumption of railway construction was partially to provide rail transport for the newly opening dry, scrub-covered area known as the Mallee.

As the Victorian example implies, recovery in the colonies was in considerable measure attributable to diversification in a context of rising export prices. The wheat industry went on expanding, gathering its forces for the remarkable expansion in New South Wales and Western Australia after the turn of the century. However, the recovery was not exuberant. Unemployment was rife and wages declined. The export price index did not reach the level of 1889 until after the outbreak of World War I. There was no encouragement for immigration and in 1894 the authorities of New South Wales took notice of the fact that the rate of natural increase had declined. Yet the devastating consequences of the adverse developments in credit, prices, climate, and wages did not permanently dampen Australian optimism about the potential. High expectations survived.

CHAPTER XVI

A Congeries of Colonies

For forty years after the gold rushes the vision of a continental Australian nation was obscured by colonial particularism. During the high noon and afternoon of the Victorian era, the six colonies were preoccupied with their own affairs. True, they gave some attention to intercolonial co-operation, as we shall see, but it was a minor theme indeed for most of the years in question. Yet this minor theme adumbrated the future and when, late in the period, men of vision recaptured the continental ideal, essentially what they proposed was to co-ordinate the particularistic colonies, not abolish them, and to enforce the co-ordination through a government with powers to deal nationally with specified matters. This left Australia with a heritage of particularistic governmental powers and emotional loyalties centered in the colonies, rechristened states, which functioned to a marked degree after the fashion of sectionalism in the United States. Though progressively moderated by the effluxion of time, Australian sectionalism, like American sectionalism, has shown a powerful capacity to survive the steady pressure for continental unity.

Yet however constricted the vision of the people and most of the leaders in the era of colonial particularism, they were willy-nilly building a nation, even though in discrete fragments. That a continental economy was the result of their efforts has already been made fairly clear. That their politics, in its detailed expression, also pointed toward a continental vision is rather harder to demonstrate, but if attention is directed toward the larger questions of political orientation and approach, it will be possible to show how out of the political goings-on of the colonies, the orientations and approaches of the Commonwealth era finally emerged.

D3

The six colonies came to be divided into two categories: inner and outer, a classification carried over into the Commonwealth period. The inner group consisted of Victoria and New South Wales and this correctly suggests that the differentiating criterion was population, for these were the most populous colonies, while Queensland, Tasmania, South Australia, and Western Australia were the "outer" colonies. Of the outer colonies, Western Australia was the most isolated from all its fellows, both in fact, feeling, and self-conception. Not until the 1890's was any great progress made toward integrating Western Australia with what the Western Australians called, with a sense that they were remote, the eastern colonies. If the outer colonies had varying senses of "outness" vis à vis Victoria and New South Wales, the two inner colonies were not intimates but rather fierce rivals and some of the more grotesque examples of colonial particularism in action grew out of this rivalry, notably with regard to tariffs. The insults exchanged by Sydney and Melbourne have become imperishable items of Australian folklore.

Within the colonies the colonists were divided politically into urban and rural groups and interests, with the urban groups normally producing the most significant politicians and having the greatest political successes. This may comport oddly with the great common colonial emphasis on rural development in this period, but it should be recalled that the politicians concentrated their attention on the promotion of agricultural settlement as against pastoral development. The urban politician was ordinarily critical of the pastoral rural interest and handled agricultural development like a weapon against the pastoral oligarchy. The building of railways, from the standpoint of money cost the greatest single developmental undertaking by government of the time and the most basic, was largely conceived of as providing for the extension and underpinning of agricultural development. Moreover the urban-oriented politicians were encouraged and strengthened by the fact, emphasized earlier, that urban growth was a natural concomitant of general economic growth under Australian conditions. They acted to encourage that growth in planning the railway networks. And as the cities grew, urban-style political demands upon the politicians were increasingly made and responded to, a fact reflected in the evolution of the content of the liberalism that characterized the most successful politicians of the time. When these urban-oriented liberal politicians came to be challenged by urban radicals closely identified with the trade unions, themselves essentially urban phenomena in spite of their early extension into rural industries, they were forced to define in a rough way the limits of their liberalism, a task not finally completed until the Commonwealth period. The end result of this was the differentiation of the two principal parties of twentieth-century Australia. Both came to be strongly urban-oriented parties, one right and one left, both deeply infused with liberalism of a kind, but one deeply tinged with a kind of conservatism, the other with a kind of socialism. After a time a rural-based party appeared which allied itself with the old liberals to gain office, for while it could survive it could not achieve full national stature, since it made a minimal appeal to the predominant urban electors.

The Australian colonies were democratic socially before they were fully democratic politically, defining full political democracy to mean universal suffrage and the election under it of at least all the legislators. The democracy that W. C. Wentworth and likeminded conservatives feared was really a limited democracy. It early saw to it that the urban interests of which it was fundamentally an expression got more representation than the Wentworths of the time thought proper; it also soon liberalized the franchise, but not conclusively. South Australia showed the way with regard to the franchise by providing from the beginning that there should be manhood suffrage in voting for the lower house. Victoria followed suit in 1857, New South Wales in 1858, Queensland on establishment, but Tasmania not until 1900. However this meant one-man-one-vote only in South Australia, for in the other colonies plural voting—the the extra votes based on property holdings—continued for some time, New South Wales until 1893, Victoria until 1899, Tasmania until 1900, and Queensland until 1905. The only colony to grant women the suffrage was South Australia in 1894. Otherwise Australian women only won the vote after the Commonwealth was instituted. The so-called "Australian" or secret ballot, designed to purify elections, which eventually migrated to the United States, was adopted in South Australia and Victoria in 1856, New South Wales and Tasmania in 1858, and Queensland on its founding. Quite early, also, the term of parliaments was reduced from five to three years, then a warmly advocated reform, except in Queensland, where the five year term was retained. Quite as significant as broadening the franchise in shifting the character of politics was payment of members, introduced in Victoria in 1870, Queensland 1886, South Australia 1887, New South Wales 1889, Tasmania 1890, and Western Australia in 1900. It is quite apparent, however, that until the pressure of the radicals began to be exerted on the Australian politicians they functioned within, and were quite satisfied with, a limited political democracy. One would never gather this from the adverse comments passed on Australian politics and politicians by worried British observers. They saw the faults as a consequence of "extreme" democracy. In their eyes, many of the innovations were identified with Chartism, to them a questionable paternity.

For about thirty years after responsible government was instituted in the middle 1850's, it was a politics without parties. Until 1900 most of the men who achieved political leadership and high office were immigrants of whom a few had arrived young and had been formed in Australia. Of the seven most conspicuous premiers of Victoria between 1857 and 1900 only one was Australian-born; in New South Wales only two. Victoria was ruled by immigrants from England, Ireland, and Scotland; New South Wales by immigrants from England and Scotland. The men who rose to the premiership were storekeepers and merchants, lawyers, journalists and newspaper proprietors, and landowners. Some passed through a variety of occupations before entering politics. It was a politics in which success went to politically masterful individuals who won temporary command of followers whose loyalty remained contingent, subject to withdrawal without notice. The political struggle was between groups and factions which freely dissolved and reformed. A man might lead several ministries during his political life, serve in another man's ministry after having been premier himself, or combine with a rival to form a coalition ministry either led by himself or his erstwhile opponent. The political instability was extraordinary, quite "South American." Victoria had twenty-eight ministries in this period, New South Wales twenty-nine, South Australia thirty-seven, Tasmania twenty-two, and Queensland twenty-one. The cause of this political instability appears to have been the absence of fundamentally differing political ideologies, or points of view, around which parties could be formed. Although men were discernibly "liberal" or "conservative" the difference does not appear to have struck very deep, or to have embraced in many cases the whole range of issues that arose, and policies identified as "liberal," such as protection in Victoria, are only understandable today as such when evaluated in the historical context. Moreover, the content of liberalism changed over time and so did the content of conservatism so that men whose minds ceased to move at a certain moment from either position could find themselves political eccentrics, as happened to the "liberal" Bruce Smith of New South Wales. On the other hand many men identified as liberal or conservative tended to exhibit a large measure of flexibility and it was not unknown for a conservative to introduce a measure in which ostensibly he did not believe, and for a liberal, after years of loyalty to his position, to join a ministry headed by an avowed conservative or vice versa. This was not exactly illustrative of that movement from left to right that political men so often exhibit over a lifetime, though examples of this are numerous enough in Australia, as an accommodation to achieve political stability. Except on the question of fiscal policy, the politicians were ordinarily pragmatists, rarely dogmatic theoreticians. Since in the colonial period their shifting and turning took place in six different contexts, it is difficult to illustrate the points summarily.

Remarkably few of the politicians whose careers were transacted wholly within the colonial period have remained vivid, even in the imaginations of the historians. The single most conspicuous figure among them is Sir Henry Parkes (knighted 1877) of New South Wales, and he more because of his work for federation than for his long labors in colonial politics. In fact most of the colonial politicians who are still esteemed are men whose careers carried over into the federal sphere, such as Samuel Griffith of Queensland, Edmund Barton and George H. Reid of New South Wales, Alfred Deakin and Isaac Isaacs of Victoria, Charles Cameron Kingston of South Australia, and John Forrest of Western Australia. Their careers will chiefly be examined in that context later. Yet in addition to Parkes there is profit in glancing at such men as McCulloch, Service, and Berry in Victoria, McIlwraith in Queensland, and W. R. Giblin in Tasmania. Nobody gained much glory merely marching in the ranks of the parliamentarians.

D3

Parkes was born in extreme poverty in England in 1815, gained but a meager formal education—his self-education became various and considerable—and arrived in Australia in 1839. He became by dint of practice a forceful public speaker, though aspirates gave him trouble to the end. His voice was almost absurdly odd: high and piping. All his life he was essentially a spokesman for the urban middle-class democracy of Sydney. Himself a fabulously bad businessman—his life was punctuated by bankruptcies and he died in poverty—he had a strong bias in favor of entrepreneurial types. He distrusted squatters. His equality was equality of opportunity. His first political identification was with the antitransportation movement; he strongly favored responsible government with more of a democratic emphasis than Wentworth offered, but he became essentially satisfied with the "limited democracy" that was realized by the late 1850's. He opposed payment of members. All his political life a member of the lower house of Parliament he operated in a membership consisting of squatters, farmers, merchants, and lawyers— a middle-class group. Like all politicians of his orientation he had his difficulties with the upper house, but in common with the other New South Wales politicians he settled for control by "swamping" or threat of swamping—that is, by the appointment of additional members to erode a hard core of political recalcitrance. Parkes would have preferred an elected upper house, but he could not get it. Although in his reflective moments Parkes wanted to be a statesman and on occasion came as near to achieving that stature as any of his Australian contemporaries, he was ordinarily a politician among politicians and both gave and took the rough and hard verbal knocks that were then regularly exchanged. He could be scurrilous, and vituperation came all too easily. He participated in intrigues of doubtful respectability. He was guilty of raising some of the most bogus bogies of his time. As a statesman, his contemporaries compared him, somewhat recklessly, to Sir John Macdonald of Canada and W. E. Gladstone. He was one of the very few colonial politicians well known outside the colony in which he made his career. Parkes suffered as many ups and downs as any politician of his day and he added the eccentricity of periodically announcing retirement from politics in disgust, but he invariably returned and died trying to keep in. Possessed to a striking degree of charisma, he early emerged as a faction leader and by 1866 it was expected that he would be chosen premier, but he had to take his first ministerial office under James Martin, next to Charles ("Slippery Charley") Cowper, with whom Martin alternated in office, the most potent politician of the time. Parkes finally won the premiership in 1872 and during the ensuing twenty years was premier no less than five times for a total of twelve years, finally leaving office in 1891. While moving into and out of office, Parkes had successfully made the transition from faction to party, taking leadership of the free traders in the middle 1880's. In his time Parkes jousted with many strong men but with none more persistently and more bitterly than Sir John Robertson who had first been premier a decade before Parkes achieved that office. Then in 1878 these contemptuous enemies joined forces in a government of which Parkes was premier in order to put an end to a period of extreme political instability. Parkes lost his seat in Parliament in 1895 and died early the following year. It is indicative of Parkes's hold over the public imagination that more of his speeches and other occasional utterances were put between hard covers than of any other public man of his period; he wrote quite the best political autobiography of any colonial politician; he had literary aspirations, published six volumes of indifferent verse, and was proud of his friendships with Carlyle and Tennyson. He was married three times and had twelve children; his third wife was not considered a fit person to be received at Government House. For posterity, his image is of a man with a great, craggy face crowned by a heavy head of snow-white hair, a snow-white beard depending. He complained in old age that while the liquor dealers kept his cellar full, nobody thought to send him anything to eat. Altogether Parkes was an eminent colonial Victorian whom it is a pity Lytton Strachey missed.

Sir James McCulloch (knighted 1870) was four times premier of Victoria between 1863 and 1877. Glasgow-born in 1819 he obtained a primary school education and then was apprenticed to a merchant firm. Diligent in the business, he was sent to Melbourne in 1853 to establish a branch. He promptly entered politics. After serving in earlier ministries, he formed, in 1863, the first stable Victorian government; it lasted five years. A conservative and a free trader—the fiscal policy of the merchants and squatters—McCulloch nevertheless introduced a mildly protective tariff under pressure from David Syme, proprietor-editor of *The Age* newspaper, whose political influence, allegedly decisive, has yet to be candidly assessed by historians. At any rate, this action brought McCulloch into conflict with the less supple conservatives of the upper house and a fierce political struggle ensued during which McCulloch only paid the government's expenses by borrowing from a British bank of which he was a local director and then arranging that the bank sue for recovery of the loan, a highly ingenious but also dubious expedient. When the lower house tried to reward with a money grant the governor who had been recalled for his role in the foregoing actions and was blocked again by the upper house, McCulloch, premier for the second time, took up the quarrel but it ended inconclusively when the governor refused the grant. Actually McCulloch's visible talents were those of a stubborn fighter and an obstructionist. Aside from the curious deviation toward protection, McCulloch was not an innovator. He became leader against the upper house only because it tried to frustrate the will of the lower house, this in itself being offensive regardless of the question at issue. He was not disposed to be overnice about choice of weapons in political war. His last two governments were revealingly uncreative. In his rough and hearty way he was and remained a conservative most adequately showing his ability as a merchant, banker, and squatter. One of his pastoral properties included Broken Hill in New South Wales. McCulloch left Australia in 1886 and died in England in 1893.

Sir Graham Berry (knighted 1886) was also closely identified with a celebrated altercation between the two houses—a kind of political exercise to which Victoria was prone—but otherwise he was a very different character from McCulloch. He was, indeed, the archetypical liberal of his time. It has been suggested that he was the Victorian analogue of Henry Parkes, but this does less than justice to Parkes. Berry was a London cockney, born in 1822. His formal education was limited, his self-education less various than Parkes's and chiefly designed to sophisticate him politically and correct his faults of speech—wild aspirates especially—and public deportment. He arrived in Melbourne in 1852 and became a small retail merchant, dealing in general merchandise, wines, and liquors. In 1860 he bought an interest in a newspaper and held such an interest in one or another paper for several years. He entered Parliament as a protectionist and Syme of *The Age* was one of his supporters during his political career. He achieved ministerial office in 1870 and in 1875 formed his first ministry, which was short lived. In 1877, after an election, he again became premier, this time with the heaviest majority behind him achieved to that time in Victoria. It was his boast that his was the first government in Victoria not beholden to any of the big interests of the time, pastoralist, importing merchant, or banking. However Berry proved to be a petty bourgeois, not a labor radical, and he drifted to the right. He quickly aroused the ill will of the upper house by forcing through a land tax bill—anathema to those who were landholders, proof of Berry's dangerous radicalism—and precipitated a crisis between the houses by including an appropriation for payment of members in a general appropriation bill instead of submitting it separately as hitherto. The upper house thereupon rejected the appropriation bill. This cut off funds for government salaries and Berry, to economize, dismissed government servants in large numbers. Whether in doing so he purged political opponents by design became a matter of bitter dispute. This was contention between the houses in excelsis, but after negotiations the upper house passed both a payment-of-members bill and an appropriation bill separately. Berry thereupon undertook to reform the upper house. The upper house rejected his bill and Berry appealed to the Colonial Office, making a trip to London for the purpose, only to be told that he had all the powers he required. During all this political contention Berry's majority had steadily dwindled and for a few months in 1880 he was out of office and James Service, leader of the opposition, was premier. Later in the year, however, after an election, Berry returned to the premiership and put through a bill increasing the membership of the upper house and reducing the property franchise to a nominal amount. He finally lost the premiership in 1881 but in 1883 so far recovered his political position that the house was evenly divided between his followers and those of James Service. They joined to form a coalition with Service as premier. Service, Scottish-born in 1823, arrived in Melbourne in 1853—the same year as McCulloch—and became a very successful importing and wholesaling merchant. He was in and out of politics from 1857 and sat in opposition to both McCulloch and Berry at one time and another. The Service-Berry coalition was a most successful government, neither conservative nor liberal, which passed legislation designed to improve governmental efficiency and also tentatively explored the field of social legislation. Service was, taking him all around, probably the most cultivated man to be premier of Victoria in this era. His active political life practically ended in 1886, but he lived on in ill-health until 1899. Meanwhile Berry had served a term as agent-general in London, had returned to Melbourne and politics, served as treasurer in a government, and finally was elected speaker of the house. In 1897 he retired on an annuity granted him by the government and died in 1904. While it cannot be argued that these three men exhibit all the facets of the many different personalities who held the Victorian premiership in this period, they can reasonably be said to be typical of the successful politicians of the colonial era.

Sir Thomas McIlwraith (knighted 1882), three times premier of Queensland between 1879 and 1893, was essentially a speculator and promoter, in or out of government. An admirer once suggested that he had the elements of a Cecil Rhodes, an exceedingly hasty judgment. Strongly biased toward the pastoral interest but favoring big operators and inflated views of possibilities in any activity, he had as his opponent Sir Samuel Griffith (knighted 1886), who was Queensland's great liberal and urban-oriented politician of this time. Born in Scotland in 1835, McIlwraith was trained as a civil engineer and on emigrating to Australia in 1854, worked for a time at his profession on the Victorian railways. In the early 1860's he acquired pastoral interests in Queensland, settled there, and entered politics in 1868. By 1874 he had risen to ministerial office and first became premier in 1879. On this occasion he had his longest and most memorable term of office, not being ousted until 1883. Griffith led the opposition. Queensland was booming and McIlwraith was in his element encouraging immigration, borrowing for development, brow-beating Parliament into accepting a contract for a Brisbane-London mail steamship service via Torres Strait, attempting the annexation of New Guinea, proposing to build on the land-grant system a railway west of the coastal mountains from the New South Wales border to the Gulf of Carpentaria, and speculating privately in land, mines, and a bank. Griffith brought him down on the land-grant railway proposal. His second term of office as premier began early in 1888 and lasted but five months, not because he had lost his political grip but because his health had weakened. By 1890, however, he felt well enough to return to active politics and there was then performed in Queensland one of those political miracles which so clearly showed how fluid colonial politics was. McIlwraith took office in a government of which Griffith was premier. Contemporaries saw this as a mythological monster, the Griffilwraith. In 1893, when Griffith resigned to become chief justice of Queensland, McIlwraith succeeded to the premiership.

Seven months later, however, he handed it over to Sir Hugh Nelson and before the year was out he had resigned from Parliament. His private speculative empire had been thrown into disorder by the panic of 1893. He died in London in 1900 still trying to fit the pieces together again.

In Tasmania until 1879 when William Robert Giblin began his second and most significant term of office as premier—it lasted five years—politics exhibited in striking degree the stigmata and consequences of factionalism. Not only had it proved impossible to establish stable governments, but it was impossible to carry out public policies upon which there was widespread agreement. Politically and economically Tasmania was locked in a stalemate. Factionalism was rooted in personal and family animosities which had retained their vigor in Parliament long after the public at large had become tired of them. Giblin, born in Tasmania in 1840, was an able and hardworking barrister and solicitor, a liberal-minded man who approached politics by way of the presidency of the Hobart Working Men's Club, a philanthropic enterprise, the patronage of a Sunday school and of football as a corrective of delinquency, and the wish to get railways built to lower the transportation costs of primary producers. He was first elected to the lower house in 1869 and achieved ministerial office the following year. A decade in the house and in and out of office taught him that only a coalition government could stabilize the situation. Giblin's coalition gave Tasmania an orderly financial system, improved the roads, and began a railway system. His example of creative public service brought like-minded men into the house, but Giblin was forced by ill-health to retire from politics in 1884. He was appointed chief justice only to die in 1887 in his forty-seventh year.

These men conducted their political lives in a political environment which, while it has never been reconstructed in detail, was quite certainly raffish indeed. In a sketch of Giblin of Tasmania it is remarked, "... he had none of the qualifications then regarded as necessary to win a seat in Parliament, which included ample financial resources to pay for election campaigns and for 'treating' [i.e., large-scale buying of free liquor] and substantial subsidies to the smaller newspapers." From other sources we learn that while the support of newspapers was very important—for Victorian liberals, the support of Syme's Melbourne *The Age*—this was the era in which newspaper editors wielded great political power—direct contact with the electors was indispensable, involving, especially in rural electorates, much hard travel and endless speech-making to innumerable tiny audiences. In town and country a favorite platform for speakers was the balcony of a hotel—that is, saloon. Handbills and posters were used to advertise candidates and meetings. Heckling of a definitely crude kind was the order of the day and no wise candidate stood up to speak without assuring himself that he had a supporting claque and some burly and efficient chuckers-out. To a very important extent the formation of political opinion was a word-of-mouth operation and a political aspirant had to discover and influence the opinion leaders if he could. They were often exceedingly knobby individuals. It was useful to drink with these fellows. In New South Wales and Victoria there was dissidence over religion—Protestants versus Catholics, and while this came to be focused on the school question, as we shall see, it nevertheless influenced how men voted even when that question was not a major campaign issue. It is also apparent that too elevated and elegant a conception of the proper role of the politician was definitely a handicap, as George Higinbotham found out when he tried to take a high-minded line while opposing an exceedingly earthy candidate, Thomas Bent. It strikes one that colonial politics was a rather solemn business for there apparently was a dearth of political jokes. Only Sir George Reid of New South Wales enjoyed a reputation as a wit and his departures from gravity were not always advantageous to him. Deakin of Victoria had some humor but "silver-tongued" oratory was his forte.

In Parliament, aside from bad manners, disrespectful interruptions, and a willingness to impute corrupt motives, as Deakin was accused of corruption in his dealings with the Chaffeys, and the resulting low tone, the most commonly cited curse was the "local member." This character, known to all democratic parliamentary bodies, was the member whose horizon was limited by the boundaries of his electorate. It was he who turned railway building and other public works into pork-barrel operations, thus corrupting the centrally important developmental activities of government. Peculation seems to have been uncommon, though not utterly unknown, and the public service was more inefficient because of its use in the payment of political debts by appointments to it than corrupt, though a profitable favoritism by ministerial direction was not unheard of. No Australian politician was cynically witty enough to talk defensively about "honest graft." Parkes, Service, Berry, George Reid, and others took legislative steps to eliminate the blots on politics. The New South Wales Parliament seems to have hit bottom in the time of the so-called "wild men" at the end of the century and the beginning of the next. But assiduous attention to these blots no more produces an accurate portrait than omission of them. It must therefore be heavily emphasized that men of very considerable stature emerged from the political morasses to give parliamentary services of inestimable value to their colonies. If a high-minded man like George Higinbotham became alienated from politics, which he patently did not understand, rather early in life, others who were in their individual ways also men of distinguished ability spent many years and fully employed their talents in the political arena, even if occasionally protesting that the game was hardly worth the toll it exacted. In colonial politics, as in any politics, to be successful was not necessarily to be right and to be right might militate against success. It is interesting to observe how many of the numerous lawyers chose to escape from politics, early or late, into the judiciary: for example, Higinbotham, Griffith, Giblin, Barton.

The bitterest critics of Australian colonial politics, mostly visiting Englishmen, were antidemocratic in outlook. As a politics the Australian variety was hardly so bad as to demand a retreat from democracy. This, as their actions indicated, was the verdict of the Australian people. They pushed forward to more democracy, not less.

D3

The issues with which the politicians had to deal were both numerous and complex and considering that many of the men, including some who rose to the top, had but limited educations, it is remarkable that in general they were decently handled. Specialized or professional knowledge was rare among them, aside from the law, unless business and journalism can be alleged to bring valuable and relevant specialized knowledge. Only two of this time can be regarded as having any professional understanding of economics—both Victorians, the university professor W. E. Hearn, whose political influence was peripheral, and the newspaper editor David Syme, the influential outsider—and yet many central political issues were economic. From this time dates the characteristic economic emphasis of Australian politics.

Some of the cleverest and best educated men in the parliaments never achieved the first rank, illustratively Bruce Smith and B. R. Wise of New South Wales, both of whom wrote rather good books on public questions, and the English historian C. H. Pearson, who was in politics in Victoria as an associate of Sir Graham Berry. Those who, regardless of the extent of their formal education, had cultural interests tended to be concerned with literature, philosophy, or theology—one might instance Griffith and his long preoccupation with translating Dante, Deakin's literary and religious concerns, Service and philosophy, Parkes and his poetry. However, most of the politicians tended to be expert, if at all, only in politics, the only professional activity for which, it was remarked, there was no formal educational preparation, an art still in the folklore stage of development, open for practice to the self-confident of any degree of wisdom.

As the focus of politics was the development of the country in terms of an expanding and diversifying economy and increasing the population, so the ordinary focus of thinking about development was the land and its uses. The thinking was heavily influenced by a very florid conception of the quality of the available resources. Even the politicians who were urban-oriented and took up policies which helped sustain urban growth, like the protectionists of Victoria, usually felt strongly that the land and how it was to be used was centrally important. As has been shown already, this resulted in an antipastoralist, pro-agriculturalist outlook. Even the railways, which were an instrument of general development, were so handled that they closely promoted the spread of agricultural settlement and also supported urban growth, though the pastoralists inevitably profited from cheaper and faster transport. While not all the politicians who devised land policies were men of the cities—some were landed men of a liberal turn of mind—most of them were, if only because the most powerful rural interest, the pastoralist, was opposed to the alternative use of the land for agriculture. While in larger part the pastoralists acted from obvious self-interest, there was also involved the conviction that much of the land coveted for agricultural use was not suited for it. Sometimes but not always the pastoralists were correct, but they were usually unable to sustain their point against the general optimism about the Australian potential. Many men became closely identified with particular land legislation, but few or none gained an enduring reputation for astuteness and insight in this crucially important matter. There was always somebody who could, with a show of reason, allege that the legislation was bad, or while perhaps good in principle, was being worked in a disastrous fashion, or was being maladministered either at the ministerial or the staff level or both. The pressure for fruitful favoritism in administration both from actual and aspiring landholders was constant. The politicians had more success in dispersing the public estate than they had in getting the land into the hands of those to whom other politicians felt it properly belonged. Partly this was due to the fact that land dealing was permeated by chicane, partly because technological and economic conditions were not wholly favorable to the spread of agriculture. Even Sir John Robertson of New South Wales, whose name is imperishably associated with the pioneering of the dispersion of the land to agriculturalists, ended his lengthy political career with his reputation in this respect sadly tarnished, in large part because he persisted with remarkable pertinacity in supporting his legislation long after it had been conclusively demonstrated that his intention and the results achieved were very far apart. His great opponent, Sir Henry Parkes, did no better. In 1872 Parkes declared with characteristic grandiloquence, but making a point he felt deeply, that the dispersal of the public estate was "a work of more sacred and tremendous consequence than anything that could fall to the lot of the statesmen of old countries like England and France. As we perform this work, so will rise the structure of society, when we are dead; so will our descendants be free, independent and prosperous men or the reverse..." Yet Parkes never found it possible to upset Robertson's bedraggled legislation and replace it with a better designed scheme, though he tried. In New South Wales, from the 1870's, the selectors organized themselves as a political pressure group. In the end the task of redoing land legislation in New South Wales had to be undertaken as a principal task of an administration with no association with either Robertson or Parkes, that of Sir Alexander Stuart (knighted 1885), banker and merchant, which followed the Parkes-Robertson coalition in 1883. However, Stuart did not find the definitive solution and as land legislation was a staple during the colonial period, so it continued to be into the Commonwealth era. The most radical innovation introduced by the colonial liberals was the land tax. When the working class came into politics, it pushed the land tax hard.

While the population of the colonies increased steadily between 1860 and 1900, the years of greatest increase from immigration were 1881–89. Consistently natural increase was more important than immigration in increasing the population, the reverse of the pre-gold rush period. From 1860 to 1900 immigration supplied only 28 per cent of the increase. The immigrants were largely from the British Isles and mostly from the working class. The British emphasis was given by conscious policy to preserve the British character of the population and colonial institutions. It was supported by the distance of Australia from Europe and the relative costliness of transportation there as compared to North America. Of the continental nationalities, Germans were by far the most important, in 1891 constituting over half of all the continental-born residents and having a history in Australia running back for over fifty years. The second most conspicuous group of non-English-speaking continentals was the Italians who, however, did not exceed a thousand until 1881. Other non-British immigrants were few in numbers and the non-British taken together were hardly numerous enough to color at all markedly the British character of the population or its works. Far more important as a differentiating factor was, as the proportion of native-born rose, place of birth as between "Home" and the colonies. The consequences of this will be examined when the rise of nationalism is discussed. The colonial governments all made use of one or another or several devices for assisting immigrants to make the passage to Australia but beyond underwriting the cost of transportation, paid little heed to the economics of the matter. While prosperity stimulated the interest in assisting immigrants, there was an inevitable lag between providing the finance and the arrival of the people, so that jobs in prospect at the earlier moment might have vanished when the immigrants actually reached the colonies. There was some effort to correlate assisted immigration and the labor needs of authorized public works, but in general the incoming people were left to find their own way to jobs. Other than in exceptional cases, such as the irrigation project on the Murray, no great effort was made to tie immigration to land settlement. When, as in Queensland, this was attempted through the issuance of land orders, it was not successful. A high percentage of the immigrants settled in the cities. Perhaps the most pronounced effect of government intervention was to throw an emphasis on young, able-bodied males, indicating a belief that the newcomers should be available for hard, probably unskilled, work. Tradesmen were usually welcomed by employers, but specialized skills were not constantly in strong demand. The conventional classical higher education of Victorian England was at a heavy discount, except for professors in the universities and clergymen; while men with higher technical training were brought out as individuals to run the railways and for similar tasks. In the ordinary immigrant, brawn was more important than brains.

There was a sharp difference of opinion about immigration between the employers and employees, naturally most active and marked in periods of depression and unemployment. The workers were in general opposed to immigration, alleging that its primary purpose was to flood the labor market, create an unemployed reserve, and bring down wages, while the employers and politicians ordinarly favored it as necessary to the "prosperity and future greatness" of the colonies. After peaks achieved in the early gold rush years money wages declined a bit but real wages nevertheless remained good. Whether or not the stimulation of immigration by government action actually menaced labor standards, the fact remains that it was in this period that working-class hostility to assisted immigration was confirmed, an attitude taken up and maintained by organized labor for many years. This made immigration policy a political issue. The argument was continued into the Commonwealth period unresolved.

However, the acutest difficulties over immigration and the resulting composition of the population arose over the question of the place of Asiatics and Pacific Islanders in the spectrum of national and racial origins. Among the Asiatics, the Chinese were by far the most conspicuous. They were first attracted to Australia in numbers during the gold rushes. This immigration, while soon unwelcome, was from the Australian point of view voluntary in that no Australian agency encouraged it. At a later stage, however, the introduction of Asiatics became involved in the question of labor supply, and employers, occasionally with the collaboration of a government, induced Asiatics—Chinese, Japanese, Indians, Javanese, Afghans, Malayans—to enter Australia to work at tasks and in industries such as railway building, camel transport, pearl fishing, sugar-cane growing, and sugar manufacture and so on, mostly carried on in the far outback and the tropical north from the Queensland sugar country via Thursday Island and Darwin to Broome on the Indian Ocean. The Pacific Islanders, called the kanakas, although first brought to Australia experimentally to work in the pastoral industry of New South Wales, became after 1863 closely identified with the plantation sugar industry of Queensland, though they worked in other industries in small numbers. Their introduction involved Queensland in the scandalous island labor trade. Only the Chinese, and far from all of them, showed a marked tendency to settle in the great cities. Alternatively the Chinese scattered themselves in the near and far outback as market-gardeners and petty merchants. In the cities they formed their own quarters and engaged competitively in certain trades such as furniture making, opened restaurants, and as a conspicuous minority with strikingly un-British customs and habits, inspired the hostility reserved for "out groups" the world around. In the colonial period hostility to Asiatics and kanakas was strongest in the southern continental colonies of New South Wales and Victoria, least virulent in Queensland and Western Australia. The South Australians for a time so administered Northern Territory as to allow the entry of Chinese for menial work such as railway building. At Darwin, a Chinese community became a permanent feature of the town.

The Chinese first caused alarm in the gold rush decade. The Chinese miners tended to earn a living by working over areas and claims abandoned by the European miners, thus not frustrating the Europeans by occupying rich ground. But this did not save them from hostility for their collective earnings appeared substantial and their customs offended. As early as 1855 the Chinese on the Victorian fields were numerous enough and the objections of the European miners strenuous enough to induce the government to legislate to restrict their entry into the colony. This legislation was administratively effective only at seaports and the Chinese continued to enter Victoria overland from South Australia. In 1857 a savage and destructive riot took place at the Buckland River gold field during which the Chinese were driven away, their tents burned, and their personal possessions tossed into the water. The Victorian government thereupon induced the South Australians to pass and enforce restrictions upon Chinese entry into their colony and thence into Victoria. An identical appeal to New South Wales failed to produce results, but when in 1861 there was a violent anti-Chinese riot on the Lambing Flat gold field in that colony, the authorities promptly legislated on the Victorian model. As the gold fever died down these acts were repealed, in South Australia in 1861, Victoria in 1865, and New South Wales in 1867.

Late in the 1870's the anti-Chinese agitation resumed, first in Queensland in 1877 when the appearance of thousands of Chinese on the Palmer field in the north led to the passing of restrictive legislation of the established kind. Then the following year the European workers of the Australian Steam Navigation Company struck in protest at the employment of Chinese seamen on the company's ships, a move that had widespread public sympathy. When, therefore, it was suspected that with the barring of the Chinese from the United States, the tide of Chinese emigration would run heavily toward the Australian colonies, the stage was set for a new spate of restrictive legislation. At that time the resident Chinese population of the colonies had reached 50,000, its historical peak. The indictment of them as a component of the population was various: there was ordinary race and color prejudice at work; they were suspected of harboring dread diseases, specifically smallpox and leprosy; their vices were loathsome, especially opium smoking; their housing was bad and disgustingly dirty; their economic competition, as in the furniture trade, was ruinous; they not only did not conform to colonial economic and social standards, they undermined them, especially in their guise of cheap labor; they were unassimilable, physically and socially, and such miscegenation as occurred was allegedly the result of disgusting vice; they were, in short, a highly objectionable element in the population on many and various grounds. The lead against them was taken by Sir Henry Parkes who, while professing admiration for the ancient Chinese civilization, denied that the resident Chinese really represented it, and elaborated the conventional indictment of them as a component of the colonial population. At an intercolonial conference which opened in Melbourne in 1880 and concluded in Sydney early in 1881, Parkes convinced the politicians of Victoria, South Australia, and Queensland to join his colony in passing fairly uniform legislation designed to stem the inflow. Western Australia did not conform until 1886, and then not too exactly, for while it forbade the entry of indentured Chinese, the entry of voluntary immigrants was permitted—the eastern colonies protested this to the Colonial Office—while Tasmania, where the problem was not acute, did not fall into line until 1887. As it happened it was in 1887–88 that a Chinese influx into Northern Territory was at its height. This provoked a second intercolonial conference on the Chinese problem which brought about not only fairly uniform legislation but also legislation of increased stringency. The Chinese population then began to decline, falling to 32,000 by 1901 and reaching its lowest point in 1947 when it was 6400. At an intercolonial conference in 1896 it was agreed to extend the restrictive legislation to all Asiatics, but Queensland arranged a loophole to allow the maintenance of a body of about 4000 Japanese indentured laborers in the sugar industry. The loophole was closed within five years.

During the four decades of the continuance of the traffic in kanaka laborers, perhaps 50,000 were introduced into Queensland. The practice was initiated by Captain Robert Towns, a brother-in-law of W. C. Wentworth, whose business headquarters were at Sydney but who was interested in island shipping and trading and Queensland pastoral properties. He experimented with cotton production on a large scale during the American Civil War with the idea of supplying the British market and it was to obtain field labor for this enterprise that he turned to the islands. When cotton failed, the rising sugar industry found island labor not only useful but long alleged that it was indispensable. Queensland became, along with Fiji, New Caledonia, and Samoa, a principal base from which recruiters operated, a principal market for island labor. Until 1868 the traffic in kanakas was not subject to any governmental regulation but in that year the Queensland government passed legislation which, however, did not deal with the situation in the islands where recruitment took place and the fouler abuses had developed. To remedy this defect, provision was made in 1870 for government supervisory agents to go in the recruiting vessels to the islands and in 1872 the imperial government took a hand in the regulation of the traffic, concentrating on the supervision of recruitment and using the naval vessels of the Australian station in the work. However, it became apparent that not all the evils were at the island end, for in Queensland conditions on the plantations were often bad, as exemplified by a high death rate.

The kanaka question inevitably became a domestic political issue. Ranged on one side were the defenders of the system, politically conservative in temper, believers in a plantation economy involving extensive landholdings which, they argued, was the only way to develop the tropical country, with kanakas as the indispensable labor force, represented in politics by men of the orientation of Sir Thomas McIlwraith. Ranged on the other side were the domestic critics of the system, including those who were sensitive about the bitter attacks upon it and the honor of Queensland by persons in the southern Australian colonies and Britain, mostly urban-based liberals like Sir Samuel Griffith. While the indictment of the kanaka traffic was moral in essence, the animus of some critics was against the presence in the colony of cheap colored labor competitive with white labor, and of others against the aggregation of land in the hands of a few great owners. It was argued before it was proved in practice that sugar cane could be profitably grown on small holdings and by white labor. Into the 1880's, however, the liberal politicians were content to try to regulate the system both at home and in the islands, the latter in co-operation with the imperial authorities. Their only reward was a series of scandals, some with international reverberations. So in the mid-1880's it was provided by law that recruitment should cease in 1890, Sir Thomas McIlwraith finally concurring. The idea was to use the transition period to introduce workers from Europe, teach them sugar-cane growing and settle them on small holdings when their apprenticeship had been completed. However, both the plantation owners and the trade unionists opposed this, the former in the hope that they could force the resumption of the traffic in kanakas, the latter on the ground that the immigrants would offer severe competition in the local labor market. While the government brought in a few hundred Italians, the unions enticed them from the cane fields, alleging that their pay was far below the Queensland standard. The prospect then was that there would soon be no inflow of kanakas and equally no significant transfer of cane growing to European small farmers. And this impasse came at a time when the industry was beginning to feel the impact of the depression of the 1890's. The result was that a liberal government headed by Sir Samuel Griffith felt that to save the sugar industry it had to authorize the resumption of the kanaka traffic. This was done in 1892, with the expectation that the change-over from kanaka to white labor and from large to small holdings could be accomplished in ten more years. Thus the kanaka system carried over from the colonial into the federal period.

D3

After the gold rushes and for the rest of the nineteenth century Melbourne successfully advertised itself as the financial center of the colonies. However, it is plain from the reconstructed record that more capital was formed in New South Wales during the period. But Melbourne sustained its reputation because it was indeed the center of *speculative* finance and because a good deal of Victorian money was invested outside the colony. For example, Victorians invested in sheep stations in New South Wales, both in the Riverina, which was a kind of economic appanage of Melbourne, and west of the Darling River, in western Queensland and even in the western Kimberley country of Western Australia. Melbourne was also a conspicuous source of speculative mining capital. It was the headquarters of the great Broken Hill mines, even though they were located in New South Wales, and Melbourne capitalists and speculators took a conspicuous part in financing the mining developments in Tasmania, notably Mount Lyell, as well as Mount Morgan in Queensland. The vigor of the Melbourne stock exchange helped give the city its self-cultivated reputation as the center of high finance. Around the exchange circled the famous and not always scrupulous promoters and share-pushers of the times. It was in Melbourne that the greatest paper fortunes were built; it was there that the most patently jerry-built financial institutions were erected; and it was there during the 1880's that the colonial speculative fever rose to its greatest height. Logically it was in Melbourne also that the effects of the inevitable crash were most devastating. A raffish Sydney paper speculated as to how far the scandalous disasters in Melbourne reflected unjustly upon the financial probity of the rest of the Australian colonies.

Of the private money available for investment in Australia perhaps two-thirds was of British origin, the rest representing Australian savings. The money of British origin and ownership was mobilized by banks which were either British banks operating in Australia or locally formed institutions with British connections, including stockholders and depositors. Only one foreign bank operated in Australia in this period, a French institution. The practice of mobilizing British deposits for Australian banks, begun about 1880, seems to have been imitated from New Zealand where it was established during the Vogel boom of the 1870's, and it was pursued with ever increasing vigor as the Australian boom pursued its course, continuing indeed even after the signs of a collapse were visible. Some of this money appears to have been what in a later era was to be called "hot money." As the temperature of the speculative fever rose in the 1880's much British money was also introduced by institutions which often called themselves banks but which really were engaged in speculative ventures in land and buildings, both modest and expansive. Ever increasingly this investment was concentrated in urban properties. When the crash came quantities of "hot money" were caught on deposit and were frozen as a phase of the reconstruction of salvageable institutions.

What role the politicians played in stimulating and sustaining the boom in its private aspects is not too clear. Graham Berry had an antibank bias, but other political figures were closely identified with institutions deeply penetrated by the boom psychology. The truth seems to be that the politicians, generally speaking, were not equipped to take a truly discerning view of what was going on. They might be critical of the banks but they did not see any way to discipline the financial institutions by legislation or treasury policy. Mostly they appear to have had confidence in the private bankers, believing that all were as wise as some of them unquestionably were. They did not notice when the wiser bankers had lost effective control. They did not understand the situation well enough to perceive either the falsity of the values that were being developed by speculation or the unsoundness of the financial structures that were supposed to sustain them. When the crisis came the Victorian politicians did not quite know what to do.

On the other hand, the great contribution to the boom by the politicians was the railway building boom which they initiated and sustained, piling up a heavy burden of debt. When David Syme attacked the grandiose plans of the Victorian politicians for railways he unquestionably touched a vital nerve, for the railways were at the center of the borrowing-for-development policy which had become the common property of all the politicians in every colony. Apparently Sir Henry Parkes initiated the policy in the Australian colonies by imitating Vogel's gambit in New Zealand. He did so in the 1870's before the risks were apparent. It is significant that the Australian politicians concentrated their attention on transportation, like Vogel, though this emphasis was strongly recommended to them by Sir Hercules Robinson who advocated a "spirited program of public works" when he was governor of New South Wales; it was he who conveyed the idea to Parkes. Of course the politicians hoped to gain the sweets of rapid development while avoiding the sours of depression. But while concentrating their minds on bringing colonial resources into more intensive use, debt-burdened, they neglected to devise any criteria for judging the soundness of the development and equally failed to take account of the factors in the international economic context, such as prices for primary produce, which could by adverse movement upset their calculations. Hence the strong disposition to poorly devised planning and extravagance, both accentuated by the pork barrel approach.

The fact that the private and the public booms ran concurrently meant that one helped sustain the other. The ex post facto judgment is that the public boom was the stronger of the two and that government investment, even when ill-advised, was usually in works expected to be "reproductive," not real estate "values." The booms were also competitive, of necessity in a fashion that intensified the general inflationary effects, both in London and in the colonies: in London by virtue of the fact that both made demands upon the money market at the same time, in the colonies by calls on labor and materials at the same time. This was understood by some during the course of the boom but it seems not to have suggested any conscious policy of accommodation to either the private or the public financiers. Definite signs of a slowdown came in the late 1880's, the crash in its financial aspects in the early 1890's. But the disaster, assessed as catastrophic, especially in Victoria, did not make an end to borrowing-for-development. It survived to become a conspicuous item in both the state and Commonwealth inheritance from the colonial politicians.

While the borrowing-for-development policy appealed to the majority of the colonial politicians in all the colonies, early or late as local circumstances dictated, they differed decisively about what they called fiscal policy, especially in Victoria and New South Wales. All the colonies had inherited from earlier times a tradition of using the tariff for revenue purposes, and all in one way and degree or another continued the practice, but Victoria beginning in the late 1860's began to develop the tariff protectively, while New South Wales accepted free trade doctrine. The only colony besides Victoria to move to protection was South Australia, under Charles Cameron Kingston's leadership. Tasmania teetered on the brink. Free trade was, of course, the orthodoxy of the Empire and in the Australian colonies the policy of the squatters and the importing merchants. Although there were protectionists in Victoria before Syme of *The Age* newspaper, it was Syme who did the missionary work for the doctrine and made it a practical political question. He appears to have been motivated by two considerations, first by a powerful conviction that no first-class people should remain forever "hewers of wood and drawers of water"—that is, wholly occupied with primary production, and hence but a market for the manufactures of others, in this case the British, and second by the conviction that factories would absorb the excess labor which tended to accumulate in Victoria, especially Melbourne. It has been suggested that the doctrine caught on in Victoria because revenue from land sales declined rather early in that colony, necessitating a search for an alternative source of income for the government. Protection was fortuitously at hand. As has been pointed out already, the protective tariff operated to confirm and support the urbanizing forces in work in Australian society. It was in effect and in genesis an urban doctrine or at least by encouraging industrialization it established the most powerful urbanizing influence of them all. In the Victorian situation it was a doctrine of the political liberals, chiefly because free trade was the doctrine of the importing merchants and squatters who were political conservatives. Their voice was *The Argus* newspaper which ably fought their rear guard action. Some of the liberals, for example Alfred Deakin, a Syme-indoctrinated protectionist, even gave the doctrine a laboristic twist by arguing that it was a people's policy in that it generated much-needed jobs. How Deakin sophisticated this argument in the Commonwealth period with curious consequences for the labor politicians, will appear later on. That it also inevitably developed another capitalist interest, normally conservative in politics, was not then too apparent. But clearly protection was not liberal by inherent character; it was rather liberal in Victoria because of local circumstances.

In New South Wales free trade was the dominant doctrine politically, with protection the minority view. Interestingly enough, free trade had an association with liberalism in New South Wales, this showing how fortuitous the association of protection with liberalism in Victoria really was. The paladin of free trade in New South Wales was Sir Henry Parkes, a convert to the doctrine, for early in his career he flirted with protection. It was around free trade that he was able to build a party and depart from factionalism in the middle 1880's. But whereas in Victoria free trade sank slowly into inanition, in New South Wales protection slowly gained life and strength, though it never in the colonial era was able to achieve political dominance. In New South Wales politics, protection was identified with Sir George Richard Dibbs. Sydney-born, Dibbs had had a checkered career in business before he entered politics in 1874 as a free trader. He had a brother, to whom he was close, who was a banker. Dibbs associated himself with the groups that opposed both Sir Henry Parkes and Sir John Robertson and, while serving in short-lived governments formed when neither of these formidable leaders could command support in the premiership, moved over to protection. He was able to increase the customs duties but not to install protection as an established policy. He first achieved the premiership in 1885 in succession to Sir Alexander Stuart who had resigned because of ill-health. Dibbs was thereafter in and out of office until 1894 when he was defeated at the polls and left politics. Until 1891 his free trade opponent was Sir Henry Parkes, and afterward Sir George Reid. Not until 1891, when Sir Henry Parkes lost the premiership for the last time, was Dibbs able to form an avowedly protectionist ministry, but even this did not mean that New South Wales had become a protectionist colony, for when Dibbs went out of office in 1894 he was succeeded by Sir George Reid, as ardent and doctrinaire a free trader as one could hope to find. Reid indeed not only kept New South Wales in the free trade column but represented the free trade position in the discussions of federation and went on to lead the free traders in the federal Parliament when it was constituted. It was only after federation that the intercolonial differences over fiscal policy were finally settled in favor of protection. It has been suggested that free trade had such a long run in New South Wales because its land revenues held up to high levels long after they had fallen in Victoria, but this ignores that inadequate customs revenues obliged the New South Wales politicians to search for alternative sources of revenue to supplement income from land sales and they also freely borrowed for development.

The difficulty in discerning the effect of free trade as against protection on the economic development of New South Wales and Victoria was pointed out in discussing the rise of manufacturing. The differences in fiscal policy between the two colonies seem definitely to have been rooted in political ideology, not related to fundamental differences in economic structure or economic consequences—a politics deeply tinged with a doctrinaire devotion to differing approaches, David Syme's economic "heresy" on the one hand, the free trade position of the British Cobden Club by which both Parkes and Reid were singled out for honors, on the other.

D

The colonies tempered their separatism by periodical conferences, held from the early 1860's to the late 1890's, at which they discussed matters believed by some at least to be of common interest. Usually the intercolonial conferences were attended by the premiers—they thus became historical precedents for the Premiers' Conferences under the federation—but ordinarily they were accompanied by the cabinet members directly in charge of the matters discussed and sometimes the lesser officials met by themselves. All the Australian colonies were participants, and occasionally New Zealand and Fiji. The topics canvassed at meetings covered a fairly wide range, including tariffs, defense, immigration including Asiatic exclusion, the idea of a common court of appeals, overseas postal services including the ports to be served, the terminal port for the ships and branch services to outlying points, cables, lighthouses, the arrest of offenders and their extradition, the handling of absconding debtors, wife and child desertion, the recovery of debts and damages, patents and trade marks, the problems that would arise when the railway systems met at borders, and control of pleuropneumonia in cattle. In no single case was uniformity easily achieved. Not only did conferences break up without a final meeting of minds, but all colonies were not represented at all the conferences, even when this appeared to be vital, and an agreement made at a conference might fail of acceptance by one legislature or another, the delegates who made the agreement might go out of office before the matter could be dealt with legislatively and a renegotiation be required to meet the ideas of a new administration, or one or another party might prove apathetic about a matter on return home, resulting in frustration by procrastination. Rivalries between the colonies might muddle seemingly neutral matters badly as when Victoria tried to make Melbourne the terminal point of the overseas mail service at the expense of Sydney. Even Chinese exclusion was achieved only at the cost of a protest by the eastern colonies to the Colonial Office against Western Australian reluctance to conform. But no matter gave half the trouble, or was so fundamentally divisive as tariffs.

It will be recalled that the imperial authorities sought uniformity of tariffs in the Australian colonies, but the colonies insisted on exercising their fiscal autonomy independently. The essence of the contention among the colonies became a struggle to achieve a reasonable uniformity, or mask the effects of difference, after the differences had become well established. Three colonies were chiefly involved in this effort, Victoria, New South Wales, and South Australia. Their differences rose to plague proportions, not so much with regard to international trade (the imposts on which could be collected at their ports of entry), as with regard to trade across their inland borders. Traffic on the Murray River caused most of the trouble. Quite apart from trade between the colonies across the river, imports reached destinations in Victoria and New South Wales by coming upriver through South Australia and exports from both went down river and abroad through South Australia. As sharp differences in tariffs developed both the cross-river, or intercolonial, and the international trade via the river caused trouble. When there was no free trade between the colonies, an internal transport artery like the Murray compounded the difficulties. The colonies such as Tasmania, Queensland, and Western Australia, whose trade, whether intercolonial or overseas, moved chiefly or wholly by ocean transport, also had a stake in the questions at issue, but their actions were less spectacular. Tasmania asserted that the Victorian tariff depressed its natural trade with Victoria and the industries that grew up behind the Victorian tariff barriers, when their products were sent into Tasmania, also hindered her economic progress. Even remote Western Australia eventually felt that it had to set up tariff barriers against goods from the eastern colonies. With regard to the crucial problem of the trade on the Murray, South Australia, to guard her interest in it, tried hard to arrange a modus vivendi between Victoria, New South Wales, and itself, without ultimate success. The two principal opponents tried various expedients of adjustment, including lump sum payments by Victoria to New South Wales, the establishment of customs houses on the river, and periodic efforts to arrange tariff uniformity, the latter usually ending in utterly futile attempts of one colony to impose its tariff on the other. As already noted, they built railways to divert traffic from the river into channels they could control directly. The customs houses were the most conspicuous and offensive symbols of the absurdity of the situation and they suggested to some clever phrase-maker the expression, "the barbarism of borderism." But in the absence of a massive change of heart and policy, the prerequisite of both being the establishment of the vision of a continental nation, the problem was insoluble. In the late 1860's a way out was thought to have been found by the Tasmanians through the device of a customs union, but the Victorians quashed the idea by insisting that the tariff of the union be its tariff and that it have sole right to make changes in the imposts. This was, of course, an unacceptable proposition, though a measure of Victoria's provincial arrogance. By obvious logic, Tasmania then proposed that such colonies as were interested, including New Zealand, might adopt a policy of reciprocity, in effect trading tariff concessions for mutual support and benefit. This proposal ran afoul of the imperial policy of free trade between the imperial units but imperial resistance to a colonial policy tended to unite all the colonies. They protested to the Colonial Office this limitation on their right to manage their own affairs, as the Canadians had earlier protested in a similar situation, and eventually established their right to negotiate reciprocal arrangements among themselves. The permission was given formal shape in an imperial act, the Australian Colonies Duties Act, 1873. It did not solve the problem of intercolonial trading relations and, as a matter of fact, the basic argument between free trade and protective tariff was passed on in a fairly virulent form by the colonies to the federal Commonwealth.

However, no amount of contention and divisiveness could quite destroy the realization that the Australian colonies and perhaps also New Zealand and Fiji had common interests and needed uniformity of legislation even when the record showed that agreement on policy was difficult or impossible to achieve. Thinking that the problem might yield to different machinery from the *ad hoc* intercolonial conference a new tack was taken in 1883. Inspired, significantly, by a realization that the representations to the imperial authorities about policy with regard to the islands, specifically New Guinea and New Caledonia, would have more weight if they proceeded from a united group of colonies, it was suggested at the 1883 intercolonial conference that a Federal Council be formed. At the conference James Service of Victoria advocated federation "pure and simple," but this was running too far ahead of prevailing sentiment and on the motion of Sir Samuel Griffith of Queensland the proposal for a Council was accepted. Sir Samuel drew up a bill to give the idea form. His council had limited legislative powers, but no executive and no control over revenue and expenditure. It was a weak body; Sir Henry Parkes later called it "rickety." It was authorized to deal with certain matters on its own motion: fisheries in waters outside territorial limits, service of civil process and enforcement of judgments in criminal process beyond the borders of a colony, extradition of offenders, and, to the points immediately engaging the attention of the current conference, "relations of Australasia with the islands of the Pacific" and "prevention of the influx of criminals." In addition the colonial legislatures might refer matters to the Council upon which the Council could legislate but only with effect in the referent colonies: defense, quarantine, patents and copyrights, bills of exchange, weights and measures, marriage and divorce, and in fact anything about which the colonies could legislate upon which uniform legislation might be wanted. Many of the matters specified had already engaged the attention of the intercolonial conferences with no effect. Since a body like the Council could only be formed after imperial legislation, the colonies of Victoria, Tasmania, Western Australia, and Fiji "prayed" that the imperial parliament so legislate, which it did in 1885, inserting in the bill certain provisions designed to facilitate growth into a truer and firmer federal form. The legislation was then accepted by Western Australia, Tasmania, Queensland, Victoria, and Fiji. Fiji, however, attended only the first meeting of the Council; South Australia joined and participated for two years, 1888–90; while New South Wales and New Zealand never joined. Meetings were held periodically from 1886 to 1899, the first meeting being held in Hobart, the last in Melbourne. Little was accomplished at any meeting. Failure was really to be attributed to the weakness of the instrument but it was popularly ascribed to the fact that New South Wales, the acknowledged senior colony, stood aloof and the blame for this was placed on Sir Henry Parkes. However, Parkes, like Service, had come to want a federation "pure and simple" (whatever that was) and was prepared to wait and work for it, not compromise and hope that an amoebic instrument would be transformed into a higher organism over time, as Service had for some reason chosen to do.

If their relations with one another were uneasy and occasionally difficult, the relations of the colonies and the imperial authorities were also. The colonies, after the middle 1850's—Western Australia after 1890—were engaged in discerning the meaning of responsible government. Responsible government, meaning the responsibility of the local executive to the local legislature from which it had emerged, was not mentioned by name in any of the constitutional instruments. It was a convention rather than a constitutionally described or prescribed form and the pattern of the convention was that worked out in Britain and still, as it happened, fluid. The establishment and development of responsible government in the Australian colonies was therefore a matter of the transit of a fluid institution from one country to another, from a metropolitan country to a colony, and its adaptation to local requirements. In the colonies the burning issue was not the detail of established practices in working responsible government—these were accepted and adapted with reasonable reverence—but the extent of the power to govern that had passed to the colonials. The colonials tended to claim all the power they felt they needed to deal faithfully with their internal affairs, and to claim it pragmatically as required, arguing each case as it arose. They conducted their arguments with the Colonial Office in London of which the governor, though viceregal, was effectively the local agent. Confronted with the forward moves of the liberal and radical politicians, the conservatives of course resisted them, often supporting their position by alleging that it represented "loyalty" to Britain while that of their opponents represented "disloyalty." This rather crass exploitation of patriotism for strictly political ends became an established conservative political tactic and carried over into the Commonwealth period. The tactic is more understandable when it is realized that to the more fearful conservatives, every move that loosened, or appeared to loosen, the ties with Britain was regarded apocalyptically as forecasting the breakup of the Empire. Occasionally imperial legislation was needed to give legal effect to a colonial wish, as just noted with regard to reciprocal tariff deals and the Federal Council. A landmark in consolidating the legislative capacity of the colonial parliaments was the Colonial Laws Validity Act, 1865, passed by the imperial parliament and applicable throughout the Empire, of which the inspiration was a desire to settle a protracted conflict in South Australia between the eccentric Mr. Justice Boothby and the local legislature over the validity of certain local legislation, alleged by Boothby to be "repugnant" to the law of England. The act defined repugnancy in a fashion favorable to the colonial freedom to legislate as seemed fitting and proper in the local context. Because of its role, the Colonial Office was regarded as hidebound by tradition, unable to move with the times, with a desire, imperfectly concealed, to maintain a relation to the responsible governments more proper with regard to crown colonies. In the vituperation of the Colonial Office in this period there are precise echoes of the vituperation directed at it by Charles Buller and the colonial reformers of an earlier time.

Among the colonial theoreticians of the powers properly to be claimed and exercised by a colony enjoying responsible government none was more vigorously forward than George Higinbotham of Victoria. It is useful, therefore, to note the limits of colonial power Higinbotham recognized. Writing to Sir Henry Holland in 1887, Higinbotham stated in the course of a very long letter (italics supplied):

By the terms of the Victorian Constitution Act power is given to the Crown, the Legislative Council, and the Legislative Assembly to make law in and for Victoria *in all cases whatsoever* . . . Questions involving Imperial interests, including the control of Her Majesty's military and naval forces, and questions affecting relations with foreign states, do not come within the purview of the Constitution Statute . . . I conceive it to be an object of the very highest importance . . . that Her Majesty's Imperial Government, while giving its earnest attention to the wishes and views of the Australian colonies, should convey to them in unmistakable terms its determination to perform its own duty to the empire by refusing to recognize or permit any direct interference with international questions by the Government or the people of any part or parts of the empire.

The full text of Higinbotham's letter makes it clear that his reference to international affairs covered such episodes as McIlwraith's attempt to annex New Guinea, the resolutions of the intercolonial conference of 1883, Alfred Deakin's assertion of the desirability of giving primacy to colonial policies in the islands, and similar Australian efforts to deal with international questions. Higinbotham, then, conceived of an Australian colony *circa* 1887 as a part of the Empire with full power to govern its internal affairs according to the best light it could generate but with no power whatever to deal with international affairs. The latter were exclusively for the imperial authorities to handle. If Australian colonies wanted to deal with them they wanted to be independent countries, a question separate from that of the absolute right of domestic self-government. It was Higinbotham's view that most of the difficulties that arose from the colonial efforts to make good his view of their powers were attributable to the antiquated nature of the instructions issued to the governors by the Colonial Office.

Higinbotham's conclusions—which he felt were largely his own because, he said, "Australian politicians have been, as a rule, perfectly indifferent to the highest questions of public law," careless of it both positively and negatively while pursuing their chosen courses—were, in the judgment of a later expert, less law than statesmanship. He transformed a vision of what was logically possible into something that he asserted to be. It only came into being in time. But the point here is not whether Higinbotham was right in law; it is that he brought to elegant expression a point of view that complemented the nationalistic aspirations of the Australians, except in their international expression. It turned out that it was with regard to their domestic concerns that the Australians became most nationalistic in the colonial and early Commonwealth period. They eventually came to accept in large measure Higinbotham's conception of their position imperially and internationally. Their nationalism was most vociferous and radical before they launched a continental nation, as we shall see, so that, paradoxically, they were most nationalistic when they were also most particularistically colonial. Only a tiny and ineffectual minority of Australians ever identified their nationalism with independence.

CHAPTER XVII

Toward a Continental Commonwealth

"Bourgeois" is the word that springs spontaneously to mind to describe the society that developed in Australia, a "new world" society without a hereditary aristocracy—no feudal background—and but a limited capacity for accepting and maintaining either a *soi-disant* local or imported aristocracy. It was a society which was, on the whole, content with its colonial status. Even the most extreme assertion of local autonomy left the colonial political position fundamentally undisturbed and in cultural affairs and manners, colonialism was unalloyed. It was of course a society in which the bourgeoisie was divided between the city and the bush—in the city between the politically conservative and the politically liberal, in the bush between the well-established squatters and the struggling agriculturalists, divisions moderated but not eliminated by political maneuvers. By the same token it was not monolithic ideologically; it was not, for example, rigorously devoted to the principle of private enterprise in economic affairs; neither was it 100 per cent laissez faire. Under the colonial middle class the state could and did engage in the construction and management of railways, telegraphs and water supply, not because anyone believed in state socialism—if they knew the term—but because it had been decided, pragmatically and realistically, that this was a proper way to give aid to private enterprise and to strengthen meaningfully the prevailing dogma of equality of opportunity. Equality of opportunity—the emphasis falling on opportunity to accumulate income-producing property —in a relatively "open" society was the ideal, the state *assisting* in the ring as well as holding it, and in the case of advanced liberals, the way open to the use of the state power to protect and advance the interests of those far back in the race for economic success, or those who were of an age to drop out of it unsuccessful.

The conclusive justification for this kind of society was believed to be the wide diffusion of wealth. As early as 1854 this was asserted to have been accomplished in the colonies and during the rest of the century it was frequently reasserted. Sir Henry Parkes waxed rhetorical on the theme; the great statistician Sir Timothy Coghlan supported it in these words: "Wealth is widely distributed, and the contrast between rich and poor, which seems so peculiar a phase of modern civilization, finds no parallel in these southern lands. That there is poverty in these colonies is undeniable and inevitable; but no one in Australia is born to poverty and that hereditary pauper class which forms so grave a menace to the freedom of many states has therefore no existence here." With regard to the working class the assertion was usually given substance by citing high wages, low cost of living, savings bank accounts, and home ownership. Indeed one defense of Australian democracy against its critics was that it was not menacing to the higher social interests precisely because it was a property-holding democracy. However, those on the lower levels of the economic pyramid took a rather more critical view of the general social situation and the particular situations in which they found themselves. They early resorted to trade unions to protect and improve their position, at first accepting the prevailing ideology but gradually working around to a radical critique of it.

D3

Organizations of free workingmen, small, weak, and usually transient, existed in Australia before the gold rushes. Indeed combinations of convict laborers are known to have existed, severely repressed though they were if discovered by the authorities. And it is useful to summon from the shades those Dorsetshire laborers who were transported to Australia in 1834 for attempting to form a trade union. They had no direct influence on Australia, but the example of the English unions that followed after and honored them certainly did. These things had been forgotten when the Australian workingmen turned to unionism after the rushes.

Unions began to be formed in the 1850's but the years of consolidation and growth were the 1870's and 1880's. The early unions were, like their pre-gold rush predecessors, a mixture of trades unions and benefit societies. Their legal position was highly ambiguous both in law and before the courts since the masters and servants acts dating back in origin to the days when the labor force was a mixture of convict and free workers were still in force. Not until the late 1870's did any colony update its legislation with regard to unions by adopting the new English acts of that decade. South Australia led the way in 1876.

During the 1880's New South Wales (1881), Victoria (1884), Queensland (1886), and Tasmania (1889) took the same step. Western Australia delayed until 1900. But even this improved legislation, when taken in conjunction with other acts dealing with employer-employee relations and relevant matters, left the unionists still in considerable jeopardy in severe strike situations, as was discovered in the 1890's.

With rare exceptions the early union spokesmen had little to propose or allege that was alarming to the colonial liberals. It took several decades and much heavy pressure from the left, beginning in the 1880's, before the trade unionists and their political associates reached a final parting of the ways with the liberals. While many of the older liberals drew a line rather early, and others showed clearly where they stood when the great strikes occurred in the 1890's, men like Alfred Deakin found it possible to work closely with labor into the Commonwealth period. The early labor leaders were within the liberal ideology in their thinking, bent upon promoting their interests but expressing no class consciousness of the radical kind and making no programmatic proposals that implied radical social reconstruction. Class consciousness seems first to have become noticeable in the colonies during the 1880's, as a robust assertion of the worth and rights of the men-of-no-property, in part envy of the successful, anticapitalist, even anticapital, but rarely revolutionary. The labor revolutionaries were of the movement, but peripherally, irritants to the usually very moderate leadership, bogies to its opponents.

Until the middle 1870's the labor organizations were mostly mixed benefit and craft unions, strongest—purely relatively—among the urban skilled workers, the "aristocrats" of labor. It was these urban craft unions that pioneered interunion co-operation through trade and labor councils—the first was formed in Melbourne in the 1870's—and also intercolonial conferences of unions, the first held in Sydney in 1879. However, in the 1870's a change came over the union scene, called the New Unionism. Organizationally this meant the formation of unions designed to bring into a single fold all the workers in an industry, regardless of specialized skills or crafts. Pioneered in gold mining in Victoria in 1874 this type of mass union was extended to include the coal miners of Newcastle and the base metal miners of Broken Hill in New South Wales. It was established among the seamen in 1876 and, finding entry through the shearers in 1886, it was the basis for the organization of the pastoral industry. This extended unionism into rural industry, a most remarkable accomplishment—in other countries rural workers have only been organized belatedly—explicable largely by the fact that a shearing shed was like a factory manned by itinerant hands who traveled to their work in groups, usually from a common place or district of permanent residence. These new unions were not only industry wide, they were intercolonial and had connections with the unions of New Zealand. By a process of amalgamation there eventually emerged an Australian Workers' Union, the largest and occupationally the most inclusive union in Australia. The new unions were by emphasis trade unions, with the benefit society character subordinate and fading. The great figure in the organization and development of the "new" unions was William Guthrie Spence who had been brought to Australia from Scotland as a child. By trade a miner, he was by gifts a skilled organizer and negotiator. He became a politician. Spence's unions were the strongest built in the colonial period.

At no time in the colonial period were the majority of the workers unionized, nor all in any trade or occupation. There were always outside the unions great numbers of nonunion workers, not regarded as a menace as long as employment was plentiful, but who gave the union leaders a keen interest in the state of the labor market. They correctly saw in an excess supply of workers or the availability of any special kind of cheap labor a menace to their positions. This led them to take up such positions as opposition to assisted immigration and opposition to Asiatic, particularly Chinese, immigrants. They also tried to obtain a preferential position for unionists in employment—the closed shop. It was efforts to rule out the use of nonunion labor alongside union workers in an industry in which the union believed itself strong that led to the bitterest of strikes. Out of this arose also the virulent hostility to "scab" or blackleg labor and, at a later time than this, the campaign for compulsory union membership. The unions thus early tried to control the supply of labor in the organized trades. In the colonial period they never came near a monopoly and, indeed, their failure to calculate correctly how far short of it they were led to a great disaster.

The first important labor campaign was for an eight-hour day. The masons of Sydney led the way, alleging that the established ten-hour day of their trade was, in the hot Australian sun, damaging to health. However, so moderate were some of the workers that to gain their end they were willing to give up the wages for the two hours they proposed not to work. Others asked ten hours' pay for eight hours' work, arguing that the last two hours were unproductive due to fatigue. It is interesting, too, that some were touched by "knowledge chartism" and argued they wanted the time to improve their minds, a prerequisite to rising in the world. The movement was nevertheless ordinarily supported by the simple slogan, eight hours' labor, eight hours' recreation, eight hours' rest. As in New Zealand the boon was won trade by trade, location by location, and did not become universal or permanent. There were retrogressions in bad times. As a matter of fact the eight-hour demand became a permanent demand of the unions, raised recurrently during the colonial period, steadily on their agenda. No legislation in support of it was passed and at best it was a widely accepted convention, supported by agreement between employers and employees, recognized in government enterprises. Statutory prescription was regarded as wrong, an abridgement of the freedom of the workers. Sir Henry Parkes, who had supported the eight-hour movement in its early stages, felt so strongly about legislating the reform that he parted company with labor and the premiership in 1891 when labor proposed to legislate an eight-hour day for coal miners.

The heritage of wage scales from the gold rush period was good but there was a downward drift as the shortage of labor characteristic of the rushes gave way to surpluses and general economic conditions became poor. The early unions were therefore as much concerned with resisting reductions of wages as with increasing them and more concerned with shortening hours than increasing pay. In the 1880's, when boom conditions obtained, attention was given to improving the wage scale with considerable success in some occupations. However, there appeared at this time the phenomenon of pockets of low wage, low standard employment, chiefly associated with manufacturing in the cities. "Sweating," a combination of low wages, long hours, bad conditions, and out-work, appeared most famously in Melbourne behind the tariff barriers but also in free-trade Sydney. In the sweated trades, while unions of male workers existed and the tailoresses pioneered the unionization of female workers, they were not able to combat and control sweating from their own strength. An Anti-Sweating League was formed in Melbourne by liberal politicians, Samuel Mauger president, Alfred Deakin treasurer, and parliamentary interest was enlisted in an attack on the evil by legislation. This was an early example of an association between labor and political liberals to achieve a social end important in the eyes of both.

The colonial leaders were ambivalent about the use of the strike weapon. They used it freely but they found it deplorable that they had to. In organizing and building the "new" unions he brought into being, W. G. Spence authorized and sometimes personally directed several thousand strikes and in the outback developed the useful device of the "strike camp" where striking itinerant workers could congregate. But Spence held no brief for strikes. He would have much preferred to discuss his demands across the table with the owners and indeed offered to do so. But faced with refusals, strikes were resorted to—to enforce demands. Leaders of the craft unions also disliked strikes. The workers rarely had any personal resources to sustain themselves and their families during strikes and the unions were decidedly low-budget affairs without large strike funds. Some of the union leaders publicly took the line that workers and employers had common interests of a kind and magnitude that should, once employers' minds were disabused of misconceptions about the unions, lead them into peaceable collaboration. Since this proved more or less a pious hope, not a reality, some leaders thought they had found a way out through conciliation and arbitration by neutral disinterested bystanders, without government participation. However, it was not until the 1890's after tremendous strikes had occurred that conciliation and arbitration were given a real trial and, significantly, then under government direction and control, sponsored by liberals sympathetic to labor seeking, as it was put later on, to establish a new province for law and order.

There was a steadily increasing interest in politics among the colonial unionists. It originated in the personal interest taken in such issues as land legislation by the pioneer union leaders. It gradually became accepted that some union concerns—regulation of the condition of work-rooms and machinery, the terms of compensation for accidents, the conditions of work in the mines and on the railways, etc.—could better be dealt with through legislation than through union-employer negotiations. Legislation on these matters was obtained from the parliaments beginning in the 1870's. A scattering of working-class members early appeared in the lower houses of Victoria and New South Wales, commonly elected by constituencies where legislation of this type was a matter of public interest. In the 1880's it was recommended at intercolonial trade union conferences that efforts be made to win parliamentary representation. While experiments were made in organizing for political action, no party of the workers emerged in any colony until after 1890. Various reasons have since been adduced to explain why so characteristic an expression of the Australian labor movement as it eventually developed was late in emerging. It has been pointed out, *inter alia,* that the unions lacked the requisite size and strength successfully to organize politically, that the workers were disadvantaged under the laws governing the franchise, that in colonies other than Victoria legislators were not paid until the late 1880's, that in Victoria the workers were politically under the spell of the liberals, that heavy enough concentrations of workers within constituencies did not exist even in the cities, where union strength was greatest, and that it was hardly possible in good times to induce the needed middle-class voters to support labor candidates. Significantly, the unions played a role in advocating and supporting the moves made to liberalize the franchise, pay legislators, and so on, in the late 1880's and early 1890's. But the rise of labor parties had to await a social crisis or something like one. This came in the early 1890's.

D3

The building of trade unions was decisive evidence of widespread discontent at the bottom of the colonial economic and social pyramid and proof of the insufficiency of the prevailing colonial bourgeois idea of a desirable society. Between the 1880's and World War I a new "idea" of Australia was hammered out in an atmosphere of contentious innovation and controversy. The innovations were undertaken and the controversies conducted at several levels in a variety of fields, most of them clearly related one to the other by the underlying forces at work. The outstanding dynamic forces were states of mind, nationalism and social reform. Here we are concerned with the impact of these states of mind up to 1900.

An outstanding peculiarity of the Australian scene was that nationalism and social reform found their expressions within the separate colonies and therefore in a little different fashion in each. They found expression also in an intellectual climate in which the idea of national independence as the ultimate end of the nationalist aspirations failed in all the colonies to achieve any significant acceptance—in a climate in which the accepted compromise was the maintenance of the established position of the colonies as members of the British imperial community. So strong was the particularistic nationalism of the separate colonies that when in the late 1880's it was proposed to substitute for the separate colonial nationalisms an inclusive continental nationalism, still within the imperial community, the resistances were considerable.

Colonial political nationalism chiefly found expression in the drive for the rights needed for the fullest domestic self-rule, approaching more or less completely the advanced position taken up by George Higinbotham. Colonial economic nationalism found clearest expression in protectionist tariff policy, most fiercely in Victoria, least vigorously in New South Wales. The way forward from these stances came to be identified with federation.

The intensification of nationalistic sentiment was associated with, but not identified with, an increase in the proportion of native-born in the population. The qualitative importance of being native-born was the intensification of identification with and acceptance of Australia in all its peculiarities, including the environmental, as one's own, one's native land. The first influential organization of the native born, the

Australian Natives' Association, was founded in Melbourne in 1871, almost precisely the year when Australian residents born overseas ceased to predominate. Although always established most firmly in Victoria, it at least tried to establish itself in the other colonies. It identified itself with the struggle to achieve continental nationalism through federation. The native-born nationalists, colonial and continental, were always quite willing to join with and even follow nationalists born overseas if they were going in their direction. At its core, Australian nationalism was a temperate affair. Extremists in ideas of any origin ordinarily suffered defeat except in the free expression of their ideas. Their contribution, both with regard to nationalism and social reform, was to enliven and vividly color the intellectual market place.

There was a tension in the minds of the Australian nationalists between the claims on their loyalty of Australia on the one hand and on the other to what was variously denominated "the British connection," "the Crown," Britain, or the Empire. This tension they were regularly able to reduce to a tolerable level by definitions of the proper relation of the two claims, consciously formulated or lodged unexamined in the subconscious, which varied between individuals and over time as the circumstances of Australia changed, domestically and within the British community.

The most intense reactions against "the British connection" were associated historically with hostile reactions to the policies and attitudes of the imperial authorities toward the colonies. An early extreme reaction of this kind was that of John Dunmore Lang. It drove him to the advocacy of the ideas of independence and republicanism. Lang took up these causes as early as 1845 and published a book-length defense of them as early as 1852, with revised and extended editions in 1857 and 1870. These ideas were integral elements of Lang's general radicalism and as such were passed along to his radical heirs and assigns. Most of them dropped them, and while he was a patron saint of the few advocates of independence and republicanism of the 1880's and 1890's, much of the wind had by then been taken out of these sails by the progressive expansion of local autonomy that had been achieved by pragmatic politicians not concerned with either—by politicians, indeed, to whom George Higinbotham was something of an extremist. The independence-republicans of the 1880's and 1890's were rarely practical politicians, as Lang certainly was in his time, but rather were, characteristically, hole-in-corner radical journalists riding a hobby-horse in transient, obscure periodicals. If they attained political success, it was other horses they rode, and they abandoned their independence-republicanism, as for example, George Dibbs did, who found protectionist tariff a more rewarding political gambit—he eventually became Sir George; and George Black later became a pioneer of the political Labor Party. It is significant that the only influential publication that ever advocated republicanism was the nationalist weekly, *The Bulletin* (founded 1880), and it, too, gave it up in due course.

The really serious struggle within the nationalist camp was not between the independence-republican advocates and the "British connection" partisans, but between the particularistic colonial nationalists and the continental nationalists whose chosen instrument was federation. It is significant that all advocates of continental organization for Australia suffered defeat until the end of the nineteenth century as much or more because they were continentalists as because of the unacceptability of items of their programs. Thus John Dunmore Lang failed of majority influence as much because his vision was continental as because of his advocacy of republicanism and independence, and the Irish nationalist, Sir Charles Gavan Duffy, who was active in Victorian politics for a number of years, failed to achieve anything substantial in his advocacy of federation from 1857 to 1870 as much because of his continentalism as because he injected the idea of neutrality for Australia in Britain's wars into his case. Indeed it can be argued that particularistic colonial nationalism was so strong that it practically forced the continentalists to advocate federation so that the identity of the old colonies could be preserved. It is revelatory of the situation that the alternative of continental unification, though argued, was decisively rejected during the federal campaign, as it has been rejected ever since. The inheritance by the federation of the old colonial nationalisms accounts for the persistence in Australia of a "sectionalism" which is, for all practical purposes, identical with state (i.e., colonial) as against all-Australia loyalties.

D3

It proved far easier to devise a moving, working compromise satisfactory to all but the extremist nationalists in politics than in the cultural fields. The economic and social conditions for a securely founded efflorescence of nationalistic cultural expressions were far more difficult to achieve than satisfactory nationalistic political and economic arrangements. It takes a long time and much uncomfortable experimentation for the enculturation to which all are subjected in the home and at school to achieve a creative balance between a solid apprehension of the extra-national cultural tradition to which the individual owes allegiance and the national ethos struggling to expression. The cultural tradition, flowing from a source overseas, tends to overwhelm the more sensitive—sometimes also the most creative—minds, implanting in them a conviction that full cultural expression can only be achieved at the source—in the Australian case, in Britain. This was all the more likely because most of the individual carriers of the tradition—the parents and the teachers, especially at the university level—were born overseas, feelingly in "exile" from the British source, a sense they conveyed to their charges. Expatriation—what has been called the "export of talent" —became a characteristic fate of a proportion of the talented of every Australian generation and if permanent expatriation and absorption into the parent culture was impossible to manage, then a visit of length to Britain—even several in a lifetime—was a coveted salve for the wounds of the aspirant compelled by uncontrollable circumstances to stay most of his life in his native land. A characteristic visit became to obtain higher education at Oxford, Cambridge, or London. However, expatriation was not exclusively a consequence of misbalanced encul-turation; it was also a way out of a genuinely intolerable entrapment. Expatriation was also a consequence of the lack of opportunity for full personal development along lines for which the underdeveloped Australian society had no crying need, offered no satisfying rewards, or did not tolerate at all. Australia exported talent, not only because the talent was culturally deracinated, not because it was hostile to it or it was hostile to Australia, but because Australia was not in a con-dition to make full or any use of the talent. At the same time, Aus-tralia persistently imported talent, especially to staff the universities, and also practitioners of the arts and the scientific professions, not to mention politicians and businessmen. On balance, however, it seems that Australia exported more talent than it imported, and talent prob-ably qualitatively superior, to its impoverishment. Oddly, while a good deal is known about Australia's exports, nobody has yet written a study of the impact of the incoming talented Australians on the cultural life of metropolitan Britain. While the exported British talent early felt "exiled" in colonial Australia, it was only as Australian culture be-came more mature that talented Australians in Britain began to feel "exiled" in their turn. It was then that expatriation as it functioned within the British community became a conscious issue to the individ-ual Australians experiencing it. However, the tension of loyalties in the cultural fields has continued largely unresolved for the Australians into the sixth decade of the twentieth century.

Though the volume of writing increased decade by decade, as did the volume of writing of Australian national reference beginning in the 1880's, none of it was produced by men and women to whom litera-ture was a primary career or by writers who earned their livings essaying literary production. Publication remained a problem, although the number of newspapers and periodicals increased, for the newspapers quite properly filled their columns with news and political comment, not literature, and the periodicals which best succeeded were not literary by the editors' primary intent. George Robertson pioneered book publishing in Melbourne in the 1850's and did his best for Australian literature, but it was not until the middle 1890's that Angus & Robertson in Sydney established the publishing of Australian writers on a reasonably sound footing. Publication in London was still the fundamentally satisfying criterion of success and the indispensable preliminary to acceptance by a vitally important segment of the Australian audience. The thriving British-Australian book trade brought these works to Australian readers along with a flood of books of British and foreign origin. The "colonial cringe," not yet unexampled, was then the common attitude of readers of taste. The writer in Australia inevitably rowed against the cultural tide as it flowed into the colonies from Britain and floated on its bosom the majority of the reading public; he rowed all the harder in proportion as he felt himself trying to be an *Australian* writer. As in the case of all overseas colonial countries with a strong and constantly reinforced attachment to a metropolitan literary tradition, the effort to produce national literature introduced ambiguities into the evaluation of local literary productions. A tone and temper that was agreed to be Australian, and exploitation of the Australian environment ("local color") tended to be prized beyond literary excellence as a rigorous literary critic would define it. Indeed, so effectively did the nationalistic critics operate that the use of "Australian" as a primary criterion of excellence only began to falter seriously in the 1960's as Australian writing *qua* literature was achieving greater maturity, forcing the more dubious nationalistic writers out of literature into culture history, a process which, for obvious reasons, will never be as complete as the more insistently aesthetic critics would like. All literatures are more casually mixed than the aestheticians care to admit.

Of the many writers who plied their trade in Australia from the 1850's through the 1880's, nine illustrate adequately and perhaps overabundantly the literature of the period: Catherine Helen Spence (1825–1910), Henry Kingsley (1830–76), Mrs. Campbell Praed (1851–1935), "Tasma" (Jessie Fraser Couvreur) (1848–97), Ada Cambridge (1844–1926), Adam Lindsay Gordon (1833–70), Henry Kendall (1839–82), Marcus Clarke (1846–81), and "Rolf Boldrewood" (Thomas Alexander Browne) (1826–1915). Of these only two were Australian-born, Mrs. Campbell Praed and Henry Kendall, while Catherine Spence, Tasma, and Boldrewood had arrived in the colonies as children. The rest arrived from England as more or less mature young men or women. Kingsley's Australian career was but an episode in a life lived mostly in England, while Mrs. Campbell Praed completed her career in England and France, and Tasma and Ada Cambridge returned to Europe for periods. Miss Spence, Gordon, Kendall, Clarke, and Boldrewood completed their lives in Australia. Of these figures Clarke and Gordon must be regarded as English "exiles" in Australia; Kingsley treated Australia as a locale of "colonial experience," and while all the women contributed to assimilating Australians and the Australian scene to literature, only Kendall and Boldrewood made truly significant contributions to this indispensable operation, while only Kendall of the nine seems in retrospect to have been a truly *literary* figure. All were "colonial" writers, but Kendall and Boldrewood were crypto-nationalists.

Although Catherine Helen Spence published several novels early in her life, all are today "rare books" difficult of access and only one, *Clara Morrison* (1854), is now regularly referred to in surveys of Australian writing as a competent narrative, Australian in point of view and substance. Miss Spence rather is more significant as an early pioneer in establishing a link between literature and political and social reform. By far the greater part of her life was spent in agitating and writing about voting procedures, the impact of law on individual welfare, and the problems of children. This linkage became especially characteristic of the early nationalistic writers. Henry Kingsley, for his part, contributed a novel, also in the 1850's, entitled *The Recollections of Geoffry Hamlyn* (1859). Kingsley was drawn to Australia by the gold rushes and spent four years in Victoria engaged in a miscellany of occupations, began to write *Geoffry Hamlyn,* and completed it after his return to England. Well received in its day, it stands as a classic novel of "colonial experience."

Mrs. Campbell Praed, Tasma, and Ada Cambridge, all of whom wrote several novels with Australian settings, exploited the Australian scene and its denizens in a slightly different fashion. They used the novel to explicate Australia and the Australians to home-dwelling British readers, "with the hope," as one of them wrote, "that I may in some slight degree aid in bridging over the gulf that divides the old world from the young." The three women thus on the one hand showed that fiction could be made out of Australian materials, a very useful object lesson for aspiring writers, but their motivation was not literarily "pure," so their books have been downgraded by later critics. Each, however, wrote one allegedly superior book: Mrs. Campbell Praed contributed

Longleat of Kooralbyn (1881); Tasma, *Uncle Piper of Piper's Hill* (1889); and Ada Cambridge, *Not all in Vain* (1892).

The most characteristic writers of this general period, however, were the four men, Kendall, Gordon, Clarke, and Boldrewood. They tried, with varying resoluteness, to lead the literary life in colonial Australia and their careers demonstrated that it was a fringe activity. Writers were odd men out and many showed their acceptance of this by indulgence in a very theatrical bohemianism. For a brief period Kendall, Gordon, and Clarke were members of the same bohemian literary club in Melbourne. However, one of the peculiarities of the Australian literary scene was, and has remained, the lack of a dominating center. The writers have normally been scattered widely, the largest clusters usually being in Melbourne and Sydney. Some of the enduring rivalry of these cities has rubbed off on them.

At one stage Gordon was regarded as the greatest of Australian poets, and as late as 1934 a bust of him was placed in Westminster Abbey in recognition of this. The author of pseudo-Swinburnian verse which at its worst became jingle, Gordon's philosophy was simple and popular. He celebrated courage in adversity, the loyalty of man to man, the associations of men and horses. Most of his Australian life he dealt professionally with horses as steeple-chase rider and stable keeper. His mnemonic manner made his verses easily retained and they passed by word-of-mouth to a wide audience. But substantively they were thin, uneven, fustian. There was a deep streak of melancholy in Gordon and given the difficulties he encountered in an ill-regulated life, it is not surprising that he committed suicide in 1870 at thirty-seven. Clarke was more decidedly the writing type than Gordon and more the poseur bohemian. After rather feckless efforts to adapt to business and squatting, Clarke became a general writer for the newspaper and periodical press. Clarke's talent did not run deep but it often sparkled as it ran. His literary facility was considerable, allowing him to write essays, dialogues, short stories, and novels and to carpenter plays and pantomimes. But he regularly mismanaged his finances and occasionally was legally bankrupt. His abilities found fullest scope in a novel of convict life which he wrote as a serial for a fiction paper and republished, after it had been edited and partly rewritten, as a book, *For the Term of His Natural Life* (1874). (The full original version was not published as a book until 1929.) With this novel—he wrote others—Clarke established his claim to being "the novelist of convict life," though what he had written was a Victorian melodrama of convict life. However since nobody had done as well, or has done as well since, Clarke's novel has stood as a classic-by-default of anything better about the convict era. It won a world audience.

Henry Kendall, grandson of Thomas Kendall the missionary to the Maoris, began to publish poetry in 1859 and brought out three important books in 1862, 1869, and 1880. Less disposed to bohemianism than Clarke, less of a harum-scarum than Gordon, but equally unfitted for a humdrum living-earning occupation, Kendall led a hard life, made harder by addiction to drink. Although Sir Henry Parkes eventually found him a post in the public service, it gave him a hard-earned income but no freedom to write. Essentially a lyric and nature poet, Kendall was more dedicatedly literary than any other writer of his time. However, his product was uneven; he survives by virtue of a handful of appealing minor poems and an assortment of brilliant lines and stanzas. In perspective, however, the significance of Kendall's career and accomplishment is very great. None other of the literary pioneers draws the critics back so regularly for reassessment. His career, given a sound foundation by his dedication to literature, better exemplifies the difficulties of the literary life in Australia in his day than any other. Kendall bore with his troubles to the end, dying in hospital of consumption.

Like Kendall, Boldrewood "accepted" Australia. He was born in England but brought to Australia as a child of four and he became completely naturalized. Boldrewood started out in life as a squatter, had some success, but was in the end defeated by drought. Thereupon he became a police magistrate and gold fields commissioner. Borrowing a writing name from Sir Walter Scott, he began to contribute to the magazines in 1865 and published books from 1878 to 1905, most frequently in the 1890's. The most prolific writer of his time of any quality—Australia has produced a goodly number of fiercely prolific popular fiction writers like Fergus Hume, author of the classic detective story, *The Mystery of a Hansom Cab* (1887)—Boldrewood poured out a long succession of books of short and novel-length stories, mostly at the level of "yarns." He had considerable powers of observation and his books can be read as social history, but his most pronounced gift was for narrative. However, not more than two or three of his books outlasted their moment and only one proved enduring. This was another classic-by-default, *Robbery Under Arms* (1888), as much *the* novel of bushranging as Clarke's was of convictism. Characteristically *Robbery Under Arms* was also originally written as a serial in a popular weekly magazine, as though to say that in this period the best an Australian writer could hope to do was to produce a rattling good *divertissement.*

None of these writers, except possibly Boldrewood, came anywhere near to coming to terms with the outback bush and its working-class denizens. This is important because the nationalist writers took as one of their principal tasks the imposing of a legend of the bush as the locale of the true Australia and of the bush workers as the autochthonous Australians. They played a strategic role in imposing a rural image of Australia even on the urban-dwelling majority. The outback and the outback workers were glorified as against the cities and their inhabitants. Hence the curious downgrading of the cities and urban influences in the histories of Australia. Hence the imposition of a working-class image of the Australian, and working-class values, as against a middle-class image, and middle-class values, which were imposed in equally fluid and pioneer United States. In line with their political ineptitude the squatters proved powerless to impose *their* image as the authentic masters of the outback world, and the urban middle class failed to establish a priority in social legend over the working class. It is as though the American cowboys had obliterated the ranchers, the people on the wrong side of the tracks the social image of those on the right side.

Very early in Australian history it was noticed that the native-born were different from the immigrants, convict and free, in physical appearance, character structure, and "values." Commissioner Bigge commented on this in 1820. As the majority of the native-born were closer, physically and in social status, to the convicts than to the free, an Australian character and its accompanying value system came to be conceived as having originated among the lower orders, not among the convicts exactly, though with carry-overs from them, but certainly to be more closely associated with the convicts, thought of as victims of a malign system, than the ruling respectables. (Here is probably the origin of the Australian contribution to the invidious and untrue legend that the Australians are all descendents of convicts.) This autochthonous Australian character developed in a society dominated until around 1870 by immigrants. The immigrants, of course, were predominantly working class, thus diluting or at least obscuring the true Australian character until it could assert itself in a predominantly native-born society. Thus the legend makers alleged that it developed chiefly in the outback, where the native-born predominated long before they did in the cities, not in the persons of owners of stations, but in those of the workers on them.

This autochthonous Australian was alleged to be a person of upstanding independence, an autonomous individual aggressively conscious of his own worth, a Jack who was as good as his master if not a bit better. He was aggressively egalitarian. He was hostile to authority, especially to bosses, policemen, and bureaucrats, a stance well exemplified in the popular reaction to bushranging which led to the romanticizing of this rather sordid crime in Australian popular and high culture. In its early expression a by-blow of convictism—a practice indulged in by convicts escaped to the bush—it reappeared after the gold rushes as an activity of the freeborn in a disturbed time and reached a kind of climax in the late 1870's. In the convict period the classic bushranger was Jack Donahoe, in the post-gold rush period, Frank Gardiner, Ben Hall, and, climactically, Ned Kelly and his gang.

In a tradition established in Donahoe's time and re-established in the 1860's, the people of lower status were normally sympathetic with the bushrangers, concealing their hideouts and warning them by bush-telegraph (grapevine) of the movements of the pursuing police. This sympathy was generated in an atmosphere of social war, of struggling, impecunious selectors against the squatters, in which many selectors condoned the ignoring of the property rights of the squatters. Horse lifting, cattle duffing, sheep stealing were tolerated dishonesties. Those who indulged in them, or tolerated them, were normally, "agin the guvnment" as the ally of the propertied class, and the police as its visible agents. They were often Irish nationalists. To them the bushrangers figured not as menacing criminals, but as men of their own class of uncommon dash, pluck, and daring, operating on their side in the class war. This version of the bushrangers passed into the popular imagination. The character of the bushrangers as rebels against authority triumphed over their criminality.

The autochthonous Australian similarly sophisticated the urban counterparts of the bushrangers and bushranging, the larrikins and larrikinism. Larrikins, who flourished in Sydney and Melbourne 1870–1900, were city hoodlums, the products of slum living conditions, loose parental control, irregular and poorly paid employment. In the absence of guidance and creative outlets for youthful energies, the larrikins fought vicious street battles with fists, stones, belts, and bottles and "put in the boot" to an enemy who went down. Aggression against their betters took the forms of vandalism and assault, especially on policemen. The terms larrikin and larrikinism were adapted to denominate a generally tolerated strain in the Australian character which found expression as a crass aggressiveness and impudent assertiveness in relations with their betters, domestic and foreign. A larrikin streak came to be tolerated, even admired, in the most surprising people, and larrikinism colored Australian conduct in the most remarkable circumstances. It is significant that the Australians romanticized the bushrangers and the larrikins, the criminals and delinquents, not the lawmen. There is no equivalent in Australian song and story of Wild Bill Hickok or Wyatt Earp. But the bushrangers found their way into ballads and songs, poetry, painting, and ballet.

At his best vis à vis life, the legendary autochthonous Australian was a battler; he fought hard to sustain his independence. However, work with him was never an end of life; it was a means to *survival,* the supreme value. The classic alternative to work was leisure for hard drinking, in time the alternative became leisure for sport, especially spectator sports like horse-racing, with gambling and drinking as accompaniments. At work, at play, at dissipation, this character was a hard swearer, blasphemous and obscene, whose most reportable epithet was bloody. In the outback he was an itinerant, forever "humping his bluey"—or carrying his "swag"—in search of work. As a worker he was a versatile performer, though specialization, as in shearing, crept up on him. He could perform under harsh and primitive conditions and a conspicuous expertness was in improvisation. Although in one of his guises he was a lone nomad, he more characteristically traveled and worked with a mate, sometimes with a team of mates. Out of the convenience of having a mate with whom to deal with the perils of environment and work grew a veritable secular religion of mateship, a form of loyalty of man to man transcending mere association for companionship or on the job. Mateship carried over as solidarity into the labor movement.

Obviously this autochthonous Australian was not this Australian or that, but a legendary figure. All Australians could participate to some extent in his character. He was adopted by the labor movement and projected as an authentic Australian in popular and high literature. One poet saw him successfully "slouching down the centuries." Actually, insofar as he ever existed, he began to fade away as the structure of Australian society shifted, bequeathing elements of his character to posterity. But in his heyday he was *the* Australian, the "dinkum Orstrylyun," obscuring the many who did not at all conform to the pattern. His great days were from about 1870 through World War I. In World War I he was that type of Australian soldier called a "digger."

Although in literary legend associated with the 1890's, some of the best nationalist writers, while they may have begun to publish during the decade or earlier, did not bring out their most characteristic books until after 1900 and many of those who did achieve book publication in the decade continued to publish well into the Commonwealth period. Here we are concerned only with those who published their first *books* in the 1890's.

To a peculiar extent the rise of nationalist Australian writing was associated with the weekly magazine, *The Bulletin,* founded in Sydney in 1880. At first rather insecure in its aim, by the late 1880's it had found its way to a full-blown, somewhat strident political nationalism closely allied to social reform and was concerned to assault critically all obstacles to the free expression of Australianism, whether political, social, cultural, or simply manners and style of living. It was anticolonial, anti-imperial, often anti-British. Although by aspiration a continental journal—it also had influence in New Zealand—it was in its beginnings an organ of the colonial nationalism of New South Wales, so decidedly so that it only espoused the continental nationalism of federation belatedly. It was too leary of the imperial British influence in the Australian colonies to embrace federalism under the Crown without hesitations. In writing style it favored pungency, the aboriginal Australian flavor, factuality, the needling observation, the sardonic comment, with brevity as a sovereign virtue. The vivid paragraph was its favored form. The tone and line of the publication were set by many hands, but probably the most influential single editor with regard to manner and matter was Victorian-born J. F. Archibald (1856–1919). Archibald was a journalist's journalist. On literature, once the paper had struck its stride, the greatest single influence was that of Queensland-born A. G. Stephens (1865–1933) who, however, actually edited the paper's Red Page (i.e., the inside of the back red cover) of literary criticism and comment, not entirely directed to Australian writing, only from 1896 to 1906. Stephens, however, continued for several decades to dominate literary criticism through his own journal, pamphlets, and correspondence, functioning, whatever his vehicle, as an extraordinary, if constrictive, critical Grand Cham. He was a literary journalist of genius, but a crabbed and scrappy writer. His most substantial separate publication was named with a bad pun, *The Red Pagan* (1904), but he also brought out numerous small brochures, usually devoted to a single writer. If from the late 1880's until World War I *The Bulletin* was the most influential single paper in the literary field, it was not, as sometimes represented, the whole of Australian literature, for there always remained, even in Sydney, writers only tangentially related to *The Bulletin* and the writers of Melbourne were never wholly at *The Bulletin*'s command. Much of *The Bulletin*'s literary influence arose from the fact that it was the best market for Australian writing.

It was outstandingly a market for short fiction. In the 1890's a great many people wrote stories for *The Bulletin* which were thought to be worth more than a single printing, as can be seen from a collection of them made by A. G. Stephens and published in 1901. No writer who was represented in Stephens' *Bulletin Story Book* was more enduringly important than Henry Lawson (1867–1922). Lawson, the child of a Norwegian father and an Australian mother, was born in the bush, meagerly educated, and was a writer of natural talent more than cultivated skill. The most gifted writer of fictional sketches of his time, permanently a front-line figure in Australian literature, Lawson has been represented as a man who expressed a continent. He was, as a matter of fact, a far more subjective writer than the tribute implies, for while he was closely in tune with the laboristic social radicals of his time and accepted most of the legend of the autochthonous Australian character, with especial allegiance to the secular religion of mateship, he was plagued by ambivalences which found expression in his work. He was a highly articulate common Australian but a common man of febrile temperament. His stories are clearly etched, the environmental circumstances intensely real, his characters stand out vividly, his values are indubitably Australian, but he is of two minds about both the environment and the people. He had the feeling that the bush was the real Australia, but he did not particularly like the bush, as many of his stories show, and spent most of his time in Sydney. He disliked the conditions of city life, especially for the poor, but it was his personal locale. He glorified mateship but he saw the limitations of it in practice. He was melancholy and euphorically humorous—both of which qualities found full expression in his work. Personally maladjusted, unhappy and unfortunate in his private life, with a weakness for drink, he was nevertheless a first-rate artist who redeemed the squalor of his life by his inherent gallantry of spirit. He deserved the public monument that was erected in his memory in a public park. His first book of collected stories appeared in 1894 and the strongest single collection, entitled *While the Billy Boils,* in 1896. He wrote perhaps twenty-five stories of the highest quality, more that are good, and a quantity of verse that is more interesting as a study in popular sentiments and sentimentality than as poetry.

Three other writers represented in Stephens' *Story Book,* and a fourth who was not, can be cited to help fill out the literary picture of this time if it is kept in mind that they were environed by a veritable army of minor figures: Price Warung (1855–1911), Louis Becke (1855–1913), Steele Rudd (1868–1935), and A. B. Paterson (1864–1941). Warung, a journalist by profession, wrote stories of the convict era, reconstructions of Australia's deplorable past, more firm-minded than Clarke's melodrama but subtly distorted by a "victims of circumstances" bias. The first book of them appeared in 1892. Louis Becke, a drifter who became a professional writer by accident, brought the islands into Australian literature with a long series of fictional and nonfictional sketches, by and large reflecting the intruder's point of view. The first collection has remained the best known, *By Reef and Palm* (1894). Steele Rudd (Arthur Hoey Davis), journalist, writer of humorous sketches and novels, published in 1899 a book called *On Our Selection,* a wonderful comedy with two characters, Dad and Dave, who walked out of its pages into a prolonged, if sometimes debased, life of their own. A. B. ("Banjo") Paterson was a very different character from any of these, professionally a lawyer, a writer and journalist by choice. Paterson gave the ballad form its enormous prestige at this time and helped, perhaps decisively, in making the ballad the people's poetry. There are those who contend he was more popular with the bush workers than Henry Lawson. Far from being alone in devising ballads, and not the first to use the form—Gordon, for example, had preceded him—Paterson nevertheless wrote some of the best and most enduring of the contrived ballads and had the perception to link them back to the authentic oral ballads by making a classic collection of the latter, *Old Bush Ballads* (1905). Paterson had his first rousing success with *The Man from Snowy River* (1895) and later in life he devised a ballad that, because it was taken up by the Australian soldiers, achieved world currency in World War II, "Waltzing Matilda."

The Australianness of these writers was readily perceptible and of a character to please both readers and critics. It was much harder to establish the literary worth of writers who made no show of Australianness, however intense their identification with their country. Standing out monumentally from his contemporaries, towering above them intellectually, academically and self-educated in classical and modern languages and literatures, a faltering bridge when it was difficult to build one between the writers and the academics, was Christopher Brennan (1870–1932). Challenging, though probably by following his star rather than by conscious intent, the ruling dogma that an outward and visible Australianness was an essential quality, dogged by misfortunes in his private life that spoiled his academic career, Brennan began to publish in the late 1890's, giving limited circulation to two small books in an environment crowded with minor poets and poetasters. Heavily influenced by French symbolism, his fate was to suffer a rather esoteric *succès d'estime* because of the physical inaccessibility of his work—though he published much more after 1900—and its inherent difficulty for readers accustomed to homespun utterance. Alone among the poets of his time he had depth.

But if the Australians could manage fiction and poetry, they could not manage playable drama, heavy or light. The theater, which was in an exceedingly lively condition in the 1880's and 1890's, was dominated by imports, both plays and players, chiefly but not exclusively British and American. Sarah Bernhardt played in Australia in 1891. In 1890 there were sufficient serious theatergoers to support a season of Ibsen. But plays made of Australian materials—*For the Term of His Natural Life* and *Robbery Under Arms* were both put on the stage—did not catch on. From 1882 the leading actor-entrepreneur was an American,

J. C. Williamson (1845–1913), who conformed to the established theatrical pattern. Vaudeville, chiefly in the hands of Harry Ricards, similarly made only incidental use of Australian materials and talent. The Australian players who showed ability went abroad for short or long stays. Nellie Stewart (1858–1931) who became the First Lady of the Australian theater—she played from 1873 to 1927—spent years abroad like the rest. There was nothing the matter with the theater as a playhouse, but even after there were Australian stories and poems to read, there were no Australian plays to see. It is doubtful, however, that many theatergoers felt deprived.

Musically Australia gave its attention chiefly to choral music and opera. For forty years opera was surprisingly popular. Up to about 1880 the leading impressario was the Irish-born soldier of fortune W. Saurin Lyster (1828–1880) who arrived in Australia in 1861 with a company with which he had been touring western United States, while after 1880 opera was one of the provinces of J. C. Williamson, first Gilbert and Sullivan and following 1893 Italian opera sung by a company brought out from Italy. The public response continued strong, though not altogether discriminating. Much was made of music in connection with expositions held in Melbourne and Sydney and the high place given it among the arts was indicated by the fact that endowed chairs of music were established in the universities of Melbourne (1887) and Adelaide (1897), and conservatories were established. The first occupant of the Melbourne chair, G. W. L. Marshall Hall (1862–1915), made an enormous contribution to music in Melbourne, especially orchestral music, and scandalized the proper middle class with his personal eccentricities and his poetry. It was out of this musical environment that Nellie Melba (1861–1931), Percy Grainger (1882–1961), and other figures emerged as Australian contributions to the international musical world.

The nationalism of the Australian painters found expression through the "conquest of the landscape," and the use of Australian episodes in genre painting. The former was the more significant achievement. "The main problem in Australian Art," wrote Sir Lionel Lindsay in retrospect, "was the conquest of the landscape. Until that was resolved the actual appearance of the country as seen by the eye of the native-born could never be satisfactorily established." (While the native-born played a role in the "conquest" immigrants also participated, as in all Australian nationalistic enterprises.) The central problem of landscape was the rendering of color and light, to capture on canvas the Australianness of a landscape of prevailingly pastel colors bathed in vivid light. Once a satisfying visual image was established, the habituation to it of an audience able and willing to buy pictures at remunerative prices followed.

This took about twenty years. It was then a relatively simple matter for painters to keep their temperamental variations of style and vision within the broad boundaries of the accepted. However, Australian painting was never all landscape. It also, as noted, embraced genre painting—most of the pioneer landscape painters essayed it. Portraiture remained exceedingly popular. The artists retained an abiding devotion to drawing as the sovereign skill of the pictorial artist. They were all representationists. Many did magazine and book illustration not only in color but also in black and white. From the 1860's on the Australians were especially skilled in black and white. In the 1890's etching, pioneered by John Shirlow (1869–1936), and woodcutting were established. Many of the painters were closely associated with the photographers who were creatively active in Australia at this time, doing excellent portraits, landscape studies, and a good deal of their version of genre, even as far afield as New Guinea by the middle 1880's. The net effect of the bias of mind and evaluation of the Australian workers was that they rather quickly academicized the open-air impressionism that had allowed them to conquer the Australian landscape. It became in due course as stoutly defended an orthodoxy as the academic studio painting it displaced. And Australian painting remained within the British tradition. As the impressionism that released the painters properly to do the landscape was introduced into a provincial world dominated artistically by immigrant British academicians and the second-rate Victorian British pictures in the galleries and homes, so it was developed within the British tradition. Many Australian painters sought training and recognition in London, few in Paris. From the middle 1880's until the 1920's, academic impressionism ruled.

The principal precursors of the genre and landscape painters were S. T. Gill (1818–80) and Louis Buvelot (1814–88), the one an English immigrant, the other a Swiss who arrived in Melbourne in 1865 after having lived and painted in Brazil and the East Indies. Although Gill was a painter, his studies of men and the man-made environment, especially of the gold fields, gained widest circulation, and remain best known, in lithographic reproductions. At his peak during the rushes, he died an almost forgotten man on the steps of the Melbourne post office in 1880. Buvelot, whose European eye had been trained to see exotic landscape before he ever reached Australia, made more than tentative steps toward getting the Australian landscape on canvas. All the major impressionists came to regard him as a sound forerunner and inspiration.

The putative father of impressionism in Australia was Tom Roberts (1856–1931) who began as a photographer, had some training in painting in Australia and more in London, and picked up impressionistic ideas from two minor French painters he encountered in Spain. Roberts was English-born but arrived in Australia in his 'teens. Bringing back from Europe the emphasis on capturing the subtleties of color and light in the open air, he had an enormous influence on his Melbourne contemporaries. He and they carried the gospel to Sydney where it chimed in readily with the plein-air approach of Julian Ashton (1851–1942) who after training in England had emigrated to Australia at twenty-seven. Roberts and Ashton were born teachers and their influence, both individual and intertwined, was very great. In addition to landscape, Roberts was also keenly interested in genre and portraiture. It would be wrong to convey the impression that the painters who felt the influence of Roberts or Ashton or both became simply epigoni of these "masters," but without them it is difficult to imagine that Australian painting would have taken the course it did.

At any rate, before the nineteenth century was out many men whose names still loom large in the story of Australian painting had emerged into notice. To name a few: Sir Arthur Streeton (1867–1943), the first major Australian-born landscapist and genre painter; Charles Conder (1868–1909), English-born, whose Australian career is a relatively unknown phase of his story as a "decadent" decorative painter of the English 1890's—he joined with Roberts and Streeton in the first impressionists' exhibition in Melbourne in 1889; Frederick McCubbin (1855–1917), a successful genre painter who worked closely with Tom Roberts in establishing artists' camps near Melbourne; George Coates (1869–1930) who became a fashionable portraitist in London; Sir John Longstaff (1862–1941), knighted in 1938, a talented figure who became trapped in portraiture; and Rupert Bunny (1864–1947), a brilliant painter influenced by Puvis de Chevannes who was one of the few Australians to make a career in Paris. Aside from painters who made incursions into the field, black-and-white men whose careers were launched in this period were the American Livingston Hopkins (1846–1927), Ohio-born, who arrived in Australia in 1883 and began an association with *The Bulletin* that only concluded with his death—his "favorite" subject in the early years was Sir Henry Parkes—and the Englishman Phil May (1864–1903) who was with *The Bulletin* from 1885 to 1888. Sir Bertram Mackennal (1863–1931)—first Australian elected R.A., first Australian whose work was purchased by the Tate, and the first Australian artist knighted (1921)—began his career as a sculptor in the 1880's. Like so many Australian professionals, Mackennal lived and worked much of his life in England, illustrating once again the ambiguous character of much of Australia's cultural expression. It is even more clearly illustrated by those figures who once they left Australia practically lost any identification with it, like the philosopher Samuel Alexander (1859–1938) and the classicist and liberal publicist Gilbert Murray (1866–1957), both of whom were awarded the Order of Merit in England.

If nationalism was the dominant state of mind from the 1880's through World War I, it had a close competitor in social reform. As a matter of fact, the two were inextricably mixed together and the nationalism of the reformers was in a sense a vision of a reformed nationalistic society, an outlook shared by a wide range of persons from liberals to socialists who differed, of course, as to what the vision actually signified and how it could, whatever its nature, best be realized. On balance, however, the more radical or leftist reformers tended to be colonial nationalists because they suspected that they had a better chance of realizing their ideas within the colonial setting than within the complexities of a federalism they did not clearly understand. This left the drive for a continental nationalistic federalism largely in the hands of the liberals and the conservatives. It tells us a good deal about the prevailing temper of mind in the colonies that they were able to put it over and that their most difficult opponents were not the leftist social reformers but the devotees of colonial particularism.

The discontent that both provoked the expression of ideas about social reform and provided the constituencies for the ideas was unquestionably generated in the colonies from local conditions, but the ideas propagated were rarely of local origin. They originated in England, on the Continent, and in the United States, and filtered into the colonies through the book trade, or were brought in by immigrants. Local advocacy and discussion domesticated them. Overseas they were generated out of prevailing discontents provoked by the conditions of industrialized societies. The economic and social analysis which accompanied and supported the proposals for reform thus related to societies very different from those of the Australian colonies in which industrialization was a fringe development and the prevailing organization was pastoral-agricultural. Yet the colonial social reformers felt that both the analyses and the prescriptions were relevant to Australia. There was general agreement that men worked too hard, too long, under bad conditions, for unfeeling, tyrannical bosses, for nothing better than a poor living. These reactions generated a good deal of class feeling and, as far as the laboristic reformers were concerned, supported the advocacy of class-angled change. The capitalists were the enemy. They were altogether too powerful. There was a widespread feeling that "Europe" was establishing itself in Australia with regard to class relations and conditions and that this should not be allowed. Australia should be different from and better than "Europe"; it should be a "millennial Eden," "Delos of a coming Sun-God's race."

The effective mechanism for sorting out the positive proposals for change was politics. This great "digester" of rhetoric and practicalities tended to erode or eliminate the irrelevancies, particularly those of a truly revolutionary character, forcing their proponents into the position of fringe pressure groups of the labor movement. The operations of the digester were greatly influenced by the fact that some of the most astute liberal politicians saw very clearly the need to deal with points raised by the radicals and brought forward proposals for handling those questions. The legislative solutions were thus as much a product of liberal willingness to meet demands as laboristic pressure. The resultant compromise was the more readily achievable because Australian society was still fluid—congealed and resistant conservatism had but limited and easily circumvented political strength. There was therefore a break-through in the welfare direction much earlier in the colonies than in overseas societies in which the conservative resistances were better founded and of greater political significance.

The radical social reformers were normally close to the trade unions, though not always members of them. They were usually self-educated intellectuals who enunciated and defended their ideas in small circulation periodicals, leaflets, pamphlets, and speeches, including soapbox talks. They circulated books from overseas. As their ideas were predominantly laboristic, or they felt their most receptive audience was the working class, their papers were ordinarily addressed to the workers and some were trade union organs. These people took a keen interest in politics but were hostile to the established politicians. They had linkages with some of the writers—for example, Henry Lawson, a labor hero—and with some of the artists, but at this stage with only a few members of the professional class, had few university contacts, and had very little acceptance by the big newspapers. Insofar as the social reformers were participants in a movement, it was in the working-class movement. Their caste of mind was secular.

These writers, propagandists, unionists, and potential politicians were influenced by a variety of currents of thought and a wide assortment of nineteenth-century books protesting social conditions and advocating reform. They read Carlyle's *The French Revolution* (1837) and *Past and Present* (1843), Ruskin's social writings, Disraeli's novels, including *Sybil* (1845), Kingsley's *Alton Locke* (1850), and Dickens' *Hard Times* (1854). They read Robert Blatchford's *Merrie England* (1894) and Max Nordau's *Conventional Lies of our Civilization* (1883). Participating in the traditional Australian preoccupation with the land problem, they read Henry George's *Progress and Poverty* (1880) and also his *Social Problems* (1883) and *Protection or Free Trade* (1886). They read Ignatius Donnelly's *Caesar's Column* (1891) and Laurence Gronlund's *The Cooperative Commonwealth* (1884). A few of them read Karl Marx's *Das Kapital* (1867), many, many more read Edward Bellamy's *Looking Backward* (1888). They were influenced by Pope Leo XIII's encyclical on labor questions, *Rerum Novarum* (1891). They read John Stuart Mill. The greatest impact was achieved by Henry George and his single tax and Edward Bellamy and his utopian socialism, both, interestingly enough, American (as also were Gronlund and Donnelly). George visited Australia and lectured in 1890. (He had been in Australia as a sailor in 1855.) Thus the two most powerful currents were land reform and "socialism," but by the middle 1890's the incompatibility of George's ideas with trade unionism and "socialism" was clear and "socialism" captured the field. It was a socialism which was not only utopian but also a socialism mixed up with a bread-and-butter unionism, the advocacy of very specific political and social reforms by parliamentary action, and embarrassed by the challenge to choose between protection and free trade. Of the early socialist propagandists none left a more vivid legend than William Lane (1861–1917), an English immigrant of the early 1880's. While he had read Marx, Lane was fundamentally a romantic utopian. From his headquarters in Brisbane he did a great deal to infuse the spirit of mateship into Queensland unionism and to convince the readers of his clever journalism that the socialism he advocated for "our time" was mateship expanded to a way of life. Although he was swept off his feet by Bellamy's industrial utopia, his personal utopia was anti-industrial and sentimentally bucolic, a throw-back to the sort of thing that flourished in the United States during the 1840's under the inspiration of Robert Owen, Fourier, and similar thinkers. In its origins, Australian laboristic socialism was not, as the Frenchman Métin put it in 1901, *le socialisme sans doctrines,* but a socialism compounded out of a multiplicity of often incompatible doctrines. This is what went into the political digester.

The Australian colonies were deeply influenced by the forces which secularized the European mind in the nineteenth century. A clear indication of the power of the secularists was the establishment of state school systems, in another aspect an essentially nationalistic move, first in the colonies in Victoria in 1872, in Queensland (by Sir Samuel Griffith) in 1875, and in New South Wales (by Sir Henry Parkes) in 1880, as free, compulsory, and *secular*. The schools fulfilled the design of insuring a literate population for the colonial democracies and between 1861 and 1901 the percentage signing the marriage register with marks declined from 18.5 for males and 30.7 for females to 1.4 for males and 1.3 for females. The triumph of secularism in the state schools did not mean that the churches—mostly still staffed from overseas—or the religious point of view suffered a decisive defeat in society at large but rather that the secularistic outlook was insured of constant reinforcement. The victory was achieved only at the expense of a rancourous row between the secularists and the churches, the Church of England and, above all, the Roman Catholic Church. The new approach centrally involved the withdrawal of state subsidies from the church schools with which the government schools had hitherto run in tandem. As the church with the most vigorous conviction that it was its duty closely to control the education of its communicants, the Roman Catholic was naturally the most strenuous opponent of the change, having most to lose by it, criticized the proposal most savagely and in return received the angriest abuse from both the secularists and the anti-Catholic Protestants. It was undoubtedly Roman Catholic intransigence that accounted for the complete secularization of state education, for had the Catholics been prepared to compromise on nonsectarian religious exercises in the schools, it would have been supported with effect by the other churches. As it was the Roman Catholics were forced to go on with the building of a comprehensive system of schools of their own, constantly complaining of the inequity of having to support both it and, through taxes, the state system. The Catholic campaign to get tax support for their schools introduced into politics a highly explosive, divisive issue. For their part the Protestants turned attention to building up their grammar schools— "public" schools—chiefly to be patronized by their social elites. No church in Australia sponsored a university. The universities remained state supported institutions with a few private benefactions like the Challis estate received by Sydney in 1890, but without church affiliation. However, the churches—Church of England, Roman Catholic, Presbyterian, and later on Methodist—adopted the permitted practice of building "colleges," usually but not always residential, within the universities.

After Sydney in 1850 there were established to the end of the century the University of Melbourne (1853), the University of Adelaide (1874), and the University of Tasmania (1890). All were "first degree" institutions, without graduate schools. At first granting only the B.A. they added at various dates, beginning at Sydney in the 1850's, degrees in law, medicine, and engineering (in that order) and took on the character of teaching schools for the professions with "arts" (chiefly the classics) as the core. In 1901 the four universities had 1376 matriculated students, Melbourne the largest student body. In 1884 evening lectures for part-time students were instituted at Sydney, this greatly expanding the reach of the university, and in 1886 Sydney pioneered adult education in the form of university extension lectures in the city and the bush to help satisfy the lively intellectual curiosity of a considerable segment of the population.

In the forty years after 1860 the colonies also followed the precedent set earlier by Tasmania and established a repertory of other cultural institutions: central reference libraries, museums, galleries, and learned societies, conceived of and sometimes named "national" institutions, illustrating how each colony then thought of itself as a separate nation. From a more or less tangled background of earlier establishments, central reference libraries, called public libraries, emerged in Victoria in 1853, New South Wales 1869, Tasmania 1870, South Australia 1884, Western Australia 1886, and Queensland 1895. Art galleries were established in Victoria in 1861, New South Wales 1876, South Australia 1881, Queensland 1895. Museums devoted to geology, ethnology, and natural science, in which New South Wales had been the pioneer in 1836, were established in Victoria in 1854, Queensland 1855, South Australia 1856, while Victoria established a museum of applied science in 1870, New South Wales in 1880, and South Australia in 1893. Royal societies (not to attempt to specify specialized learned societies), foci for those interested in the sciences, were established in Victoria in 1859, New South Wales 1866, South Australia 1880, and Queensland 1884. New South Wales also had a center for the study of natural history, called the Linnean Society (1874), supported generously by Sir William Macleay. An Australasian Association for the Advancement of Science held its first meeting at Sydney in 1888. In membership and management these cultural institutions were linked to both the university communities and to the general educated public, while in the case of the museums and galleries the general public, educated or not, was assumed to profit from visits to them.

In the absence of close historical studies of the higher intellectual life and of detailed biographies of more than a few significant participants in it, it is impossible accurately to indicate either its breadth or depth or, perhaps more importantly, its contribution to the general intellectual climate of the time in Australia. The impression one gets is that in spite of the elaboration of the institutional structure, individual workers, self-starting and self-sustaining, were peculiarly the mainstay of the higher intellectual life. The cultural institutions were ordinarily financially undernourished.

As in the universities the emphasis was on the teaching function, so in the extra-mural cultural institutions the emphasis was on dissemination, not creation. Even so, they suffered severe handicaps. For example, very little natural history collecting was financed by them; they were dependent upon the generosity of foreign collectors and local amateurs. The institutions tended to be governed, speaking by and large, by amateurs and dilettantes, of whom in Victoria Judge Sir Redmond Barry (1813–80), first chancellor of the University, first president of trustees of the Public Library, the judge who sentenced Ned Kelly to be hanged, was the exemplary figure. The men of genuine distinction of mind and accomplishment were divided in some proportion which is not clear between the university staffs and nonacademic employments. Men of exceptional ability and drive were on the staffs of the universities from their beginnings but some of the most memorable figures of the intellectual life of this period were public servants.

Without pretending that the men to be mentioned were all the scholars who lived and worked in the Australian colonies 1860–1900, twenty individuals, ten academics and ten nonacademics, may be cited as probably characteristic of the period and in some instances of the succeeding early Commonwealth period as well. The academics: W. E. Hearn (1826–88), Irish-educated polymath, at the University of Melbourne from 1855, remembered as a political economist and legal scholar; Charles Badham (1813–84), a leading classical scholar of his day, at the University of Sydney from 1867; Sir Edgeworth David (1858–1934), geologist, with the geological survey of New South Wales from 1882, professor at the University of Sydney from 1890; E. E. Morris (1843–1902), scholar of languages, at the University of Melbourne from 1883; Sir William Bragg (1862–1942), physicist, at the University of Adelaide 1886–1908; David Orme Masson (1858–1937), professor of chemistry at Melbourne from 1886; Sir Mungo MacCallum (1854–1942) at the University of Sydney as professor of modern languages from 1886; Sir Baldwin Spencer (1860–1929), anthropologist, professor of biology at Melbourne from 1887; Francis Anderson (1858–1941), philosopher and educationist, at Sydney from 1888; G. A. Wood (1865–1928), historian, at Sydney from 1890. The nonacademics: Sir Ferdinand von Muller (1825–96), botanist to the government of Victoria from 1852; Julian Tenison Woods, (1832–89), geologist, Roman Catholic priest; A. W. Howitt (1830–1908), anthropologist, explorer, government administrator; Lorimer Fison (1832–1907), anthropologist, Methodist missionary to Fiji, journalist; E. H. C. Oliphant (1862–1936), scholar in Elizabethan drama, journalist specializing in mining affairs; Sir Timothy Coghlan (1856–1926), statistician to the colony of New South Wales, historian, civil engineer, public servant; H. H.

Hayter (1821–95), statistician to the colony of Victoria, public servant; G. E. Morrison (1862–1920), journalist, specialist in Chinese affairs, London *Times* correspondent, Peking, from 1897; F. J. Gillen (1855–1912), anthropologist, collaborator with Sir Baldwin Spencer, telegraphist; Lawrence Hargrave (1850–1915), specialist in aerodynamics of heavier-than-air machines, retired explorer, and public servant. Of these—perhaps by accident of selection—only three were Australian-born: Morrison, Coghlan, and Oliphant, all nonacademics. The day of the Australian academic in Australia was yet to come.

However, "the distinguishing note of Australian character" at this time was not considered to be devotion to literature, art, church, education, science, or social reform but "an enthusiastic predilection for sport and outdoor amusements," explained, as to the present day, by reference to "equable temperature and pleasant climate." Racing was the universally popular spectator sport and that greatest of Australian folk sport festivals, the Melbourne Cup Race, was first run at Flemington as early as 1861. No city, hardly any smallest bush town, was without a race course. Cricket too was firmly established as both a participant and spectator sport. It first became competitive between colonies when New South Wales met Victoria at Melbourne in 1856 and the first English team arrived to play the colonials in 1862. Football—the outside rivals here were the New Zealanders—bowls, lawn-tennis, track, aquatic sports including swimming and "surfing," rowing and yachting were popular, not to mention such exotic diversions as kangaroo hunting (as distinguished from drives to kill off the beasts as vermin of the outback) and rabbit coursing. Bicycling was in vogue. So fervent was the devotion to sport that the suspicion that it was being overdone, as unsporting visitors hinted, had frequently to be brought up to be knocked down as an absurdity of foreign critics.

D3

When in 1889 Sir Henry Parkes once again raised the question of federation, he was obviously playing a hunch that the time was ripe for making it a serious political issue. As he pursued the matter he thought of it as peculiarly a question to be dealt with by members of the colonial legislatures. For years the idea of federation had been discussed not only at the political level, as by Gavan Duffy and his friends, but also more or less theoretically by a variety of interested persons. Sir Henry uncovered a surprising number of persons well informed about federal constitutions, especially Canadian and American. Sir Henry himself, while not a constitutional expert, had toyed with the idea from time to time for several decades. His view was that continental federation would

at a stroke raise Australia's prestige among the nations far beyond anything the colonies taken separately could achieve.

What led Sir Henry to speak out at the particular time he chose was
a report by a British army officer on the organization of the land forces
of the colonies. While Australian defense was viewed as basically a naval
problem and, beyond territorial waters, an imperial responsibility, from
1870 when imperial troops were withdrawn, the colonies had provided
—somewhat sporadically in response to "scares"—for their domestic
defense on land. By an agreement made in 1887 the imperial authorities
had increased the number of ships of the imperial navy assigned to
the Australian station and at the same time the colonies jointly became
responsible for a subsidy and provided a few ships for harbor and
coastal waters. Following these arrangements, the position with regard
to the land forces—the armies—obviously needed review. After studying the situation Major General Sir Bevan Edwards made a series of
observations and recommendations in a report to the colonial governments of which the most significant were those which suggested that
no satisfactory scheme could be devised on the basis of each colony
separately and laid down that troops available in any colony (either
the small permanent forces or the larger volunteer reserves) should in
an emergency be available for service where needed in any of the colonies; that the troops available should be centrally directed and centrally serviced, as by a school for officers and a munitions factory; and
that for the efficient movement of troops and matériel, the unification
of the railways was required. It had by this time been established that
Australia would contribute land forces to imperial wars. The vital
precedent was the sending a small body of troops from New South
Wales to the Sudan in 1887. The policy was confirmed before federation was achieved when all the Australian colonies sent forces to the
Boer War. (No Australian leader made as much of the Boer War as
Richard Seddon did in New Zealand, and there was far more important criticism of it in Australia than in New Zealand, but Australian
popular support was strong, sustained by the Australian spirit of adventure and a vigorous imperial patriotism.) It was the suggestion that
the colonial land forces be centrally controlled and directed that set
Sir Henry Parkes off on the quest for federation.

However, organization and control of land defense, even with the
unification of the railways added, was not sufficient to justify a superstructure of federal government. Sir Henry, therefore, soon added items
of public business which by general consent of the intercolonial conferences and the Federal Council had been agreed to be of concern to
the colonies collectively, including the one most likely to cause dissen-

sion, fiscal policy—the tariff. To these he made an abortive attempt to add the public lands. But he never envisioned any distribution of powers as between the federal authority and the member-colonies that would diminish the primary responsibility of the colonies for growth and development. His emphasis was on aggrandizing them collectively rather than diminishing them individually. Nevertheless he wanted a strong and comprehensive federal machinery of government: legislative, executive, judicial. And he wanted the new federation to have its being "under the Crown." He was extremely sensitive to any hint or expressed suspicion that *he* was leading the colonies on toward independent nationhood, either by design or inadvertence, though he recognized that it might someday come.

Sir Henry's first task was to get the colonial leaders committed to the *idea* of federation. The first obstacle he encountered was loyalty to the existing Federal Council. It was alleged that the Federal Council could deal satisfactorily with all common colonial questions, including defense, especially if New South Wales would join it. This was embarrassing to Sir Henry for not only was he convinced that it was politically impossible to get his colony to join the Council but also, in spite of the fact that he himself had first proposed the Council idea—he was absent from politics and Australia when it was finally constituted—he had long since come to the conclusion that it was inadequate to its ostensible purpose. He now wanted a stronger and more elaborate federal instrumentality. He therefore had to argue around and by his own brain child to get his fellow politicians committed to his enlarged vision of federation.

Sir Henry had his triumph at Melbourne in 1890. He there got the assembled politicians committed to the idea of federation and to the calling of a meeting to discuss a constitution at Sydney the next year. At Melbourne were gathered representatives of every Australian colony and New Zealand, the only colony of Australasia which, in the end, did not join the federation. Such distinguished federalists as Alfred Deakin of Victoria, Sir Samuel Griffith of Queensland, and Inglis Clark of Tasmania were present. Sir Henry, warned by James Service of Victoria that the fiscal question was the "lion in the path," made clear that he, as a free trader, was prepared to put federation above fiscal policy and leave the fiscal decision to the federal legislators. He argued from the disorders which beset the United States under the Articles of Confederation, equated roughly with the condition of the Australian colonies under the Federal Council, to the conclusion that a strong federal constitution was required to save the Australian situation, as one had saved the United States. He referred feelingly to Gavan Duffy's remark that

"Neighboring States of the second order inevitably become confederates or enemies." He referred to the necessity for a common determination on the racial composition of the population; he referred in his classic phrase to the common national origin of the Australian colonists: "the crimson thread of kinship runs through us all"; he referred expansively to Australia's future as master of the islands; he conjured up an impressive vision of the prestige a federated Australia would enjoy among the nations of the world. Sir Henry made clear that in his view the creation of a federated, continental, Australian nation was the next step toward the realization of Australia's manifest destiny. If he did not sweep all before him, he at least established that it was not "some day" that the federation of the colonies was desirable, as the reluctant alleged, but now.

In 1891 the constitutional convention at Sydney opened on March 2 and ended on April 9. It brought together in addition to the federalists who had been at the Melbourne meeting—Parkes, Deakin, Griffith, Clark—Edmund Barton of New South Wales, Charles Cameron Kingston of South Australia, and Sir John Forrest of Western Australia, all destined to have distinguished federal careers. From New Zealand came Sir George Grey, chiefly to preach "one man, one vote." Parkes, as host and president of the convention, laid out the task before the gathering in a comprehensive resolution. This document began by stating: "That the powers and privileges and territorial rights of the several existing colonies shall remain intact, except in respect to such surrender as may be agreed upon as necessary and incidental to the power and authority of the National Federal Government." It then went on to assert: "That the trade and intercourse between the Federated colonies, whether by means of land carriage or coastal navigation, shall be absolutely free" and that the federal government should alone have the power to impose customs duties, but since this would deprive most colonies of their most important source of revenue and require free-trade New South Wales to assume new burdens, the disposal of the income thus derived among the colonies was to be agreed upon. Finally, it was laid down that the military and naval defense was to be undertaken by federal forces "under one command." It then set out the requirements that there should be a parliament of two houses, the lower house alone to have the power to originate and amend money bills, a judiciary, and an executive of the British parliamentary style headed by a governor-general representing the Queen. The guiding principles were debated for eleven days, while twelve days were devoted to drafting the text of a bill and other committee work. The final draft of the bill was the work of Sir Samuel Griffith, the principal architect, Edmund Barton, Charles Cameron Kingston, and Inglis Clark. Of these men Inglis Clark was the most ardent admirer of the American federal system, but it is generally agreed that the 1891 constitution was the creation of men all of whom were heavily influenced by American precedents. In effect the bill represented what could happen when one mixed together American constitutional ideas, British parliamentary forms, and the Australian experience of working responsible government. The creation was dubbed, at Parkes's suggestion, the *Commonwealth* of Australia, not without hesitation because of the association of the term with Oliver Cromwell, a doubt in part assuaged by the fact that the word was used with favorable connotation by Shakespeare.

Although some antifederal politicians—for example Sir George Dibbs of New South Wales—attended the 1891 convention, the constitution that issued from it was the fullest expression of the ideas of the profederalist politicians yet achieved. It was expected that when the bill was submitted to the colonial legislatures it would be amended in particulars but not modified in any fundamental respect. It was not anticipated that the bill and the federal question would become entangled in the politics of the time to the disaster of both. Yet within two years it was necessary to start the campaign for federalism all over again on a new basis. The 1891 constitution survived as a foundation document for those who wrote the instrument eventually accepted, but only because the federal question was taken from the charge of the parliamentarians and placed in the hands of men who had their mandate directly from the voters.

Politics in the Australian colonies underwent a great shake-up in the 1890's, caused in large measure by the appearance of labor as a political force in the parliaments. Although the trade unionists had taken an interest in politics earlier, it was not until the organized workers had been defeated in a series of great strikes that an organized effort was made to win parliamentary seats for members of labor parties. In four great strikes, a maritime strike in 1890 which affected the ports of Australia and New Zealand, strikes in the pastoral industry of Queensland in 1891 and 1894 primarily involving the shearers, and a strike of the miners of Broken Hill in 1892, the unionists tested their strength against that of the employers organized in associations. All the strikes spread beyond the place or industry or type of employment in which they originated by the sympathetic action of related unions. All provoked the governments of the day to use the police power, ostensibly to guarantee the public peace but in a fashion that the unionists inevitably interpreted as hostile and oppressive to them. All the newspapers were hostile to the strikers. The strikers indulged in destructive action against employers' property; strikers were arrested, prosecuted, and jailed for violations of laws, sometimes laws they had not realized were still in force. The strikes were of the nature of social war. The unionists thought of themselves as striking—or being locked out—in defense of the *principle of unionism,* but in the eyes of the employers the big question at issue was "freedom of contract," or the right to hire any labor, union or nonunion, on terms determined by direct discussion between employer and worker, as against the assertion of a monopoly claim over labor and terms of employment by the unions. The conflicts were bitter and embittering. They were class warfare, open and avowed. Caught in the middle, the politicians stood with their governments for law and order: Parkes in New South Wales, Deakin in Victoria, Griffith in Queensland, not because they were hostile to labor or in the pockets of the employers, but because they were the guardians of the public peace. Actually as the subsequent political actions of the younger liberals showed, they were prepared to concede much to labor, though not in response to direct action. The ugliness of the strikes appalled all but the most reckless of the laborites and the most rigid and hardboiled of the capitalist employers. Open class warfare was too much for the Australian temperament. The strikes thus became a most effective argument in favor of political and social reform. When labor turned to politics, it therefore commanded support at the polls beyond its organized ranks and indeed it smartly angled for that support with platform planks designed to capture it. And if labor appeared to think of politics in its first approach as a continuation of class warfare by other means, reversing the Clausewitz maxim, actually its first gains were made because of the disposition of the established politicians to grant some of the concessions labor demanded in return for supporting the leaders in office. The established politicians appeased labor, but by accepting the discipline of parliamentary democracy the rather inchoate utopian radicalism which characterized the labor movement of the time was shaped into a kind of left-wing liberalism, or a catch-as-catch-can *social* democracy, almost wholly compatible with the established social order. Labor did not vault to power with its radicalism untempered. It did not basically change the rough and tumble character of Australian politics, though it introduced a new intensity of organization into it. It took labor twenty years to gather the voting support that would give it office and power at the same time, though it gained office without power, or shared office and power, earlier, for example, in Queensland in 1899 and in South Australia in 1905. By the time labor came to power its radicals were either transformed into left-liberal politicians or were operating in the trade unions and labor-associated outside organizations, constantly pressuring the parliamentarians, trying to dictate to them, often embarrassing them, but only exceptionally dominating them. Labor in the 1890's introduced the social democratic note into the Australian political chorus. It has waxed to a shout and waned to a whisper ever since. Australia was the first British community to experience this more or less inevitable development in democracy under capitalism.

In its first appearance as a separate force in politics, labor achieved its greatest strength in New South Wales. In Queensland, where it was most radical, or "socialistic," because of the influence of William Lane, it was a politically isolated group, not only from the dominant conservatives but also from the liberal minority; in Victoria its parliamentary representatives continued to work with the Liberals; and in South Australia it collaborated effectively with liberals such as Charles Cameron Kingston. In New South Wales in 1891, however, it immediately gained the balance of power as a third party in the legislature and exploited its position by offering at "auction" to support in office that leader who would promise it most by way of legislative "concessions." While pursuing this course it consolidated its ranks by initiating the practice, subsequently one of its hallmarks, of shedding lukewarm, dissident and ideologically uncongenial associates—the Henry George-ites were early dropped—and securing its voting strength by the highly controversial (in view of the conventions of British politics) innovation of exacting a pledge from all candidates for office under its auspices that they would unfailingly, on pain of expulsion, vote in Parliament as decided by the party in caucus, except on issues specified not to be party questions. Of all the men who came into politics under the labor banner in the first decade, none was more fated and fateful than William Morris Hughes, exponent and later ruthless violator of the pledge. Hughes entered Parliament in 1894. The 1891 platform was a shrewd document, illustrative of the peculiar nature of the new political force, at once declaring its working-class orientation, demonstrating its willingness to support reforms which, while obviously beneficial to the working class, were yet sure of a welcome by a larger constituency, its willingness to identify with, whether pragmatically or from weakness of ideological perception, small capitalist entrepreneurs, especially in farming and mining, thus confusing its collectivist bias, and its nationalism, at this stage more colonial than continental. In pursuit of its objectives, Labor began by supporting Parkes and then precipitately toppled him from office—finally and forever as it turned out—on the question of legislating the eight-hour day; it then supported Dibbs the protectionist and in due course dropped him in favor of Reid the free trader, only to be trapped into turning him out in favor of the radical liberal Sir William Lyne, perhaps their best "friend" before federation. Labor got something it wanted from all these old-line politicians except Parkes, but in the perspective of history their most important early gains were old age pensions and conciliation and arbitration of labor disputes, first voluntary, then compulsory, the one, ex post facto, the seed of the future Australian welfare state (which was a long time coming), the other the foundation, along with related but not identical legislation in Victoria, of a system that institutionalized state participation in the determination of wages, hours and conditions of labor, hopefully but not actually to eliminate strikes. Both of these innovations were based on New Zealand precedents and were essentially *liberal* in genesis and social meaning. Neither was a labor-originated measure. Indeed, what was striking was how little of what was put on the lawbooks by way of reform at this time could be claimed *ab origine* by labor. Labor was, however, reasonably clever in its eclecticism. As in New Zealand across the Tasman—as in the long run in Britain—the Liberals led the way, with labor encouraging, prodding, and supporting them, though on specific questions often hesitantly and with limited perception of implications. The great political unknowns at this stage were how far the Liberals—or the opportunists—would go in the direction labor was pointing and how far labor would go, and where, if and when it won power.

The irruption of Labor into the parliamentary politics of New South Wales had a fateful effect on the federal cause. Labor, while declaring in its 1891 platform for "the Federation of the Australian colonies on a National as opposed to an Imperial basis"—a form of words designed to declare its opposition to imperial federation—was really not much interested in the national federal question. It was rather interested in social reform in the colony of New South Wales. Therefore the federal cause suffered a severe reverse when Labor tumbled Parkes from the premiership on a social reform question before he was ready to bring in the 1891 constitution for legislative discussion. Since the other colonies waited upon the leadership of New South Wales, this was a signal to mark time generally. Dibbs, who succeeded Parkes, was not interested in federation—he toyed with unification—and though he allowed his ardently federalist associate Edmund Barton to try to do something about the 1891 instrument, he did not personally assist him and Barton soon fell victim to political misfortune and resigned from office. When Reid followed Dibbs, that extraordinarily pliable man, firm about very little except free trade, was maneuvered into doing something about the matter—a rather extraordinary something it turned out to be—only because the federalists were able to shake him out of his rather supercilious indifference by the thrust of the popular movement for federation, stemming from Victoria with its New South Wales leader, Edmund Barton, blessed by Sir Henry Parkes. The question was taken up again at the highest level in 1895.

The organized popular movement in support of federation originated in Victoria in close connection with the Australian Natives' Association. The Association carried on federalist propaganda in its own name and assisted in the formation of federal "leagues." In mid-1893 the Victorians asked Edmund Barton to establish in Sydney, and head, a "central" league to link up and direct the local leagues then coming into existence. This Barton did. It gave him effective leadership of the federal movement. Local leagues were formed in Victoria, New South Wales, South Australia, Queensland, and even New Zealand. Also in 1893 a conference of then existing leagues was held at Corowa, New South Wales, at which Dr. (later Sir) John Quick, a Victorian federalist, obtained adoption of a proposal of fundamental importance to the eventual success of the federalist campaign. The idea was not new, nor was it peculiarly Dr. Quick's at the moment, but what he proposed was that "each Australasian colony should pass an act providing for the election of representatives to attend a statutory Convention or Congress to consider and adopt a Bill to establish a Federal Constitution for Australia, and upon the adoption of such Bill or measure it to be submitted by some process of Referendum to the verdict of each colony." It was this proposal that Reid picked up when it was made apparent to him that he had to do something about federation. At a conference of premiers at Hobart in January 1895 Reid obtained an agreement to carry through essentially what Dr. Quick had proposed. The required enabling acts were passed by New South Wales, South Australia, Tasmania, and Victoria in late 1895 and early 1896, but in Queensland the bill failed, while in Western Australia it was decided to keep the matter in the hands of the legislators until a constitution had been approved by Parliament. The New South Wales act specified that to be declared adopted any constitution had to get at least 50,000 affirmative votes in a referendum.

The elected delegates held three convention sessions, in Adelaide, Sydney, and Melbourne, between March 1897 and January 1898, of which the most fruitful from the standpoint of constitution writing was that at Melbourne. At the sessions federalists of established reputation, Barton, now the unquestioned leader, Deakin, and Charles Cameron Kingston—Parkes was dead, and Sir Samuel Griffith as chief justice of Queensland could not have participated even had Queensland arranged participation—were joined by men who subsequently made federal history such as Reid, Lyne, and R. E. O'Connor of New South Wales, Sir George Turner, Dr. John Quick, Isaac Isaacs, and Henry Bournes Higgins of Victoria, P. McMahon Glynn of South Australia, Sir Edward Braddon of Tasmania, and Sir John Forrest of Western Australia, as well as many figures of lesser distinction. Of the delegates, five were currently colonial premiers, three were speakers, and twenty were or had been ministers. The only individual present who was identified with the labor movement was W. A. Trenwith of Victoria, and in the end he was repudiated by the organized workers for supporting the resulting constitution. After the coming of Labor into parliamentary politics as before, therefore, the federal movement was a liberal-conservative affair. It tells much about the state of colonial public opinion that it consistently commanded a majority of the electors voting. The opposition was partly expressed in active voting but more in nonvoting apathy.

At Adelaide the 1891 constitution was accepted as the basis of discussion. The constitutional committee, the most important of the three committees, the others being the judiciary and finance, consisted of twenty members. It was dominated by Barton and O'Connor of New South Wales and Deakin of Victoria; the actual drafting was done by Barton and O'Connor and Sir John Downer, a lawyer and former premier of South Australia. Attention at Adelaide was concentrated chiefly on the basis of representation in the federal Parliament—the proposal for equal state representation in the Senate was contentious—the structure of the judiciary, the method of amending the constitution—there was a fear of a rigid constitution, with the United States constitution as the horrid example—and finance, the distribution of revenue as between the federal government and the states. Between the Adelaide and Sydney meetings, the constitution as it then stood was debated in the legislatures and all told no less than 286 amendments were proposed. At Sydney, by agreement, only the larger issues of finance, representation in the Senate, the powers of the Senate with regard to money bills, and deadlocks between the houses, were discussed. It was now apparent that a strong tide was running in favor of federation—unexpectedly strong as far as the opposition was concerned—and the New South Wales antifederalists tried to stem it by trickery by raising the statutorily required affirmative vote from 50,000 to 80,000. At Melbourne the text of a constitution was finally fixed. A bicameral legislature had been provided for consisting of a Senate in which all the states were equally represented, the members popularly elected by state-wide constituencies and a House, also popularly elected, but in constituencies marked out on a population basis, the House to have twice as many members as the Senate. The House was to have sole power to originate money bills; the Senate could only suggest amendments, not make them. Elaborate machinery for solving deadlocks, fear of which was widespread because of colonial experience, was provided. The executive was constituted on the British parliamentary model and was headed by a governor-general, representing the Queen. This was an attempt to marry British "responsible government" under the Crown with federalism. The judiciary was capped by a federal supreme court, called a High Court. Finance was handled by providing that the excess of federal revenues to be derived from a tariff, estimated at three-quarters of the probable total, was to be handed back to the states. The formula for this bookkeeping operation was provided by Sir Edward Braddon of Tasmania; it became known derisively as the "Braddon Blot." The powers of the federal government were specified; they numbered, by accident one assumes, thirty-nine and included matters which had been considered common since the days of the intercolonial conferences. However, the railways were not unified. And two items were added that directly reflected the newer politics of the 1890's: "xxiii Invalid and old age pensions" and "xxxv Conciliation and arbitration for the prevention and settlement of industrial disputes extending beyond the limits of any one State." A late insertion into the preamble, made under pressure from outside the convention, was "humbly relying on the blessing of Almighty God."

The constitution fixed and polished at Melbourne was submitted to the people in a referendum conducted in New South Wales, Victoria, and Tasmania on June 3, 1898, and in South Australia on June 4. Western Australia, Queensland, and New Zealand were at this stage on the sidelines, and while it was still likely that Western Australia and Queensland would eventually join the federation, it was felt doubtful that New Zealand would. There had been no participation in the discussions by New Zealand since 1891. Majorities for federation were obtained fairly easily in Victoria, Tasmania, and South Australia, but in New South Wales the calculated roadblock of 80,000 affirmative votes proved effective: 71,595 voted yes and 66,228 no. In New South Wales, as in the other colonies, a wide variety of highly particularistic considerations, founded in fear of economic competition from the other colonies, or of economic or political disadvantage to be suffered from association with them—that is, narrowly colonial, even parish-pump, considerations—explained the no vote, while a very generalized continental nationalism, rather than considered judgment of the technicalities of the constitution, accounted for the yes vote. But there were special factors in New South Wales which accounted for the failure to top the 80,000 minimum affirmative votes required by statute. New South Wales had the most violently parochial opponent of federation—a lawyer-politician named J. H. Want; it had the most consistently antifederal newspaper, the Sydney *Daily Telegraph* to balance a consistently federalist paper, the conservative *Sydney Morning Herald;* it had a Labor party trapped in a decidedly populist point of view with regard to the franchise, representation in the Senate, and the uses of referendum, which made it antifederal, with an effective spokesman in W. M. Hughes; and it had —perhaps most importantly—George Houston Reid. Reid seized the opportunity to outdo himself in his favorite ploy of masterly indecision. He opened the prereferendum campaign with a speech in which he severely criticized the constitutional instrument as disadvantageous to New South Wales and concluded nevertheless by announcing that he would vote yes in the referendum. This was one of the most famous political speeches in Australian history—Reid's yes-no speech. It undoubtedly influenced the vote just sufficiently to put Reid where he had aimed to get, in a position to ask amendments to the constitution favorable to the interests of his colony. The requirement of 80,000 affirmative votes was thus used by Reid for his—and New South Wales's? —political advantage.

Reid's first reaction to his success was to assume a dictatorial attitude. He named amendments he would exact. But before he could act in this fashion he barely weathered a general election and moderated his tone. And when he finally met with the other premiers in Melbourne in January 1899 to discuss the questions, he settled for less than he started out to get. At Melbourne Western Australia also asked changes as did Queensland which, at this point, returned to the federal discussions. All told, seven amendments were agreed to, six proposed by New South Wales, one by Queensland. Of the seven, four were minor and three major; the latter all asked by New South Wales. The provision governing deadlocks was improved, the life of the Braddon Blot was limited to ten years when federal-state financial relations would be open to review, and it was provided that a permanent federal capital would be established someplace in New South Wales not less than one hundred miles from Sydney. The temporary federal capital would be at Melbourne.

In this amended form the constitution was accepted by the people in a second referendum held in mid-1899 in the colonies of New South Wales, Queensland, Victoria, South Australia, and Tasmania. Comfortably over 100,000 affirmative votes were cast in New South Wales and there were heavy majorities in all colonies except Queensland where the affirmative margin was but 7000 out of 69,000 votes. The Western Australian legislators were still considering "conditions" for joining the federation when the other five Australian colonies made their decisions. The New Zealanders, while apparently keenly interested in what was going on in Australia, were in a practical sense inactive.

Up to this point the constitution making had been an exclusively Australian affair without even the "permission" from London that had authorized the constitution making of the 1850's. True, the secretary of state for the colonies, that redoubtable imperialist Joseph Chamberlain, had spoken about the business to certain of the colonial premiers when they were in London in 1897 to attend the Diamond Jubilee of Queen Victoria, but apparently only casually, though he had sent Reid a confidential memorandum about appeals to the Privy Council. Now the time had come to submit the instrument to the Queen—really to the imperial government—with a prayer that it be enacted by the imperial Parliament. As the separate political units of Australia were individually colonies, so collectively as a federal Commonwealth the legal status would remain colonial. At Chamberlain's request the colonies sent delegates to London to discuss the instrument and see it through Parliament, Barton for New South Wales, Deakin for Victoria, Kingston for South Australia, J. R. Dickson, a liberal politician currently premier for Queensland, Sir Philip Fysh, liberal politician currently agent-general in London, for Tasmania, and S. H. Parker, after Sir John Forrest the most powerful political figure of the colony, for Western Australia. For New Zealand the spokesman would be her agent-general, Pember Reeves, acting on instructions from Prime Minister Seddon in Wellington. The Australian delegates were under instructions to see to it that the constitution was enacted unchanged, since it had in its current form been accepted by referendum by the people, and they put up a powerful struggle to that end. They early discovered, however, that Chamberlain and his advisers were bent on changes, the implicit motive for which was a resolution that nothing in the Australian national federal constitution should prospectively interfere with imperial federation, in their eyes the next great development in the British community. This was more implicit than avowed, though met head-on by the Australians. Avowedly what Chamberlain proposed was to see to it that the old distinction between imperial and colonial authority and responsibility was observed in favor of traditional imperial prerogatives. Chamberlain insisted upon closely examining the meaning of anything that appeared to cast doubt upon the continuance of imperial authority and responsibility with regard to Australia, considered as a colony, and he succeeded in modifying or eliminating many, to him, doubtful phrases, but serious contention occurred only over appeals from the Australian courts to the Privy Council in London. In the 1899 constitution these were severely limited. Chamberlain insisted upon liberalization as essential to the preservation of the imperial connection. He was successful, partly because of the defection to his side of Dickson of Queensland, partly because when consulted by telegraph the colonial premiers acquiesced, but only after the High Court was given the task of granting leave for appeal instead of the governor-general and the state governors as Chamberlain proposed. Along the way Chamberlain's emphasis on appeals as a vital and indispensable link of Empire was rebutted by the Australian delegates in rhetorical irony: "The consciousness of kinship, the consciousness of a common blood and a common sense of duty, the pride of their race and history—these are the links of Empire; bands which attach, not bonds which chafe. When the Australian fights for the Empire, he is inspired by these sentiments; but no patriotism was ever inspired or sustained by the thought of the Privy Council."

Meanwhile other matters were brought up for discussion. Reeves of New Zealand submitted a memorandum asking that New Zealand be preserved the right to join the federation as an "original state," that while she remained outside the federation her litigants have the right to appeal to the Commonwealth High Court as an alternative to the Privy Council, and that the Commonwealth and New Zealand be empowered to concert their military and naval defense. (However, what was really on Prime Minister Seddon's mind was trade relations with Australia which involved no constitutional relationship; and he was currently seeking to fortify his position for such negotiations by attempting to bring island groups into closer relation to New Zealand.) The Western Australians, for their part, asked that the constitution be modified to allow the colony to maintain its full tariff for five years after joining the federation, chiefly to protect its infant agriculture, instead of having progressively to reduce the tariff over five years as the constitution provided. After the Australian premiers had been consulted, these requests were denied. However, New Zealand, while now definitely out of the federation, remained one of the colonies named in the definition of "state" in the constitution (as it does to the present day).

The amended bill went through the House of Commons and House of Lords without any very searching debate. Campbell-Bannerman, leader of the opposition, criticized Chamberlain's handling of the matter, especially his insistence on amending after the Australian people had accepted the constitution by referendum, while having foregone many opportunities to make clear his position at earlier stages. On July 9, 1900, Queen Victoria gave her assent, signing two documents so that one could be returned for preservation in Australia.

There was then a short delay while the Western Australians made up their minds whether or not to join the federation. On July 31 a referendum was held in which the urban voters of Perth and Fremantle and the gold fields voters of Kalgoorlie and vicinity gave the proposal an affirmative majority, but in which the tariff-protected crop agriculturalists voted no. The most ardent federalists were the people of the gold fields. In large proportion from the eastern colonies, they apparently saw in the continental nationalism of federalism a way of escaping from the isolation they felt in Western Australia and from political domination by the politicians in Perth whose views were, by inheritance, essentially isolationist, and reintegrating themselves into the larger Australian community then, as today, centered in the east. With the personal element favoring integration progressively lessened, integration into the Australian community, not automatically achieved by federation, has remained a chronic Western Australian problem. The gold fields people felt so strongly about the matter that at one stage they attempted to secede from Western Australia and form a colony of their own which would promptly join the federation. The antifederalist farmers feared the competition of eastern suppliers of foodstuffs if the tariff barriers were lowered. Many off the gold fields who voted affirmatively were of two minds about the question. Sir John Forrest, who had dominated Western Australian politics since the colony had achieved responsible government in 1890, finally declared for federation, but frankly said that he could not see it doing much good for Western Australia for some years in the future, yet, on the other hand, it did not seem wise for the colony to attempt to stand out of the continental union. The affirmative decision of Western Australia therefore concealed a troublesome ambiguity that found expression now and again down the years and in especially dramatic fashion thirty-odd years later.

Assured that Western Australia was to be an "original state," Queen Victoria on September 17, 1900, finally signed a Proclamation that "on and after the first day of January, 1901, the people of New South Wales, Victoria, South Australia, Queensland, Tasmania and Western Australia should be united in a Federal Commonwealth under the name of the Commonwealth of Australia."

NEW ZEALAND

CHAPTER XVIII

The Pakehas Take New Zealand

The Treaty of Waitangi did not provide an unassailable basis for ordering the relations of Maoris and pakehas, nor did it, in the eyes of international lawyers, provide an absolutely sound basis for British sovereignty. It was rather a statement of intent. The intent was to establish a biracial society in New Zealand with equality of rights for both races.

It was assumed that the Maoris possessed a capacity for cultural growth and adaptation which made equality under law with the intruding whites a reasonable ideal. It was assumed that while the Maoris had clear priority rights in the land, they knew enough about what systematic settlement by the whites would mean to part with some of the land if their material stake in it were protected. Provision was therefore made for orderly transfer of title to land from one party to the other.

Plainly, the treaty was viable only if the assumptions underlying it were accepted both by the Maoris and the incoming whites, and if the machinery for transferring title to land was worked with the most careful regard for the interests of both parties. The necessary conditions failed immediately to materialize. The intent survived as an ideal.

While the government instituted in New Zealand by the British, acting under instructions of the Colonial Office, had the responsibility for initiating general policy and tried valiantly to do so in the spirit of the Treaty of Waitangi, it was not in a position to act as though it were writing on a clean slate. It was not only that it inherited the situation created by the intruders from the earliest days, but it was also that it confronted the New Zealand Company, the principal promoter of systematic settlement. It is the common verdict of historians that the Company must be given great credit for establishing the British in New Zealand, but its contemporary pretensions were much larger than was comfortable either for the local or the London government. While the

Company never seriously disputed the ultimate authority of the colonial government, it nevertheless resisted its policies, especially as to land and the Maoris, both in the colony and in London, constantly vituperating the governors and exerting strong pressure on the Colonial Office, directly and through Parliament. The Company was irked by the assumptions of the treaty. It tried hard to get the British government to repudiate it insofar as its spirit influenced public policy; its legality was attacked in an effort to make its principles inoperative. The government's policies were thus not only criticized, but their very foundations were assailed. In large measure this campaign was motivated by land-hunger, naked and hardly to any degree ashamed. The Company's position was, by the implication of land-hunger and often by open avowal, rather anti-Maori, and from being upstanding individuals capable of participation on a footing of equality in a biracial state, the Maoris became "naked savages" destined, happily, to disappear from the face of the earth. Many settlers not beholden to the Company shared these views for their own reasons, while a few honorable men with responsibilities to it did not do so. As a form of government evolved which allowed the settlers a voice in policy making, anti-Maori views influenced the line taken in general and in critical specific situations. Step by step the situation was created that led to the Maori-pakeha wars of the 1860's.

The New Zealand Company, it will be recalled, began its activities in the country without the authorization of the British government, without a charter—it only got one early in 1841—and when New Zealand was not yet part of the Queen's dominions. Its settlers began to arrive before British sovereignty was proclaimed in New Zealand and before a government was inaugurated. The precipitate action of the Company led it to introduce settlers before the land it proposed they should occupy had been explored and assessed, let alone surveyed. Indeed, it was not known in England that any land at all was available to them for settlement; it could only be presumed that the Company's advance agent had succeeded in buying some. He had, but on a land-sharking basis. He eventually claimed he had purchased 20,000,000 acres, in parcels chiefly around Cook Strait in both the North and the South islands. But the rapidity with which the British government moved to acquire sovereignty and define its land policy threw into doubt the validity of the Company's claims even before it could give the settlers the benefit of possession. Nevertheless, it proceeded to place some of its settlers on the land, though after long delays while the surveyors did their work, leaving the argument over title to pursue its course. It was in many ways an even worse performance than that in South Australia, and it had a similar consequence: it tended to coop up many of the intending settlers in Wellington for long periods, during which they lived on their capital, as in South Australia they had been cooped up in Adelaide while similarly occupied.

As a place from which to spread settlement, moreover, Wellington had its peculiar deficiencies. It was a hilly place, with hills back of it, though on an excellent harbor admirably situated in relation to the eventual development of the North Island. But as a center from which to spread agricultural settlement, it was a doubtful choice. It was better suited as a trading town for settlements at varying distances from it, with communications by sea. Fortunately, it took firm root and grew on that basis.

The first settlement made under Company auspices apart from Wellington, and what may be called its suburbs (like the Hutt Valley), was at Wanganui, 120 miles to the north, late in 1840. This involved some 200 settlers and was a swarming from the original hive of people frustrated by the situation in it. Then, in the following year the settlers of the New Plymouth Company, a subsidiary of the New Zealand Company, arrived from England and were placed on land in Taranaki at the foot of Mount Egmont, about 200 miles north of Wanganui. And while the Taranaki settlement was in process still other people arrived from England before an argument between the Company and Captain Hobson as to where they should be established had been settled. Hobson wanted the new settlement in the north of the North Island, while the Company favored the South Island at Canterbury. Eventually, they settled at Nelson in the north of South Island.

Meanwhile, Captain Hobson, not having found any satisfactory location at the Bay of Islands, had established his capital at Auckland in the north, far removed from the Company settlements (to the Company's arrogantly expressed annoyance), but convenient to country occupied by great numbers of Maoris, to whom Hobson naturally felt special obligations. Many of the settlers attracted to Auckland were from Australia. And meanwhile the protracted drama of French interest in New Zealand ended when a handful of Frenchmen and a few Germans were settled by a French colonization company at Akaroa on Banks Peninsula in the South Island. Obviously intended to effect a French claim to the island by occupation, and to live by selling goods and services to French whalers, these people had arrived too late, and their sponsors had no choice but to recognize that England was sovereign. Some of the French drifted away to Tahiti and the Marquesas, but the rest settled down and were soon joined by stray British settlers, either in their immediate or more remote vicinity, who turned out to be pioneers of a great body of British who were to enter the island at about this point later on.

D3

There had been trading for land with the Maoris for over a quarter-century before the British took sovereignty in New Zealand. The earliest purchases by white intruders were modest in acreage and were quite clearly for use. By the middle 1820's, however, a speculative element appeared in the trading, but it is probable that up to the end of 1838 the Maoris had not sold much more than 2,000,000 acres. At that time the imminence of large-scale settlement was apparent, and land sharks, mostly from Australia, began to buy millions of acres. W. C. Wentworth, as already mentioned, claimed he had bought over 20,000,000 acres. The New Zealand Company, employing land-sharking methods, accumulated claims to 20,000,000 acres also. By the time the British government got around to the claims, about 46,000,000 acres were involved. The total acreage of the two islands of New Zealand is only about 66,000,000 acres.

When the British authorities stepped into this situation in 1840 they had two purposes in view: they proposed to investigate and allow or disallow all claims to land dating from prior to their assumption of sovereignty, and they proposed to set up machinery for acquiring land so as to make the government the sole broker of land between the Maoris and the pakehas. As to the first, many claims were, when formally examined, either thrown out completely or drastically reduced. The bulk of these were claims of the land-sharking variety. A fantastic claim like W. C. Wentworth's never got off the ground; it was promptly quashed by Governor Gipps of New South Wales after a brilliant and bitter verbal battle between the two in the Legislative Council. Others, however, especially those dating from the mid-1830's or earlier, including missionary claims, dragged through the courts for many years. The New Zealand Company's claim, which by virtue of the Company's special position had a special status, was eventually, after negotiations between the Company and the British government, compromised in such a fashion that the Company ended up with only 283,000 acres. The worst disadvantaged of all in this unhappy business were those who had purchased land from the New Zealand Company and then found that the Company could not give them a clear title to it. This led many to accuse the Company of fraud, and it certainly lowered the Company's prestige, not to mention the delay it occasioned in developing the settlements.

As to the other aspect of the matter, the government set up machinery for acquiring land from the Maoris, but in fairly short order that machinery became less a means of protecting the Maoris from exploitation such as had accompanied direct sales, than of "legally" parting the Maoris from their lands. Governor Hobson started confusion by setting up a Protectorate Department charged both with the duty of "protecting" the native race *and also* buying land. A factor in discrediting this machinery was the government policy of buying land from the Maoris at one price and immediately selling the same land to whites at a much higher price, pocketing the profit. Not its intent, but its perversion in working, played a large role in disillusioning the Maoris with pakeha government, especially as it was not accompanied by any compensating benefits. It became the common Maori belief that about the only time the government officers appeared among them was when they wanted to buy some of their land.

D3

The disputes over the land were not, even if our focus is closely on the North Island, carried on in naked isolation. They must be thought of in a complex context of pakeha settlement and development, of Maori adventures in agriculture, of struggles of the whites for a greater share in the government (with the Maoris excluded, in spite of the promise of the rights of British subjects). Thus far, aside from references to Nelson and Akaroa, little mention has been made of the South Island, but it is an important fact that by the fortunes of history the balance of strength shifted from the North to the South Island in the 1860's and remained there until the turn of the century. At this point it is necessary to take note of the founding of two settlements in the South Island before reverting to a discussion of economic and political matters involving both islands and recounting the role of violence in Maori-pakeha relations up to 1860.

The two South Island settlements are accounted the greatest successes of the New Zealand Company, which initiated them through subsidiary companies. The first was made in Otago in the south of the island in 1848, the other in Canterbury in the center of the island in 1850. In both cases the Company was not in direct control—it went out of active existence in a state of bankruptcy in 1850—but its principles were followed and improvements in practices suggested by experience were profitably used. Both colonies were identified with sponsoring churches, the Otago settlement with the Free Church of Scotland, the Canterbury settlement with the Church of England. However, the echo of the religious motivation which inspired settlements in North America in the seventeenth century was modulated, for while the religious element was conspicuous, it was not narrowly exclusive in spirit and neither settlement was ever legally theocratic.

The settlements in interesting ways reflected the character of the people founding them, the Scotch in Otago acting in the light of a dour, cautious seriousness, the English in Canterbury displaying a greater expansiveness and acting out their characters as middle-class English. The one was a settlement of relatively poor people seeking to improve their condition, the other a settlement dominated by people self-consciously "capitalists" seeking to enlarge their stake. Canterbury was very close to Wakefield's ideal of what a colony should be. Both, like the earlier settlements which the Company directly managed, displayed an imported class structure, with a "select" and "well-connected" upper class over a larger group of laborers. The Canterbury settlement was more quickly and directly a success. The Otago settlement went through fearfully hard times in its earliest years. The founding leader at Otago was Captain William Cargill, who had retired from the army after serving in India and Spain and who then had made a career in banking, while at Canterbury it was John Robert Godley, an Anglo-Irishman long interested in colonization, a Colonial reformer, New Zealand Company director, friend of Wakefield, an ardent Church of England communicant, and a Tory, who, after a brief tour of duty in New Zealand, had a distinguished career in United Kingdom politics. Both of these settlements were prepared by survey in advance and land sales were on the Wakefield principles. The settlements were facilitated by the fact that Maori title to the land was extinguished before they were begun, and by the circumstance that Maoris in their areas were few. Both, too, benefited by the fact that their areas had been pioneered beforehand—Otago by John Jones, the Sydney whaler-capitalist, Canterbury not only by the settlers of Akaroa but also by the Deane family on the plains the Canterbury people aimed to occupy—and their establishment was much assisted by the early arrival of pastoralists from Australia to occupy the land outside the agricultural blocks. These people, rather than the Canterbury immigrants, came to constitute the landed aristocracy. The principal settlement of Otago was Dunedin (ancient name of Edinburgh), of Canterbury, Christchurch (an inland town with its port at Lyttleton).

In accordance with the Wakefield theories, the several colonies to be planted in New Zealand were to be built on the basis of crop agriculture. It is one of the oddities of the Wakefield experiments that with all the emphasis on crop agriculture, Wakefield and his fellows paid so little attention to the nature and quality of the land they proposed to occupy. The Wakefieldians acted as though land was land and that was that. And it is equally odd that they paid so little heed to the problem of remunerative markets, especially markets available in the pioneering period. The first markets were practically limited to the small urban centers in the settlements. The North Island settlers, moreover, immediately confronted the difficult task of hewing farms out of the forests, a laborious and costly process in the course of which they were reduced to hoe-culture among the stumps. The net consequence was that in their various circumstances the Cook Strait settlers quickly reverted to a rather primitive subsistence farming. In the Cook Strait settlements, too, unemployment early plagued the laborers and after a period while the Company exhausted its funds in providing special employment on public works at reduced rates of wages, there was nothing for it but to assign the men small plots of land on which to raise some of their food. This, of course, was to ignore the Wakefield theory that easy access to the land by laborers was ruinous of the prosperity of the "capitalists." It had the consequence of making labor scarce for capitalist farmers, and they had to work on the land themselves, with but casual assistance. All were subsistence farmers together. The difficulties of the Cook Strait settlers during the 1840's were, however, mitigated by the establishment of sheep stations in areas where the character of the country made it possible. Pastoral pursuits, which Wakefield took so lightly, saved the Cook Strait settlements, and when Otago and Canterbury were occupied, notably facilitated their sound and rapid development. There was an export market for wool.

The Maoris supplied a certain amount of labor to the settlements, particularly for work of the rougher kind. Maori workers took a hand in land-clearing, track- and road-cutting and road building, even house-building. But while this contribution was important, their most remarkable economic accomplishment was in farming on their own account. They had been learning something of pakeha farming methods for a good many years; they had early adopted pakeha crops; but the great era of Maori farming before the wars came in the 1840's and 1850's. When the pakeha farmers were still struggling to establish themselves, the Maori farmers, working on a communal basis traditional and congenial to them, were thriving and sending quantities of foodstuffs to market, especially the market at Auckland, of which they were the chief suppliers. This enthusiasm for farming for market was one phase of the Maori aspiration to a position of equality in the new society. The most famous Maori areas in which such farming throve were the Waikato, south of Auckland and north of Taranaki, and Taranaki itself. Not only did the Maoris cultivate great acreages of wheat, grow quantities of potatoes, and raise many pigs, but they built gristmills to turn out flour. When they kept sheep for wool, they immediately strove to learn weaving that they might produce cloth. To carry their products to market, they acquired a fleet of boats and nearly dominated the local carrying trade. When demand for foodstuffs boomed in Australia at the time of the gold rushes, it was more the Maoris who supplied that market—conspicuously with flour—than the struggling pakeha farmers. All in all, the Maoris demonstrated their capacity to participate greatly in the field of commercial crop agriculture and to engage to a lesser extent in the pastoral industry. But in 1856 the Australian gold-fields market collapsed; the price of wheat fell sharply. Having but a limited understanding of market forces, though shrewd traders, the Maori farmers were deeply discouraged.

Ambitious Company settlers, not finding quick profit in crop farming, turned their hands to whaling and to dealing in flax, but above all to depasturing sheep for wool. As in Australia, the first basis for a viable New Zealand economy was woolgrowing. There were sheep in New Zealand, even flocks, before the Company people arrived, but the sheep to stock the runs they established were brought from Australia. The Australian-type merino was the earliest characteristic sheep of New Zealand. The early New Zealand pastoralists were as much squatters on the runs they established as were their Australian opposite numbers, even though many of the North Island pioneers paid a nominal rental to the Maoris whose lands they used. The sheep, they found, throve on the tussock grasses and on certain edible shrubs. The shorn wool was sent to Wellington in open boats for export, at first via Sydney to England, later on directly to England.

The men who pioneered woolgrowing from the Wellington settlement were of the class called "capitalists" and almost invariably the better-off members of the group. They alone had the money to embark upon such an undertaking, especially after the erosion of capital suffered by so many while waiting in the town for access to their land. The first area opened up by the pastoralists was the Wairarapa, a district to the east of Wellington, but practically inaccessible from it overland because of the heavily forested precipitate hills.

The Wairarapa was pioneered by the sheep people in 1844. Within three years the more adventurous people of Wairarapa were looking for pastures new, though the district was far from overcrowded or overstocked. A dominant characteristic of the pastoralists in both Australia and New Zealand was a passion for spreading into new country. In 1847 two of the Wairarapa people crossed Cook Strait to the vicinity of Cape Campbell in what was to become Marlborough Province. Also in the middle and late 1840's pastoralists established themselves in the Wairau Valley in Nelson. Thus, before Otago and Canterbury were settled, the pastoralists were active in the South Island and, indeed, were running more sheep than their North Island fellows. With the opening up of the country at Otago and Canterbury, the numbers of sheep rapidly mounted and the predominance of the South Island in this basic industry was confirmed.

D₹

New Zealand remained subordinate to New South Wales until May 3, 1841, when it was proclaimed a separate colony. However, the laws of New South Wales, insofar as they were applicable in New Zealand, remained in force until April 25, 1842, when it was decided that the New Zealand government had fully provided for the "good government" of the country and the laws of New South Wales were repealed. In form the government of New Zealand was a Crown Colony. Captain Hobson as governor was assisted by the Executive Council consisting of himself and the senior officials of the government (appointed in England) and the Legislative Council consisting of the same officials plus three senior justices of the peace. The country continued as a Crown Colony until 1852 when representative government, quickly transformed into responsible government, was introduced. From the beginning it had been recognized at the Colonial Office that it would be excessively difficult to govern New Zealand from a distance. Sir James Stephen had been explicit about this even before the final decision to take sovereignty in New Zealand had been made. This was the reason why New Zealand was so quickly separated from New South Wales; it was 1200 miles away, obviously too far for the authorities there to have the detailed knowledge required to govern successfully. And it was the reason why New Zealand gained responsible government within sixteen years of Waitangi.

Although the Crown Colony government had charge of everything, even the regulation of the dog nuisance in the towns, its major concerns were the land and the Maoris. Hobson, as the founding governor, carried into effect the land policy laid down in general terms by the Colonial Office and given specific definition and a machinery for executing it by Governor Gipps of New South Wales. This policy, as we have seen, was received with hostility by the claimants of land. It threw occupation plans into chaos, but it appeared at first to be acceptable to the Maoris. In his short term of office—he died in September 1842—Hobson was subjected to merciless abuse by those who could see no good in government policies which did not serve their private interests. His recall was insistently demanded. Yet his course won the approval of the Colonial Office, as appeared from a dispatch that arrived in New Zealand after his death. The Maoris, for their part, considered him a just man.

Hobson's successor, Captain Robert FitzRoy, R.N., a brilliant but emotionally unstable man (he eventually committed suicide), was in office from December 1843 until November 1845. He won more acclaim as commander of the "Beagle" on the voyage on which Charles Darwin was a member of the company, carried out before his tour of duty as governor, and as a meteorologist afterward, than in New Zealand. Not only did FitzRoy receive the abuse that all the Crown Colony governors attracted, but he decided upon policies that were clearly contrary to his instructions, and he finally was recalled by the Colonial Office.

To the central problems of the land and the Maoris were now added the government's financial troubles. Hobson had drawn on New South Wales for £45,000 and borrowed £10,000 more from the Bank of Australia in Sydney to meet his expenses in New Zealand. He was unable to carry on his government after the separation from New South Wales without accumulating a deficit. This deficit was inherited by Fitz-Roy who also found that current revenue was still far short of necessary expenditures. In dealing with this difficulty FitzRoy issued debentures to the amount of the accumulated deficit and made them legal tender, thus unconsciously invoking Gresham's Law. To close the gap between revenue and expenditures, he increased the customs duties, and as this did not suffice, he issued more debentures. This was illegal, unwise, inept. He compounded his folly, when he found that both the Maoris and the settlers objected to increased customs duties, by repealing them and substituting a property tax, but the property tax did not work and he had to revert to customs duties. This infirmity of economic understanding and purpose told against him. Moreover, FitzRoy arrived at a time when the troubles of the Company settlements were worsening. The people were assailing the Company, but they were also venting their wrath more savagely on the government as an available whipping boy. Their complaints were echoed in London in Parliament. For their part, the Maoris were beginning to question the good faith and justice of the pakehas, government people and settlers, both with regard to general policy and land policy.

FitzRoy's problem was to govern a country in which both of the principal parties, the Maoris and the pakehas, were to some extent disaffected from the government. FitzRoy interpreted his mandate to require him to mete out even-handed justice to Maori and pakeha alike, but neither party saw his acts in that light. Before his arrival there had been violence between pakehas and Maoris over the land. FitzRoy tried to hasten the settlement of land claims as a way of pacifying all hands; he even tried to facilitate the passing of land from Maoris to pakehas by waiving the government's right to be sole purchaser and allowing direct purchases on payment of a fee of ten shillings an acre to the government. Finding that the high fee stopped dealings, he reduced the fee to a pence an acre. This, however, was illegal and was condemned by the Colonial Office. It did not, in any case, either ease or solve the land problem; it simply created more land claims difficult to settle. The drift was toward chaos. The violence between the races, variously provoked, became worse. FitzRoy did not succeed in putting it down. He was recalled and replaced by Captain George Grey who had demonstrated his capacity for bringing order out of chaos in South Australia.

Grey arrived in New Zealand in November 1845 and continued in office for eight years. He ordered the finances by funding FitzRoy's debentures and obtained loans and grants from England; the imperial treasury paid off New Zealand's debts to New South Wales and the Bank of Australia; and he justifiably depended upon the growth of customs returns for the bulk of current income. Soon no aid was needed except to pay the costs of the military forces. He declared his belief in the principles of Waitangi which he interpreted to require the rapid Europeanization of the Maoris in accordance with an idea he had evolved from observation of the Australian aborigines. He was early successful in getting on friendly terms with important Maori chiefs, acquired great mana in their eyes, learned the Maori language, and published a classic study of the Maori mythology which embodied much of their wisdom. His policies were generally favorable to the Maori interests—he along with Chief Justice Sir William Martin and Anglican Bishop G. A. Selwyn made an influential philo-Maori team. However, he was not successful in translating his excellent intentions into equally vivifying action, and he never carried the majority of the settlers with him on Maori questions, let alone on other public questions of the time; and his influence on the Maoris was peripheral—many, especially those in the interior, totally escaped it, as much because of the weakness of Grey's effort as because of their own resistance. He merely provided a few hospitals, schools, and vocational training institutes, and tried to facilitate their use of pakeha courts. Grey suffered the vituperation of the settlers, then considered the proper reward for anyone so misguided as to attempt to govern them.

Grey's initial task was to put down Maori violence. He first addressed himself to what has come down in history as Hone Heke's war, named for the Maori chief who took the initiative in challenging the government. Heke was a Ngapuhi of the Bay of Islands country, missionary educated, but disaffected by the deterioration in the economic welfare of his people occasioned by the decline in trade at Kororareka attributed to the imposition of port fees and customs duties. As the difficulties developed,

Heke and his associates began to fear that their lands would be taken from them. Heke first indicated his defiance by cutting down the pole from which the British flag was flown over Kororareka—a symbolic act against a symbol. He first performed this ritual on July 8, 1844, while FitzRoy was still in power. FitzRoy attempted to compromise the issues with Heke, but with no success. He was assisted in this effort by a Maori chief named Waka Nene, friendly to the government. Waka Nene thus became one of the first of the many Maori chiefs to make it clear that there was a division of opinion in Maori circles about Maori-pakeha relations. This continued to be true all through the troubles that followed in the ensuing two decades; there never was, it is important to notice, a general Maori rebellion, though friends of one period might become rebels of another time. In January 1845 Heke resumed his rebellion by twice in the course of the month cutting down the offending flagpole. At this stage he was joined by another chief, Kawiti, the two commanding 700 fighting men, the maximum of the whole war. The government responded to the new affront by not only re-erecting the flagpole but by building a blockhouse at its base. On March 11 Heke and his followers succeeded in capturing the blockhouse and cutting down the flagpole for the fourth time. But this time more followed: the town of Kororareka was assaulted and destroyed and its defenders, military and civilian, were forced hastily to evacuate the place and retreat by ship to Auckland. This ominous development forced Governor Fitz-Roy to put a combined pakeha and Maori military force into field against Heke. Heke administered two defeats to it in fairly rapid order. It was at this point that Grey intervened.

Warfare with the Maoris always circled around their fortified *pas;* as military engineers the Maoris won the respect of the British experts who operated against them; but while destruction of a *pa* could be a decisive event, this was not always true, for the Maoris might evacuate successfully at a critical moment and retreat to build a new *pa* elsewhere. However, the *pas* did serve to focus what would otherwise have been endless indeterminate bush skirmishing. In warfare with the Maoris, assault and defense of *pas* were the nearest thing there was to formal battle on the European pattern. In the present instance, Grey ended Heke's war by a successful attack on his principal *pa,* called Ruapekapeka (or Bat's Nest), on January 11, 1846. Heke acknowledged defeat, although he made no formal surrender, least of all of his person. He "retired" and never took up arms against the British again.

This victory in hand, Grey turned to deal with the troubles in the south of the island. These troubles arose directly out of disputes over the land between the Maoris and the Company. The first serious collision had taken place in June 1843, in Nelson across the strait, between the death of Captain Hobson and the arrival of Governor FitzRoy. The Nelson settlement had proved to be at a location where there was simply not enough land to meet the needs of the settlers. In their search for additional land, they found the Wairau Valley and were proceeding with a survey of it when they were warned off by Te Rauparaha and his nephew Te Rangihaeata, of the Ngati-Toa people. Te Rauparaha, as spokesman, contended that the Wairau had not been included in the original purchase of land made by Colonel Wakefield. He insisted that all action be suspended, pending examination of the case by the land commissioner. When a surveyors' hut was burned (after their belongings had been carefully removed) by the Maoris, the settlers undertook to arrest Te Rauparaha for arson, and in the course of the attempt firing broke out, people were killed on both sides, and the whites driven back. White prisoners were then killed by Te Rangihaeata in revenge for the shooting of one of his wives. FitzRoy, with the concurrence of the Colonial Office, treated this affray as a consequence of ill-advised and illegal action by the whites.

At Wellington, particularly in the Hutt Valley, contention early arose over what land the pakehas had purchased and what they had not. The local chief, encouraged by Te Rangihaeata (and more remotely by Te Rauparaha), had created a situation that required the settlers to build blockhouses on the American style at strategic points. This quarrel Te Rangihaeata eventually took up as his own, with Te Rauparaha's support. Governor FitzRoy thought he had composed the differences with a money payment to the Maoris, but this proved not so. The Maoris would not quit the disputed areas. Grey at first attempted a settlement by negotiations, but not succeeding captured Te Rauparaha by a stratagem (considering him the ultimate source of Maori resistance) and carried him off into a two-year extra-legal disciplinary detention. Then, with the help of a friendly Maori named Wiremu Kingi (of whom we shall hear more later in quite another role), Te Rangihaeata was gradually forced back into the interior until he voluntarily retreated to a place beyond the easy reach of the pakeha forces. There he "retired" à la Heke and gave no more trouble, though maintaining his aloofness.

The final episode in this series occurred at Wanganui between April 1847 and February 1848. A pakeha military man accidentally shot a Maori chief. In revenge the Maoris massacred a pakeha family. The guilty Maoris were seized by friendly Maoris and turned over to the pakeha authorities, who hanged four of them. The disaffected Maoris thereupon attacked the town but were repulsed. Grey then arrived accompanied by Waka Nene and another northern chief named Te Whero

Whero, and the hostile Maoris were blockaded in their own country until they voluntarily sued for peace. After the Wanganui episode, there was no more violence of high political significance for a dozen years.

But if Grey by following his own inclination and taking the principles of the Treaty of Waitangi seriously, in his fashion, could conciliate the Maoris even while employing force against a rebellious minority, he was almost by the same token unable to win the warm support of the pakehas. It was one thing to satisfy the needs of the Maoris, quite another to satisfy the aspirations of the whites. Yet Grey used his prestige with the Maoris to buy more land from them for white settlement than anyone previously had managed under Waitangi principles. He had ordered the finances of the government, and he certainly kept steadily in view the need for greater participation in the government of the local people. Unfortunately, Grey was by temperament an autocrat, a "hero" of the Carlyle variety, as a New Zealand writer has suggested, and under the conditions of Crown Colony government, full play to his autocratic tendencies was allowed. It was not so apparent then as later that whatever he was by temperament, he was by intellectual conviction always something of a liberal and that his liberalism was intensifying as he grew older. The real difficulty was that Grey was given to employing devious expedients, was never reluctant to wave aside inconvenient facts and play his brilliant verbal spotlight on those which favored his purpose, and, being inordinately suspicious of others, found it difficult to work with them. Since at this time the others in New Zealand were, with the notable exceptions of the chief justice and the bishop, more or less hostile to his ideas, he was unable or unwilling to communicate his real purposes to the public.

Thus, in 1846 when Earl Grey, the colonial secretary, sent out a new constitution providing for representative government and, because it was both ludicrously cumbersome and contradictory in spirit and letter to the Treaty of Waitangi, Governor Grey set it aside, the settlers saw nothing in the step but an effort on Grey's part to deny them representative government and to hang on to his autocratic powers. They thereupon put on an ill-mannered, ill-tempered, campaign, of which Grey was the unfortunate butt, for a constitution. The settlers failed to notice that Governor Grey was risking his position and career by ignoring the instruction to introduce the dubious constitution, hardly the act of a man bent on retaining his autocratic powers at all cost. Fortunately, Earl Grey had, along with his other and less admirable characteristics, the ability to admit he was wrong. He saw the force of George Grey's arguments and arranged, as Grey asked, for a delay of five years in bringing the constitution into force. George Grey thereupon set about devising a more reasonable constitution, and his suggestions were in large measure embodied in the constitution of 1852.

The constitution of 1852 set up a pseudo-federal system in New Zealand, establishing a scheme of six provinces with legislatures and a central government with an upper house, called the Legislative Council, the members appointed for life, and an elected House of Representatives. The six original provinces (the number later varied) were Auckland, New Plymouth (Taranaki), Wellington, Nelson, Canterbury, and Otago. An elected superintendent was to run each province in conjunction with a council (of at least nine members) elected on a property franchise. The governor retained the Crown's sole right to buy land from the Maoris; and he also assumed responsibility for native policy, though he was expected to listen to the advice of his ministers. Originally designed to provide representative government, this was challenged when the first House and Council met in 1854. Responsible government—government on the British parliamentary model, with the ministers chosen from the House and responsible to it—was demanded. This was conceded in 1855 and in May 1856 New Zealand was launched upon its career as a self-governing colony.

Grey had finished his term as governor and departed for England before the first elected House assembled, but as a principal author of the constitution, it is not astonishing that he took the opportunity to show his bias of mind about it. He took care to launch the provinces on their careers before the machinery for setting up the central government was put in motion. This was a most surprising move for one allegedly passionately devoted to autocracy; it was rather the move of a convinced democrat who believed that the most vital government was that closest to the people. But his critics did not interpret his going in this light at all: they said he ran out rather than work with the elected representatives of the people! However, the settlers in time learned that Sir George's—he was knighted in 1848—devotion to the provinces was not a passing whim. He also favored democracy when in 1853 he reduced the price of land to ten shillings per acre for good land and five shillings for less promising land. His purpose was to make land more accessible to the poorer settlers excluded from the land by the higher prices obtaining under Wakefieldian principles. But as his favored provinces outlived their usefulness within a quarter century, as we shall see, so his pricing of land also failed of its purpose. It rather facilitated the aggregation of land by the wealthy than made it more freely available to poorer people. But if his departure caused hardly any sorrow among the pakehas, the

Maoris were sincerely grieved. Grey was their friend. It was not yet apparent to them that he had not left behind him any firmly founded policies or any institutions that would make the spirit of Waitangi live on.

D3

Between Grey's departure at the end of 1853 and 1860 when war broke out, the strengthening of the pakeha hold on New Zealand went on apace and the Maori disillusion with the consequences of this intensified. The reciprocal process was, of course, a North Island affair, for the South Island Maoris were too few to provide such a sour counterpoint to pakeha progress. Sir Thomas Gore Brown, who succeeded Grey in September 1855, kept native policy in his own hands, and while he was well-intentioned he never achieved any real knowledge of the Maoris—not learning the language—or any insight into their social structure, particularly their land law. He was in effect in the hands of his advisers, particularly Donald McLean, the government's land purchase agent, who was not above using foul methods if fair ones did not work. Moreover, there was the never-solved question of what weight he should give to the advice of his ministers. The government from its initiation, both in its provincial and central aspects, was controlled by the large landholding class, land speculators (particularly from Auckland), squatters, and professional men more or less sympathetic to them. The era of rule by a landed "colonial" gentry which was to continue to 1890 had begun, a gentry whose sense of *noblesse oblige* tended to be Roman rather than "humanitarian," and often did not extend at all to the lesser Maori breed without the law. The pressure the ruling gentry exerted on Maori policy might often be directed against the Brown-McLean line for factious reasons, but it was never philo-Maori in any but the most superficial, and often deceptive, way.

The position of the Maoris was onerous by its very nature: they were "natives" in a country being rapidly taken over by whites. Moreover, action to protect their position along the lines suggested in the Treaty of Waitangi had consistently been ill-conceived (from anthropological ignorance as much as from conscious malice) and certainly had not done much to enable them the better to withstand the competitive pressures of the whites and their civilization. No intelligent use had been made of self-generated Maori efforts at adjustment and adaptation, and no wise efforts had been made to assist them to do either. Grey's activities were vitiated by their limited scope and effect and by the subtle falsity of their premise: rapid "Europeanization." In effect the Maoris, by the early 1850's, were being forced back upon themselves rather than being brought forward into partnership. Under the constitution of 1852 they were denied the franchise because they did not hold their land individually, as Europeans did, but communally. Not represented in Parliament, they were nevertheless heavily taxed. As consumers of European goods, supplied by traders in Auckland, they paid perhaps half the customs collected. Moreover, the profit from the resale of land bought from them was a most important item of government revenue. But only about one twenty-fifth of the revenue was devoted to Maori purposes. There was provision for setting up Maori districts where the natives could organize their lives under their own customs, subject to European guidance. No such reserves were proclaimed before the outbreak of war.

The consequence of failure—pakeha failure quite as much as Maori failure—might on historical analogy have been forecast, but it was not. Since the Maoris were a virile and intelligent people it was improbable that they could be mistreated without making some effort to fight back. Inevitably, the first effort at resistance was centered upon the land. The Maoris themselves were divided as to whether to continue to sell land or to cease selling it. The whites, to whom land was the be-all and end-all of their interest, suspected that the widespread refusal to sell land was an organized conspiracy controlled and directed by an intertribal league, but this was not so. The Maoris were never able to agree on any concerted policy. At about the same time, unable any longer to believe that the pakeha government was going to find the policies and an administrative structure that would assimilate them to the general community, certain intelligent, mission-educated Maoris began to talk in favor of a plan for self-government. They proposed to accept the Queen, but otherwise to go their own way as a separate community in New Zealand. Basic to this proposal was the conquest of the divisiveness of tribalism and the achievement of Maori unity (kotahitanga), the unity to be signified by common allegiance to a Maori king. The so-called King Movement was initiated in 1853 by two Maoris named Tamihana Te Rauparaha and Matene Te Whiwhi, both former pupils of a great Church of England missionary, Octavius Hadfield. About 1857 the idea was taken up by Wiremu Tamihana to whom goes the credit for turning it into a reality. But by the time Wiremu Tamihana was active there were two currents of opinion among the Maoris: that represented by Tamihana himself which supported a constructive effort to solve the problem without active enmity to the pakehas but definitely apart from them, and that represented by a Maori named Rewi Manga Maniapoto which favored active warfare against the pakehas. The strength of the movement in both its aspects was among the Waikato Maoris south of Auckland whose chiefs had not signed the Treaty of Waitangi. After a blundering failure of the government to treat Wiremu Tamihana with decent respect at a critical moment, and the too-little-too-late failure of a last minute effort to gain control of the Waikato Maoris, the two groups agreed upon a king, their policy differences unreconciled, and the ancient and revered warrior Te Wherowhero was chosen in 1858.

But the decisive event in Maori-pakeha relations proved to be a land transaction in Taranaki. Land buying had been accelerated under Grey and, in the hands of Donald McLean, had continued very actively under Gore Brown. However, it had never proved possible to satisfy by purchase the land hunger of the people of Taranaki. They felt—and were—frustrated and deprived, while what little land they held was contiguous to rich land still in Maori hands. The difficulty went back to the shabby land sharking of the New Zealand Company, for the government had been unable conscientiously to validate any but a small portion of its original purchase in Taranaki. Not even McLean with his infinite capacity for cajolery and chicanery had been able to move the Taranaki Maoris. When, therefore, a dissident follower of Wiremu Kingi, the local paramount Maori leader, offered to sell an especially attractive block of land on the banks of the Waitara River, the offer was not only welcomed but embraced with a remarkable lack of discrimination. Wiremu Kingi's right, under the Maori laws of communal title, to veto the sale was waved aside. Governor Gore Brown did not understand Maori land law; his people advised him badly; and insofar as the ministry played a part, it rather encouraged him than emphasized his egregious error. When surveyors were sent to the block, they encountered opposition. Maori women pulled up the surveyors' pegs. Troops were sent in; martial law was proclaimed. Wiremu Kingi's *pa* on the disputed land was attacked and destroyed on March 17, 1860. This was war.

In June of the following year a rich gold find was made at Gabriel's Gulley in Otago in the South Island. While the North Island became entangled in war with the Maoris, the South Island enjoyed the excitements of a great gold rush.

CHAPTER XIX

War and Gold

The Maori wars, which occurred discontinuously from March 1860 to February 1872, consisted of a loosely linked series of outbursts of bush fighting in different parts of the North Island, involving different tribes and associations of tribes at different times. Never at any time were all the tribes that sooner or later went to war active simultaneously; there was never a general Maori uprising. Engagements were fought between a line drawn across the island just below Auckland in the north and a line across the island just south of Wanganui in the south, and from coast to coast within these limits. The fighting never came nearer to Wellington than Wanganui. To name only the principal campaigns, the wars began in Taranaki in 1860–61, flared up there again in 1863, became active in the Waikato and near Tauranga on the Bay of Plenty on the east coast in 1863–64, broke out in the Taranaki-Wanganui area in 1864–66, continued on the east coast in 1865, in the Taranaki-Wanganui area once more in 1868–69, and concluded with an east coast campaign which ended in the Urewera Mountains in 1868–72. The wars stopped rather than arrived at a formal conclusion. On the pakeha side both imperial troops and local militia (and rangers and constabulary) were employed, with "loyal" Maori collaboration. After 1864 the imperial troops were gradually withdrawn and the burden of the fighting fell on the colonial troops and the loyal Maoris. No engagement of the wars ever involved more than a few hundred on either side; the pakeha and loyal Maori losses by death in battle 1860–72 probably totaled no more than 700, while the hostile Maoris lost perhaps 2000 men.

The author of the most detailed study of the Maori wars opens his volumes with an invocation of the parallel with the American Indian wars but refers indiscriminately to the Indian wars of the eastern forests, the midwestern prairies, and the western plains. The wars in New

Zealand were unquestionably something like the smaller Indian wars of the eastern American forests, but nothing like those of the prairies or the plains. At the outbreak of war in New Zealand in 1860 the pakehas occupied footholds on the seacoasts, while the Maoris held the wooded interior of the island. This gave the Maoris the important advantage of possession of interior lines of communications with which the pakehas were then very little familiar. In the early years the pakehas were reluctant to pursue the Maoris into the forests; but the colonial troops, beginning in 1863, learned the art of mobile forest fighting with its scouting, ambushes, skirmishes, sudden strikes, and quick moving retreats. However, while the Maoris were from the beginning adept at such activities, the earlier phases of the wars were characterized by a warfare of and for *pas* of the kind discussed earlier in connection with Hone Heke's rebellion. In this *pa* warfare the imperial troops made good use of artillery and "sapping" operations. Though the pakehas built forts and blockhouses *à la* American both to protect their coastal settlements and the lines established against the Maoris, they never purposely drew the Maoris to them, as the Maoris drew the pakehas to their *pas*. It is significant that the wars began with the pakehas being drawn to attack a Maori *pa*. As time passed, however, and especially after 1864, for reasons to be adduced later, guerilla-like bush warfare became increasingly prominent, until in the last campaigns it predominated. The imperial officers who directed operations derived their ideas about how to fight from their campaigns in India and on India's frontiers; the colonials gradually developed methods analogous to those used in Indian warfare in the eastern forests of North America.

D3

After Wiremu Kingi's people were forced from their *pa* on the Waitara they began raids upon the isolated farmsteads, killing those pakehas who had not taken refuge in the newly fortified town of New Plymouth, burning all that was combustible, and carrying off much plunder. In the ensuing months the Maoris devastated the Taranaki country, sparing only the churches, all of which were still standing when the war ended, as clergymen were also spared if encountered. The pakehas in Taranaki were reinforced by troops from Australia in April; the Taranaki Maoris received contingents of the followers of Rewi from the Waikato in May. (Wiremu Tamihana, consistently with his feeling that war would bring disaster to the Maoris, opposed Rewi's fatal decision to fight.) The first pakeha expedition to punish the Maoris for their raids almost ended in disaster. In a joint effort of imperial troops and local militia, the militia was caught in a battle with the Maoris without firm imperial support. The contingent was saved from annihilation only by the arrival of a scratch naval contingent which not only supported the militia and assisted its retreat but also captured the *pa* on which the Maoris were based. General Pratt, who had come across from Australia to direct operations, eventually retaliated by invading the Maori farming country and burning crops and buildings and destroying equipment. He also assaulted Puke-ta-kauere *pa*, occupied by followers of Kingi and Rewi, but was repulsed; however, soon after at Mahoetahi he administered to the Maoris a sharp defeat of which the chief sufferers were the Waikatos. Pratt's warfare was marked by his reliance upon sapping as the most effective approach to a *pa*. His last major move before returning to Australia was directed at Te Arei *pa*, where he dug a sap extending over 1600 yards, which caused its capitulation. The success at Te Arei coincided with negotiations for a truce. Wiremu Tamihana had initiated the discussions with the encouragement of Chief Justice Martin and Bishop Selwyn. The final terms, however, were accepted by the Maori chief in charge at Te Arei after Tamihana had left. But since it proved impossible to commit either Wiremu Kingi or Rewi to the terms, aside from agreement to cease fighting, what was achieved was less peace than a truce. Wiremu Kingi now associated himself with the bellicose Waikatos under Rewi, and the key to the situation was with the Waikato, not the Taranaki Maoris.

The war had broken out while Parliament was in recess, and when it reassembled there was a lively debate about it. A significant minority attacked the government for its handling of the Waitara purchase for, having knowledge of Maori land law, they suspected that the position taken by the governor and his supporters was unsound. However, the majority supported the authorities, not entirely because they agreed with them on the legality of the purchase, but because they felt that the Queen's authority had been challenged and must be upheld. On the other hand, the Colonial Office demonstrated its disapproval of what had occurred by recalling Sir Thomas Gore Brown late in 1861 and sending Sir George Grey from the Cape Colony in South Africa, where he had been governor since 1854, to deal with the situation. Grey continued in office until February 1868. Gore Brown was appointed governor of Tasmania.

The truce lasted from May 1861 to May 1863, when fighting was begun again in Taranaki on the advice of Rewi. The immediate cause for the renewal of hostilities was an attempt on the part of the pakehas to occupy a block of land called the Tataraimaka, which earlier had been properly purchased but which the Maoris now claimed by right of conquest. A few days after the fighting was renewed, Grey announced that investigation had shown that Wiremu Kingi's position with regard to the Waitara land had been sound; the government's position was legally incorrect and indefensible. The disputed land was therefore to be returned to Wiremu Kingi and his people. Unluckily, the announcement came too late; Grey blundered badly in scheduling his moves at Tataraimaka and Waitara. The fighting over Tataraimaka had to be pursued to its inevitable conclusion in the defeat of the Maoris. However, the new war in Taranaki was less significant than the course of events in the Waikato.

Grey took office with the purpose of pursuing a peace policy. A government not associated with the blunders over the Waitara purchase came to office with the same policy. Grey began by attempting to conciliate the Waikato people, proposing to develop a system of local government with Maori participation, the government's interests represented by pakeha commissioners. More money than formerly was to be made available for schools, hospitals, farming equipment, and other things of benefit to the Maoris. However, the Maori king was not to be recognized for Grey contended that the king and his flag were a challenge to the Queen's sovereignty.

What Grey did not clearly perceive was that the time had passed when the Waikato Maoris would welcome institutions savoring so strongly of pakeha paternalism and so obviously designed to insure to the pakeha general direction and control of Maori affairs. Grey's personal mana was now sharply diminished in Maori eyes, and pakeha mana was dropping toward zero. The king had become the symbol of the determination of the nationalistic Maoris to control their own affairs, if not in hostility to the pakeha at least apart from him. Moreover, Grey's new institutions and officers appeared in Maori country after the more disaffected Maoris had experienced the ancient pleasures of warfare, pleasures they were not disposed lightly to abandon for possibly delusive institutional reforms. And finally it did not escape attention that at the same time that he was preaching peace, Governor Grey was also preparing for war, not least by building a military road south from Auckland into the Waikato. When Grey issued a proclamation to the chiefs of the Waikato in July 1863 notifying them that because of harassment of pakeha farmers and other illegal activities, it was necessary to establish military posts on the Waikato River in the heart of their country, it was taken as equivalent to a declaration of war. When Lieutenant General Sir Duncan Cameron (successor to Pratt) moved his forces into the Waikato, fighting inevitably ensued. Significantly, it was at this point that Wiremu Tamihana finally threw in his lot with the war party. Cameron, an exceedingly cautious soldier—he moved so slowly that he exasperated the settlers—systematically and inexorably reduced the Waikato people to submission.

Cameron's first victory occurred at Koheroa on July 17, but it was not until October that another significant step was taken. This was the reduction of Rangiriri *pa,* a defeat which cost the Maoris more fighting men, dead and prisoner, than any collision with the pakehas to that time. It forced the Maoris to abandon their "capital" very soon after, a matter perhaps of greater symbolic than practical significance. The Maoris then divided their forces between two *pas,* Paterangi on the Waipa River, which was very strongly fortified, and Tiki-o-te-Ihingarangi on the Waikato, but Cameron attacked neither. Rather he moved to destroy their chief source of supplies at Rangiaowhia. This drew the garrison out of Paterangi; it was defeated in the open near Rangiaowhia. One Maori force under Wiremu Tamihana was then concentrated at Maungatautari *pa* on the Waikato River, while another began to build a *pa* at Orakau, to counter one of Cameron's principal troop concentrations a few miles away. The Orakau *pa,* commanded by Rewi in person, was surrounded, but the defenders eventually broke out by suddenly rushing through the pakeha lines into a great swamp, though at the cost of many lives. The defeat at Orakau broke the Waikato will to resist. Tamihana, dispersing the people at Maungatautari *pa,* voluntarily gave himself up, while Rewi "retired" in the fashion of Hone Heke of old. But there still remained the problem of dealing with the restless east coast sympathizers of the Waikato. While friendly Arawa Maoris kept some of the disaffected tribes in check, and pakeha troops others, a force under Cameron was sent to Tauranga on the Bay of Plenty to deal with the Ngaiterangi people who controlled the easiest way of access into the Waikato from the coast. This was a ridge between two swamps on which they had built a most skillfully designed *pa,* known from its position and purpose as Gate *pa.* Cameron attacked this stronghold with forces of overwhelming numerical superiority and after heavily bombarding it, rushed it, only to be repulsed when the defending Maoris swarmed out of their underground refuges. This was the worst defeat administered by Maoris to pakehas since Hone Heke's time. But for the Maoris it was futile, for they had to abandon their *pa* and, unable to build another in the brief time allowed them, were disastrously defeated in improvised entrenchments at Te Ranga to the rear of Gate *pa.* The Ngaiterangi immediately surrendered, June 21, 1864.

D3

After the defeat of the Waikato Maoris at Orakau and of their allies at Te Ranga, the character of the war changed. The king movement which sustained the Waikatos (and which did not die at Orakau) was a relatively benign ideology of nationalistic resistance, largely political and cultural in expression, but there now appeared on the scene a new and fiercer ideology called *Pai Marire* ("goodness and grace") by the Maoris and Hauhauism (from the recurrence of the word *hau* in the chants and cries of the devotees) by the pakehas. *Pai Marire* was religious both in genesis and expression, but it supported a fanatic racial hostility to the pakehas, as well as a politics of unrelenting resistance. Composed of elements drawn from the Bible, especially the Book of Revelations—for the inventor, Te Ua Haumene, to whom it was communicated by the Angel Gabriel, had been educated by Methodist missionaries—it also revived ideas and practices associated with the old Maori *tohungas* (priests) and involved rituals (notably dancing around a tall pole to generate excitement) and magic incantations to ward off pakeha bullets. It stimulated, whether by design or accident is not clear, the bloodlust of the communicants, facilitating reversion to old Maori practices in warfare, such as cutting off the heads of defeated enemies, curing them, passing them around the countryside, and drinking the blood of enemies.

An excellent example of the curious consequences that have followed when two strong cultures have met and clashed, *Pai Marire* arose out of Maori despair at the defeats in arms they had suffered and which had been emphasized by the pakeha policy of confiscating huge acreages of land as a punishment for rebellion. As land was not only life to the Maoris, but possession of it their highest patriotism, the confiscations (to be discussed later on) were a crushing blow indeed, so crushing as to inspire the wiser pakehas themselves to objection. Hauhauism arose in the Taranaki-Wanganui area. It never gained many adherents among the followers of the Maori king, but it spread to the east coast, especially among tribes that had had little contact with the whites and, with a personal variation of a remarkable Maori leader, lasted on as a vital cult and church for many years after the wars had ended.

The coming of the Hauhau rebellion also signalized a change in the character of the war apart from the injection of fanaticism. From being a war for *pas* in a context of mobile forest fighting, it became more and more a true guerilla war, and in its final phases a guerilla war marked by diabolical skill on the Maori side. Moreover, as the character of the Maori participants changed, so a change also came over the pakeha formations. The wars in New Zealand had never been well received at the Colonial Office, and constant pressure had been exerted on the New Zealand government to take over responsibility for them, thus releasing the imperial troops supplied from Australia, India, and

Ireland to the maximum number of 10,000. The Colonial Office drew a distinction between the maintenance of "internal tranquility," which was a responsibility of the colonial government, and the repulsing of an external menace, which was an imperial responsibility. The Maori wars were seen as primarily involving the maintenance of internal tranquility, and the colonial government was pressed to take full responsibility. This became mixed up with an imperial policy of reducing the imperial garrisons in all self-governing colonies, which came to a climax in 1870. As we shall see, this led to the New Zealand government's acceptance of a policy of self-reliance in 1864, the consequence of which was that in the next few years the number of imperial troops in New Zealand was progressively reduced and the burden of fighting the Maoris was gradually taken over by the militia or constabulary and the friendly Maoris. However, the gradualness of the change was such that imperial troops were used in the initial phases of the protracted campaign against the Hauhaus.

The Hauhaus first appeared as warriors in April 1864 in Taranaki when they ambushed a patrol of imperial troops, killed the commander among others, and cut off and after drying it by ancient Maori method circulated his head for propaganda purposes. Shortly after the Hauhaus attacked a small fort near New Plymouth which was garrisoned by imperial troops and received a sound lesson in the worthlessness of incantations and gestures against pakeha bullets. They then turned south toward Wanganui, but their way was barred by loyal Maoris.

These disturbances brought imperial troops into the area in force under General Cameron, who by this time was thoroughly bored with the war. He held the lowest opinions of pakeha motives, ascribing their keenness for war entirely to land hunger, and developed a profound distaste for the use of his forces in support of such purposes. His relations with Governor Grey worsened progressively and reached the breaking point when Cameron's letters of complaint to the War Office (to which, rather than to the Colonial Office, he was responsible) came into Grey's hands and were shown by him to the colonial government. When Cameron was sent into the Wanganui-Taranaki area in 1865 his objective was supposed to be to clear hostile Maoris from a block of land known as Waitotara, defended by the Weraroa *pa*. But Cameron considered the Waitotara claim as even worse founded than that to Waitara, and he was deep in his ever more acrimonious correspondence with Governor Grey. He therefore put on a display of dilatoriness which was in its fashion a masterpiece. He made a slow progress north from Wanganui along the coast, but he resolutely refused to enter the bush to attack Weraroa, which was soon to his rear. In exasperation,

Grey himself took the field—he was, of course, a military man by profession—and, by getting in the rear of the *pa,* forced the Maoris out of
Weraroa. Cameron for his part continued his leisurely coastal progress,
having minor brushes with the Maoris and building small forts to hold
his line, until he reached Patea. He then went to Auckland and early
in 1865 resigned his command and returned to England. By this time
the number of imperial troops in New Zealand was in process of reduction.

Cameron was succeeded in command by Sir Trevor Chute who came
across from Australia. Chute tackled the Taranaki-Wanganui problem
forthrightly. He marched from Wanganui to New Plymouth and back
to Wanganui, circling Mount Egmont by marching along the inward
side on the journey north and returning on the seaward side. In this
notable demonstration that the pakehas could succeed in bush fighting,
he reduced no less than seven *pas.* His invaluable Maori associate and
adviser was the famous Keepa Rangihiwiuni—known as Major Kemp.
This exploit freed Taranaki from the incubus of war, but it left unfinished business in the vicinities of Wanganui and Patea. This was handed
over to colonial forces under Colonel Thomas McDonnell and friendly
Maoris. However, the year 1867 saw a lull in the fighting as the Hauhaus
brooded on their reverses.

Among the pakehas, though, affairs were lively, for in this year Governor Grey was recalled, never again to hold proconsular office. As
we shall see, he wore out the patience of the Colonial Office by his
quarrel with Cameron (and with Chute), by his arrogance in defending his position, and by usurping military authority in taking the field
against Weraroa. His successor was Sir George Bowen, transferred from
Queensland.

As 1868 wore on the restlessness of the Maoris near Patea became
more and more marked, but trading relations with them were maintained even after it was apparent that they were hostile. The Hauhaus
of the vicinity developed a stronghold, not exactly a *pa,* at Te Ngutu-o-
te-manu in the bush, under the leadership of Titokowaru. Colonel Mc-
Donnell, a brave and impetuous soldier, made two efforts to destroy
Ngutu-o-te-manu. The first assault was repulsed with losses, the second
in September 1868 was a major disaster. This pakeha defeat increased
Titokowaru's prestige, brought many adherents to his cause, and de-
moralized McDonnell's followers, who succumbed to indiscipline and
drunkenness. A vast stretch of country from close to Patea to the north
passed into Hauhau control. McDonnell resigned and was replaced by
Colonel G. S. Whitmore. Whitmore, who had fought Kaffirs in South
Africa and had regular army training, discharged soldiers mutinous be-

yond redemption and rebuilt the force. He then moved against Tito-kowaru at Moturo, but on the verge of victory mistakenly withdrew his forces.

At that point Whitmore was summoned to take part in the fighting on the east coast. He left his men to hold a line near Wanganui, and they were reinforced against the day when the campaign against Tito-kowaru could be renewed. That day came when in January 1869 Whitmore returned to Wanganui accompanied not only by some militia but also Keepa Rangihiwiuni and his Maoris. Titokowaru had taken refuge at Tauranga-ika *pa*. Whitmore and his forces attacked the *pa* on February 1 and by a quirk of Maori logic that had nothing to do with the fighting, but with honor under the Maori code of sex ethics, Titokowaru evacuated it and took to the bush. He and his people were tenaciously pursued and defeated wherever they were able to make a stand. Tito-kowaru's mana was destroyed and war on the west coast was, for all practical purposes, over.

The troubles on the east coast began as a result of the activities of Hauhau emissaries. Their fanatic preaching led step by step to a particularly brutal and senseless hanging of a missionary named Volkner. It was utterly unprecedented for Maoris, no matter how disaffected, to deal out death to a missionary. But not only did the Hauhaus kill Volkner, the leader of them cut off his head and exhibited it at a parody of a church service and also ate his eyes to appropriate his mana. This atrocity was a prelude to a protracted series of Hauhau-pakeha fights in the country to the north, south, and west of Opotiki which culminated in the exploits of Te Kooti. The Te Kooti campaigns were true guerilla warfare, turning wholly upon the mobility of the participants, on clever ruses, daring adventures, and feats of superhuman endurance in rough, mountainous, and snowy country. They brought Te Kooti the accolade as the greatest Maori strategist and tactician and parallel laurels to pakeha leaders, notably Colonel Whitmore, and friendly Maori associates of the pakeha, such as Ropata te Wahawaha (Major Ropata), probably the greatest of the "friendly Maori" leaders.

In the first phases of the Hauhau troubles Te Kooti enjoyed the reputation of a friendly Maori and fought with the pakehas, but he was indiscreet, incurred the dislike of the pakehas, and eventually was accused of communicating with the enemy. In 1866 he was sentenced without trial to exile with other Maoris in the Chatham Islands. The sentence was undoubtedly illegal. At the Chatham Islands Te Kooti (who was not a chief) exhibited marked qualities of leadership. He became the leader of the Maori exiles; he preached the *Pai Marire* religion to them; and it was he who, impatient of unjust detention, devised a scheme of escape. With his fellows he seized a visiting schooner and forced the captain to take the 300 Maori prisoners back to New Zealand. Te Kooti took charge of all the arms and ammunition he could find. The party landed at Whareongaonga, south of Poverty Bay, July 10, 1868, and started overland for their homes.

Almost immediately they were challenged to stand and surrender, but Te Kooti refused, alleging in his reply that he was on his way to set up a new Maori king. This reply, seeming to indicate that he intended the marrying of *Pai Marire* and the kingship idea, was an indication that he was developing an ideology peculiarly his own. In time it became known as the Ringatu religious cult which still has adherents among the Maoris. Te Kooti was not, however, a *tohunga,* any more than he was a chief; he was, in Maori terms, a man of great mana and he was in pakeha terms a charismatic personality. Within ten days of landing at Whareongaonga, he defeated his pakeha pursuers by clever tactics. The disaffected of the east coast began to flock to his camp. He drew his greatest support from the Urewera Maoris who had had little contact with the whites.

Te Kooti established an armed camp at Puketapu in the hinterland of Poverty Bay at which his adherents could gather. They were a mixed group, partly back-country Maoris who joined him voluntarily, partly coastal Maoris coerced into fighting for him, and so his following remained throughout the four years of his campaigning. Other than to give vent to a rancorous hostility to the whites and the Maoris friendly to them, expressed in Biblical terms from the Old Testament, it was not clear what he was fighting for, unless it was their expulsion from New Zealand. At no time did it appear that he could expel the whites even from the districts he invaded. His first action from Puketapu and its sequel set the pattern afterward followed. On November 10, 1868, he directed a raid on Matawhero, inland from Poverty Bay, in which thirty-three Europeans and thirty-seven friendly Maoris were ruthlessly butchered, while houses were burned. These were very high figures for Maori killings—the worst since the massacre of the *Boyd* in 1809— but the whole affair was only an episode, not decisive in any respect whatever, for Te Kooti promptly retreated into the hinterland again and established himself in an improvised but very strong *pa* at Ngatapa. There early in January 1869 he was attacked by forces under Colonel Whitmore and Ropata te Wahawaha and forced to make a night-time evacuation down a steep cliff. His losses on this occasion surpassed those of any other engagement in the entire Maori wars; they were almost three times as numerous as at Rangiriri in the Waikato War. Te Kooti

fled into the Urewera Mountains, establishing a camp on an upper reach
of the Waioeka River.

From there in March he made another fierce and destructive raid
into the valley of the Whakatane River, toward and into the small town
of Whakatane on the Bay of Plenty. This raid, too, fell as brutally on
friendly Maoris as on the whites. And its sequel was another retreat
into the Urewera Mountains, followed the next month by a similar raid
into the valley of the Mohaka River, and another retreat into the mountains.

Between Ngatapa and Whakatane, Colonel Whitmore was on the
west coast dealing the final blows to Titokowaru. On his return he directed a concerted incursion into the Ureweras by several columns of
mixed pakeha and Maori troops in an effort either to capture or kill
Te Kooti. This was an extraordinary undertaking, for very few whites
had ever been into the Urewera Mountains and detailed knowledge of
them did not exist. (It proved to be so difficult that the expedition broke
Whitmore's health.) Te Kooti was not captured; his capacity for being
elusive was one of his distinctive characteristics; but he was forced out
of the mountains into the country around Lake Taupo, from where he
made an unsuccessful effort to reach the Waikato and the king. His
greatest success in the Taupo country was a surprise attack on a cavalry
patrol at Opepe, but his effort to coerce the local Maoris into supporting him failed. When he made a feint at the Maori center of Rotorua,
he was attacked and driven back by a mixed Maori-pakeha force under
Gilbert Mair (of a family prominent in New Zealand from the old days
at Kororareka). Once more a hunted fugitive in the Urewera Mountains, Te Kooti now had to concentrate upon eluding his pursuers and
the possibility of managing an escape into the king country. The last
armed collision of this game of hide and seek, and of all the Maori
wars, occurred deep in the bush on February 14, 1872. Te Kooti escaped
from it and finally achieved refuge in the king country where the government decided to let him "retire" in peace.

D3

Running parallel with the Maori wars during the 1860's was the story
of gold in New Zealand. It opened with individual miners and small,
intimate teams of miners, winning the coveted metal on alluvial diggings,
and closed with the establishment of quartz crushing and the beginning
of the era of mining by companies which, with downs and ups, continues
to the present day. The great rushes to California had drawn a quota
of adventurers from New Zealand and the Australian rushes had drawn

more. Gold was known to exist in New Zealand very early, but the first alluvial gold field of even passing significance was not discovered until 1852, when Charles Ring washed out gold at the Kapanga stream on the Caromandel Peninsula, in Maori country near Auckland. Alluvial mining at Caromandel proved, however, to be but a come-on, for the real riches were won by deep mining later on. In 1857, however, alluvial gold was found in Nelson Province and while the finds were rich enough to persuade the colonists to abolish Tasman's old place-name of Massacre Bay in favor of Golden Bay, they proved not to be of the first magnitude. The central government, however, was sufficiently confident of the shape of things to come in 1858 to pass a Goldfields Act modeled on that of Victoria, with a miner's license and an export tax on the metal. Anticipations were fully justified when in 1861 a "professional" gold hunter named Gabriel Read came across from Tasmania where he had been living after experience in California and Victoria and, with local encouragement, found payable alluvial gold at Tuapeka in Otago. This discovery was the real thing and set off a sequence of rushes that did not peter out until the early 1870's. Otago proved to be the gold-rich province of New Zealand, but rich finds were also made on the west coast of the South Island beyond the high mountains in what was then the province of Canterbury, as well as new finds in Nelson, a lesser find in the province of Marlborough (formed from a part of the original Nelson), and again at Caromandel in Auckland province. The heaviest impact of the rushes was on the South Island, but it is an indication that progress in the North Island was not completely halted by the wars that rushes were also feasible there.

The Otago rush to Tuapeka was in its initial phases a local rush which emptied the town of Dunedin and drew many from the farms and sheep stations, but it was rich enough quickly to attract the attention of the miners of Victoria where, by that time, alluvial mining was about over. Once the Victorians came to believe that the Otago finds were a reality—they at first dismissed the news as propaganda of shipping companies desperately drumming up trade—they flocked through Dunedin by the thousands and dispersed over the back country toward and into the high mountains in the west of the province. The largest influx in any one month occurred in March 1863. Many of the men were not only veterans of the Victorian diggings but a proportion had also been in California, and a sprinkling of these were Americans. The New Zealand rushes, then, may perhaps be seen as a phase of the gold hunting which began in California in 1849, continued in Australia in the 1850's, moved to New Zealand in the 1860's, and completed its circuit of the Pacific in the Klondike at the end of the century, with the tremendous byblow in Western Australia in the 1890's, and the activities in islands such as Fiji and New Guinea later on. It was an American, Horatio Hartley, working with an Irishman, named Christopher Reilly, with whom he had teamed up in California, who in August 1862 disclosed in Dunedin their fabulously rich find on the upper Clutha River and thereby insured the continuance of the Otago boom and the full investigation of the rough country to the west. The miners, who were but a little behind the pastoralists in exploring the interior of Otago, tackled the mountains with vigor, reaching the permanent snow fields, and early beginning the search for a pass to the west coast. 1862 was the *annus mirabilis* of gold strikes in Otago. All this development was closely linked with Melbourne, for not only did the greater proportion of the incoming miners come from there, but Victorian businessmen quickly followed them, establishing new concerns or branches of their Melbourne houses, not to mention liquor peddlers, "entertainers," and even a few bushrangers. Dunedin as the principal place of entry had a rapid and extremely disorderly growth. Otago boomed in a decade into the most populous and richest province in the country. But while the search for gold galvanized this development, and the gold won put money into some pockets and was invested locally, the capital brought in by the newcomers was probably equally important, and the growth was given what solidity it had by expansion of farming and grazing. Gold duties gave Otago a fine current income, but land sales (which also brought income) were more significant for the future.

Some of the Otago miners took part in a rush to Wakamarina in Marlborough province in early 1864—more than the field could support—and many from Wakamarina, and more direct from Otago, went to the west coast of Canterbury province later the same year. Prospectors had been working down the west coast from Nelson for some time and no single discovery started the rush to the coast in 1864. Rather, it was a case of a cumulation of small discoveries raising the expectation that something big was to be found. This was an all the more potent appeal in that in Otago alluvial mining was in its final phase. Large numbers of miners reached the west coast by ship, but some crossed by the pass over the mountains in Canterbury discovered by Sir Julius von Haast, the provincial geologist, in 1863. The west coast was a wild country—the mountains were close to the sea—which had never attracted many Maoris and had drawn very few whites as settlers prior to the coming of the gold miners. Far more than in the case of any other province, the gold miners pioneered and opened up the west coast (or Westland). Hokitika became the principal port. In this rough and inhospitable country, gold was found on the beaches and in the turbulent streams coming down from the mountains, both north and south of Hokitika. Profitable alluvial mining did not last long; the last significant rush occurred in 1867, after which the next stop for many of the miners was Gympie in Queensland; but quartz crushing prolonged significant activity into the 1870's, and alluvial miners continued to work into the 1880's. In its next stage, Westland was the principal coal mining district of New Zealand.

The gold excitement was renewed in Auckland Province in 1867 when attention was once more paid to the Caromandel field. Numerous small crushing plants were built. But the great days in the North Island had not yet arrived. New Zealand's richest gold mine, the Waihi, was not discovered until 1878 and development of it did not begin until a decade after that. Waihi, however, was to New Zealand what Kalgoorlie was to Australia, or Johannesburg to South Africa, the outstanding example of capitalist gold mining unless the practice of dredging in the South Island rivers be granted the accolade.

D3

By 1869 the alluvial rushes were effectively over, so decidedly that the course was clearly set for an economic depression. This was avoided for a decade by extraordinary political action, as we shall see. Meanwhile it is necessary to take a brief look at the New Zealand economy after a decade of war and gold strikes. Obviously the South Island had been booming, but the North Island had not, as is often implied, been standing still. The figures clearly show that the contrast between the two islands was far from absolute.

New Zealand had led up to the gold discoveries in Otago through a decade which opened with farming experiencing a useful stimulation from the demand on the Australian gold fields for grain and vegetables. When this stimulus slackened around the middle of the decade, wool, which had been steadily expanding since the middle 1840's, became the principal New Zealand export. It was sent to market in Sydney. The provinces at that stage were decidedly separate settlements, though the central government was established. (Regular communication among them and to Australia by steamer did not begin until 1865.) Auckland was the premier province by all indices—population, exports: timber, grain, vegetables (but little wool). It was outside the influence of the Company theories and closely linked to Australia. Wellington was next to Auckland in importance and the center of Company influence. Its principal export was wool. Taranaki, the remaining North Island province, was the smallest and poorest of all the colonies in New Zealand; its exports were mainly vegetables. Across Cook Strait in the South Island Nelson was next to Wellington in population and at the moment possessed the largest flocks in New Zealand. Canterbury, a very new settlement, was pushing Nelson hard in population and in numbers of sheep depastured. Otago was still small and poor; it had but few more people than Taranaki; its export reliance was upon wool and grain of about equal value. With Auckland and Wellington, the North Island, therefore, possessed the most populous and economically strong provinces of New Zealand. Their strength compensated for Taranaki's weakness. The South Island around the end of the 1850's was in the process of becoming a great center of wool production.

The wars had a very uneven impact on the North Island provinces but only Taranaki, the poorest, suffered devastation. However, it began to rebuild, on an expanded area of available land, before the fighting was wholly over. Taking Wellington as originally constituted—before Hawke's Bay was separated—it suffered from the war only when the Hawke's Bay area was sharply depressed during the east coast Hauhau disturbances. Auckland about compensated for the loss of trade with the Maoris by sales of provisions to the imperial army's commissariat. As we have seen, it was in a position to do something with gold mining. Taking the North Island as a whole, the war period was one of steady progress. Between 1858 and 1871, the pakeha population rose from 34,000 to 97,000, houses from 8000 to 21,000, cattle from 76,000 to 180,000, sheep from 411,000 to 1,853,000, cropped acreage from 100,000 to 468,000, while exports per head multiplied about three times in value and public revenues expanded notably. The most difficult years were 1864–67, but the difficulties of those years were smothered over the longer term.

The South Island in the same years—1858–1871—exceeded the North Island in progress by every index and this swung the economic balance in its favor for thirty years. Population rose from 25,000 to 159,000, houses from 5000 to 36,000, cattle from 61,000 to 257,000, sheep from 1,112,000 to 7,848,000, cropped acreage from 41,000 to 574,000, while exports per head better than doubled in value and public revenues, larger than the North Island's at the beginning of the period owing to sales of land at higher prices, increased almost three times. Without minimizing the impact of gold on the South Island, special emphasis should be placed upon the vast increases in cattle, sheep, and acreages under crop, all based on the land.

D3

The political life of New Zealand during the era of wars and gold rushes was dominated by questions arising from the wars and the relations of the central government and the provinces. Sir George Grey, it will be recalled, favored the provinces and had set their governments going before the central government began to function. Because New Zealand was occupied as a series of isolated settlements the minds of most of the people were inevitably focused on local affairs, and it was within each settlement, as far as most men were concerned, that effective action was being taken. It was easy in such a climate to propose and evaluate policies designed to advance provincial interests, but it was hard in such a fragmented country to think nationally. Only when a vision of a nation seated in the islands taken as a whole became common and its realization appeared an immediate possibility did it become feasible to take the drastic step of abolishing the provinces and establishing a unitary government. Yet even in the period under discussion here there were some men who clearly perceived that there were national problems that should be handled nationally. They, however, had to advance their position in a context of great provincial strength which found full expression in the central government. On the other hand, even the most devoted provincialists, when they rose to national power, had to govern nationally. New Zealand never worked out a sound balance of provincial and central powers.

Toward the wars, once they had begun, there were two possible positions: either they could be prosecuted with force without stint within the limits imposed by finance and manpower, or a conciliatory line could be taken toward the disaffected Maoris in the hope of putting an end to the struggle. But as the decision as to the use of violence was equally in the hands of the Maoris and the pakehas, and the disaffected Maoris elected violence even when some of the pakehas were talking conciliation, the paradoxical situation arose of conciliators prosecuting active fighting. Only when the fighting ceased did the conciliators become dominant and even then it took a long time for a really satisfactory policy to be evolved—if any ever has been. But the questions arising from the war could not in any case be neatly divided under the headings suggested, for the Colonial Office injected into the situation issues of magnitude that were profoundly divisive of colonial opinion. What the Colonial Office wanted was to hand responsibility for native policy to the central government of New Zealand and also the intimately associated responsibility for the prosecution and the financing of the wars. This was because the Colonial Office took the position that the wars were not an imperial responsibility (since they involved no external enemy either for New Zealand or the Empire), but rather were a matter of "domestic tranquility" for which the colonial government was wholly responsible. This position led on to the conclusion that the financial burden of the war was also a colonial responsibility. The colonists tried to argue, however, that since the wars had been started while native policy was in the hands of the governor (Gore Brown), they *were* an imperial responsibility. There was a solid basis for the protracted wrangle that ensued. And the whole question became involved with the resolution of the imperial government to reduce the imperial garrisons in the self-governing colonies as a measure of economy and to make effective the new doctrine that part of the responsibility of colonial governments was considerable local responsibility for local defense. New Zealand had the misfortune to have to deal with this development in a time of serious domestic disturbances, but Australia, the Cape Colony, and Canada had to face it also at the same time under *their* peculiar contemporary circumstances. In the New Zealand context it meant the withdrawal of the imperial troops assembled in the country to fight the Maoris. The withdrawal was completed in 1870, the year the new imperial defense policy was intended to be in full force.

Since the franchise was restricted by a property qualification, only about one out of every five pakehas was able to vote in the elections of this period. The quality of the men elected to the House of Representatives (and who chiefly manned the ministries) was high. No parliaments in the history of New Zealand have had so many well-educated men. Of the six men who were premier one or more times between 1856 and 1872 four were eventually knighted. They were predominantly young men (under fifty). Three were lawyers by education, two by principal occupation in New Zealand, one a man-of-letters turned civil servant, and two pastoralists. One became governor of other British colonies. All of them were conservative and sympathetic to the landowning class, but they often had interesting crotchets. One was an ardent temperance advocate. Most of them had had experience in government before being elected to the House, several as superintendents of provinces, or comparable office. But with all the political and administrative ability available, it was very difficult to maintain a ministry in office—a condition which continued in New Zealand to 1890. The fundamental trouble was that there were no organized parties and while the members of the House associated themselves on particular questions, the groups were far from cohesive. At times the House was but a collection of individuals, not even a congeries of groups. Governments maintained themselves, or were voted out of office, by grace of a single vote. There were three governments formed within the first year and nine in the first sixteen years of responsible government. However, some continuity was obtained from the fact that some men served in several successive ministries, even ministries of slightly different complexions. The dominant figures in this period were Edward W. Stafford and William Fox. Stafford was the more successful in retaining office for reasonable periods; he was premier 1856–61 and 1865–69. Fox was a skilled oppositionist who was premier in his own person in 1856, 1861–62 and 1869–72, while he was the recognized power behind another man's premiership in 1863–64. Stafford was a moderate centralist and, more by force of political circumstance than personal choice, of the war party. Fox was an ardent provincialist and a conciliator. Oddly neither made one of the most fundamental policy adjustments of the period, the acceptance of full colonial responsibility for native policy and the war. This was carried out by Frederick Weld. Others who were premier during the period were Henry Sewell, the lawyer who initiated responsible government, held office but two weeks, and thereafter was a member of many succeeding governments; Alfred Domett, poetaster and civil servant, notable for his strong anti-Maori sentiments; and Frederick Whitaker who fronted for Fox in a short-lived administration, and was reputed to be the Bank of New Zealand's man.

The wars began as a consequence of bad advice tendered Governor Brown by civil servants and members of a ministry headed by Stafford. Stafford himself was absent in England at the time, and while he was never held personally responsible for the fateful misstep, he accepted its consequences. He supported the pro-war policy of Governor Brown. Fox, giving expression to the conciliationist position, managed to engineer Stafford's defeat in the House (by one vote) and took office. His assumption of the premiership coincided with the arrival of Grey to resume the governorship. Grey initiated his peace policy. When Fox attempted to get a resolution through the House in favor of the transfer of native affairs to the colonial government, as the Colonial Office wished, but without accepting full colonial responsibility for the cost of the wars, he was defeated (by one vote). His successor was Domett who had been anti-Maori since the Wairau affair in Nelson and who surrounded himself with men of similar mind. Domett was a poor poet, a bitter and vituperative newspaper writer, a first-rate bureaucrat, but a weak premier. It was only with difficulty that Domett was persuaded to accept Grey's finding that the right was with the Maoris in the matter of the Waitara purchase. He stubbornly resisted the pressure to take over full responsibility for native affairs and when he finally recommended it to the House, coupled it with a policy of hard war and land confiscation. Land confiscation, first injected into politics by Governor Grey, was designed to punish the Maoris for rebellion, while the sale of the land would produce funds to pay for the war. It was authorized by the New Zealand Settlements Act of 1863. However, Domett's weak government fell before that. His logical successor was Fox, but while Fox was unquestionably the dominant figure in the new government, the premiership was held by Whitaker. Under the circumstances of the moment this created the curious situation in which Fox, a conciliationist, had strongly to support the war in the Waikato, now in full flood. To compound the irony, the Whitaker ministry introduced confiscation on a sweeping scale—so sweeping Grey now opposed the practice, as did the Colonial Office—which caused injustices to the Maoris formally admitted by the government in 1928, when compensation was granted; and it suspended the Waitangi principle of land purchases only by the government in favor of free trade in land (a suspension that lasted thirty years from 1862). Whitaker, as a land speculator, was suspected of hoping to profit personally from confiscation. But the Whitaker-Fox government fell and was succeeded by Frederick Weld's government which faced up to the crucial political issue. On the theory that only if the colonial government took full responsibility for native affairs and the war could peace be achieved, Weld proceeded to implement the so-called policy of self-reliance. This meant, among other things, that the imperial troops would be withdrawn and responsibility for the fighting would fall on the colonials. But Weld's self-reliance did not mean any softness toward the Maoris: he intended to fight; and he continued confiscation. His was essentially a South Island policy that originated in public discussions in Canterbury. It was his financial policy that defeated him. He saw that war meant higher taxes and asked for them. The provincialists resisted and turned him out of office. Stafford now returned to office and more by administrative dexterity than brilliance of policy guided the country during the Hauhau disorders on the west and east coasts. He was brought down by Fox in 1869. Fox now shifted the emphasis from aggressive warfare against Te Kooti to an effort to abate the violence, a line feasible after Te Kooti's defeat at Rotorua, and placed great reliance upon a policy of pacification and conciliation under the direction of Sir Donald McLean as native minister. The wars ended in Fox's administration.

Turning now to the question of provincialism versus centralism, which threaded its way through the war period, the first thing to note is that Stafford, the most successful centralist politician of the period, was not an extremist in the matter (or any other matter). His thinking was oriented toward centralism and he eventually struck some solid blows for it, but at this time he did not raise the question in any defiant way. Rather, the initiative was taken by the provincialists, chief among them William Fox. It was Fox who in 1856 defined and got accepted by the House, and eventually by Stafford's government, what became known as "the compact." Under this arrangement the provinces received substantial shares of the customs revenue and in large measure the control of the lands within their borders including returns from sales, aside from two shillings sixpence an acre paid to the central government. As the provinces also controlled immigration, constructed public works, had their own police, managed education, and (after Domett's time) borrowed money on their own credit, their powers were comprehensive. If they were doing well economically, provincial patriotism tended to rise in fervency, even to flirting with secession from the federation, as happened in Otago during the gold rushes and in Auckland after the capital of the federation was moved to Wellington in 1865. (This long-wanted change, made the more compelling by the isolation of Auckland by the wars, was finally engineered by Weld after the choice of the new site was made by a committee of Australians!) On the other hand, there was restlessness in the outlying parts of some provinces which alleged neglect of their interests and supported agitation for separation and erection into independent provinces. Hawke's Bay was separated from Wellington in 1858, Marlborough was carved out of Nelson in 1859, Southland out of Otago in 1861 (only to return to it in 1870), while the west coast became a province in 1873. This concession to ultra-provincialism at once weakened the provinces that gave up the land and people and usually failed to create economically viable units of government. The poorer provinces had to ask for subsidies from the central government, introducing an unhappy ambiguity familiar in almost all federal systems. And the misuse of the borrowing power by the provinces, combined with heavy borrowings by the central government to finance the war, led to a weakening of New Zealand's credit. To correct this the central government assumed responsibility for all outstanding loans, and took control of all future borrowings, thus compromising provincial autonomy, and strengthening the central government's position. New Zealand was plagued not only by provincial-central pulling and hauling, but also by some North Island-South Island dissension. The South Island felt that while the war was obviously being fought for the benefit of the North Island, the South Island was in large measure paying for it. Voices were raised in favor of divorcing the islands governmentally. At the bottom of William Fox's conciliation policy was a provincial conviction that the war was not worth its cost to the South Island provinces which were not directly and unmistakably involved in it; that it was not, in the true sense, a national war, and so the issues should be compromised. New Zealand emerged from the wars and the gold rushes still an uneasy association of provinces. It is remarkable how soon afterward the idea of New Zealand as a single nation won acceptance.

CHAPTER XX

Progress and Poverty

The 1870's and the 1880's in New Zealand stand in marked contrast. The 1870's were years of boom, the 1880's of depression. Both boom and depression were essentially phenomena of the pakeha world and episodes in the history of the pakehas in New Zealand, for with Te Kooti's escape into the king country and the end of the fighting, the Maoris of the tribes that had contended against pakeha mastery of the country attempted to withdraw into themselves and stand apart from the pakeha world. From the pakeha point of view relations with the Maoris became the pacification of the rebels to facilitate the fullest possible occupation and exploitation of the North Island. The boom through which New Zealand passed was in part a matter of a politician's plan for stimulating development, in part a matter of private capital investment and the expansion of credit. Its impact was chiefly, but not wholly, on the South Island. Australia across the Tasman went through an analogous cycle in this same general period, but the timing was different and Australia was still booming in the 1880's when New Zealand was depressed. Behind colonial events was the United Kingdom depression of the 1870's and especially the long-continued decline in the prices for primary products, particularly wool and grain, that then began. The New Zealanders were feeling their way in the dark toward the status of one of the principal suppliers of foodstuffs to an industrialized and urbanized United Kingdom. However, the commodities on which they were to build their economy to high levels of productivity and prosperity only *began* to be exported in the two decades discussed here and this delay is part of the explanation for the frustrations of the 1880's. The full exploitation of them waited upon developments in technology as much as on a change for the better in prices, especially the technology of refrigerated transport. One of the new industries led to the successful occupation of the North Island and the initiation of its march to predominance in the domestic economy. Ex post facto it is apparent that while the troubles with the Maoris slowed the pakeha mastery of the North Island, equally important was the slow appearance of a sufficiently productive industry based on the land which would fully justify the great cost of removing the forest cover. Dairying provided the answer.

D3

McLean had been associated with Maori affairs, particularly land buying, from 1844. Scottish-born, he had spent two years in Australia before he went to New Zealand in 1840 as agent for a timber firm. His occupation brought him into intimate contact with the Maoris and taught him how to deal successfully with them in trading operations, not excluding the use of chicane. This knowledge he put at the service of the government and in Gore Brown's time he was, as noted, the chief land buyer. His experience gave him the conviction that pakeha ends could be achieved by negotiation and guile with less cost than by war, once the Maori will and power to make war had been broken. His great chance came when he associated himself with Fox in opposition to Stafford's war policy. By that time his mana as a manager of Maoris was very great and it continued little diminished until his death. His policy was founded on the premise that mastery of the Maoris was best to be achieved by promoting pakeha settlement and thus effectively submerging the natives, dressing up the harsh realities by encouraging the Maoris to associate themselves with the pakeha government and to participate in the pakeha economy, at least in a peripheral fashion.

What McLean did was to leave the Maoris of the two great centers of smoldering discontent and disaffection—the king country of the Waikato and southern Taranaki—as much to themselves as possible to allow time to effect a healing. Meanwhile he actively promoted the building of roads and bridges, telegraphs, and eventually railways from the established coastal settlements into the interior where the Maoris had been supreme and where pakeha settlement would have to spread if the island was to be mastered, concentrating first on the utilization of the confiscated land and then, as the 1870's wore on, buying additional tracts. As the Maori leaders of the rebellion showed that they were firmly inclined toward peace, they were formally pardoned. All Maoris were encouraged to adapt themselves to the pakeha world: they found employment as laborers on the public works; on the east coast in the grazing country they became shearers and station hands; and so on. From 1867 the Maoris had the privilege of electing four members of the House of Representatives, three from the North Island, one from the South; and from 1872 the Maoris were represented by appointment of two members in the upper house. From 1872 also one or two Maoris were almost always included in the successive ministries as members of the Executive Council.

McLean's policy was in essence a personal policy and its success was guaranteed largely by his personal prestige with the natives on the one hand and the pakeha politicians on the other. At the time of his death he had gone about as far as it was possible to go using his methods. Further progress required active efforts to dissolve the hostility of the Maoris of Waikato and Taranaki. In 1881 the Maori king, Tawhiao, made voluntary submission to the pakeha authorities in the Waikato by surrendering rifles and although in 1884 he made a trip to England to obtain redress of grievances directly from the queen—a futile journey since native affairs were wholly in colonial hands—his submission meant an end to the threat of violence from the Kingites. In 1883 even Te Kooti was given a pardon. In 1885 a railway was built into the king country.

Affairs in Taranaki took a different turn. Here it was made abundantly clear that the land continued to be the prime bone of contention between Maori and pakeha and that this also meant a Maori resistance to pakeha life-values. The Taranaki Maoris fell under the spell of a prophet named Te Whiti, who made his headquarters at Parihaki on the slopes of Mt. Egmont. He, rather than the old warrior Titokowaru, also settled in the vicinity, led the last stand of his people. Te Whiti preached nonresistance, with mystical and Biblical flourishes. He advised his followers, who were found far and wide in the Maori world, simply to resist without violence all efforts of the pakeha to assimilate them economically or otherwise, to take their stand on the ancient Maori values, in the expectation that one day the pakehas would have a change of heart and leave the Maoris in peace. This was not to be, for in the late 1870's the pakehas began to make roads into the area Te Whiti controlled and to plan pakeha settlement of confiscated lands which, to that time, Te Whiti's people had occupied undisturbed. In opposition Te Whiti's people, on his advice, resorted to the old tactic of pulling up surveyors' pegs and also building fences across the roads. Step by step the struggle moved to a climax—the dispatch of a force of armed constables to Te Whiti's town of Parihaki to arrest him, to disperse members of other tribes assembled there, and to destroy the houses. This caused a sharp political crisis among the pakeha politicians (during which Sir George Grey, for some odd reason, supported this resort to violence), but in the end the treatment of Te Whiti, in spite of the illegality of his detention, was supported. It broke the back of Maori resistance, for while Te Whiti resumed leadership of his cult after his release from jail, he had lost his effectiveness. After the raid on Parihaki in November 1881 the Taranaki Maoris offered no significant resistance to the wishes of the pakehas.

By the middle 1880's the Maori people were close to a low point in their history and once more there was talk that they were going to die out. Their numbers declined until in 1896 there were but 42,000 of them; and they continued to sell land until 1929, when they possessed a remnant of but 4,300,000 acres, of which only half was of any use for farming. But in the late 1890's they found new leadership and began a new career in New Zealand.

D3

The boom of the 1870's is imperishably associated with Sir Julius Vogel (knighted 1875); and the ideology of the boom is known as Vogelism. Julius Vogel was a London-born Jew, early orphaned and intended by an uncle to follow him into the export trade to South America. At seventeen in 1852, however, Vogel chose to join the gold rush to Australia, preparing himself for eventualities by short courses in chemistry and metallurgy. He did not find success as an assayer in Melbourne, but rather drifted into journalism in inland gold-fields towns. He revealed a marked flare for newspaper work, especially the composition of opinionated "leaders." But he did not find what he wanted in Australia and in 1861 he followed the rush to Otago. He was twenty-six years old. Within a month he was editor and part-owner of the first daily paper not only of Otago but of New Zealand. He delighted in the manipulation of ideas, not necessarily his own, but always presented in a bravura fashion that was exceedingly effective. All his life he wrote a good deal, in later life chiefly for United Kingdom publications; and he wrote one novel, a fascinating utopia (very bad as fiction, "wonderful" for its ideas) called *Anno Domini 2000*, published in 1889. When he could find no other outlet for his ideas he freely resorted to that refuge of the intellectual *manqué*, the "letter to the editor." Vogel tended to be discursive rather than solidly ratiocinative; he sought to dazzle his readers (or his hearers, though he was a much less accomplished speaker than writer), as an easy way to "convince" them. His favorite ploy was to support his arguments with figures in which he himself implicitly believed. His way with figures was the basis of his reputation as a financier. But underlying his character as newspaperman or statesman was his character as promoter, speculator, or gambler. His conspicuous private vice (aside from ill-advised eating and drinking, he was a classic nineteenth-century case of victimization by gout) was, significantly enough, card playing. He was a terrifyingly reckless poker player. Yet his intentions were always excellent; his ultimate political objective was neither power nor the emoluments, but the development of a prosperous New Zealand. Few ever suspected Vogel of evil purposes. They indicted him for extravagance of ideas and with public money—his expense accounts on his ceaseless travels abroad on public business were extraordinary—but the solid objections to him were different: he was all too willing to have the built-in safeguards in his schemes set aside; and he was a fascinatingly bad administrator. He lacked the patience to carry out even his own most cherished schemes. He was a financial lepidopterist who was almost entirely concerned with *chasing* lovely butterflies, not with the patient but dull laboratory work that should have followed. Sir Julius, his ills overtaking him, was old at fifty; he died at sixty-four in poverty in a London suburb. His adored Gentile wife had to take in sewing to support him.

Hardly had Vogel settled himself as the leading journalist in Otago when he went into politics. In 1862 he was elected to the Provincial House; the next year he won a seat in the central legislature at Auckland as much by total default of opposition as by merit. This colonial edition of Disraeli entered the House while Alfred Domett was insecurely premier: the poetaster met the writer of "think-pieces." He was a vigorous, often violent, provincialist, even a "separationist," if not of Otago then of the South Island, apparently on the analogy of the successful separation of Port Phillip from New South Wales. He was antiwar and anticonfiscation. Beginning as an unpopular member he slowly won the respect of the House and was taken up by Fox who, when he won office in 1869, made Vogel his treasurer. Aside from the expectation that Sir Donald McLean would be successful in pacifying the Maoris, Fox was largely without a policy. The country was moving into a depression. It was Vogel who produced the policy; it was Vogelism. Where Vogel got his ideas is obscure. He had, to be sure, already a reputation as a man of figures; he had, for example, published a pamphlet of complaint and exhortation arguing that United Kingdom money going abroad should go to the colonies, not foreign countries; and if he remembered it, he knew of a scheme for borrowing for development which Domett had outlined. Aspects of his plan—the disregarded aspects as it happened—appear to have been suggested by the American land-grant system for getting railways built. He may simply have been thinking of a stimulant comparable in effect to gold rushes. At any rate, what he propounded was a scheme for borrowing heavily in London for the construction of public works, chiefly roads and railways—the transportation problem was basic in New Zealand—coupled with the bringing in of immigrants on a large scale to do the work, and *guaranteed* primarily by blocks of land totaling six million acres set aside along the railways on which the government would collect the increment in value when sold off to small settlers, most of whom would be immigrants who had built the railways, the proceeds from sales to pay for the railways. At that time the public debt of New Zealand was about £8 million; Vogel proposed to borrow £10 million to finance his program. It actually cost £16 million. "We shall be told," he ended his presentation of the scheme, "that these proposals will entail on posterity an enormous burden. Granted—but they will give to posterity enormous means out of which to meet it."

Although Vogel's scheme was promptly attacked by members of that unexterminable tribe, the folk who do not believe that men and governments can borrow their way to prosperity—they talked of "Vogel's Bubble" in ominous reference to the South Sea Bubble of John Law—it was accepted by the House of Representatives and Vogel began the restless travels which ever after characterized his career by leaving for London to "find" the money. While he was away the preliminary work on the projected railways was put in hand. Surveying went forward in the Canterbury and Otago provinces. On his return what may be called the contextual troubles were becoming evident. Wool prices were unsteady; the budget showed a substantial deficit; and, worst of all, the provinces, which had controlled the land since 1856, had failed to follow Vogel's scheme of setting aside reserves for future sale to pay for the railways.

Moreover he was immediately involved in administrative difficulties for which he was no hand at all at finding satisfactory solutions. The contracts—or alternative contracts—he had made in London for building the railways were bad, not least because they gave a single contractor a monopoly of railway building in the country. Railway building in New Zealand, as elsewhere, was a speculation as well as a problem in engineering. In the long run the New Zealand solution was to take railway building into the hands of the government. Meanwhile endless administrative difficulties had to be faced. Estimates of cost per mile for building railways under New Zealand conditions—exceptionally difficult in many parts because of the rough topography—were too low (the same error was made in Australia), and the railways therefore demanded a far higher initial capitalization than had been intended. Costs were further increased by the fact that bridging the fast-flowing New Zealand rivers was an engineering problem not immediately understood in all its implications. Many bridges constructed had to be rebuilt. There was incipient trouble over gauges before the 3' 6" gauge was finally made standard. And while Vogel had thought in terms of trunk lines for both islands, the pork-barreling of the provincialists led to the construction of numerous isolated lines. A partial South Island trunk line, Christchurch-Dunedin, was completed in 1879, but it did not reach Cook Strait until

1945. A trunk line from Auckland to Wellington was not completed until 1928.

The flow of immigrants regarded as indispensable to the scheme's proper operation began slowly. What Vogel and his associates wanted was physically sound and ambitious laborers, or people willing to begin as laborers on public works; what he got was all too often citified factory workers, often from light industries, the "sweepings" of charity institutions, and marvellously inappropriate persons, such as a company of French ballet dancers. It took time to devise a method of selection that insured the dispatching of appropriate persons. The agents in London had to look outside Britain as well as inside; incursions were made into Scandinavia (with small but excellent results) and Germany. The mechanics of moving the people to New Zealand caused trouble; a shipping monopoly had to be fought both to keep down costs and to insure that the conditions aboard ship were up to a reasonable standard. It was slow work ironing out the kinks, and Vogel was a poor administrator who issued sweeping orders and left it to his agents in England to find the ways of carrying them out. Eventually most of the problems were solved in reasonable fashion, but there was no escaping the fact that the Vogel scheme required concentration on a working-class emigration, not a mixed one on the Wakefield pattern. In due course this had an impact on social politics. The failure to facilitate the eventual settlement of these people on the land led to their concentration in the towns.

Nor did the course of politics run smooth. The conflict between groups and factions (not parties), divided as often as not on the basis of personalities or fringe questions, not on fundamental issues, continued. An innovation was the introduction of the secret ballot in 1871, but the suffrage was not changed and voting was still a minority privilege. Only about 20 per cent of the population could vote. A debate on the *administration* of the Vogel scheme in September 1872 led to the defeat of the Fox government in which Vogel was treasurer, and the installation of Stafford as premier for what proved to be the last time. Stafford lasted only a month. He was replaced by a ministry led by G. M. Waterhouse in which Vogel was again treasurer, but it lasted only five months, when Fox returned to power, with Vogel still at the Treasury. Fox's new government lasted but a month and was replaced by an administration with Vogel as both premier and treasurer. This government lasted for two years, but Vogel went abroad on one of his official trips and his absence was so prolonged that it became necessary to reconstruct the government. Daniel Pollen took the premiership and Vogel was assigned the office of postmaster general. On Vogel's return Pollen stepped down and

Vogel once more became premier and treasurer. He stayed only from February to September 1876 when he left the country to become agent-general of the colony in London. He held this post for five years and when he finally left it he was entirely divorced from New Zealand politics for a period. After a six-year absence he returned to the country in 1882 as promoter of electric lighting schemes and shortly entered politics again, but by this time Vogelism had little effect. Vogel finally left New Zealand in 1888 and died in England in March 1899.

Vogel was the dominant figure in all the successive governments before his appointment as agent-general except that of Stafford and even Stafford had no alternative policy; he simply tried to administer Vogelism more astutely. However, the social and economic context constantly changed. Vogelism, designed to escape an incipient depression, pursued its course through a period of inflation into a period of depression that originated overseas and which, since it involved a steady decline of prices for New Zealand's exports, was adjudged beyond New Zealand's power significantly to mitigate. It was Vogel's own incapacity to find an answer to the depression, in spite of his pretense to the contrary on the hustings, that led to his New Zealand career ending in an unimpressive afterclap. The factors which defeated Vogelism were the difficulty of borrowing in a disturbed London money market and the slow and uncertain tempo of economic development in New Zealand under the depressive impact of falling prices.

Vogel's own political orientation is difficult to define. His association was with the conservatives of New Zealand, but if he himself was conservative, his was a conservatism with a difference. His great contribution was to use government credit to build government-owned railways. He was not, plainly, the kind of conservative who shied away from state action, of whom there were many in New Zealand at that time—as well as many liberals who took a comparable line and confined their liberalism to questions of the suffrage, taxation, and access to the land. Vogel betrayed no interest in the suffrage, tried to use taxation to perform political conjuring tricks, and was blind to all but one aspect of the land question. That aspect was his demand for land reserves to pay for the railways.

The land reserves were, plainly, indispensable to his plan. The provinces, which controlled the land, persistently refused to give up sufficient quantities to meet Vogel's needs. Each province had a different reason for not complying with Vogel's plan, but the net effect was the same. Vogel, it will be recalled, had begun his career as a violent provincialist and his early days in the House had launched many a vituperative attack on proposals to tamper with provincial prerogatives. But Vogelism was nothing if not a *national* policy. Confronted therefore with the incorrigible provincialism of the provincialists, Vogel the nationalist had no real choice but to repudiate Vogel the provincialist. He could, if he had known it, have dismissed his inconsistency with Emerson's phrase about consistency being a hobgoblin of small minds. He proposed resolutions abolishing the provinces of the North Island and they were passed. The handwriting had long been on the wall with regard to the provinces for all to see, though there were still fierce provincialists—Sir George Grey entered politics in 1875 in Auckland Province, after living there in retirement since 1871, expressly to defend that and the other provinces— but they were partisans of a lost cause. Chronic financial difficulties, only to be met with money begged from the central government, had discredited the provinces with the public. While Vogel's was the voice that attacked the provincial system, the hands that insured him success were those of Sir Edward Stafford who, working behind the scenes with his followers, insured that Vogel's resolutions would not be victimized by factional voting. Stafford was an old-time centralist. Vogel left on a trip to London before legislation could be submitted giving statutory form to the abolition. It fell to Sir Harry Atkinson, treasurer in the stand-in Pollen government, actually to submit the legislation. It was he who, acting on the antiprovincial sentiment prevailing in the House, broadened the legislation from the North Island provinces to include the South Island provinces as well. Sir George Grey led the last stand of the provinces in the House, but the victory for abolition was a foregone conclusion. The legislation, passed in October 1875, provided that the provinces cease legally to exist on November 1, 1876. However, if the provinces disappeared legally, provincialism continued to be an active force, at first as the inspiration of the pork-barreling of public works appropriations, more enduringly as the basis of a differentiation of character and personality among New Zealanders and the constituent of their primary loyalty within the New Zealand nation.

Vogelism thus led to a fundamental change in the structure of the government of New Zealand. A unitary system was substituted for a federal system. It also was Vogelism, or at any rate its father, that supported another enduring innovation. Vogel planted the first seeds of *étatism,* or state socialism, or the willingness to have the government undertake tasks that earlier—and in many governments for a very long time after—were not regarded as within a government's proper ambit. *Étatism* inaccurately and rather prejudicially overstates what eventuated. Two institutions, aside from the railways, established the precedent. The first, the legislation for which was introduced by Vogel himself, dates from 1869. This was the government life insurance office. At that time there was no New Zealand life insurance company in operation. United Kingdom companies controlled the field. Vogel's proposal, suggested and supported by Gladstone in England, encountered no particular opposition and but little interest. It passed easily. The second, originally the creation of John Hall, but taken up and pushed by Vogel, was established in 1872. This was the Public Trust administration, a scheme for taking care of the estates of deceased persons who either had appointed the government officer to do so in their wills, or of persons who had failed to make any provision at all for the service. Both proved successful and enduring innovations. It is interesting that both of these innovations were readily accepted by conservative legislators. Near the end of his career, Vogel passed the tradition of such innovations to the liberals, in the person of his associate, Sir Robert Stout, and it was the liberals, or the "lib-labs," of the 1890's who finally made it a characteristic aspect of New Zealand's politico-economic administration.

But with all his power of persuading his colleagues to innovation, Vogel could not convince them of the necessity for land reserves to finance the railways. The abolition of the provinces did not lead to a solution of his difficulty. His final effort to accomplish his goal was made in 1873 when he tried to persuade the provinces to set aside forest reserves and have them managed in such a fashion as to insure perpetual yield. Vogel had observed that not only were the settlers "mining" the forests for commercial purposes, carrying out the lumbering with maximum destruction of the unmarketable trees, but fire was also wreaking havoc. Not only did intending settlers "burn off" to clear their land, but forest fires were not fought and often destroyed acres and acres before dying out. This waste of a resource appalled Vogel, and though he made a masterly speech in defense of his forest reserves bill, it was rejected by the provincialists who professed to see nothing in it but an attempt to get hold of their land by underhanded means. All that Vogel got out of it was the reputation as pioneer of forest conservation in New Zealand.

When Vogel left New Zealand in 1876, the economy still appeared buoyant, but there were nevertheless indications that not all was well. Vogel could not yet be assailed as one who was hastening to leave a sinking ship. He was not, of course, wholly responsible for the buoyant economic conditions; his inflationary policy ran parallel to heavy private investment and a concomitant (and badly managed) credit expansion by the banks and other lending agencies. The banks rode the wave sustained in part by deposits of funds from the United Kingdom in search of high "colonial" returns. Private investment was not only in land—there was a land boom on—but, also, in factories to produce boots and shoes, iron and brass articles, clothing, furniture, woolen goods, and beer. These factories used coal from the mines of Westland, first opened in the late 1860's, but for several decades demand outran supply from Westland and large quantities were brought in from New South Wales. There was a premonitory economic shiver in 1874 when an English financial crisis led to withdrawal of deposits in the New Zealand banks. Prices for exports were at this time already falling. Local credit was suddenly constricted. But the setback was temporary. Not until 1880 when the land boom collapsed did hard times really begin. Then for a time Vogel was the villain of the piece.

D3

On Vogel's departure political power passed to Sir Harry Atkinson who held it, with interruptions characteristic of the New Zealand scene, until the beginning of 1891. Atkinson was in a sense the inheritor of Vogelism, but economic circumstances turned him into its liquidator and political circumstances into Vogel's opponent. Atkinson had settled in Taranaki in 1853 and first came to public attention as a guerilla leader in the Maori wars, and as such was considered the equal of G. S. Whitmore. He first entered the House of Representatives in 1861. His earliest contributions were as an expert in military matters. He sympathized with Weld's self-reliance policy and was Weld's defense minister. He early perceived that Taranaki was not a viable economic unit and was thus prepared to see the province incorporated into a larger neighbor or abolished. His association with Vogel began when he accepted a ministerial post in Vogel's government of 1873–75. Although Pollen took the premiership to hold it for Vogel, he was a member of the upper house and Atkinson in the House of Representatives (and holding the office of treasurer) was the real leader of the government. He piloted the abolition of the provinces through the legislature. When Vogel left the country to be agent-general, Atkinson was his logical heir. He took office as premier and colonial treasurer on September 1, 1876, and held it until October 1877.

Atkinson was unseated by a clutch of oppositionists, among whom provincialists and liberals (some both, some not) were conspicuous, who had as their leader Sir George Grey. Grey held office for two disorderly years. The significance of this irruption is that for the first time in the political history of New Zealand an alternative to the conservatism that prevailed in the ruling group (and which continued to prevail for a decade after Grey went out of office) was at least adumbrated. The weakness of Grey's performance is attributable in part to his personal idiosyncrasies as a leader and in part to a lack of coherence in his following. As a provincialist—though a provincialist with no hope of restoring the provinces—Grey drew his support chiefly from Auckland and Otago. As a liberal he made more of a national appeal, though a spotty one, more in the towns than in the rural areas. Programmatically Grey founded his case on universal manhood suffrage, a national system of education, a "free breakfast table," and an assault on the land problem by the use of the tax mechanism. As a liberal, Grey was in the tradition of John Stuart Mill, with whom he corresponded. He believed that with national education, the vote, low tariffs on necessities, and a tax on land that would force the breaking up of large holdings the way would be open to a prosperous and socially desirable New Zealand. As a provincialist Grey was expected to extend "favors" to the provinces, especially Auckland and Otago, on more or less a pork-barrel basis. Grey's primary strength as a politician was in his capacity as a demagogic orator. Personally awkwardly inflexible, he did not see politics as the art of the possible, but as a conflict of absolutes. He knew very little about how to manage men, either the small group in the cabinet, or the larger group in the House. Moreover he led what was not yet a party, but still a loose association of persons perhaps capable of amalgamation into a party, some of whom were more interested in pork than liberalism, some of whom were more intelligently liberal than he was, and many of whom were far better politicians, though no match to him in oratorical demagogy. In two years Grey led his followers on an obstacle race in which he stumbled over most of the hurdles, alienated his wisest and strongest cabinet associates, and turned a following that was at least incipiently a party once again into a collection of inchoate factions.

Grey nevertheless got a land act passed in 1877 that provided for land boards in the old provincial areas which administered policies laid down by the central legislature and the Department of Lands. The income from land sales was "colonialized" (that is, nationalized). Vogel's idea of reserves was ignored. Grey also passed an education act which left administration in the "provinces" and initiated a long-continued struggle between local and national control of education but established it as free, compulsory, and secular. He levied a land tax, but this became a political football for some years, being booted out in favor of a property tax, and then in again not only for income but to influence the size of holdings. And one of his cabinet ministers, Sir Robert Stout, put through an act giving sound legal status to trade unions. The result was, however, that Grey failed to demonstrate that liberalism was as yet a viable alternative to the prevailing conservatism, that liberalism in fact offered anything by way of ordering New Zealand's affairs that the conservatives could not equally well supply. It took another decade of conservative rule—and the depression that was closing in as Grey fell—to temper

New Zealand liberalism intellectually and politically into the extraordinary instrument it became in the hands of other men, some of whom Grey had alienated in 1877–79.

Grey was overthrown by a close vote and was succeeded by a ministry led by John Hall in which Atkinson was treasurer. Between the installation of the Hall government in October 1879 and January 1891 when a political revolution was consummated by the accession to office of the "lib-labs," Atkinson was the key figure in politics. Under Hall and Hall's successor Whitaker—the same Whitaker who had been premier during the Maori wars—Atkinson ruled from the Treasury, but for a year in 1883–84 he was both treasurer and premier and it was from that position that he was dislodged by Vogel (in alliance with Sir Robert Stout) in his late incursion into New Zealand politics. Vogel himself followed precedent by ruling from the Treasury, assigning the premiership to Stout. Atkinson formed a short-lived administration between the two Vogel governments and, when Vogel finally fell in October 1887, succeeded to the premiership and the treasurer's office, holding power continuously for the rest of the decade.

These turns of the political wheel can hardly be said to have involved any profound conflicts of political principle (aside from the Grey episode) until the very end of the decade when Atkinson was finally challenged and disposed of. As long as the money was available, Atkinson followed a policy which was in essence Vogelism, that is, heavy expenditures of borrowed money on public works, but as the depression deepened and borrowing in volume ceased to be feasible, Atkinson adopted a policy of penuriousness and standing pat, of pinching pennies while waiting for something to turn up, of grinning and bearing what appeared to be punishment for past extravagance. Vogel's return to office in 1884 was not based on anything more negotiable than the hope that since he had once made New Zealand prosperous, he could do so again. Vogel himself believed the crisis to be psychological: what was needed was to restore "confidence." Confident you are if you say you are. He tried to provide a material basis for confidence by resuming the building of railways, taking incidentally an unfortunate flyer in having a line built as a private enterprise on the American land-grant system, and he attempted to generate the confidence that arises from falling taxes by reducing the levy and spending a sinking fund. In the end, however, he was forced to *raise* taxes, an intolerable affront to the electors, and in 1887 he was defeated on a budget. This finished him; it was clear he possessed no magic formulas. However, Vogel was not entirely barren of constructive ideas. He perceived that New Zealand needed to diversify production and exports, but with all his active canvassing of possibilities, he failed to find any satisfactory answer. Most of his suggestions, duly embodied in parliamentary papers, came to nothing. His favorite was the growing and processing of sugar beets. Already in Vogel's time New Zealand had achieved the highest per capita consumption of sugar in the world; and that sugar was being imported. To the end Vogel revealed himself as a most prolific "idea man."

New Zealand's conservatives have rarely been out-and-out reactionaries. Not only have many of them had their private reformist foibles, as Fox had temperance, but they have rarely been unwilling to "dish" their opponents by going them one better, and they have, like their British colleagues around the world, usually ended by incorporating their opponents' innovations into their own orthodoxy. A remarkable example of "dishing" as a political technique took place in the Hall administration. Grey had failed in his effort to liberalize the franchise; he had, as a matter of fact, shown a strange reluctance to go as far in his suggested legislation as he had advocated in appealing to the electors: he was a "one man, one vote" partisan. But Hall tackled the franchise problem—a condition for elevating him to the premiership was that he would do so—and established universal male suffrage, with the property qualification and plural voting continued, a definite step toward "democracy" which increased the proportion of the electors to the total population. Hall also reduced the life of a parliament from five to three years. It was not until 1889, however, that the "one man, one vote" principle was given legal expression by abolishing plural voting. (The property qualification remained until 1896.) This was achieved when a conservative administration accepted an amendment from Grey to that effect. (In 1881 the practice of weighting the country vote as against the town vote was established. In 1889 the weighting was fixed at a 28 per cent addition to the rural population and so remained until it was abolished in 1945.) Probably the most extraordinary case of a conservative essaying a liberal innovation was Sir Harry Atkinson's advocacy of old age pensions in 1882. This came to nothing; the idea was denounced by Sir George Grey as an affront to Christian charity; but the proposal from such a source was very curious. Yet however willing the conservatives might be to liberalize the franchise, and even to adumbrate the welfare state, they were not so agile with regard to the problem of land reform.

As the years passed in the 1870's and 1880's it became more and more obvious that the land problem was a central economic and political question. For years—at least since Sir George Grey's unfortunate essay in land policy of 1853—more and more land, the greater part of it the best land in the country, had been "aggregated" as freehold in the hands of individuals and companies. A veritable landed aristocracy had come into existence and in politics the defense of this class was the ultimate essence of political conservatism. The land boom of the 1870's was in large measure a matter of land aggregation and the protection of aggregation by turning leasehold into freehold. The banks and other lending institutions (some of them subsidiaries of banks) lent large sums on the security of the land, and after the collapse of the boom in 1880, came into possession of vast acreages by default of mortgages. Aggregation kept people off the land, especially those who aspired to be small holders engaging in intensive farming rather than large holders of grazing territories. Vogel, whose ideas about the land were often obtuse, had intended that many of the immigrants brought in to build his public works should eventually go on the land. Such people and others had a genuine land hunger which could not be appeased. It was clear that a more intensive use of land was feasible in New Zealand, but aggregation and extensive use was the ruling practice. The liberals were unable for some time to arrive at any really satisfactory land policy. Sir George Grey's policy of a land tax—an idea he had borrowed from John Stuart Mill and his talk about the state recapturing through a tax what he called the "unearned increment" on land—lasted but a moment (though it was returned to later) and never made too direct a contribution to breaking up the great estates. A more drastic policy was needed. A conservative named William Rolleston suggested a lease-hold system making small holders permanently Crown tenants but his associates amended the bill so that leaseholders could buy freehold. As the 1880's wore on the liberals slowly evolved a position on the land question which contributed to their victory at the polls in 1890. Their success in implementing their policy undermined their political strength.

They also evolved an attitude, sympathetic in essence, toward the labor movement. The Wakefieldians plainly supposed that the laborers they introduced into New Zealand would quietly play the role assigned to them in the theory of colonial development. They were soon disabused of this notion, for not only did the laborers, in the Cook Strait settlements, as was noted earlier, claim as a right employment at Company expense and finally win the appeasement of small grants of land in violation of Company principle, but they also in certain trades early enforced an eight-hour day. They were not strong enough, however, to make the eight-hour day universal either by legislation or combination. The carpenters pioneered the organization of trade unions, closely followed by the typographers, but the first unions were, like their British counterparts, chiefly benefit societies. The unions for several decades came and went and as depression intensified in the late 1870's they suffered severe reverses, especially in 1879. For a time labor activity was chiefly a business of protests from the unemployed trapped in the towns. By 1883 it was politically necessary to appoint a royal commission to study unemployment in New Zealand. After the bankruptcy of Vogel as an economic magician was exposed in 1877, emigration from New Zealand had set in which continued until it reached a peak in 1891. Australia, then booming, was the goal of most of the immigrants. Late in 1888 the Reverend Rutherford Waddell exposed sweating in Dunedin as it was practiced in the clothing industry, then operated on the putting-out system. The burden of this fell most heavily on women. About the same time it was also revealed that the apprenticeship system was being exploited to provide cheap labor and that child labor, both male and female, was being used at starvation wages in preference to adult labor. Trade unionism had a new growth in the early 1880's, this time permanent. By 1885 it was feasible to hold the first nationwide trades and labor congress. Some of the most significant new unions had close ties with their Australian counterparts, or were offshoots of them. Australian organizers, like William Guthrie Spence, were active in New Zealand. As in Australia, the writings of Edward Bellamy, Henry George, and the late Victorian British socialists provided an ideological background for the activity. The American Knights of Labor gained a following. Strikes occurred sporadically during the 1870's and 1880's, but until the New Zealand maritime unions became involved in the great maritime strike in Australia in 1890 on a sympathetic basis, no major upheaval took place. This strike ended with the defeat of the unions and the circumstance, as in Australia, led to the trade unionists placing increased emphasis on political action to achieve their goals. But instead of moving directly into politics, as in New South Wales, the New Zealanders at first backed the liberals, many of whom had shown themselves sympathetic to them, notably Sir Robert Stout in Dunedin, and especially William Pember Reeves, the journalist and parliamentarian of Lyttleton in Canterbury. The liberal association with labor was intimate enough to make "lib-lab" an accurate shorthanding of the orientation, especially in contrast to the passive neutrality of the conservatives under Atkinson.

The increasingly firm policy definition of the liberals in the late 1880's was matched by a struggle for an equal cohesion in political organization. In the last years of Atkinson's rule, the liberals, as the opposition, felt it the better part of wisdom to keep Atkinson in office even in the face of the willingness of many of his own nominal followers to turn him out. The divisive question was the use of the tariff for protective purposes (and to increase revenue) which was heresy to the conservative free-traders. Only liberal votes for Atkinson's tariff saved it. The basic trouble of the liberals (as indeed of the conservatives opposite them) was that they were still not a properly organized party but rather an aggregation of individuals. After the fall of Grey, this was illustrated by the action of Stout in closely associating himself with Vogel and of John Ballance in accepting cabinet office in the Stout-Vogel governments. Vogel, whatever else he was, was no liberal. With the election of John Ballance to leadership of the parliamentary liberals in 1889, the process of consolidating the groups into a party began, and shortly after the liberals took office in January 1891 the party was cohesive enough to accept and thrive upon the somewhat autocratic management of a highly skilled politician named Richard John Seddon, which insured its continuance as the ruling party for over twenty years. Political stability had arrived in New Zealand.

CHAPTER XXI

King Dick's Realm

The victory of the Liberals in the election of 1890 was a nasty surprise to the conservatives who had held office so long that they regarded themselves as the "natural rulers" of the country. They tried hard to disbelieve in the reality that confronted them, predicted the early disintegration into hostile factions of the Liberal following, and attempted to fortify their position by having the governor appoint six additional members to an upper house already overwhelmingly conservative, thus increasing the house's power of obstruction (and forecasting an outbreak of upper house trouble in New Zealand).

The Liberal victory was in truth less a party triumph than an upsurge of more or less blind rebellion against conservative rule. It brought into Parliament, ostensibly under a common label, an apparently discordant association of land reformers on the one hand and labor sympathizers on the other, with vaguer humanitarian reformers in between. The conservatives, past masters of the art of doing little, were replaced by men who at least proposed to do something, specifically about the depression which still continued unabated. There was no obvious reason to suppose that a farmer-labor alliance under Liberal auspices would be any more enduring in New Zealand than elsewhere in the world. It could not immediately be foreseen that it would take some time for the incompatibilities to work themselves out disruptively in politics, that there was, in addition to land reform and laboristic legislation, a rich middle ground of humanitarianism to be prospected before the incompatibilities became dangerously divisive. Above all it was not known that among the Liberals was one of the most astute political managers New Zealand has ever seen, Richard John Seddon, "King Dick." And of course it was not possible to foresee that Seddon, once installed in office, would operate in a period of prosperity, founded on a rise in the prices of exports and strongly supported by the expansion of the pro-

duction of meat, cheese, and butter which it was possible to export because of the application of refrigeration to ocean shipping. Seddon was
prime minister—he himself shifted to this designation from premier—
from 1893 to 1906, when he died. The Liberals continued in office,
with diminishing élan, until 1912, when they succumbed to one of the
two potential opponents they as adventurous Frankensteins had done so
much to create—the farmers. Labor was much longer in finding an independent road to power.

John Ballance led the Liberals to victory. Ballance was of Anglo-
Irish stock, born in Ireland, son of a farmer, who grew to maturity
in Birmingham, England, where he gained his education in evening
adult schools and at the lively political meetings of that city. He arrived
in New Zealand at the age of twenty-six in 1865 and established himself as owner-editor of newspapers, served in the Maori wars, and entered the House in 1876. He was a member of Sir George Grey's government, but resigned after a personal quarrel with Sir George. With
his friend Sir Robert Stout, who had an identical experience with Sir
George, Ballance was associated with Sir Julius Vogel's "afterclap"
administrations. He was elected leader of the Liberals in the House in
1889, thus signalizing the increasing cohesiveness of the group, which
he carefully fostered; and at the victory of the Liberals in 1890, he
became premier. He brought into his cabinet Richard Seddon, William
Pember Reeves, John McKenzie, and Joseph Ward. Although Ballance
had a clear majority of six in the House, stated the Liberal program with
clarity, and demonstrated that the Liberals could govern, he was able
to go but a short distance in legislation because of the organized obstructionism of the upper house. Ballance passed legislation changing
appointments to that house from life to seven years, as indeed the conservatives had proposed to do earlier, and he then attempted to overcome the obstructionism by recommending to the governor the appointment of twelve new members, but as the governor (or rather two successive governors) resisted the advice, a constitutional crisis occurred.
The crisis was eventually resolved in Ballance's favor: the governor
was instructed by London in a classic statement of the position to follow the advice of his ministers. By the time the constitutional trouble
was surmounted and the Liberals were in a strong position legislatively,
Ballance was ill. His parliamentary deputy was Seddon but his heir
as leader was Sir Robert Stout, not then in the House. On Ballance's
death on April 27, 1893, Seddon took and held the prime ministership
in spite of the efforts of Stout's friends to displace him, and when Stout
returned to the House he was reduced to leading a small liberal faction
hostile to Seddon. Eventually Stout went to the Supreme Court as

chief justice. Seddon took seriously the point that he was successor to Ballance, but he felt more strongly that he was heir of Grey.

Seddon was like neither of his mentors. He was by birth a Yorkshireman. At fourteen he was apprenticed as a mechanic; and at eighteen he emigrated to Australia where he followed his trade in the railway workshops at Melbourne. He had a brief go at gold mining, but without success. In 1866, at the suggestion of an uncle, he migrated to the west coast of the South Island and, while not successful as a miner there either, established himself as a storekeeper, hotel (that is, saloon) keeper, and miners' advocate in the Warden's court, although without legal training. He entered local politics in 1869 and was elected to the House of Representatives in 1879 as a supporter of Grey. Seddon was an assiduous student of parliamentary procedure, a constant reader of newspapers but of little else, a prosy and longwinded speaker, an indefatigable traveler among his constituents, a man who turned personal accessibility into a public policy, a gargantuan consumer of public banquets, and a master of all the arts of winning political support, including the insurance of votes by carrying out public works in constituencies and tactically apt appointments to public jobs, no matter how trivial. He was not anti-intellectual so much as determinedly unintellectual; he had a suspicion of experts of any kind; he had a Jacksonian belief in the omnicompetence of the average man, especially himself as a noble specimen of the species. As Seddon saw it, he was simply first among equals and his political task was to ascertain (by the use of trial balloons) what the people wanted and then to deliver it to them by the use of the political arts. He worked like the proverbial horse at the tasks set before him; and as his term in office lengthened, he did more and more himself and the quality of his cabinet deteriorated. Like so many imperious democrats in office, he set no store on gathering strong and able men around him. "Le gouvernement," he might have remarked, "c'est moi." His confidence in his abilities grew from what he fed on: power; and his widening horizons—from the west coast, to New Zealand, to the Pacific islands, to the Empire—simply brought into view new worlds to run. He was an imperialist of the *fin de siècle* Joseph Chamberlain-Rudyard Kipling-Cecil Rhodes outlook: the British over all. Above everything he had a perfect passion for being liked, especially by voters, and he was widely liked: he was King Dick, people's monarch of God's Own Country, New Zealand. His vulgarity was so remarkable that it endeared him to the British connoisseurs of that estimable human quality.

In view of Seddon's political equipment, it is rather straining a point to insist that he have a social philosophy, but as it was the New Zealand of his time that acquired a world-wide reputation for experimental social legislation, it is necessary to indicate where Seddon stood. His native shrewdness kept him close to the middle of the road. It was rumored around the world at the time that something extraordinary was going on in New Zealand—and about the same time in Australia—which was variously described as state socialism, *étatism,* or in the words of a French investigator, "socialisme sans doctrines," and in any case to be regarded as very "advanced." Given the intellectual climate of the time, what was going on in New Zealand was certainly "advanced," but the basic character and especially the implications of the experiments were widely misapprehended, usually with the result that an anticapitalist intent was ascribed to them. The intent, as a matter of fact, was not purposefully to weaken capitalism or capitalists but to make capitalism function with greater justice to the poor by using the state power to protect and advance their interests. The intent was to bring into being a democratic capitalism as a lower middle-class person who was more equalitarian than libertarian might conceive it. It was the range and peculiarity of the purposes for which state power was used in this connection that made New Zealand appear "socialistic" in the world of the end of the nineteenth century, when any degree of sophistication in these matters was uncommon. It was therefore often overlooked that private capitalism not only remained virile in New Zealand but that some of the state programs were capitalist in purpose, while others focused on redistribution of income earned by capitalist means, and that the land and money-lending operations were aimed at enlarging the capitalist class. The New Zealanders invented, with no great self-consciousness as to theory, a variety of socialized capitalism which forecast developments during the twentieth century in other and far more complex societies.

Seddon himself was hardly the inventor of any of the measures, either as to basic idea or particular form, and he was responsible on occasion for putting on the statute books acts embodying ideas for which he personally had no great use. He faithfully followed Ballance's program even as to items about which he was distinctly indifferent, notably women's suffrage, which was legislated with an important measure of conservative support (especially from Sir John Hall) in 1893. His experimental labor legislation was the creation of William Pember Reeves; the land legislation was the special care of John McKenzie. What Seddon took a personal interest in, though administratively he had a finger in everything sooner or later, was humanitarian legislation, of which the old age pensions of 1898 are a prime example; and when in his latter years he began to feel hard pressed by political opponents, it was to humanitarian legislation that he instinctively turned to build up his political strength. In a famous speech he exalted what he called his "humanities" and set them out seriatim in four categories: (1) Humanity for the mother and the infant [to insure a healthy and growing population for the country]; (2) Humanity for the young [to protect their physical and intellectual well-being—health and education—and to prevent their exploitation economically]; (3) Humanity for the worker [to protect him from exploitation and give him a "fair shake"]; and (4) Humanity for the old and feeble [chiefly by granting them pensions and other benefits]. Economically he laid great store by order in the national finances, including a balanced budget and care in public borrowing (which was resumed in 1894)—a policy made easier for him by continuing prosperity during most of his regime; and by seeking the middle way between favoring labor and capital. "Extremes on the part of either the labourites or the capitalists must lead to disaster," Seddon wrote in a very revealing letter. "To exalt labour and to improve the conditions of the workers is noble, but at the same time it is wise and just to give security to capital, to ensure its profitable employment, and the corollary of the development of the resources of the country." The only capital Seddon actively disliked was "big" capital organized in trusts and "rings." He had many affinities to the middle-class populist-progressives of the United States of his time; and in the United States the New Zealand program was ardently publicized by them, notably Henry Demarest Lloyd.

D3

In the foreshortened perspective of Seddon's time and immediately after there was an intense interest, in New Zealand and overseas, in the details of the Liberal legislation, including the amendments to the principal acts which were made from time to time, but after sixty years much of this necessarily appeals only as a variety of political archaeology. What is of enduring interest and importance is the general intent of the legislation and its long-range consequences to New Zealand. Legislatively the wonderful year was 1894. By that time Ballance's effort to temper the obstructionism of the upper house had achieved success, although the Liberals did not *control* the upper house until 1899, and the Liberals, led by Seddon, had for the second time won a general election, thus making it clear that the country supported the Liberal program. The era of conservative frustration had begun; it was to last for two decades during which they forgot the meaning of political success.

In attacking the land problem the Liberals aimed to facilitate closer settlement, to establish more small holders on the land. The animus was against the large holders of the so-called "aggregations" of land. John Ballance, long identified with land reform, was more particularly concerned with the problem of land taxation; and it was he who reinstalled the land and income tax in place of the property tax long favored by the conservatives. Ballance's move was in the tradition of Sir George Grey. But the land tax by no manner of means solved the closer settlement problem; it was but a minor factor in forcing great estates onto the market. A more direct attack on the problem was required. The Liberal evangel of closer settlement was John McKenzie, born in Scotland, but a small holder in Otago from 1865. McKenzie's program included compulsory "resumption" of large estates by the government and their division into small farms to be held on long-term leases. The purpose was to substitute lease for freehold, since the latter was identified with aggregation. The leasehold tenure was also to be used in dealing with sales from the public estate. To assist in establishing the new people on the land, government advisers working a kind of agricultural extension service were provided, the railways were operated and extended in support of land development, rather than for profit, a shift in policy dating from 1895, and the treasurer, Joseph Ward, added the Advances to Settlers Act of 1894. This act put the state in the money-lending business. State credit was used to borrow money overseas for lending to settlers at rates lower than those prevailing with private lenders. In the long run McKenzie's leasehold proved unpopular and less significant in promoting closer settlement than the other policies. Even men who got their foothold in farming by taking out leases eventually coveted freehold and the push for freehold played a strategic role in driving the Liberals from power. Leasehold as a permanent tenure proved best adapted to the poorer lands occupied on an extensive basis for grazing, this guaranteeing that in terms of acreage, great quantities of land should be held on leasehold. For the better land, freehold was strongly favored, not least because it enabled the farmers to participate in speculative trading in land values, after the fashion of farmers the world around. However, McKenzie operated in a climate generally favorable to the multiplication of small holders. It is especially to be noted that the North Island was at this time being rapidly opened up and much of the so-called Maori land was being brought into use by pakeha settlers. (In 1892 the Liberals reverted to the old policy of allowing purchases of land from the Maoris only by the government. Seeing what appeared to them to be a disproportion between the Maori population and the land held by it, the Liberals freely bought and quickly resold Maori lands.) But the effective economic development which supported closer settlement was the rise of the dairy industry.

The opening up of the North Island, especially on the basis of dairying, was less a consequence of a change in land policy than of technological developments and a rise in prices for foodstuffs on the London market. The Liberals, of course, did not break the depression which had gripped New Zealand since the early 1880's; they were indeed in office for five years before it even began to lift, as indicated by the improvement in prices which began in 1895. Significant technological developments began earlier, however; the most important one as far as New Zealand was concerned dated from 1882, though it went back further elsewhere. This was the application of refrigeration to ocean-going ships. In 1882 a cargo of frozen mutton was successfully transported overseas and profitably marketed in London. The experiment was suggested by the manager of the largest (absentee) land-owning company in the colony and handled in New Zealand by the company's resident representative. The success it achieved opened up an outlet for what had hitherto been a source of very limited profit to the pastoralists: the carcass of the sheep; and it led them to develop a cross-bred sheep which provided better meat than the merinos that had been standard up to that time. Before export of meat became important, profit or loss in grazing was practically determined by the price of wool, and wool only. Freezing works to prepare carcasses for export were promptly established at the ports serving pastoral districts of the South and North Islands. This development strengthened the economic position of the holders of large properties, but in the long run the applicability of refrigeration to the transportation of perishable foodstuffs other than meat did have repercussions on the pattern of land use and holding, not least by making dairying for export possible. It was the same company that demonstrated the feasibility of exporting meat that showed dairy products could be handled the same way. The important technological changes more particularly influencing dairy production came along before and after refrigeration. These were the cream separator in 1879 and a method for determining the butterfat content of cream, invented by the American, Stephen M. Babcock, professor at the University of Wisconsin, in 1890. Dairy production, beginning with cheese and proceeding to butter, was organized with governmental encouragement in co-operative factories on an American plan: farmers of a district, the size of which was determined by the mode of transport employed, brought or sent their cream to a central factory for processing. The first factory of the kind was built by the same land company that had pioneered refrigeration. By 1900 a veritable boom was underway in cheese and butter production and there was thus established the basic foodstuffs industry of New Zealand, the greatest single earner of export income, and a prime factor in closely integrating New Zealand into the imperial trading and financial systems.

On the labor front the spurs to action felt by the Liberals were, on the one hand, the harsh poverty of the town-dwelling workers that had come to light in the 1880's and, on the other, the rise of the trade unions and their expectation of the use of the strike as a weapon. The spokesman for the Liberals on labor questions was William Pember Reeves, New Zealand-born (at Lyttleton in Canterbury), well educated, the most radical of all the members of the cabinets of Ballance and Seddon, as well as by far the most articulate. He was more sympathetic to Stout than to Seddon and was in fact outmaneuvered by Seddon when the succession to Ballance was determined. Reeves was appointed agent-general in London in 1896 and there is a suspicion that he was deliberately "exiled"; it was after Reeves's departure that Seddon settled into the character of King Dick. Reeves thus held cabinet office in New Zealand for but five years—not long enough to administer the great experiment he had initiated. He gained greater contemporary and subsequent fame from his writings about New Zealand and its experiments than from his political career as an experimentalist. He was, par excellence, the intellectual of New Zealand liberalism. In London he was long closely associated with Beatrice and Sidney Webb and the Fabians with whom he shared that love affair with the state so devastatingly satirized by Max Beerbohm in the cartoon entitled "Arranging Society" (the state as pinup girl), and from 1909 to 1917 he was full-time director of that Webb creation, the London School of Economics.

The mere mention of items in his remarkable record does not make his politics particularly clear; his ideas seem as murky as those of his New Zealand contemporaries, though they were incisively expressed. In England he appears to have stood somewhere between the Liberals and Labour, while in New Zealand his reputation as the real radical of his time seems to have been based upon his warm interest in labor's aspirations, his conviction that any check upon the total freedom of capitalists was somehow "socialism," a position which gave his every move something of an anticapitalist bias, and his belief that state paternalism was always a "good thing," especially in matters involving the welfare of the wayfaring citizen. But as the measures for which Reeves the cabinet member took responsibility were hardly socialism by any proper definition, his radical reputation appears founded on his rhetoric rather than his actions. Apart from initiating or burnishing up elementary protective legislation such as that requiring the payment of wages in money and not in "truck," that insuring that payments were not unduly delayed or wholly evaded, that making employers feel proper responsibility in accidents to employees, or that raising the standards enforceable as to workplaces (this a matter of revising a law dating back to 1873), and so on, Reeves is more particularly identified with the establishment of conciliation and arbitration of disputes between capital and labor.

In the wake of the great strikes of the 1890's, in which the repulsive face of the "class struggle" was clearly seen, many middle-class liberals in New Zealand and Australia thought they had found in conciliation and arbitration, separately or in combination, a way of evading acceptance of "class warfare" as the normal way of settling differences between employers and workers. As Reeves and his fellows saw it, conciliation and arbitration would on the one hand encourage the formation of trade unions and thus improve the bargaining position of the workers, while on the other they would protect the public against the high social costs of strikes. It was not proposed by these people fundamentally to change the structure of society in a socialist or any other direction, but rather to create (in the words of the Australian, Higgins) "a new province for law and order" within the existing society. That those who held this view were truly men of the middle is shown by the fact that they had to spend considerable energy converting both workers and capitalists to support of the system. It was then rather uncommon for governments to intervene in disputes between employers and workers with a view to effecting a mutually tolerable settlement. In New Zealand a proposal to do so stood in contrast to the established conservative policy of rather frigid neutrality, followed by Sir Harry Atkinson in the maritime strike of 1890. However, state intervention was not utterly unprecedented in other parts of the world. What Reeves proposed was to make such intervention customary instead of exceptional. He rather expected that most disputes would be settled by conciliation, but in practice it turned out that even under New Zealand conditions, little could be accomplished by conciliation. Most cases of any moment to either party went inevitably to arbitration by a justice of the Supreme Court, who had powers of compulsion. Thus under Reeves's inspiration—he wrote and rewrote his bill several times before it was finally passed—the government in New Zealand acquired a powerful influence over the cost of labor to employers, thus conditioning the economics of capitalist enterprise, and over the standard of living of the workers (especially as reflected in *money* wages) presumptively to be exerted always by a paternalistic state to raise and fortify the standard. He did not, however, in spite of his own expectation and that of other enthusiasts, put an end to strikes, for it proved impossible always to render judgments acceptable to both parties and in any case both the unions and the employers developed ideologies inimical to the very idea of allowing the state finally to settle fundamental questions. The arbitration system as a system with the purpose defined became itself a bone of contention between the parties and among the unionists a rock upon which they split into left- and right-wingers. This Reeves clearly did not foresee, but by introducing arbitration he, for good or ill, made a permanent contribution to the way in which employer-employee relations would henceforth be defined, especially as they involved the division of the social product. In this sense, Reeves's scheme for the intervention of the state in the relations of capital and labor became an important constituent element of great significance in New Zealand's vague ideology of socialized capitalism.

Assumption of responsibility for wage-rates by the state led logically to a concern about the incidence of certain costs on wage earners. The particular cost to which Seddon gave special attention was that of housing. It was pointed out to him that rents were absorbing an undesirably high percentage of the earnings of low-paid workers and that they were nevertheless getting very inferior accommodations. He tried to meet the difficulty first by having the state build and rent houses (1905) and, when this seemed unlikely to work out properly, tried a scheme for advancing money to workers to build their own houses (1906). Either way, the proposition that the state had a responsibility for housing was established.

Reeves's experiment can readily be classified as a Seddonian "humanity," though it is rather doubtful that Reeves himself ever thought of it in such a vaguely sentimental fashion. It is also doubtful that Seddon, who was an eminently practical character, ever acted from truly sentimental motives, however he may have chosen to advertise his intentions. When in 1900 his health policy was given legislative form, the immediate spur to action was an outbreak of bubonic plague in Australia. A system of health officers was set up. The officers were charged with the tasks of studying the incidence of diseases and preventing epidemics; inspecting slaughter houses and dairies to insure the cleanliness of the meat, cheese, and butter they turned out; inspecting foodstuffs generally to protect consumers; and controlling the handling of dangerous drugs. Similarly when Seddon became disturbed about the possibility that the rate of natural increase of the population of New Zealand was declining—this had been demonstrated to be true of the population of New South Wales—he established a state register of nurses (1901), a register and training scheme for maternity nurses (1904), and a system of maternity hospitals. Seddon saw this as an insurance that as few as possible of the children born would be lost to the community.

All the Seddonian innovations were undertaken in a highly pragmatic spirit. It is improbable that any of the Liberals could have ordered them into a system reflecting a clear philosophy of government, save perhaps Reeves. Nor did the capstone of Seddon's arch of "humanity," old age pensions, really clarify the situation philosophically, though looking back the pensions appear to forecast the welfare state. But many of the other innovations proved assimilable by the state without giving it what to our latter-day sense is a welfare character. In the Seddon repertory, however, old age pensions appear to have been but another pragmatic move in a series.

A pension for the indigent old was first proposed by Sir Harry Atkinson, an extraordinary deviation from his normally conservative line. The point made by Atkinson about the almost inevitable indigence of elderly working-class persons in New Zealand was ever more fully illustrated and understood as time passed. But up to the moment Seddon resolved to put a scheme on the books, there was no movement for old age pensions in New Zealand. In a peculiar way the old age pension scheme was Seddon's personal venture into experimental social action. It was his thesis that a pension paid from the general revenue was no more than a just reward to the deserving elderly poor for valiant service in pioneering. In 1894 Seddon got a Select Committee of the House appointed to examine the idea; its view was sympathetic. Two years later he introduced a bill into the House just prior to the general election as a kind of trial balloon. This provoked widespread discussion and clarified the proposal. A survey to determine the probable number of persons likely successfully to claim pensions was made later that same year; it was figured that about 5600 claims would be successful. A new bill—or a rewriting of the 1896 bill—was introduced into the House in 1897; it passed the House but failed in the upper house. In July 1898 an act was finally put on the books and in November the system came into operation. To get the bill through Seddon had to put on an extraordinary demonstration of his power as a political boss during which he held the House continuously in session for a longer time than ever before in New Zealand history. The basic pension allowed was £18 (or about $90) a year, obtainable only after meeting a means test. The next move in the field of pensions did not come until 1911. But the act of 1898 clearly marked the acceptance of the principle of state responsibility for the condition of the old.

It was in the Seddon era that one of New Zealand's most famous private enterprises in the welfare field had its origin and that another reached a climax of political strength. The latter was the temperance movement which had overtones of prohibition. Although it was not exclusively led and supported by women, it was conspicuously a women's affair. In essence it was a reaction against the free-wheeling drinking associated with every frontier of the nineteenth century and thus inevitably New Zealand also. As a man with a gold rush background who had been a saloonkeeper, Seddon was not the ideal person to deal with this agitation. It gave him, as a matter of fact, a good deal of serious trouble until he was able to reduce the head of steam it had built up by legislating "local option." And since the temperance people usually also favored women's suffrage, the granting of suffrage also assisted in the decline of temperance as a separate political force. At any rate the forward fringe of prohibitionists never gained the power they achieved in, say, the United States. The other private enterprise in welfare was more clearly of a nature to win Seddon's approval. This was the promotion of infant welfare by the Society for the Promotion of the Health of Women and Children, established in 1905 by (Sir) Truby King. From a small beginning in Otago, the society became national and the principal force in defining the methods of baby care in the country. Dr. King was a powerful advocate of breast feeding.

It is odd how often the Liberals accepted responsibilities for the state—in health, housing, pensions, industrial peace, wages, etc.—and yet when confronted with an opportunity to take control of a "commanding height" of the economy they drew back as if to demonstrate that they were not, after all, socialists. The chance came in 1894. On June 25 of that year John Murray, speaking on behalf of the Bank of New Zealand (though not then an employee of it), told Joseph Ward, the government's treasurer, that unless aid was immediately forthcoming from the government, the bank would collapse into bankruptcy in a few days. Rumors that the Bank was in a shaky condition had been circulating for some five years; and a year previously Ward himself had asked it some searching questions which only elicited vague answers; but this sudden avowal that bankruptcy was imminent was nevertheless sensationally startling. The Bank of New Zealand (founded in 1861) was then by far the largest and most influential banking institution in the country; it handled the government's accounts; its collapse could not fail to precipitate a devastating panic. The Bank had come into possession of vast landholdings on the collapse of the boom in the early 1880's and the ensuing prolonged depression had left it heavily loaded with frozen assets. It had been badly jolted by the financial troubles in Australia, where it did considerable banking business. To maintain "face," it had regularly paid dividends not warranted by earnings. In effect, it had reached the end of a rope that had been rather foolishly paid out. It was, moreover, more than just a financial institution; it had long been an important political power in the land, though New Zealand writers have thus far failed to deal with the point in detail. Sir Frederick Whitaker, sometime premier, and perennial attorney-general in Atkinson's governments, is believed to have been the Bank's spokesman at the cabinet level for many years. At any rate Ward as treasurer and Seddon as prime minister had to decide whether to put government money and credit behind the Bank, or let it crash, and on what terms to help if they decided to do so. They chose to act to save the Bank, since the collapse of the country's financial fabric simply could not be faced, holding the legislators to four o'clock in the morning to pass the necessary laws; and while they placed government representatives on the Bank's board, they allowed it nevertheless to remain essentially a private bank in which the government held a large interest rather than take steps to nationalize it. Even when the ramifications of the Bank's affairs took the government deeper and deeper into its business, no move was made to make the Bank permanently responsible to the government through the treasurer or prime minister. In fact many years were to pass and the relations of governments and banking were to be transformed even in the most capitalist of countries, before the Bank of New Zealand was anything other than a private bank in which the government had inadvertently acquired an interest. It was not nationalized until 1945, by which time it hardly mattered. The episode clearly demonstrated that the Liberals were willing to have the state assume obligations of peripheral but not of central significance to the capitalist system, chiefly those involving protection of the wayfaring citizen, the redistribution of income in his favor, and the sustaining of his position as a small capitalist.

D3

The New Zealanders took an exuberant satisfaction in the figure they cut, and the world-wide attention they were given, as bold experimentalists in social action, even during later times when the experimental impulse was curbed by the antithetical impulse of conservatism. Indeed in historical perspective it is an open question as to which aspect of the New Zealand temper is thesis and which is antithesis, judgment depending to some extent on the observer's own temperament. There is, however, less room for doubt about the fact that in Seddon's hands and in the perspective of history, the synthesis was a variation on capitalism, not socialism. Seddon was to a marked degree the synthesizer and moderator of the three strands of land reform (McKenzie), laboristic reform (Reeves), and humanitarianism (his own favorite) into the vision of New Zealand as God's Own Country—one of Seddon's favorite locutions—in which the common man's interests were dominant, though not rampant. All such syntheses are unstable, for the world changes, and when Seddon suddenly died in 1906 while homeward bound from a visit to Australia, the stage was set for an attempt to stabilize the Seddonian synthesis, the task of his successor as prime minister (Sir) Joseph Ward, and for the increase in political power of conservatism, leading to the eclipse of the Liberals in 1912. Because of the changing world, Liberalism as the antithesis to conservatism slowly lost its force and its position was eventually yielded to organized labor. It was thus revealed that New Zealand's Liberalism was actually a synthesis which contained the seeds of its own destruction, but since ideological purity is rarely achieved in democratic politics, it can be said that Liberalism influenced its successors both in spirit and method. The Seddonian synthesis, therefore, was not entirely an aberrant factor in New Zealand's history, but rather loosely outlined a comprehensive pattern from which the country has not to the middle of the twentieth century fundamentally departed.

As a domestic politician Seddon was definitely "colonial." His flamboyant pride in the New Zealand of his time which, in his eyes, he had in large measure created, was accompanied by a firm resolution fully to control the internal affairs of the country but it was not accompanied by the kind of colonial nationalism which flourished in Canada and, to a lesser extent, in Australia. Many things Seddon did and said seem at a casual glance to imply a strong colonial nationalism, but actually he took a stand on intra-imperial relations which was not only more moderate than that of his fellow colonial leaders but was, as we can now see, in opposition to the currents running most strongly in the Empire. He was a colonial imperialist, not a colonial nationalist.

Thus when we come to deal with the politics of the islands 1850–90 we will find that Seddon was devoted in a fiery fashion to the views expressed by Sir George Grey, Bishop Selwyn, Sir Julius Vogel, and Sir Robert Stout. He thought and brashly said that Britain should take sovereignty in all the island groups which still remained masterless and to get them he was prepared to have them annexed to New Zealand. However, he no more than his predecessors had the power to act extraterritorially, for by definition colonial self-government stopped at the defined boundaries of the colony, so his only course was to try to influence United Kingdom policy in the direction he wanted to go. Imperialism as a policy of territorial expansion was the prerogative of the

imperial authorities who were subject to pressure from the colonial leaders but not bound to respond favorably to their proposals. No matter
how fierce the territorial covetousness of the colonials might be, it had
to be bottled up if the imperial authorities were hostile or indifferent
to specific proposals for action. Actually Seddon got very little of what
he wanted in the islands, because the imperial authorities chose to act
on imperial and not colonial assessments of the successive situations as
they arose. Few colonials, and Seddon was certainly not one of them,
had more than the vaguest knowledge and understanding of how the
imperial authorities weighed up the factors involved, especially when
the factors were in the area of foreign relations.

Seddon's problem was how to gain greater influence over imperial
policy. He wanted to preserve New Zealand's position as a self-governing colony; he would certainly welcome any change of law or nomenclature that would enhance New Zealand's status and reputation within
the Empire; but at the moment he was most interested in gaining a
strategically stronger position in imperial counsels. This meant getting
closer to the United Kingdom. The objective was to tighten the bonds
of empire, to give institutional expression to what was taken to be an
inherently organic relationship. Seddon favored any scheme that contributed to the end he had in view, whether it was designed to integrate
more firmly the imperial trading system by preferential tariffs or to
bring colonial statesmen more directly into imperial counsels by federation or by contributing to the support of the Royal Navy. He gave
tongue to his ideas at the Imperial Conferences of 1897 and 1902 and
his successor, Sir Joseph Ward, repeated them in a confused way at
the Conference of 1907. Seddon's man in United Kingdom and imperial
politics of the day was Joseph Chamberlain: the Radical turned Conservative and Imperialist: the Chamberlain of the closely integrated
and administered Empire and tariff reform. But while Seddon failed
to win over his colonial colleagues, and while Joseph Chamberlain's
brand of imperialism was but a passing phase in United Kingdom politics, New Zealand's politicians continued to follow the gist of the Seddonian line long after the colonies had moved away from satisfaction
with things-as-they-were and indifference to the Seddon-Chamberlain
orientation, to support of the aggressive positions of Canada and South
Africa which led on to the great formal statements and legislation on
intra-imperial relations of the 1920's and 1930's.

Seddon as imperial statesman was, therefore, in effect reduced to
becoming a colonial jingo, not that he or those who shared his position
regarded that as a low or benighted condition, though some deplored
Seddon's extravagances in its expression. After all, it had its roots in

the fundamental loyalty of the New Zealand people, loyalty to the Empire, transcending any secondary nationalistic loyalty to New Zealand as their own country. Seddon's jingoism found full voice in the South African War which he in effect adopted as his and New Zealand's war. For the first time New Zealanders left their country to fight in an imperial war. It was not a question of the Empire right or wrong; it was assumed without question that the Empire was right, except when the managers of the war made it difficult for New Zealand exporters to sell on the war-created market in South Africa, or sentimentalists proposed to treat the Boers with a modicum of decency. Seddon knew just how the war should be fought, how the Boers should be treated. He looked benignly on Kitchener's more primitive acts and proposals. But if the details were peculiarly Seddonian, the larger implication was of higher significance: fervent participation in the war in South Africa established the point that New Zealand could be counted on to fight in support of imperial policies, even if she had no influence upon their formation and the constitutional position was such that she had no choice but to be at war when war was declared by the imperial authorities. She was "loyal." Participation in the South African war intensified that sentiment. Imperial federation was not necessary to its existence, as the people of New Zealand, even if not Seddon, had rather quickly perceived. Loyalty was the root, federation a gaudy, exotic flower, mostly attractive to theorists, but also to a few politicians, though most voters found it scentless.

D3

The "capitalists" who emigrated from the United Kingdom to New Zealand in the early days of systematic settlement were in many instances men of university education, graduates of Oxford, Cambridge, Edinburgh, or Dublin. They often brought sizable private libraries with them and arranged to be supplied with the current publications from London. Before the first year was out at Port Nicolson, a Public Library had been established, though it was a rather exclusive public that was served, for the membership fee was £5 per annum. One of Alfred Domett's more memorable services to New Zealand was to lay firmly the foundations of a parliamentary library, with special attention to the collection of classical texts. At the other end of the social scale, perhaps three-quarters of the laborers brought out were literate. They often had a few books in their huts and they sought to improve their condition by associating themselves together to sponsor library facilities, lectures, and discussions. Mechanics' Institutes appeared quite early. In the period of crown colony government George Grey gave legislative encouragement to the establishment of primary schools for all, complementing the intention of the Wakefieldian settlers, and as premier, he established the tradition of free and secular education under local boards. The superior attainments of the minority of pioneers were in due course transformed into a compensatory legend which undoubtedly exaggerated both the attainments and the contribution the individuals made to the cultural tradition of New Zealand. As a matter of fact the pioneers seem to have exhausted themselves culturally in political speeches, pamphlets, and newspaper articles, many of which are not very flattering to their tempers, whatever they may tell about their strength of mind.

Writings about New Zealand of a kind out of which a tradition could ex post facto be constructed, a usable past, began as reportage— whether it was a matter of explorers' reports (mostly in English, sometimes in French, and once at least in Dutch), the accounts of early visitors (John Savage contributed the first book of this kind in 1807), or the narratives of pioneers. Books of this description dominated the literature of New Zealand until the 1860's at least and ordinarily were produced by amateurs, though they were often none the worse substantively or literarily for that. Naturally the Maoris and their ways figured largely in this literature.

Closely allied to it in intent were the books of scientific observers, professional and amateur, which also were until at least as late a time fundamentally occupied with inventorying the country. This tradition was established in New Zealand, as it was in Australia, by Sir Joseph Banks, but it was re-established by the systematic settlers. The Company sent out the refugee German scientist Ernest Dieffenbach, a man of general competence, whose two-volume report ranged from geology to anthropology. From the time of Dieffenbach, a succession of distinguished scientists labored at the inventory of New Zealand, mostly as government servants, including Sir Julius von Haast (1822–87, born in Bonn, Germany), James Hector (1834–1907, born in Edinburgh, Scotland), and Frederick W. Hutton (1836–1905, born in Lincolnshire, England). Hector and von Haast were chiefly identified with geology, Hutton with biology, but all were competent workers in more than one field. Hector and von Haast also made important contributions to institutional culture, von Haast establishing an important museum in Canterbury, Hector the New Zealand Institute, a general scientific society, and he was influential in the University of New Zealand, founded in the 1870's.

The first artists in New Zealand were also concerned with the inventory function. Probably the most distinguished early artist, Charles

Heaphy (1822–81), was sent out by the Company as a surveyor but also to make pictures. That he had a small surplusage of talent for art was all to the good for New Zealand; his pictures were "representational" but they were good.

In the 1860's New Zealand had two temporary residents who qualified as professional writers. One was Samuel Butler (1835–1902), the great Victorian dissenter, famously the author of *The Way of All Flesh,* and the other was Lady Barker (1839–1911). Both lived for a time on their own sheep stations in Canterbury. Butler's reminiscences of his stay in New Zealand were published as *A Year in the Canterbury Settlement* (1863), edited from his letters home by his father. He also contributed some prophetically contentious essays to local newspapers. But his most memorable use of New Zealand materials was in his fascinating utopia, *Erewhon* (1872), sometimes called the first New Zealand novel. Lady Barker wrote two books, both classics, *Station Life in New Zealand* (1870) and *Station Amusements in New Zealand* (1873) as well as a number of fictional sketches. These writers thus at once continued the tradition of reportage, raising it to a higher level of literary expertness than it had hitherto attained, and helped in the transition from reportage to fiction. Another distinguished contributor to reportage of this general period, though not a professional writer, was F. E. Maning (1811–83), author of *Old New Zealand* (1863). Maning had begun life in New Zealand, to which he went from Australia as a young man, as a pakeha Maori, and ended it as a respectable civil servant under the pakeha government. His tales of the old days, told artfully, have entranced all except those who see that he distorted the values of Maori life for the sake of the fun of a story.

But if Butler, and Lady Barker to a lesser extent, could make successful fiction out of New Zealand materials, it proved much harder for less talented writers to do so. For a long time the novelists arbitrarily mixed fiction and reportage, or tricked out reminiscence as fiction by not sticking to the facts as experienced; and these were succeeded by didactic novels in support of causes such as women's rights and temperance. It was not until after 1900 that a writer appeared who tried the novel *qua* novel. Nor were the poets any more successful. Until at least 1900—some authorities insist until the 1920's and 1930's—it was a matter of an occasional good poem by an amateur rather than a body of good work by a true poet. And similarly with the painters. John Gully (1819–88) produced some impressive water colors of the romantic kind, but it is doubtful if he ever really saw New Zealand plain.

The trouble was twofold: on the one hand life in New Zealand failed to take a shape that stimulated the aesthetically inclined but rather encouraged an emphasis on material progress and material well being, whether in the fashion of Vogel or of Seddon, while on the other New Zealand took pride in its cultural colonialism, and sought to enforce it, as by having the examinations for degrees in the University evaluated in England, as the University also enforced it by importing the staff from the old country, this delaying the appearance of that aspect of nationalism that leads to a struggle to express the uniqueness of a country (and the artist) aesthetically. Concurrent with the triumph of the Liberals in 1890, there was momentarily a nationalistic stirring among the New Zealand intellectuals, but instead of heralding a literary renaissance, it was rather an isolated event which, ironically, occurred at the beginning of four decades during which the New Zealanders sought, consciously and unconsciously, to sink their identity in the imperium. Seddon was the prophet of this orientation, with its peculiar mixture of intense local pride unvexed by nationalistic sentiment, and vigorous imperial patriotism. It was this that led to the long-established verdict that New Zealand was the most "loyal" of the colonies, while even the Australian version of nationalism was sufficient to consign her to second place in the hierarchy.

Insofar as New Zealand's intellectual energies were not satisfied within the areas of economics, politics, and public administration, they went into increasingly expert studies of the Maoris (the Polynesian Society was founded in 1892) and studies of pakeha history, mostly carried on outside the University, science, and colonial-provincial essays in painting, music, and writing. The arts were at least a generation behind the English tastes and standards by which they were measured, for while the image of "Home" weighed heavily on the New Zealand mind, it was uncommonly an up-to-date image, or one that bore invariably accurate relation to the reality of any time. And there was a steady "export of talent"—expatriation, especially to the United Kingdom. Australia, itself exporting talent, drew talent from New Zealand as though by contrast it were a "metropolitan" country.

While expatriation was chosen by many who suffered the illusions of talent without possessing the reality, it was also the choice of many of New Zealand's finest spirits. While the colony imported brains to insure her steady enculturation as a British country, it exported brains because the resultant cultural situation could not satisfy the aspiring talents that had been bred there. They could not, under the prevailing conditions, find or persuade themselves that they could find scope in New Zealand. The society was not complex enough to find use for all the brains it produced; it encouraged their departure by persistently romanticizing Home. The departure of William Pember Reeves (1857–1932) for London in 1896, whence he never returned, was a symbolic act of fateful implications: it appeared to show that the brilliant native son could best fulfill his talent not in the colony but at the center of Empire. Powerful currents of sentiment, conscious and unconscious assumptions and judgments, impelled them to the imperial center. "Home" was more than the locale of imperial power; it was equally the reality and the utopia of the mind and spirit. In literature the symbolic figure was Katherine Mansfield (1888–1923) of Wellington; in painting, Frances Hodgkins (1869–1947) of Dunedin; in anthropology, Te Rangi Hiroa (Sir Peter Buck, 1880–1951), who, however, chose the United States, not the United Kingdom; in physics, Lord Rutherford (1871–1937), a fruitful part of whose career was spent in Canada; and in cartooning, David Low (1891–   ), who used Australia as a waystation on the road to London. The theme of expatriation is a persistent and poignant one in New Zealand cultural history; and one of the most brilliant examinations of it ever written was penned by a New Zealander around the career of Frances Hodgkins.

THE ISLANDS

CHAPTER XXII

The Partitioning of the Islands (1)

The partitioning of the Pacific islands began before 1850 and it continued after 1900 in the sense of reassignment of responsibility or possession, but between 1850 and 1900 the first and primary distribution of them among the powers—Britain, France, Germany, the United States—was completed. The partitioning was not a planned operation; it was in execution and result a disorderly, illogical operation characterized by a general lack of plan on the part of all the participants. The only thing inevitable about it was that, given the world of the nineteenth century, ultimate control or possession of the islands should pass from the natives to the governments of the intruders. By logic but not by choice or assertion at this time the predominant power in the area was Britain, but the British were not moved to impose an over-all division. Indeed they largely lacked a policy toward the islands and it has proved difficult to disinter a policy line ex post facto from the record of their action and inaction. Alternative characterizations of the British line are "minimum intervention" and "inaction punctuated by crises, of solutions slowly imposed by events and finally accepted under the threat of impending chaos." The British colonists of Australia and New Zealand can be argued to have had a policy—that of keeping the islands British, at minimum by declaring protectorates, at maximum by taking sovereignty, but the colonists lacked the legal power to give effect to their external aspirations, being only colonies, and they are therefore better viewed as "pressure groups" operating on the imperial authorities. As the British had no firm line and the French, Germans, and Americans none of a comprehensive kind, either because of lateness of arrival, indifference to the fate of most of the groups, or lack of power to follow a comprehensive line. The result was that the fate of each group was the consequence of special circumstances which had arisen in that group or outside—as far outside as Europe, America,

Africa, or Asia. Hence the very disorderly and illogical end result which has troubled so many commentators and has frustrated the orderly and logical of both good and bad intent ever since.

D3

King Louis Philippe's territorial imperialism in the islands was largely frustrated by the British. The French were allowed sovereignty over the Marquesas but only a limited protectorate over the Society Islands (Tahiti), specifically over those islands in which the Tahitian queen had been exercising authority. The French had tried not only for sovereignty in Tahiti but also to extend their control farther afield, not only to groups near Tahiti, like the Gambiers, but to Wallis Island, with the "king" of which a treaty was made on November 4, 1842. French Catholic missionaries were well established there; they were the chosen vanguard of French imperialism. And in 1843 the French made their first move toward taking over New Caledonia in Melanesia when a naval officer, having landed Catholic missionaries at the port of Balade, negotiated with the local chiefs for the transfer of sovereignty over the whole island to his king.

Far more clearly than elsewhere this was a case of acquiring a *point d'appui* for the benefit of French merchants, merchant-shipping, and the royal navy. The large island of New Caledonia was very strategically located indeed. It was also climatically very suitable for white settlement, unique in Melanesia in that respect, though its agricultural resources were unevenly distributed. Only 900 miles from the British in Sydney, it was an important stepping stone toward Australia approaching from the east via Tahiti 3000 miles away. Moreover, in the days when an important approach to eastern Asia from Europe was via Cape Horn, New Caledonia was strategically related to any route running up the west side of the Pacific. Indeed New Caledonia has retained its strategic significance into the middle of the twentieth century, for as the Japanese perceived, it is indispensable in any plan to isolate Australia from North America; while in reverse it proved valuable to the United States in keeping communications with Australia open from North America.

The first French attempt on New Caledonia in 1843 was too precipitate and ill-conceived to come to anything and, moreover, the French government was not then prepared to support forward moves in that part of the world. In 1844 Guizot even disavowed the treaty with the "king" of Wallis Island. Moreover, the French missionaries had trouble in establishing themselves among the Melanesian savages. It was soon obvious that Melanesia in general was going to be a far harder "nut to crack" for all hands than Polynesia. Not only were the savages more savage, but in most of the islands the climate was markedly worse, the menaces to health of Europeans more devastating, especially malaria, and the trading possibilities, on the basis of visible resources, more speculative. It was obviously going to take a considerable time to bring the Melanesian islands into the Western economic system, though a decision as to who should control them politically need not wait on that. A great attraction of New Caledonia was that it was so much more hospitable for white men than the islands north of it.

The penetration of Melanesia was the work of missionaries, "gatherers" of sandalwood and *bêche-de-mer*, petty traders, labor recruiters, and planters. The pioneers appear to have been the gatherers. The traders and labor recruiters came in after the missionaries. Finally there came the planters. All these people, like the explorers before them, chiefly confined their activities to the coastal areas of the islands, a point that is important with regard to sizable islands, for it meant that life in the interior pursued its accustomed way while that of the coastal natives suffered the impact of Westernization.

D3

Missionary pioneering in Melanesia is peculiarly associated with the first Anglican bishop of New Zealand, George Augustus Selwyn. By the error of a clerk, the Melanesian islands were included in Bishop Selwyn's diocese of New Zealand, together with much of the Pacific farther north. Selwyn was never disposed to evade responsibility and he used the error in geography to justify his incursion into missionary work. When he made his first visit to Melanesia in 1849 he found not only gatherers at work—most notably Captain Paddon, an Australian who eventually based his economic activities on New Caledonia—but also Wesleyan Methodist, LMS, and Roman Catholic missionaries; and he traveled part of the time in company with Captain J. E. Erskine, R.N. and his ship "Havannah," then on a famous tour of the islands "showing the flag" and critically observing the activities of the white intruders. The missionaries were active only in the southernmost islands of Melanesia, reached by most of the Protestants from the established missionary headquarters in Samoa, but the trend was north and west. The Anglicans, in fact, reached the Solomons within seven years. Protestant missionaries of other denominations than Anglican played a notable role in Melanesia. Like their Anglican associates, they came to their task from far places—England, Scotland, Nova Scotia in Canada, Australia —and their names, for example John G. Paton in the New Hebrides and George Brown in New Guinea, continue to exude the peculiar odor of sanctity missionaries cultivated. But the Anglican effort—known simply as the Melanesian Mission—overshadowed all the others and in Anglican narratives they are definitely satellite undertakings. They all had in common a preoccupation with the preaching of the Word and the suppression of savage customs.

Whereas the missionaries of the lesser denominations and sponsorships ordinarily began their work by taking up residence in Melanesia, directly struggling with the climate as well as the savages, often with results fatal to themselves, the Anglicans established the pattern of visiting the islands and inducing boys and girls on the verge of manhood and womanhood to return with them to New Zealand—later Norfolk Island—where they were schooled in the secular arts of reading and writing, simple carpentry and agriculture, and steeped in a rather primitivistic Christianity, with emphasis on belief rather than intellectual comprehension, against their early return to their islands as teachers and leaders of their people. Only at a later stage of the activity did the Anglican missionaries go to live in the islands and then usually at points where they could exercise supervision over the well-established churches of the natives and with reason establish schools to forward the work. The story of the Melanesian Mission is to a peculiar extent the story of the voyages of the bishop of Melanesia for visitation, supervision, and the searching out of new islands from which to draw native recruits. It is thus presented to us as the story of outstanding leaders, rather than of outstanding field workers as in the case of the others, notably among them to *circa* 1900, after Selwyn the pioneer, John Coleridge Patteson who was killed by the natives of Nukapu Island in the Santa Cruz group, Robert Henry Codrington the great specialist on Melanesian languages, and Selwyn's son John.

Since they believed themselves bearers of divine truth to the heathen, practically no missionaries, until a very late stage of the island story, saw themselves also as agents of social change and hence on equal footing in that respect with the gatherers, traders, labor recruiters, and planters. Actually they were simply in charge of one phase of the Western influence on native life. However, they were confronted with the problem of how to deal with the other agents of influence. Ordinarily they recognized that it was impossible to fence off native life from all Western influences but their own. They saw that traders, gatherers, planters, and even labor recruiters, acceptance of whom was most difficult, were among the inevitabilities. They therefore tried to believe that if trade, etc., was in the hands of good men it was good for the natives, but if in the hands of bad men, then evil. Conditions in the islands in a later era are as much a charge to the missionaries as to their fellow agents, "good" and "bad."

D3

Napoleon III was able to do with regard to New Caledonia in 1853 what Louis Philippe had found it impossible to do in 1843. By his direction the island was brought under French sovereignty. Napoleon's calculations were on the devious side, but they proved correct. He reasoned that the British had no fixed view of the future of New Caledonia, least of all any intention of taking sovereignty over it, and that the colonial views on the point, which favored British sovereignty, would not rule. Moreover, he felt that the British would be disinclined to make anything out of a French action, even to satisfy colonial opinion, for Britain and France were allied against Russia, a more important consideration to Britain than any South Sea island. France still held to the calculation of New Caledonia's strategical importance—indeed the strategical argument was stronger in 1853 than 1843; she was under pressure from the missionary interests to provide a secure base for mission activities in Western Oceania; and Napoleon had the notion that New Caledonia would make a useful place of exile for criminal and political deportees. New Caledonia was taken first and developed later, the reverse of the order in other islands. As far as the French were concerned, its "prehistory" was the story of Roman Catholic missionary activity.

Nevertheless the French felt it necessary to proceed with caution. They were not absolutely sure that the British would not suddenly take New Caledonia if they had reason to suspect that the French intended to act. In 1850 they sent an exploring expedition to the island which closely surveyed the coasts and probed the interior, and the French missionaries, who had weathered a serious native rebellion in 1847, were there to support French actions. Orders to take New Caledonia were quietly sent from Paris to the commanders of the South American, Indian Ocean, and Pacific squadrons. Rear Admiral Febvrier-Despointes of the Pacific squadron received his copy at Lima, Peru, in mid-June, sailed immediately, and became the effective agent of the Emperor's wishes. He was instructed to consult with the missionaries to make sure that the British had taken no action, and then to proceed to proclaim French sovereignty. This he did at Balade on September 24, 1853, specifying that his action included the dependencies of New Caledonia. He then proceeded to the important "dependency," the Isle of Pines, where he found His Majesty's ship "Herald," as he had had information he might. Nevertheless Febvrier-Despointes managed to carry out his orders, if by strategem to avoid a direct challenge to the British, and gain sovereignty there too. The British may have coveted Isle of Pines as a coaling station—the evidence is inconclusive—but the French outmaneuvered them. Beyond Isle of Pines no clear definition of "dependencies" was given and thus was missed a chance to take the New Hebrides group to the north, an error of procedure long regretted. Over a period of a quarter-century the dependencies were defined as including, in addition to Isle of Pines, the Loyalty and the Chesterfield groups.

As one of their historians has remarked, the French proved not, in New Caledonia at least, to have the "colonial vocation." Nor did they prove in any hurry even to begin experiments in exploitation. As the Australians had begun the utilization of New Caledonia's resources, so they continued it. Such exports as became available went to Sydney, such imports as were required came from there. Finally in 1863 New Caledonia was designated a place to which convicts might be transported from metropolitan France. Between 1864, when the first convicts arrived, and 1894 when transportation ceased, a total of perhaps 40,000 persons were sent out, the predominating types varying from time to time. However, there were at the peak usually no more than 7000 convicts on the island at any given moment, of whom perhaps 5000 were employable. As under the old Australian system, the labor power of the convicts was assigned to free settlers who, naturally, were a numerical minority of the total population. As an aftermath of the famous Paris Commune of 1871, so conspicuous in the historical mythology of communism, there was an influx of political offenders the next year, a development which probably made convict New Caledonia more famous than any other single episode in its history. Under a law of 1875 chronic recidivists were sent to the island, distinctly lowering the moral tone. The economic results of the system were negligible in spite of a tremendous effort in the 1880's to achieve success. As the 1880's wore on the numbers began to increase, but so did the British (really Australian) protests, inspired by the alleged menace of escapees to the Australian colonies. The system was finally abandoned in 1897. No more convicts were sent out and then began the slow process of the fading away of the convict population which extended through World War I.

By 1870 free settlers numbered around 1500, some Australians, some Creoles from the island of Réunion. A cattle boom which lasted roughly from 1871 to 1876 approximately doubled the free population. A dramatic check to progress occurred in 1878 when the natives revolted. About 200 settlers lost their lives. The fundamental cause of the uprising was the land question. The crowding of the natives off the best land had begun very early by the missionaries who thus became great landowners. By 1855 nine-tenths of the land had passed from native hands; and their precipitate decline in numbers was by no means proportionate. The French record with regard to the natives was bad and the inevitable consequence was rebellion. Much menacing unrest continued for some years after 1878. In the middle 1890's Governor Feillet—in office 1894–1902—tried to establish a solid and vigorous rural democracy on the island, but his effort failed. Agricultural development was a thing of shreds and patches. But in the 1870's the great mineral riches of the island began to be uncovered and from 1875 New Caledonian production of nickel dominated the world market until the Canadian deposits were discovered and exploited. Chrome and cobalt were also produced. It was minerals, therefore, that made New Caledonia a source of great wealth, not agriculture, even if largely to the profit of the great capitalist exploiters domiciled overseas and their industrial customers. By 1900 there were 23,500 white persons in New Caledonia, by far the largest white population in any South Seas island group.

D3

The colonists of Australia and New Zealand had begun to be conscious of New Caledonia as an island of potentially special value around 1840 when the prospects were still wholly agricultural. In that year sandalwood was discovered on the Isle of Pines and its exploitation was immediately begun. A "wasting" resource, it was nevertheless with customary heedlessness rapidly cut out and as early as 1849 Captain Erskine of the "Havannah" noted that it was nearing exhaustion. The most famous of the sandalwooders was the Australian Paddon who set up a headquarters in the Loyalty group in 1843, shifted to the Isle of Pines in 1847, and in 1851 established himself on l'Isle Nou close to what became the site of Noumea. (L'Isle Nou was eventually acquired by the French as their principal place of close detention of convicts.) There Paddon dealt not only in sandalwood but in coconut oil, whale oil, *bêche-de-mer,* and other products, a true exemplar of the gatherer. Another famous Australian enterpriser in the New Caledonian sandalwood trade was Captain Robert Towns.

In 1842 a man named Sullivan outlined a scheme for the systematic colonization of New Caledonia from Sydney and Governor Gipps was so impressed by it that he forwarded it to the imperial authorities with an indorsement. John Dunmore Lang's eagle eye fell upon the island and *he* proposed that it be colonized by the Germans, then reckoned a people friendly to the British. But the imperial authorities said and did nothing. It was the Australians and New Zealanders who took a proprietary attitude toward New Caledonia, though not markedly more so toward it than toward any island in the Southwest Pacific.

When the French actually took over in 1853 the Australians and New Zealanders were exceedingly upset and sharply castigated the imperial authorities for their negligence and apparent indifference. Newspaper comment in Sydney was especially bitter and the French came to regard this as the first clear expression of Australian imperialism, ignoring the historical roots of the position.

The French action came at a time when the situation in the Pacific was manifestly changing but into exactly what shape was not clear. The British obviously did not foresee a menacing shape. The demand for island products was active and appeared to be rising. The plantation system of production was creeping in for coconut oil, cotton, sugar, coffee, and other products. That curious episode the guano trade brought gatherers into the Pacific islands on a new errand and the American government in supporting its contingent adopted the policy of taking sovereignty over any island they found worth their attention, though this turned out to be more a temporary expedient to guard rights while an exhaustible resource was abstracted than a tack for establishing permanent American rights. The policy, however, complicated the sovereignty history of numerous eastern islands of the Southwest Pacific. There was also at this time a revival of the expectation that a canal would be cut at Panama, revolutionizing transport to and in the Pacific. A railway was completed across the isthmus in 1855. In 1854 the Americans engineered the opening of Japan; the French were about to address themselves seriously to the "problem" of Indo-China; steamers, first introduced into the Southwest Pacific in 1830, were undertaking longer journeys into the ocean than hitherto, raising the question of coaling stations. One was at New Caledonia in 1854. A line was established from San Francisco to Honolulu in the same year and an experimental voyage was made from Sydney to Panama. The Australian gold rushes were rapidly augmenting the British colonial population. The British, therefore, were being subjected to mounting colonial pressure for a forward policy in the islands, regarded as British but liable nevertheless to fall into the hands of objectionable foreigners if the imperial authorities were not alert. At this stage, however, the British were not responsive. They ignored the Australian and the feebler New Zealand pressure *before* alleged facts; and they endured complacently the reproaches *after* facts, as in the case of New Caledonia. Their maximum response was to expand the consular service in the islands. In 1857 consuls were appointed at Samoa and Fiji, and later Tonga was placed under the care of the Fiji officer. At that time these three groups seemed likely to be the principal foci of Western interest.

After annexation as before the Australians predominated in the trade of New Caledonia. The great island was unquestionably politically French but economically it was almost British. But New Caledonia was nevertheless permanently out of British colonial reach. Attention in the western Pacific shifted to the New Hebrides. A Gallicized Australian led the economic way there.

D3

Although the Fiji group was to become by far the most important British colony in the islands, the British were not persuaded to take sovereignty there until 1874, two decades after the French had secured New Caledonia. A Melanesian group, though on the border of Polynesia and subject to Polynesian influences, Fiji was long considered difficult of access because of the reefs in the seas about the islands, and risky in any case because of the savagery of the natives. For many decades Fiji became a classic locale of South Sea cannibalism in the Western imagination. However the gatherers began to work in the islands beginning around 1800 and the missionaries, after some preliminary gestures earlier, established themselves there in the middle 1830's. Nevertheless as late as 1857 it was estimated that no more than thirty to forty Europeans were resident in the group. It was during the third quarter of the century, however, that developments in Fiji took a turn which made the absorption of the group into the Western political and economic system an inevitability. In the 1850's the contenders for possession appeared to be the French, the Americans, and the British. The French soon left, leaving only a minor missionary group; the Americans remained rather ambiguously in the picture until around 1870, chiefly as traders and planters; and the British proved to be the heirs of the chiefs of whom the most notable were the Fijian Cakobau and the Tongan interloper Ma'afu.

The effective cause of the taking over of Fiji by the British was the establishment of plantations in Fiji by colonial, British, American, and other adventurers. Fiji first attracted their attention in the 1860's and there was something of a rush to Fiji in 1870–71. Although solid and responsible individuals took part in the penetration of Fiji, a considerable number of dubious and definitely shady characters were attracted there also, particularly to the trading headquarters of the group, the village of Levuka. The islands had always had a fateful attraction for riffraff and when overtaken by law and order in one place they tended to migrate hastily to another. From Fiji, after British rule was established, there was a migration to Samoa. The planters were attracted by the tracts of usable land, especially on the large islands, notably Viti Levu. The immediate inspiration for the invasion of Fiji was the American Civil War which, by cutting off England's cotton supply, led to experiments in cotton growing in various places overseas, among them Fiji. Plantations required labor and Fiji was a focal point of the island labor trade which became a scandal of considerable proportions, to the shame and chagrin of the authorities in Britain. Fiji entered the British official consciousness as a "problem."

In its aboriginal state Fiji was a country ruled by chiefs whose authority within their districts was limited only by the extent to which they acknowledged the paramountcy of other and more ambitious and powerful chiefs. However, no Fijian chief had ever achieved mastery of the whole group; there had never been a "king" of Fiji—or in the native language, a Tui Viti. Chief Cakobau was, however, remarkable among the leaders of his generation in that he adopted the title Tui Viti and managed, especially after intruding whites found it convenient to accept his pretensions, to sustain the position, with ups and downs, for over twenty years. His rule over the other chiefs was, however, never absolute and his position was particularly and regularly challenged by the Tongan interloper, Ma'afu. The Tongans had been in contact with the Fijians for many generations; they were the principal carriers of Polynesian influences into Fiji. From Fiji the Tongans particularly obtained canoes in the building of which the Fijians were highly skilled. It was while visiting Fiji on presumably peaceful trading missions that the Tongans perceived that by throwing their weight to one party or another of a current quarrel, they could not only assist their "friends" but gain power for themselves. Ma'afu was resident leader of the Tongans in Fiji, established at Lomaloma on Vanua Balavu Island in the eastern islands of the group, collectively known as Lau. Ma'afu was unquestionably a man of ability—in some respects superior to his great rival, Cakobau—but his unwillingness honestly to collaborate with Cakobau in any form of government based on the assumption of native sovereignty contributed heavily to the collapse of the governments Cakobau headed as "king." Until 1869 Ma'afu was agent in Fiji of King George of Tonga, but in that year George took alarm at the dangers inherent in his position, now that Fiji was a matter of interest to European governments, and formally transferred his interest to Ma'afu. This temporarily strengthened Ma'afu's position, but Cakobau proved to be an obstacle in his path to supreme power in Fiji he could not remove. In the end Ma'afu had to join Cakobau and it was as his nominal subordinate that he signed the Deed of Cession transferring sovereignty to the British.

Up to 1854 Cakobau was a paladin of heathenism, but in that year he was converted to Christianity by the Wesleyan missionaries. At the moment he was surrounded by enemies, for intertribal warfare had been fierce for some years. In part it was a struggle between Christian and heathen natives, with the Tongans participating on the side of the Christians, for they had been converted earlier and had both a religious and a political motive for thus opposing Cakobau. Cakobau's conversion caused a realignment of forces, for it was regarded by his friends as often as by his enemies as a "political" development. He was thought to have accepted Christianity as a means of saving his skin now that the impotence of the heathen gods was so painfully clear. He was promptly besieged on his island stronghold of Bau, off the coast of Viti Levu, and his fall seemed inevitable. The white traders at Levuka, conspicuous among them the American J. B. Williams of Salem, Massachusetts, warmly advocated his destruction in the interest of peace in Fiji, but a visiting American trader helped save him. Defying the blockade, the trader sailed his ship to Bau and landed desperately needed food, guns, and ammunition. At this point King George of Tonga attempted to mediate the quarrels of the Fijians, but his envoys were fired upon by tribesmen at Levuka and the Tongans then joined Cakobau as *his* allies. Together they won a notable victory over the enemy at Kaba on the mainland of Viti Levu, a victory which marked a turning point in the history of western Fiji, for after Kaba outbreaks of tribal fighting among the natives were of minor significance, whether provoked by Tongan activities, brought on by reversions to savagery in the remoter parts of the group, or attributable to resistance of the hill tribes of the interior to the pretensions of the coastal tribes or the incursions into the great island of the whites. Although Cakobau had thus escaped total destruction by virtue of the actions of an American trader and the Tongans, and was then able to impose a fairly general peace by virtue of the almost universal exhaustion after a period of rather desperate warfare, he did not abandon his pretension to being Tui Viti. He not only snatched victory out of the jaws of almost certain defeat, but he retained his ambition intact.

It was in the midst of this turmoil that the Wesleyan missionaries engineered the first offer of sovereignty over Fiji to the British authorities. Their motive was not to invoke external authority to put an end to tribal warfare, though they may have hoped for that result, but to frustrate what they thought were the designs of the French and the Roman Catholics whom they suspected of fishing in the troubled Fijian waters. With the example of Tahiti before them, they had visions of being ousted from Fiji. But the offer was based only upon the alleged wish of a minor chief, involved only the minor island of Ovalau on which Levuka was located, and though transmitted to London by the missionary Calvert, it was rejected by the authorities as "premature and unauthorized."

Nevertheless the situation in Fiji was now so obviously changing that the powers began to take formal notice of the group. Not only the British from their naval station in Australia but also the French and the Americans sent warships into the group to show the flag and treat with the natives. For some years the United States had been represented in the group by J. B. Williams with the title of commercial agent. In June, 1857, the United States negotiated a treaty designed to insure its nationals freedom from molestation in Fiji. The French negotiated a similar treaty a year later. These treaties were negotiated with Cakobau, this bringing him white support for his pretension to being Tui Viti. He was soon to learn that the recognition brought onerous responsibilities as well as honors. The British regularized their position in Fiji by appointing a consul there. The first occupant of the office was W. T. Pritchard, son of George Pritchard of Tahitian fame, who came from Samoa to take up his duties in September 1858.

Pritchard was the son of his father in more ways than one for he was not satisfied to perform the routine duties of a consul but was immediately deeply involved in Fijian politics and in the engineering of a new move to bring Fiji into the British Empire. He got an offer of cession from Cakobau within eight weeks of his arrival. The immediate cause of Cakobau's action was his difficulties with the Americans, especially J. B. Williams. Williams and others had suffered property losses from various causes which at the end of 1858 totaled $45,000. A visiting American naval captain in October 1858 demanded of Cakobau, who in accordance with his pretension to be Tui Viti had accepted responsibility for such claims beginning in 1855, that he pay up within a year. Cakobau knew very well he could not raise such a sum to satisfy the Americans, so he asked Pritchard, who believed his allegation that he was Tui Viti, to accept a deed of cession of the group to Britain, one of the conditions being that the British pay off the Americans, in return for which Cakobau promised to transfer title to 200,000 acres of land to the British Crown. With this document in hand, Pritchard left for London to put the case to the British government.

Pritchard was absent in London for a year. He was ordered back to his post with no more than the message that the request for annexation was under consideration. On his arrival at Levuka he found that Fijian politics had taken a shape he had not anticipated. Nobody, least of all Cakobau, had pointed out to him that Cakobau was Tui Viti only by pretension and not in fact. On his return he discovered that Cakobau had all along lived in fear that his Tongan allies who had insured his position by decisive assistance in the battle of Kaba would turn against him and take supremacy in Fiji themselves. That his fear was well founded was demonstrated by the actions of Ma'afu and the Tongans while Pritchard was in London. Ma'afu had only pretended to agree with Cakobau's offer of cession, and as soon as Pritchard had left Fiji he set about systematically depriving Cakobau of the support of the lesser chiefs until he was isolated. Ma'afu pretended friendship for Cakobau up until the very moment he was ready to strike against Cakobau himself at his stronghold on Bau. At this point Pritchard stepped into the picture and summoned the chiefs, including Cakobau and Ma'afu, to a meeting in the British consulate in Levuka. He there extracted from Ma'afu a renunciation of his political claims in Fiji, obtained a new offer of cession from the chiefs jointly, devised a document setting out rules for relations between the whites and the Fijians, and arranged that the "controlling power" in the group be placed in his hands. While this was a remarkable performance on any grounds, it was a venture far outside the bounds of consular authority and was, naturally, not well received in London.

Meanwhile the London government had dispatched as a mission of inquiry to Fiji, Colonel W. T. Smythe of the Royal Artillery and Dr. Berthold Seemann, a skilled botanist. Smythe was to judge the general situation, while Seemann was to study the prospects of cotton growing and the economic uses of indigenous plants. Seemann got to Fiji without too great difficulty and formed a friendship with Pritchard which survived subsequent difficulties, while Smythe after a delay in Sydney awaiting transportation, crossed over to New Zealand in the hope of doing better, was unfavorably impressed by the Maori-pakeha war, and annoyed that in the end he had to charter a vessel to get to Fiji at all. Seemann not only adopted Pritchard's politics and opinions about annexation, but he arrived at favorable conclusions about the prospects of growing cotton in Fiji and identified many indigenous economic plants, compiling a valuable essay in Fijian botany. Smythe on the other hand came to the conclusion that not only was Fiji isolated from its nearest British neighbors but that the chances were good that systematic occupation would lead to a costly war with the natives, as in New Zealand. Moreover he thought that Fiji would never produce more than insignificant quantities of cotton, and probably little of anything else. Although the Admiralty had, from the study of maps, arrived at the opinion that the possession of Fijian harbors would be useful in the transpacific trade that would probably develop once a canal was built at Panama, and defensively along the line Sydney-Fiji-Hawaii-British Columbia, Smythe concluded that the Sydney-Panama run would probably follow a track either south or north of Fiji (which was a correct guess) and in any case the islands were enmeshed in dangerous reefs that were a menace to navigation. And Smythe's sizing up of the political situation in Fiji was contrary to Pritchard's. He established to his own satisfaction that Cakobau was not Tui Viti, but only a dubious pretender to the position; and he was influenced by missionary opinion to take a favorable view of Ma'afu's position and influence. He concluded that Cakobau did not have the 200,000 acres he had offered to transfer as compensation for payment of the $45,000 to the Americans (which was true). The missionaries, while deploring Ma'afu's frequent resort to violence, could not forget that he had long been pro-Christian. Moreover, Smythe felt that Pritchard had gone much too far in interfering in the domestic politics of Fiji and should have confined his activities exclusively to the prevention of actual warfare. When Smythe's report reached London in August 1861 the authorities read it as supporting a refusal of the offer of cession. The decision, conveyed to Fiji via the governor of New South Wales, reached the islands July 7, 1862.

While the Smythe report was proceeding through channels, Ma'afu had contrived another of his upheavals in Fijian affairs but Pritchard succeeded once again in getting him to renounce his ambitions. That Ma'afu was a double-dealer to whom agreements were but scraps of paper was quickly revealed, for he soon again menaced Cakobau whom he said he would make his cook, while he himself became Tui Viti. Moreover other disturbances took place, involving punitive visits from both British and French warships. The former burned a few villages; the latter exiled to New Caledonia a follower of Ma'afu's who had mistreated a Roman Catholic missionary. Ma'afu was not subdued by these events but again renewed his campaign against Cakobau and, moreover, stirred up King George of Tonga actively to support him. This menacing situation Pritchard disposed of by visiting King George at his capital, Nukualofa, and exacting a scrap of renunciatory paper from *him*.

The official decision to refuse cession was accompanied by an instruction to the governor of New South Wales to appoint a commission of inquiry into Pritchard's conduct, particularly his role in native affairs. The commission reported unfavorably and Pritchard was removed from office. However, the consulate was maintained. Pritchard proceeded to London but was unable to change the government's mind either about his conduct or the annexation of Fiji. In the end he went to Mexico and disappeared under unknown circumstances while on an overland journey to California.

D3

The situation in Fiji in the early 1860's was that, while the number of white residents was increasing, a considerable number having arrived in response to Pritchard's representations made in letters to colonial newspapers, there was no visible prospect of orderly government by annexation by the British or any other government. It has been estimated that at the time there were at least forty chiefs in Fiji exercising despotic power over areas of greater or lesser size, of whom perhaps a dozen were of some importance in relation to the affairs of incoming whites, and of these Cakobau was the most important in relation to Viti Levu and Ma'afu elsewhere. The incoming whites, insofar as they established plantations, were chiefly interested in cocoanut oil and cotton, with the latter of rapidly rising importance. Sugar was a reserve possibility.

Naturally the country could not get along without some kind of formal government. Colonel Smythe had suggested that a native government be encouraged, guided by the advice of the resident consuls. The first move in this direction was made in 1865 when seven of the principal chiefs, including Cakobau and Ma'afu, formed a confederacy with Cakobau as elected president. However, Ma'afu wrecked this within two years by standing for president. Much as the chiefs disliked Cakobau, they disliked Ma'afu more and rather than accept him as their president, they withdrew.

Ma'afu thereupon gathered around him a few chiefs and set up a confederacy of his own which claimed and maintained authority in the north and east, in Vanua Levu and the Lau Islands, and was known as the Lau Confederacy, while Cakobau set up the Kingdom of Bau with a constitution modeled after that of Hawaii to control Viti Levu. Ma'afu's area was better administered, but Cakobau's had the most white settlers. Both native rulers relied heavily on white secretaries for guidance. After 1869, when King George of Tonga transferred his interests in Fiji to Ma'afu, Ma'afu assumed the title of Tui Lau. In 1871, however, he abandoned all claims outside Lau, acknowledged Cakobau as king of Fiji, and became lieutenant-governor of Lau. He was, however, a very restless subject of the triumphant Cakobau.

D3

Of the classic three—land, labor, and capital—the white intruders in Fiji expected the Fijians to supply the first two cheaply and in abundance, while capital investment was to be held to a minimum. By and large the investors were impecunious men, long on a willingness to take risks, short on cash and capital goods. They looked for support to quick returns from annual crops, sought their profit in a fairly crude "primitive accumulation"; they saw in a fling in Fiji an opportunity to clean up and get out. Those who rode the cotton boom and bust, however, mostly ended up too poor to move on and became compulsorily resident micawbers waiting for something to turn up. The pioneers had no understanding of the Fijian system of landholding and the Fijians had but a limited understanding of what was involved in transferring land to men who thought they were acquiring indisputable freehold rights. Although efforts were made, on the advice of more disinterested whites, to control transactions in land, titles remained irregular and insecure until Fiji became a Crown Colony, when the task of reviewing claims was undertaken by the British authorities. On the whole the land situation in Fiji did not get entirely out of hand. But with regard to labor the situation was different. It got out of hand to the point where it was adjudged a major scandal. Fiji became involved in the labor trade scandal because the Fijians resisted recruitment for plantation work.

Plantations could not be operated without an abundant supply of cheap labor. This was the universal experience. Where there was no resident labor supply, or where the prospective members of it were reluctant to work, it appeared entirely logical to bring labor from elsewhere. There thus grew up as a phase of plantation development a "trade" in labor, the essence of which was the bringing of workers from places where they were abundant but "unemployed," to places where a demand for their services existed.

All of them were islanders, most of them Melanesians. The men who went into the islands to obtain laborers—the recruiters—were not the ultimate employers of the workers they assembled and transported to "market." The custom was to sell the labor to the planters at a price which recouped the recruiter's expenses and left him a profit. The planters, for their part, assumed responsibility for the maintenance and reward—£2 or £3 a year in trade goods—of the workers obtained, usually for some fixed period, say three years, as well as the cost of transporting the workers back to their islands. Fiji was simply one of several places in which a market for recruited island labor developed. Queensland in Australia was another, as has been noted. The French recruited for New Caledonia and Tahiti, the Germans for Samoa, the Peruvians for a brief period for plantations and mines on their mainland and on coastal islands, the Chileans practically denuded Easter Island of inhabitants during their incursion into the trade. Americans were involved as recruiters, but not for any American market for labor. The trade was predominantly a British affair. The principal markets were British: Queensland and Fiji; most of the recruiters were British operating British-flag boats. The laborers brought to Fiji came from the New Hebrides, the Solomon Islands, and the Ellice and Tokelau Islands. The trade began in 1864.

What turned this induced migration to economic opportunity into a scandal at all its stages—recruitment, employment, and repatriation—was that the islanders involved were really pawns in a white man's game in which they began by having but a limited understanding and ended by fearing and hating. Labor under the system was a commodity and since it was impossible under the conditions to draw any distinction between the laborer and his labor-power, the natives were in essence treated as commodities. There was, of course, no tradition among the islanders of going abroad to work—least of all to work in the steady and systematic fashion the planters required. The laborers were at best induced to "sign on" by arousing their desire for trade goods, or more often by arousing the desire in a chief whose *quid pro quo* for possession of the articles was to hand over a few warriors to the recruiter, and at worst there was literal kidnapping, often by ruses like sinking canoes and scooping the survivors out of the water. The plantation employment assumed the character of forced labor under conditions of housing, clothing, and diet unfamiliar to the natives, leading inexorably to sickness and a high death rate. Recruiting was thus an efficient agent of depopulation. Repatriation—often not honestly carried out because of the poverty of the planter, or because it was easier for the recruiter to deposit his charges on a convenient island rather than the natal island, whereupon the unfortunates were promptly killed by their hosts—was not in any case a net gain for the worker. Chances were he would quickly be deprived of the fruits of his labor, tawdry trade goods, and forced to share them out among his fellow-tribesmen, or, if he brought a gun home, an outbreak of uncommonly destructive warfare would ensue. A common justification of the trade was that it "civilized" the recruits. In what sense was the reduction of natives to the status of unskilled laborers in white enterprise—that is, to the condition of low-grade "economic men"—a civilizing experience? Only a nineteenth-century entrepreneur could find a positive answer to the question. The labor trade beyond a doubt was a major facet in the Western impact on Melanesian society in the nineteenth century, but any effort to make out that it had a creative influence on the natives, or native society, is doomed to failure. Since it took individuals out of the context of their society, breaking up patterns of family life, labor, and warfare, it contributed to the disintegration of native life. Returned laborers were, in effect, deracinated men let loose in tightly organized societies. Whatever creative consequences followed from the labor trade must be sought, if sought anywhere, in the history of white enterprise. What happened was that a virgin pool of labor was systematically raided to supply the manpower for the establishment of the plantation system in Fiji, Queensland, and elsewhere. This was "good for" the white entrepreneurs, who could not have realized their purposes without such labor. However, it was a crude method of economic advancement and it was rather early condemned not only by the missionaries but also by naval observers and men of good will in Australia, New Zealand, and England. They commonly found it uncomfortably like slavery. The native protest against the system took the form of miscellaneous barbarities, including cold-blooded murder, motivated by revenge on the tribe of white men. Vengeance was taken on unwary recruiters and innocent bystanders, often pronative, alike. Conspicuous among those who suffered equally but unwarrantedly for the trade were Bishop Patteson in 1871 and Commodore J. G. Goodenough of the Australian station in 1876. Patteson was clubbed to death by natives among whom he had trustingly gone, Goodenough by poison arrows showered on his party. Both fell victim to Santa Cruz natives, but this was an accident, for natives on other islands than these were equally infuriated against the whites.

Between June 5, 1871, when Cakobau's Constitution of 1867 was suddenly rescued from innocuous desuetude and a new ministry of white men was announced at Levuka and October 10, 1874, when the Deed of Cession transferring sovereignty to Queen Victoria was signed, the rather sordid drama of "native government" was played out to its end. The discredit for the failure by no manner of means fell wholly upon the natives. The fundamental difficulty was that the Cakobau government could not establish its legitimacy with either the whites or the natives; its authority was persistently challenged by dissident natives and whites alike. To be sure the problems with which it had to deal were complex and recalcitrant, but failing of recognition of its legitimacy and plagued by its inability to reconcile conflicts of interest among the whites, it was reduced to a dangerous insecurity from which no escape could be found. The government, for example, could not fully collect its taxes; it weakened its position by trying to survive on borrowed money. Dissident whites failed to pay up, Ma'afu withheld from the central authorities moneys he had collected in Lau. The collapse of the cotton boom made general economic conditions very difficult; the planters faced an uncertain future. Not even the elevation of a man of the ability of J. B. Thurston to the position of chief secretary could save the situation.

Cakobau's decision to support the transfer of sovereignty to the British was a recognition that it was quite beyond his power and the abilities of such whites as he could collect around him to provide the government the situation required.

The situation the ministers confronted was remarkably complex. About 2500 whites and 135,000 natives were involved. By a revision of the Constitution of 1867 it was arranged that while Cakobau was something of a figurehead, the ministry was nevertheless responsible to him and not to the elected Assembly. Nevertheless it was a white man's government, in spite of native participation, not a native government asserting its power over white men, though it had, or came to have under Thurston's prompting, a sense of responsibility to the natives. The place of the natives in politics and government was, indeed, one of the basic issues of the time. Many whites wanted to exclude them altogether and establish a white man's government exclusively, reducing the natives to the role of voiceless subjects. In one of his gambles with destiny Thurston sought to reverse this and establish a government whose authority would be based on the native vote, the white men to be treated as "foreigners." However, not until the very end of its career did the Cakobau government stop the recruitment of Fijian labor for plantation work and it, of course, never mastered the problems created by the importation of labor. The natives for their part, however, did not always willingly acknowledge Cakobau's authority, especially the hill tribes of the interior of Viti Levu, armed conflict with whom periodically broke out. The hill tribes resisted Cakobau and the white intruders alike. But the divisions among the white settlers were far more threatening to the government's authority. There was little unity of purpose in any group of them. Some planters rather favored central government, provided it served their purposes with regard to land and labor, while others thought they could best make a go of it by dealing on a catch-as-catch-can basis with local chiefs. One group so far resented central authority that it fomented armed rebellion against it. The trader-service group in Levuka also had a party favorable to central government, provided its policies were "right," but a sizable contingent of Levuka residents, not the most reputable, appeared to favor anarchy structured only by systematic exploitation of the natives. At one stage these people organized themselves into what they called a Ku Klux Klan, complete with the use of violence to defy and reverse the government's policies and actions. Even when less provocatively styled, they were recklessly antigovernment. To compound confusion the centralists, whether planters or of the trader-service group, tended to disagree on policy and were lacking in a disposition to compromise. All in all it was a situation that only a strong, rather authoritarian government could hope to master. No Cakobau government ever acquired the requisite strength, though Thurston reached for it. At no stage was a Cakobau government independent of outside support, chiefly supplied by the naval authorities of the Australian Station whose law and order attitude led them to respect it, and insist to all parties that it be respected, as the *de facto* government of Fiji. Unluckily the resident representative of the most prestigious foreign government—the British—was through most of these years anti-government in attitude and policy. As time passed, opposition to the Cakobau government tended to intensify until it was almost literally beleaguered by its opponents. Cession came out of crisis in Fiji.

On January 31, 1873, Thurston addressed a letter to the United Kingdom government asking, "Will Her Majesty's Government entertain a proposition from the Government of Fiji to cede the Kingdom to Her Britannic Majesty if its King and People, once more, and now through the King's responsible advisers, express a desire to place themselves under Her Majesty's Rule?" This was repeated telegraphically through the governor of New South Wales. Shortly before this Thurston had outlined the Fiji situation to Sir Hercules Robinson, governor of New South Wales, and asked that a ship be sent to quell a rebellion of planters. Robinson agreed and Captain Chapman of the "Dido" arrested the rebel leaders and, at Thurston's particular request, deported them from Fiji. Shortly thereafter, however, the Cakobau government was defeated in the Assembly on a financial question. Instead of dismissing the ministers, Cakobau retained them in office, as was constitutionally permissible since they were responsible to him, not the Assembly, but the whites chose to stigmatize the action "unconstitutional." The effect was to intensify the opposition to Cakobau's rule and practically render his government impotent. Nevertheless a visiting naval officer chose that moment to emphasize that it was still the *de facto* government of Fiji.

The United Kingdom's reply to Thurston's inquiry of January 31 was the appointment of a commission to study the situation and make recommendations for action. The two commissioners were to be Commodore J. G. Goodenough, newly appointed to the Australian station, and E. L. Layard, newly appointed British consul at Fiji. The commissioners were to assemble evidence relating to the relative wisdom of four possible courses of action: (1) to take control over British subjects in Fiji by investing the consul with magisterial powers, a course often suggested since the time of Pritchard; (2) to grant recognition to the Cakobau government, thus moving a step beyond the acknowledgment that it was the *de facto* government of the country; (3) to establish a protectorate over the country, and (4) to annex the islands. The letter of appointment referred to the likelihood that annexation would make possible the suppression of the objectionable labor trade.

In spite of the fact that the Gladstone government was known not to favor such a course, the Goodenough-Layard inquiry became in effect a canvassing of the reasons why annexation was the only possible course. When the inquiry began it appeared that Thurston had retreated from the idea of annexation, but events moved him back to that position, though behind a hedge of elaborate provisions for the protection of native rights. Cakobau, for his part, favored annexation not only as a way of correcting an impossible political situation, but as a safeguard against any move by Ma'afu to take advantage of the chaos to gain supreme power. Ma'afu himself, however, also favored annexation, though it meant the death of his old ambition; he apparently did not believe he could conquer the impending chaos. The lesser chiefs, for their part, began by opposing annexation for two reasons: they feared loss of the power they had as officials in Cakobau's government; they suspected Ma'afu of devious purposes in supporting annexation and therefore opposed it instinctively. The prevailing sentiment among the whites was in favor of annexation, though a minority was opposed, for it was hoped that British government would favorably transform the economic situation.

The position in Fiji was such that there was very little hope that Cakobau and his ministers could regain control. Goodenough and Layard in effect found that the government was financially bankrupt. They implied that it was constitutionally bankrupt as well. They indicated their disbelief in its future by ordering all British subjects but one to withdraw from its military service; and emphasized their judgment that it was incompetent by forcing the transfer of control of the labor trade to the British consul.

If nothing else did, this put Cakobau in a box from which the only escape was cession. The alternative was the probability that Ma'afu would take over supreme power. Cakobau therefore formally offered cession on March 21, 1874. The commissioners completed their report and dispatched it to England on April 13. It concluded: "We beg to assure your Lordship that we can see no prospect for these Islands should Her Majesty's Government decline to accept the offer of cession, but ruin to the British planters and confusion to the Native Government." On April 11 Thurston had played his last card in defense of native rights as he saw them by setting out sixteen conditions for cession in a letter to the commissioners, most of them designed to protect the rights of the chiefs, particularly with regard to perquisites of status and ownership and sale of land.

Pending the reply from London, Fiji was put into the hands of an interim government in which Thurston was the principal figure. Its task, apart from caretaker functions, was to try to bring order into the finances. Surprisingly, in this it had some success.

D3

Of the 2500 whites who were in Fiji from 1870 on, probably 2300 were of British nationality. Americans were the most numerous nationality among the remaining 200, some of whom had resided in Fiji for decades, arriving as whalers from New Bedford and Nantucket, or gatherers or traders from Salem. Of the 2300 British it is a safe guess that most of them were Australians and the next most considerable group New Zealanders, men who, if not born in the colonies, had resided there for a number of years. The Fiji rush of 1870–71 was almost wholly a rush from Australia—from Sydney and Melbourne. It was notorious for including considerable numbers of men of dubious character, absconding debtors perhaps predominating. These types, experienced at living by their wits, congregated at Levuka and manned the Ku Klux Klan when it was formed. They injected a note of ultra-unscrupulous rowdyism into the rowdy politics of Fiji and were unquestionably among those to whom Cakobau was to refer to as cormorants who aimed to swallow the Fijians. They contrasted violently with honest men like J. B. Thurston and his associates in the later stages of Cakobau's government.

The interest of the home-staying Australians in Fiji was primarily an interest in an island frontier, an interest which had continuously expressed itself from the earliest days. Attempting to put the best face possible on his demand that Fiji be annexed, a speaker in the House of Commons *circa* 1870 cited as favoring the step missionaries, colonists, and merchants. He might later have added holders of the debentures of Cakobau's government which borrowed most of its money in Australia. He did cite Australian parliamentarians. It was the latter who, beginning in 1870, rather continuously pressed the imperial government to annex. As a matter of fact, they had favored the step since it was first seriously proposed in 1859. At a Premiers' Conference held in Melbourne in 1870 the following resolution referring to Fiji was passed: "That it is of the utmost importance to British interests that these islands should not form part or be under the guardianship of any other country than Great Britain . . ." This was simply to apply to Fiji a line of reasoning applicable, to Australians, to any island group at all. It was a standard, well-established argument; it was reiterated at odd moments until Fiji was finally annexed. It was supported not only by parliamentarians but by resident imperial officials sensitive to colonial public opinion, by newspaper editors, by inveterate advocates of British expansion in the islands such as John Dunmore Lang. But while this illustrates persistent Australian interest in the islands, its nature, and particularly its rationalization in terms of imperial interest—even, by the support of it by resident imperial officials, its persuasive character in the Australian atmosphere—it does not prove that the Australians had much direct influence on the annexation of Fiji that eventually took place. Theirs was an ancillary, a contingent influence, even when they had played such a large part in creating the mess the imperial authorities felt they had to clear up. Annexation was an imperial decision and act and while the cession of Fiji was negotiated by the governor of New South Wales, he was chosen for the task largely because as New South Wales was senior colony in the Southwest Pacific, its governor was naturally regarded as the senior imperial official there, obviously the man to carry out a special and reasonably delicate assignment, especially as he was well known to be able indeed.

D3

By the time the Goodenough-Layard report on Fiji reached London Disraeli had replaced Gladstone as prime minister, but though the Conservatives stood for a revival of imperialism, it was duly noted by Colonial Minister Carnarvon in discussing the report in the House of Lords that the commissioners for Fiji had exceeded their instructions in advocating annexation. Only the possibility of putting down labor trade by taking Fiji struck the minister as a really strong argument for taking that course. He noted only in passing the Australian-New Zealand interest in annexation and then chiefly to say—wrongly it turned out—that the colonies could be expected to contribute to the cost of establishing a Crown Colony government. He announced, in concluding, that the whole question was to be referred for final decision to Sir Hercules Robinson, governor of New South Wales, "as not being committed to any view and so able to act firmly and independently." Robinson was a distinguished imperial servant who had begun his colonial career in the West Indies, moved from there to Hong Kong where in 1861 he had negotiated the cession and later formally annexed Kowloon, succeeded then to the governorship of Ceylon, and become governor of New South Wales in 1872. Subsequently he was briefly in New Zealand and extendedly in South Africa. He became Baron Rosmead.

Robinson arrived at Levuka on September 23, 1874. He carried out his commission like a man thoroughly convinced that annexation was the only proper course; his cues were apparently all to that effect. His first move was to reject all sixteen of Thurston's conditions, good and bad—and some of the recommendations of an economic character, such as a banking monopoly, were bad—insisting that cession must be unconditional or it was not acceptable. To this Cakobau readily assented, alleging that he had never favored conditional cession, for "conditions are not chieflike." Cakobau further seized the occasion to remark that "The whites who have come to Fiji are a bad lot . . . if we do not cede Fiji, the white stalkers of the beach, the cormorants, will open their maws and swallow us." "By annexation," he added, "the two races, white and black, will be bound together, and it will be impossible to sever them . . . the stronger nation will lend stability to the weaker." This, alas, was only to be imperfectly realized.

On September 30, one week after Robinson's arrival, four chiefs including Cakobau signed the unconditional Deed of Cession at Levuka. Ma'afu signed later at Lomaloma in Lau. In all thirteen chiefly signatures were finally obtained, or about a third of those of chiefly rank ultimately signed. Cession Day was held at Levuka on a rainy Saturday, October 10. As a final gesture of good will Cakobau presented Robinson for delivery to Queen Victoria "the only thing he possesses that may interest her," his favorite war club. After a long absence in England, this club was returned to Fiji in 1932 by King George V and it is now the mace of the Fijian Legislative Council.

CHAPTER XXIII

The Partitioning of the Islands (2)

When the formalities of cession were completed in Fiji, Sir Hercules Robinson assumed the office of governor, but he himself promptly returned to Sydney. Actual administration was placed in the hands of resident appointees, the senior official being the former British consul E. H. Layard, but the officers most experienced in Fijian affairs were John B. Thurston (colonial secretary) and R. S. Swanston (native affairs). Following the New Zealand precedent, the laws of New South Wales were adopted to apply, except when otherwise specified by special proclamation. To deal with the native labor problem the law of Queensland was adopted, with provision for local variations. The first resident governor, Sir Arthur Gordon, arrived in June 1875 and assumed office on September 1, when a Charter of the Colony was proclaimed. Gordon remained in office until 1880, when he became governor of New Zealand.

During his five years in office, Sir Arthur Gordon took steps which decisively influenced Fiji's future. Forty-six years old when he took up his post, he was son of the Earl of Aberdeen, had been his father's private secretary when he was prime minister, and a member of Parliament. Before serving in Fiji he had headed the governments of New Brunswick, Trinidad, and Mauritius. After New Zealand, he was to serve in Ceylon. He retired from the colonial service in 1893, when he was created Baron Stanmore, and died in 1912. By temperament a scholar, he chose the tasks of a man of affairs during most of his life. Today he is considered to have contributed largely to the development of that complex of attitudes, ideas, and policies known to students of colonial government as "indirect rule," more commonly identified with the African administrator, Lord Lugard (1858–1945). By position and inclination an autocrat (except in New Zealand), he nevertheless had a liberal outlook. His nearest analogue among the figures of the nineteenth century in the Southwest Pacific was Sir George Grey.

Gordon faced the task of establishing an efficient government in a tropical colony where, he felt, the rights of the natives could not properly be denied and in which the claims of the intruders, bent on establishing a western-style, plantation economy could not be denied either. At the moment of his assumption of office the western-style economy was in a doldrums caused by the collapse of the cotton market. The natives had just experienced a devastating measles epidemic and shortly the government would be confronted with a bush-war with the hill tribes of the principal island, Viti Levu. Gordon set about devising a scheme which would, on the one hand, secure the position of the native population and which, on the other hand, would enable the western-style entrepreneurs to find security. It was up to the planters to find the export crop that would bring them prosperity.

His general approach is well illustrated by his policies with regard to land claims, taxes on natives, and the provision of labor for the plantations.

As to land, the Fiji situation paralleled that which existed wherever land purchases had been made from natives before a Western government had taken control. The claims totaled 854,000 acres out of 4,500,000 acres, of which only 16,524 acres were actually under cultivation. After the machinery of examination and validation of claims had been worked, 414,615 acres were confirmed to their European claimants. This halving of the European claims was largely the consequence of Gordon's resolute defense of the moral, in addition to the legal, rights of the natives—though technicalities, including those arising from the communal landholding system of the Fijians, were closely examined. However, the significance of the European residue was enhanced by the fact that it included much of the most useful agricultural land in the colony, particularly on Viti Levu. On it a western plantation economy could be established. On the other hand, the result left the overwhelming bulk of Fiji's land in the hands of the Fijians, communally held, and this pattern of landholding as between the Fijians and any alternative owners, became a heritage of the colony which in the twentieth century turned into a difficult problem.

Tax policy was, of necessity, linked with native policy. A consequence of money taxes under Fijian conditions was to draw natives into the labor market in search of the money to pay them, or to bring them to work by force by selling their labor after arrest for failure to pay the money taxes. These techniques had been used by the Cakobau government, but the selling of labor power had been abandoned by Sir Hercules Robinson, who instituted a tax in labor which could be redeemed in money if the taxpayer chose. In practice this meant the government was under constant pressure to provide work by instituting public works. For this it lacked finance. Money taxes thus opened up the Europeanization of the natives. Gordon took a different tack. He started out with the idea of protecting the natives and preserving their social organization, especially the lines of authority in it—its chiefly character—in accordance with the "indirect rule" approach. Whether he nevertheless envisaged a slow assimilative evolution of the natives, as J. B. Thurston certainly did, is not clear. As to taxes, he devised a system of payment-in-kind, levied on districts, apportioned by the native's own authorities, produced by communal effort in line with the native Fijian economic organization, but collected and sold by the colonial government. Commodities involved included copra, cotton, candlenuts, tobacco, maize, and coffee. Only copra long retained its commercial importance. This method of taxation advanced the economic development of Fiji, encouraged direct native participation in that development, and pointed out to the natives a way of access to the European commodities they needed, while offering minimum disturbance to their social organization. It allowed them largely to avoid serving in the labor force of the European economy; and it kept them from getting too intimately involved in the European economy in any other way.

But if Sir Arthur Gordon was concerned to protect the Fijians, he was not prepared to do so by excluding European enterprisers from Fiji, not that his native policy endeared him to them, for they preferred a direct exploitation of the natives for their benefit. His land policy had left them with a substantial base for agricultural operations. He favored their firm establishment. His primary concern was to insure them a labor supply. He began with the premise that the sources of the island labor were drying up, though at the time of his arrival this was hardly apparent. Rather, the Fiji planters could not fully use the island labor they had, nor could they afford to repatriate it. Gordon was also concerned in any case to deal critically with the island labor trade. In any event it continued to supply islanders to Fiji for some years to come. Sir Arthur's mind turned to a source of supply outside the islands. He proposed that indentured laborers be obtained from India.

Aside from his work as protector of the Fijians, no act of Sir Arthur Gordon's had such enduring and none a more fateful consequence than the introduction of the Indians. The Indian indentured labor trade was a British substitute for the slavery they had abolished in 1833. It was nearly fifty years old by 1879 when it was adopted in Fiji, and about a third of a million Indians were in that year working in such

British colonies as Mauritius, British Guiana, the West Indies, Natal, and Malaya. As early as 1875, Gordon let it be known that he was thinking of Indian labor. The planters were, in their depressed condition and strongly prejudiced as they were in favor of cheap island labor, opposed to it, but the government proceeded with the idea. The first ship arrived at Levuka on May 14, 1879, a sailing ship that had traveled to Fiji via the south of Australia carrying laborers assembled at Calcutta from the northeast of the United Provinces. This was the vanguard of a total of 60,500 Indian indentured laborers brought to Fiji.

The rise of the sugar industry guaranteed the success of Sir Arthur's solution of the labor problem. Sugar was first produced in Fiji in 1857 by the Americans Dr. Isaac Brower and David Whippy and R. S. Swanston, a British subject, who were farming the island of Wakaya at the time, experimenting with sugar cane and cotton. But it was not until 1872 that the first commercial sugar was produced on the site of Suva, subsequently the Fijian capital (founded 1882), and in 1873 ten tons of sugar were exported to Australia. The Australian market was long the chief outlet for the Fijian producers. The shift to the locale of Suva indicates that already at that time the sugar-cane growers and the millers had their eyes on the wet Rewa River valley, where cotton growers had also been concentrated. They persisted there for many years, although a sugar expert has recently noted the "Early planters mistook the general lushness of the wet zone for fertility . . . The importance of sufficient sunlight for the plant to manufacture sugar was not appreciated." At any rate, by the end of the 1870's, and many independent ventures in canegrowing and milling later, it was apparent that sugar had a future in Fiji, a very important conclusion in view of the prevailing slackness of the European economy. Subsequently both growing and milling were established at what turned out to be more suitable points elsewhere on Viti Levu than the Rewa Valley, and on Vanua Levu, but Viti Levu remained the principal site of the sugar industry, as it has in general remained the heart of economic Fiji.

The central problem in the late 1870's was capital and expertise in sugar production. J. B. Thurston was charged by Sir Arthur Gordon with inducing Australian investors to enter the Fiji industry. On the other hand, interested Australians studied the situation in Fiji on their own initiative. In 1879 the Colonial Sugar Refining Company of Sydney sent a man to Fiji and, after negotiating an agreement with Thurston in Sydney the following year, invested £50,000 in a mill at Nausori on the Rewa River and purchased 1000 acres of land. This introduced into Fiji the company that over the subsequent years became dominant in Fiji sugar by virtue of its capacity to weather periods of economic difficulty in the sugar trade, absorb competitors, and extend its operations by expanding its capital investment from local earnings and its Australian resources. Exports of sugar from Fiji rose from 593 tons in 1880 to 32,961 in 1900. C.S.R. began to mill sugar in 1882.

Colonial Sugar became the largest employer of labor in Fiji and while it continued to use islanders until after the turn of the century, and in 1894 experimented unsuccessfully with Japanese laborers, it became the principal reliance for the absorption of the indentured Indians. Indeed, one of the objectives of the government in inducing Colonial Sugar Refining to establish itself in Fiji was to provide private employment for Indians. The Fijians themselves never occupied any more than a peripheral position in the sugar industry in any of its phases. Sugar became peculiarly a European-Indian industry and, as the most important single industry in Fiji, became inextricably interwoven with the general history of the group.

Sir Arthur Gordon's view that the sources of island labor were drying up by 1875 was only partially true. The depopulating effects of the trade were certainly then visible in the New Hebrides and in other groups where the recruiters were early active, but this merely forced the recruiters farther afield, to the Solomons and then to the New Guinea area. In dealing with the trade, the British authorities were handicapped by the facts that the French and the Germans continued to engage in it, particularly to get labor for New Caledonia and Samoa, that it necessarily ramified into groups not under the jurisdiction of any European power, and that not even within the British areas was complete identity of view achievable, for example as between the governments of the colonies of Queensland, New South Wales, and the government of the United Kingdom. The United Kingdom sought to enforce its view—essentially that it was necessary closely to regulate but not stamp out the trade—by the use of the naval vessels of the Australian station for patrol of the recruiting areas and by establishing, in 1877, a high commissionership of the western Pacific, a post usually occupied by the governor of Fiji. Sir Arthur Gordon was the first high commissioner.

The establishment of the office of high commissioner was a logical outgrowth of the protracted British effort to find some way to enforce law and order, carry out judicial functions, supervise the labor trade, and conduct relations with native governments in the islands. The high commissioner was expected to carry out these tasks with due regard to the powers of the other British authorities in the islands in relation to the labor trade, for example, the powers of the naval authorities and the courts and political authorities of New South Wales and Queensland. His powers were never comprehensive. Moreover, his ability to function effectively was circumscribed by the fact that he had jurisdiction over British subjects only, while the Europeans in the islands were of many or no avowed nationality. It would have helped if all had been represented by consuls, or if all consuls present had accepted British regulations. British control was always limited by the nature of the total situations in which the British subjects were acting. When the British regulations curbed conduct in such a way as to put British subjects at a competitive economic disadvantage, or curbed conduct which other nations did not attempt to regulate at all, they were naturally evaded by the more raffish British subjects, the very characters the high commissioner was allegedly seeking to control. The high commissioner was also frustrated by a chronic shortage of officers to assist him over the vast area for which he was responsible. The very fact that there were probably no more than ten or twelve thousand Europeans in the islands under the high commissioner's jurisdiction was no consolation in view of the scatter of their residences and the presence of a high proportion of unreliables among them. Moreover, many of the worst characters were peripatetic in the islands, or made incursions into them from elsewhere. All this was particularly true in relation to the labor trade.

In spite of all efforts to deal more or less faithfully with the labor trade, the high commissioner, often not seeing eye to eye with the navy and the Australian courts and political authorities, made but irregular progress toward its regulation. Even after twenty years of effort—at the end of the century—British participants in the trade were still guilty of fraud, injustice, and even barbarity. However, the high commissioner was also charged with loftier duties than keeping the more raffish British subjects in the islands in some kind of order. As long as the fate of groups of islands remained a high political question, it was he who represented the London government on the spot, as the governor of New South Wales had done occasionally earlier. In such work, however, he assumed another of his titles, consul-general, to bring him under the authority of the Foreign Office. The high commissioner was a Colonial Office official, as was the governor of Fiji. Sir Arthur Gordon was active in Samoa and Tonga especially, but also in New Guinea.

D3

The story of the absorption of Fiji into the Western—or British—political and economic systems is straightforward and pellucid as compared to that of Samoa. Yet the central point about the Samoan situation was the same as the Fijian: after a certain position had been reached in the development of Western contacts with and activities in Samoa, a stable, strong, central government became the paramount need if order was to be maintained and progress made. This proved to be more difficult to achieve in Samoa than in Fiji because, on the one hand, native politics in Samoa, though not complicated by any native intrusion such as that of the Tongans in Fiji, was peculiarly vigorous and productive of the disorders of war—a continuation of politics by other means, so to speak—while on the other hand *three* foreign powers—Germany, Great Britain and the United States—had a stake in Samoa which they proved tenacious in maintaining. The Samoans have a claim to being the most ardent politicians of all the island peoples, and the reputation for being the best mannered.

That three powers were entangled in Samoan affairs was a fateful accident of history. The British interest was, as usual, dual—metropolitan and colonial. The colonial interest was chiefly New Zealand's. Originating in a missionary interest, the British stake was broadened with some trade, particularly with Sydney and Auckland, landholding, the problems of communications between the Southwest Pacific and Canada and, after 1874, a conception of the relation of Samoa to Tonga and Fiji. While participating in the Samoan contention, the British also came into collision with the Germans elsewhere in the Southwest Pacific, in New Guinea and the Solomon Islands. For the Americans the Samoan episode was something of an extension of their North Pacific concerns, centered on Hawaii, with a fairly remote connection with their interest in Panama and the projected canal. Basically a communications interest, it was centered on the superb harbor of Pago Pago in the island of Tutuila, the smallest of the principal islands of the group. They did, however, have a small interest in trade and landholding. The German interest, early conceded to be the most substantial in material terms, was in trading, landholding, and land exploitation. The island of Opolu, not the largest but the richest of the group, was the locale of Samoan politics, and the town of Apia the point at which the Europeans were concentrated.

The Germans, comparatively late-comers, arrived as traders but soon bought land and established plantations. At first private enterprisers only, they became territorial imperialists when Bismarck was induced to change his mind about colonies. The pioneer German company was Godeffroy and Son of Hamburg, a trading and plantation company which had first appeared in the Pacific at Hawaii in 1845 and quickly spread its activities from Valparaiso in Chile to Cochin China and Australia. It arrived in Samoa in 1857 via Valparaiso and Tahiti and established a headquarters at Apia for operations in the islands to the south and north: the Marquesas, Tahiti, Fiji, Tonga, the Gilbert and Ellice islands, and New Guinea. Godeffroy's rivals were, until the 1880's, smaller companies operating out of Sydney, Auckland, or San Francisco, as well as the more considerable independent traders in the islands.

At first its primary interest was in native-produced coconut oil, exported to Europe for use in soap- and candle-making. But it was the Germans who revolutionized this industry in the late 1860's and early 1870's by introducing the practice of sun-drying the meat of the coconut to produce copra. The copra was bagged and shipped to Europe where the oil was extracted and the residue made into cake for feeding to cattle. As the natives proved not enthusiastic about copra-making, the Germans devised a system of establishing agents, many of whom were British and American beachcombers, at likely points in the islands to trade European goods supplied by Godeffroy to the natives for coconuts which they dried. The copra was then carried to Apia and forwarded to Hamburg. This system was, obviously, the basis of the life of one important group of the considerable number of traders who spread through the islands at this time, providing the natives with access to European trade goods. Others were independents who sold their copra to any visiting trading vessel. The small independents were a transient phenomenon, by and large, retrospectively romanticized by Louis Becke, the fiction writer, before the century was out. One aspect of the romance was the fathering of numerous half-castes.

The agent system became the basic organizational form of island trading, with the independence of the agent progressively diminished. From being dealers, Godeffroy and Son became plantation operators, for example in Samoa, and this inevitably involved them in landholding. They also dealt in other island produce; they handled coffee, cocoa, and rubber. During the American Civil War they began to grow cotton between the rows of coconut palms on their plantations in Samoa, first exporting it in 1864. This pattern of undertaking actual production and producing and trading in any island produce that offered also became generally characteristic of island traders. However, copra was the most commonly available product in all the islands, the only one in many islands, and the one continuously available, with seasonal variations in quantity. It was the foundation of most island economies and important in all. Other produce tended to flourish and fade away, either because of disease, as in the case of coffee and cocoa, or in the face of world market conditions, as with cotton and rubber. Only sugar in Fiji sharply contradicts this generalization.

Production and trade in most of the islands involved remarkably few resident whites. Probably more were employed on the shipping which serviced the traders and planters than on the islands. At Apia, the center of white residence in Samoa, there were in 1874, after about two decades of fairly intensive attention to the group, only 181 Europeans: 75 British, 33 Germans, 22 Americans, the rest French (chiefly Catholic Missionaries), Portuguese, Spanish, Danish, Swedish. Until 1864 the Germans were led by August Unshelm, who died in that year, after that by the famously redoubtable Weber brothers. At later stages the German consuls were the leaders in local politics. The British and the Americans were represented by consuls and the British on occasion by the visiting high commissioner for the western Pacific.

At the time that the Germans were gaining their foothold in Samoa, the British were continuously interested, while the Americans, largely because of the Civil War, were for years not officially represented. From 1859 to 1864 no United States consul was stationed in the islands, and from 1856 to 1869 no United States warship visited the islands. It was in the early 1870's that the Americans really became involved in Samoan affairs, during President U. S. Grant's administrations (1869–77). Although the Americans had long managed to hold a fairly strong position in Samoan trade, especially in imports, carried by their own shipping from San Francisco, by the middle 1870's they were not entirely secure. In 1875 United States Consul Foster reported the American resident traders at a disadvantage as to credit and merchandise and handicapped by the lack of a good copra market in the United States. Nor were they any more secure as landholders. As a matter of fact, their landholding never became much more than a speculation, chiefly promoted by what the Germans correctly called *"aventuriers californiens,"* operating as the Central Polynesian Land and Commercial Company of San Francisco, headed by James B. M. Stewart, an Australian, brother and erstwhile associate, until they quarreled, of William Stewart of Tahiti. In the late 1880's, they held highly dubious claims to about 300,000 acres, a total second only to the British claims of 1,250,000, and twice as large as the German claims to 130,000 acres. Only the German claims were strengthened by the considerable development of actual plantations.

In 1872 the Americans added what proved to be the crucial item to the list of their interests in Samoa: the harbor of Pago Pago. It had been carefully examined by Wilkes in 1839 and assessed by him as "the one best adapted for the refitting of vessels." In time it acquired the reputation as the best in the islands. However, as Wilkes had clearly implied, it lacked a rich hinterland, which Apia had, and this important point was consistently overlooked. Pago Pago was valued as a harbor *qua* harbor, not as a *point d'appui* for the penetration of a rich hinterland. As long as the sailing ship was the sole reliance, the Americans paid no particular heed to Pago Pago, but when the steamship began to come into use, its value as a possible coaling station was perceived. When planning his steamship service from San Francisco via Hawaii to New Zealand and Australia, W. H. Webb had Pago Pago called to his attention and in 1871 he had it especially surveyed and determined to make use of it. The next year the navy took notice of it and evaluated it in relation to communications to and from the North Pacific via Cape Horn and in relation to the expected canal at Panama, 5660 miles away.

The navy's entry into the picture came about because Henry M. Pierce, the United States minister to Hawaii, an ardent expansionist, had had his attention drawn to Pago Pago by the Webb people and he suggested to Commander Richard W. Meade of the "Narragansett," at Hawaii en route for a tour of the South Pacific, that he be the agent to obtain Pago Pago for the United States. At Pago Pago on February 14, 1872, Meade concluded a treaty with the local chief granting the United States "the exclusive privilege of establishing in the said harbor of Pago Pago, island of Tutuila, a naval station," though most of the discussion was about the use of Pago Pago as a coaling station by Webb's commercial line. Meade sent his treaty to the secretary of the Navy, and via the State Department and President Grant it was submitted to the Senate with a favorable recommendation from Grant, in accordance with his expansionist attitude. The Senate let it die.

As commercial considerations had really been paramount in Meade's actions, so the next move in American-Samoan relations was also commercially inspired. It led to a deep American involvement in Samoan domestic affairs, the international politics of the Samoan group, and the definition of an American attitude toward the islands that made it difficult for the United States to "let go" of Samoa had it wanted to do so. As a matter of fact, it never really did. The bauble that led the Americans on was Pago Pago. While the Meade treaty was being stifled in the Senate, the Samoans made the standard gesture of native politicians who found themselves in difficulties, or under pressure, hostile or friendly, which made them doubt their capacity to manage their own affairs: they petitioned the United States to annex the islands. The petition, rather significantly, reached Washington through Stewart's California land company and W. H. Webb in New York. The Washington reaction to the petition was to arrange for a firsthand survey of the islands.

The agent selected was Colonel A. B. Steinberger, a friend of both W. H. Webb and President Grant. Steinberger's report was reasonably intelligent but his sojourn in Samoa, during which he perceived that the great need of the country was stable government, inspired in him the ambition to provide such government himself. The native politics of Samoa was made excessively difficult by the fact that there were five legitimate claimants of the kingship; these were, so to speak, several equally legitimate prospective heads of state and normally at least two claimants were in the field at critical moments. The Samoans dealt with this problem by war. The intruders tried various devices, including intrigues, to promote the fortunes of one group over the other, not only to achieve stability of native politics but to advance their national interests, a tactic which further exacerbated an already difficult situation. Steinberger aspired to establish a stable native government with himself as prime minister, a pattern suggested by the Hawaiian, Fijian, and Tongan situations. The United States government refused to support his project so he turned to the Germans and offered economic favors in return for support. The Germans agreed. On his return to Samoa, Steinberger kept secret both that he had no American support and that he was involved with the Germans, but the damaging facts soon leaked out. On July 4, 1875, he set up the government he had planned. It lasted five months, but it did not fall because of native troubles; it fell because, at the instigation of the United States consul and with the acquiescence of the British consul, Steinberger was arrested and deported by the captain of a British man-of-war from the Australian station. Steinberger was taken to Levuka, Fiji, and from there went on to Auckland and Europe. The upshot was that the American consul was removed from office, the British captain was dismissed from the service, and the British consul was transferred elsewhere. All this contributed nothing to the solution of the problem of Samoa.

The first essay at a solution came during the late 1870's when the three intruding powers separately made treaties with the Samoan native authorities. The Americans were the first. Reacting to strong German pressure upon them, the Samoans appealed to the Americans and the British simultaneously. The Americans responded with a treaty signed in Washington on January 17, 1878, negotiated by a Samoan representative with President Rutherford B. Hayes's secretary of state, W. M. Evarts of Boston. In gist, this treaty recognized the native government and promised it advice and help on request. Use, but not exclusive use, of Pago Pago was provided for. In January 1879 the Germans signed a treaty fortifying their position, while the British, with Sir Arthur Gordon as spokesman, concluded a treaty in August of the same year. Moreover, Sir Arthur took the initiative in establishing a system of government by the consuls for the municipality of Apia. The Convention outlining the system was signed on September 2 by the three consuls and the captains of the German and American warships then in port. On the Samoan side, the arrangement was accepted by the Malietoa faction. The government of Apia was placed under the three consuls. They were given power to make and enforce regulations, to tax buildings and lands for community expenses, and to appoint a magistrate. In times of native civil war, Apia was to be neutral territory. Thus was established a peculiar institution which lasted for twenty years, but like the three treaties it was an evasion of the point, only to be sustained so long because the three powers found it difficult to agree upon the extinction of Samoan sovereignty and the distribution among themselves of the "loot" Samoa represented.

The fundamental point was that the pace of the partitioning of the islands was accelerating. It was becoming increasingly impossible to treat any of the islands as no man's lands, or to sustain the legal fiction of native sovereignity anywhere. It was not because all the island groups were equally affected by European penetration, for exacerbated conflict over islands hardly touched at all by the whites was developing, but that European overseas territorial imperialism was making itself felt in the area. What happened in the islands of the Southwest Pacific *circa* 1880–1900 should be seen in relation to what happened in Africa, and the Middle and Far East, and the foreign political relations of the powers of Europe during those years, especially Great Britain, Germany, and France. The direct participation of the Americans in the Samoan struggle illustrates nothing so much as that the United States was not entirely immune to the virus of overseas territorial imperialism, even before it came down sharply with the sickness in McKinley's presidency at the end of the century.

There were wide differences of attitude and action in the islands among the powers. Broadly speaking, the initiative was with the Germans, to a much lesser extent with the French, while the British rather lethargically responded, usually after violent prodding by the colonies. The British lethargy was partly derived from a conception of the islands as of peripheral importance in any terms to the Empire or any division of it, in part, at least to the middle 1880's, from an acute sense of being a surfeited power which simply had no use for more territory. This the Germans and the French clearly recognized and the Germans especially thought the ambiguities of the composite British attitude as they put it together stemmed from British hypocrisy.

D3

Although New Guinea was by far the largest island south of the equator and was early known to the Portuguese during their involvement in the East Indies, it was in effect largely derelict until the nineteenth century. Little was known of the coasts of the great island—they were only roughly and partially surveyed—and the interior was utterly unknown. Of the natives it was understood that they were stone-age savages, for they actively repelled all efforts to make contact with them, and that they were not uniform as to stature, pigmentation, customs, or language.

The Dutch, who approached New Guinea from the west from their East Indian empire, first made contact with New Guinea while on their exploring expeditions in the seventeenth century but they did not assume that they had any sovereign rights over the island until 1714 when they inherited the rights of the Sultan of Tidor. With their customary indifference to the portions of the Indies beyond Java and closely associated islands, they were in no hurry to assert even these shadowy rights, for it was not until a century later, in 1828, that they formally claimed even the western portion of the island. In that year they established a fort called du Bus on Triton Bay and on August 24 by proclamation took over the western portion. Fort du Bus was, however, abandoned in 1836 and the eastern boundary was not defined until 1895, by which time Britain and Germany had divided the rest of the island. The 1895 boundary was the 141st degree of longitude, save where the course of the Fly River was followed as the border between Dutch and British territory. However, the Dutch move to establish possession did not mean that they now had knowledge of the island, least of all its interior. Such Europeans as were active in Dutch New Guinea at this stage and for the ensuing seventy years were the naval personnel who carried out coastal patrols, with incidental scientific investigations, in Dutch ships of war, traders along the coasts operating as individual enterprisers, adventurous scientists of one discipline or another, and missionaries. The very famous Alfred Russel Wallace was at Dore Bay on the northwest coast of the Vogelkop Peninsula for five months in 1858 collecting birds, insects, etc. The first missionaries had arrived only three years before, in 1855, Protestants of the Utrecht Society, and had established themselves at what became known as Manokwari, also on Dore Bay. Catholic missionaries did not follow until 1894 and were not considered to be established until 1905—at Merauke on the south coast near the British border. The coastal trade did not become extensive enough to lead the Royal Packet Steamship Company to establish a service until 1890. The first government administrative post was not attempted until 1892. It was short-lived and it was not until 1898 that administrative posts that proved permanent were established at Manokwari on the north coast and at Fakfak, a little west of due south from Manokwari on the south coast. A third post was set up at Merauke in 1902.

The British, whose association with New Guinea can be dated from Dampier's visits to the associated islands of New Britain and New Ireland in 1699, had in the 1790's made short-lived efforts to establish trading posts on the north coast. These were largely private ventures, though supported by the East India Company, and were related to the British struggle with the Dutch, forerunners of the settlements the British made in northern Australia for the same purpose later on and with equal lack of success. In the 1840's private petty traders out of Australian ports were beginning to visit the southern coast of New Guinea, but the British interest was more significantly illustrated by the surveys along the southern coast by Blackwood in the "Fly," Yule in the "Bramble," and Owen Stanley in the "Rattlesnake" during the same decade. Thomas Henry Huxley was a naturalist in the latter. However, there was considerable interest and activity in the Torres Strait area before there was much in New Guinea and it can be argued that the British were drawn to New Guinea by the uses of the Strait, its waters, and the islands therein. For one thing, there was a shipping route to and from the ports in the southeast of Australia along the passage inside the Barrier Reef via the Strait and west of New Guinea to China, Singapore, India, and England. For another the *bêche-de-mer* and then the pearl shell fisheries, and the labor trade drew men and vessels to the Strait. And finally the islands were useful to adventurers on the far northern mainland of Queensland who traveled by sea. These were dangerous waters and in 1863 the Queensland and imperial authorities established a port of call at Somerset on the northern tip of York Peninsula as a general utility and supervisory station for mariners and enterprisers, distressed and otherwise. This settlement throughout its history was a shabby, fever-ridden affair, but it served as a *point d'appui* for southern New Guinea. In 1879 it was abandoned in favor of a station on Thursday Island which has ever since been the focal point of the area on the Australian side. It was from Somerset that Captain Moresby, R.N., of the Australian station, made his tours of the pearl shell fishing grounds and from which he departed on his surveying expeditions to the coasts of New Guinea in the 1870's.

Moresby's principal contribution to knowledge of the coast was a close survey from the eastern tip, the precise nature and position of

which he established, westward along the northern coast to Astrolabe Bay. He also had the good luck to discover and give his name
to Port Moresby, by far the best port on the *southern* coast. He developed and publicized the conviction that New Guinea was a pre-
destined field for Australian enterprise; he was an imperial servant
who adopted the colonial point of view on the islands.

The colonial enterprisers began to talk about ventures in New Guinea
in the late 1860's and in the mid-1870's were mooting plans that included colonization. At this time the center of the agitation was Sydney,
also the center of the gathering trades pursued in Torres Strait. The
leading, or a least the most florid, theoretician of colonization of New
Guinea was John Dunmore Lang and his point of view was consistent
with his view of the islands in general. The core of the interest was
economic and New Guinea was envisioned in terms derived from the
Netherlands East Indies, not from knowledge of New Guinea, and included expectations of all the spices and gold. The illusion of richness
of the tropics dominated men's minds. Politicians like Sir Henry Parkes
and Sir John Robertson were New Guinea enthusiasts. Political pressure
on the Colonial Office in London to take over New Guinea began in
1874 when a Victorian lawyer resident in London, F. P. Labilliere, initiated it. In 1875 a Sydney man, the wealthy squatter Sir William Macleay, who was devoting his time and money to natural history collecting, led an expedition to the southern coast of New Guinea which was
successful scientifically but disappointing to the prospective exploiters.
Macleay pointed firmly to the bad climate of the island—especially the
prevalence of "fever," or malaria, the etiology of which was not then
known—the difficult nature of the low-lying coastal country, the absence so far of any known way to penetrate to the presumably healthier
interior, and the probable resistance of the natives to white settlement
and to working for the whites. Macleay believed the imperial government should annex New Guinea, but to facilitate exploration and scientific study before occupation. About the time of Macleay's expedition,
other scientific investigators were active, including the Italian D'Albertis,
the Russian Miklouho-Maclay and the Englishman Stone.

The real pioneers of the *occupation* of New Guinea were the missionaries. The workers of the London Missionary Society approached
the southern coast of New Guinea via Somerset and the Torres Strait
islands. The missionaries themselves traced their interest to a trader
who was active in the islands of the Strait and knew something of New
Guinea. He told a missionary in the Loyalty Islands that New Guinea
offered a wonderful field for them. As the missionaries were having
trouble with the French authorities in the Loyalties, the suggestion was

taken up with support from England. The pioneers were Samuel Macfarlane from the Loyalties and A. W. Murray from Samoa. They started
from the Loyalties in May 1871 and set up a headquarters at Somerset.
Aside from the European leaders, the first workers were natives of the
Loyalties, while the next year a second native contingent came from
Rarotonga. Macfarlane went on a visit to England where he stayed
for three years soliciting support for the mission, while Murray prosecuted in the field the task they had jointly undertaken. Native teachers
were first distributed over the islands of Torres Strait, but in 1872 teachers were left at Redscar Bay on the New Guinea mainland. This proved
a desperately unhealthy place and the following year they were established at Port Moresby. At the end of 1874 they were joined by W. G.
Lawes, who had earlier worked on Niue, a dedicated missionary whose
great work was in learning the local language, reducing it to writing,
translating the Bible into it, and printing the version. His house was
the first European-style building at Port Moresby. Lawes began work
on establishing outstations along the coast to the east. In 1877 he was
joined by James Chalmers, who had worked at Rarotonga, an athletic
Christian, keenly interested in exploration and the establishment of new
mission stations. Chalmers prosecuted this task along the coast both
east and west of Port Moresby until he was killed by hostile natives at
Gaoribari Island in 1901. Lawes died in retirement at Sydney in 1907.
Lawes and Chalmers were the true pioneers of mission work in the
southern mainland of New Guinea. They witnessed the tortuous moves
made to absorb southern New Guinea into the British Empire.

Meanwhile traders pioneered an approach to New Guinea through
the islands to the north. The German Godeffroy organization sent its
people from Apia into the islands north of New Guinea beginning in
1871. They chiefly collected copra, trochus shell, and tortoise shell. A
smaller German company, Hernsheim's, was chiefly concerned with
trade in this area and in Micronesia. Permanent trading stations of these
companies were established on New Britain and the Duke of York
islands. It was from this vicinity that the Germans came to draw most
of the native labor for their plantations in Samoa and, when in the
early 1880's recruiters for Queensland also invaded the area, the Germans regarded them as interlopers and their traders tried to frustrate
them. A few Australian petty traders were also active by that time.
Mission work was pioneered by the Methodists, led in the first instance
by Dr. George Brown, who had made his reputation in Samoa, later by
Benjamin Danks. The Roman Catholics arrived in the 1880's.

By the early 1880's Australian suspicion about what the foreigners
were up to around New Guinea was mounting constantly. The Ger-

mans, the Italians, the Russians, and the Americans were all alleged to have designs on the great island and its outliers, but the Germans were most steadily under suspicion. The British missionaries, still devoted to their policy of not really favoring a protectorate or annexation for any islands in which they were operating, nevertheless always, as patriots, favored British control to any other. Missionaries were apt, therefore, to be in the forefront of campaigns against non-British powers they suspected of having ambitions in the islands. It was entirely natural that they cultivated anti-German sentiment in the emerging New Guinea difficulties. They whispered into politicians' ears, wrote pseudonymously for Australian newspapers, and generally acted to advance their cause. They thus stimulated and in particular instances focused, or helped to focus, the natural suspicions of the Australians—not the LMS missionaries in this instance, for they were neutral, but the Methodist George Brown who had worked in the areas where the Germans were most active, Samoa, and was now active in the islands north of New Guinea. Here was the genesis of the fierce anti-Germanism that characterized Australia, so remote from Europe's quarrels, in World War I.

The Australian concern that New Guinea come into British possession, first expressed in the middle 1870's and rising to a crescendo in the 1880's, was based on economic expectations and alleged need for an outlet for enterprisers, not on any existing economic stake, plus a frenetic suspicion that it would be dangerous to Australia's security if it came into non-British hands, not upon a hard knowledge of anybody's strategy of attack or of their own defense. The metropolitan British understood no part of the Australian case, perceiving none of its elements of sound sense. What was more extraordinary, they discounted the Australian appreciation of German intentions.

What the London authorities missed was the shift in Bismarck's attitude on the colonial question. It cannot be said that the Australians were better informed on this point, or about the intricacies of European international relations. Indeed they advocated action from premises and in situations that showed they were insensitive to, or ignorant of, the posture of the powers. However, their interest in keeping foreign powers away from their shores made them extremely sensitive to any developments interpretable as hostile to their interests. Thus they seized upon and unquestionably exaggerated the intrinsic importance of an article in the *Allgemein Zeitung* in 1883, translated and republished in the colonial press, advocating German colonization of New Guinea. This, rather than any prevision of Bismarck's change of attitude, was the basis of their action.

It was Sir Thomas McIlwraith, premier of Queensland, who in 1883 brought the New Guinea question to a boil. A Queensland leader was not the ideal person to deal with New Guinea because he was open to the suspicion of seeking to guarantee a supply of island labor—a suspicion immediately expressed by the missionaries and Sir Arthur Gordon—but on the other hand Queenslanders had a special interest in communications through Torres Strait, and they were directly involved in administration in that part of the world at and from Thursday Island, from whence indeed their representative had been visiting Port Moresby. It turned out, however, that McIlwraith's position enjoyed all-Australian support. After asking London for permission to annex all of New Guinea east of the Dutch portion, and offering to bear the expense of administering it, but not waiting for a reply, McIlwraith instructed Queensland's police magistrate at Thursday Island, H. M. Chester, who had been advocating annexation, to proceed to Port Moresby and there take possession in the name of the Queen. W. G. Lawes assisted in the ceremony, but his reaction was highly critical. He not only suspected that the move had something to do with the labor trade, but he put his finger on the fatal flaw: "that an Australian colony should be allowed to take this step is to us most surprising." Having directed that the step be taken, McIlwraith set about getting the support of the other eastern colonies, asking that they direct their agents-general in London to express their support at the Colonial Office. This they uniformly did. In spite of this, the Colonial Office not only repudiated the Queensland act as unconstitutional—annexation was an imperial, not a colonial, power—but it went on to stigmatize the action as unnecessary, for it stated firmly that it had no evidence of German designs. A newspaper article was not convincing evidence. The imperial government, therefore, did not immediately substitute its authority for Queensland's in New Guinea but returned the territory to *status quo ante*. Its maximum concession was to accept Sir Arthur Gordon's diagnosis that New Guinea required no more than the posting there of a high commission representative.

The repudiation of McIlwraith unaccompanied by any imperial action to regularize the annexation produced a violent reaction in Australia. As has been pointed out in another context (see Chapter XVII), the seeming imperial indifference to Australian wishes caused the Australians to begin to explore the uses of federation. It also stimulated them to confer together to assert their outlook on the islands; and before and after the meeting Australian leaders savagely attacked the London authorities for not conforming to Australian wishes. In retrospect this period appears as a highwater mark in Australian efforts to influence —nearly to attempt to dictate—imperial policy in their area. Geographical determinism was at work as it was fifty years later when the Australians began seriously to explore the possibilities of an Australian foreign policy. But in the 1880's the way was not even theoretically open to independent action and their position was necessarily that of a strident, vociferous pressure group operating within the imperial fold.

Because of developments in Queensland's domestic politics, Mc-Ilwraith passed the leadership of the agitation to James Service, premier of Victoria, but the meeting to define island policy was finally held in Sydney, behind closed doors. While supporting the McIlwraith line on New Guinea, Service was deeply involved in an agitation over the New Hebrides, a matter to which he had been introduced by the Presbyterian missionaries, notably J. G. Paton. The objective was to prevent the French from taking over the islands as a logical extension of their New Caledonian possessions and to stop France from dumping more criminals into the Pacific islands. At Sydney, Queensland, Victoria, New South Wales, Tasmania, South Australia, Western Australia, New Zealand, and Fiji were represented. While the colonial leaders varied widely in the intensity of their interest in the islands question—Queensland and Victoria being most fervent on this occasion—they nevertheless managed to agree on some exceedingly forthright resolutions. Queensland led with regard to New Guinea, Victoria with regard to the New Hebrides and the convict question, while New South Wales and Tasmania exercised a restraining influence—New South Wales in spite of the fact that it was the center of the island trade. The spokesman for Fiji, Governor Sir William DesVoeux, attended with permission from London, to see that the importance of the high commission's authority and activities was not overlooked. He was also concerned to issue a warning that, in his opinion, the economic potential of the islands was widely overestimated. He had no vote. The resolutions constituted a major declaration on "foreign policy." New Zealand's association with the resolutions was indicative of the fact that its outlook was by virtue of geography usually close to the Australian. The principal resolution, unanimously adopted December 5, 1883, was:

That further acquisition of dominion in the Pacific south of the Equator, by any Foreign Power, would be highly detrimental to the safety and well-being of the British possessions in Australasia, and injurious to the interests of the Empire.

The British government's reaction to the Sydney resolution was a mixture of disapproval and disbelief, while the London press, reflecting the rising imperialist sentiment, was quite favorable. Lord Derby, the colonial secretary, commented, in a letter to his prime minister,

W. E. Gladstone, "What can be said in favor of the Monroe Doctrine laid down for the whole South Pacific . . . ? . . . . This is mere raving . . . The notion that other Powers . . . may have rights which an Australian is bound to respect, does not seem to have entered the Colonial mind." Nevertheless Derby saw that if some concession were not made to the Australians, disaffection would result. He therefore proposed that Britain formally claim the *coasts* of New Guinea not in the hands of the Dutch. But Gladstone, the exemplar of anti-imperialist sentiment, was not prepared to make any concession at all. A little later, however, Derby suggested that if the colonies would provide £15,000 toward expenses, a high commission representative would be established in New Guinea.

The Germans resolved the imperial government's doubts and hesitations about New Guinea but in a fashion that outraged the Australians, made the imperial authorities look "imbecile"—a word used by James Service to describe them—and left the Australians with but half the loaf they coveted. From the early 1870's Bismarck's policy had been to support and protect German overseas traders, but not to seek overseas territorial possessions beyond coaling stations. The treaty of 1879 with Samoa was in this tradition. In 1878 Godeffroy formed its South Seas interests into a joint stock company, Der Deutschen Handels und Plantagen Gesellschaft der Sudsee Inseln zu Hamburg, known to English-speaking Pacific hands as "The Longhandle Firm." The Godeffroy family held most of the shares, but it was embarrassed by unlucky mining speculations in Europe and heavily in debt to the British banking firm of Baring Brothers, the security being Gesellschaft shares and Samoan land claims. At the end of 1879 the Godeffroys went bankrupt. The Gesellschaft took over the Godeffroy debts to Baring to prevent the British from gaining possession. At this time the Longhandle Firm was the principal German interest in the islands. It was commonly conceded that the Germans were in a very strong position as island traders. Above all they were highly organized, whereas their principal competitors—the British colonials—were not, though Sydney was unquestionably the chief center of island trade nevertheless. Not until the 1880's was an Australian firm launched that proved capable of entering the island trade in a really big way. This was Burns, Philp and Company, set up in 1883, with a capital of £750,000. It originated out of trading and sea transport enterprises on the tropical Queensland coast. From a headquarters at Sydney it then began to extend its activities in both fields to the islands, starting with New Guinea and the New Hebrides. It got into almost everything profitable in the islands without ceasing to be involved in a variety of enterprises on the Australian mainland. What the Germans in the islands feared, however, was not trade competition so much as Australian territorial ambitions, as epitomized in the 1883 resolutions, for the Germans assumed that if the British took sovereignty in islands, they could not hope to survive economically especially insofar as their activities involved landholding and plantations. This they deduced from the experience of being squeezed out of Fiji after cession. They therefore appealed to Bismarck in this sense and got a favorable response. Bismarck was changing his outlook on the colonial question, largely as a consequence of German experiences in Africa, and was now prepared for territorial imperialism not only in Africa but also in the Pacific. Like the Germans in the islands, Bismarck took the colonial imperialists seriously. He was informed of Australian opinion and action directly from Sydney by the German consul, not through the moderating muffle of London.

Not Samoa, where German interests were considerable, but New Guinea, where they were more potential than actual, became the focus of contention. In April 1884, after a long, inconclusive discussion with the British, the Germans took Angra Pequena in Africa. In May German banking interests formed a Neuguinea Kompagnie to engage in trading and planting in the northern part of the island and associated islands. The company dispatched the German scientist Otto Finsch to Sydney with orders discreetly to spy out the land and establish claims. Bismarck's interest in this was engaged. In early August the German ambassador at London sounded out the British on the New Guinea question but so ambiguously that the situation was fogged rather than clarified. On August 19 Finsch in Sydney was informed by cable that he should proceed on his mission with the backing of his government as well as the company. In September the British felt they had to redefine their position. They decided to assume a protectorate over the unclaimed coasts of New Guinea except on the northern coast between 141° East, the Dutch border, and 145° East. The Germans objected, alleging that this was contrary to their understanding of the situation. The British then agreed to confine themselves to the south coast. The Germans were now using the Egyptian question as a weapon, hinting that they would move toward the French position if the British did not curb their intentions in New Guinea. Further to confound the situation, when the British sent a deputy high commissioner to New Guinea in November he thought he was to take possession with one set of boundaries, while the naval commander of the Australian station, who also had New Guinea instructions, arrived a little later to perform the ceremony and define a different set of boundaries. Port Moresby thus witnessed two ceremonies within ten days.

In December the Germans took the north coast and the Bismarck Archipelago. The British then tried to extend their claim to include the north coast to Huon Gulf. The Germans objected and the British retreated east to 148°. The boundaries were finally established in June 1885.

The following year the Germans and the British signed a declaration in Berlin which defined their respective spheres of influence in the islands. In effect the Germans were given a free hand, up to the level of establishing protectorates, to the north of New Guinea west of the Gilbert Islands. Samoa was declared to be a separate matter since it was affected by treaties with the United States as well as Germany and Britain. Tonga and Niue, affected by German and United Kingdom treaties, were declared neutral territory. The Australians were enormously displeased.

D3

The Australians received no satisfaction from developments in the New Hebrides either. There the opponent was France. As the 1883 resolutions made clear, the Australians had two bones to pick with the French: the question of who was to possess the New Hebrides, and the matter of convicts in the New Hebrides and New Caledonia, especially the prospect of a flooding of the islands with recidivists and their escape to the Australian colonies. The French came to regret that they had not taken the New Hebrides as logically a dependency of New Caledonia. However, the penetration of the group was largely a British enterprise, first by the sandalwood gatherers, then by the missionaries, notably the Presbyterians, the labor traders—the New Hebrideans were peculiarly the victims of the labor traders—and finally planters. In the mid-1870's the British living on the island of Tanna petitioned the French authorities to annex that island. These people were engaged in production and trade in copra, *bêche-de-mer,* pearl and turtle shell, cocoa, cotton, and foodstuffs for labor vessels. They felt themselves within the economy of New Caledonia. But the British missionaries were hostile to the French because of the difficulties they had made for them in the Loyalty Islands. With J. G. Paton at their head, they turned the full force of their propaganda on the Australians, particularly on the Victorians, specifically on Premier James Service, who responded vigorously. This was in 1877. How this linked up with the New Guinea agitation we have seen. The first result of the contention over the New Hebrides was Australian pressure on Britain for annexation. To this the British responded in 1878 by an agreement with the French to the effect that both would respect the independence of the New Hebrides.

About the same time the British in the New Hebrides came under the high commissioner's jurisdiction, this tempering their feeling that they were living precariously in a no man's land. However, the agitation for annexation to Britain continued.

To establish the French position and if possible make it paramount, an Irish-born French subject named John Higginson, once a resident of South Australia, who for years had been a principal figure in the management of the New Caledonian nickel mines, in 1882 launched the Compagnie Calédonien des Nouvelles Hébrides to colonize the group. The British consul at Noumea, E. H. Layard, formerly of Fiji, thought he was also interested in a labor supply for the mines, where the wastage was very high. Higginson's associates in the field soon got control of thousands of acres of land and began settling colonists on twenty-acre plots to raise the usual line of commodities. So effectively did they gain control of the useful land that they largely frustrated the competitive Anglo-Australian Company. Higginson alleged that the New Hebrides was a second Fiji, a proposition difficult to support, but suggestive of the contemporary illusions about the islands. Higginson began again to pressure Paris for annexation. Since the British were already under pressure to the same end—Paton still in the vanguard of the Australian annexationists, with E. H. Layard in Noumea from his angle supporting him—the two governments corresponded freely about the matter. The question was complicated by a rumor that France was going to send convicts into the islands, which the British agreed with the Australians was highly objectionable. It was further complicated when the French sent in marines to protect their nationals against murderous natives and other enemies, a most provocative gesture. But because of the disturbed condition of Anglo-French relations—Suez, Somaliland, Morocco, Newfoundland (fishing rights), the German question—it was no time for the British to get tough with the French, even had the stake been worth it, as the British felt it was not.

The Australians thought the New Hebrides to be of great economic importance. The British did not agree. The Australians thought it extremely objectionable that a foreign power should extend its holdings so near their continent. They had never liked having the French in New Caledonia, although they held a strong position in the trade of the island. To have them also in the New Hebrides was intolerable. The British did not see it that way. The Australians defined imperial interests as interests as they conceived them, especially in the immediate Australian vicinity, while the British defined imperial interests in the Australian vicinity as they conceived them, taking a global view from London. The Australian case at its most vehement was stated at the Colonial Conference of 1887 by Alfred Deakin of Victoria in a speech, a principal point of which was that the colonial view of imperial interests should prevail. It was a speech of high emotional content, the emotion generated by the New Guinea and New Hebrides issues. "We hope," Deakin declared, "that from this time forward, Colonial policy will be considered Imperial policy; that Colonial interests will be considered and felt to be Imperial interests; that they will be carefully studied, and that when once they are understood, they will be most determinedly upheld." This was a view of international politics which the British were simply not in a position to adopt.

Quite definitely, the British did not act upon the Deakin ideas in the New Hebrides, for when they came to settle with the French, the established game of trading this for that to fortify a compromise was played. The compromise of November 16, 1887, was the establishment of a joint naval commission of British and French officers to deal with the interests of their respective nationals in the islands. This led, with some experiments along the way, to the condominium of 1906, the basis of government to the present day. To get what was in effect a stalemate in the New Hebrides, there was trading: the British agreed to the abrogation of the Declaration of London of 1847. This had chiefly been designed to stabilize the position in the Society Islands on the basis of a French protectorate over the dominions of Queen Pomare. Release from it, specified to apply to the Îles sous le Vent, enabled the French to consolidate their position in eastern Polynesia on the basis of sovereignty.

D3

The Tahitian adventure of France had not been a "success." It had begun with a war with the Tahitians not concluded until 1847. In the 1850's there began a process of bringing Tahiti under the direct rule of France. This naturally undermined the authority of the native monarch and the people alike. Moreover, the French subjected the protectorate to an exaggerated multiplicity of officials—to a *fonctionnarisme hypertrophié*—most of whom, especially at the higher levels, served very short terms. In the 1860's, Tahiti was the site of the elaborate speculation in cotton planting of the Australian William Stewart, a phase of which was the introduction of island and Chinese labor, which, in 1873, was a nasty and spectacular failure. William died and his brother James fled to San Francisco to play a role in American affairs in Samoa. Commercial agriculture failed to find its feet and Tahiti suffered a deficit economy based precariously on copra and vanilla, introduced in 1846, and some cotton, coffee, sugar, bananas, and oranges. On the basis of pearl shell, the Tuamotu Archipelago was more prosperous than Tahiti. Papeete was a town of about 3000 inhabitants with the whites a small minority. External trade was chiefly with San Francisco, Auckland, and Sydney. The Americans had a continuing special interest in Tahiti. Steamship lines between the Southwest Pacific and the United States west coast made Papeete a port of call in the islands. Even with Melville in eclipse, American literary men continued to be interested in Tahiti, though the most famous of all creative artists who responded to Tahitian romance in this period was the French painter Paul Gauguin, who was in Tahiti from 1891 to 1893 and again from 1895 until just before his death in the Marquesas in 1903. Gauguin was appalled by what he felt to be the Europeanization of Papeete and retired to the hinterland—see his *Noa Noa*—and in his last period carried on as spokesman for the natives extraordinary journalistic warfare with officialdom.

Symbolically, Gauguin was in Tahiti to witness the funeral of Pomare V, the last of the native Tahitian monarchs, who had been deposed by the French in 1880; which led immediately to the "cession à la France de la souveraineté pleine et entière de tous les territoires dependent de la couronne de Tahiti," this meaning the islands of Tahiti and Moorea and the Tuamotu Archipelago, a step the British accepted on being granted boundary revisions in West Africa. The Marquesas were then brought under the government at Tahiti. Suspicion of German and American traders was a galvanizing factor in the French anxiety to tighten their hold at this time, and they were thinking of the position of Tahiti vis à vis Panama. In 1881 the French took over the isolated island of Rapa, coveted by the Australians as a useful coaling station on the route Sydney-Panama. In 1888 they annexed the Îles sous le Vent (or Leeward Islands), in 1889 the Austral group, and they brought the Gambiers, part of the Tuamotu Archipelago, under their political control after it had been the scene of a Roman Catholic experiment in intensive enculturation comparable only to the Protestant experiments of John Williams and his fellows. They reaffirmed their protectorate over the Wallis group, but they let Easter Island pass to the control of Chile and Pitcairn Island to remain under the British. In effect the French became dominant in eastern Polynesia, but in spite of this activity they were not at this time primarily interested in the Southwest Pacific; they were primarily interested in Africa and Indo-China; and they allowed their eastern Polynesian possessions to be separated from New Caledonia by British-held groups, and New Caledonia from Indo-China by German-held groups, something unlikely to have happened at an earlier stage of their activity in the Southwest Pacific. It turned out, however, that this did not matter very much.

D3

Samoan affairs 1879–99 were marked by a great deal of disorder. Stability of government proved impossible to achieve, either by the natives acting alone, or by the natives with European assistance. As a matter of fact, the native instability was considerably increased by interference in their affairs by the powers, especially the Germans, who thus sought to fortify their inherently strong position as traders and planters. The Americans also took a hand in native politics, usually to counter the Germans, and so to a lesser extent did the British. The British soon came to the conclusion that the best solution of the Samoan problem was to turn control of the country over to a single power and that power, in the light of the facts, should be Germany. Although the New Zealanders still advocated that Britain take Samoa—in the middle 1880's as a *quid pro quo* for the German sharing of New Guinea—and the Australians resented any foreign power gaining a position in the islands, they never really had much influence on British Samoan policy. The Americans were the only active party in Samoan affairs who had a strong vested interest in the maintenance of native sovereignty. They erected their defense of native independence into a moral imperative. It was the American stubbornness about this that for twenty years prevented the Germans and the British from settling the Samoan question in the accepted nineeenth-century fashion.

In 1880, after certain constitutional arrangements had been made to define the relation of the Samoan government and the intruding powers, Malietoa Talavou emerged as king. (Malietoa, a family or clan name.) On Talavou's death shortly after, Malietoa Laupepa succeeded him, but he was unacceptable to some Samoans who thereupon set up Tamasese as king. Civil war was averted by the Americans who in 1881 arranged a compromise: Laupepa would be king, Tamasese vice king.

Three years after, the Germans, alleging that they were seeking to reduce to writing what was implicit in their treaty of 1878, imposed a convention on Laupepa to which he so strenuously objected that he, Tamasese, and the other leaders tried to counter it by secretly sending an offer of cession to the British. Incensed by this double dealing, as it appeared to them, the Germans withdrew their recognition of Laupepa as king and turned to Tamasese. Laupepa set up his headquarters in Apia while Tamasese occupied the traditional Samoan capital of Mulinu'u, on a peninsula adjacent to the town. In December 1885 German sailors tore down Laupepa's Samoan flag at Apia.

This brought on an investigation of Samoan affairs by three commissioners, one for each power, George Bates for the United States, J. B.

Thurston for Britain, and Travers, the German consul at Sydney. They all saw the same facts and the same problems, but they differed as to how to handle the situation, so on June 22, 1887, a conference of the powers was held in Washington, with Secretary of State Bayard representing the United States, Sir Lionel Sackville-West, British ambassador to Washington, the United Kingdom, while Germany was represented by her minister to Washington von Alvensleben. The Germans proposed the abandonment of the attempt at loose tripartite control and the substitution of control by a single power. The British supported that position. Bayard stood out for a continuation of the tripartite system. He recognized Laupepa as king but, taking notice of the opposition of Tamasese, suggested that the kingship be vacated and an effort be made to ascertain the real choice of the Samoans. The conference adjourned on July 26 to allow the negotiators to consult their governments. Bayard suspected that Britain and Germany were seeking to deal the United States out of Samoa. He insisted on staying in—to protect native independence, and Pago Pago.

Meanwhile, the Germans sent into the situation a certain Captain Brandeis. He first appeared in Samoa as a clerk of the Longhandle Firm but was soon installed at Mulinu'u as Tamasese's political, governmental and military adviser. The German consulate then struck at Laupepa. It demanded immediate payment of a $1000 fine for an insult to the Kaiser which had occurred during a drunken riot at Apia for which Laupepa was held responsible, and $12,000 as compensation for native thefts from German plantations back to 1883. When Laupepa temporized, the German consul brought Tamasese to Apia, recognized him as king, and later induced the Samoans formally to accept him as their king. Laupepa, rather than take responsibility for civil war, gave himself up and was deported to Jaluit in the Marshall Islands. However, he bequeathed his political prestige to a third legitimate claimant of the kingship, Mata'afa, considered by his contemporaries to be the greatest Samoan of his generation. By combining his followers with those of Laupepa, Mata'afa had an effective majority of the Samoans. He also enjoyed the support of the Americans and, less aggressively, the British. Tamasese was a minority king. Brandeis by his strong, though always well-meant and often sensible policies, completed the alienation of the Samoans. They saw small point in Brandeis' road building, less in his insistence on collecting taxes in full.

Mata'afa was, vis à vis the Tamasese-Brandeis government, unquestionably in rebellion and that government was obligated to attack him. It initiated the war on August 31, 1888, with a weak foray against Mata'afa's camp just back of Apia. Thus challenged, Mata'afa formally accepted leadership of Samoa and adopted the title Malietoa To'o Mata'afa, thus signalizing his representation of the Malietoa interests. On September 11 he attacked the Tamasese forces, deployed on either side of Apia, and succeeded in penning them up at Mulinu'u. By complicated maneuvers, in which the Americans played a part, the Tamasese forces were eventually ousted from Mulinu'u and moved elsewhere. Mata'afa continued his siege at the new position. At this point everybody, including Brandeis, knew that Tamasese was beaten, but the German consul refused to admit it. He ordered German sailors to attack Mata'afa's camp. They were badly defeated. Thus the first victory of Samoan over European armed forces was accomplished. It raised Mata'afa's prestige to new heights.

These disorders, when reported to their governments by the consuls, led to the dispatch of warships to the scene. Early in March of 1889 Germany had the "Eber," the "Olga," and the "Adler" at Apia, the United States the "Nipsic" and the "Vandalia," while Britain had the "Calliope." On March 11 Rear Admiral L. A. Kimberly, U.S.N., arrived from Panama in the "Trenton." Thus the powers had ships of far greater value than the Samoan Islands committed to the defense of their interests in them. On March 15 a stupendous hurricane which lasted twenty-nine hours struck Apia. All of the ships save Britain's "Calliope" were sunk, and only Germany's "Olga" and America's "Nipsic" could be refloated and taken for rehabilitation to Sydney and Honolulu, respectively. Germany's "Eber" had disappeared *under* the overhang of a coral reef, her "Adler" was *on* the reef, where it still can be seen. America's "Trenton" and "Vandalia" were dismantled and destroyed where they lay and the spoil given to the Samoans. Britain's "Calliope" managed to steam out to the open sea and safety in the teeth of the gale. It returned briefly to Apia after the storm and then left for Sydney.

On April 29, 1889, the conference on Samoa which had been adjourned at Washington in 1887 was resumed in Berlin at the initiative of Bismarck. At Berlin tripartite government was given another try in a new form. This was a triumph for the Americans because the Germans and the British went into the conference unmoved from their positions of 1887. What emerged was essentially a condominium. It was provided that the powers would maintain only one warship each in the islands; that sales of arms and liquor to the Samoans were to cease; that the municipality of Apia was to be reconstituted; that a permanent president of the municipality, to preside over the consuls representing the powers, should be an outlander appointed by the powers; that an outlander should be appointed chief justice by the king of Sweden; that a commission to examine land claims should be constituted; that the king-

THE PARTITIONING OF THE ISLANDS (2)

ship of Samoa should be continued; and that the person chosen president of the municipality should be adviser to the king. Thus the American policy of recognizing Samoa as a sovereign nation was continued but at the price of involving the United States in an entangling alliance for the first time in ninety years.

While the competence, or incompetence, of the new European officials was of great importance, the crucial question was whether or not the Samoans could be persuaded to bury their differences and agree on a king, at the moment and in the future when succession was in question. The powers bungled the matter at Berlin by a grave ambiguity in the phraseology dealing with the question and in Samoa by their choice of the man to start off the royal line. Tamasese was obviously out of the question. The Germans could not accept Mata'afa, the man who had humiliated them, in spite of his obvious ability. So the British suggested Malietoa Laupepa, and he was brought back from exile to be king once again.

The new regime was not fully functional until early in 1891. Meanwhile Laupepa had resumed the kingship. Mata'afa appeared to be prepared to co-operate but he was not disposed to relinquish his claims which not only he but also many Samoans, Americans, and Britons considered to be superior to Laupepa's. In traditional Samoan fashion, Mata'afa could be eliminated only by war, so war was waged against him. He was defeated in battle at Malie on June 28, 1893, and again on the island of Savaii, where he had fled, a month later. On the latter occasion he was captured and was sent into exile on Jaluit in the Marshalls where Laupepa had been before him.

Meantime the regime staggered from error to error, led by the president of the Municipal Council who was, of course, entangled in the affairs of both the municipality of Apia, the focus of foreign interests, and of the Samoan king. Laupepa was a weak king and was relegated to an inferior position vis à vis the outlanders and the outlander officials. Only the land commissioners did good work. After ascertaining that claims totaled more than the land area of Samoa, they—the commissioners of Germany, the United States, and Britain—found that German claims were valid to 56 per cent of the land claimed, or 75,000 acres; to 7 per cent or 21,000 acres in the American case; and to 3 per cent or 36,000 acres in the British case. However, 19,000 of the 21,000 acres adjudged really to belong to the Americans were awarded to the thoroughly bankrupt Central Polynesian Land and Commercial Company of San Francisco. But all three powers were thoroughly disturbed by the state of things in Samoa, though they were pro tem prisoners of their own policy.

The opportunity to break the stalemate came in 1899. In the previous year King Malietoa Laupepa had died. As successor, Malietoa Tanu was elected. Mata'afa, back from exile, challenged. Civil war loomed. To deal with the situation, which critics of the Berlin settlement had forecast as very likely, the powers sent special commissioners to Samoa. In June 1899 they agreed that the kingship of Samoa should be abolished by obtaining the resignation of Malietoa Tanu and that the natives should be forced to surrender their guns to render their fighting less lethal. This, however, did not solve the problem of Samoa. The Germans began by sounding the British about dividing the islands with the United States, the latter to get Pago Pago, the British to take Tonga as compensation. On another occasion they suggested the British take compensation in Africa and Zanzibar. The British were reluctant to make a deal in the face of New Zealand and Australian opinion, but the Germans considered using British embarrassment in South Africa. When the kingship commission held its sessions the Germans became aware that the American commissioner thought tripartite control impossible. The Germans then proposed partition to John Hay at Washington, thus linking the question to the settlement of Pacific Basin affairs after the Spanish-American War. American Ambassador Choate at London proposed to the British that the United States take Tutuila (Pago Pago) and Britain and Germany divide the rest. The British and Germans could not agree on how to work this out, but they did, on November 14, 1899, agree to a deal whereby Germany took all of Samoa except Tutuila and small associated islands, which went to the United States, while Germany (a) resigned all her rights in Tonga and Niue in favor of Britain; (b) changed the distribution of the islands in the Solomon group to give the British all islands east and southeast of Bougainville and Buka; (c) adjusted boundaries between German and British territories in West Africa; and (d) renounced her extraterritoriality in Zanzibar. This done, a convention dividing the islands between Germany and the United States was signed in Washington on December 2, 1899, and ratified by the United States Senate on February 16, 1900. Three days later President McKinley by executive order put American Samoa under the control of the navy for use as a naval station. The American objective was achieved.

D3

The German renunciation of rights in Tonga allowed the British to regularize their relations with that group.

Tonga at that time was a fairly well ordered constitutional monarchy with a native king, prime minister, and legislature. It had not achieved the position without trials and tribulations. The first modern-style native monarch was George Tabou I who came to the throne in 1845 and ruled for 48 years thereafter, until he was ninety-five years old. For the first seven years of his reign there was civil war in the land as rival chieftains challenged his position, but in 1862 he felt strong enough to grant a constitution on the Hawaiian style which left him absolute ruler but granted the common people a considerable measure of freedom. In 1875 George proclaimed a constitution which provided for a constitutional monarchy. The principal pressure for modern innovations came from the Wesleyan missionaries.

Wesleyan Methodists were in a strong majority in Tonga, with a minority of Roman Catholics and a few rugged unconverted heathens. From 1857 the Methodists were under the direction of the Board of Missions of the Australian Wesleyan Church. Tonga was a model mission, giving special emphasis to education. In 1860 the Reverend Shirley Waldemar Baker was assigned to Tonga and within ten years he was head of the mission. An ambitious man, keen on power, Baker developed a career in Tonga that made such Samoan characters as Steinberger and Brandeis look silly and inadequate indeed.

The position as chief of the Methodist mission, and thus principal adviser to King George, proving insufficient, Baker in 1880 resigned from the mission and took the post of prime minister. This shift was occasioned by difficulties between King George (on cue from Baker?) on the one hand and the Australian Wesleyan Board of Missions on the other. The Methodists had great success in raising funds in Tonga— Baker was the most successful of all fund-raisers—and considerable sums of money beyond those needed to support the local mission flowed into the coffers of the Board in Australia. As early as 1874 King George asked that the Tongan church be made an independent, self-governing, self-financing organization. The Australian Board took no action. Tongan discontent mounted. To demonstrate his independence in one direction at least, King George in November 1875, with Baker's collaboration, signed a treaty with the Germans which largely had to do with trade but also granted a coaling station at Vava'u, an excellent harbor. In 1880 relations between the Board and the Tongans came to a crisis. The previous year the situation in the church in Tonga had been investigated by representatives of the Board. The 1880 Australian Conference, after investigation had shown him to be a thoroughly black sheep, voted to recall Baker. He countered by resigning and accepting the post of prime minister.

By 1883 it was so clear that Baker was at the bottom of the trouble in Tonga that the British high commissioner for the western Pacific, then Sir William DesVoeux, wanted to deport him. Nothing was then done and Baker continued his course, manipulating the law, the constitution, and the finances, all to feed his lust for power. In 1885 he played a major card: he set up a Free Church of Tonga which was in effect a state church, Methodist still but with a difference. He equated membership in the Free Church with loyalty to King George, a potent appeal, and soon reduced the traditional Wesleyans to a tiny minority. An attempt of some escaped convicts to shoot him, in 1887, for which Baker placed the blame on the Wesleyans, led to a furious outburst of persecution. About 100 Wesleyans, a loyal remnant, fled to, or were deported to, Fiji. An investigation by the high commissioner, Sir Charles Mitchell, resulted in a recommendation of the restoration of freedom of worship but Baker was left in office, in spite of the poor opinion Sir Charles formed of him, because it was supposed that without him Tonga would fall into hopeless disorder. It was not perceived that Baker's specialty was ordered chaos.

At any rate, any improvement in Tongan affairs was only temporary and partial for within three years the news out of Tonga was of such a character that the high commissioner, now Sir John Thurston, had again to investigate the situation. This time decisive action was taken. Baker was dismissed as prime minister and deported to New Zealand on July 17, 1890, forbidden to set foot in Tonga for two years. The exiles in Fiji were brought home. Mr. Basil Thomson was sent to Fiji to disentangle the snarled affairs of the kingdom.

King George Tabou I died on February 18, 1893, and was succeeded by his great-grandson, styled King George Tabou II. Insured of sound advice by the British protectors, the Tongan monarchy proved to be the only durable native government in the islands.

D

While these events were transpiring, the New Zealanders were standing hungrily by, their appetite for islands unappeased. Recalling that Sir George Grey had first formulated the idea of an island empire centered on New Zealand in the 1840's, the promotion of the idea came naturally to Sir Julius Vogel in the 1870's and 1880's, and appealed equally strongly to "King Dick" Seddon in the 1890's. Vogel's facile imagination first embraced the notion when, in 1871, it came to his attention while dickering for a steamship service across the Pacific that there was no British port of call between Auckland and Vancouver. From then on he was recurrently interested in the acquisition of island groups—Fiji, Tonga, Samoa. When the future of Fiji was under discussion, he pressured Britain for favorable action, preferably in a form that would give New Zealand a role in Fijian affairs. After Fiji became British, he concentrated on Samoa but never achieved a higher status than that of an irritant of Britain and an object of suspicion of Germany. In the late 1870's Vogel gave New Zealand's island policy a commercial twist, highly characteristic of the man. Cued by New Zealanders who had been adventuring in Fiji, he conjured up the vision of a vast island trading company along the lines of the East India Company, centered on New Zealand, that would not only develop the islands but bring them sooner or later under British political control. First suggested in 1876, the vision was rehabilitated for another and final run in 1884. Even beyond the average of his time, Vogel believed there was wealth to be had in the islands. His approach was politico-speculative.

Richard Seddon's line was almost purely imperialist. He saw the islands as proper objects of white exploitation. He wanted Samoa British. As late as 1899 when there were difficulties about the kingship between Malietoa Tanu and Mata'afu, Seddon wanted to send a New Zealand expeditionary force to Samoa to clean up the place once and for all. The colonial secretary, Joseph Chamberlain, restrained him. Seddon's imperialism in the islands reached a peak in 1900 when, in search of health, he made a semiofficial tour which took him to Tonga, Fiji, Niue, and Rarotonga in the Cook group. Samoa had just then passed beyond his reach. The Cooks New Zealand had long coveted; Niue, lately freed from its involvement with Germany, might be associated with them, while Fiji might be attached to New Zealand federally. Only Tonga, at the moment of Seddon's visit about to become a British protectorate, appeared to escape the net and even with it, looking to the future, close relations might profitably be cultivated. In the end Seddon got the Cooks, a British protectorate from 1888. By an Order in Council under the Colonial Boundaries Act of 1895, dated May 13, 1900, they were transferred to New Zealand and in June the boundary of New Zealand was extended to embrace them and Niue.

This was, in a way, a part of a general tidying up the British had in hand, to which the Samoan settlement was a very useful assist. In 1888 the British substituted sovereignty over their portion of New Guinea for the protectorate status, in 1889 they assumed protectorates over the Phoenix and Tokelau islands, in 1892 over the Gilbert Islands and the Ellice Islands, and in 1900 they took charge of Ocean Island. Back in 1881 they had attached Rotuma to the Fiji government. The partitioning of the islands was, pro tem, for all practical purposes, complete.

ANTARCTICA

CHAPTER XXIV

Era of Limited Interest

During the second half of the nineteenth century there was great interest and activity in the Arctic, but much less of both in the Antarctic. The Arctic appeared to absorb almost all the polar energy available. Not until the 1890's was there any very clear sign that systematic work in Antarctica was in for a revival, even though a few voices were raised in favor of such a course in the previous three decades. The era of minimum activity extended roughly from Captain Ross's great voyage to the Borchgrevink expedition of 1898–1900. When the attack on Antarctica was resumed in full force after the turn of the century knowledge and experience gained in the Arctic was, of course, a bank upon which the venturers into the Antarctic could try intelligently to draw. Not all of what they drew, relying on analogical reasoning, was to their advantage, as will appear, not only because the Antarctic was a very different place from the Arctic, in spite of superficial resemblances, but also because the items chosen were not always of the best. Of the many individuals whose Arctic knowledge was freely drawn upon, the most influential was unquestionably the Norwegian, Fridtjof Nansen. However, many of those who ventured into Antarctica had previous personal experience in the Arctic, and Antarctic hands often subsequently visited the Arctic. There thus grew up a small group of specialists in the polar regions.

The first journey into Antarctica after Ross's came just after it and was really a pendant to it. It was designed to fill a gap in magnetic observations left by Ross. It was not a complete success but has the special importance of being the last made in a ship wholly dependent upon sails for propulsion. This was the "Pagoda," commanded by Lieutenant T. E. L. Moore, R.N., who had been mate on Ross's "Terror." Moore sailed from Capetown, South Africa, on January 9, 1845, and proceeded south to work eastward, thus traveling against the winds prevailing south of 60°, so he had little success in carrying out his instructions as to positions to be achieved, while getting badly battered by the winds. Moore emerged from the low latitudes in late March and put into King George Sound in Western Australia, where he stayed for three weeks. He then proceeded to Capetown via Mauritius, concluding his voyage on June 20. The magnetic work had been done as well as possible under the adverse circumstances, but the contribution to geography was small. Why Moore was instructed to sail from west to east instead of east to west as knowledge of the winds dictated, is unknown.

Moore's was the last purposeful voyage of discovery for thirty years. Sealers, and merchantmen using Matthew Fontaine Maury's wind charts, continued to work along the northern limits of Antarctica, making minor discoveries and rediscoveries, as of what eventually was named Heard Island, 900 miles from the continent, halfway between Africa and Australia, but no exploratory ventures to the far south were made until the 1870's.

Using a steam whaler, Captain Eduard Dallman, sailing from Hamburg on a voyage sponsored by the German Society for Polar Navigation, combined sealing and exploration southward along the west coast of the Palmer-Graham Peninsula during the 1873–74 season. He did some useful charting and made some minor discoveries but did not cross the Antarctic Circle. A fleet of American sealers from Stonington, Connecticut, was found working in the area. In February 1874 the British ship "Challenger," while making a world-wide oceanographic cruise, proceeded south well beyond the circle from Heard Island, where it had arrived via South Africa and the Marion, Crozet, and Kerguelen islands (where it too had met Stonington sealers) after an extensive Atlantic Ocean voyage. Because it approached the continent at a point of deep indentation, explored and named Prydz Bay by a Norwegian expedition eighty years later, land was not seen. Nor was any seen as the ship was navigated eastward to a point off what is now known as Queen Mary Coast at 99° East. From there the "Challenger" proceeded to Melbourne. After covering the Pacific as thoroughly as it had the Atlantic, the ship returned to England via the Strait of Magellan and the east coast of South America. The "Challenger's" voyage is chiefly memorable as marking a point of revival in the history of the science of oceanography. As to Antarctica, the men of the "Challenger" proved from a study of materials dredged from the ocean floor that a continent almost certainly existed close to where they had been. They demonstrated, too, that the waters south of the circle were rich in life. And their ship was the first steam vessel to cross the Antarctic Circle.

During the 1870's and 1880's there were also other occasions on which scientific interests took men toward if not quite to Antarctica. In 1874–75 no fewer than three expeditions to observe the Transit of Venus, the phenomenon that had originally brought Cook into the Pacific, made their winter headquarters at the Kerguelen Islands: a United States expedition at Baie du Moribihan, a British at Baie de l'Observatoire, a German at Anse Betsy. The French, oddly, did not base their expedition there but at St. Paul and Amsterdam islands. In 1882–83, as a contribution to the first International Polar Year (ancestor of the International Geophysical Year), a German expedition wintered at Royal Bay, South Georgia, making magnetic, meteorological, and astronomical observations.

This slow and in some respects gingerly return of the scientists to Antarctica preceded that of the whalers—who did not begin to arrive until the 1890's, but the earliest economic exploiters, the sealers, were still on hand when the scientists renewed their probing. As it had been the great German mathematician and astronomer Karl Friedrich Gauss (1777–1855) who revived interest in the study of magnetism on a world-wide basis and in a sense stood behind the voyages of D'Urville, Wilkes, and Ross, so now it was scientists who asked for answers about Antarctica and, on occasion, tried to obtain them.

Matthew Fontaine Maury (1806–73), the great American student of the seas who published the first edition of his great work *Physical Geography of the Seas* in 1855, tried several times between then and the outbreak of the Civil War, when he went with the Confederacy, to stimulate exploration in the far south. His first published work had been an essay entitled "On the Navigation of Cape Horn" and he had plotted the Great Circle route in the south which took commercial ships to and from Australia to the borders of Antarctica. He needed more meteorological knowledge of the far south in his work and he tried to stimulate interest in obtaining it, first in the United States and then internationally. "Ho for the South Pole" was his slogan:

It is enough for me when contemplating the vast extent of that unknown region, to know that it is part of the surface of our planet and to remember that the earth was made for man; that all knowledge is profitable; that no discoveries have conferred more honor and glory upon the age in which they are made, or been more beneficial to the world than geographical discoveries; and that never were nations so well prepared to undertake Antarctic exploration as are those I now solicit.

Particularly he emphasized that: "The gold of Australia has built up among the Antipodes of Europe one of the most extensive shipping ports in the world [Melbourne]. By steam, it is within less than a week's sailing distance of the Antarctic Circle"; and it offered a wonderful base for exploration in the far south. But no heed was paid to Maury's reasoning.

Georg von Neumayer (1826–1909), a German disciple of Maury's, took up also his idea of Antarctic exploration. After a university education, von Neumayer pursued his studies of the seas at first as a common seaman. He then spent two years on the gold fields of Victoria and in 1856, with the intellectual support of German colleagues and with funds supplied by King Maximilian II of Bavaria, he set up a magnetic and meteorological observatory at Melbourne, practicing what later became known as geophysics, and systematically collected all the data he could on the navigation of the seas to the south. Returning to Germany in 1865, von Neumayer developed oceanography and marine meteorology at the Deutsche Seewarte (Marine Observatory) at Hamburg. Although he never actually made a trip into Antarctica, he several times came very near it, as when the observation of the Transit of Venus was planned in the early 1870's. And he unquestionably influenced the decision of the German Society for Polar Navigation to send Captain Dallman south. Von Neumayer also carried on propaganda for Antarctic exploration in England. After the "Challenger" voyage he was supported by some but not all of the scientists of the expedition, particularly Sir John Murray. He was elected president of the International Polar Congress which met at Hamburg in 1879. To give his statements focus, von Neumayer emphasized the high importance of magnetic and meteorological studies in the polar regions.

By the middle 1880's Antarctic exploration had begun to gain powerful advocates in England. Founding his position largely on von Neumayer's statements, Admiral Sir Erasmus Ommanney vigorously advocated action. In 1885 a committee of the British Association was formed to which Ommanney was appointed along with Sir Joseph Hooker, who had been with Ross, Sir George Nares of the "Challenger," Sir John Murray who had also been with the "Challenger," Sir Leopold McClintock, Sir Clements R. Markham, and others. Ommanney, Nares, and McClintock all had had Arctic experience. But while this committee grew in size, its effectiveness was very limited because of general and especially governmental indifference. When in due course the Colony of Victoria in Australia, which had been induced to offer a premium to whalers and sealers landing cargo in Melbourne from south of 60°, offered £5000 toward the guarantee of £150,000 estimated to be necessary for an expedition, the committee was not able to persuade the United Kingdom Treasury to act. Rumors then flew around that the Australians in their impatience with English procrastination were negotiating with

Baron Nordenskjold, the great Swedish Arctic explorer, then with Fridtjof Nansen, the Norwegian, to lead an expedition. It was even rumored that Professor von Neumayer had actually found a backer in a millionaire German-American brewer!

Then came men to examine the possibilities of whaling in Antarctic waters. The British whalers were of Dundee, Scotland. The supply of whales in the Arctic had been dwindling for some time and the price of bone had risen to great heights. The desirable whale was, therefore, that of which the bone was of commercial value, the so-called bowhead whale. It was in search of bowheads that the Dundee whalers resolved in 1892 to send four ships south, taking their cue in large part from the remarks about whales in the narrative of Captain Ross. The ships were the "Balaena," the "Diana," the "Active" and the "Polar Star," captained respectively by Alexander Fairweather, Robert Davidson, Thomas Robertson, and James Davidson. All the ships and men had spent the immediately preceding season in the Arctic. The "Ballaena" was the largest ship (400 tons), the "Polar Star" the smallest (216 tons). Aboard the "Ballaena" as surgeon was Dr. W. S. Bruce who was also a naturalist and meteorologist. Bruce was accompanied by an artist, W. B. Murdoch. The purpose of the expedition was strictly commercial, however, and in the end only one ship, the "Active," attempted anything in the way of exploration, and this was because of the captain's private interest in the business. On the way south, the "Active" met an American whaler off the coast of Brazil and learned that the Norwegian steam whaler "Jason," Captain C. A. Larsen, in the service of Oceana Company, Hamburg, and Christen Christensen, Sandefjord, Norway, was also bound to the Antarctic like the Dundee contingent for the Weddell Sea area. About the same time the Frenchman, Lieutard, was making a hydrographic survey of the much-visited Kerguelen Islands in the South Indian Ocean.

Having arrived in the northwest of the Weddell Sea via the Falkland Islands, the Scottish whalers searched for bowheads with no success and to fill the ships turned to sealing. None of the ships crossed the Antarctic circle. No landings were made except from the "Active." Dr. Bruce on the "Balaena" had to make what scientific observations he could while at sea. Captain Robertson sharply examined the coast of Joinville Land, Erebus and Terror Gulf—the association was thus with both Dumont d'Urville and Ross—and discovered that it was really two islands, the southernmost of which, as new land, he named Dundee Island. A landing party went ashore on the south coast of Joinville. This was on January 8, 1893.

At that time the Scottish ships were in company with Larsen in the "Jason." Larsen was also an old Arctic hand—he it was who had landed

Nansen from the "Jason" on the coast of Greenland—and he had the explorer's itch. He went ashore at the South Orkneys, and again at Ross's Cape Seymour, Erebus, and Terror Gulf. The latter he determined to be an island and on it he found fossils for the second time in Antarctica, helping to open the way to the eventual determination of climatic changes in the area. Larsen also had a glimpse of land to the west, as had the men in the "Balaena," probably the east coast of the Palmer-Graham Peninsula. Like the Scots, Larsen had to turn to sealing to fill his ship.

The Scottish whalers did not return to the Antarctic, but Larsen did. In the 1893–94 season he was back in the "Jason," accompanied by Captain C. J. Evensen in the "Hertha" and Captain M. Pedersen in the "Castor." All were in the employ of the Oceana Company and Christen Christensen. Larsen worked on the east coast of the Palmer-Graham Peninsula, while Evensen and Pedersen worked on the west coast. Larsen contributed most as an explorer. All were forced to turn to sealing from a failure to find suitable whales.

Larsen found seals and at the same time gratified his interest in exploration along a considerable ice shelf bordering the eastern shore of the Palmer-Graham Peninsula. It began about 64° 30′ and Larsen followed it to 68° 10′ South. Subsequently it was found to end at 69° 30′ South and was named for Larsen. In pursuing it the "Jason" was taken across the circle, the second steamship thus navigated. Back of the shelf Larsen could see high land, part of which he named Foyn Coast and another part Oscar II Coast. On his return from the south he discovered and named Robertson Island, an ice-covered island some distance from land and the Seal Nunataks scattered westward of Robertson in the contiguous ice shelf. He then went north to the coast of Tierra del Fuego looking for whales and, after a visit to Port Stanley in the Falklands, spent some time looking around the Erebus and Terror Gulf. All told, Larsen's voyage of 1893–94 was the most remarkable sealing-cum-exploration voyage since Balleny's of half a century earlier.

On the western side of the peninsula Evensen in the "Hertha," with the "Castor" as consort, worked his way south beyond the circle to 69° 10′ South and got closer to Alexander I Land than either Bellingshausen, its discoveror, or Biscoe had ever done before him. However, the voyage was remarkable only because of its achievement of a high latitude.

To survey whaling possibilities was also the purpose of Henrik Johan Bull in promoting an expedition to the south. A Norwegian resident of Melbourne, Bull found it impossible to raise funds locally for a journey into Ross Sea, although there was a continuing interest in whaling and the Antarctic. He therefore journeyed to Norway and obtained a ship and funds from Svend Foyn of Tonsberg, inventor of the grenade harpoon, a major advance in whaling technology. It was Foyn, acknowledged chief of the Norwegian whalers, for whom Larsen had recently named a coast of the Palmer-Graham Peninsula. At eighty-four Foyn was, after a lifetime in Arctic whaling, still keen on the possible discovery of new resources. The ship he provided Bull was a whaler of the kind used by Larsen and his companions. It was renamed "Antarctic." Captain Leonard Kristensen was given command. Sealing was to be the insurance against too great a loss of money if suitable whales were not found.

The "Antarctic" left Norway in September 1893 and reached Melbourne the following January after a stop at Kerguelen Islands for some sealing. It remained in port for nine months, awaiting the proper season for a venture south. Finally on September 26, 1894, the "Antarctic" put to sea to engage in sealing at Macquarie Island, but it was frustrated there by the weather and while a few seals were taken at Campbell Island, nothing economically encouraging was accomplished, but specimens of plants and birds' eggs were gathered. A start for the far south was made on November 28, but damage to the ship on its first encounter with the ice caused a retreat to Dunedin, New Zealand, for repairs. Everything in order, a passage through the pack was made and the Balleny Islands were sighted on December 14 and on January 16, 1895, Cape Adare was sighted for the first time since Ross's original sighting of 1841. Serving as a somewhat privileged ordinary seaman on the ship was Carsten Egeberg Borchgrevink, a young school teacher of Norwegian-English origin, educated at Oslo University, who had lived in Australia for some years. It was Borchgrevink who, when a party from the "Antarctic" was landed on Ross's Possession Island, near Cape Adare, discovered lichen growing on rocks, the first vegetation ever to be found within the Antarctic Circle. However, the party found no suitable whales, at least none with which the existing technology could cope. At 74° South, near Coulman Island, Captain Kristensen gave up his search. But on the way north, on January 24, 1895, at one o'clock in the morning a small party from the "Antarctic," consisting of Captain Kristensen, the ship's second mate, Bull, and Borchgrevink, went ashore on Cape Adare and spent two hours on the mainland shore of the continent. This was the first landing on the main continent, as distinguished from the Palmer-Graham Peninsula, where Captain Davis' men established a first in 1821. A pole was erected to which a box painted in Norwegian colors was attached and on which was printed the date and the name of the ship. Some rock specimens were collected, lichens were found, and some penguins captured. It was agreed that Cape Adare was a suitable site for a land headquarters of some future expedition and that the particular beach they had chanced upon was a good place for a house, observatory, etc. Homeward bound an attempt was made to do some whaling off the coast of Tasmania, but without success. Melbourne was reached on March 14. Commercially the voyage was a failure, but that the Ross Sea and its coasts were accessible was conclusively demonstrated, a valuable encouragement to exploration. While the ship was in the Antarctic, Sven Foyn died, so Bull lost a patron for future work. Bull also suffered the chagrin of seeing Borchgrevink get more of the credit for what had been accomplished than was granted him.

It was Borchgrevink, for example, who delivered the lecture on the expedition at the Sixth International Geographical Congress in London; and it was at this congress that a forward step was taken in the protracted campaign for a renewal of systematic exploration in the Antarctic. Professor von Neumayer gave a historical paper on what had been done to date and a vigorous discussion ensued which was actively encouraged by Sir Clements Markham as president of the congress. Sir Joseph Hooker, Sir James Murray, and Sir Erasmus Ommanney took part. A resolution was passed: "That the Congress record its opinion that the exploration of the Antarctic Regions is the greatest piece of geographical exploration still to be undertaken. That in view of the additions to knowledge in almost every branch of science which would result from such a scientific exploration the Congress recommends that the scientific societies throughout the world should urge in whatever way seems to them most effective that this work should be undertaken before the close of the century." It took rather longer than that to get national expeditions underway, but before the century was out two important private expeditions were launched, one by the Belgian, Lieutenant Adrien de Gerlache, the other by Carsten Borchgrevink. In Sir Clements Markham, moreover, Antarctic exploration found a vigorous exponent and patron, but he was a jealous and partial man, taking the same proprietary attitude toward Antarctica as a British preserve as had appeared in Captain Ross and, indeed, often seemed to narrow his sympathies to one British explorer, Captain Robert Falcon Scott. In 1899 Sir Clements proposed that Antarctica be divided into four quadrants to all of which he assigned strictly English names, ignoring, as the American scholar Edwin Swift Balch promptly pointed out, Bellingshausen, Wilkes, and Dumont d'Urville, all of whom had made important history in Antarctica, but were, alas, a Russian, an American, and a Frenchman.

Lieutenant de Gerlache's expedition is more commonly known by the name of his ship, the "Belgica," formerly a Norwegian sealer. The expedition was by design strictly scientific; its personnel was strikingly international; its finances were of the shoestring order. The Norwegian Roald Amundsen, then at the beginning of a great career, was mate; the American Dr. Frederick A. Cook, who had already been with Peary to Greenland, subsequently notorious for an unsubstantiated claim to the discovery of the North Pole, was the doctor; the naturalist was a Romanian, Racovitza; the geologist and meteorologist a Russian Pole, Arctowski. The expedition won an extra fillip of fame because of the circumstance that the "Belgica" became frozen in the ice and drifted about for many months and the expedition was thus the first ever to live through the Antarctic night. Hitherto all visits to the Antarctic had been made in the summer months. Now it was to be shown, by accident, that men could survive the dark winter. Oddly enough, the same point was about to be made on land and by calculated design by Borchgrevink.

After spending some time at Tierra del Fuego, the "Belgica" arrived at the South Shetland Islands on January 20, 1898. Proceeding south, the first discovery was of a strait separating Palmer Archipelago (then for the first time so identified) from the Palmer-Graham Peninsula. Many landings were made along the strait, positions were accurately determined, geological specimens in abundance were gathered, and Belgian names, still retained, were freely scattered. Continuing southward, though the season was now far advanced, the party crossed the circle on February 15 and moved toward Alexander I Land, but was unable to get nearer than twenty miles of it because of ice. Nevertheless De Gerlache continued to push south, though his scientists were getting worried, and by March 3 had reached 71° 30′ South. An attempt to return north was then made, but it was too late; the ship was quickly frozen in. For thirteen months thereafter it drifted in the ice of the Bellingshausen Sea, one of the iciest of the world, south of Peter I Island, mostly over "continental shelf," as was determined by soundings. 71° 36′ South was the farthest south the "Belgica" drifted, the eastern limit of drift was 80° 30′ West, and the ship got free of the ice in 103° West. Important oceanographic and meteorological observations, the latter for the first time covering a full year, were systematically made during the drift; the psychiatric and physiological consequences of confinement in the dark were carefully observed by Cook; and dietetics was given close attention, leading to the use of seal meat as a specific against scurvy. The ship was finally freed in part by sawing a channel by manpower at the suggestion of Cook whom Amundsen always considered one of the best "ice men" he had ever known. The pack was left at 70° 45′ South, 103° West; and the "Belgica" arrived at Punta Arenas, Chile, on March 28, 1899. The Belgian government undertook the publication of the scientific results.

While the "Belgica" was in the ice, a German expedition finally clarified a geographical point that had been obscure since 1738. In that year, as stated earlier, Bouvet de Lozier had discovered an island in the far south of the Atlantic Ocean which he had named for himself. Many a search had subsequently been made for it without success. Now a scientific deep sea expedition led by Professor Karl Chun in the ship "Valdivia" of the Hamburg-Amerika Line successfully hunted it down at 54° 26′ South, 3° 24′ East on November 25, 1898. The "Valdivia" was then taken south, in spite of the fact that it was a light steel vessel, and a point about 100 miles off Enderby Land was reached. Dredging results made it clear that a continental landmass was near, but no land was seen. Turning north the Chun party visited the Kerguelen Islands and then continued its deep sea work in the Indian Ocean. As in the case of the "Challenger," the Antarctic work of the "Valdivia" was but an episode in an extended oceanographic cruise almost wholly in temperate and tropical waters.

Carsten Borchgrevink had hoped that the warm interest shown in his lectures in Australia on the Kristensen-Bull expedition could be translated into funds for the support of a new expedition under his leadership. But while he evoked plenty of moral support, money proved elusive. Schemes for supporting a voyage by commercial ventures also proved abortive. In London in 1896, however, Borchgrevink found a wealthy patron in Sir George Newnes, the publisher; and in the next two years he set up an expedition on a pattern that was, in its fundamentals, to become classic. Obtaining an old Norwegian whaler which was renamed the "Southern Cross," he gathered around him a group of scientists and other useful personnel whom he proposed to transport to Cape Adare along with housing and gear, including equipment for land travel, not forgetting dogs, and establish them there in fit condition to spend the winter. The ship meanwhile would go to New Zealand to winter and early in the next Antarctic summer would return to Cape Adare to pick up the men and their scientific results and bring them back to civilization after a bit of exploration by sea. Aside from the leader, the most enduringly famous member of the party was Louis Charles Bernacchi, a Tasmanian-born scientist trained at Melbourne as a meteorologist and physicist.

The expedition sailed from London for Hobart, Tasmania, on August 22, 1898, and left Hobart for the Ross Sea on December 19. An attempt was made to reach the continent at the Balleny Islands. However, ice was encountered exceptionally early in the voyage and while the objective was nevertheless retained, it proved impossible to reach the Ballenys. At the nearest approach they were forty miles away across impenetrable ice. Working northward to the open sea after forty-eight days in the ice, the ship was navigated eastward in open water until the pack was re-entered where the ice seemed lighter. On February 16 land was sighted and the ship entered Robertson Bay of which Cape Adare formed the eastern side. Next day a camp site was selected and for the first time in history a ship dropped anchor in Antarctic waters. Working under pressure and badgered by bad weather, unloading was accomplished by the use of whaleboats from ship to shore. Two buildings were erected, one for living quarters, the other for storage, and the space between was roofed over. On March 2 the Union Jack was hoisted. The ship sailed that day for New Zealand with instructions that on returning the pack should not be entered west of 170°.

Even before the ship's departure Borchgrevink had discovered an imposing glacier at the head of Robertson Bay which he named Sir George Newnes Glacier; and a party had climbed 3000 feet up into the mountains and obtained valuable rock and moss samples. Throughout their stay, except in the very worst of weather, the party made periodic forays into the surrounding country, but the area was very ill-adapted for land travel and no way into the interior could be found. Most of the field work was done in the Admiralty Range, named by Ross. It was extremely rugged. For seven weeks an out-station was maintained at Mt. Sabine; Geikie Ridge was visited and charted; and the Duke of York Island was closely studied and found mineralized. Bernacchi thought he detected geological similarities between Cape Adare and Australia. Meteorological observations were carefully made, though at times during the winter it was too windy for the men to get to the weather board from the hut. Knowledge of the storm pattern was gained, the high velocity of the winds was noted as well as the low temperatures ranging down to −52°F, and the fact that prior to storms winds out of the south often brought a sharp rise in temperature. The doctor of the expedition found three distinct types of insects in the mosses he was studying on Geikie Ridge. The penguins were studied, exceptionally large jelly-fish (up to ninety pounds) were observed in the shore waters, diatoms were found abundant, and also the crustacea making up the "krill" on which whales, seals, and penguins fed. The tragedy of the stay at Cape Adare was the death of the zoologist. He was the first man ever to be buried in Antarctica.

The ship returned from New Zealand on January 28 and the party left Cape Adare on February 2, 1900. The huts, a coal supply, and provisions were left in good order for any subsequent visitor to the locality. The party then went southward into the Ross Sea. They investigated the shore in the vicinity of Cape Washington and found what they thought was an excellent site for a camp, dominated by Mt. Melbourne. Mounts Erebus and Terror came in sight and they landed at the foot of Terror. Landings were made for the first time also on Coulman and Franklin islands and at Woods Bay. Coasting along the Ross Ice Shelf (or Barrier) from Cape Crozier, on February 17 they discovered a break with low ice at 164° 45′ West and landed sledges, dogs, and instruments. (This indentation was later named Bay of Whales by others.) The ship was now at 78° 34′ South, farther south than Ross had achieved; a brief sledge journey out on the ice to 78° 50′ South, established the southward record. The journey home was begun on February 19 and the first contact with civilization was made at Stewart Island, New Zealand, on March 30. A telegram was sent to London announcing success.

However, Borchgrevink's accomplishments were not heartily acknowledged, for unluckily the scientific records proved not to be in the best of order and results when printed seemed meager. Moreover Borchgrevink had never won Sir Clements Markham's approbation. He had to wait for thirty years before he was rewarded with the Patron's Gold Medal of the Royal Geographical Society. Markham thought that Borchgrevink, who had not sought his patronage, had interfered with the plans then being laid for the National Antarctic Expedition under Scott and therefore snubbed him. But Borchgrevink had certainly confirmed his title as an Antarctic pioneer in more ways than one.

This is not an inclusive, exhaustive, bibliography. Rather, an attempt has been made to list and sometimes comment upon only those books which provide more detailed information about matters treated in summary fashion here. Very few articles are cited, though readers with specialist knowledge will recognize that I have read a great many in my time, but periodicals rich in relevant articles are mentioned at appropriate points. Many of the books cited have useful and sometimes elaborate bibliographies, these opening the way to the ultimate details for those who want and can use them. Where a specialized bibliography exists, it is cited, but no attempt is made to reproduce its details here. No effort has been made to provide exhaustive lists of those books which are now "sources" from which history is made, even though I happen to possess a good many of them. They are mostly "rare books" and in any case immerse readers in problems of fact and evaluation. These books are selected from the author's past reading as supporting the foregoing narrative or opening avenues to detailed knowledge. Where a book covers more ground than might be assumed from its place in this listing, that fact is noted; this list is cumulative, only occasionally repetitive. There is some cross-referencing.

D3 INTRODUCTION

I. THE AREA DISCLOSED: THE EXPLORERS

Professor J. C. Beaglehole's *The Exploration of the Pacific* (2d ed.; London, 1947), a tour de force in organization and expression, is indispensable. In the bibliography the primary documents and the principal modern works are named. It may here be observed that there is no real substitute for reading the "primary documents" if one wishes to gain an accurate sense of "what it was like" when the explorations were being made, but few have the detailed geographical knowledge required to relate the texts to the facts as they are now established. Hence the need for modern annotated editions and secondary works summarizing the stories and putting them into context and perspective. L. C. Wroth's *The Early Cartography of the Pacific* (New York: Papers of the Bibliographical Society of America, 1944) reproduces numerous maps. R. A. Skelton's *Explorers' Maps* (New York, 1958) contains relevant text and reproductions. Professor Ernest Scott's *Australian Discovery: By Sea* (London & New York, 1929) provides a collection of explorers' narratives. Peter H. Buck (Te Rangi Hiroa), the distinguished Maori anthropologist, compiled the exceedingly useful *Explorers of the Pacific: European and American Discoveries in Polynesia* (Honolulu: Bishop Museum Publication, 1953). It covers all the discoveries until the middle of the nineteenth century. A companion work of identical plan on Melanesia is much needed. The standard work on the discovery of Australia is G. A. Wood, *The Discovery of Australia* (London, 1922), but the story is now ripe for retelling in the light of later research. On the discovery of New Zealand the standard work is J. C. Beaglehole, *The Discovery of New Zealand* (2d ed.; London, 1961). For Tasman's journal see *Abel Janszoon Tasman and the Discovery of New Zealand* (Wellington, 1942). See also E. H. McCormick, *Tasman and New Zealand: A Bibliographical Study* (Wellington, 1959). On Cook there is an inclusive bibliography, *Captain James Cook: A Bibliographical Excursion* by Sir Maurice Holmes (London, 1952). Cook's *Voyages* have been popular reading since their appearance, but in heavily edited and rewritten versions. The original texts are to be restored and annotated in the Hakluyt Society's edition under the direction of Dr. Beaglehole. Two volumes have thus far appeared: *The Journals of Captain James Cook on His Voyages of Discovery: The Voyage of the* ENDEAVOUR *1768–1771* (Cambridge, 1955) and Vol. II, *The Voyage of the Resolution and Adventure 1772–1775* (Cambridge, 1961). The editorial material in these volumes must unfailingly be read. In addition to the three *Journals,* each in its own volume, there will be a fourth volume in this publication consisting of scholarly papers on aspects of Cook's work. The set also includes a portfolio, R. A. Skelton, ed., *Charts and Views drawn by Cook and his Officers and reproduced from the Original Manuscripts.* When this undertaking is completed, a sound life of Cook for the nonspecialist reader will be a possibility. (On Cook see also below, Part I, Australia, General.) On Cook's place in the history of navigation, see E. G. R. Taylor, *The Haven-Finding Art* (New York, 1957). On Sir Joseph Banks, see Sir J. D. Hooker, ed., *The Journal of Sir Joseph Banks* (London, 1895); J. H. Maiden, *Sir Joseph Banks* (Sydney, 1909); Edward Smith, *The Life of Sir Joseph Banks* (London, 1911); G. Mackaness, *Sir Joseph Banks: His Relations with Australia* (Syndey, 1936); H. C. Cameron, *Sir Joseph Banks* (London, 1952); and W. P. Morrell, ed., *Sir Joseph Banks in New Zealand, from his Journal* (Wellington, 1958). Banks' *Journal,* which Sir Joseph Hooker cut rather ruthlessly, has now been edited from the manuscripts by J. C. Beaglehole (2 vols.; Sydney, 1962).

PART I AUSTRALIA

General: A bibliographical work specifically designed to orient the newcomer to Australian history in the truly vast accumulation of printed matter that exists, to say nothing of the materials still in manuscript, would be a welcome addition to the "apparatus" available. For the time being, use can be made of the bibliographies of certain works around which prestige has gathered, for example, E. Scott, ed., *The Cambridge History of the British Empire,* Vol. VII, Part I, *Australia* (Cambridge, Eng., & New York, 1933), a book now somewhat out of date in this respect; Grattan, ed., *Australia* (Berkeley, 1947); and G. Greenwood, ed., *Australia: A Social and Political History* (Sydney

& New York, 1955). The first and last include references to manu-
·script sources. John Alexander Ferguson's *Bibliography of Australia
1784–1850,* 4 vols. (Sydney, 1941–1955) lists all printed materials
in all languages for the years specified, with valuable critical annota-
tions on occasion. As far as this user has determined, only certain
American editions of works of Australian reference are missing from
it. Naturally enough, all of the most significant material about Australia
is in English, but material has been appearing in other languages from
the earliest days. For guides to this material see the bibliographies by
L. L. Politzer: *Bibliography of French Literature on Australia 1596–
1946* (Melbourne, 1952); *Bibliography of German Literature on Australia 1770–1947* (Melbourne, 1952); and *Bibliography of Dutch Literature on Australia 1642–1950* (Melbourne, 1953). These books
were published in limited editions and may now be difficult to come
by. A general description of the resources of the richest single collection of Australiana is *The Mitchell Library, Sydney* (Sydney, 1936).
For references to the Australian resources of another great collection,
see *The Public Library of Victoria 1856–1956* (Melbourne, 1956).
A third great collection is in the National Library, Canberra. All the
state libraries, located in the capital cities, have rich holdings relating
to the states they serve and sometimes also to Australia in general.
The collecting of Australiana is a widespread private interest, or sport,
pioneered by David Scott Mitchell when he was forming the library
that now bears his name. For public documents, mostly official, to
around 1840, see *Historical Records of Australia,* 33 vols., (published
by the Commonwealth Government, 1914 ff). To initiate this project
the government published a volume of facsimile reproductions of documents entitled *The Beginnings of Government in Australia* (1913).
Another collection which in part parallels and in some respects supplements the foregoing is *Historical Records of New South Wales,* covering the period 1762–1811, 7 vols. (Sydney, 1893–1901). Part I of
Vol. 1 of this series deals with Captain Cook; it is accompanied by
a volume entitled, *Charts, Plans, Views and Drawings taken on board
His Majesty's Bark* ENDEAVOUR (Sydney, 1893). Different in intent
and coverage are Professor C. M. H. Clark's two volumes *Select Documents in Australian History 1788–1850* (Sydney, 1950) and *1851–
1900* (Sydney, 1955). These books are designed for university
students of Australian history and include selections from a wide
variety of printed sources. A listing of the quoted works and documents, plus references in critical notes and in short bibliographical
notes, would make a useful bibliography indeed, but Professor Clark
did not cumulate his items in this fashion. Since 1935 Dr. George
Mackaness has been issuing in Sydney what he calls Australian Historical Monographs. They are reprints of rare pamphlets, printings of
manuscript materials, etc., some of which are of high interest to historians. Documents of Australian reference are to be found in collections designed to illustrate Imperial history, e.g., A. B. Keith, ed., *Selected Speeches and Documents on British Colonial Policy 1763–1917,*
2 vols., (London: World's Classics, reprinted 1933); V. Harlow and

F. Madden, eds., *British Colonial Developments 1774–1835* (Oxford, 1953); and K. N. Bell and W. P. Morrell, eds., *Select Documents on British Colonial Policy 1830–1860* (Oxford, 1928). Other such collections will be noted as relevant. For the Parliamentary Papers of the Commonwealth 1901–1949, see *First Consolidated Index to the Papers Presented to Parliament* (Canberra, 1955). See also D. H. Borchardt, *Checklist of Royal Commissions, Select Committees of Parliament and Boards of Inquiry*, Pt. I: *Commonwealth of Australia 1900–1950* (Cremorne, N.S.W., 1958). Articles on Australian history can turn up in almost any journal devoted to modern history, but the journals to which the inquirer should first turn are *Historical Studies: Australia and New Zealand* (Vol. 1, No. 1, 1940–) and *The Australian Journal of Politics and History* (Vol. 1, No. 1, 1955–). *The Journal and Proceedings* of the Royal Australian Historical Society (founded 1901) contains a host of useful articles but a critical guide to the vast accumulation (47 volumes to 1961) is much needed. A *Journal of Religious History* began to be published in Sydney in 1960 and what had hitherto been a society bulletin became *Business Archives and History* in 1962. *The Australian Quarterly* (Vol. 1, No. 1, 1929–) rather frequently prints historical articles of good quality and other magazines do so occasionally in relation to their specialist interests, for example, *The Economic Record* (Vol. 1, No. 1, 1925–) and *Public Administration* (Vol. 1, No. 1, 1938–). *Historical Studies* regularly prints lists of documents recently acquired by the chief libraries and annual surveys of publications of historical interest, in addition to reviews of the more substantial books. For articles on Western Australian history see *University Studies in Western Australian History*, sponsored by the University of Western Australia (Vol. 1, No. 1, 1934). *The Australian Encyclopedia*, 10 vols. (Sydney and East Lansing, Mich., 1958) contains a wealth of historical material, including numerous biographies. A biographical dictionary is P. Serle, *Dictionary of Australian Biography* (Sydney, 1949). The best collection of interpretative biographical essays is Vance Palmer, *National Portraits* (1st. ed.; Sydney, 1940) which opens with a sketch of John Macarthur. General, comprehensive histories of Australia are quite numerous and selection is invidious, but perhaps the most useful are the Scott, Grattan, and Greenwood volumes cited above. A good example of a short history which takes account of recent research is A. G. L. Shaw, *The Story of Australia* (London and New York, 1955). In 1962 Professor C. M. H. Clark published Volume I (Melbourne) of what will be a four-volume *History of Australia*. It must unfailingly be read. Well-regarded interpretations of Australia, all strongly historical in content and emphasis are Sir Keith Hancock, *Australia* (London and New York, 1930); G. V. Portus, *Australia: An Economic Interpretation* (Sydney, 1933); R. M. Crawford, *Australia* (London and New York, 1952); and C. Hartley Grattan, *Introducing Australia* (New York and Sydney, 1942, 1947). In the bibliographical notes on the chapters which follow, reference to the foregoing should be taken as implied as long as any work referred to is relevant. As other works of extended coverage are introduced, it should be assumed that they too are implied in the bibliographies of chapters that follow. This bibliography is cumulative rather than repetitive, though some repetition is inevitable.

II. THE BRITISH FOOTHOLD

The best specialized account of the founding of Australia as a "penal colony" is Eris O'Brien, *The Foundation of Australia 1786–1800* (London, 1937; Sydney, 1950). However, O'Brien says too little about the economics of convictism. The structure of government is normally analyzed as part of constitutional history: see, e.g., A. C. V. Melbourne, *Early Constitutional Development in Australia: New South Wales 1788–1856* (London, 1934); F. L. W. Wood, *The Constitutional Development of Australia* (London, 1933); and E. Sweetman, *Australian Constitutional Development* (Melbourne, 1925). For the American view of the story of convictism see A. E. Smith, *Colonists in Bondage 1607–1776* (Chapel Hill, N.C., 1947). A useful collection of documents of the founding is Owen Rutter, ed., *The First Fleet* (London, 1937). A kind of register of passengers of the First Fleet is H. J. Rumsey, ed., *The Pioneers of Sydney Cove* (Sydney, 1937). An account of the hulks through which so many convicts passed is W. Branch-Johnson, *The English Prison Hulks* (London, 1957). On the ships, see Charles Bateson, *The Convict Ships 1788–1868* (Glasgow, 1959). There are two good studies of Arthur Phillip: George Mackaness, *Admiral Arthur Phillip 1738–1814* (Sydney, 1937), and M. Barnard Eldershaw, *Phillip of Australia: An Account of the Settlement at Sydney Cove 1788–1792* (London, 1938). Information on La Pérouse at Botany Bay is to be found in E. Scott, *Laperouse* (Sydney, 1912). The standard life of Macarthur is M. H. Ellis, *John Macarthur* (Sydney, 1955). A valuable documentary collection is S. Macarthur Onslow, ed., *Early Records of the Macarthurs of Camden* (Sydney, 1914). On the peopling of Australia in the early period see R. B. Madgwick, *Immigration into Eastern Australia 1788–1851* (London, 1937). On economic history, books which differ in purpose, content, and interpretation, and therefore force a personal assessment of the evidence are T. A. Coghlan, *Labour and Industry in Australia 1788–1901*, 4 vols. (London, 1918); E. O. G. Shann, *An Economic History of Australia* (Cambridge, 1930); B. Fitzpatrick, *British Imperialism in Australia 1783–1833* (London, 1939); and S. J. Butlin *Foundations of the Australian Monetary System 1788–1851* (Melbourne, 1953). The last three are explicitly critical of one another. Finally this is surely the place to call attention to the great narratives of the "founding fathers": Arthur Phillip, *The Voyage of Governor Phillip to Botany Bay* (London, 1789); John White, *Journal of a Voyage to New South Wales* (London, 1790); John Hunter, *Historical Journal of the Transactions at Port Jackson and Norfolk Island* (London, 1793); Watkin Tench, *A Narrative of the Expedition to Botany Bay* (1789) and *A Complete Account of the Settlement at Port Jack-*

son (London, 1793); and Lt. Col. Collins, *An Account of the English Colony in New South Wales 1788–1801* (London, 1804). Only the Tench books are available in a popular annotated edition: *Sydney's First Years* (Sydney, 1961), but others have been reprinted in recent years in costly, limited, fine editions, and more in popular editions are promised.

III.   SEARCH FOR A VIABLE ECONOMY

Of the three governors mentioned in the opening paragraph of this chapter only Bligh has thus far commanded a book-length study and he largely because of the "Bounty" mutiny: George Mackaness, *The Life of Vice-Admiral William Bligh* (rev. ed.; Sydney, 1951) is the standard work. There is, however, a life of Mrs. King: Marnie Bassett, *The Governor's Lady: Mrs. Philip Gidley King* (London, 1940). H. V. Evatt *Rum Rebellion* (Sydney, 1938), Foreword by C. Hartley Grattan, is a study of the crucial episode in Bligh's Australian career. Edgars Dunsdorfs, *The Australian Wheat Growing Industry 1788–1948* (Melbourne, 1956) first becomes useful here. The standard history of the land problem, a matter also freely treated in the economic histories, is S. H. Roberts, *History of Australian Land Settlement 1788–1920* (Melbourne, 1924). S. M. Wadham and G. L. Wood, *Land Utilization in Australia* (Melbourne, 1939 and later ed.) has its uses for the historian quite apart from its explicitly historical passages. On the history of exploration see Ernest Favenc, *The History of Australian Exploration 1788–1888* (London, c. 1889). A new history of exploration by a professionally adequate hand is very much needed. On Flinders see E. Scott, *The Life of Captain Matthew Flinders* (Sydney, 1914). On Bass, Keith Bowden, *George Bass 1771–1803* (Melbourne, 1952). On the French explorers see E. Scott, *Terre Napoleon* (London, 1910). For the narratives of exploration (discussed more fully below) see E. Scott, ed., *Australian Discovery: By Sea* (London and New York, 1929). Flinders' book is now an exceedingly rare item of Australiana. For the early history of Van Diemen's Land see James Fenton, *A History of Tasmania* (Hobart, 1884); R. W. Giblin, *The Early History of Tasmania,* Vol. 1 (London, 1928), Vol. 2 (Melbourne, 1939); and J. B. Walker, *Early Tasmania* (Hobart, 1914). M. H. Ellis, *Lachlan Macquarie: His Life, Adventures and Times* (Sydney, 1947) is a fine biography of a remarkable man. Marjorie Barnard, *Macquarie's World* (Sydney, 1941) is an impressionistic picture. *Lachlan Macquarie: Governor of New South Wales* (Sydney, 1956) reprints for the first time Macquarie's journals of tours in New South Wales and Van Diemen's Land 1810–1822. On Macquarie as an autocrat the pioneering study is Marion Phillips, *A Colonial Autocracy* (London, 1909). A comprehensive history of the wool industry has yet to be written, strangely enough. See the Ellis life of Macarthur, the S. H. Roberts book and the economic histories cited above; also E. W. Cox, *The Evolution of the Australian Merino* (Sydney, 1936) and R. D. Watt, *The Romance of the Australian Land Industries* (Sydney, 1955). A first-class specialized study is Alan Barnard, *The Australian Wool Market 1840–1900* (Melbourne, 1958). On the crossing of the Blue Mountains, a key episode in the history of inland exploration, see for narratives G. Mackaness, ed., *Fourteen Journeys Over the Blue Mountains*, in 3 parts (Sydney, 1950). For explorers' narratives generally see K. Fitzpatrick, ed., *Australian Explorers* (London, World's Classics 1958) and E. Scott, ed., *Australian Discovery: By Land* (London and New York, 1929). The Bigge investigation is worth a book in itself, tracing out all its ramifications, but none has yet been written. The reports must still be read in their original editions, save for excerpts, as in Clark, Vol. 1.

IV.   TOWARD CONTINENTAL OCCUPATION (1)

Practically all the major explorers of the Australian continent, by land and sea, wrote and published elaborate narratives and solid reports of the others, major and minor, have been put into print. Few of the great narratives have ever been reprinted and the original editions are now collectors' items. A useful list of them, of lives of the explorers, and histories of exploration, is given as a "Note on Sources" in the Fitzpatrick compilation cited above. The opening up of Queensland is told as a personal story with documentary support in H. S. Russell, *The Genesis of Queensland* (Sydney, 1888). The first volume of a monumental editorial job is F. K. Crowley, *The Records of Western Australia* (Perth, 1953). The standard history of Western Australia is J. S. Battye, *Western Australia* (London, 1924), but F. K. Crowley, *Australia's Western Third* (London, 1960) supplements Battye generously throughout and carries the story forward to the present day. A geographer's collection of documents on Western Australia, contemporary in emphasis, is T. P. Field, *Swanland* (Lexington, Ky., 1957). A study of James Stirling is Malcolm Uren, *Land Looking West* (Melbourne, 1948). On northern Australia see A. G. Price, *The History and Problems of the Northern Territory of Australia* (Adelaide, 1930). Additionally on Tasmania see R. M. Hartwell, *The Economic Development of Van Diemen's Land 1820–1850* (Melbourne, 1954); the oddly defensive life of Arthur, M. C. I. Levy, *Governor George Arthur* (Melbourne, 1953); and W. D. Forsyth, *Governor Arthur's Convict System* (London, 1935). An admirable account of Franklin's Australian career is Kathleen Fitzpatrick, *Sir John Franklin in Tasmania 1837–1843* (Melbourne, 1949). On politics in Van Diemen's Land see W. A. Townsley, *The Struggle for Self-Government in Tasmania* (Hobart, 1951). The best account of whaling in Australian waters is W. J. Dakin, *Whalemen Adventurers* (Sydney, 1934). Useful for the "feel" of whaling is C. R. Straubel, ed., *The Whaling Journal of Capt. W. B. Rhodes 1836–38* (Christchurch, 1954). The classic American document on sealing in Bass Strait is Amasa Delano, *A Narrative of Voyages and Travels* (Boston, 1817). For references on American whaling and sealing in the South Pacific, see Chapter XI, below.

V.   TOWARD CONTINENTAL OCCUPATION (2)

A documentary collection on early Victoria is J. J. Shillinglaw, ed., *Historical Records of Port Phillip* (Melbourne, 1879). On the Hentys, see Marnie Bassett, *The Hentys* (Melbourne and London, 1954). An account of Batman and company that freely quotes the documents is James Bonwick, *Port Phillip Settlement* (London, 1883). The standard history of Victoria is still H. G. Turner, *A History of the Colony of Victoria 1797–1900,* 2 vols. (London, 1904). R. D. Boys, *First Years at Port Phillip* (Melbourne, 1935) is a mine of detail, arranged chronologically, covering the years to 1842. R. V. Billis and A. S. Kenyon, *Pastures New* (Melbourne, 1930), deals with the pastoral occupation. See also on this vital matter, T. F. Bride, ed., *Letters from Victorian Pioneers* (Melbourne, 1898); E. M. Curr, *Squatting in Victoria* (Melbourne, 1883); G. F. James, ed., *A Homestead History* (Melbourne, 1941); P. L. Brown, ed., *The Narrative of George Russell* (London, 1935); and *Clyde Company Papers: Prologue* (London, 1941), Vol. 2 (London, 1952), Vol. 3 (London, 1958), Vol. 4 (London, 1959). There is no throughly satisfactory study of E. G. Wakefield, either as a "life" or monographically, but his Australian impact is well assessed in R. C. Mills, *The Colonization of Australia 1829–1842* (London, 1915). The most recent study of Wakefield, P. Bloomfield, *Edward Gibbon Wakefield* (London, 1961), though it brings together many personal facts, cannot be regarded as a good book because of the author's limited knowledge of colonial history. As to the other Colonial Reformers, the books about them will be found listed in the bibliographies of United Kingdom or imperial history. On their butt, Sir James Stephen, see P. Knaplund, *James Stephen and the British Colonial System 1813–1847* (Madison, Wisc., 1953), truly a study in historical justice. The founding of South Australia is dealt with in A. G. Price, *The Foundation and Settlement of South Australia 1829–1845* (Adelaide, 1924); A. G. Price, *Founders and Pioneers of South Australia* (Adelaide, 1929); G. V. Portus, *et al.*, eds., *Centenary History of South Australia* (Adelaide, 1936); and D. Pike, *Paradise of Dissent: South Australia 1829–1857* (London and Melbourne, 1957). Much documentary information about William Light, including his journal of the selection of the site of Adelaide, is to be found in Thomas Gill, *Colonel William Light* (Adelaide, 1911) and a later life is M. P. Mayo, *The Life and Letters of Colonel William Light* (Adelaide, 1927), but the best life so far is Geoffrey Dutton, *Founder of a City: The Life of Colonel William Light* (Melbourne, 1960). The best life of Grey is J. Rutherford, *Sir George Grey* (London, 1961). A document on the overlanding of stock is *The Journal of a Journey from New South Wales to Adelaide performed in 1838 by Mr. Joseph Hawdon* (Melbourne, 1952). See, too, George Sutherland, *The South Australian Company: A Study in Colonization* (London, 1898). Dunsdorfs on wheat is especially important here.

VI.   THE PASTORAL ECONOMY

On squatting, see S. H. Roberts, *The Squatting Age in Australia 1835–47* (Melbourne, 1935). An older book on the same subject is James Collier, *The Pastoral Age in Australasia,* this taking in New Zealand (London, 1911). In addition to the books dealing with the pastoral development of Victoria cited above, see also such books as James Backhouse, *A Narrative of a Visit to the Australian Colonies* (London, 1843); A. Harris, *Settlers and Convicts* (1847, reprint ed. by C. M. H. Clark; Melbourne, 1953), a vivid and valuable book; C. P. Hodgson, *Reminiscences of Australia* (London, 1846); Rolf Boldrewood, *Old Melbourne Memories* (London, 1896); R. D. Barton, *Reminiscences of an Australian Pioneer* (Sydney, 1917); W. A. Brodribb, *Recollections of an Australian Squatter* (Sydney, c. 1884), F. J. Meyrick, ed., *Life in the Bush 1840–1847* (London, 1939). A social history of a pastoral district, of which many more are needed, is Margaret Kiddle, *Men of Yesterday: Social History of the Western District of Victoria 1834–1900* (Melbourne, 1961). Insight into the social structure of New South Wales can be gained from Ralph Mansfield, *Analytical View of the Census of New South Wales for the Year 1841* (Sydney, 1841). The Madgwick book cited above is, of course, indispensable here. See also F. H. Hitchins, *The Colonial Land and Emigration Commission* (Philadelphia, 1931) and Margaret Kiddle, *Caroline Chisholm* (Melbourne, 1950). Although there is much in print about the convict system—see the general and economic histories and the collections of documents—there is as yet no single, comprehensive book that traces its evolution as a phenomenon of overwhelming importance during the first six decades of Australian history and studies its consequences in moral, social, economic, and political terms. An interesting book that recently came to light is T. J. Lemprière, the *Penal Settlements of Van Diemen's Land,* originally written in 1839 but not published until 1954 (Launceston, Tas.). On the penal reformer Maconochie, see J. V. Barry, *Alexander Maconochie* (Melbourne, 1958).

VII.   A STRUGGLE FOR FREE GOVERNMENT

The Evatt book cited in Chapter III is essentially a study in politics. Barron Field, incidental to his judicial work, published a book of poetry (see text of Chapter VIII) and edited *Geographical Memoirs of New South Wales* (London, 1825), a book of interest for its records of exploration and scientific observations. A study of Wentworth is A. C. V. Melbourne's very brief *William Charles Wentworth* (Brisbane, 1934). M. H. Ellis is understood to be at work upon a full-dress biography. The famous book was W. C. Wentworth, *A Statistical, Historical, and Political Description of the Colony of New South Wales and its dependent Settlements in Van Diemen's Land with a particular enumeration of the advantages which these colonies offer for emigra-*

tion and their superiority in many respects over those possessed by the United States of America (London, 1819 and later editions). There is no comprehensive history of the Australian press. A facsimile of *The Sydney Gazette: March 5, 1803–February 26, 1804* was issued in 1899 in an edition of 100 copies. See as the most comprehensive newspaper history in print, *A Century of Journalism: The Sydney Morning Herald 1831–1931* (Sydney, 1931), a full report on a paper steadily influential throughout its history. A fascinating book on the early Tasmanian press is E. Morris Miller, *Pressmen and Governors* (Sydney, 1952; ed. of 250 copies). A historical account of magazines is Frank S. Greenop, *History of Magazine Publishing in Australia* (Sydney, 1947). See here again the books on political and constitutional history cited above. See J. M. Ward's excellent *Earl Grey and the Australian Colonies 1846–1857* (Melbourne, 1958). The three famous books of 1837 were: Anonymous (but by James Macarthur assisted by Edward Edwards), *New South Wales: Its Present State and Future Prospects* (London, 1837); James Mudie, *The Felonry of New South Wales* (London, 1837); and John Dunmore Lang, *An Historical and Statistical Account of New South Wales* (London, 1837). Lang, who has been mentioned in earlier chapters and will be mentioned again, was a very prolific writer and practically everything he wrote has its intrinsic interest and importance if only as *his* statement on a public question. A large compilation of Lang writings is A. Gilchrist, ed., *John Dunmore Lang: Chiefly Autobiographical 1799–1878* (Melbourne, 1951, edition of 300 copies). Unfortunately the very length of Lang's career and its almost innumerable ramifications has discouraged the writing of a biography, a book which, when it does come, will, if it is properly done, vividly illuminate a long stretch of the history of the Southwest Pacific.

VIII. A TRANSIT OF CIVILIZATION

On the idea of federation, see Ward's book just cited. The roots of Australian nationalism, about which more is said later, are explored in R. Ward, *The Australian Legend* (Melbourne, 1958). The anthropological literature on the aborigines is very extensive. Good introductions are A. P. Elkin, *The Australian Aborigines* (Sydney, 1938 and later editions) and R. and C. Berndt, *The First Australians* (Sydney, 1952). On policy and action with regard to the aborigines, see E. J. B. Foxcroft, *Australian Native Policy: Its History, Especially in Victoria* (Melbourne, 1941); Paul Hasluck, *Black Australians: A Survey of Native Policy in Western Australia 1829–1847* (Melbourne, 1942); and Clive Turnbull, *Black War: The Extermination of the Tasmanian Aborigines* (Melbourne, 1948). On Australian housing, see Robin Boyd, *Australia's Home* (Melbourne, 1952) although it is mostly concerned with later periods. There is a very brief account of early town planning in Australia in A. J. Brown and H. M. Sherrard, *Town and Country Planning* (Melbourne, 1951). M. H. Ellis has written a life of Greenway, *Francis Greenway* (Sydney, 1949). Morton

Herman's *The Early Australian Architects and their Work* (Sydney, 1954), admirable in its text, is excellently supplied with pictures and plans. On Tasmanian buildings, see M. Sharland, *Stones of a Century* (Hobart, 1952). On Melbourne buildings, see Maie Casey, *et al.*, *Early Melbourne Architecture 1840–1888* (Melbourne, 1953). A sumptuous and classic book of drawings of early buildings is Hardy Wilson, *Old Colonial Architecture in New South Wales and Tasmania* (Sydney, 1924). No history of science and technology in Australia has yet been written. A life of Richard Johnson is James Bonwick, *Australia's First Preacher* (London, c. 1898). On the early history of education in New South Wales, see S. H. Smith and G. T. Spaull, *History of Education in New South Wales 1788–1925* (Sydney, 1925); Part I of C. E. W. Bean, *Here, My Son* (Sydney, 1950); and C. C. Linz, *The Establishment of a National System of Education in New South Wales* (Melbourne, 1938). The best single book on the early history of public education is A. G. Austin, *Australian Education 1788–1900* (Melbourne, 1961). For documents, see D. C. Griffiths, *Documents on the Establishment of Education in New South Wales 1789–1880* (Melbourne, 1957). There is no thorough history of the University of Sydney. On Marsden the best book so far is S. M. Johnstone, *Samuel Marsden* (Sydney, 1932). On Broughton, see F. T. Whitington, *William Grant Broughton* (Sydney, 1936). See also E. C. Rowland, *A Century of the English Church in New South Wales* (Sydney, 1948). The best account of the rise of the Catholic Church is Eris O'Brien, *The Dawn of Catholicism in Australia,* 2 vols. (Sydney, 1928). On Therry, see Eris O'Brien, *Life and Letters of Archpriest John Joseph Therry,* 2 vols. (Sydney, 1922). See also James G. Murtagh, *Australia: The Catholic Chapter* (New York, 1946). On the Australian language the authoritative work is Sidney J. Baker, *The Australian Language* (Sydney, 1945). For samples of some of the protean manifestations of popular culture excellently reproduced see G. C. Ingleton, *True Patriots All, Or News from Early Australia as told in a Collection of Broadsides* (Sydney, 1952). A study that investigates the situation in both "popular" and "high" culture is George Nadel, *Australia's Colonial Culture,* Foreword by C. Hartley Grattan (Cambridge, Mass., and Melbourne, 1957). For the books produced at home and overseas to 1850, see the Ferguson bibliography. For books of literary pretensions see E. Morris Miller, *Australian Literature From its Beginnings to 1935, A Descriptive and Bibliographical Survey,* 2 vols. (Melbourne, 1940). The standard history of Australian literature remains H. M. Green, *An Outline of Australian Literature* (Sydney, 1930), but there are several others. The struggle to use Australian themes and situations in drama is recounted in L. Rees, *Toward an Australian Drama* (Sydney, 1953). A history of Australian theaters is Paul McGuire, *The Australian Theatre* (Melbourne, 1948). On music, see W. A. Orchard, *Music in Australia* (Melbourne, 1952). The most comprehensive factual record of painting and painters is William Moore, *The Story of Australian Art,* 2 vols. (Sydney, 1934); while the best interpretative history is Bernard Smith, *Place, Taste and Tradition* (Sydney, 1945), but it is weakened by the author's attempts to use a Marxist approach. An admirable account of the gradual habituation of the European eye to the Southwest Pacific, including the beginnings of art in Australia, is Bernard Smith, *European Vision and the South Pacific 1768–1850: A Study in the History of Art and Ideas* (Oxford, 1960). There are numerous books of color reproductions. An interesting book about the convict artist Wainewright is Robert Crossland, *Wainewright in Tasmania* (Melbourne, 1954). On Martens, see Sir Lionel Lindsay's classic monograph, *Conrad Martens, The Man and His Art* (Sydney, 1920).

D3 NEW ZEALAND

General. A most useful orientation in the materials about New Zealand, historical and otherwise, can be obtained from John Harris, ed., *Guide to New Zealand Reference Material* (2d ed.; Dunedin, 1950), with supplements. This work lists bibliographies. The richest collections of books about New Zealand are to be found in the Alexander Turnbull Library and the Hocken Library. Some notes on the holdings of the Turnbull are to be found in an essay by C. R. H. Taylor, in Barrett, ed., *The Pacific* (Melbourne, n.d., c. 1950). A *Guide to the Dominion Archives* (Wellington, 1953) has been followed by a pamphlet series of preliminary inventories of the period 1840–1899 (Wellington, 1953–58). Robert McNab, *Historical Records of New Zealand,* Vol. 1 (Wellington, 1909), Vol. 2 (Wellington, 1914), contains a great deal of useful documentation up to 1842. A valuable mimeographed collection of documents is *Select Documents relative to the Development of Responsible Government in New Zealand 1839–1865* (n.p., 1949). For the period to c. 1840 documents of New Zealand reference are to be found in the historical records collections of Australia. The documentary collections on imperial history, cited earlier, contain New Zealand documents. A fascinating collection of pictures, arranged topically, with textual and bibliographical notes, is *Making New Zealand: Pictorial Surveys of a Century,* 30 Parts in 2 vols., indexed (Wellington, 1940). The history of New Zealand is normally told in one volume and the story has rather frequently been told. The most useful volumes are William Pember Reeves, *The Long White Cloud,* first published London, 1898 and subsequently in revised and extended versions—the latest 1950—a classic without doubt but to be read today with caution both as to facts and judgments; G. H. Scholefield, *New Zealand in Evolution* (London, 1909), A. W. Shrimpton and Alan E. Mulgan, *Maori and Pakeha: A History of New Zealand* (Wellington, 1930); J. Hight, ed., *The Cambridge History of the British Empire,* Vol. VII, Part II, *New Zealand* (Cambridge, Eng., and New York, 1933); J. C. Beaglehole, *New Zealand: A Short History* (London, 1936); Harold Miller, *New Zealand* (London, 1950); J. B. Condliffe and W. T. Airey, *A Short History of New Zealand* (Wellington, 1953); W. P. Morrell and D. O. W. Hall, *A History of New Zealand Life* (Wellington, 1957); Keith Sinclair, *A History of New Zealand* (London, 1959); and W. H. Oliver, *The Story of New Zea-*

land (London, 1960). The standard economic history is J. B. Cond-liffe, *New Zealand in the Making: A Study of Economic and Social Development* (2d rev. ed.; London and New York, 1959). An excellent symposium on New Zealand is Horace Belshaw, ed., *New Zealand* (Berkeley, 1947). The Cambridge History, Morrell-Hall and Belshaw have useful bibliographies. An excellent interpretation of New Zealand life is F. L. W. Wood, *This New Zealand* (3d ed.; Hamilton, 1958). An excellent atlas, complete with text, pictures, maps, and gazetteer, is A. H. McLintock, ed., *A Descriptive Atlas of New Zealand* (Welling-ton, 1959). Articles on New Zealand history appear in many journals devoted to modern history, but the best place to begin searching for them is *Historical Studies: Australia and New Zealand*. This periodical also provides occasional bibliographical reviews of the newly published books. Occasional articles of historical reference appear in *New Zealand Geographer* (Vol. 1, No. 1, 1945–), *Political Science* (Vol. 1, No. 1, 1948–), *The Economic Record* (Vol. 1, No. 1, 1925–), the quarterly *Landfall* (Vol. 1, No. 1, 1947–), and the biannual *Historical News* (Vol. 1, No. 1, 1960–), both published in Christchurch.

IX.   NEW ZEALAND IN POLYNESIA

As remarked several times earlier, this bibliography is cumulative and items cited under the successive chapters are additional. Although the plan of this book does not allow the exploration of Maori history and society, the emphasis rather falling upon the doings of the intruding whites, the opportunity may be seized to call attention to such fasci-nating books as Sir Peter Buck (Te Rangi Hiroa), *The Coming of the Maori* (Wellington, 1949) and Raymond Firth, *Economics of the New Zealand Maori* (Wellington, 1959). The editions cited are the latest and fullest of these two classics. On the general subject of the white "invasion" from Australia see E. J. Tapp, *Early New Zealand: A De-pendency of New South Wales 1788–1841* (Melbourne, 1958). Useful sources of information on early white activities in the South Island are A. H. Clark, *The Invasion of New Zealand by People, Plants and Animals* (New Brunswick, N.J., 1949); A. H. McLintock, *The History of Otago* (Dunedin, 1949); and J. Hight and C. R. Staubel, *A History of Canterbury*, Vol. I (Christchurch, 1957). Robert McNab wrote a number of gossipy books concerning both islands in this general con-nection of which *From Tasman to Marsden* (Dunedin, 1914) is repre-sentative. A detailed study of the successive situations at the Bay of Islands c. 1790–1840 is very much needed. A study chiefly concerned with the impact of the incoming whites on the Maoris of the North Island is H. M. Wright, *New Zealand 1769–1840* (Cambridge, Mass., 1959). Some conception of how the impact appeared to the Maori can be had from such books as L. G. Kelly, *Tainui* (Wellington, 1949) and Pei te Hurinui, *King Potatau* (Wellington, 1960), the latter a biography of the first Maori king (see text of Chapter XVIII). Rich documenta-tion of the coming of the missionaries is provided in J. R. Elder, ed., *The Letters and Journals of Samuel Marsden 1765–1838* (Dunedin,

1932) and J. R. Elder, ed., *Marsden's Lieutenants* (Dunedin, 1934). The Yate book referred to in the text is William Yate, *An Account of New Zealand* (London, 1835). See also E. Ramsden, *Marsden and the Missions* (Sydney, 1936). On Henry Williams, see Hugh Carleton, *The Life of Henry Williams,* ed. and revised by J. Elliott (Wellington, 1948), and, better still, L. M. Rogers, ed., *The Early Journals of Henry Williams 1826–1840* (Christchurch, 1961). On the Roman Catholics, see Lillian Keys, *The Life and Times of Bishop Pompallier* (Christchurch, 1957). An amusing, unfortunately undocumented, account of life among the missionaries is A. Sharp, *Crisis at Kerikeri* (Wellington, 1958). On the pakeha Maori, the classic work, not entirely reliable, is "A Pakeha Maori" (F. E. Maning), *Old New Zealand* (orig. ed., 1863, but often reprinted). A vivid account of the situation in 1820 as it appeared to a member of a timber-getting expedition is Richard A. Cruise, *Journal of a Ten Months' Residence in New Zealand* (orig. ed., 1823, reprinted Christchurch, 1957). Another, briefer, journal is Alexander McCrae, *Journal Kept in New Zealand 1820* (Wellington, 1928). On the early comers as explorers, see W. G. McClymont, *The Exploration of New Zealand* (Wellington, 1940). How early New Zealand appeared to the French explorer Dumont d'Urville appears in the translations from his journals by Olive Wright, *New Zealand 1826–27* (Wellington, 1950) and *The Voyage of the Astrolabe—1840* (Wellington, 1955).

X. TOWARD BRITISH SOVEREIGNTY IN NEW ZEALAND

A life of Busby is Eric Ramsden, *Busby of Waitangi* (Sydney, 1942). There is light on the United Kingdom background in J. S. Marais, *The Colonization of New Zealand* (London, 1927), P. Knaplund, *James Stephens,* cited earlier, and much in the documentary collections mentioned above. See also A. J. Harrop, *England and New Zealand* (1926). Specifically on Waitangi, see J. Rutherford, *The Treaty of Waitangi and the Acquisition of British Sovereignty in New Zealand* (Auckland, 1949); T. L. Buick, *The Treaty of Waitangi* (New Plymouth, 1936); G. H. Scholefield, *Captain William Hobson* (London, 1934); and H. H. Turton, ed., *Facsimilies of the Declaration of Independence and the Treaty of Waitangi* (1st ed., 1877; reprinted Wellington, 1960). See also J. C. Beaglehole, *Captain Hobson and the New Zealand Company: A Study in Colonial Administration* (Northampton, Mass., 1928). For an early American account of Waitangi and New Zealand of that time, see Charles Wilkes, *Narrative of the United States Exploring Expedition,* Vol. II, Chapter xii (Philadelphia, 1845).

D3 THE ISLANDS

General. A comprehensive list of the bibliographies of the islands is Ida Leeson, ed., *A Bibliography of Bibliographies of the South Pacific* (Melbourne, 1954). Miss Leeson lists not only separately printed bibliographies but bibliographies in books, thus in effect supplying also a useful list of the books of substance about the islands which are not, really, too numerous. A very large proportion of the literature of the islands, aside from the voluminous anthropological literature, is reportorial, autobiographical, polemic, or of the variety called "travel" and discriminating evaluation is badly needed as an aid to the writing of history. A book of mildly critical essays by and for bibliophiles fascinated by Pacificana is Charles Barrett, ed., *The Pacific: Ocean of Islands* (Melbourne, n.d., c. 1950). Attention must be called specifically to J. W. Davidson, "The Literature of the Pacific Islands," in *The Australian Outlook* (a periodical), Vol. 1, No. 1, March 1947, since it is critical in intent. C. R. H. Taylor, *A Pacific Bibliography* (Wellington, 1951) is a bibliography of the anthropological literature but includes many references highly useful to the historian and reader of history. This suggests what is very true, that the historian must read as much anthropology, especially social or cultural anthropology, as his energies and opportunities allow, even when his emphasis is upon the doings of the white intruders. Such reading will sharpen his insight into the consequences of white intrusion and into the kinds of societies that resulted from it. Therefore it may be useful to call attention to F. M. Keesing, *Social Anthropology in Polynesia* (Melbourne, 1953) and A. P. Elkin, *Social Anthropology in Melanesia* (Melbourne, 1953), books designed to survey the anthropological research done bibliographically and to suggest topics for future investigation. The principal general histories of the islands are G. H. Scholefield, *The Pacific: Its Past and Future* (London, 1919); J. I. Brookes, *International Rivalry in the Pacific Islands 1800–1875* (Berkeley, 1941), the only one of the four that makes extensive use of the literature in French; J. M. Ward, *British Policy in the South Pacific 1786–1893* (Sydney, 1948); and W. P. Morrell, *Britain in the Pacific Islands* (Oxford, 1960). A rather brief but highly useful French history of the islands is Ch-André Julien, *Histoire de l'Océanie* (Paris, 1951). No book of island documents, i.e., deeds of cession, treaties, basic policy statements and recommendations, etc., has ever been compiled. Such a volume would be highly useful. Early documents can be found, however, in *Historical Records of Australia* and others are to be found as appendices to various books. Some early French documentation is to be found in Marcel Dubois and Auguste Terrier, *Les Colonies Françaises: Un Siècle d'expansion coloniale* (Paris, 1902). There is as yet no periodical devoted to historical studies of the islands, but articles of this character are to be found in the periodicals covering the area or the Pacific in general.

XI.   THE ISLANDS AS NO MAN'S LANDS

On what the explorers discovered in Polynesia, see the Buck book listed in Chapter I above. On the mutiny of the "Bounty" the literature is enormous. See, in addition to the Mackaness life cited in Chapter III, Owen Rutter, ed., *The Court-Martial of the "Bounty" Mutineers* (Edinburgh, 1931), which has a useful bibliography. Professor J. W. Davidson of the Australian National University has a study of Dillon in hand which should revolutionize our conception of him and cast much light on the French penetration of the Southwest Pacific. The Darwin reference is to the *Journal of Researches . . . during the Voyage Round the World of H. M. S. Beagle* (Various editions). On the voyage Darwin also visited New Zealand and Australia. A little on what the Russians discovered in Polynesia, and more on the general context of their activities in the Pacific is to be found in A. I. Andreyev, *Russian Discoveries in the Pacific and North America in the 18th and 19th Centuries,* translated by C. Ginsburg (Ann Arbor, Michigan, 1952; U.S.S.R. ed., Moscow, 1944). A classic narrative of life in the islands in the very early days is John Martin, ed., *An Account of the Natives of the Tonga Islands . . . compiled . . . from . . . communications of Mr. William Mariner* (1st American ed.; Boston, 1820). On American maritime enterprise, a bibliographical guide is Robert Greenhalgn Albion, *Maritime and Naval History: An Annotated Bibliography* (Rev. ed.; Mystic, Connecticut, 1955). See especially Samuel Eliot Morison, *The Maritime History of Massachusetts 1783–1860* (Boston, 1941) and Edouard A. Stackpole, *The Sea-Hunters: The New England Whalemen During Two Centuries 1635–1835* (Philadelphia, 1953), the first volume of a two-volume history, the second of which will deal with the great days of whaling in the Pacific. On colonial sealing and whaling, see Chapters IV and IX above. On sandalwood-gathering, see Sir Everard Im Thurn, ed., *Lockerby's Journal* (London, 1925). The economic historian who will sort out and rationalize the activities of the early gatherers and traders has not yet appeared. Missionary narratives, not the most thrilling reading, are exceedingly numerous. A mildly critical discussion of them is to be found in the Barrett volume cited above. A book about the missionaries which has a very useful bibliography of the literature is L. B. Wright and Mary I. Fry, *Puritans in the South Seas* (New York, 1936). On the "Duff," see William Smith, *Journal of a Voyage in the Missionary Ship Duff* (New York, 1813). A Quaker view of the missions is *Extracts from the Letters and Journal of Daniel Wheeler* (Philadelphia, 1840). The Williams story is told by himself in John Williams, *A Narrative of Missionary Enterprises in the South Sea Islands* (London, 1838). Williams' biography is Ebenezer Prout, *Memoirs of the Life of The Reverend John Williams* (New York, 1843). An account of the Methodists in Fiji is J. W. Burton and W. Deane, *A Hundred Years in Fiji* (London, 1936). After my text had been fixed there appeared C. W. Newbury, ed., *The History of the Tahitian Mission 1799–1830* (Cambridge, Eng., 1961). This history, written by John Davies, one of the missionaries, edited for the Hakluyt Society, must unfailingly be read. A French study of this general period is Jean-Paul Faivre, *L'Expansion Française dans le Pacifique de 1800 à 1842* (Paris, 1953).

XII. THE ISLANDS ENTER WORLD POLITICS

On the American activities in the Southwest Pacific in their larger context, see J. M. Callahan, *America in the Pacific and the Far East*

(Baltimore, Maryland, 1901); C. O. Paullin, *Diplomatic Negotiations of American Naval Officers 1778–1883* (Baltimore, Maryland, 1912); and F. R. Dulles, *America in the Pacific* (Boston, 1938). A classic narrative of American gunboat diplomacy in this period is C. S. Stewart, *A Visit to the South Seas . . . during the Years 1829 and 1830,* 2 vols. (New York, 1833), but there are several others. See, e.g., the Wilkes *Narrative.* Probably the most famous British narrative of this kind is J. E. Erskine, *Journal of a Cruise Among the Islands of the Western Pacific* (London, 1853).

D3   ANTARCTICA

General. The indispensable materials for a history of Antarctica are the narratives, or other records like logbooks, of the various expeditions. These are now of a formidable number and bulk and I can not pretend that I have read all of them. Frankly, however, I have read all the major narratives, I think, and many of the shorter accounts of other expeditions (usually magazine articles). Some of the book-length narratives are now, as books, fairly elusive, impenetrable because of the language barrier, or I have not read them because of shortage of time. Of course I intend to go on reading in this particular field and will catch up with all the basic narratives in due course. Here I will not attempt to list them—see the *Bibliography* below for a list— but will from time to time indicate which for particular reasons should be read by anyone more than casually interested in Antarctica.

In my experience the best periodical sources are *The Geographical Review* (New York), *The Geographical Journal* (London), the *Smithsonian Reports* (Washington), and the more popular accounts in *The National Geographic* (Washington). The best bibliography is *Antarctic Bibliography* NAVAER 10-35-591 (Washington, Department of the Navy, 1951). Sections 22 and 23 cover narratives of expeditions, most of the rest list scientific materials. This suggests a prime problem that confronts anybody who attempts Antarctic history: how to indicate in a balanced way the progress of scientific research. Obviously knowledge and understanding are cumulative, but my information is that nobody has attempted to tell the history of scientific endeavor in Antarctica either over the whole range of the sciences practiced or within any particular science. Only a few essays with any such historical content exist and the usual tactic is sketchily to indicate the background while concentrating on the state of knowledge as cumulated to a particular date. Yet it is very obvious that a history of Antarctica is incomplete unless the theme of scientific progress is developed; and since in our time science has become dominant in Antarctic affairs, signalized bravely by the treaty of 1959, such incompleteness is serious. I am quite aware of the imperfections of my own narrative in the light of these considerations. Like most such narratives it is strongest, I think, where it is dealing with geographic discovery—who got where first—and when it is developing the historical continuities, but obviously weakest when dealing with the progress of science. The ideal historian of Antarctica needs more knowledge of science than is in the possession of men like me. There is but one history of Antarctica that has achieved classic stature: Hugh Robert Mill, *The Siege of the South Pole* (London, 1905) and it, it is worth noting, was produced as the Heroic Age began and before scientific endeavor became of central importance. There are other histories of later vintage of varying worth, some of which will be cited as the narrative develops. There is no satisfactory anthology of Antarctic narratives. Documents are where you find them. Works of great use to the understanding and writing of the history are *Sailing Directions for Antarctica* (U.S. Navy, Hydrographic Office, Washington, 1943) and its supplements and *Geographic Names of Antarctica,* Gazetteer No. 14, U.S. Board on Geographic Names (Washington, 1956).

XIII. QUEST INTO ANTARCTICA

A study of the American activity in Antarctica from the earliest sealers through Wilkes is Philip I. Mitterling, *America in the Antarctic to 1840* (Urbana, Illinois, 1959). My chapter was written before this book appeared. A British history of the American sector of Antarctica is E. W. Hunter Christie, *The Antarctic Problem* (London, 1951). The classic source of the story about Palmer and the Russians is Capt. Edmund Fanning, *Voyages and Discoveries in the South Seas 1792–1832* (Orig. pub. 1833; Salem, Massachusetts, 1924). The best presentation of Palmer's case—a presentation that ultimately failed—is W. H. Hobbs, *Discoveries Within Antarctica* (Philadelphia, 1939). Edouard A. Stackpole, *The American Sealers and the Discovery of the Continent of Antarctica: The Voyage of the Huron and the Huntress* (Mystic, Connecticut, 1955), put the whole question in a new and unquestionably sound perspective. The English-language edition of the Bellingshausen book is Frank Debenham, ed., *The Voyage of Captain Bellingshausen to the Antarctic Seas 1819–1821,* 2 vols. (London: Hakluyt Society, 1945). There is a considerable literature on the subantarctic islands of Australia and New Zealand. The classic scientific study is Charles Chilton, ed., *The Subantarctic Islands of New Zealand,* 2 vols. (Wellington, 1909). See also, e.g., F. B. McLaren, *The Auckland Islands* (Wellington, 1948) and R. Redwood, *The Forgotten Islands of the South Pacific* (Wellington, 1950). See also John Cumpston, ed., *Macquarie Island: A Bibliography* (Cremorne, N.S.W., 1958). For Wilkes, Clark and Dumont d'Urville, see their narratives. The only life of Wilkes is an indifferent performance, Daniel Henderson, *The Hidden Coasts* (New York, 1953).

D3 PART II AUSTRALIA

XIV. THE GOLD RUSH DECADE

This is as convenient a place as any to bring together some general histories of the colonies which cover the period 1850–1900. Only a few are satisfactory as histories. It is therefore useful to know that a series of state histories is now in the planning stage, each designed to bring out the distinctive character of the state in question, the common character of all being inevitably apparent. This will be a most valuable contribution to the understanding of Australian "sectionalism." The most comprehensive review of Australian colonial history is G. W. Rusden, *History of Australia,* 3 vols. (Melbourne, 1897). Rusden's bias, fantastic at the time of composition, is now curious indeed; his idea of organization something to behold; his self-confidence in judgment delightful; but the result often hilariously absurd. Other general surveys covering this period are G. Tregarthen, *Australian Commonwealth* (London, 1893), A. W. Tilby, *Australasia 1688–1911* (Boston, 1912), and T. A. Coghlan and T. T. Ewing, *Progress of Australasia in the Nineteenth Century* (Philadelphia, 1903), by far the best of this lot. Oddly there is no satisfactory, comprehensive, general history of New South Wales, a gap which becomes very noticeable at the time that New South Wales ceased to be the sole Australian colony, and hence not the only point of reverence in Australian history. A volume that is called an "official and political" history—in its latter pages a parliamentary history—is T. Richards, *An Epitome of the Official History of New South Wales . . . 1788 . . . 1883* (Sydney, 1883). As a factual record it has its uses. For Victoria there is H. G. Turner, *A History of the Colony of Victoria 1797–1900,* 2 vols. (London, 1904). This is a substantial work of obvious political bias by a literary banker. A book covering a later span of time more discursively, valuable for its facts and its wonderful pictures, is E. A. Doyle, ed., *The Story of the Century in Victoria 1851–1951* (Melbourne, 1951). See also, but use with caution, A. Pratt, *A Centenary History of Victoria* (Melbourne, 1934). For Queensland there is an official government publication, Anon., *Our First Half-Century* (Brisbane, 1909). See also Bernays on politics, referred to elsewhere. On Tasmania, James Fenton, *A History of Tasmania* (Hobart, 1884). On South Australia, a book by many hands, *The Centenary History of South Australia* (Adelaide, 1936). On Western Australia, the Battye and Crowley books cited earlier. On Northern Territory, A. G. Price, *The History and Problems of the Northern Territory* (Adelaide, 1930). There is a very great deal of topical journalism in hard covers dealing with the colonial period. William Westgarth of Victoria contributed some of the best. English visitors whose assessments are worth weighing include Anthony Trollope, J. A. Froude, and Sir Charles Dilke.

Edward Jenks, *The Government of Victoria, Australia* (London, 1891), a work by a sometime professor of law at Melbourne, a mixture of law, political science, and history, can be read with profit for information about and insight into politics.

The classic assessment of the gold rush decade is the late Prof. G. V. Portus' essay in the *Cambridge History.* I feel that the rushes are exaggerated in importance when they are made a turning point in Australian history. For the world context, W. P. Morrell, *The Gold Rushes* (London, 1940). On Hargraves' discovery, W. R. Glasson, *The Romance of Ophir* (Orange, N.S.W., 1935). Classic histories are W. B.

Withers, *The History of Ballarat* (2d ed.; Ballarat, 1887) and George Mackay, *The History of Bendigo* (Melbourne, 1891). There is a voluminous literature of personal reminiscence, from which may be selected more or less at random such items as C. R. Read, *What I Heard, Saw and Did at the Australian Gold Fields* (London, 1853); J. Sherer, ed., *The Gold-Finder of Australia* (London, 1853); Anon., *The Gold Fields of Victoria in 1862* (Melbourne, 1862); A Bank Official, *Banking under Difficulties: Life on the Goldfields of Victoria, New South Wales and New Zealand* (Melbourne, 1888); E. Scott, ed., *Lord Robert Cecil's Gold Fields Diary* (Melbourne, 1935); and C. D. Ferguson, *The Experiences of a Forty-Niner during Thirty-Four Years Residence in California and Australia* (Cleveland, 1888), by general consent the best American book on the episode. Books about the rushes still continue to appear, for example, D. G. Moye, ed., *Historic Kiandra* (Cooma, N.S.W., 1959); especially good for documents and pictures relating to a rush to the high snow country. On Charles Thatcher and entertainment on the gold fields of Australia and New Zealand, Hugh Anderson, *The Colonial Minstrel* (Melbourne, 1960). There are books on practically all the rushes in colonies other than Victoria and New South Wales, but they cannot be listed here, even in careful selection. However, notice must be given to the excellent history of gold-hunting in Western Australia, Malcolm Uren, *Glint of Gold* (Melbourne, 1948). On Eureka Stockade, for the conservative view see H. G. Turner, *Our Own Little Rebellion* (Melbourne, 1913); for the laboristic view, R. S. Ross, *Eureka! Freedom's Fight of '54* (Melbourne, 1914); and for a portrait of Peter Lalor, Clive Turnbull, *Eureka: The Story of Peter Lalor* (Melbourne, 1946). Carboni Raffaelo's curious narrative, *The Eureka Stockade* (Melbourne, 1855), was republished in a very plush edition, with a preface by Dr. H. V. Evatt (Sydney, 1942) and as a paperback, with an introduction by Brian Fitzpatrick (Melbourne, 1947)—both sponsors supporting the laboristic view of Eureka. As an example of how specialized study of Eureka can become, see C. H. Currey, *The Irish at Eureka* (Sydney, 1954). For a wide-ranging survey of fact and opinion, see the "Eureka Centenary Supplement" of *Historical Studies* (December, 1954), including R. D. Walshe, "Bibliography of Eureka."

On the writing of the new constitutions see F. L. W. Wood, *The Constitutional Development of Australia* (London, 1933); E. Sweetman, *Australian Constitutional Development* (Melbourne, 1925); A. C. V. Melbourne, *Early Constitutional Development in Australia: New South Wales 1788–1856* (London, 1934); and since the colonial constitutions carried over to the states, K. R. Cramp, *The State and Federal Constitutions of Australia* (Sydney, 1914). On the background of constitutional changes in Tasmania, W. A. Townsley, *The Struggle for Self-Government in Tasmania* (Hobart, 1951) and in Victoria, E. Sweetman, *Constitutional Development of Victoria 1851–6* (Melbourne, 1921).

XV. A NEW ECONOMIC PATTERN

Although a great deal has been written about the period 1861–1901 the professional historians have only lately begun a searching reanalysis and reinterpretation of it. Here are the roots of contemporary Australia. A major contribution to the understanding of the period in its all-important economic aspects, our concern in this chapter, is being made by Noel G. Butlin, reader in economic history at the Australian National University, in a series of articles (published in *Historical Studies, The Economic Record,* and the book, H. G. J. Aitken, ed., *The State and Economic Growth* [New York, 1959]), and two statistical monographs, *Public Capital Formation in Australia 1860–1900* (Canberra, 1954) and *Private Capital Formation in Australia 1861–1900* (Canberra, 1955). Mr. Butlin is reported to have in progress a general economic history of the period. Meanwhile, relevant here are the books by Coghlan, Fitzpatrick, Shann, Roberts, Dunsdorfs, and Watt which deal with economic development in one or another or several aspects. See also C. J. King, *An Outline of Closer Settlement in New South Wales 1788–1956* (Sydney, 1957) and J. D. Bailey, *Growth and Depression, Contrasts in the Australian and British Economies 1870–1880* (Canberra, 1956), both mines of specific economic data. On sheep numbers and wool production, *Statistical Handbook of the Sheep and Wool Industry* (Canberra, 1956). Reminiscences by pastoralists of this period are useful and fairly numerous but secondary studies of the industry are uncommon and much needed. The best secondary study is A. Barnard, *The Australian Wool Market 1840–1900* (Melbourne, 1958). On technological changes, diseases, pests, etc., the information is where you find it—e.g., for fencing in J. Gregson, *The Australian Agricultural Company 1824–1875* (Sydney, 1907); for machine shearing in A. D. Fraser, ed., *This Century of Ours* (Sydney, 1938), a company history of Dangar, Gedye & Malloch; on the rabbit D. G. Stead, *The Rabbit in Australia* (Sydney, 1935), really a specific proposal for dealing with the rabbit with a historical preface, in pastoralists' handbooks, in articles in *The Australian Encyclopedia,* and incidentally in discussions of the industry otherwise focused. On the droughts which plagued the pastoralists and farmers alike, the standard source is now J. C. Foley, *Droughts in Australia: From the Earliest Years of Settlement to 1955* (Melbourne, 1957). Light on conditions in the early days on the remoter frontiers (aside from that to be gleaned from reminiscences) is to be gained from such books as M. M. Bennett, *Christison of Lammermoor* (London, 1927); M. J. Costello, *Life of John Costello* (Sydney, 1930); Hudson Fysh, *Taming the North* (Sydney, 1933); Gordon Buchanan, *Packhorse and Waterhole* (Sydney, 1934); and Mary Durack, *Kings in Grass Castles* (London, 1959). On wheat farming, see D. W. Meinig, *On the Margins of the Good Earth: The South Australian Wheat Frontier 1869–1884* (Chicago, 1962). See also Dunsdorfs, Callaghan and Millington, J. D. Bailey's monograph, King's monograph, and the general histories. On water conservation and irrigation, see C. S. Martin, *Irrigation and Closer Settlement in the Shepparton District 1836–1906* (Melbourne, 1955); J. A. Alexander, *The Life of George Chaffey* (Melbourne, 1928); H. E. Dare, *Water Conservation in Australia* (Sydney, 1939); E. Hill, *Water into Gold* (Melbourne, 1937). On the sugar industry, see H. T. Easterby, *The Queensland Sugar Industry* (Brisbane, n.d.); A. G. Lowndes, ed., *South Pacific Enterprise: The Colonial Sugar Refining Company Ltd* (Sydney, 1956). The history of mining enterprise has yet to be written. By far the best book about an Australian mining enterprise is G. Blainey, *The Peaks of Lyell* (Melbourne, 1954). On the discovery of the wealth of Broken Hill see the early pages of R. Bridges, *From Silver to Steel* (Melbourne, 1920), a company history of BHP, or *Fifty Years of Industry and Enterprise 1885–1935*, a publicity publication of the BHP. For other aspects of Broken Hill see the bibliography of Chapter XVII. On Mount Morgan, B. G. Patterson, *The Story of the Discovery of Mount Morgan* (Brisbane, 1948). There are no comprehensive, solid books about the rise of manufacturing or the evolution of transportation and communications. Such material on these subjects as has passed through my hands has been fragmentary in coverage, uncommonly written historically, and rarely perceptively interpreted. In effect, these important stories are still buried in the archives. For example, *The Railways of New South Wales 1855–1955* (Sydney, 1955), which contains much useful information, valuable charts, and magnificent pictures, is really a conventional "company history," though it deals with a public enterprise, historical chiefly because the bulk of its material is presented chronologically, but hardly at all as economic history. Useful on the origin and history of the railway gauge muddle is Eric Harding, *Uniform Railway Gauge* (Melbourne, 1958). As a matter of fact one has to pick up one's information about transport *incidentally*. More is to be learned about transport by bullock wagon from reminiscences and novels than any other way. On roads, H. H. Newell, *Road Engineering in Australia 1788–1938* (Sydney 1938). On the river traffic, see Eric Irvin, ed., *Letters from the River, A Boat Trip down the Murrumbidgee in 1875* (Wagga Wagga, N.S.W., 1959). On the pioneer of steamboating on the Murray, M. Kinmont, *Family Portrait of W. R. Randell* (Adelaide, 1951); the passage on Randell in A. G. Price, *Founders and Pioneers of South Australia* (Adelaide, 1929); Allan Morris, *Rich River* (Echuca, Vic., 1952); and Ian Mudie, *Riverboats* (Adelaide, 1961). See also C. E. W. Bean, *The Dreadnought of the Darling* (London, 1916). A contemporary geographical survey of the Murray Valley with some historical data, J. MacD. Holmes, *The Murray Valley* (Sydney, 1948). (A history of the Murray Valley could, if perceptively done, be a wonderfully illuminating story of inland Australia in all its aspects: original exploration, traversing by pioneer overlanders of stock, occupation by squatters, mining, the river traffic, the coming of the wheat farmers, of the irrigation agriculturalists, the extension of the railways to the rivers, the political struggle over the waters, the Snowy River project, etc.—the whole sweep of Australian history!) The role of transport and communications in binding Australia into the Empire has never been fully investigated, though the historical importance of shipping in maintaining Britain's trading position is well understood in general terms. On the clippers, Basil Lubbock, *The Colonial Clippers* (Glasgow, 1955 reprint). The few pages of historical background in Woodruff and McGregor, *The Suez Canal and the Australian Economy* (Melbourne, 1957) are very useful. Histories of British shipping companies throw some light. On the Pacific cable, see George Johnson, ed., *The All Red Line* (London and Ottawa, 1903). There are numerous articles in *The Australian Encyclopedia* which contribute facts about most of the foregoing subjects. All the general and economic histories give an account of the difficulties encountered 1889–93 *et seq.* See also G. Blainey, *Gold and Paper: A History of the National Bank of Australasia* (Melbourne, 1958); Gordon Wood, *Borrowing and Business in Australia* (London, 1930); Roland Wilson, *Capital Imports and the Terms of Trade* (Melbourne, 1931). On the recovery, see the excellent specialized study, W. A. Sinclair, *Economic Recovery in Victoria 1894–1899* (Canberra, 1956). On the cities the writing from the angle taken here is very meager, but see on urban architecture Maie Casey, *et al.*, *Early Melbourne Architecture 1840–1888* (Melbourne, 1953) and Morton Herman, *The Architecture of Victorian Sydney* (Sydney, 1956). On the use of cast iron for decoration see E. G. Robertson, *Victorian Heritage: Ornamental Cast Iron in Architecture* (Melbourne, 1960). The most elaborate city history is Gordon Greenwood and John Laverty, *Brisbane 1859–1959: A History of Local Government* (Brisbane, 1960). A city history in the form of excerpts from the literature, with commentaries, is J. Grant and G. Serle, *The Melbourne Scene 1803–1956* (Melbourne, 1957). A similar book on Sydney is Birch and Macmillan, *The Sydney Scene 1788–1960* (Melbourne, 1962). A brief sketch, C. H. Bertie, *The Story of Sydney* (Sydney, 1933).

XVI. A CONGERIES OF COLONIES

Now that I come to compile a bibliography, I realize that this chapter is in large part based on bits and pieces from a great variety of sources, including journal articles.

For information about and light upon colonial politics see the histories cited above, Chapter XIV, and the biographical sketches in Serle and *The Australian Encyclopedia*. Of the figures selected for special attention, only Parkes has commanded a full-length biography, but it was published sixty-five years ago! Inadequate when published and now antiquated, it is C. E. Lyne, *Life of Sir Henry Parkes* (Sydney, 1896). Subsequent books about Parkes have not repaired the deficiencies of Lyne, but rather have battened upon him. See Sir Thomas Bavin, *Sir Henry Parkes: His Life and Work* (Sydney, 1941). A collection of Parkes's early speeches is David Blair, ed., *Speeches on Various Occasions Connected with the Public Affairs of New South Wales 1848–1874* (Melbourne, 1876). It is time for a thoroughgoing restudy of Parkes's career; and full-dress biographies of other colonial premiers would be most valuable.

On the "wild men" of New South Wales politics, Cyril Pearl, *Wild Men of Sydney* (London, 1958). Since Mr. Pearl's principal character also published something called a newspaper, his book is additionally a study in the history of Australian gutter journalism.

The standard history of "White Australia" is Myra Willard, *History of the White Australia Policy* (Melbourne, 1923).

On fiscal policy, see C. D. Allin, *A History of the Tariff Relations of the Australian Colonies* (Minneapolis, Minn., 1918) and also his *Australasian Preferential Tariffs and Imperial Free Trade* (Minneapolis, Minn., 1929). On Syme, A. Pratt, *David Syme: The Father of Protection in Australia* (London, 1908). On Syme as an economist, see the essay on him in J. A. La Nauze, *Political Economy in Australia: Historical Studies* (Melbourne, 1949).

I know of no study of the intercolonial conferences or the Federal Council. A Ph.D. thesis of first-class importance could well be written on them to illuminate intercolonial relations.

For an interesting glimpse of the egregious Mr. Justice Boothby, see A. J. Hannan, *The Life of Chief Justice Way* (Sydney, 1960). (Way of South Australia was an almost classic example of a colonial big-wig with a well-stuffed shirt.)

On Higinbotham, including the full text of the letter quoted, see E. E. Morris, *A Memoir of George Higinbotham* (London, 1895).

XVII. TOWARD A CONTINENTAL COMMONWEALTH

On the rise of the trade unions, J. T. Sutcliffe, *A History of Trade Unionism in Australia* (Melbourne, 1921). On the history of the labor movement, Brian Fitzpatrick, *A Short History of the Australian Labor Movement* (Melbourne, 1944) and E. W. Campbell, *History of the Australian Labor Movement: A Marxist Interpretation* (Sydney, 1945), essentially a communist rewrite of Fitzpatrick. See also W. E. Murphy, *History of the Eight Hours Movement* (Melbourne, 1896). *The Book of the Martyrs of Tolpuddle 1834–1934* (London, 1934) and H. V. Evatt, *Injustice Within the Law* (Sydney, 1934) deal with the transportation of the Dorsetshire laborers. The classic statement of the argument associating labor with the liberal tradition is H. V. Evatt, *Liberalism in Australia . . . to the Year 1915* (Sydney, 1918). A classic account of labor's entry into New South Wales politics is George Black, *A History of the New South Wales Political Labor Party*, a series of pamphlets (Sydney, n.d.). W. G. Spence tells his own story in terms of the movement in *Australia's Awakening: Thirty Years in the Life of an Australian Agitator* (Sydney, 1909, 1962).

On literary developments, see the Morris Miller bibliography cited in Chapter VIII above and H. M. Green, *An Outline of Australian Literature* (Sydney, 1930). (In 1962 Green published *A History of Australian Literature* [2 vols., Sydney], using a most inclusive definition of literature.) See for particulars, J. F. Young, *Catherine Helen Spence*

(Melbourne, 1937); C. Roderick, *In Mortal Bondage: The Strange Life of Rosa Praed* (Sydney, 1948); T. T. Reed, *Henry Kendall* (Adelaide, 1960); Brian Elliott, *Marcus Clarke* (London, 1958); K. Burke, *Thomas Alexander Browne (Rolf Boldrewood): An Annotated Bibliography, Checklist, and Chronology* (Cremorne, N.S.W., 1956); E. Humphris and D. Sladen, *Adam Lindsay Gordon* (London, 1912).

On the autochthonous Australian probably the best single reference is R. Ward, *The Australian Legend* (Melbourne, 1958), but much of what is said here is gleaned from the "sources." There are many, many books about bushranging, early and late, some of them classics of the literature of crime. On the early outburst in New South Wales is John Meredith, *The Wild Colonial Boy: The Life and Times of Jack Donahoe* (Sydney, 1960). Another is F. Clune, *Wild Colonial Boys* (Sydney, 1948). On Ned Kelly, Clive Turnbull's bibliography, *Kellyana* (Melbourne, 1943), but the "items" have gone on multiplying since it appeared. For Kelly in literature, see Douglas Stewart, *Ned Kelly* (Sydney, 1946); in painting see the sequence of pictures by Sidney Nolan; and there is a ballet. Nobody has yet thought to write a book-length socio-historical study of the larrikins. There is no book, though an accumulation of essays and a multiplicity of references, on *The Bulletin* and its influence. (M. Clark's source books have excellent quotations from the paper.)

There is a good deal of writing about Lawson but no "life" as yet, though Colin Roderick is at work on one. Paterson's ballads have been collected. There are numerous books of ballads but for a very convenient introduction see Douglas Stewart and Nancy Keesing, *Old Bush Songs and Rhymes* (Sydney, 1957) which reprints Paterson's *Old Bush Songs* and adds to it; and Stewart and Keesing, *Australian Bush Ballads* (Sydney, 1955) which selects the best of the "contrived" ballads, including Paterson's. A series of lectures on the Australian novel using Australian-ness as a criterion is Miles Franklin, *Laughter Not for a Cage* (Sydney, 1956). After years of delay there appeared A. R. Chisholm and J. J. Quinn, *The Verse of Christopher Brennan* (Sydney, 1960) and *The Prose . . .* (Sydney, 1962).

Vance Palmer, *The Legend of the Nineties* (Melbourne, 1954) must be read as a corrective to overemphasis on the period.

On the theatre, drama, and music in this period see the McGuire, Rees, and Orchard books cited above, Chapter VIII.

On the artists, see Moore and Smith, Chapter VIII above, and the following for details: R. H. Croll, *Tom Roberts: Father of Australian Landscape Painting* (Melbourne, 1935); R. H. Croll, ed., *Smike to Bulldog: Letters from Sir Arthur Streeton to Tom Roberts* (Sydney, 1946); Julian Ashton, *Now Came Still Evening On* (Sydney, 1941); Amy Lambert, *Thirty Years of an Artist's Life: G. W. Lambert* (Sydney, 1938), Dora Coates, *George Coates* (London, 1937); Nina Murdoch, *Portrait in Youth: A Biography of Sir John Longstaff* (Sydney, 1948); Ursula Hoff, *Charles Conder: His Australian Years* (Melbourne, 1960). On the black-and-white artists, see D. J. Hopkins,

Hop of the "Bulletin" (Sydney, 1929); *On the HOP!: A Selection from the Australian Drawings of Livingston Hopkins* (Sydney, 1904); and *Phil May in Australia* (Sydney, 1904). (There are many books of color reproductions of Australian paintings, organized on historical principles.) On photography, Jack Cato, *The Story of the Camera in Australia* (Melbourne, 1955). (An attempt to tell the story of "Australian life" using the vast photographic record is Irma and Cyril Pearl, *Our Yesterdays: Australian Life Since 1853 in Photographs* [Sydney, 1954].)

There is as yet no study of expatriation as a prime factor in Australian cultural history, though the materials for one are abundant. Most of the writing about the matter is in terms of complaint about the "export of talent" or rationalizations for leaving Australia, the easiest way out. On the dis-ease of colonial expatriates, see W. K. Hancock, *Country and Calling* (London, 1954), who, wisely, eventually returned to Australia. Of the impact of colonials on metropolitan Britain we also lack a study, but see the suggestive little essay by the historian of Rome, R. Syme (a New Zealand expatriate), *Colonial Elites: Rome, Spain and the Americas* (London, 1958). On the impact of the "imported" Britons on Australia's cultural life, see the history of that cultural life *passim*.

The best single book on the social reformers and their miscellany of ideas is Robin Gollan, *Radical and Working Class Politics: A Study of Eastern Australia 1850–1910* (Melbourne, 1960). For quotations from the writings, see M. Clark's source books and R. N. Ebbells and L. G. Churchward, *The Australian Labor Movement 1850–1907* (Sydney, 1960). On William Lane, see Lloyd Ross, *William Lane and the Australian Labor Movement* (Sydney, 1938). (Dr. Ross is a most astute interpreter of the history of the movement but his work is mostly essays not yet collected into a book.)

A study of the establishment of the state schools as free, compulsory, and secular is much needed. The tendency in the histories is to skip by this crucially important development under the cover of careful generalizations. See S. H. Smith and G. T. Spaull, *History of Education in New South Wales 1788–1925* (Sydney, 1925); E. Sweetman, J. Smyth, and C. R. Long, *A History of State Education in Victoria* (Melbourne, 1922); T. H. Smeaton, *Education in South Australia 1836–1927* (Adelaide, 1927); C. Reeves, *A History of Tasmanian Education* (Melbourne, 1935). See also T. F. Mackenzie, *Nationalism and Education in Australia* (London, 1935). For the Catholic reaction to the secularist campaign, see *Pastorals and Speeches of Archbishop Vaughan* (Sydney, 1880). There are a good many books about the Protestant "public" schools, but to my knowledge no comprehensive study of any in its historical and socio-cultural context, demonstrating its impact on the Australian scene, but some articles showing the special status of "public school" "old boys" have appeared. See, e.g., C. E. W. Bean, *Here, My Son: An Account of the Independent and other Corporate Boys' Schools in Australia* (Sydney, 1950) and E. R. Holme, *"Shore": The Sydney Church of England Grammar*

School (Sydney, 1951). On the whole complicated story of Catholic education in Australia, see Brother Ronald Fogarty, *Catholic Education in Australia 1806–1950*, 2 vols. (Melbourne, 1959).

There is no systematic study of the higher intellectual life of this period, but something can be learned and sensed from such books as G. Blainey, *A Centenary History of the University of Melbourne* (Melbourne, 1957), quite the best university history of all; R. A. Dallen, *The University of Sydney: Its History and Progress* (2d ed., 1925); or preferable on Sydney, R. B. Farrell, *et al.*, *One Hundred Years of the Faculty of Arts* (Sydney, 1952); *The Public Library of Victoria 1856–1956* (Melbourne, 1956); R. T. M. Pescott, *Collections of a Century: The History of the First Hundred Years of the National Museum of Victoria* (Melbourne, 1954); M. E. David, *Professor David: The Life of Sir Edgeworth David* (London, 1937); Margaret Willis, *By Their Fruits: The Life of Ferdinand von Mueller* (Sydney, 1949); R. R. Marrett and T. K. Penniman, *Spencer's Scientific Correspondence with Sir J. G. Frazer and Others* (Oxford, 1932); and D. B. Copland, *W. E. Hearn: First Australian Economist* (Sydney, 1935). An account of a benefactor of the University of Melbourne is C. S. Ross, *Francis Ormond* (Melbourne, c. 1912). Interesting and revealing accounts of British-Australian-British careers are William Stebbings, *Charles Henry Pearson* (London, 1900) and Spencer Childers, *The Life and Correspondence of the Rt. Hon. Hugh C. E. Childers,* 2 vols. (London, 1901).

There is no history of "fun and games" in Australia, presumably because all interested have been too busy having fun and playing games, but see A. G. Moyes, *Australian Cricket: A History* (Sydney, 1959) and M. Cavanough and M. Davies, *Cup Day: The Story of the Melbourne Cup 1861–1960* (Melbourne, 1960).

The debates at the constitutional conventions 1891–98 were published in five large volumes, but much other material is difficult to come by. The classic historical account of the coming of federation in Australia is to be found in the prefatory matter of John Quick and Robert R. Garran, *The Annotated Constitution of the Australian Commonwealth* (Sydney, 1901). Robert R. Garran, *The Coming Commonwealth* (Sydney, 1897) is a handbook of federalism. The prolonged discussion produced no *Federalist,* though one has a suspicion that excellent argumentation may be buried in magazine and newspaper files. Other useful books are Robert R. Garran, *Prosper the Commonwealth* (Sydney, 1958), an autobiography, B. R. Wise, *The Making of the Australian Commonwealth 1889–1900* (London, 1913), Sir Henry Parkes, *The Federal Government of Australasia: Speeches* (Sydney, 1890), and also Sir Henry's autobiography cited earlier; H. L. Hall, *Victoria's Part in the Australian Federation Movement 1849–1900* (London, 1931); E. M. Hunt, *American Precedents in Australian Federation* (New York, 1930); and Alfred Deakin's *The Federal Story* (Melbourne, 1944), reflecting so brilliantly Deakin's novelistic fascination with personalities. Insight can also be gained from the biographies of participants in the conventions, most of which are listed in the reading list of Volume II. This is by no means an exhaustive canvas of the books available; an attempt to make a bibliography of the writing of the constitution is Alan Gross, *Attainment, Being a Critical Study of the Literature of Federation, with Bibliography* (Melbourne, 1948). What is greatly needed is an analytical history of the writing of the instrument, dealing with each clause *ab origine* to finished version as a study in the politics of constitution-making.

D3   NEW ZEALAND

XVIII. THE PAKEHAS TAKE NEW ZEALAND

The Marais volume, *The Colonization of New Zealand,* cited above, continues to be useful, but this is a good place to note that the work is biased against the Maoris and the government in favor of the Company. A. H. McLintock, *Crown Colony Government in New Zealand* (Wellington, 1958) must unfailingly be read but this writer finds difficulty in accepting its value-judgments. John Miller, *Early Victorian New Zealand: A Study of Racial Tension and Social Attitudes 1839–1852* (London, 1958) is an excellent work. So also is Keith Sinclair, *The Origins of the Maori Wars* (Wellington, 1957). T. L. Buick, *New Zealand's First War or The Rebellion on Hone Heke* (Wellington, 1926) gives the details of that episode. John Gorst, *The Maori King,* ed. by K. Sinclair (Hamilton, 1959) is a modern edition of an indispensable classic originally published in 1864. The new edition contains in an appendix an illuminating Maori document on the king movement by Wiremu Tamihana. See the life of the first Maori king cited above. A documented book which deals with W. C. Wentworth's landsharking is Edward Sweetman, *The Unsigned New Zealand Treaty* (Melbourne, 1939). Michael Turnbull, *The New Zealand Bubble* (Wellington, 1959) is a too-brief essay in deflation of the traditional claims for the New Zealand Company which the author should expand and closely document. To the McLintock book on Otago and the Hight-Straubel book on Canterbury cited above we may here add R. G. Wood, *From Plymouth to New Plymouth* (Wellington, 1959) and J. Rutherford and W. H. Skinner, eds., *The Establishment of the New Plymouth Settlement in New Zealand 1841–1843* (New Plymouth, 1940), a book of documents, both books covering the origin and early years of the Taranaki settlement. T. L. Buick, *The French at Akaroa* (Wellington, 1928) is the established work on that episode. For detail about Otago, see the classic work, T. M. Hocken, *Contributions to the Early History of New Zealand: Settlement of Otago* (London, 1898) which has useful documentary appendices. The basic statistics for this period are collected in *Statistics of New Zealand for the Crown Colony Period 1840–1852* (Auckland, 1954). On constitutional development the traditional standard work is J. Hight and H. D. Bramford, *The Constitutional History and Law of New Zealand* (Christchurch, 1914), but see also J. L. Robson, *New Zealand,* vol.

4 of *The British Commonwealth: The Development of its Laws and Constitutions* (London, 1954). Guy H. Scholefield, *New Zealand Parliamentary Record 1840–1949* (Wellington, 1950) has many uses for the historian, not least because of its photographs of the notables. Scholefield on Hobson has been cited above. There is no life of Fitzroy. There has been a good deal written about Grey, for example, W. L. and L. Rees, *The Life and Times of Sir George Grey* (Auckland, 1898), but he is an excessively difficult subject. J. Rutherford, *Sir George Grey K.C.B. 1812–1898: A Study in Colonial Government* (London, 1961) looks like a first-class work but it appeared after my text was fixed. On Bishop Selwyn, see H. W. Tucker, *Memoirs of the Life and Episcopate of George Augustus Selwyn D.D.*, 2 vols. (London, 1879). On Godley, C. E. Carrington, *John Robert Godley of Canterbury* (Christchurch, 1950). Two fascinating collections of documents indispensable to an understanding of "what it was like" in New Zealand in these days are Nancy M. Taylor, ed., *Early Travellers in New Zealand* (London, 1959) and Alison Drummond, ed., *Married and Gone to New Zealand* (Hamilton, 1960). Several collections of letters and papers relating to this period have been published in recent years, for example, J. R. Godley, ed., *Letters from Early New Zealand by Charlotte Godley 1850–1853* (Christchurch, 1951); *The Journal of Edward Ward 1850–51* (Christchurch, 1951); C. A. Sharp, ed., *The Dillon Letters 1842–1853* (Wellington, 1954); P. B. Maling, ed., *The Torlesse Papers 1848–51* (Christchurch, 1958). A classic about the background of the Auckland settlement is J. L. Campbell, *Poenamo* (1st ed., 1881, reprinted 1953). A large collection of family papers covering the years 1841 to 1906 is G. H. Scholefield, ed., *The Richmond-Atkinson Papers*, 2 vols. (Wellington, 1960).

XIX. WAR AND GOLD

The standard account of the fighting side of the Maori wars is James Cowan, *The New Zealand Wars*, 2 vols. (1st ed., 1922; reprinted Wellington, 1955). There are numerous personal accounts of the fighting, or phases of it. On an important aspect of the political side of the wars, see A. J. Harrop, *England and the Maori Wars* (1937). As to the gold rushes in addition to the accounts in the general and provincial histories and W. P. Morrell, *The Gold Rushes* (London, 1940) see R. A. Loughman, *The First Gold Discoveries in New Zealand* (Wellington, 1906) and A. B. Ryan *Gold Discoveries in New Zealand* (Wellington, 1959). On the west coast, see R. A. Kay, ed., *Westland's Golden Century* (Greymouth, 1959) not least because it is full of interesting pictures. Like the Australians the New Zealanders have thus far failed to produce a history of the pastoral industry, but see L. G. D. Acland, *The Early Canterbury Runs* (complete edition; Christchurch, 1951). On agriculture see G. T. Alley and D. O. W. Hall, *The Farmer in New Zealand* (Wellington, 1941). Although not a historical survey, there are some historical data in H. Belshaw, ed.,

Agricultural Organization in New Zealand (Melbourne, 1936). An interesting specialized study is B. L. Evans, *A History of Farm Implements and Implement Firms in New Zealand* (Feilding, 1956). See, also, Condliffe's economic history. There seems to be no single work on the politics of this period that can be cited as convincing and exhaustive, but see the appropriate chapters in the general histories and W. P. Morrell, *The Provincial System in New Zealand 1852–1876* (London, 1932) and L. Lipson, *The Politics of Equality* (Chicago, 1948). See also the relevant remarks in L. Webb, *Government in New Zealand* (Wellington, 1940). R. F. Irvine and O. T. J. Alpers, *The Progress of New Zealand in the* [19th] *Century* (Toronto, 1902) has its uses. For the details about the regions of New Zealand, not now necessarily thought of as the old provinces, see K. B. Cumberland and J. W. Fox, *New Zealand: A Regional View* (Christchurch, 1958). Indispensable on the course of economic development is the specialized study, C. G. F. Simkin, *The Instability of a Dependent Economy: Economic Fluctuations in New Zealand 1840–1914* (London, 1951). A history of the operations in New Zealand of an Australian bank, which is an important contribution to economic history, is K. Sinclair and W. F. Mandle, *Open Account: A History of the Bank of New South Wales in New Zealand 1861–1961* (Wellington, 1961).

XX. PROGRESS AND POVERTY

On the course of economic affairs, see the books by Condliffe and Simkin and on politics Morrell, Lipson, and Webb. On Vogel, R. M. Burdon, *The Life and Times of Sir Julius Vogel* (Christchurch, 1948) is a first-class political biography. The Grey irruption is dealt with critically in T. G. Wilson, *The Grey Government* (Auckland, 1954), while the subsequent developments among the liberals are recounted in T. G. Wilson, *The Rise of the New Zealand Liberal Party 1880–1890* (Auckland, 1956). See also J. Rutherford's study of Grey. Aside from Vogel none of the principal leaders has yet been intensively studied, but there is an illuminating life of an off-side conservative, W. Downie Stewart, *William Rolleston* (Christchurch, 1940). On the rise of the trade unions, see J. D. Salmon, *New Zealand Labour's Pioneering Days* (Auckland, 1950). On social conditions see Morrell and Hall cited above.

XXI. KING DICK'S REALM

Seddonian New Zealand was extensively written about by contemporaries and many of their books are still prime sources, but lately the restudy and reinterpretation of the period, now an episode in, not a climax of, New Zealand history, has begun. Of Seddon himself the pioneer biography was James Drummond, *The Life of Richard John Seddon* (London, 1907). It must still be read for its original materials, but as a biography it has been displaced by R. M. Burdon,

King Dick: A Biography of Richard John Seddon (Christchurch, 1955), considered the best political biography yet written about a New Zealander. Mr. Burdon also has a study of John McKenzie in his *New Zealand Notables: Series Two* (Christchurch, 1945). A biography of Pember Reeves is being written by Keith Sinclair. Reeves himself helped set the standard interpretation of the period not only in the first edition of *The Long White Cloud* (London, 1898) but also in his famous *State Experiments in Australia and New Zealand*, 2 vols. (London, 1902). Of the books by contemporary foreign observers, the best remembered appear to be André Siegfried, *Democracy in New Zealand* (translation, London, 1914; orig. French ed., Paris, 1905); Albert Métin, *Le Socialisme sans Doctrines* (Paris, 1901 and 1910); Henry Demarest Lloyd, *A Country Without Strikes* (New York, 1900) and *Newest England* (New York, 1903); and Frank Parsons, *The Story of New Zealand* (Philadelphia, 1904). James E. Le Rossignol and W. Downie Stewart, *State Socialism in New Zealand* (London, n.d.) is an American-New Zealand collaborative effort. The standard reference on refrigeration is J. T. Critchell and J. Raymond, *A History of the Frozen Meat Trade* (London, 1912). On economic changes see Condliffe and Simkin as cited. On "bush settlement" generally see James Cowan, *Settlers and Pioneers* (Wellington, 1940). There are a number of widely read reminiscences which deal with the pioneering of the North Island country in this time, illustratively Harry Combs, *Growing Up in the Forty Mile Bush* (Hamilton, 1951) and Helen Wilson, *My First Eighty Years* (Hamilton, 1950). On Seddon and the islands, something of the spirit of his approach can be savored in the curious hardcover book, *The Right Hon. R. J. Seddon's Visit to Tonga, Fiji, Savage Island and the Cook Islands* (Wellington, 1900). On imperial federation and New Zealand see Keith Sinclair, *Imperial Federation: New Zealand Policy and Opinion 1880–1914* (London, 1955), an Institute of Commonwealth Studies paper. On the Boer War, see D. O. W. Hall, *The New Zealanders in South Africa 1899– 1902* (Wellington, 1949). On the transit of culture to New Zealand, there is no general study, but the standard accounts of literature and painting are by E. H. McCormick and of science, S. H. Jenkinson, *New Zealanders and Science* (Wellington, 1940). McCormick's *New Zealand Literature* (London, 1959) is a revision and extension of the literary portions of *Letters and Art in New Zealand* (Wellington, 1940). This leaves the story of painting in a curious limbo. A charming and fascinating essay by McCormick is *The Inland Eye: A Sketch in Visual Autobiography* (Auckland, 1949); it tells one much about the visual impact of the North Island of New Zealand. McCormick has also given us a most brilliant study of expatriation around the painter regarded as the best New Zealand has produced, *The Expatriate: A Study of Frances Hodgkins* (Wellington, 1954). See also E. H. McCormick, *Works of Frances Hodgkins in New Zealand* (Auckland, 1954), and there is a Penguin devoted to Hodgkins' work. The books of Samuel Butler are usually in print in England and the United States;

those of Lady Barker are kept in print in New Zealand. The life of Katherine Mansfield that best presents her New Zealand background is Antony Alpers, *Katherine Mansfield: A Biography* (New York, 1954). Low has written vividly of his New Zealand years in *Low's Autobiography* (New York, 1957). On the University of New Zealand, see J. C. Beaglehole, *The University of New Zealand: An Historical Study* (Christchurch, 1937). There is an enormous "life"— over 1000 pages—of von Haast, H. F. von Haast, *The Life and Times of Sir Julius von Haast: Explorer, Geologist, Museum Builder* (Wellington, 1948) which is very profitable reading both for the light on von Haast and the context in which he worked. For a shorter view of von Haast, see Burdon's *New Zealand Notables: Series Three* (Christchurch, 1950).

⌐⌐THE ISLANDS

XXII. THE PARTITIONING OF THE ISLANDS (1)

All the histories of the islands cited above under "The Islands: General" are still useful here but the Brookes volume concludes at 1870 and the Ward at 1893. Attention should be called to the journal *Historical Studies* for important articles on the islands in this period. James Colwell, ed., *A Century in the Pacific* (Sydney, 1914) should properly be called *A Century of Methodism . . . ,* but it has its uses. Tucker's life of Bishop Selwyn, cited in Chapter XVIII, is useful in connection with E. S. Armstrong, *The History of the Melanesian Mission* (New York, 1900). On Erskine's tour of the islands see *Journal of a Cruise of the Western Pacific* (London, 1853). Another illuminating "cruise book" is J. L. Brenchley, *The Cruise of the Curaçoa Among the South Sea Islands in 1865* (London, 1873). On the Presbyterians in the New Hebrides, see *John G. Paton: An Autobiography* (New York, 1889). On George Brown, C. Brunsdon Fletcher, *The Black Knight of the Pacific* (Sydney, 1944). On the history of Fiji to cession see R. A. Derrick, *A History of Fiji,* Vol. 1 (Revised ed.; Suva, 1950) and the books cited therein, and J. D. Legge, *Britain in Fiji 1858– 1880* (London, 1958). There is no satisfactory single volume on the labor trade. The account given here is the result of the reading of a variety of sources and commentaries. A collection of narratives of episodes in the labor trade is T. Dunbabin, *Slavers of the South Seas* (Sydney, 1935). On Patteson, see Charlotte M. Yonge, *Life of John Coleridge Patteson,* 2 vols. (London, 1894) and on Goodenough in this and the next chapter, *Journal of Commodore Goodenough 1873– 1875* (London, 1876). The account of the taking of New Caledonia is principally but not wholly based on Brookes. A French study of the partition of the islands is H. Russier, *Le Partage de L'Océanie* (Paris, 1905). A biography of J. B. Thurston integrated into a carefully developed historical context would be a most important contribution to the understanding of the islands in this time. Thurston, like so many of his fellows, had been a colonist in Australia before venturing into Fiji.

XXIII. THE PARTITIONING OF THE ISLANDS (2)

On Fiji see J. D. Legge as cited above; J. C. Potts, *The Sugar Industry in Fiji: Its Beginnings* (Suva, 1960) which has a valuable documentary appendix; and A. G. Lowndes, ed., *South Pacific Enterprize: The Colonial Sugar Refining Company Ltd.* (Syndey, 1956). On Samoa, see M. E. Townsend, *The Rise and Fall of Germany's Colonial Empire 1884–1918* (New York, 1930); S. Masterman, *The Origins of International Rivalry in Samoa 1845–1884* (Stamford, 1934); G. H. Ryden, *The Foreign Policy of the United States in Relation to Samoa* (New Haven, 1933); Robert Louis Stevenson, *A Footnote to History* (London, 1892) and his public and private letters pertaining to Samoa (an excellent life of Stevenson is J. C. Furnas, *Voyage to Windward* [New York, 1951]); J. A. C. Gray, *Amerika Samoa* (Annapolis, 1960). I know of no good historical account of the traders in the islands. A candid, solidly documented "company history" of Burns, Philp, for instance, would be invaluable. Not reading Dutch, I have had to gather and sift my information about Dutch New Guinea from where I could find it and organize it historically. At this point I shall refer the reader only to Alfred Russel Wallace, *The Malay Archipelago* (6th ed., 1877). On British New Guinea see J. D. Legge, *Australian Colonial Policy* (Sydney, 1956); S. W. Reed, *The Making of Modern New Guinea* (Philadelphia, 1943); D. C. Gordon, *The Australian Frontier in New Guinea 1870–1885* (New York, 1951); C. K. Cooke, ed., *Australian Defences and New Guinea: Papers of Sir Peter Scratchley* (London, 1887); J. King, *W. G. Lawes* (London, 1909); R. Lovett, *James Chalmers* (London, 1902); D. S. Macmillan, *A Squatter Went to Sea* (Sydney, 1957), F. S. Greenop, *Who Travels Alone*, a study of Miklouho-Maclay (Sydney, 1944). The best material I know on the German take-over is in articles in learned journals. On the New Hebrides see T. Harrison, *Savage Civilization* (New York, 1937), though the history is not wholly reliable, and S. H. Roberts, *History of French Colonial Policy 1870–1925*, 2 vols. (London, 1929). On Tahiti see Roberts and for Paul Gauguin see *Noa Noa* (various editions, for example, New York, 1957) and, on his first visit, Chapter x of John Rewald, *Post Impressionism from Van Gogh to Gauguin* (New York, n.d.), for his death in the Marquesas ending his second visit, Bengt Danielsson, *Forgotten Islands of the South Seas* (London, 1960), Chapter 6. On Tonga see Monseigneur Bishop Blanc, *A History of Tonga* (Vista, Calif., 1934) and Basil Thomson, *The Diversions of a Prime Minister* (Edinburgh, 1894), which contains "A Sketch of the History of Tonga." An expert, modern historical study of Tonga would cast light on the entire island story. Nobody has yet published a comprehensive book on the activities and aspirations of the Australians and New Zealanders in the islands in spite of their manifest importance. On New Zealand in the islands see the lives of Grey, Vogel, and Seddon and F. L. W. Wood, *New Zealand in the World* (Wellington, 1940). On Australia for the establishment of

Somerset see R. L. Jack, *Northmost Australia,* 2 vols. (Melbourne, 1922); on the Queensland political background of McIlwraith, C. A. Bernays, *Queensland Politics during Sixty Years 1859–1919* (Brisbane, n.d.); on Deakin, see W. Murdoch, *Alfred Deakin: A Sketch* (London, 1923); on Australia and the Empire, see H. L. Hall, *Australia and England* (London, 1934). For Australian-New Caledonian economic relations, see Georgette Cordier-Rossiaud, *Relations Économiques entre Sydney et la Nouvelle-Calédonie 1844–1860* (Paris, 1957). See also the relevant chapters of the Australian and New Zealand narratives.

D3 ANTARCTICA

XXIV. ERA OF LIMITED INTEREST

For Nansen, see conveniently, E. E. Reynolds, *Nansen* (Penguin, 1949) and note also the references to and conferences with him, and to his work, in the narratives of the leaders of the "heroic age." The literature of the "Challenger" expedition is voluminous, but it mostly deals with extra-Antarctica activities. See, for example, W. J. J. Spry, *The Cruise of the "Challenger"* (New York, 1877) and H. N. Moseley, *Notes by a Naturalist on the "Challenger"* (London, 1879). For the Dundee whalers, see R. N. Rudmose Brown, *The Life, Work and Voyages of Dr. W. S. Bruce* (London, 1923). The Bull voyage is recounted in H. J. Bull, *The Cruise of the Antarctic* (London, 1896). Borchgrevink tells of his adventure in C. E. Borchgrevink, *First on the Antarctic Continent* (London, 1901).